DISORGANIZATION

PERSONAL AND SOCIAL

DISORGANIZATION

PERSONAL AND SOCIAL

HERBERT A. BLOCH

[ST. LAWRENCE UNIVERSITY]

ALFRED · A · KNOPF : NEW YORK

L. C. catalog card number: 51–11104

THIS IS A BORZOI BOOK
PUBLISHED BY ALFRED A. KNOPF, INC.

 Manufactured in the United States of America. Published simultaneously in Canada by McClelland & Stewart Limited.

FIRST EDITION

TO MY WIFE

Inspiring Partner and Companion

PREFACE

THIS BOOK seeks to establish a theory of personal and social disorganization and to indicate how such a theory may be applied to various social problems. Very few fields in modern sociology offer such an abundance of materials as does the field of modern social problems. In this connection, the sociologist suffers from an *embarras de richesse*. Much of this material, however, is unintegrated and lacking the systematic frames of reference which are progressively being cultivated in other areas of sociology. The approach in this book attempts to synthesize many of the modern views in anthropology, social psychology, and psychiatry which have begun to affect so vitally the field of modern sociology. The attempt has been made to sustain throughout the volume the indissoluble relationship between culture, the group, and the individual personality.

The book is so organized that it may be used as a text in social disorganization or pathology, or as a straightforward "social problems" text. For the instructor who chooses to eliminate theoretical considerations, the student may be sent directly to the problems beginning in Part Two. If only essential phases of the theoretical introduction are required, it is recommended that the introductory section on "A Frame of Reference" and Chapters 2, 5, and 6 be read. Chapter 5, providing a sociological analysis of personality in terms of attitudes, statuses, and roles, and suggesting a new orientation, should prove particularly helpful to the student beginning to undertake an analysis of social problems. In addition to serving as a theoretical introduction to social problems, Part One offers the advantage of reviewing for the student many of the basic materials in sociology ordinarily offered in the introductory course. Of some advantage should be the organization of these materials into a basic theoretical framework.

Although the primary function of this volume is to provide the student with analytical insights and intellectual skills, the writer has been mindful of the ethical responsibility of the teacher to his students. Sociology as an intellectual discipline and a social science bears certain specific responsibilities when confronted with the demands of the classroom. For this reason, therefore, although the principal emphasis throughout the book has been upon procedures of analysis, implications for the resolution of contradictory social patterns and the relationship between social trends and social policy have been suggested. The primary emphasis, however, rests upon procedural methods of analysis and interpretation.

It is impossible to acknowledge adequately the indebtedness to the various individuals who have contributed, directly or indirectly, to the writing of this book. The debt to former teachers and the stimulation provided by tireless workers in the fields of research and theory can never be fully repaid by any author. The writer wishes, however, to acknowledge his gratitude to Mr. Julius Rabin for his initial reading of the manuscript and the helpful suggestions given during the preliminary stages of the work. For preliminary clerical assistance and the chores of typing, acknowledgement is gratefully made to Mrs. Connie McAloon, Mrs. Ann Joyce, and Miss Elizabeth J. Roberts. Professor Clarence Hurd Gaines rendered valuable service in revising the draft of Chapter Seventeen. To my wife, however, for her continued encouragement, her inspiring faith in the capacity of the human race to improve itself, and her cheerfulness in performing the arduous burdens of bringing the manuscript to completion, no acknowledgement I can make here would be adequate or sufficient. Spencer and Susan Bloch have helped immeasurably, in more ways than they can appreciate, by being themselves and for their forbearance of their father.

Canton, New York **H.A.B.**

CONTENTS

PART II

Individual and Social Disorganization

DISORGANIZATION

PERSONAL AND SOCIAL

INTRODUCTION

TODAY'S students have never known the true meaning of social stability and peace. They have made their adjustments to the contemporary scene during a major and protracted depression and a world conflict unequaled in scope, intensity, and savagery. It is this unsettled world that the youth of today may soon again be called upon to defend with their lives. This generation that until recently has been forced to defer education, postpone marriage, and delay normal entrance into vocations and professions may have to defend the "way of life" of which they are a part; and upon them will ultimately devolve the responsibility of forging those instruments, technical and social, that may satisfy the enduring hope of mankind for a just and orderly world.

The evidences of a world in catastrophe are overwhelming. The statistical pointer-signs—indices, in the professional terminology of the sociologist—are so diverse that it is difficult to piece together the general pattern of disorder. Universities, research foundations, and social agencies are producing an enormous mass of detailed statistical data indicating in their wide scope the gravity of domestic and international social disorder. They provide ample testimony for the conclusion that it may be considerably "later than we think."

The basic fabric of our institutional life seems to be undergoing transformation and modification. The American family is experiencing a period of intensive disruption, and no one knows for certain what eventual form this vital institution may take.[1] The mounting incidence of divorce and desertion is so great as to pose the threat that the annual divorce rate may soon equal the annual marital rate. The plight of the American family since 1880 can be demonstrated in formidable statistics; while the population of the country has doubled and the marriage rate has tripled, the divorce rate has increased by over one thousand per cent. The progessive increase in the rates of crime and delinquency, no longer centering in the foreign-born elements of the population, is a matter of grave concern. The "new immigrants," migrants from rural to urban areas, and the professional and white-collar classes, groups that heretofore have been involved to only a minor extent, have currently assumed im-

[1] See, for example, the rival points of view of such eminent students of American family life as J. K. Folsom, *The Family and Democratic Society* (New York, 1943), and Carl C. Zimmerman, *The Family of Tomorrow: The Cultural Crisis and the Way Out* (New York, 1949).

portant places in the consideration of crime. The rising percentage of young people engaging actively in crime draws attention to the place of crime in the pattern of disorganization among our youth. Crime is becoming increasingly a proclivity of the young in this country.[2] A large volume of our commitments to state penal institutions comprises youths under twenty-one years of age—as high as forty per cent in some states. It is estimated that in 1948–9 one-half of all automobile thefts, one-third of all burglaries, robberies, and other thefts, one out of five of all rapes, and one out of seven of all murders were committed by youths under twenty-one years of age.

Even more disturbing, perhaps, is the appalling increase in psychoneurotic disorders. A report made in 1947 by General Cooke to the Surgeon General stated that approximately 1,250,000 young men of draft age had been rejected for military service because of some emotional or psychoneurotic difficulty. Adding further confirmation to the illness of our age is the statement of Dr. Treadway of the Public Health Service that at the present increasing rate of diagnosed mental disorders, it is possible that one out of every twenty-two of today's elementary school-age children may eventually find himself in a mental hospital. Elsewhere it has been reported that approximately one-half of our public hospital beds are occupied by mental patients.[3]

For other symptoms of our disorganized times, we may look at the recent disclosures concerning the rate of alcoholism. Research reports of the Yale Laboratory of Applied Physiology, Alcoholics Anonymous, and other groups, indicate the extent of personal and social breakdown induced by this excess.[4] It is estimated that in the United States there are very likely no less than 3,000,000 alcoholics. Of this number, it is presumed that approximately one-fourth, that is, 750,000, are chronic alcoholics requiring concerted medical and psychotherapeutic care. Nor may we assume that alcoholism is an exclusively male prerogative. Dipsomania among women has been increasing during the last twenty-five years, a fact which is especially significant when viewed as a concomitant of shifts in the culture as a whole. Another dimension of the problem of alcoholism calls for comment: of our total national income, five per cent is expended annually for alcoholic beverages, as compared with approximately three per cent spent for education.

Such indices of social disorganization could be reported *ad infinitum*.

[2] John R. Ellingston, *Protecting Our Children From Criminal Careers* (New York, 1948).

[3] Albert Deutsch, *The Mentally Ill in America* (New York, 1949), pp. 455–7, 506–07.

[4] E. M. Jellinek, *Recent Trends in Alcoholism and in Alcohol Consumption* (New Haven, 1947); "Alcohol, Science and Society," *Quarterly Journal of Studies on Alcohol* (New Haven, 1945).

The significant growth of narcotism since the turn of the century and its spread among the young, the increase of sexual pathologies and inversion, the innumerable disorganizing effects of migration and mobility (particularly aggravated by the recent war), the increase of various forms of personal vice and the sporadic rise of suicide—all seem to fit the pattern of the age. Nor may we overlook the heightened tensions and struggles characteristic of the acrimonious labor disputes of the last decade. All such forms of disorder seem to be part of a general pattern of violent struggle and change, stemming from certain fundamental disorders in the social structure itself.

The clue to personal and social pathologies may no longer be sought in the individual problems themselves. Some years ago, Lawrence K. Frank, in an incisive book aptly entitled *Society as the Patient* attempted to show that the afflictions besetting mankind, diverse as they may appear in their outward forms, are simply variegated manifestations of the same basic problems.[5] The sociologists and social psychologists of today tend to affirm this thesis. If we are to understand modern social problems we must learn to distinguish between symptoms and fundamental dislocations. These dislocations are not so much in evidence as are their symptoms, whose appearance is determined by the cultural, economic, regional, and stratified differences peculiar to our society. Symptoms and basic dislocations both must be viewed in relation to the entire framework of social processes that is proper to the particular cultural milieu. In a sense there is *one* problem expressing itself through the multiple stresses and strains in the different segments of society. Social problems can no longer be studied piecemeal, that is, as mutually exclusive or separate subjects of inquiry; they must be approached as manifestations of the underlying cultural conflict and social discord inherent in the total social structure.

If the social scientist is to find a demand for his special skills and perceptions he must first make clear what he can accomplish. The laboriously accumulated techniques that have been developed in the social sciences and psychology during the past fifty years must be made meaningful on an unprecedentedly wide scale. Popular ignorance and misunderstanding concerning the social sciences and their methods must be dispelled, and in their place must be established the understanding that the scientific intelligence functions in the field of human relations as well as in the field of the physical sciences.

Despite the pressure of the times to produce conclusive results in social science researches, the findings obtained have been sparse indeed, when compared with the contemporary progress of physics or chemistry.

[5] Lawrence K. Frank, *Society as the Patient* (New Brunswick, New Jersey, 1948), pp. 1–20.

Yet, our very survival may depend upon how soon the average person becomes acquainted not only with the results of our researches but also with the methods of thought employed by the social sciences. The few techniques that we have contrived, so little understood by the layman, must be organized into procedures of analysis to enable the average person, as well as the professional researcher, to cope with the conflicts of our modern world. It is in a scientific temper that we must confront and deal with the confusion that the domination of the natural and physical sciences has produced. If "whirl is king" we must understand our social confusion so that we may stave off disaster. At the same time, we may acquire such insights that will make the recurrence of chaos less likely, or at the least, less ominous.

There is an increasing recognition of this viewpoint among sociologists and social psychologists. We may hope that eventually the student of society will be provided with a *frame of reference*, a point of view by means of which he may begin to examine for himself the problems of social disorder. The random, indiscriminate collections of facts, partial facts, and substantiated and unsubstantiated statistical data, functioning within different and frequently mutually exclusive frames of reference, will begin to be oriented around generalized and integrated points of view.

Although sociologists differ considerably in their conceptions of science and scientific methodology, a remarkable degree of consensus exists nevertheless regarding some of the basic concepts. With an integrated approach, the data produced in the various unrelated and theoretically diverse studies in the field of social pathology will show a fresh usefulness by providing affirmation or denial of many of the hypotheses that such a conceptual revision will stimulate. Finally, the abundant findings and statistical data of the field of social pathology will assume for the student a new meaning and functional coherence.

No science or discipline can be effective without a knowledge of techniques. (We do not refer here to manipulations associated exclusively with the laboratory.) A sound knowledge of techniques, as we understand them, rests fundamentally upon the theoretical usages of the field and the procedures of analysis employed. These are the most basic of techniques in the scientist's repertory. The natural and physical sciences presuppose the analysis and understanding of such procedures as an introduction to, and accompaniment of, the mastery of laboratory skills. It would be foolish to train a student of physics or chemistry in the results of research, popularized and watered down, rather than in the mastery of theoretical usages and attendant techniques. Similarly invalid is the attempt to provide training in sociology by means of a simple exposition of the randomly assorted, unrelated, and largely verbalized data of the social sciences. What is required is an integrated and systematic approach to the field of sociology as a whole.

This work will examine how the fundamental processes of social disorder manifest themselves in the separate but related areas of the individual, the family, and the community. Eventually, the perspectives gained through such an analysis may shed light upon the broader dimensions of the international world which Graham Wallas called the "great society." In Part One, a co-ordinated theory of social and personal disorganization will be established. This is to provide the student with an integrated frame of reference, an intellectual tool for the interpretation of subsequent problems. Central in this frame is a sociological theory of personality growth and development (the theory of the "p.g.p."), which emphasizes the important sociological concepts of status and role. This theory will serve as an integrative concept in our development of the duality of the individual-social equation. Part Two deals with the bearing of social disorder on the individual. Various problems of this order are discussed (adolescent tension, delinquency, crime, sexual disorders, alcoholism, mobility, the personal vices, mental pathologies, and suicide), all illustrative of our earlier point concerning the relationship between basic disorder and symptoms.

Throughout, the attempt will be made to provide a systematic presentation and analysis of the several problems falling within each area of social disorder. (1) In each instance a specific framework of disorganization will be set up, stemming from the original hypothesis and pertaining to the particular problem. (2) Following the particular frame of reference, a descriptive "statistical profile" will be presented to illustrate the dimensions of the problem. (3) Enmeshed within the complex of our statistical data is the social individual, who becomes the next focus of our investigation. (4) Fortified with theory, statistical evidence, and an understanding of the individual, a causal interpretation will be sought on the basis of the interpretive frame of reference. (5) Finally, case-study materials will be employed as a basis for illustrating the complete problem in its manifold aspects and as a means of testing the student's critical and analytical ability.

The treatment of each problem in this way, it is hoped, may lay the foundation for a persistent analytical ability, and contribute in a small way to the growing scientific perspective on human affairs, so indispensable to the furtherance of a "just and orderly world."

PART I

A THEORY OF SOCIAL AND PERSONAL DISORGANIZATION

A FRAME OF REFERENCE

THE MEANING OF A FRAME OF REFERENCE

A TERM commonly employed today in the social sciences is "frame of reference." It is important, at the very outset, for the student to become familiar with the meaning and use of this term, since (1) it suggests a new departure in the development of the sciences of human relations, and (2) it will be used widely in this text.

By a "frame of reference" we mean in general the *standpoint*, intellectual or otherwise, from which a certain social problem, fact, or issue is perceived, appraised, and analyzed. To a certain extent, everything we do is adjudged and controlled by some frame of reference. This is almost self-evident, although we may not always be aware of the framc of reference in a given social experience. If we have strong prejudices towards certain types of people, if we entertain a strong animus towards certain types of political conviction, or if we have predilections for particular associates, forms of recreation, or varieties of food—there exist certain frames of reference, although they may not be *consciously* recognized.

THE GENERAL FRAMES OF REFERENCE GOVERNING OUR LIVES

The frames of reference regulating our lives are created and conditioned largely by the social organization of which we are a part. This social organization, however, is highly complex. We are not only citizens of the United States at a given moment in its history, subject to the various currents and drifts of public opinion, as well as the several historical processes existing at the moment; we are also motivated by highly complex sectional, political, class-structured, economic, cultural, and educational interests. Each one of these various segments of the social order is *selective* in the types of social values it promotes. Each plays its contributory role in determining what frames of reference will operate in the choice-making situations confronted daily by the several groups, associations, and the myriad of social individuals comprising our social order. (The social organization in which the individual exists presents itself to him as a scarcely differentiated totality; if here we segment this totality into separate institutional categories, it is for convenience of presentation and analysis.)

The frames of reference of a given social group will largely depend upon deeply-entrenched customary usages, i.e., folkways, mores, and institutional values. By understanding these frames of reference, we begin to gain some insight into why the individuals in such a group act in the way they do. Moreover, we begin to recognize that even the sensory perceptions of individuals (that is, the very way in which they perceive the world) are conditioned by basic elements of the frames of reference, in accordance with the process which the psychologist refers to as autism.[1] In its broadest terms, this simply means that every man perceives, thinks, remembers, and reacts in terms of the needs created by his economic interests, his religious and racial bias, his social and cultural background.

THE FRAME OF REFERENCE USED AS AN INTELLECTUAL TOOL

The concept "frame of reference," however, has a more specialized meaning for us. The term as we have used it thus far is largely *descriptive*, providing insight into why we find differences among human beings in various parts of the world and why the behavior of one group is distinguished from the behavior of others. The term may be used in a more restricted and also a more *functional* and *pragmatic* sense. That is, it may be employed to indicate the nature of the intellectual tools we are using in the appraisal of a given problem. We know, for example, that any given social problem may be viewed from a variety of different standpoints. The study of a social community may focus on its economic, social, political, or territorial aspects. If we define and specify carefully the critical factors that operate from a given aspect, then we are establishing a frame of reference within which the community itself may be studied.

The establishment of such a frame of reference requires careful logic. In defining the frame of reference—and this is a prior condition in all good analysis—we determine what we will discuss within our analysis and what we will reject. We thus limit the types of facts we are interested in surveying. This is not to suggest, however, that other facts may not be important. For example, if, in studying a modern community we choose its *economic organization* as our frame of reference, it does not follow that

[1] Gardner Murphy, in his *Personality, a Biosocial Approach to Origins and Structure* (New York, 1947), and Cantril and Sherif, in their *Psychology of Ego-Involvements* (New York, 1947), furnish striking evidence of how the perceptions of the individual are formed and conditioned in relation to *socially acquired* needs. For an especially illuminating and lucid statement of this process, see pp. 362–90 in Murphy's volume. An interesting recent illustration of how perceptions and social behavior are developed through status differentiation in the social structure is provided by August B. Hollingshead in his *Elmtown's Youth* (New York, 1949). This is a study of the impact of social classes upon adolescent behavior. See particularly pp. 441–7 ("Family Background and Behavior") in which "the family and neighborhood sub-cultures" are analyzed to show differences in adolescent behavior traceable to class status.

the facts of political or family life may not also be significant in our study. Indeed, they may actually be of greater significance than the range of factual data suggested by the frame of reference we are using. However, once "pledged" to a particular mode of analysis, it is necessary to close our eyes temporarily to these other factors, and bind ourselves exclusively to *the definition of the problem as incorporated within our frame of reference.*

An effective frame of reference, devised as an intellectual tool, will indicate clearly the theoretical conditions under which the given social area or problem will be surveyed. It will indicate, furthermore, what are, from its standpoint, *the key processes functioning in the problem.*

THE FRAME OF REFERENCE AS A SET OF BASIC DEFINITIONS

Developing rigorous prior definitions is not merely an arduous academic exercise or a superfluous requirement. Rather, it is a method of analysis, an intellectual tool, by means of which we are better able to probe social problems. Furthermore, our definitions will determine, to a considerable degree, what form our analysis will take.

Adequate basic definitions of the terms we use are essential in analysis. Such definitions should be operational and functional; that is, we should be able to validate them from observed behavior and subject them, whenever possible, to quantitative proof. This proof may depend on the techniques of measurement which are known to the sociologist and the psychologist respectively as sociometrics and psychometrics. Our definitions should recognize the basic assumptions employed in contemporary researches by sociologists and social psychologists. Where they fail to agree with the findings and conclusions of such researches, the discrepancies should be carefully validated. Throughout, when we define our basic terms and set up our basic theoretical views we should indicate our general point of view.

More important, however, we should integrate the several points of view that may be used in approaching particular problems into a coordinated pattern to provide a coherent system for the study of the entire range of personal and social problems.[2] We should not be content with a means of understanding solely how crime is brought about, or a given type of sexual pathology, or some form of parent-adolescent conflict; we should try to devise a probing and analytical technique that is equally ap-

[2] Cf. Lawrence K. Frank, *Society as the Patient* (New York, 1948). In this collection of essays written by Frank during the past two decades, the writer makes clear this basic thesis. He holds that the different types of social distress confronting man are primarily manifestations of a common pattern of breakdown in contemporary society. In short, they are merely different symptoms of the same kind of basic disorder.

plicable to the understanding of crime, prostitution, adolescent tensions, or any other social disorder.[3] This type of procedure is known as the synthetic view; its goal is the production of a complete picture of an ailing society.

SYSTEMATIC AND SYNTHETIC APPROACHES

Our approach to an understanding of social problems is *synthetic* and *systematic*. This does not in any way imply that it must be one-sided, pedantic, or otherwise limited in character. On the contrary, in view of the fact that the approach attempts to employ several of the well-established and more widely accepted current points of view, its scope is broad and comprehensive. Its advantage lies in its goal of putting diverse points of view into some kind of order. By organizing the highly complex and diversified approaches of sociology into a coherent and systematic structure, the student should be enabled to see not only the several different perspectives, but also how they are related, and how they may be used conjointly in the understanding of social disorder and pathology. Nor is the attainment of such a comprehensive view a matter merely of academic concern. The average student will find it valuable in analyzing problems that directly concern him in his daily life and that he will have to confront later, not as a professional sociologist but as a citizen of his community and of the world.

THE SCOPE OF OUR FRAME OF REFERENCE

The dimensions of our frame of reference, as well as the effectiveness of our analysis of any social problem, will depend upon the adequacy and validity of the theoretical propositions we present. Does the theoretical concept we are employing adequately resolve the major questions raised by the problem? Or, to put it another way, after our theoretical interpretations have been applied, are there many loose entangling ends left in the form of facts unaccounted for, dubious data, and unresolved issues? If so, does the theoretical view we are following provide any suggestions as to new directions of research to be pursued, new types of data to be sought?

If many crucial questions remain unanswered after a sociological analysis has been made, are they due to the insufficiency of the theory itself, or are they due to the immaturity of our science? If the latter be the case,

[3] For an analysis of some of the fundamental problems necessary to develop such a co-ordinated point of view from the standpoint of "structural-functional" theory, see Talcott Parsons, "The Prospects of Sociological Theory," *American Sociological Review*, Vol. 15 (Febr., 1950), pp. 3–16. Cf. also Talcott Parsons, *Essays in Sociological Theory, Pure and Applied* (Glencoe, Ill., 1949), Ch. II, "The Present Position and Prospects of Systematic Theory in Sociology," and the application of his systematic view to several "problem areas" in Part II of the same volume.

then we may say that *for the present* the theoretical explanation we are employing is sufficient as simply a temporary vantage point, one capable of providing partial answers until our insights are clarified and enlarged on the basis of future investigations.

The scope of the frame of reference we will develop here must be sufficiently broad to serve the diverse problems we are about to consider. To meet this requirement, our frame of reference will seek to fulfill the following terms:

(1) it will attempt to set forth the general conditions under which social change is brought about together with the effects of change upon the social structure;
(2) it will attempt to describe the varied and obscure ways in which individual and social change are related;
(3) it will attempt to lay down the basis upon which may be developed a general theory of personality as it is related to the conditions of the changing world.

We will try to indicate *first* how social change is brought about, how society is transformed as it passes from one set of conditions to another, and how changes may produce either social disorder or social stability. *Second*, we will try to point out how the individual is affected by social change, and how, reciprocally, changes in his personality may have certain effects upon the social structure itself. And *third*, we will try to show how the modern personality itself is organized in our culture, and how this personality may be affected by the type of world in which we live.

With the aid of this analysis, we hope to provide an intellectual tool to be used in understanding and analyzing the problems of social disorder and pathology considered in this book. The student should be enabled to discover for himself, through understanding gained in carefully controlled, systematic training, how social problems are to be approached. In this way, he is apprised of the "logic" of the socio*logic*. The goal of his study is no longer the mechanical mastery or memorization of a large amount of unrelated material but instead, the acquisition of a method by means of which he may discover for himself how the scientific intelligence functions and how the scientific temper may create for us a genuine science of social relations.

CHAPTER ONE

CHANGE AND THE SOCIAL ORDER

(1) SOCIAL CHANGE—A CONSTANT FACTOR IN ALL SOCIETIES

IF THERE is anything of which we can be sure in this all too uncertain world, it is that life is in a continual state of change and movement. The things which men once held to be immutable and timeless, have been replaced, lost, or transformed in the course of human history. Never has a people or a period of history not been subject to continuous, relentless change. This, then, must be regarded as a fundamental axiom: one of the most basic elements in all social life is the process of change itself. In fact, we may say that virtually the only unchanging element in all human existence is the factor of change.

Social Change Proceeds at Varying Rates of Speed

Not all peoples and cultures, of course, are subject to change at the same rate. During certain periods, such as the present, the forces of change have been so multitudinous and so swift that the source and the pattern of change have been very difficult to describe. In some societies, on the other hand, change has been so slow and imperceptible that its presence has occasionally gone undetected. For example, it has been commonly thought that some of the great civilizations of antiquity, particularly those of the Orient, were virtually static. Primitive peoples have been frequently referred to as part of an unmoving backwash, undisturbed by the rest of mankind's development. But the recognition that social change may proceed at a very slow pace which at first is difficult to detect does not signify that change is absent. Careful analytical study of the characteristics of changing social structures, as well as more precise examinations of the data of history, are not in accord with such a view. All societies change, whether slowly or rapidly. It is our faulty perception of history that has endowed some periods with perfect constancy.

(2) SOCIAL CHANGE COMPELS CONTINUOUS ADJUSTMENT

In a world that is continually changing, adaptation and readjustment are constantly necessary. Life demands a flexible strategy to meet the novel situations that emerge from the continuous interaction of social institutions and natural environment. All life, in fact, is dependent upon this process of adaptation; it constitutes the irrevocable condition upon which all biological and social existence proceeds.

In modern psychology and sociology, we speak of human adjustment as taking place within a "field situation," a concept which draws attention to the functioning of persons in their environments. This concept describes the highly interdependent but precarious states of balance and imbalance between the individual and his environment and the altered structure of such relationships occasioned by changes in either the human individual or the environment.[1] Human existence is said to be dependent upon the capacity of the organism to respond to features of the environment. Such features are said to be meaningful when they demonstrate the ability to elicit effective responses from the active organism. If death is to be avoided, the organism must have the capacity to sense its requirements and pursue them, while the environment must afford satisfaction. It is for this reason that we say "to live is to adjust."

There are two factors in the process of complying with this law of biological and social existence. They are (1) the adjustment-capacity of the individual himself, and (2) the adjustment situation of conditions of the environment, both natural and social. Both of these factors must be carefully examined in order to determine whether or not the adjustment-effort itself will be successful.

Under the best of circumstances, some individuals fail—individuals who, because of some reason of environment or defect of personality, are unable to confront successfully the demands of adjustment.

The Conditions of Adjustment

(1) *The adjustment-capacity of the individual or group.* Failures in adjustment may result from obvious physical defects or from intellectual deficiencies; but men fail, or succumb to the pressure of living conditions, for innumerable reasons, some of which may be extremely complex. Men fail not because they want to fail but because of innumerable personal reasons covering the entire range of human experience, including their own

[1] See Gardner Murphy, *Personality, A Biosocial Approach to Origins and Structure* (New York, 1947), pp. 4 ff.

ambitions, prejudices, habit-patterns, desires for wish fulfillment, lack of insight, loyalties, and social convictions.

(a) *Psychological elements: inability or failure to comply with external conditions.* Men who ordinarily possess great resources for meeting extremely difficult conditions may nevertheless be inadequate in certain situations for reasons of conscience, political or social idealism, or ideological conviction. Some individuals may have acquired, or be endowed with, unusual sensitivity and demand too much of themselves or of the times in which they live. Some men may strive for too much and eventually may be betrayed by their own ambitions. Others, like the "envious Cassius" in Shakespeare's *Julius Caesar* may be constantly stirred by a gnawing and discontent which makes it difficult for them to abide success in others or the sense of futility and failure in themselves. Irrespective of the impulses and motivations which characterize human conduct, these individuals, in one sense, represent failure to adjust to conditions generated by the process of social change.

(b) *Biological basis of adjustment.* One cause of maladjustment seems to lie in the incapacity of the human organism, or biological mechanism, to adapt successfully to conditions shaped by the physical and social environment. The biologist has used this concept in the study of biological structures. Life is conceived of as existing within a structured field in which the elements of the environment elicit those capacities within the organism which automatically ensure adaptation. Adaptation depends, therefore, upon the existence of these inherent capacities; it is largely a mechanical process of evocation by the environment. If the capacities are not present, in the form of hereditary mechanisms or acquired patterns, adaptation cannot proceed and the organism is not acted upon; stagnation and death result. Both survival and the character of the survival depend upon the nature of the biological process of adaptation.

(2) *The nature of the adjustment-situation.* We shall later examine in detail how the several factors of the social environment—psychological structure or conditions and the natural environment—combine to produce successful or unsuccessful adjustment. Here we are interested primarily in the nature of changing social situations and the qualitity of those situations which causes some individuals to succeed and others to fail in meeting the requirements of group living.

Each social situation consists of three basic elements: the physical, the social, and the psychological. Each of these elements, operating alone or together with others, may create situations ranging from catastrophe to beneficence, depending upon the adjustment capacity of individuals within a culture. Thus, (1) a *physical* disaster, such as a typhoon, a prolonged drought, or a tidal wave, may produce a situation that makes it impossible for individuals to continue their usual social lives. (2) *Social* changes, such as a political revolution or the introduction of new methods of economic production and distribution, may have effects upon masses of people which may not alone alter the fundamental fabric of their lives, but which, for some, may even signify extinction. (3) The same may be said for changing *psychological* conditions which may exert such strong social pressures that masses of human beings are unable to make adjustments.

Each of these major levels of adjustment—physical, social, and psychological—may be further subdivided and classified into elements that produce the changing patterns which bring about separable problems of adjustment. The *physical* conditions of human life, for example, include climatic changes and territorial differences; each produces certain types of structural potentiality and growth. Similarly, *social* factors include group structure, cultural attributes, technological achievement, class and status differences, kinship organization, and a myriad of other facets which determine human relations, to a greater or lesser degree. Likewise, *psychological* conditions comprise intelligence, emotions, attitudes, and instincts. They must all be considered, separately and jointly, if we are to understand how adjustment is brought about.

Our major concern, however, is primarily with the social situation. To understand how a complex social situation is created and developed, we need to evaluate and measure the separable weights of all the complex elements—physical, social, and psychological.

The importance of each element is always relative. What may be primarily a physical concern, as in the case of vast erosion of a once arable region, may eventually become secondary to certain types of psychological and social problems after irrigation projects and soil rehabilitation programs have been carried out. A social problem—the refusal or inability of individuals and groups to co-operate in meeting a common physical calamity—may eventually be found to be a psychological problem.

(3) *The interrelationships of physical, social, and psychological elements.* These separable forces will have variable effects according to different pressures of the moment. But in practice, when groups are confronted by these problems, the elements are likely to appear as a *totality* in which all factors play a vital part. Regardless of ingenuity in overcoming physical obstacles, if men lack the capacity for social organization the physical problems themselves may not be surmounted. Similarly, the most effective type of social organization and the highest order of psychological accommodation will be of no avail if we lack adequate knowledge to meet the emergencies created by a physical disaster. Even when men have reasonable assurance that they have devised the best scientific solutions, there is never any guarantee that their recommendations will be accepted in the face of political or ideological resistance, social apathy, or cultural inertia.

If we consider further the process of adjustment to changing conditions, two questions arise: (a) what are the various conflicting standards in the social situations produced by change? and (b) how do individuals adjust to the standards of social life which are never static, but change during the very process of adjustment itself?

(a) *The conflicting standards of the social situations.* Adjustment is highly complex and involves many diverse psychological, social, and physical elements. As an example of the composite character of all situations of adjustment, let us consider an individual starting work in a factory. From the very beginning, he is called upon to respond to manifold, new requirements. The adjustment problem extends far beyond the simple relation of a man to his machine or a man to his paycheck. The new employee must accustom himself not only to the new routine, but also to his fellow-workers, the mode of operation of his plant or office, the temperament of his employer, the physical conditions of his surroundings, and a host of other factors. Furthermore, willingness and the ability to perform his task satisfactorily do not in themselves guarantee acceptance by his fellow workers nor promotion by his superiors. Religion and race, peculiarities of taste and mannerisms, and even location of his residence may enter into the situation to promote or to hinder the efficient performance of his job. These latter "irrational" factors must all be taken into account by the new worker.

The intricate network of ties and expectations that run through every society (grouped into institutional patternings by the sociologist) involve the individual in a multitude of adjustment processes. Family life, politics, economic modes of behavior, and religious, cultural, and educational usages impose conflicting standards upon the individual. In our everyday life we are not accustomed to analyze social experience into such institutional components. But the multiplicity of these components becomes apparent when we approach scientifically such problems as crime, alcoholism, or the rising incidence of mental disturbances. An understanding of these disorders may require a consideration of the varied social (not to mention physical and psychological) factors that are instrumental in their development. When these factors, which have been isolated for the sake of analysis, are recombined in their original form, the complexity of their interconnections appears to be endless.

There are many difficulties inherent in the task of dissecting total social experiences or situations into their parts and establishing the nature of their connections. Yet, dissection must be undertaken if we are to determine the characteristics of the adjustment process. The difficulties of analysis appear even greater when we realize that in current sociological research only the most crucial and salient factors are dealt with; innumerable other factors may significantly affect the processes and results of social change.

The obligation to master such wide ranges of data in their complex relationships may dismay the student and cause him to question whether it will ever be possible to formulate even the first principles of a science of human relations. In reply, we may say that as formidable as the task may appear, considerable progress has already been made. Furthermore, the problem of complexity is essentially one of developing adequate methods by means of which *crucial* factors may be handled.

(b) *The dynamic quality of components in the adjustment-situation.* From an analytical standpoint, the individual seeking adjustment faces two types of problems. The first of these we have already dealt with, namely, the multiplicity of conflicting elements within the adjustment-situation. In this section we shall discuss the problems posed by the continuous flux of elements within the adjustment-situation.

No situation ever stands still. While the individual plans how to accommodate himself to demands of the present, circumstances may be so altered that the action he eventually initiates is hopelessly inadequate. The situation is analogous to that of the traveler, who, upon finally reaching his destination, finds that his prospective host is not there. Numerous difficulties arise from the fact that our best-intentioned plans and adjustment-efforts, once consummated, are often ill-suited to the situation towards which our efforts were originally directed.[2] Ours is a slippery and precarious kind of stability at best; the solutions of yesterday are forever being outmoded by the changes of today.

To see the problem of adjustment in clear perspective, we must recognize that the several aspects of a situation may be changing at different rates of speed. Three considerations must be taken into account in studies of adjustment: (1) the adjustment-situation is a complex of many parts; (2) these parts are in a state of continuous change; and (3) the rate of change is not the same for all parts. We may take as a demonstration of these considerations the case of the farmer who plans carefully for the year how he will work his land, distribute his crops, and repair certain of his out-buildings. The execution of his plan is dependent upon the weather, market conditions, the confidence of his banker, the state of his personal health and that of his family, and so on. Most of these conditions are beyond his prediction or control. In the course of the year, the farmer will be compelled repeatedly to readjust his program according to unfolding circumstances.

(3) THE IMPERSONAL NATURE OF SOCIAL CHANGE

The social scientist, like the natural scientist, must learn to restrict his inquiry to certain key factors. The world of fact is infinitely large; to

[2] See Robert K. Merton, "The Unanticipated Consequences of Purposive Social Action," *American Sociological Review*, I (1936), 894–904.

trace out in detail all the ramifications of a problem would take many lifetimes. Common sense is in accord with scientific method in directing that we consider only those crucial factors that we have discovered to be most directly instrumental in producing the conditions under study. We have already touched on this in our previous analysis of the role that the frame of reference plays in establishing a good scientific study.

Because of the complexity of social life, the untrained individual is unable to fulfill one of the initial requirements of analysis, namely, to designate which factors in a social situation are of key significance. Common sense, in the person of the untrained observer, has erred in suggesting that social disorder is directly an effect of human volition. Our present understanding of social change emphasizes the impersonal forces making for change.

Rarely do men willfully seek distress and discomfort. Men have been known to bring about willingly—or so it has seemed—their own destruction, whether by suicide or by some less dramatic action; but self-destruction is, on the whole, a rare occurrence. To understand the recurrent calamities that beset mankind, we must look, for the most part, to absences of intention. We should recognize, furthermore, that even when men have presumably "willed" their own destruction, the possibility exists that this step was taken with a larger end in view—that of gaining a more successful adjustment for others. In general, we may say that men usually seek to improve their physical and social positions, although we know all too well that "the road to hell is paved with good intentions."

The point we wish to establish here is that social change is largely *impersonal. Vast social forces are continuously in operation regardless of the motivations of individuals. Whether individuals or groups meet with success in their actions depends upon how these forces reinforce or thwart their intentions.* This is not to say that the universe is conspiring to defeat man in the accomplishment of his essential purposes. The impersonal forces to which we assign so important a place may be understood as *resultants,* whose weight and direction are determined by a combination of the innumerable factors of which social situations are composed—conflicting group interests, technological arrangements, personal bias, and the like. In the final analysis, to be sure, these forces are the work of persons; yet, they are only rarely reflective of the *intentions* of persons. The combined effect, or resultant, of the activities of numerous individuals or groups is almost always different from what the various participants might have contemplated. For this reason we say that any course of action we may undertake within human society transpires in a setting that has already been structured by forces that are for the most part beyond our control, forces that we may safely designate as impersonal. These forces, which stand sometimes advantageously and sometimes disadvantageously between men's objectives and their achievement, may be broadly subdivided into two major categories: (1) the *ideological and volitional,* and (2) the *physical and technological.* The former refers to the contradictory and conflicting objectives, ideas and orientations of groups and individuals, each intent upon promoting its own interest; the latter refers to physical limitations of the environment and to technological situations that block the attainment of desired human ends.

Because the social milieu is so intricate, men often find themselves confounded in the pursuit of both their remote and immediate goals. The situation resembles that of a man in a sailboat who is unable to reach port when overtaken by unforeseen squalls or winds, despite his most skilled efforts and calculations.

(4) THE IMPERSONAL FACTORS OF SOCIAL CHANGE INDUCE TRENDS

The known and unknown factors of social situations create drifts and trends which, from certain standpoints, seem largely unalterable. However, the naturalistic interpretation of human events, which asserts that there is a cause-and-effect relationship between what goes before and what ensues in human society, provides us with the assurance that the political, social, and economic events of today may, eventually, be read out of the complex web of conditions which preceded them. In the present state of the social sciences, it is virtually impossible to ascertain with accuracy what are the trends of our time. Yet, it is becoming evident that with the attainment of greater precision in our instruments of measurement and analysis, this goal will be brought closer to realization.

Can Social Trends Be Controlled?

Knowledge of a trend does not necessarily signify a recognition of the inevitable. Such knowledge can provide us with a greater capacity for control and self-direction, and enable us to temper or avoid the misfortunes that might otherwise befall us. Just as knowledge of tides and winds enables a navigator to control the direction in which he is going, so a knowledge of the social forces influencing a trend may enable men in general to deal with them in their early stages and redirect them.

Whether a trend may ever be completely controlled poses another question. The complete checking of a trend or the complete transformation or reversal of its direction appears to be a self-contradictory operation. What has already been set in motion may be deflected or modified, but it cannot be completely reversed. Trends, as we understand them, are representative of deeply implanted attitudes, values, and emotions that play basic roles in the relationships of men. As our knowledge becomes more precise, and as our tools for measurement and analysis become more incisive, we will gain greater power in redirecting trends according to the requirements of public welfare and policy.

An illustration of what we have been proposing here may be found in certain recent attempts to deal with economic problems. No longer do we believe, for instance, that economic depressions are inevitable. Instead, we have learned that a knowledge of how depressions come about may enable us to forestall their worst effects. The measures we take, however, do not completely eliminate the effects of the depression cycle. So long as forces making for depression, such as inflation, excessive consumers' borrowing, and unregulated currency distribution, go unaltered, various symptoms of periodic depression will be with us. However, given a knowledge of how the factors of depression operate, we may be able to prevent the most serious effects of a depression.

The recognition of a trend in no way indicates that it must be endorsed, accepted, or justified. The origin and characteristics of a trend may be *explained* and *analyzed,* but such understanding does not compel justification of its existence. *Analysis* and *justification* are two distinct intellectual processes.

The impersonal nature of social change and the "great man" theory. The process of social change provides us with a valuable insight into the role of the "great man" in history. No individual of and by himself can direct or control the course of human history. The impersonal nature of the historical process, and the profusion of personal, social, natural, and technological factors indicates how limited is the role of the individual in the introduction of change. Sociological analysis assumes that an individual may be related to a social trend in several ways: he may endorse it, he may identify himself with it, or he may oppose it. But the fact remains that the role he may play in its creation and development remains strictly limited.

(5) THE PRINCIPLE OF LATENT ALTERNATIVES IN THE CHANGING SOCIAL SCENE

From time to time dominant personalities or groups of personalities may seem to ride rough-shod over the course of human development, causing it to take certain directions in accordance with their dictates. Such a notion, however, is highly deceptive. What has actually occurred is that the decisive individual or group has functioned as a vehicle through which a trend or a phase of a trend has found expression. Thus, contrary to the ardent protestations of loyal Nazis, Hitler did not in effect create the National Socialist revolution by himself. Corporate state control was already latent in the stormy social conflict leading up to his accession to power. Hitler asserted himself at a time when there existed in Germany a potentiality for success of just such an organization as he could lead. Only to this extent may we say that men such as Hitler have "controlled" the forces of history. The imprint of the leader on a historical movement has a real existence only in a special sense. It is not that the leader makes his mark on history so much as that, when he arrives on the scene, he finds his mark already present in the tendencies of his times. *Latent within every trend are certain limited alternatives and possibilities. The possibility of bringing one of these alternatives to crystallization lies within the function and capacity of the great leader.* To use an analogy, the leader may be regarded as a human catalyst causing the precipitation of the possibilities inherent in the chemical solution of human attitudes, motives, and social considerations.

To a certain extent, the function of the leader is meaningful and highly significant. At times, he may stimulate in the social situation a latency which reflects a particular benevolent or sinister aspect of his own prejudices and antipathies. Anti-Semitism, for instance, already existed within the German social structure as a covert social force when Hitler capitalized on its reflection of his own violent attitude. In this sense, he "mirrored" the view of large sections of the German masses.

Devotion to a leader and willingness to follow him do not, of course, necessarily indicate a rational estimate by the followers. The observation has been made repeatedly that the docility of the masses in our own civilization has a deep-seated sociological basis. We may find in the very fact that men persist in the belief that a great leader can direct the forces of history affirmation of a latent willingness to be led. Nazism was not the exclusive product of a small band of conspirators who seized political control and duped the masses into following them. That the seeds of Nazism were long present as *one of the possibilities* within the social structure of the German state is strikingly apparent to anyone familiar with German history since the time of Frederick the Great.

(6) SOCIAL CHANGES AND THE DEVELOPMENT OF SOCIAL TENSIONS

In any rapidly changing social order not all segments of the population are affected in the same way. The complex nature of the social order, as well as the peculiar and predominant *character* of the change at any given time, creates for various groups different kinds of problems. We must now examine two considerations: (1) *the particular structure of the social order* at a stipulated period of social development, and (2) *the nature of the changing forces themselves.*

(1) When we refer to the social structure, we have in mind *the pattern of its organization,* the way in which its several parts are held together. This pattern includes manifold elements which the sociologist has come to regard in certain standardized ways. Incorporated within the social structure are such related elements as age-groupings; status-differences determined by family, political, and economic considerations; specialized class and organized group interests; regional or territorial groupings; occupational differences; and similar components. Subsumed under such major classifications as the foregoing are related structural, or what are occasionally termed *morphological,* characteristics, comprising such factors as status-differences based on sex, and complementary and conflicting determinants of status engendered by educational, religious, ethnic, and cultural differences.[3] All such status-differences, and the way in which they reflect the structural groupings of the social order, must be considered. No vital change in the social order could conceivably affect in the same way all individuals and groups.

(2) Correlatively, we must assess with extreme care the *character of the social change.* The change induced within the social order may be essentially political, technological, economic, or ideological. As we analyze such forces, we perceive that their nature and direction will affect different groups in diverse ways. While certain groups may be vitally affected, the existence of others may be hardly disturbed. Thus, if the change happens to be fundamentally ideological (for instance, the propagation and dissemination of new points of view), the chief focus or target for such novel ideational patterns may be any one or any group of a variety of major institutions—the church, the state, or the mode of economic life. Thus, the forces of social change must be seen in conjunction with (a) the peculiar and unique form of the social structure at a given moment in its historic evolution, and (b) the nature and character of the change itself, whether it be physical, technological, ideological, political, economic, or religious.

The structural characteristics of social groups are always changing, whether rapidly or slowly. As social change occurs, it alters the structures of the groups affected, causing some individuals to lose or modify their status and others to enhance their relative positions. In one sense, thus, social life is a continual jockeying for power. If changes are particularly cataclysmic and pervasive, as during a great political revolution, large sections of the population will find their positions drastically and suddenly altered. In general, when the pace of change is rapid, life becomes a precarious enterprise of maintaining hard-won gains and consolidating one's position against immediate and possible future deprivations.

[3] See Talcott Parsons, *Essays in Sociological Theory, Pure and Applied* (Glencoe, Illinois, 1949), chs. VII, X, XI, and esp. XII.

(7) SOCIAL CHANGE AND GROUP DEPRIVATIONS

An unavoidable result of rapid and pervasive change appears to be deprivations for masses of people. These deprivations are felt not only in the reduction of physical standards. Deprivations include the categories of socially structured interests, basic value-satisfactions, and status-determined physical comforts—categories which are of key importance to *social* man.

A wealthy industrial or managerial class may find that its fundamental standard of living has not been appreciably altered by particular social changes; yet it may object strenuously should these changes curtail its control of business affairs. In Nazi Germany changes in the pattern of economic control actually strengthened and improved the position of certain groups; yet opposition arose because of the accompanying restrictions imposed by the Third Reich.

(8) THE PERSISTENCE OF DEPRIVATIONS RESULTS IN GROUP FRUSTRATIONS

Changes producing deprivations will frequently bring in their wake, sooner or later, frustrations for masses of people. The newly created frustrations will seek outlet for the needs that are denied. In well-organized societies, there are conventional patterns, techniques, or channels by means of which individuals may express tensions. In our society, we do not murder people we fear or hate, although as Clarence Darrow once remarked, we can, on occasion, "read the obituary columns with considerable relish." In every society there are approved procedures, legitimized by law and custom, by which some of our animosities may be expressed. We may sue in our courts of law, we may exclude people from our clubs and societies, we may plot their downfall by means of legally accepted practices.

Under the cumulative impact of social change, we frequently find that mounting frustration and tensions strike with particular severity certain classes and groups. Such tensions must inevitably find an outlet. A principle in the field of human relations is closely analagous to the physical law concerning the equilibrium of forces. This principle may be expressed roughly as follows: *If the repression of functioning social forces renders them incapable of finding accustomed outlets or expression, there results a strain within the entire system, leading to disruption of the prior state of equilibrium.* In short, outlets or expressive channels will most assuredly be sought. If socially approved channels are not available, explosive action will take place in the form of anti-social aggression and violently emotional outbursts against whatever targets happen to be most convenient.

The "Scapegoat" as a Focus of Social Frustration and Resentment

A common illustration of how such misplaced antagonism operates can be seen in the familiar "scapegoat" behavior. The power of this mechanism becomes more apparent when we recognize how difficult it is for even the most intellectually disciplined elements of the population to act rationally during periods of great social stress. If the relatively well-educated and more stable groups of the population are prone to intense emotional outbursts during periods of great social travail, how much more readily will the economically and socially underprivileged—the marginal and poorly adjusted elements—fall prey to social dissension.

The impersonality of the social setting plays its part in the development of widespread social tensions. An individual who has suffered a severe deprivation can hardly understand the reason for his plight in terms of the impersonal forces of social change. The "sweet reasonableness" of logic can hardly give an effective explanation of the passions of frustration held too long in restraint. When the impulse to strike out is uppermost, it appears foolhardy to attempt to stem pent-up emotion with the simple counsel of reason.

For the harassed and frustrated man-on-the-street, recognition of the impersonal factors producing his difficulty lies beyond his grasp; *personification* of this abstract entity is, however, possible, and seemingly imperative. The "social system," a meaningless and abstract entity, cannot be smashed in the face, nor can blows be rained upon the "body politic." It is possible and feasible, however, if only to reduce one's own tensions, to strike an individual or a group of individuals. Even an inanimate object, such as a church, a bank, or a stone that one has tripped on may prove a satisfactory butt of aggression.

Since a "system" cannot be smashed in the nose or obliterated, while a person or thing can, it proves relatively easy to find such social escape-valves within societies where classes of people are defined as pariahs. Thus, Negroes, Jews, Catholics (in predominantly Ku Klux Klan country), and other groups become recognized targets of social opprobrium and animosity. The need for an immediate, preferably personal, focus for emotional expression appears to be one of the factors in the broad social-psychological basis of the "scapegoat" philosophy. When practiced on a sufficiently wide scale, such irrational vehemence may play a part in the development of revolutionary or anti-social activities.

(9) UNRELIEVED SOCIAL TENSIONS FOLLOW FRUSTRATION-AGGRESSION PATTERNS

Continual thwarting may produce aggressive designs. The development of aggressive patterns is not a simple process. Many psychologists agree that the emotions of anger and aggression in some form are always provoked by thwarting experiences. The social and psychological sources of such thwartings, however, may not always be immediately apparent; they may be extremely devious in their development and manifestation. John Dollard has analyzed certain selected aspects of the class-structure with the aid of the frustration-aggression hypothesis. He concludes that the greater the social area in which frustration may operate and the more unstable the socio-economic status of those concerned, the greater the possibility for mob violence and other forms of social hostility.[4]

Frustration, therefore, may lead to aggression, and as we have already suggested, aggression may in some cases find satisfactory outlets along socially approved channels. When the opportunity for expression through such channels is lacking, there remain two possible courses for aggressive action. (1) As previously stated, the aggression may find some outward focus in the form of a "scapegoat" group or institution. In this category fall international conflicts in which the enemy is portrayed as the malignant source of all domestic evil (the socio-psychological basis for chauvinism). (2) The aggression may be directed inwardly, that is towards the self.

Aggressive Designs Directed Inwardly

A current psychiatric view, oriented towards a closer consideration of the social and cultural determinants of behavior, suggests that the directing of aggression *inwardly, towards the self,* is a commonplace in modern society, particularly among certain classes. Discipline, fear, or the inability to find conventional outer foci for growing resentment may lead individuals to inhibit their natural impulses towards aggressive self-expression. Subsequently they experience what the modern psychiatrist refers to as an "anxiety-state"—a state of nervous tensions, fears, and insecurities induced by the failure to find normal avenues of self or group expression. Karen Horney and Erich Fromm have endeavored to give emphasis and historic confirmation to this view.[5]

[4] John Dollard, *et al., Frustration and Aggression* (New Haven, 1939); *Class and Caste in a Southern Town* (New Haven, 1937). Although the thesis that frustration must inevitably produce aggression has been criticized by certain sociologists and psychologists (cf., for example, Ellsworth Faris' review of *Frustration and Aggression, American Journal of Sociology,* XXXXV (Jan., 1940), 595–8), there is no attempt here to indicate that frustration is the *only* or even the principal source of aggression in all cases. Most recent evidence, however, appears to concur in the view that persistent frustration does constitute a valid basis for aggressive activity which may take any number of subtle and disguised, as well as overt, forms. Faris' critique appears to have overlooked the subtle varieties of the aggression pattern.

[5] Karen Horney, *The Neurotic Personality of Our Time* (New York, 1937); also by the same author, *New Ways in Psychoanalysis* (New York, 1939), and *Our Inner Conflicts* (New York, 1945). Erich Fromm, *Escape From Freedom* (New York, 1941).

According to these writers, the emotions of anger and rage are natural and healthful accompaniments in defense of our persons and positions. If the means of self-defense are cut off, and if we find ourselves increasingly in the position of being unable to protect ourselves through the effective channeling of our anger and rage, we become anxious about our security and our persons. Something of this sort apparently happens to countless persons in present-day society. We would like to storm back at our employer when we believe that we have been unjustly put upon; we would like to shower abuse on our partners and associates, but we know the consequences may be highly unpleasant. From one standpoint, all social relations may be considered to be under the control of socially required inhibitions.[6]

Subject as we are to highly competitive forces in our social life, we often find ourselves suffering setbacks without adequate opportunity to find satisfactory and realistic compensations. The cumulative effect of such stress and tension develops, for some individuals, acute anxiety. The fact that increasing numbers of the middle class, particularly the educated and professional middle class, appear to suffer from various psychoneuroses might in itself be considered a partial validation of this principle. Members of the middle class are ordinarily more highly self-disciplined, subject to greater cultural restraint, and less likely to give vent to sudden and spontaneous flurries of temper and violence than marginal and socially underprivileged groups. Consequently, the intensity of repression is greater, and thus more likely to produce states of anxiety.

SUMMARY *

(1) Fundamental to all social existence is the factor of continuing change. (2) Change, however, necessitates a process of continuing adjustment between man and his physical and social environment. The adjustments, themselves, are dependent on two major conditions: (a) the adjustment capacity of the individual or group, involving requisite physical, biological, and psychological propensities; and (b) the nature of the situation to which adjustment is being sought. The adjustment-situation is invariably highly complicated. Its complexity consists only partly in the network of its many factors, physico-environmental, cultural, social, and psychological, any one of which may be prominent or subordinate at a given time. We must further take into account the varying rates of speed at which the factors themselves undergo transformation. (3) The complicated pattern of social change is essentially an *impersonal* process in which

[6] Sociology may be defined as the study of socially acceptable, culturally processed, and group-sanctioned inhibitions.

* Numbers in the chapter subheadings correspond to numbers in the chapter summaries.

the motivations of individuals and groups play a limiting and contributory role. (4) The combination of such factors, however, conduces towards the development of social drifts or trends. A knowledge of the crucial factors in the development of a given trend may enable us to modify and partially control its direction. Great leaders may play a role in crystallizing social forces, but the function of such leaders is largely that of "catalytic agent" rather than that of creator and undisputed arbiter of social change. (5) Implicit within the changing social scene are a number of *latent possibilities*, any one of which may be developed, depending on the historic and social circumstances. Thus, every social trend reveals in itself a number of alternative possibilities. (6) Social change will invariably affect different parts of the social structure in different ways. The results of change will be determined by (a) the nature of the social structure at a given time in its history, and (b) the *character* of the change itself. (7) These results frequently constitute deprivations of various sorts for different levels and segments of the population and produce social tensions and dislocations of the social structure. (8) Social tensions, if prolonged, in turn promote a *dynamic* in the form of frustrations whose manifestations may be highly devious and diversified. (9) Frustration may eventuate in aggression, either crudely in the form of "scapegoatism" and mob violence, or more subtly, in the form of quietly maintained prejudice. The suppression of aggression, induced by cultural restraint, may be deflected inwardly, towards the self. Thus are produced widespread anxiety-states, whose impact on different segments of the social order varies according to the nature of the social structure. Such covert tensions may constitute one component in the driving forces of social change.

CHAPTER TWO

SOCIAL CHANGE AND THE LATENCIES

(1) INHERENT CONTRADICTIONS AND THEIR MEANING IN THE SOCIAL ORDER

OUR complex social order continually generates contradictory patterns of behavior.[1] These patterns create conflicts among the several institutional practices comprising the social structure and, at the same time, expose individuals to dilemmas of social and personal choice. No one wills such conditions; they are by-products of the complexity of modern society. Paradoxically, society does not function in accordance with the wishes of its members; in their final effects, the ends scarcely resemble the original intentions of the individuals. As a result, the actions of given groups and individuals frequently run counter to their own institutional interests and the interests of others. Men may deliberately intend to do certain things, but the conditions of their social, economic, and political living frequently compel different actions.

(2) ILLUSTRATIONS OF SOCIAL CONTRADICTIONS

The concept of contradictory social patterns has long been recognized by sociologists as a basic tool in the analysis of social forms and processes. Max Weber has dealt with these conflicts by developing the categories of "formal rationality" and "substantive rationality." He distinguishes between the conflicts inherent in the formal institutionalized patterns and the needs which they purport to satisfy.[2] An investigation of any modern social order discloses an enormous number of contradictions in virtually every phase of social life. Individual and group rationalizations enable nor-

[1] The presence of such contradictory patterns gives rise to what Karl Mannheim has referred to as the "ideologies," the systems of thought sustaining the social order, and the "utopias," those critical systems of thought which attempt to establish new social goals. Mannheim regarded such cleavages as constituting a fundamental dynamic of social change. See Karl Mannheim, *Ideology and Utopia*, trans. by Louis Wirth and Edward Shils (New York, 1940).

[2] For an extended treatment of this entire thesis, see Max Weber, *The Theory of Social and Economic Organization*, trans. by Talcott Parsons (New York, 1947).

mal social activities to continue for long and relatively stable periods. Eventually, however, the mounting tide of contradictions impels us to seek some type of *rapprochement*. The dynamic flow of human society has for its source just such contradictions.

An example of these contradictions may be seen in the economic life of our society. According to the capitalist ideology, individuals must be unrestrained in their economic practices and in their drive towards private profits. Nevertheless, those very entrepreneurs who support most vociferously the doctrine of *laissez faire* are continually forced to seek assistance, governmental and otherwise, in restraint of free trade by means of preferential tariffs, taxes, monetary controls, and other forms of economic protection.

Such social contradictions are to be found not only in the conduct of our business and economic affairs; they are located in every institutional sphere of social life. The patterns of our family life, for example, are full of such contradictions. We are eager to defend the continuance of the traditional authoritarian and patriarchal family, but harrowing social conditions make its survival dubious.[3] The status of women in contemporary society provides us with another illustration of how social contradictions operate. According to a poll of average male Americans concerning attitudes toward the employment of women in industry, particularly married women, the orthodox opinion still prevails that "a woman's place is in the home."[4] Yet the record shows that even before the recent war, a rapidly rising percentage of women, both married and unmarried, have been employed in industry. One estimate places the figure of women in industry at almost 30 per cent, of which number approximately 45 per cent are married.[5] A considerable number of the problems we encounter in family life (delinquency, child-neglect, adolescent-tensions, marital friction) may be attributed in part to this dual attitude toward the employment of women.

Additional social contradictions may be cited endlessly. The ambivalence in attitudes created by the contradictions has been effectively shown by Robert and Helen Lynd in their compilation of the value-judgments

[3] This contradiction keynotes the controversy between C. Z. Zimmerman and J. K. Folsom concerning the survival of family forms. Although differing in their estimates of surviving family forms, they agree in the main on the nature of the contradictory rifts in the contemporary family. See Carl Z. Zimmerman, *Family and Civilization* (New York, 1947) and *The Family of Tomorrow* (New York, 1949) by the same author; also, Joseph K. Folsom, *The Family* (New York, 1934) and by the same author, *The Family and Democratic Society* (New York, 1943).

[4] See Robert S. and Helen M. Lynd, *Middletown in Transition* (New York, 1937), p. 410; also, Clifford Kirkpatrick, "The Measurement of Ethical Inconsistency in Marriage," *International Journal of Ethics*, 46 (1936), 444–60; and Eleanor Coit and Elsie Harper, "Why Married Women Work," *Survey*, 64 (1930), 79–80.

[5] *Facts on Women Workers, January, 1949* (Women's Bureau, U. S. Department of Labor, Washington, February 28, 1949).

which comprise "The Middletown Spirit." [6] From the lengthy list which they have gathered, some samples may be drawn at random to indicate the orthodox Middletown view.

The strongest and best should survive, for that is the law of nature, after all.

"American ways" are better than "foreign ways."

Middletown will always grow bigger and better.

Economic conditions are the result of a natural order which cannot be changed by man-made laws.

Ordinarily, any man willing to work can get a job.

Everybody loves children, and a woman who does not want children is "unnatural."

"Culture and things like that" are more the business of women than of men.

The Constitution should not be fundamentally changed.

Human nature being what it is, there will always be some graft in government.

In every instance, the test for social contradiction should be: Is the reality of the situation not in accord with the stated institutional attitude and alleged practice?

(3) THE BASIS OF CONTRADICTIONS: THE LATENCIES

What lies behind social contradictions? What produces these contradictory patterns of potential change and disorder? At this point we may begin to consider the basic causal factors in the development of inherent social contradictions. If contradictions lie in the inconsistencies between institutional belief and practice, there must be present within the individual and the social group certain elements that are resistant to the acceptance of objective necessity and reality.

Particular latent elements within the personality make it difficult for the individual to confront and acknowledge certain conditions of realistic social change. These elements we refer to as *latencies*. Latencies are behavioral practices that the individual is unable or reluctant to abandon. Every contradiction which the social analyst studies in society is attributable to the existence of a latency, singly or in combination with other latencies.

[6] *Middletown in Transition* (New York, 1937), chap. 12, especially pp. 405–15. This contradiction between social ideal and social practice is becoming an accredited element in sociological analysis.

A latency is an adjustment effective in the past and persisting in present behavior tendencies even though it may not be appropriate in contemporary situations. In the individual, latencies may be regarded as basic habit-patterns or attitudinal-sets which have enabled adjustment in the past but which may no longer be adequate. On the social level, a latency may be said to constitute the complex of social traits which has enabled a group to make a satisfactory social adjustment in the past, but which may not prove effective in the present.

It is not enough, however, to say that latencies are simply adjustments to past situations. Human adjustments, as we have learned, are complex entities. Each adjustment in the past consisted of a number of elements which were related to the varying requirements of the situation. These latency elements continue to function as phases or parts of our contemporary adjustment procedures. Latencies thus refer not only to the total adjustment but also to the several significant elements which comprise such adjustments. Seen in this light, latencies are closely interwoven with the habitual and contemporary adjustment-procedures of individuals and groups. Every present adjustment contains elements of the past which may mitigate or impede a present adjustment. Any attempt to adjust to a novel situation thus brings to the fore latent elements of our adjustment-procedures which may, or may not, be in keeping with the demands of the new situation. Furthermore, these elements determine the manner in which we *perceive* the particular situation which confronts us; they comprise the psychological phase of our social and cultural frames of reference.

An individual or group which has learned to respond in a specific way to a given type of social situation has developed certain expectancies or perceptive elements upon the psychological level. They channel behavior into procedural forms that automatically define and approve the habituated or accustomed behavior. In effect, the person comprehends the situation solely in terms of such accustomed elements of perception. Thus, a group that has grown accustomed to certain economic practices develops a frame of reference which orders the elements of business situations. For example, businessmen in certain parts of the Near East and the Orient find that "normal" business practice in those parts of the world includes deceit and chicanery. "Normalcy" is determined by prevailing latencies.

Latencies "bind" the individual to a situation; the object of the situation and the perception itself are contained within a common frame of reference. The meaning of a situation is determined by how it has been perceived. The conditions under which a given situation has been perceived—that is, the elements entering into the formation of a given latency—depend upon psychological, social, and cultural configurations that have played a part in the socialization of the individual and the group.

Every latency creates in the mind of the individual the proper type of "normal" conditions which relate to it and which comprise the outer form of its existence; every latency calls forth an appropriate expectancy of what is fitting. The world is perceived through our latencies.[7]

The concept of latencies is valuable in the analysis of social problems provided we are aware of certain important characteristics. Fundamentally, every latency involves (a) the attitudes which indicate the evaluation an individual places upon a given situation, and (b) the objective conditions of the situation to which the perceived situation and its evaluation conform. They exist as two faces of the same coin. The subjective evaluation (a) has relevance only in relation to the objective conditions (b) it denotes.

Using the dominant aspects, inner and outer (the evaluative and the denotative), of the latency situation, we begin to understand the source of social difficulties arising from the adjustment-techniques that are employed in novel situations. This approach, however, may seem deceptively simple. When we try to use the concept in analysis, the problem of determining just what specific latency produces what problem-configuration becomes exceedingly difficult. Nevertheless, we are quite safe in saying that virtually every problem which individuals confront may be attributable in part to the existence of certain specific latencies or groups of latencies.

As adjustments which have been previously effective, latencies are attributes of groups as well as of individuals. The distinction between individual and group latencies is one primarily of scope and complexity. For an individual, latencies involve the dominant evaluative attitudes together with the objective situation. For a group, such subjective attitudes depend upon a basic framework consisting of inter-personal attitudes and values as well as inter-group relationships. Even in the analysis of a group latency, we refer to the predominant evaluative judgment and the objective events that relate to such a group evaluation. For the group as well as the individual, our analysis of problems is thus two-fold.

In appraising the reaction of a group of Southern whites to a situation in which Negroes exercise civil rights which are ordinarily denied them, we may trace the bitterness which is aroused to (a) the latent evaluative judgment of Southerners in the Deep South concerning the status of Negroes, and (b) the situation itself, namely the condition under which Ne-

[7] That we do not actually see what we think we see, but rather those images which are affected by our past experiences and our subjective impressions (that is, our latencies) has recently been revealed by a series of demonstrations in visual perception conducted by the Visual Demonstration Center of Ohio State University (November, 1949). These demonstrations were based upon the experimental methods in optics devised by Professor Adelbert Ames, Jr., head of the Hanover Institute of Vision in New Hampshire.

groes are encouraged to react in an unaccustomed manner. The situation, "Negroes in politics," impels a judgment counter to the group evaluation, a judgment which is in turn completely different from that held by the civil rights proponents.

(4) LATENCIES AND THE FIELD-STRUCTURED VIEW OF SOCIETY: SOCIAL EQUILIBRIUM

If we recognize that the social and cultural conditions of a given situation impose a frame of reference, we may then regard such conditions as limiting our social activities. Social activities exist within a social and psychological field composed of conditioning social and psychological factors, which in their *constricting* influence eventuate in some sort of completed social action.[8] The actual conditions which at any given moment determine the outcome of a given social situation represent the structural aspects of such a field of action.

The type of adjustment found within a given field-structured situation represents an equilibrium of a great many forces. Thus, every adjustment is the nodal point of a number of confluent forces which have entered into the adjusted state. Latencies represent prior states of social equilibrium. Such states of equilibrium in highly differentiated societies like ours are precarious; they display constant flux and change. Each equilibrium is formed by individual attitudes, social and cultural pressures, and physical circumstances—all joining at a common meeting point of internal balance.[9]

In the following illustrative cases, the reader should keep in mind the nature of the past adjustment and the attitudes and values implicit in it. He should ask whether the needs of the habituated attitude are likely to be fulfilled or thwarted. Our attitudes are the "equipment" with which we enter the situations to which we must adjust. If the situation fulfills the need of that attitude, then we adjust; if the situation fails in fulfilling the need of the attitude, then we find ourselves in a state of maladjustment whose consequences may take innumerable forms.

Case 1: Trina and McTeague

The novel *McTeague*, by Frank Norris, provides an example of how latencies arise and how, in specific situations, they may produce acute problems and even tragedy.

[8] This modern point of view was worked out some years ago by the late G. H. Mead in his general theory of perception and social behavior.

[9] The elaboration of this view may be found in J. F. Brown's *Psychology and the Social Order* (New York, 1936), pp. 43–62. More technical treatment is afforded in the appendix of the same volume, pp. 469–502. This concept is derived from Kurt Lewin and has been ably treated in his *A Dynamic Theory of Personality* (New York, 1935).

The central character is a simple, hulking individual named McTeague. When the story opens he is practicing dentistry in San Francisco during the period of its early, lusty growth in the middle years of the nineteenth century. McTeague's knowledge of dentistry has been obtained casually from a traveling side-show charlatan. Despite the meagreness of his training, he is able to maintain himself in some decency and comfort in the sprawling young city.

McTeague's wants revolve about two sets of primary needs: the need to satisfy his modest economic requirements and provide the minor luxuries to which he has become accustomed, and the need to attain a position of status and prestige. The pride he takes in his dental office provides ample satisfaction for this latter need. In keeping with McTeague's undiffuse and elementary character, the pattern of his life is simple. One of his chief delights, occurring regularly on Sundays—to him an unhallowed day of rest—is to visit a nearby saloon, return to his office with a container of beer, drink himself into a stupor, and then retire blissfully for the remainder of the afternoon to his dentist's chair. McTeague is not vicious or villainous. His wants are uncomplicated, consisting in his harmless Sunday recreation and his yearning for a large gilded dentist's tooth, emblematic of his profession, which he could hang outside his window. His horizons do not extend far beyond these elementary wants.

McTeague falls in love with a rather prim, ingenuous middle-European girl named Trina. Before she met McTeague her life was conditioned within a narrow and rigorous mold. Coming from a home with rigid parental discipline and marked by a Teutonic sense of order and frugality, her life was oriented around a primary set of values which laid special stress upon attitudes such as economy, orderliness, and the need for routine.

Note: (1) In any set of latencies the individual develops a number of basic needs and techniques for satisfying these needs through certain social arrangements, which apparently are sufficient to satisfy some of the principal requirements of the personality.

(2) These adjustment-techniques, to be discussed later in detail, may be considered to be latencies within the personality, ready to be released upon the occasion of primary inter-personal relations, and inducing frustration and tension when the conditions of expectancy within which they operate are not satisfactorily fulfilled.

Thus, when an individual like Trina desires a sense of order in a great variety of basic social situations, the failure of the social situation to comply with such an expectancy must necessarily create tension. The student should not infer that the entire pattern of the personality of Trina revolved wholly about such value-systems. These, however, did become predominant patterns of social adjustment and the basis of much of the motivation of her behavior. (In Chapter IV, in which the psychogenetic basis of social behavior will be discussed, a detailed analysis of such basic behavior patterns will be given.)

McTeague's prior adjustments (that is, his latencies) were premised upon a set of psychological needs involving basic patterned social arrangements designed to satisfy the simple, day-by-day, creature-comfort satisfactions previously described.

The temperament which stresses the need to secure one's self against the proverbial "rainy day" (as was the case with Trina) involves a latency which runs counter to the latencies implicated in a casual attitude towards economic affairs and improvidence.

In the marriage we begin to see what happens between two people when their adjustments are not mutually complementary. Between Trina and McTeague there developed mounting tensions because of the inappropriate and antagonistic expectancies contained in their different latency-structures.

Note: In this process, a common phenomenon is disclosed. This phenomenon expresses itself in the continual exacerbation and frustration of each other's personality, since their basic adjustment tendencies do not find adequate fulfillment and satisfaction in their shared experiences. Under the stress and strain of this type of relationship it is not surprising to find unfolding a secondary socio-psychological process, one of *intensification* of these basically antagonistic adjustment-procedures.

The simple needs of McTeague, expressed in the type of relaxation which had become an indispensable requirement of his personality, become intensified; he changes from an easy-going, benign, and simple individual into a man of violent rages and stormy temperament. The insistent presence of his wife, grimly intent upon conserving their small income, planning for their future, and building an orderly life according to the pattern set down by her parents, incites him to increasingly uncontrollable rage. We notice at the same time a degenerative transformation in the otherwise pleasing personality of Trina. Constantly harassed by the profligacy and imprudence of her husband, she becomes zealous in the conservation of the small income he earns. Her frugality becomes parsimony,

parsimony becomes niggardliness, niggardliness entails abnormal deception and the craving to save, saving becomes abnormal hoarding, which in turn degenerates into pathological miserliness. In Trina's case, the intensification process results in her becoming first, a person of extreme parsimony, and eventually a pathological miser.

As the tragic story unfolds, the continual frustrations brought about by latent tendencies, *which in themselves were neither dangerous nor harmful* and which under other circumstances might have proceeded without any problem or disaster, produce intense hostility between the two. McTeague's recurrent outbursts toward his wife culminate in his murder of Trina. The novel concludes with the flight of McTeague from his accustomed surroundings and from the authority of the law, and with his search for some type of sanctuary. The end finds him a completely disillusioned and dissolute character.

(5) PRIMARY IMPLICATIONS OF THE LATENCIES

We should keep in mind for future reference the following notes on the processes that occurred in the development of this fictional case:

(1) Latencies in themselves cannot be adjudged as good or bad for adjustment. *Successful or unsuccessful adjustments depend upon the nature of specific social situations in relation to a particular latency or set of latencies.*[10]

(2) The latencies involve expectancies which specific social situations may satisfy or deny.

(3) In inter-personal relationships, non-complementary latencies initiate a process of *intensification;* they emphasize and bring into sharp focus certain potentialities of previous adjustments frequently productive of discord and disharmony.

(4) Human behavior in social situations involves a set of latencies in relation to the capacity of the socio-cultural and physical environment to draw out certain latencies. Aside from social situations, human behavior is difficult to classify from the standpoint of its problem-potentialities, except for certain limited and well-marked

[10] Modern psychiatric theory is tending more and more in the direction of such an observation as this, rather than in the direction which describes the source of behavior difficulties as emanating from unitary and nuclear elements within the individual personality. Primary interest centers today on the analysis of the situation, moving away from the earlier type of studies which viewed individuals in isolation. The stress by Harry Stack Sullivan upon interpersonal relations within each social situation productive of maladjustment is particularly notable in this respect. See *Conceptions of Modern Psychiatry* (William Alanson White Psychiatric Foundation, Washington, 1946).

physical and intellectual disabilities. Thus, as the novelist Sinclair Lewis once put it, in describing the difficulty of categorizing individuals in relation to their psychological characteristics, there are "no doctors—only men studying and practicing medicine; there are no authors—only men writing; there are no criminals and no prisoners, but only men who have done something that at the moment was regarded as breaking the law." [11]

These inferences, drawn from the operation of the latencies, may be broadly summarized under two principal categories: (1) latencies may be complementary, that is, congruent or synchronous; and (2) latencies may become intensified through conflict. Congruent or synchronous latencies are those which, in a given situation, fulfill or "fill out" the behavior-tendencies of a person. Thus, an individual whose recreational adjustments call for satisfactions in the field of sports may be uncomfortable and dissatisfied in social situations where the predominant topic of discussion is contemporary poetry or the existentialist movement. Even here, however, if the dominant need of the latency is for social acceptance, the individual may profess an interest in such subjects. An adjustment tendency is a highly complex entity, and the matter of synchronization concerns the inter-locking of its several parts, with the result that although the dominant aspect of its evaluative attitude is highly significant, the related phases must also frequently be taken into consideration. These secondary aspects (emotional affects, feeling-tones, percepts, secondary values, and related interests) may likewise play an important role in determining the outcome and character of the final situation. The intensification of the latencies occurs when the evocative capacities of the total situation give no scope for the release of expected fulfillments in behavior, with the result that there follows a process of tension, thwarting, and friction.

Latencies in the Total Situation

The case of McTeague and Trina was more or less an idealized version of latency conflict; the novelist was able to highlight and emphasize certain aspects of character and situations. However, the following case illustrates how the types of actual problems we face, whether they be serious or negligible, result from the presence or absence of certain latencies. Habitual procedures of adjustment contain latent elements which have become integrated in the entire personality. A problem will manifest itself only if the types of life situations, social areas, or individuals with whom the personality comes into contact, fail to elicit the proper type of response. With this understanding, let us examine the following case.

[11] *Ann Vickers* (New York, 1933), p. 305.

Case 2: The Case of S. N.

The problem of marital conflict in this case is striking because both individuals were seemingly adequate and well-integrated personalities.

Note: (1) Here again we notice that the prior adjustment-techniques are not necessarily to be considered "good" nor "bad" in an ethical sense.

(2) It is the evocative potentialities of such adjustments *when confronting new or emergent situations* which may create a particular problem.

S. N.'s mother died before he was five. The family was governed almost exclusively by an older sister who was zealous in exercising her responsibilities towards the younger children in the family, particularly S. N., the youngest. A considerable portion of the problem which emerges can be seen to reside in the personality dictates of the eldest sister herself. Characteristic in the development of S. N.'s personality were traits reflective of the sister's dominating relationship. Conspicuous were an excessive desire for esteem and the necessity to observe the proprieties of the "better" social groups with which he mingled; they caused him to be referred to as a "model young man." Also notable was his undue concern about his appearance and the impression he made upon others. Pivotal to the entire development of his personality was his inability to make any decisions for himself, even those of a minor nature. Nevertheless, having a high order of intelligence and strong incentives towards self-improvement, he gave considerable promise for a successful career.

The "silver cord" binding him securely to his sister stultified some of the most normal impulses of self-action. After completing college, he became engaged to a young woman whose background, as far as the character of her own previous adjustments were concerned, was highly similar to his own. If the young man in the case resembled the cartooned figure of "Casper Milquetoast" in certain respects, this young woman might be considered his female counterpart. She was incapable of making even the most minor decisions for herself. After their marriage the most elementary decisions which married people are called upon to make for themselves—handling of income, naming the baby, and other common issues of marital co-operation—fell beyond their abilities and created consternation and crises. This was particularly surprising because both of them were highly intelligent. The result was in every sense a very dismal and static marriage, expressing itself not only in their personal contacts and in their sex lives, in the acute emotional discomforts of regression experienced by each, but in a wide range of social relationships outside of the marriage as well. An acute marital disaster was averted only by the patient and devoted efforts of individuals very close to the couple, who felt themselves constrained to intercede in behalf of salvaging the marriage.

Note: (1) The problem of conflict must be seen in relation to the entire situation which evokes it.

(2) Each situation contains a great many associated elements which, in their interrelated effects, may render the study of any such case extremely subtle and complex. *However, such problems inhere in the nature of the latencies involved.*

(3) An uncovering of the latent elements within the complex of adjustment will reveal the several connective strands, psychological and sociological, which play a part in producing such problems.

(4) Latent traits in interpersonal relations must be complementary if tensions are to be avoided. For example, "Casper Milquetoast," although ordinarily an innocuous and ineffectual personality, may nevertheless, in conjunction with a dominant personality, prove to be a successful or even a highly effective type of human being. An understanding of such interlocking roles suggests the configuration which the sociologist refers to as *superordination* (dominance) and *subordination* patterns in various kinds of social relationships.

(6) THE INTENSIFICATION OF THE LATENCIES

In the processes of maladjustment revealed in both of these cases there occurred a continual heightening and intensification of certain latent tendencies imbedded within the individual personalities. Latencies with no effective outlet undergo a process of intensification that may aggravate the problem created and lay the basis for a resultant crisis. The fundamental source of problem-situations lies not in the essential disutility of a given latency but in *its disutility in a particular field* which, as structured, is unable to satisfy the demands of personality functioning within its dimensions.[12] Psychiatrists and other personality consultants frequently find that such difficulties arise not *necessarily* because of any inherent or acquired defects of personality, but because of the effects which such latencies induce.

[12] Brown, *Psychology and the Social Order*, pp. 43–62, 278–304.

Latencies and the Psychological Principle of Adience. The process of intensification which we have described is closely akin to the concept of *adience* developed by the psychologist, E. B. Holt, and many others.[13] This concept suggests that individuals tend to become most deeply involved in situations in which certain needs are implicated, despite the fact that resistances and thwartings may become manifest in the situations. In being impelled to enter certain situations, the individual perceives them in terms of the positive drives which the latencies have accustomed him to expect. *Thus, the compelling force of the need still functions despite the inability of the situation to satisfy it.* The result is that the individual falsely envisages the situation in terms of what he expects, rather than in terms of what the situation may accomplish or do for him.

Implicit within the process of adjustment are certain needs for which the individual seeks satisfaction. *The "needs" related to the latent elements within our adjustment procedures constitute a driving force.* When confronted with a frustrating situation, there is both a heightening of these needs in the face of the continued frustration, and, frequently, increasing resentment towards those individuals and those aspects of the social situation which are conceived as impeding the satisfaction desired. (This feeling resembles in part the attitude which the psychiatrist refers to as *ambivalence.*) Consequently, we frequently witness individuals who become hopelessly embroiled in situations which appear to defeat the very drives they are trying to satisfy.

Hostility-patterns, deep-seated acrimony, resentment, and tensions may manifest themselves in unsatisfied latency-situations. A successful adjustment-effort that concerns itself with the fundamental drives of personality tends to persist. Efforts to adjust become integrated with many other phases of the total personality, so that what may appear to be a unitary striving towards a given objective may actually entail a great many phases of the personality. *The deeply frustrated person is amazed to find how many segments of the personality may be involved in a problem which seems to have a single and unitary source.* The intensification of human relations in situations such as these remind us once again of Santayana's observation, that "fanaticism is zeal which has lost cognizance of its end."

(7) ILLUSTRATIONS OF LATENCIES: SOCIAL

Just as the concept of the latency may be applied to the interpretation of problems of personality-situational conflict, so it may be utilized

[13] Cf. *Animal Drive and the Learning Process* (New York, 1931); Gardner Murphy, *Personality: A Biosocial Approach to Origins and Structure*, pp. 167, 235–9, 298, 319, 374 ff.

for insight into broad social problems. The chief difference lies in the degree and complexity of the two rather than in the basic attitudinal mechanisms. Problems examined in broad social perspective—the breakdown of the family, industrial disorder, minority group problems, and problems involving the widespread conditions producing crime, delinquency, and adolescent tensions—arise from discrepancies between group attitudes (attitudes entertained by large groups of the population) and contemporary situations which make the exercise of such attitudes difficult or impossible. The development of new situations and novel conditions imposes demands upon our institutional modes of thought and behavior for which such accustomed practices are not geared.

Such institutional practices are nothing more or less than attitudes and behavior patterns shared in common by large masses of people who have come to regard certain forms of behavior as normal and proper. The conditions of change encounter resistance with the result that frequent gaps or lags may be perceived between the inescapable compulsions of contemporary practice and the traditional viewpoints of our ideologies. These lags or gaps, to be discussed more fully later, are referred to in one sense as the *cultural lags*. The discrepancies tend to create what Read Bain has called a "schizoid culture," a culture deeply riven between two phases of its existence, the present and the past.[14]

The social latencies are manifest group attitudinal complexes which reflect the conditions of past methods of adjustment. Having become a part of the customs and folkways, they exist as attitudes held in common by several groups of the social order and as such carry the weight of group opinion in obstructing change. To illustrate the cleavage between the behavior requirements created by modern conditions and the resistance of our acquired attitudes let us turn to a problem that has created tension on the American scene for many years, the so-called "farm problem."

A Social Latency: The "Farm Problem"

Although there is no single "farm problem" in the United States, there is a series of specific farm problems reflecting regional conditions in many different rural areas and containing certain common elements. This problem particularly concerns the situation of the "dirt farmer" or "cash-crop" farmer of the Middle West and the South who produces the great "cash crops," such as wheat, grain, cotton, and other important basic crop staples.

During the nineteenth century, and until the time of the First

[14] Read Bain, "Our Schizoid Culture," *Sociology and Social Research*, XIX (1935), 266–76.

World War, farm produce was sold in the open market, with price returns largely determined by supply and demand. With no controls over agricultural production, if the farmer overproduced during periods of a relatively constant demand, the prices of agricultural produce declined. The industrialist, on the other hand, maintained strict production schedules according to "fixed-price scales" as dictated by his "costs of production." Modern industry could have developed only upon some such basis. The result was that the income accruing to industrialists was relatively high as compared with the dwindling and shrinking income of large masses of the farm populace.

Agrarian economics, however, had been conditioned until recently by the system of that early period which promoted unrestricted freedom of exchange on the open market to the end that the sale of any product, and its resultant price, were determined under the "sanctified" principle of supply and demand. Here were laid the seeds of a profound antagonism in economic life. *The previous attitudes concerning economic practice were generated during a period where unrestricted freedom of economic enterprise was considered a normal phase of the social order.* The development of large-scale industry, however, necessitated a completely different set of arrangements if industry was to grow and prosper. The industrialist inadvertently created a set of new conditions to which the adjustment-techniques of nineteenth century economic practice were inappropriate. In order to reconcile this situation to contemporary life, continual pressure has been exercised by farm groups and their lobbies to ameliorate the problem through various types of governmental assistance, e.g., price-controls, liberal credit allowances, agricultural price subsidies, tax rebates, low interest rates on borrowed capital, and the like. *Such assistance involves changes not only in economic operation but also in economic thinking.*

Note: (1) In examining this complicated social problem the latency-situation must be regarded as consisting not solely of a specific kind of economic and market practice, but as an entire series of interrelated and supporting institutional practices. These institutional practices are resident in the attitudes of large masses of people and reflect normal adjustments of the past.

(2) Such a "latency-situation" is complicated and complex. It contains not only specific customary habits of adjustment relative to economic life but also a great many related practices closely associated with a variety of other institutional usages in the highly diversified aspects of our cultural life.

(3) The latency concept helps to focus attention upon the salient habitual factors of prior adjustment which underlie the given problem.

(4) Further analysis sheds light upon the several related adjustments, in the form of group practices and customary usages which, in their reciprocal interrelations, support and reinforce the broad area of adjustment-techniques which are involved. Efforts to correct the "farm problem" involve an entire series of related institutional adjustments inherent in such behavior conceptions as "freedom of enterprise," "individual initiative," the degree of governmental control, legal procedures in relation to business affairs, and constitutional traditions.

Our analysis of the farm problem shows that the source of the difficulties inherent in such a social problem lies in the contradictory attitudes provoked by our traditional usages and the new demands which a contemporary situation presents. This conflict in attitudes can be seen in the *psychological bases* of the traditional usages and accustomed ways of facing problems which have become ill-adapted to the conditions imposed by the new situation. The development of new industrial techniques and concepts has forced us into a position where we are compelled to entertain new outlooks and engage in certain social practices *irrespective of the hold which historic attitudinal complexes may exercise.* The dead weight of our past traditional adjustments continually serves as a brake, conscious and unconscious, upon the ready adoption of such new alternatives.

Nevertheless, we are always meeting situations whose implications are affecting and transforming our lives. How to adjust our basic attitudinal orientations to the complexities of the new demands is an unchanging problem of human advancement and effective social progress. Each personality is compelled to move forward, whether willingly or not, on the basis of certain habitual usages, attitudinal complexes, and social values, which may or may not be synchronous with the changing demands of the new social scene.

SUMMARY

(1) Implicit within every changing social structure are maladjustments which arise because of the specialized interests and group pressures reflecting the growing differentiation and particularism of the several institutional forms of social life. These are unwilled and unpremedi-

tated, and may be recognized as inherent social contradictions, the inevitable by-products in any changing social order. Such inherent social contradictions have a psychological basis in the form of the attitudes shaped by our institutions and the patterns of group life, which have contributed to the procedures of past social adjustments. (2) Such social contradictions may be illustrated by the discrepancies which exist between the realities that are encountered and dealt with from day to day, and the evaluative judgments, grounded in past attitudes, by means of which we try to describe them. This is manifested by a kind of self-deception, commonly expressed in a contradiction between belief and practice.

(3) The psychological basis for such contradictions may be sought in the latencies, adjustments which, while once effective, may be inappropriate in meeting a contemporary situation but whose elements persist in contemporary behavior. Such latencies may be employed to account for personal-situational problems and for the broader problems of a group nature. (4) In every situation involving adjustment, an accommodation of social and psychological factors occurs in which latency elements, viewed as components of adjustment-procedures, function within the conditions established by such factors. These limiting conditions under which human adjustment takes place may be regarded as the conditioning frame of reference, or as a circumscribed field of operations. The harmonious confluence of forces entering into such situations may be regarded as establishing successive states of social equilibrium which may be unbalanced by the introduction of new elements within the field or by the incapacity of such conditions to satisfy the needs of latent elements within individuals and groups.

(5) The latency, although a complex structure involving many phases of the personality entering into adjustment-states, may be characterized by two predominant phases: (a) the evaluative attitude of the individual, reflecting past modes of adjustment, and (b) the objective conditions of the situation which conform to such an evaluation. In seeking new adjustments, the outcome depends upon whether or not the confronting situation is able to satisfy the latent expectancies and needs of the individuals and the groups concerned. Thus, in problems involving the adaptation of individuals and groups to their social environments, there are two primary implications: (a) latencies may be congruent or synchronous, i.e., they may satisfactorily fulfill the conditions of the situation, or (b) they may become intensified in the face of situations which are not in accord with the requirements of the striving attitudes involved. (6) Such intensification frequently leads to hostility-patterns, disharmony, and social and personal conflict. The intensification process arising in conflict situations is primarily aroused because the latent needs of the

individual are thwarted by a situation towards which he entertains expectancy of fulfillment and satisfaction.

(7) Since latencies may be viewed as attitudinal structures within the individual, they may be applied in the interpretation of broad social problems as representative of those attitudes of past adjustment in which there is broad group consensus, as manifested in the folkways, mores, and other institutional usages.

CHAPTER THREE

SOCIAL CHANGE AND THE CULTURAL LAGS

(1) THE LATENCY-STRUCTURE

SO FAR we have dealt with latencies as methods of adjustment that were once effective but later fail to meet current situations. Such adjustment-procedures have three fundamental parts: 1) the implicit structured attitude through which the individual or group seeks adjustment, 2) the actual procedures of adjustment, and 3) the conditions to which adjustment is sought.

The first of these parts, the implicit structured attitude, consists in the tendency of the individual to respond in rather consistent ways to situations that are meaningful to him. We call such attitudes "structured" because they involve a great many elements in the social environment and within the individual that have become a pattern associated with the situation to which the individual is seeking adjustment. Thus an employer who is strongly prejudiced against labor unions may have a structured attitude that involves not only his prejudicial judgment about a specific labor union but also, frequently, strong animosities toward related organizations and personalities. These sentiments may be bolstered by his emotions and psychological needs. The broad structured attitude is a pattern ready to be released wholly or in part when cues suggestive of "unions" are given. It is not surprising, therefore, that bitterness toward labor unions is reflected in a number of related emotions and intellectual judgments in business and social life. In short, structured attitudes tend to determine the perceptions of the individual. Structured attitudes, in their psychogenetic development, are related to, and derived from, fundamental needs and organic drives of the personality.

Secondly, latencies imply procedures through which the adjustment is made. An attitude of dislike, for example, may be expressed in a wide range of activities, extending from open coercion to subtle connivance.

Finally, the conditions to which adjustment is sought form the physical and social setting that impels the attitude and the appropriate procedures to manifest themselves. These procedures, it should be recalled, tend to be in keeping with the views of the members of the individual's group, who have come to agree upon the efficacy of such practices. This consensus provides a frame of reference within which the agreed-upon activity takes place.

These three aspects of the latency—namely, the structured attitude, the procedures of adjustment, and the conditions to which adjustment is sought—are the latency-structure.[1]

(2) THE LATENCIES AS STRUCTURED ATTITUDES

The latencies as structured attitudes are an important aspect of the inherent social contradictions previously discussed. As accustomed ways of doing things, they may not always be in keeping with changing circumstances. Each social contradiction has two features: 1) a structured attitude that is inconsistent with existing social reality, and 2) resulting conditions that reflect the disparity between the accustomed attitude and social reality. The latter discrepancy constitutes a cultural lag—a widening rift between the demands of the novel situation created by social change and the viewpoints from which we ordinarily approach such situations. The term "cultural lag" is usually employed to indicate a special kind of rift—that between the conditions produced by our technology and the accustomed practices in dealing with them. Here we give the term a wider meaning, applying it to any gap between traditional attitudes and current circumstances.

(3) THE CULTURAL LAG: MATERIAL AND NON-MATERIAL PHASES OF THE CULTURE

The cultural lag is one of the most important concepts developed in sociology during the present century. First introduced by William F. Ogburn in his volume entitled *Social Change*,[2] despite some criticism and modification since it was introduced, it remains substantially sound. One must, however, bear in mind that maladaptations in society have a wide variety of origins.

The term, as originally conceived by Ogburn, refers to the discrepancy in the rates of development of the material and the non-material phases of our culture. By material culture, we mean every physical thing, natural or manufactured, which has meaning or use in the culture. In contrast,

[1] It is interesting to note that this concept of the latency-structure is becoming widely used under different names by sociologists and social psychologists and resembles the concept of "the simple need aggregate" developed by Kluckhohn and Murray. See their "Outline of a Conception of Personality" in *Personality in Nature, Society, and Culture*, edited by Kluckhohn and Murray (New York, 1949), chap. I, p. 14.

[2] William F. Ogburn, *Social Change* (New York, 1922), pp. 200–13. See also *Recent Social Trends in the United States* (New York, 1933), Vol. 1, pp. viii–xiv.

non-material culture refers to all the theories, scientific doctrines, ideologies, values, social sentiments, and ideas that are necessary for living within a given social order.

Relationship between material and non-material phases. Except for convenience in analysis, it is virtually impossible to separate the material and non-material phases of a culture. A given industrial device invariably suggests an associated idea about its use, benefit, or value. The existence of a religious object, such as a crucifix, invariably presupposes some conception as to why the particular object has become ceremonially important. Any object is meaningful to the members of a culture only in terms of some related non-material conception within the same society. In our culture, for example, we can immediately associate an appropriate use with physical items.

Levels of understanding within a culture. There are, of course, in all societies different levels of understanding of items in the physical culture. The radio engineer has an entirely different image of the use of the radio tube than does the untrained individual who enjoys the results of its functioning but recognizes it solely as an object belonging in a radio cabinet. Moreover, many of the physical appurtenances of other societies would be meaningless to us. For example, a medicine bundle, as used by the Crow Indians of the Western Plains, would seem to us a weird assortment of battered relics, old bones, and similar paraphernalia. Yet, in the culture of which it was a part, the mystical and magical properties of such items would be immediately understood.

(4) CULTURAL LAGS AS MALADAPTATIONS BETWEEN MATERIAL AND NON-MATERIAL CULTURE

Cultural lags reflect (a) differences in the rates of development of social institutions, and (b) maladjustments between the spheres of interest such institutions represent. As an illustration of (a), the rapid rate of our technical progress since the Industrial Revolution has created problems for which much of our current thinking in other fields is outmoded. Item (b) refers to the fact that the specialized interests of the institutions involved in social life—the family, the church, and so forth—frequently come into conflict. Although cultural lags are usually thought of in the former, or temporal, sense, particularly with respect to our technological institutions, the term may also refer to any type of maladjustment between different spheres of social interest.

Since an indissoluble relationship exists between the material and the non-material phases of a culture, the student may ask why every new material object does not immediately suggest a functional use or value that becomes integrated with the rest of the culture. The answer is that societies are extremely complex, and the meanings of specific material items refer only to certain aspects of the culture. Science, for example, may produce a number of objects and interests with little or no relevance to other phases of social life.

The many physical uses to which such innovations are put create numerous secondary meanings and practices that, cumulatively, broaden the gap between the thought-patterns not directly related to them. Our technology has a dynamic of its own whose effects carry over into the non-material culture. These effects are not calculated, nor can their character be foreseen from the technological processes which gave them life. A knowledge of radio theory and manufacture does not enable us to predict such non-material consequences as the right of a father to determine his children's listening habits and the belief of Mr. Petrillo in the right of every union musician to have a job.

The idea of the cultural lag has sometimes been expressed more simply by stating that difficulties arise because we try to meet the problems of a streamlined, industrial age with minds still geared to "horse and buggy" thinking. But to put the situation in this way is not completely accurate, since the process of maladaptation may also work the other way around. Our technical practices may be maladapted to the conditions of our family and religious life. Technical progress has created an enormous rift in our social life; but whether this means that we must alter other significant aspects of society to suit the technical order, or redirect technical innovations to meet the interests of other phases of our lives, is a question that only time and the latent alternatives in the trends of time can answer. The orthodox view of the cultural lag which suggests that men must learn to think in terms of the necessities of the machine and the machine age overlooks the fact that it is equally important for men to think in terms of the other requirements of their culture. The maladaptation process is a two-way road.

Nevertheless, it is important to view the social discord of our times in relation to the unprecedented growth of our technical culture. Technical achievements have an immediate impact in many unforeseen ways upon the life of the people, who are daily forced to make important decisions concerning their use. The effects and implications of these decisions soon influence a wide range of habits and patterns of behavior within the culture. Eventually these expedient, day-to-day decisions and the behavior-patterns they generate become incompatible with attitudes and values reflecting a previous era and other sectors of society. The problem then becomes one of reconciling these opposing elements of the social process. The effect is to lay the basis for compromise-practices, new forms of social behavior that may become the social patterns of the future.

Emotional Resistance to the Changes Required by Cultural Lags

Adjustments to the times cannot be made without considering the emotional reorientations involved. If adjustment were simply a matter of devising new laws, it would be relatively simple. The problem is acute, because even when the soundness of a new solution is seen rather clearly, many emotional resistances persist. We may cite the violently emotional resistance to attempts to deal rationally with phases of the Negro problem in American life by passing fair employment practice acts and by guaranteeing fundamental civil rights.

The transmission of culture from one generation to another, which occurs particularly in the early conditioning of the child, produces an irrational substratum of emotional predispositions. Most adult men and women find it difficult to accept calmly some new technique of thinking and behaving, advantageous though it may objectively appear, if emotional attachments are jeopardized.

Men at all times and in all cultures have had to accept the necessity of making new physical adjustments to their environment. Sometimes these adjustments have presented serious problems to the societies concerned. But no other culture in human history has experienced technological progress at the break-neck speed of the Western world since the Industrial Revolution. This increase in technical achievements and the apparatus of modern living may be graphically depicted in the form of a sharply rising geometric curve.[3] The non-material phases of our culture have lagged behind, so that life has become a continual process of trying to reduce the great gaps caused by the disproportionate rates of development.

Cultural Lags and Social Policy

The recognition of cultural lags in the social order makes social planning essential, to forestall serious effects. If a given technical innovation will produce a set of conditions to which man's thinking and behavior are not geared, the obligation laid upon us is unmistakable.

Whenever technical progress is under way, we may expect a measure of misfortune. This is true even when the advantages seem self-evident, apparently outweighing any possible disadvantages. To illustrate the point, we may look at modern communications. Developments in this field have been of incalculable value in business and in the dissemination

[3] Although no satisfactory composite index has been devised to depict accurately the rate of growth of the technical and material aspects of culture, crude approximations show that the curve of progress, particularly since the Industrial Revolution, follows a geometric ratio. For an attempt at quantitative analysis of some limited aspects of technical progress, see Mildred Fairchild and Hornell Hart, "A Million Years of Evolution in Tools," *Scientific Monthly*, XXVIII (Jan., 1929), 71–9.

of news and information, but at the same time they have contributed to confusion by exposing the human mind to a myriad of conflicting standards and points of view. Labor-saving devices that free men from drudgery and increase productivity may appear a remarkable boon. But they must be assayed in the light of accompanying unemployment and other serious economic dislocations. Similarly, the increased household leisure ushered in by the machine age has not necessarily added to the aesthetic tone and solidarity of the family circle, but rather, has often contributed to divorce, desertion, and other rising symptoms of family disorganization.

To summarize briefly, cultural lags reflect discrepancies between the daily material needs of modern technological life and attitudes of intellectual and emotional resistance that reflect the psychological make-up of the human personality. We must remember that in the psychological environment in which each generation is reared, the dead hand of the past continually operates. Time can never be grasped by the forelock. While attitudes are being inculcated in the young, novel conditions produced by the machine-age technology create new crises and conflicts which the rising generation must face on the basis of its existing outlook.

Some Illustrations of Cultural Lags in Operation

We may now consider specific cases of how cultural lags operate in modern society.

Procedure of observation. Let us try to determine the structured attitude of the underlying latencies operating in each of the following cases. In each illustration, the crucial factors producing the cultural lag are readily apparent and the student should learn to identify them. All too frequently, the term "cultural lag" is loosely used and applied, but if we keep in mind the meaning of the latency-structure and its three parts, as well as the varying rates of growth in the accumulation of material and non-material culture, we may begin to bring into focus the underlying causes of social problems.

(A) In interpreting social changes caused by technological factors, the student may be guided by three queries concerning the latency-structure:

(1) Is the structured attitude lying at the core of the latency-structure able to withstand the new social practices introduced by the innovation?

(2) Are the previous, routinized procedures of adjustment compatible with the new set of conditions?

(3) To what extent are the emergent conditions able to satisfy the needs of the situation?

(B) Cultural lags such as those presented below may be viewed from three standpoints:

(1) The impersonal character of change produced by modern technology.

(2) The sporadic manner in which the cultural lag is bridged over a period of time.

(3) The possibility of anticipating the problems created by the cultural lag.

1. The Automobile and the Small Rural Community

(An illustration of the impersonal character of change produced by modern technology)

Evidences of cultural lag can be seen in the effects of the modern automobile on the small country village. As testimony to the paradoxes accompanying such change, one need only mention the attitude of Henry Ford, who fought strenuously the very results of his mass-production techniques. (Consider, for example, his valiant efforts to revive the handicrafts of an earlier day and his reconstruction of nineteenth-century village communities as "living models" of the past.) One effect of the automobile technology has been the disappearance of the small village from the American scene, particularly the older cross-roads hamlet, which has figured so prominently in the growth of our national and rural culture. One estimate in the decade preceding the depression of 1929 placed the rate of disappearance as high as 2500 small villages annually for selected years. When the "conveyor-belt" system of automobile production was introduced, these results were hardly foreseen.

To understand how the American village was affected by automotive transportation, we must examine those rural institutions about which community life revolved and observe carefully the direct effects upon them. These fundamental institutions were (a) the old-fashioned general store, (b) the village church and parsonage, (c) the one-room school house, and (d) the grange hall around which considerable recreational and political life centered. Modern automobile transportation and the development of hard-surfaced highways have slowly dealt a death-blow to each of these important rural institutions.

Impersonal Effects Upon Specific Pivotal Agencies

(1) When the villager can shop conveniently in a larger center where chain-stores provide variety and lower prices, the village store is eventually forced to close its doors.

(2) The possibility of safe and speedy transportation of school children to the larger nearby towns by means of the modern bus results in the organization of central school districts with modern buildings and improved facilities. Exit the little red school house.

(3) The same pattern affects the village church, which might have been regarded as the one bulwark able to stem the tide of events. The evening prayer meeting, the Sunday devotional and sermon, and other local church functions cannot compete with the activities of larger churches in nearby communities. Moreover, the accessibility of recreational centers to the automobile owner is important in the general decline of church attendance.

(4) The grange hall, the previous center of much rural entertainment and recreation, withers under the competition of the latest Hollywood extravaganza, the "horse opera," and the roadside tavern.

2. Workmen's Compensation

(An illustration of how the cultural lag has been bridged in relation to a specific problem)

An interesting example of a cultural lag and of attempts to close the breach can be seen in the growth of workmen's compensation legislation. In early nineteenth-century Europe, particularly in France and England, there were sporadic and violent efforts by masses of workers to do away with the machine. Not only was the machine a symbol of the destruction of their former way of life and the direct instrument of their growing unemployment, but the machine also brought a great many other problems for which the early nineteenth-century agrarian mind was unprepared. Not all of the animus toward the machine was due to the fact that it created unemployment. A great deal of the antipathy arose because the machine produced a tremendous number of accidents and fatalities.

Resistance to Change by the Latencies

Why was it not until the latter part of the nineteenth century that provision was made for the medical and physical care of workmen injured by machines? Moreover, as Ogburn has pointed out, not until the second decade of this century did a number of states in this country take any effective action. The lag existed because the conditions created by the machines were approached with an attitude that the care of the sick and the injured was a family responsibility.

We may outline the situation as follows:

1) The patriarchal and large consanguineal family organization of former days implied a family responsibility for the care of children,

the old and infirm, and family members unable to fend for themselves. (The second, or "procedural" aspect of the latency-structure.)

2) This mentality persisted into the nineteenth century even though the family was broken up and became fragmentary in its organization, with local conjugal units living in the overcrowded tenements of the new factory cities. (The third, or "changed conditions" aspect of the latency-structure.)

3) Although it was hardly feasible under the new conditions to act upon the old conception of care of the injured, the old attitudes, values, and emotional beliefs were so entrenched as to lead masses of people, at that time, to accept the fact that injuries, regardless of their cause, were the concern of the family or the individual, and not of the larger social order. (The first, or "structured attitude" aspect of the latency-structure.)

The entire procedure in analyzing this example of lag is summed up in the following three items:

(1) *The actual situation as it presents itself:* Injuries to individuals caused by industry.

(2) *Prior conditions:* Large kinship family groupings living on the land and organized to care for the injuries and other disabilities of their members.

(3) *The new conditions:* Nuclear families, uprooted from their former kinship organization, living on a cash-and-wage basis and unable to care for their ailing members.

As the problem became increasingly acute, it was seen that these two trait-complexes in the social system could not exist side by side and that they involved an inherent social contradiction. It was understood that the individual or the individual family could not cope with accidents, occupational diseases, and kindred problems.

Consequently, as a means of closing the gap, legislation to meet these problems became common in the late nineteenth century in Germany, France, England, and other parts of Europe, and belatedly, in the United States. Workmen's compensation laws were passed, so that modern industry could continue efficiently and assume its responsibility in the new order which it had created. A partial answer to the challenge of the early accident rates was the eventual development of workmen's compensation laws which are part of the legal structure of every modern industrial society. Moreover, modern programs of social security and old-age assistance may be viewed as natural outgrowths of the pioneer efforts in workmen's compensation laws. These programs represent the effort to close the gaps which the major dislocations of the industrial order continuously create.

3. Cotton-Picking Machine

(An effort to anticipate problems created by a cultural lag)

A good illustration of how social planning can solve problems created by cultural lag and forestall eventual ill-effects is afforded by the mode of introducing the modern cotton-picking machine. This contrivance, comparable in significance to Eli Whitney's cotton gin, is already beginning to revolutionize the cotton industry in parts of the South. If introduced widely without adequate social planning, its economic repercussions might seriously impair the economy not only of the South, but of the entire country. Consequently, considerable caution was used in introducing the machine in areas which it might dangerously disorganize. A research foundation has been established to determine the probable economic and social effects on areas in which the machine is to be introduced. Only after careful study of the area and after efforts to determine how the displaced elements of the population and the entire local economy may be handled effectively is the machine introduced, and then only by carefully regulated stages. The machine itself is not sold outright, but leased with the provision that part of the profits be used in planning, promoting, and rehabilitating the areas in which it will be used.

This is a good illustration, on a private level, of an attempt to plan for the integration of a new technique which might otherwise upset the pattern of economic and cultural life. The planning which preceded and accompanied the development of the T.V.A. provides a comprehensive instance of the same kind. The T.V.A. is also a good example of dealing effectively with the needs of a sub-region through the close co-operation of private and public agencies. A closely-knit program was established through which the various elements of the population and the area's economic resources, present and potential, might be rationally co-ordinated. This type of planning, called "rationalization" by Swedish social scientists, is a prerequisite of modern democratic life. In it both governmental and private agencies can play effective roles.

It is evident that, with a knowledge of proper techniques and planning procedures, we may anticipate the kinds of problems modern technology raises. Success in handling such problems will depend upon the use of sociological and other social science procedures through which alternatives may be carefully studied. Such studies as the one by Ogburn, mentioned above, can help us to cushion the impact of our changing technology. Increasingly, the federal and state governments, as well as local agencies, private and public, must employ the prediction made possible by scientific procedures. Only in this way can we anticipate cultural gaps and close them before the problems introduced by innovations deluge us.

(5) RELATIONSHIP BETWEEN INDIVIDUAL HABITS AND SOCIAL PATTERNS

All adjustments involve an intricate network of the individual's habits and attitudes. We need now to examine the relationship between such individual networks and the social patterns which they support and upon which, in fact, they are based.

Individuals vary in the extent to which they conform to customs and common behavior patterns. Furthermore, individuals sharing the same common patterns of behavior do not react to them with the same intensity and degree of acceptance. In other words, the idiosyncratic elements that appear in all behavior lead individuals to place different evaluations and emphases upon identical objective situations. Each individual is unique, having experienced differentiated conditions of birth and rearing, situations that exercised varying degreees of control and pressure, and group memberships and loyalties that are peculiar to him.

In following a common social pattern, a mass of individuals may conceal a great many individual subjective differences in response, meaning, evaluation, and intended effect. Sociologists have not always recognized these differences. Some customary usages, such as folkways and mores, have been considered simply as group habits, or to be more precise, as habits of a similar or identical nature that are carried on by a great number of individuals within the same group. Such an identification is invalid. In a study of common behavior traits, F. H. Allport seems to suggest that in any social pattern, even though the expressions of a given trait may appear to be very similar, they are nevertheless based upon unique personal elements in the individuals participating in the group practice.[4]

To illustrate our point let us consider the apparent deference that is shown an elderly person who enters a room. The individual motivations for such deference can be, and frequently are, quite diverse. One individual may rise from his chair largely because of the belief that old age deserves such special deference; another, because of the social pressure exercised by the presence of other members of the group; while a third may make this gesture primarily because he is eager to make an impression upon his companions. In short, we perceive in the execution of any common

[4] "The J-Curve Hypothesis of Conforming Behavior," *Journal of Social Psychology*, V (1934), 141–83; see also his paper " 'Group' and 'Institution' as Concepts in a Natural Science of Social Phenomena," in Ernest W. Burgess, *Personality and the Social Group* (Chicago, 1929), pp. 162–80.

social pattern an infinite variety of personalized backgrounds that support the pattern. The observance of a common form of behavior entails personalized expressions on the part of each individual.

(6) FOLKWAYS, MORES, AND SOCIAL INSTITUTIONS

Customary ways of dealing with social situations and problems by the group have long been known to the sociologist as folkways. The concept of folkways is very broad and contains many sub-divisions. Principal among the sub-divisions is the concept of the mores. Folkways are group habits or customs that represent optional actions of the group members. The mores, on the other hand, are more pervasive group usages; they are usually mandatory within certain groups, and when they are not observed, considerable group resentment and disturbance is likely to follow. We might classify the distinction between the folkways and the mores by the following criteria.

Folkways	*Mores*
1) optional;	1) non-optional (or mandatory);
2) associated with particular groups;	2) universal (or almost so);
3) no deep seated resentment if disregarded.	3) group emotion aroused if disregarded.

We must be careful in applying these criteria, however. They are general rules-of-thumb which are valuable only with reference to given groups. For example, what constitutes an optional folkway to one group, such as the custom of smoking among women, may be a breach of the mores among another. Finally, in the course of social change, folkways and mores may become so altered that previously optional practices may become mandatory and mandatory practices may come to require only casual observance. Thus, folkways and mores may become interchanged.

In every community we can observe numerous social behaviors which, while widespread, do not appear to be obligatory. Every society is marked by countless such open choices, which Ralph Linton has called "alternatives."[5] On the other hand, there are certain social practices, referred to by Linton as "universals." These are exceedingly difficult to flout because of their wide occurrence and the deep feelings associated with them. Traditional practices in connection with religion, patriotic observances, and parent-child and husband-wife relationships are frequently in this category of universals. Thus, while smoking among adults in our population may be called a folkway, the act of a parent in encouraging minor children to smoke would be considered in most American communities a

[5] *The Study of Man* (New York, 1936), pp. 273–4, 278–9.

violation of the mores. Whereas as a folkway, considerable latitude may be exercised in the type of clothing one wears, appearing in public in scanty garb (except under such sanctioned circumstances as a bathing beach or those conventional forms of undress permitted women at formal evening occasions) would constitute a disturbance of the mores.

Developmental characteristics of the folkways. Studies of the folkways, including the work of the founder of the concept, William Graham Sumner, indicate that they are distinguished by (a) irrational origins, (b) origins whose beginnings are lost in obscurity, and (c) survival largely through trial and error. This irrational basis, which makes modifying them difficult, may be likened to some of the streets and highways of New England. Beginning as cow-trails, with twists and wanderings, they eventually developed into links between towns, retaining all their original deviousness. Many of our folkways may be visualized as "cow-paths" of the mind. Lest the student think that this "trial and error" characteristic has made possible rational correction of some of these casual twists of the human mind, it should be recognized that the term "trial and error" refers to survival value. Thus, if a given practice did not knowingly impede or hinder survival, it was retained. The "trial and error" characteristic alludes primarily to value for survival rather than to the experimental process of societies consciously seeking to correct and render more rational previous errors of judgment.

Social institutions. Folkways and mores, which together satisfy social needs, eventuate in those broad patterns of behavior called social institutions. The interrelated procedures by which religious, family, economic, and other social needs are satisfied, cluster into characteristic forms and patterns—social institutions. A social institution contains (a) a basic concept, and (b) a formal and informal structure by means of which the basic social need is satisfied.[6] By "concept" we refer to the basic social needs or values that the institution exists to satisfy. In order to implement the satisfying of these needs, a number of interrelated patterns of behavior have sprung up, involving material objects and non-material phases. These interrelated patterns constitute the structure; they may be classified into four distinct component parts, two of which are material and two of which are non-material. Our discussion may be summarized in the form of the following equation:

$$\text{Social Institution} = \text{(a) Concept} + \text{(b) Structure } (1 + 2 + 3 + 4)$$

The institutional structure consists of (1) the reciprocal attitudes and behavior patterns of the participating individuals, (2) oral and written

[6] F. S. Chapin, "The Formal Analysis of a Social Institution," *Social Forces,* VI (Mar., 1928), 375–7.

specifications concerning the operation of the institution, (3) the material objects required to maintain the institution in operation, and (4) the material objects that are emblematic of the needs and values of the institution. (1) and (2) are non-material in character and form, while (3) and (4) may be classified as material culture elements.

We must bear in mind that the institution functions as a totality; all the parts are interrelated and implement each other. A reciprocal and close relationship exists between the concept and the structure of an institution. Changes in the conceptual needs and values have repercussions on the operation of the structure; similarly any alteration in the structure of an institution will eventually have an impact on the fundamental ideology contained within the concept.

Folkways, mores, and social institutions organize the diverse practices of society into well-defined patterns. They are mechanisms of social control, directing the social impulses of men towards defined objectives and giving meaning and purpose to social activities.

(7) PRIMARY FUNCTIONS OF THE FOLKWAYS AND INSTUTIONAL PATTERNS

As mechanisms of social control, folkways and institutional patterns serve two very important functions: (1) *they define normalcy for the group,* and (2) *they direct and control the processes of human interaction.* Let us consider each of these functions in some detail.

(1) On the basis of trial-and-error adjustments individuals make adaptations to their social and physical environments, which in the course of time appear to them fitting and proper. Such adjustments vary from society to society. Individuals who practice common adjustment-procedures eventually come to look upon certain activities as "normal." This consensus is nothing more or less than a particular way of looking at certain events or things; it is a way of "defining" certain events as being normal. Thus, when we speak of social normalcy we are really thinking of the two related characteristics of (a) the consensus or the shared opinion of the group as to what is normal, and (b) the "definition of the situation" (the way in which the group has come to define certain activities as being normal). We do not mean to imply, of course, that the group consciously plans and premeditates its definitions of normalcy.

Definitions of normalcy vary with place and time, from culture to culture, and within the same culture. The conception of "normal" behavior for young people which our grandfathers followed is quite different from that which we follow today. Moreover, as our discussion of folkways has indicated, even within the same area and at the same time, different groups and generations define normalcy in different ways. As we shall see later, conflicting definitions of normalcy play an important part in many social problems.

Normalcy and abnormalcy. If normalcy is the state wherein a situation is given a common definition, then abnormalcy exists in the degree with which particular individuals and groups deviate from such common definitions. Abnormalcy, thus, is a relative and variable condition. The inability to respond in a way that the group regards as normal often lays the basis for maladjustment. On the other hand, there are significantly creative individuals and groups whose definitions of common situations have been at variance with the definitions of the majority. Although abnormal with respect to their own times, the views of such persons have often been vindicated by posterity. The history of art and other spheres of creativity is studded with accounts of important figures who were spurned by their own times, only to be acclaimed by later generations. While creative deviants will often be rated as abnormal by any standards, their productions may nevertheless have undisputed merits, setting the standards for new, socially accepted definitions.

(2) In examining the function of the institutional patterns in directing and controlling the processes of human interaction, we must remember that individuals and groups are always reacting to each other according to prescribed patterns. *This reciprocal interplay of persons and groups within a given social environment (defining the "frame of reference") we refer to as the social processes or the modes of human interaction.*

(8) THE SOCIAL PROCESSES

In all human social orders, the ways in which men interact may be summarized under the following five categories: (1) communication, (2) competition, (3) conflict, (4) accommodation, and (5) assimilation. (Various sociologists have devised several intermediate categories, but these five cover the predominant forms of interaction.) This enumeration may be somewhat misleading unless we recognize that we use the categories for convenience in examining interaction; all of them may be present in some degree in all human relationships.

(1) Basic to all social processes is communication; it might be considered, in fact, not a separate process, but a condition of all modes of interaction. No interaction is possible unless there is communication—and a mechanism or medium for communication—through which the interaction may be expressed.

Communication may lead to social disruption or integration. Misunderstandings frequently arise because of confusions about the meanings of certain common situations. Even within a common culture, we have, because of stratified and segmental differences, varying "realms of discourse" which may serve as barriers to social integration and solidarity. Modern communication, with its vast networks binding all parts of the world, has been responsible for a considerable portion of the world's unrest. Before the advent of modern communication techniques, men lived in their own tightly enclosed worlds that harmoniously united their behavior. Modern communication has penetrated age-old insularities and has exposed men to a myriad of conflicting ideas.

Although communication often provokes disruption, it is indispensable for the establishment of social order. There can be no reconciliation of human differences unless the differences are conveyed through some medium of communication. Communication may disrupt the existent order of social relationship in the degree to which the objects communicated are not compatible with the group's behavior. Correspondingly, communication may be effective as an instrument of social harmony.

(2) The process of *competition*, sociologically viewed, is *unconscious* and impersonal. So many variables are always in action that the stress and strain upon the social system conspires to aid some individuals and to hinder others. Population conditions, family background, religious and social considerations are but a few of the factors in the process of obtaining an objective. Among the Manus in the South Seas, competition takes the form of a struggle for wives. In our society, the competition is for power, wealth, and rank. Whenever there is an insufficiency of things which are desired, and whenever there are present the complex elements of social choice which determine "who shall be chosen," the process of competitive activity inevitably sets in. Not all are chosen who "stand and wait."

Some societies, such as our own, have made a virtue of the competitive process. We give it a social value which everyone is encouraged to support from childhood onwards. It manifests itself in almost every facet of our lives, from the child who competes for the coveted distinction of being the "monitor of the white mouse" in his grade school to the tycoon in industry who engages in strenuous activity to attain his own special distinction in the competitive process.

(3) Unlike competition, the related process of *conflict* is *personal* and *conscious* and leads inevitably to alterations of status. In conflict, the individual is acutely aware of the significance of the contest and of the adversaries against whom he is contending. Conflict must have a vanquished and a victor. Unlike competition, conflict limits the sphere of social activity and precludes alternative social processes. Whereas competition voices tremulous hopes for the outcome, conflict speaks in the stentorian tones of finality and certainty. In any rapidly changing society the possi-

bility of competition becoming transformed into conflict and the possibility of conflict becoming modified into some competitive form is always present. The former transformation, however, is always more likely than the latter. Once conflict is set in motion, the possibility of transforming its objectives becomes very limited.

(4) *Accommodation* refers to the process of *conscious* adjustment of individuals and groups to each other and to the cultural standards according to which specific group situations are defined. It refers to both intergroup and intragroup relations. As a conscious and directive process, it must reckon with the types of resistance existing within each situation. Thus an immigrant group may have a strong desire for accommodation but if it meets with a strong hostility towards foreigners, the accommodation-effort is likely to result in failure. The accommodation-effort is usually determined by the nature of the dominant controls exerted by the principal groups of the community. The effect of such domination on the accommodation process frequently produces a stratified social order designed "to keep certain elements in their place." Such systems may congeal into rigid class or caste structures as in the South of this country or in India.

Thus, accommodation is determined by majority strength and by the social status of dominating minorities who prescribe the form and direction of the adjustment-behavior. Despite the fact that accommodation processes depend in large part on such dominating groups, the processes must be regarded as reciprocal or two-way. Even those groups that determine the essential conditions of adjustment are affected by the accommodation process. The conditions of adjustment, regardless of who imposes them, eventually affect in varying degrees all groups involved in the adjustment equation.[7]

(5) The *unconscious* absorption and interpenetration of individuals and groups within a common area of patterned social behavior is known as *assimilation.* Assimilation takes place in all social areas and on all social levels, but it is particularly marked in those areas where a minority group eventually absorbs and acquires many of the mannerisms and points of view of a dominant majority. Even when antagonisms and resistances exist between groups, a certain degree of interpenetration takes place. Unconsciously, groups and individuals identify themselves to some extent with the points of view of others, through the process known as *introjection.*

Assimilation processes are always defined by (a) the resistances to such processes by dominant groups, and (b) the rigidity with which sub-

[7] This has been well expressed, within an ethical-humanitarian frame of reference, by Booker T. Washington. He states: "If the white man pushes the Negro into the gutter, he must eventually get down into the gutter himself in order to keep him there." This is essentially the basic theme of Lillian Smith's novel on Negro-white relations, *Strange Fruit* (New York, 1944).

ordinate groups adhere to institutional practices. Finally, and of considerable significance, is the fact that as assimilative processes grow in scope and intensity, they give way to the conscious procedures of accommodation. The more individuals and groups learn to share common views, the greater is the willingness to resort to conscious adjustments to reconcile their differences. A study of immigrant behavior in this country, particularly among the second and third generations, provides ample evidence for this conclusion.

(9) THE SOCIAL PROCESSES AND SOCIAL UNITY

Accommodation and assimilation are primarily *associative* and *co-operative* procedures, tending, in the long run, to lay the basis for co-operative social enterprises and social unity. Competition and conflict may provide healthy social change if they are subordinated to the broader procedures of accommodation. If the antagonistic forces are completely dominant, however, they place the social structure in a continuous state of disequilibrium. When practiced with restraint, even competition and conflict can induce a certain degree of accommodation and adjustment and strengthen the co-operative bonds of the separate contending groups. The established rules of procedure under which competition and conflict take place themselves denote a special kind of adjustment. Even the savagery of military conflict among nations is governed presumably by the international agreement known as "The Rules of Land Warfare." Moreover, as we have learned from our own recent history, wars may often produce a degree of co-operation within the domestic order and among allies hardly conceivable in times of peace. The control of the disruptive potentialities in competition and conflict in order to produce a greater social unity is a persistent problem in modern societies. Social conflict or harmony depends upon certain factors in the changing social equation which we are now ready to appraise.

SUMMARY

(1) In our analysis of cultural lags, we have noted that resistance to change lies within the latency-structure, which consists of three parts: (a) the structured attitude, (b) the procedures of adjustment, and (c) the conditions to which adjustment is being sought. (2) The psychological aspect of this resistance is particularly apparent in the structured attitudes of individuals and groups who have come to define their situations in particular ways. (3) The discrepancies between the new conditions produced by change and the resistance of our social attitudes are known as cultural lags. (4) Cultural lags are ordinarily regarded as the disparities existing

between the character and the rates of accumulation of our material and non-material culture, especially as they appear in the resistance to the effects produced by rapid technological progress. (5) Since the bases of these resistances are to be found in the latencies existing within the individual and within the group, we have noted the complex organization of secondary attitudes, mental traits, values, social usages, and cultural practices which surround the latent attitudes. (6) This complex of enveloping traits is interwoven with the supporting social sanctions and usages in the form of the folkways, the mores, and the diversified institutional practices of the social order. (7) The combination of folkways and mores into clusters of institutional practices serves the very important basic functions of (a) defining normalcy for the group at a given time in its history and (b) directing and controlling the processes of human interaction. (8) The processes of human interaction may be broadly classed under the following five categories: (a) communication, (b) competition, (c) conflict, (d) accommodation, and (e) assimilation. (9) Accommodation and assimilation are essentially integrating processes in the social order. Competition and conflict are dissociative, unless they are harmonized within a larger framework of adjustment, serving as instruments of well-ordered change.

The important function of latencies in their relation to normal behavior and the social processes is summarized in the following diagram.

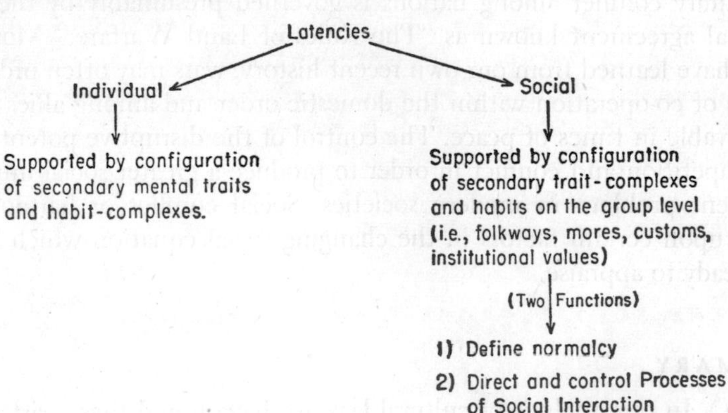

CHAPTER FOUR

INTERACTION AND SOCIAL DISORGANIZATION

(1) PROCESSES OF INTERACTION AND SOCIAL PATHOLOGY

SOCIAL life is dynamic because of the processes of human interaction described in the last chapter. These processes, we noted, may be associative or dissociative in form.[1] Now we shall analyze the factors that determine whether the outcome of any human interaction is harmony or strife, i.e., in sociological language, associative or dissociative.

Every human interaction is compounded of (a) a given personal attitude and (b) a given type of social situation. If we know the specific attitude to be expressed and the nature of the social situation which the attitude will encounter in its expression, then we should be able to predict the form of any social process. Prediction is difficult, however, because we cannot easily determine just what an individual's attitude is, and his stated attitude may be quite different from his actual attitude in meeting real situations. Yet, much progress has been made in learning the nature of personal or individual attitudes by means of psychometric and sociometric devices and by the techniques of case study. For the most common conspicuous situations an individual meets, therefore, it is possible to predict his attitudes with some certainty.

(2) THE SOCIAL PROCESS EQUATION

Personal attitudes are determined by (a) the individual's native endowment or biological inheritance and (b) the character of his past social experience. The personal attitude thus determined is one phase of the social process equation; the other is the normal social situation to which an individual is exposed. Modes of social normality are established by two leading factors, one physical and the other socio-psychological: (1) the nature of the physical environment and (2) the nature of the

[1] The dissociative or conflict element as the predominant basis of social change comprises the central concept in the sociological theorizing of many classical and recent theorists, such as Ratzenhofer, Gumplowicz, and Leopold von Weise. Von Weise, however, places this concept within the formal framework of the social processes.

social and cultural attitudes that have arisen in traditional relation to this environment.

The relationship between physical environment and social attitudes is not always easy to establish, but there is no one-way determinism between the two. The physical environment imposes limiting conditions upon the possibilities of social development, but it does not determine the actual character of such development. As A. E. Goldenweiser points out, the physical environment supplies limited raw materials from which human nature may select.

Discovering the basis of social norms and behavior patterns requires us to determine those factors of the past that enabled men to establish their early symbiotic relations with their environments, that is, those natural patterns of balance and adaptation developed within the limitations of the physical surroundings. Horse-stealing in the Far West of the United States, for example, was at one time a capital offense. When a man's horse was his only means of conveyance in a vast, sparsely settled area, stealing a horse was frequently equivalent to taking its owner's life. Consequently, the death penalty seemed a normal punishment. Social normalcy, as represented by a consensus of definitions of the situations, has thus developed out of the basic conditions imposed by the physical environment in its relation to cultural and social attitudes.

To summarize, then, we may say that *a given personal attitude in conjunction with a specific social situation defined as normal produces a characteristic social process or mode of interaction*. This principle may be expressed in the following equation:

The Personal Attitude	×	*The Social Situation*	=	*Characteristic*
[Determined by:		(Defined as normal)		*Social*
a) native endowment,		[Determined by:		*Process*
b) social experience]		a) physical environment,		
		b) reflective and reciprocal social and cultural attitudes]		

With a knowledge of the critical factors within situations involving personal attitudes and conceptions of normalcy, we may anticipate (within the limitations specified in the equation) the nature of the social processes that may emerge.

A brief examination of only one of the limitations, however, will suggest the many variables in the operation of behavioral processes. The young woman from the rural Middle West, for instance, seeking her fortune as a stenographer in New York City and settling in Greenwich

Village, confronts situations which, defined as normal in New York, run counter to the mores of her native community. The fact that in the United States there are so many diverse conceptions of normalcy provides the basis for the appearance of dissociative processes that result in social change; the encouragement of social mobility and the abundance of communication devices contribute to the rapidity of this change.

(3) SOCIAL PROCESSES AND DYNAMIC ELEMENTS

Because of structural differences present in all societies, the social processes bring about a degree of change and disorganization in every society. It is impossible for all individuals at a given time to concur in the definitions of normalcy contained within their social structure. Even in the more fully integrated social orders, such as those of nonliterate peoples, past and present, processes of disintegration have been inevitable. *Social disorganization thus exists to a degree in all societies.* The degree depends on the complexity of the social structure, the opportunities for mobility and communication, and the diversity of definitions of normalcy.

To an extent, the probability of rapid change and social disorganization may be computed statistically. Two types of data are required for such an analysis of a given society: (a) quantitative indices of mobility and (b) quantitative statements of the condition of the social order and the definitions of social situations. With this information it is possible to estimate the degree and *locus* of breakdown.[2]

Although some breakdown is inevitable in all social structures, societies differ widely as to the character of this process and the rate at which it occurs. Certain social structures appear to be relatively immune to the widespread factors of disorder that bring about rapid dissolution and change. It would be helpful if we were able in the social sciences to draw up a blueprint of the "perfect society," or one marked by the desired degree of social health. Just as the physician employs certain criteria by means of which he judges the physical condition of his patients, so we may suggest, on the basis of comparative historical and anthropological studies, the conditions of those integrated societies that present relatively negligible signs of social breakdown. The attainment of such states may not be possible or even desirable; but there are societies marked by conditions of social integration and unity that render them relatively impervious to rapid change and dissolution. From an examination of such

[2] For an illustration of suggestive techniques of this type, see Calvin F. Schmid, *Mortality Trends in the State of Minnesota* (Minneapolis, 1937), pp. 191–3; also, for a variation of such analysis, W. Lloyd Warner and Paul S. Lunt, *The Social Life of a Modern Community* (New Haven, 1941). An interesting new aspect of such analysis may likewise be found in James L. Halliday, *Psychosocial Medicine* (New York, 1948), Appendix, pp. 247–54.

social structures we may posit the existence of what has been termed the "ideal-typical" conditions of social integration, that is, a theoretical statement of what constitutes the criteria for social integration:[3]

1) Characteristic processes of social pathology exist as a matter of *degree*. They are observed in relation to the standards of social integration in all societies.
2) Even in relatively stable societies, some breakdown or dissolution is inevitable.
3) Assuming some degree of disorganization as a necessary concomitant of social change, we may note nevertheless that some societies have been marked by a relatively small degree of maladjustment. Such societies may be broadly defined as possessing social integration or social equilibrium.

(4) THE ESSENTIAL CONDITIONS FOR SOCIAL INTEGRATION

Societies and social groups that are marked by an absence of extensive tension and whose structures appear to be unified and co-ordinated are distinguished by one or all of the following characteristics:

1) The social institutions comprising the social structures are *congruent* and not in essential conflict.
2) Separate social institutions are not coerced nor are they jeopardized in their survival by the functioning of other institutions.
3) Substantial concurrence exists with respect to the group's and the individual's definitions of common and fundamental situations.

Let us examine each of these characteristics in greater detail.

1) The basic condition for social integration is implied in the first characteristic. In all cultures, certain institutions enjoy pre-eminence. This is due, in part, to the cultural and social preferences of the individuals living during a particular era. Theoretically, any institution may assume a dominant position, providing it can effectively meet the felt needs of individuals. Such dominant institutions serve an ordering function within the social structure; they determine priorities in social choice and action. Thus, the Church in medieval society served as final arbiter in the crucial matters of policy and social direction.

The question of which institutions will exercise control over the rest of society depends upon the character of the times and the social structure. For example, today, in modern American society, dominance in institutional structure is frequently a matter of economic control. Eco-

[3] Howard Becker, in H. E. Barnes, H. and F. B. Becker, *Contemporary Social Theory* (New York, 1940), p. 30.

nomic institutions, however, although playing an "ordering" role, are not capable of exerting any such coercive pressure over other spheres of social action as was the Church during the medieval period. The ordering function, therefore, may be dominant (1) by virtue of the unanimity with which its authority is recognized (as in the case of the medieval Church), thus discharging its functions as part of an organized plan of control; or 2) by virtue of its experienced and acknowledged pre-eminence in human affairs, without enjoying the popular and spontaneous support of the society (as in the case of modern economic life). It is in the case of the former type of dominance that institutions assume a congruent pattern; all institutions become subordinate to the values expressed by the dominant agency of the social order. Authority in this type of dominance is not necessarily achieved through physical coercion, but may be maintained by psychological persuasion and through the voluntary commitments of members of the social order.

In institutional dominance, such as this, the fundamental situations in the social order receive their principal meaning from the values of the dominant agency. These basic meaning-situations, dealing with all spheres of life, are co-ordinated into a common "design for living" or pattern of basic values, which we call the ethos of the society. This ethos co-ordinates the separate aspects of the social order: the values in the most fundamental and commonly defined social situations fit into a logically related pattern. The character of the structure of such integrated societies is shown below.

Diagrammatic Structure of Institutional Congruence

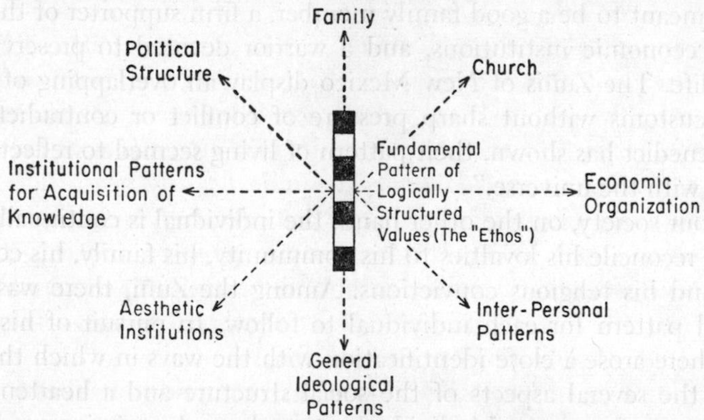

(2) Another kind of integration may be seen when separate institutions function freely irrespective of where institutional dominance lies. Although no strong unifying ethos binds such social orders together, pervasive attitudes of mutual forbearance and tolerance prevail, permit-

ting freedom of social expression just as long as the prerogatives of social choice are not hampered in neighboring institutional spheres. The continuance of such social orders depends upon the effectiveness of the mechanisms for resolving social conflict whenever it may arise. Classic democratic forms of society, the early free city-states of northern Europe, and early forms of republicanism display some of the characteristics of this type of social organization. However, such states of balance by their very nature are precarious, particularly when confronted with the rise of rapidly changing conditions and the growth of complexities within the social order.

(3) We may now consider the last condition of an integrated society—concurrence by the individual and the group about the meaning of fundamental social situations. This appears to constitute either (a) an accompanying psychological condition of the two prior forms discussed, or (b) a condition denoting a remarkable adaptive capacity of members of a society to come to terms of agreement about areas of difference. Recent history seems to make such agreement more a conjecture than an actuality; but limited historical evidence of this possibility may be seen in the willingness of men to accede to the demands of new social situations, as a means of preserving order, in the face of crisis affecting already established and integrated forms of social organization.

Examples of simple integrated societies can be found among primitive social organizations in which the routines of social behavior are well defined by the "cake of custom"; each specialized activity has implications for, and is re-enforced by, the other phases of the social order. Among the ancient Hebrews, for example, to be a religious member of the community meant to be a good family member, a firm supporter of the political and economic institutions, and a warrior devoted to preserving this way of life. The Zuñis of New Mexico display an overlapping of various sets of customs without sharp pressure of conflict or contradiction. As Ruth Benedict has shown, their pattern of living seemed to reflect "man's oneness with the universe."

In our society, on the other hand, the individual is continually called upon to reconcile his loyalties to his community, his family, his economic needs, and his religious convictions. Among the Zuñi, there was a foreordained pattern for each individual to follow. In pursuit of his private needs, there arose a close identification with the ways in which the group defined the several aspects of the social structure and a heartening correspondence of group and individual action. In such societies man "knows his place," and "there are ready-made answers to his questions and his doubts, if ever they arise." [4]

[4] Cf. Ruth Benedict, *Patterns of Culture* (New York, 1934), p. 117.

Institutional Conflict in Personal Focus

When the various institutions of a society differ in the demands they make upon the individual, the result is group antagonism and personal conflict. The individual, regarded as a *socius* (the organic center of the institutional patterns of society), becomes the battleground upon which such differences must be reconciled. Life becomes a hazardous reconciliation of the divergent claims upon the personality.

Since our lives as human beings may be fulfilled only in terms of our separate group and institutional associations, we feel personally the discord of these social aspects of our personalities. No aspect of modern social and individual life escapes these conflicts. It is seen in the college classroom where the student tries to put together into some semblance of unified order the diverse emphases of the different subject matters he is being taught; it exists in the search of countless people for a "philosophy of life," in the modern pursuit of some harmonizing principle for the separate views of science and religion, in the naturalism of modern social science, and in the conventional ethics of our social mores.

The price of institutional conflict in any society is the irresolution it imposes upon its members. Continual adjustment, readjustment, and compromise is required of both individuals and groups. Such societies are marked by their amazing capacity to improvise, if they are to survive, and their tendency to seek refuge in rationalization as an ultimate safeguard of personality.

(5) INDICES OF SOCIAL DISORGANIZATION

Discord in institutional life appears in certain unmistakable symptoms. These symptoms are to be found in the rates of problem-increase known as the indices of social disorganization. The state of social health may be determined by the frequency with which such problem-rates make their appearance. Broadly speaking, the indices of social breakdown may be classified in two categories: (1) sociological and (2) literary-ideological. Such indices are symptomatic; they resemble the symptoms observed by the physician in detecting the breakdown of the individual's physical health. Fevers and increased pulse-rates are not causes of organic disorder; they are the signs of such breakdown. Similarly, indices of social breakdown, particularly with respect to the first category, must be regarded as signs rather than causes of disequilibrium in the social order.

(1) *Sociological indices of pathology*. The sociological indices of pathology refer to the statistical rates of increase of specific problems within the social organism. If they show significant and precipitate rises,

they indicate grave problems of disequilibrium within the social order. Their graphic movements are comparable to the fever-chart which reveals to the attending physician the progress of his patient's health. Such sociological indices may be subdivided into three principal categories: (a) individual, (b) family, and (c) community. Individual indices of social disorganization are reflected in the quantitative rates describing delinquency, crime, mental pathologies, alcoholism, suicide, and the like. Family indices may be seen in such problems as those of desertion, divorce, and child neglect. Community indices are revealed in the rates of unemployment, relief, mobility, disorganized community controls, and governmental corruption.

An index of disorganization in one sphere has immediate repercussions upon, and is closely related to, the indices of breakdown in the other spheres. Delinquency might be examined as an individual index, but it may result from, and have an impact upon, the disorder within both family and community life. Conversely, unemployment as a community index has direct repercussions upon the stability of family life, which, in turn, will affect the problems of its individual members. In short, although we may logically separate these aspects of social disorganization into the three categories specified, they are actually interrelated phases of common problems of social pathology.

In scientific analysis, we are often called upon to determine the degree of social breakdown on the basis of certain manifestations. These manifestations are frequently difficult to recognize. We try, however, to find a measurable unit that is representative of the problem before us. Such a behavioral and measurable characteristic is called an operational index of the given problem.

(2) *Literary-ideological indices of social pathology*. Although the sociological indices provide concrete evidence of social pathology, we can find more indirect evidence of breakdown operating upon other levels; this evidence supplements the objective and measurable quantitative rates of problem-situations. Studies of changing intellectual drifts and social currents by the "sociologists of knowledge," such as Karl Mannheim and Maurice Halbwachs, reveal the significant literary-ideological drifts of the times. They present added testimony to the fundamental confusion in the ideologies and theoretical reflections of the individuals. They provide, furthermore, a picture of the mood and temper of the times, the so-called "feeling-tones," unlike the objective and external evidences yielded by the study of the conventional problem-rates. Although sociologists have been prone to neglect this type of evidence as largely speculative and theoretical, it nevertheless provides incisive insights into the state of man's mind during periods of disintegration. Moreover, procedures have been re-

cently worked out to put such evidence on an empirical and statistical basis.[5]

During periods of rapid change, literary and artistic expressions tend to conform to limited patterns. This is largely due to the fact that the creative artist, as an agent of social expression for his time, is unable to find a common idiom or message acceptable to all the diversified and contending groups within the social order. Consequently he must find some common ground upon which he and the public may meet. Broadly speaking, we may classify these patterns as follows: (a) themes of objective description, (b) themes of nostalgia, (c) free associational themes, (d) depictions of personal frustration, and (e) the literature of rebellion.[6]

(a) In desperation some writers resort to the objective-descriptive journalese or factual description to which the reader may impute his own subjective impressions, emotional attachments, and values.

(b) Since the writer and his audience share common memories of the past, some of which are viewed in retrospect as a kind of halcyon period, we have a spate of nostalgic writings about "father," "mother," "horse and buggy" doctors, and small town lawyers. This nostalgic mood is expressed in countless ways, in the standardized entertainment from Hollywood, the revival of interest in past history, household arts and crafts, and in such recreations as folk dances.

(c) The creative artist may describe his feelings and thoughts tumbling upon each other in a series of impressions or a "stream of consciousness," feeling that though he is describing his own emotional experiences, they reflect the universality of subjective experience.

(d) A universal characteristic of modern society being that of individual frustration, another type of literature attempts to find some common substratum of experience in descriptions of personal suffering and crisis.

(e) Finally, in the esthetic forms of social protest the author seeks a common ground with one or more of the groups that are dissatisfied with the existing social order and that are attempting to establish a new point of view or ideology. A great deal of what we call proletarian literature in modern times is of this kind. Largely designed to establish rapport with specific groups which share the convictions of the writer (possessing a common "frame of reference" or a series of common "definitions of the

[5] See, for example, Gwynne Nettler, "A Test for the Sociology of Knowledge," *American Sociological Review*, X (June, 1945), 393; also, the author's statistical examination of a twenty-year trend of rapid social change, "An Analysis of National Publication Trends and Publishers' Best Sellers As An Index of Cultural Transition," *The Journal of Educational Sociology*, XXII (Dec., 1948), 287–304.

[6] Cf. Herbert A. Bloch, "Towards the Development of a Sociology of Literary and Art Forms," *American Sociological Review*, VIII (June, 1943), 310–20.

situation"), such works center upon a limited community of interest or touch upon the frustrations common to particular groups.

Crises and Social Pathology

In appraising any state of social disorder, we must examine the critical elements within the particular situation. These elements represent both the effects of the pathological process and the dynamic stage the situation has reached, which will point to the final form the problem may take. Processes of social disorganization manifest themselves in specific forms of crisis. A knowledge of the character of the elements comprising the crisis enables us to understand the antecedent conditions which have produced it and the consequent conditions of adjustment or continuing breakdown which its several elements, in combination, may continue to sustain.

Crises represent those states of social disequilibrium, incipient or advanced, which eventually result in a continuing state of maladjustment or a state of adjustment upon a new level. Crises may be likened to those states of imbalance in nature whose elements are so precarious and unstable that a new type of configuration must take place, either through adjustment or some type of continuing disequilibrium.

Crises may be categorized as (a) *precipitate*, (b) *voluntary*, and (c) *cumulative*. For reasons to be discussed shortly, *all crises may be considered as fundamentally cumulative in form*; however, in terms of what the crisis may reveal about the resultant problem, we may recognize crises as assuming *precipitate* or *voluntary* characteristics. A *precipitate crisis*, as its name indicates, is one that appears with great suddenness and over which the individual frequently has little or no control. Such crises are of the kind called by students of jurisprudence "acts of God." Unexpected and sudden illnesses, fatalities, accidents, or disasters in nature are instances of precipitate crises. The sudden and unanticipated loss of employment or one's business might, under certain circumstances, be precipitate crises.

Voluntary crises are those sudden alterations of circumstances which the individual or group brings about through some act of volition. The decision to abandon one's family, position, or accustomed social membership, or the decision of a group of workers to go out on strike, are instances of voluntary commitment. The resolution to initiate a new policy, the consequences of which may lead to conflict and strife, may be viewed as a step toward voluntary crisis.

Cumulative crises are those situations in which, by the slow accretion of events, the social situation is thrown into a state of precarious imbalance. Thus, an individual or group may be prepared to accept certain minor calamities, but as these grow in dimension and scope, a point is reached at which the precarious state of imbalance must be resolved upon a new basis. Then there is an immediate transformation of the entire situation into a new physical form.

Basically, all crises are cumulative. Although the outward manifestations may appear to be almost wholly precipitate or voluntary, the fact remains that *not all individuals and groups break under the pressures of the same outward events*. The individual or the group that breaks under the strain must have had a long prior history which predisposed it to catastrophe. Not all individuals who face certain catastrophe in business or the loss of a beloved family member give the same manifestations of collapse or breakdown. A case in point may be seen in the suicides among stockbrokers and businessmen that followed the stock market crash in 1929. It was commonly assumed that such personal tragedies were the direct result of the loss of fortunes on the stockmarket. Yet the majority of businessmen who suffered this economic collapse survived to recoup their fortunes or to mend their personal affairs.

The deterministic character of social causation. We may gather from what has been said that precipitate and voluntary crises always occur in relation to a particular situation. The background factors comprising this situation may provide either a resiliency or an inability to cope successfully with the crisis. Consequently, the broad pattern of antecedent events, in their genetic development, must always be considered in relation to how they predispose the individual toward successful adjustment or toward failure. This broad basic pattern, cumulative in character, should be regarded as the *sufficient basis* for the creation of problem-states. Thus, disorganized families, poor schooling, bad companions, and a disorganized community may provide a *sufficient basis* for the establishment of juvenile delinquency. This, however, does not mean that *all* individuals exposed to such environments will become juvenile delinquents. The final precipitating factor, either in the shape of an unanticipated outward event or a volitional step, may be regarded as the *efficient* cause, i.e., the crucial and effective determinant which brings about the state of maladjustment.

The nature of the crisis-situation may reveal the character of the problem. The nature of the particular critical situation frequently sheds light upon the character of the resultant problem. For this reason the analysis of crisis-situations is extremely significant. Not all individuals or human groups break under the impact of the same social situations. Consequently, the nature of the crisis will frequently reveal the low threshhold of resistance in certain significant phases of the individual's or group's constitution and developmental background. It will also reveal what conditions will follow when a particular difficulty has been overcome. For example, the past history of an individual whose family is in process of disorganization may reveal a characteristic way of meeting certain difficulties through flight from his surroundings. Another individual may, in similar critical situations, feign illness. The nature of the crisis will often reveal the "chinks" in the person's "psychological armor."

(6) THE FALLACIES OF PARTICULARISTIC INTERPRETATIONS

The vastness of the network of past events and contemporary circumstances that are conjoined to produce a critical situation suggests that there are no simple explanations by means of which we may account for human difficulties in adjustment. We must be prepared to evaluate and assess each factor and its associated pattern in terms of the entire complex which produces a problem of human behavior. Nevertheless, as the history of social pathology has shown, there have been suggested repeatedly simple formulae by means of which all-encompassing explanations could be sought. Such one-sided deterministic conceptions are known as "particularistic views." The term "particularism," or "particularistic interpretation," refers to the attempt to explain a complex pattern of social behavior on the basis of one aspect of the problem. Efforts to account for delinquency and crime exclusively on the basis of bad housing, immorality in the family, low intelligence, or psychological motivations to compensate for a sense of one's deficiencies are all instances of particularistic views. Whereas each may be important as a factor, to view the situation as if each such factor was the *only* significant determinant renders these views essentially false and misleading. Nevertheless, the history of social problems is full of attempts to gain insight into social problems through particularistic interpretations.

Such cultist views have been common in the social sciences and in psychology. We have to be extremely wary of them, although each may add something to our total knowledge of the subject under examination. This has been illustrated by the history of studies in the causation of crime, beginning with the work of the celebrated classical Italian theorists, Lombroso and Ferri who, in 1876, tried to show that criminality was associated with certain physical factors. During the course of the next three decades, it became apparent that sizable percentages of the normal population, including such eminent members of society as ministers, university professors, businessmen, physicians, lawyers, and others, bore the same physical stigmata. Gradually, other views, equally one-sided, began to supplement or replace the older anthropological views of Lombroso and Ferri.

Modern criminology received its first great impetus with the classical work of Lombroso and his disciple, Ferri, who as products of their age during the latter part of the nineteenth century, attempted to lay the basis for a fully scientific crimino-biological theory of crime. . . . The basis of crime was biological and innate, like Calvinistic predestination and damnation for those marked by certain stigmata. Not only were criminals conceived as possessing different physical characteristics, prognathic jaws, low foreheads, a peculiar helix of the ear, the nasal structure and other distinguishing features, but these were conceived as outer manifestations of innate psychological characteristics. This ready and over-simplified separation of the sheep from the goats suffered not only from a lack of knowledge of modern psychological and sociological factors, but from inadequacy in evaluation of comparative data, which is so important today. . . .

The ingenuous nature of this and subsequent theories lay in the fact that their proponents sought to discover some magical touchstone, some alchemist's miracle element, by which the knotty problem of criminality might be miraculously unraveled. Hence an entire series of such particularistic views was paraded before us, each to provide the answers to our questions and each soon to be supplanted by an equally spurious doctrine. Curiosity concerning the function of intelligence and its measurement arose during the First World War. The psychologist Goring in 1913 thought he had found the answer to the sphinxian riddle of criminality in low intelligence. Hot upon the chase, Goddard came along in 1919, and through the much abused Kallikaks sought to show that the basis of crime lay in feeblemindedness. This trial balloon was soon pierced when, with a growing sophistication and temperateness, it was revealed by Herman Adler in 1918 that the intelligence scores of prisoners at Joliet Penitentiary yielded a higher average than a comparable sampling of representative groups in the United States Army. Under subsequent studies, the average intelligence of even selected officer groups suffered in comparison, a rating which apparently comes as no surprise to ex-GIs. The endocrine glands came in for their brief day, through the work of Berman, and Schlapp and Smith, heralding the day of "the new criminology," when for a brief moment we suspected that the judge's gavel might be replaced by the hypodermic syringe and the proper hormonic extract.

The discouraging quest for a unitary explanation finally led to the recent sociological emphasis upon (multiple) configurations of external (environmental) factors. We are still largely under the influence of this school of thought. . . .

At this point the circle has come full round. We have found ourselves on a theoretical merry-go-round whose spins and turns have largely been compelled by *the dominant cultural interest at the moment.*[7]

Particularistic views and the total integrated outlook. Particularistic views are essentially false because they overlook the welter of additional factors that may play a part in producing a given problem. These views, however, may contribute to our total insights into social problems by directing our attention to certain phases which may previously have been misunderstood or overlooked. Whenever particularistic views are encountered, therefore, the student should ask himself not only *to what extent* the view is wrong and inappropriate, but also, *to what degree* it adds to our understanding of the entire problem. Particularistic views frequently reflect the dominant intellectual currents of their day. Thus, the Freudian view on the causation of crime is currently enjoying a vogue. In the course of time, particularistic views frequently amend previous conceptions, both supplementing and complementing them. The gradual correction of the former biological views of Lombroso has been brought about by critical insights and modifications introduced from various other fields emphasizing different factors. Although the view of Lombroso was largely discounted by 1920, the work of Ernst Kretschmer on the study of bodily types and psychopathological traits (although also particularistic in emphasis), shed a new light on the relationship between human motivations and biological characteristics.[8] Although the modern efforts to revive the Lombrosian view have been repudiated by most sociologists, an interesting development of a related hypothesis concerning human physique and personality characteristics has been carried forward by W. H. Sheldon.[9] In conjunction with findings from other fields, these gradual enlargements of the former biological view are giving us a perspective upon the causation of crime which may eventually prove of inestimable value in the development of a unified crimino-biological theory.

SUMMARY

(1) In our analysis of the processes of interaction in their relation to social pathology, we noted that emergent social processes depended upon certain characteristic factors within the individual and the social environ-

[7] Herbert A. Bloch, "Social Change and the Delinquent Personality," in *Current Approaches to Delinquency*, 1949 Yearbook, National Probation and Parole Association (edited by Marjorie Bell), pp. 241–3.

[8] *Physique and Character* (New York and London, 1925).

[9] Cf. Ernest A. Hooton, *Crime and the Man* (Cambridge, 1939); W. H. Sheldon, *The Varieties of Human Physique* (New York, 1940). Also by W. H. Sheldon and S. S. Stevens, *The Varieties of Temperament* (New York, 1942) and by Sheldon, E. M. Hartl, and E. McDermott, *Varieties of Delinquent Youth* (New York, 1949). More recently, Sheldon and Eleanor Glueck have appraised constitutional factors in their *Unraveling Juvenile Delinquency* (New York, 1950), Chap. XV.

ment. It was noted that a given social process (i.e., accommodation, assimilation, competition, conflict, etc.) depended upon (a) the personal attitude, in conjunction with (b) a specific social situation defined as normal by a given group, giving rise to the "social process equation." (2) Factors in the determination of the personal attitude were found to be (a) the native endowment of the individual and (b) the character of his past social experience. Factors that determine the normalcy of a given social situation reflected (a) its physical environment and (b) the social and cultural attitudes generated by social groups in relation to this environment. (3) The continual operation of the social processes in all societies indicates that a certain degree of social breakdown is inescapable among all social groups. *Social pathology, thus, is largely a matter of degree.* (4) There are, nevertheless, states of relatively high social integration and equilibrium whose primary criteria are: (a) congruence of the incorporated social institutions; (b) the relative absence of coercion and the absence of threats to the functioning of individual institutions by dominant institutions or social agencies; and (c) substantial concurrence by the group and the individual in the definitions of basic social situations. (5) The increase of social disorganization manifests itself in various types of symptomatic forms or indices. Such indices may be categorized as (a) sociological, and (b) literary-ideological. Sociological indices may be seen in the statistical rates denoting the incidence of the commonly defined types of social problems. As such, they may be sub-divided into the following major classifications: (a) individual, (b) family, and (c) community. All such categories are interrelated. Literary-ideological indices afford some insight into the underlying mood, temper, and emotions of the times, and fall into the following patterns: (a) objective-descriptive, (b) nostalgic, (c) free-associational, (d) frustration, and (e) protest. Processes of social pathology eventuate in the following types of crisis-situations: (a) precipitate, (b) voluntary, and (c) cumulative. Fundamentally, however, all crises are *cumulative* in character, regardless of their outward forms, and clearly express deterministic, cause-and-effect relationships in all social processes leading to social breakdown. (6) The complex nature of the deterministic, causal chain disallows the possibility of particularistic interpretation, i.e., the attempt to appraise causal conditions in terms of single, selective aspects of the given problem.

CHAPTER FIVE

PERSONALITY AND THE CHANGING SOCIAL PROCESS

(1) THE MEANING OF PERSONALITY AND THE INDIVIDUAL LIFE-ORGANIZATION

IN ANALYZING the processes of social disorganization we have seen that the individual encounters certain situations through the medium of his personal attitudes and other personality attributes. Such attitudes and other personality characteristics, however, are not isolated and discrete aspects of his personality. The human being in his social behavior comprises a *totality* which brings together the several specialized phases of his behavior into some form of coherent structure or design. Any single attitude which the individual personality displays, reflects, to a certain degree, the entire structural composition of all the diverse aspects and phases which, in their combined form, constitute the workings of his personality. Political convictions, racial antipathies, and other social preferences are usually linked together into a complex pattern of behavior which is descriptive of the personality as a whole.

The psychologist is primarily concerned with the biological mechanisms of behavior and the way in which they have been shaped to give meaningful expression to the individual's pattern of response. He deals with such entities as perception, motivation, concept formation, and the like. The sociologist, on the other hand, is fundamentally interested in the way in which the social conditions of the individual's environment have shaped his behavior to define for him his social statuses and roles, and the effects which such statuses and roles may have upon the social structure. Dealing with the personality in this way necessitates the development of a *sociological theory or view of personality*, rather than a strictly biological or psychological view, although at many points the two conceptions will necessarily overlap. Recently, a great many efforts have been made to devise such a purely sociological conception.[1] Attempts to treat

[1] Among the several attempts which have been made to define the sociological basis of personality have been the well-nigh classical works of Charles H. Cooley, *Human Nature and the Social Order* (New York, 1922); G. H. Mead's collected papers appearing in *Mind, Self and Society*, edited by Charles W. Morris (Chicago, 1934);

personality on the psychological level *as a functioning whole* have been relatively belated. Recent efforts in this direction by Gordon Allport, Gardiner Murphy, Hadley Cantril, and Muzafer Sherif indicate the inescapable necessity of some amalgamation with the social field.[2]

To the sociologist, the meaning of personality must be defined in terms of its structural organization and the way in which this structure is related to the operating mechanisms of society. By personality we refer to the way in which the individual's habits, mental traits, attitudes, values, emotional characteristics, feeling tones, and the remainder of his individualized responses to the social processes *are organized into a unified whole to impart consistency to the behavior-reactions of the individual.* The key words in this definition are the concepts of "organization" and "consistency." We mean by organization the arrangement of the several parts of the personality into a unified whole. The concept of consistency, however, raises some problems of a different order. According to our view, each individual, on the basis of his rearing and constitution, has developed certain characteristic patterns of response that differentiate him from other individuals.[3]

Such consistent patterns of response are not always easy to ascertain. Moreover, even when they are recognized it is sometimes extremely difficult to formulate the basis and the reasons for such patterns of consistency. Nevertheless, it is possible to detect in our behavior and the behavior of others certain degrees of persistence in trait-behavior as manifested in our reactions to certain types of problems and events. The Viennese psychologist, Alfred Adler, founder of the school of individual psychology, used to refer to such consistent, distinctive patterns in the life-history of the individual as his "style of life."

and numerous works of John Dewey, primarily his *Human Nature and Conduct* (New York, 1922). More recent efforts to formulate such a conception are marked by their association with psychiatric and psychoanalytical views. Some of the more notable of these are Ralph Linton, *The Cultural Background of Personality* (New York, 1945); Abram Kardiner and Ralph Linton, *The Individual and His Society* (New York, 1939); Abram Kardiner *et al.*, *The Psychological Frontiers of Society* (New York, 1945); Karen Horney, *The Neurotic Personality of Our Time* (New York, 1937); and *New Ways in Psychoanalysis* (New York, 1939); and Clyde Kluckhohn and H. A. Murray, eds., *Personality in Nature, Society, and Culture* (New York, 1948).

[2] See Allport, *Personality: A Psychological Interpretation* (New York, 1937); Sherif and Cantril, *The Psychology of Ego-Involvements* (New York, 1947); and Murphy, *Personality, A Biosocial Approach to Origins and Structure* (New York, 1948).

[3] The emphasis upon self-consistency, which is the central theme in our sociological conception of personality, has only recently been recognized by sociologists. See Herbert A. Bloch, "The Social Individual as a Primary Datum in Sociology," *American Sociologocal Review*, VIII (Oct., 1943), 499–512. A highly effective and similar treatment of the same view may be found in Prescott Lecky, *Self-Consistency: A Theory of Personality* (New York, 1945), which has been incorporated by Kingsley Davis in his *Human Society* (New York, 1949). See particularly Chap. 9, and especially pp. 238–41, of this last volume.

This does *not* mean that everything the individual will do may be predicted and its relationship to the broad centralizing principle of consistency immediately perceived and established. Nor does it mean that the individual is incapable of developing other forms of behavior, spontaneous and independent, which do not seem to fit into the predominant conception of consistency. Least of all does it mean that the individual is foreordained by some mystical principle of predestination to walk forever upon the narrow and constricting pathway of his own peculiar type of consistency. It means simply that individuals *do* display remarkable persistence in the maintenance of certain behavior-forms and that these consistencies are bound into the central, organized structure of each personality.

Although "the doctors may wrangle," the man on the street is very quick to recognize consistencies in others. He may demur at our technical jargon but nevertheless admit freely that human beings seem to react in certain predictable ways. Much human behavior is predicated upon expectations as to how other persons will react. If the pattern of our behavior-responses differed greatly from day to day, it would be virtually impossible to achieve an ordered society. If we did not recognize the conditions under which our employer becomes annoyed and if we were incapable of detecting his annoyance, our relations with him would be made difficult indeed. In short, a fundamental attribute of human behavior is based upon the consistency we expect from others and the consistencies which we, in turn, display towards them. The determination of the principle underlying such consistencies is difficult. All we can assert, at this point, is that such consistencies exist and are apparent at every turn of ordinary human existence.

Another fact we may note is that the *mode* of consistency for different individuals varies widely under different circumstances. Moreover, certain personalities display with more candor, emphasis, and color their more consistent traits. Such individuals are easily classified in the catalog of our frequently fallacious common-sense judgments. They are readily reacted to in terms of our expectancies of what they may or may not do under given conditions. Thus, we discern the type of the "chronic worrier," the organizer, the pollyanna, the insouciant individual, and so on. These caricatured "types" are indicated as evidence of the remarkable consistencies we see and deal with in our every-day lives. That there are more subtle individuals whose elusive qualities make it much more difficult for us to denominate their consistencies is, of course, a matter of ready knowledge. Yet, repeated contact with such individuals frequently reveals outstanding characteristics of an enduring nature. It might be possible to establish a category of consistencies which would be called "consistent inconsistencies."

Personality Formation and the Social Processes

The conditions under which the personality grows and develops are always related to the social processes, which shape and fashion the human personality from birth onwards. We have already noted that social interaction as a continual process consists of *the reciprocal interplay of personalities within a given social environment.* This reciprocal interplay of personalities defining human behavior is always distinguished by the following characteristics:

(1) the unique histories of the personalities involved;
(2) the reciprocal effects upon personalities which this interaction produces;
(3) the expectancies which each interactive situation evokes;
(4) the characteristic forms which arise from specific interactive processes.

We may elaborate these characteristics as follows:

(1) Each individual trails his own "special cloud of glory and disrepute behind him." The reactive-tendencies he develops will depend upon his singular biological inheritances and the particular set of social conditions that have patterned his social behavior.

(2) Moreover, the interactive process to which the individual has been exposed since birth is dynamic in an unusual sense. This dynamic element lies in the fact that individuals, while responding to the conditions that affect them, are likewise stimulating others at the same time. To this extent, human behavior is *reciprocal. Every response we make as reacting individuals is also a stimulus to others.* The social processes, thus, enfold our behavior into recognizable moulds or forms. The situation can be likened to a tennis match in which the strokes of the players are mutually conditioned by each other's mode of service, volley, and return. One's play is "entrapped" or "grooved" by the nature of the play of the opponent. Thus, if his opponent gives him a high service towards the far side of the opposite court, he is forced to employ his backhand which, if successful, will condition the counter-stroke the opponent returns.

(3) Social interaction, however, is also marked by anticipations and expectancies. Whatever we do in response to others is based upon our *expectancies* of how they will react towards us. The consistencies, which have recently been described, cause us to develop expectancies of behavior from others upon which the regularized patterns of social life are based. If we think carefully about this for a moment, we will recognize that in all human intercourse our behavior toward others is guided by an expectancy of what they will do or say, or fail to do or say, under certain circumstances. Moreover, because we know how others may react toward

us in relation to our expectancies concerning their behavior, in approaching them we already have some conception of how we will respond when they have fulfilled our expectancy.

(4) The forms of interaction which shape our lives fall into well-established categories. We have already classified them into the conventional forms of accommodation, assimilation, competition, and conflict, which may be broken down into numerous sub-categories representative of particular aspects and phases of such behavior-forms.

(2) PRIMARY COMPONENTS OF PERSONALITY FORMATION IN THE SOCIAL STRUCTURE

If social interaction is an integral part of all personality development, it is important to recognize at the outset the fundamental psychological and cultural conditions that create it. A distinctive type of human personality always constitutes *one* phase of the social process equation. What, then, are the predominant factors that have played a part in determining the unique function that such a personality will exercise in the development of the social structure and its dynamic social processes?

The human personality is created out of three sets of conditions: (1) biological-constitutional factors of the individual's inheritance; (2) the direct behavioral relations he has had with others in the shaping of his career—what Kimball Young has called the "personal-social" factors; and (3) the cultural factors that exist all about him and define his objectives, as well as the modes of achieving them. The first and third conditions are readily apparent, but the second may not be grasped as readily. By the *personal-social* factors we mean the interpersonal factors, the direct ways in which the individual has been shaped and moulded by those with whom he has come into close, primary contact, such as his parents, teachers, and associates. The term refers to what Charles Horton Cooley has called the *primary relations,* that is, those intimate "face to face" contacts that exert influence upon the personality. We will shortly consider each of these sets of conditioning factors in their effects upon the developing social personality. We will concentrate first upon the cultural conditions that define and limit the individual's psychological growth, next focusing upon the manner in which the culture is mediated by the individual's family, and finally indicating how the biological determinants of the individual are translated into meaningful forms of social behavior by the working of the social and cultural processes.

The External Conditions Under Which Interaction Operates

The conditions imposed by culture. The culture of each society, as we have learned, consists of its values, beliefs, theories, ideological points of view, and its intellectual expressions, as well as the material conditions required for their implementation and attainment. However, in its simplest terms, human culture may be reduced to certain broad *proscriptions* and *prescriptions*. Reduced to its fundamentals, human culture tells us (a) *what we shall want* and (b) *what we shall not want*. The child in society soon learns which objectives he should desire and which he should avoid. Culture tells us (a) how we should go about attaining these desired end-objects and at the same time indicates to us (b) in what ways we should *not* proceed. Implicit in every prescription is its negative proscription. Thus, wealth may be obtained by assuming certain acceptable employments and positions, saving income, not being profligate in recreations, "marrying the boss's daughter," and learning to invest wisely. Conversely, most individuals are soon taught that regardless of the coveted award, they must not cheat, steal, or behave in any other "immoral" or anti-social manner.

Thus, in its immediate effects upon the individual, particularly in the case of the young child, culture consists of various admonitions and reproofs; they are manifested in encouragement and incitement, goadings and cajolings, physical punishment and praise, rewards and rejections, and discouragements and reproofs, which appear in countless guises in the social order. By means of such behavioral forms, the individual is restrained in the free exercise of his behavior should it be other than what is prescribed or approved.

Modes and techniques of imposing restraints and encouragements. The imposition of desired cultural values upon others is ordinarily achieved through the following forms: (a) physical coercion, (b) verbal admonishment or encouragement, (c) rewards, actual or potential, and (d) other forms of approval and disapproval. In all societies there exist techniques for imposing enjoinders and injunctions. These techniques vary considerably. Among the Manus in the South Pacific, physical punishment is rarely administered to a child; among the people of Dobu, the chief technique for gaining conformity is by subjecting the child to painful ridicule and embarrassment. In the last analysis, the young child, growing up in "a world he never made," understands the implications and the objectified meanings of the culture which is moulding him only in terms of such personal restraints and contacts.

(3) THE UNIQUE FUNCTION OF THE FAMILY IN MEDIATING THE CULTURE

In the psychogenetic development of every child, the family provides the emotional atmosphere which plays a basic and lasting role in the child's learning of cultural values. Thus, the basic cultural values "from without" are mediated or "refracted" through the individual personalities comprising his immediate circle. A sociological principle in child development emerges which is similar to the principle of refraction of light in physics. The eventual imprint of a given cultural value upon the child will depend upon two sets of factors:

(a) The personality characteristics of the bearer of the cultural value (in the case of the child, the bearer is likely to be the parent or other members of the family or those immediately concerned with his upbringing);

(b) The attitude toward the given cultural value *entertained by these same human agents.*

Institutional values are thus brought to the child only through the actions of given persons who have played a part in his development. For example, the conception which the child may receive as to religious observance will depend upon the attitude that the parent has towards the church, and secondly, upon the way in which he has brought this value to bear upon the child's life. An illustration of this second point may be shown in the case of two parents who presumably enjoy identical attitudes about religious observance. In the case of the first parent, an "enlightened individual," the child is taught to accept this value on the basis of patient

The Refraction of Cultural Values Through the Mediating Influence of the Family

(*Note:* The hatched lines of the inner circle represent the individual personalities of parents and others in the field of the child's primary relations, who "filter" the cultural values from without.)

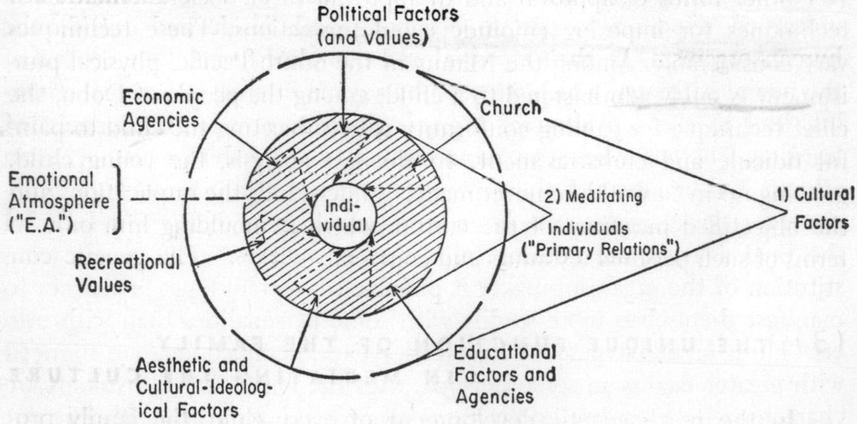

1) *Outer Circle:* Cultural factors, agencies, and institutions.
2) *Inner Circle:* Mediating personalities of family-members and others with whom the individual has "controlling" primary relations.

and sympathetic understanding and discipline. In the case of the second child, the technique employed to impress the value is one of harsh and stern discipline. The effects in the life of each of these children can be seen in the differing "emotional atmospheres" which these distinctive approaches have produced, *even though the desired objectives have been the same.* The individual personalities of the parents, teachers, relatives, and associates serve as "filters" through which the cultural values are strained. The position of the family in the stratified structure of society will determine to a considerable degree the kind of impact which the cultural values will have upon the child. This principle of "refraction of the cultural value" and the emotional atmosphere it creates may be illustrated by the diagram on page 90. To the child, a cultural value manifests itself only through the embodied form of a personality who reacts to him in certain ways. All cultural values come to the child in a form which is to a certain degree distorted.

Biological-Constitutional Factors Contributing to Personality Growth

The behavior patterns of the human agents responding to the child, and the cultural determinants that motivate their behavior, constitute a set of variable conditions contributing to the development and growth of his personality. The other "variables" in the human equation of personal growth arise from his biological endowment. These biological factors may be summarized under the following principal headings: (a) simple organic reflex-activities, (b) organic drives, (c) inborn temperamental predispositions, and (d) the intellectual capacities.

(a) The simple organic reflex-activities, the primary "atomic elements" of the physiological psychologist, consist of those automatic and unlearned responses to stimuli occurring both inside and outside the human organism. In their essential and complete forms, they consist of the neural pathways, which, aroused by a given internal or external stimulus, lead to the activation of a given gland or muscle. The process of learning, whether it be a classroom exercise, a new habit or custom, or an athletic skill, consists of the linking together of a number of such component reflex-elements into large structured arcs of behavior which, in the final analysis, are nothing but "chained reflexes." The genetic constitution of the organism makes it possible for certain types of reflexes to manifest themselves more readily with some personalities than with others. Thus, certain types of reinforced synaptic connections are induced with greater facility in some persons, with the result that individuals are characterized by diverse bodily capacities for the acquisition of different kinds of learning. The difficulty encountered in understanding the reflex stems from the fact that any given behavioral activity consists of a number of interrelated component "reflexes" that are linked into a vast and intricate chain.

(b) The organic drives are the broad instinctual and motivational patterns of human behavior. They express themselves in the powerful vital urges, impelling the internal forces of hunger, thirst, protective devices, and sexual drives, which incite the organism to activity. Fundamentally, such organic drives are complex arrangements of innumerable reflex components which operate upon broad behavioral tracts and manifest themselves in external activity. The hungry infant expresses his need by the diffuse and random actions of crying, screaming, and flailing of the limbs. Only later, through a process of conditioning, does this diffuse and random instinctual activity become "goal-directed," i.e., moving to those specific and recognizable elements within the environment that may ameliorate the "internal imbalance" which the individual experiences. The sources of our organic drives are found in those internal "tension states" of disequilibrium created by the setting up of bodily cravings whenever the vegetative functioning of the organism is disturbed.[4] Such tension-states vary in their intensity from individual to individual. Their function is to enable the organism to survive as a *biological mechanism.* As such, they are to be envisaged primarily as (a) *appetitive* and (b) *defensive or protective* in nature. On the organic level, it is difficult to conceive of "social instincts." Rather, *the early social propensities of the child are developed out of his dependencies upon the adults about him.*

(c) All individuals, infant as well as adult, appear to be marked by temperamental differences. When we speak of the "temperamental disposition" of the individual we are referring to the characteristic emotional moods which are associated with his behavior in the expression of his various wants and drives. Thus, some infants in a nursery will express hunger by sporadic wailing and thrashing about, some by continual crying, and others by rigidity and holding of the breath. Such temperamental traits, manifesting themselves shortly after birth, are conditioned by the endocrine organization of the human organism. Endocrine research, although showing remarkable progress during the last three decades, has still far to go in the study of the precise effects which the total endocrine functioning of the organism exercises upon the development of personality. However, the hyperactivity of certain glands, such as the suprarenals, can be shown to affect the behavior of children shortly after birth. It is interesting to note that endocrine functioning may be modified not only by organic measures, such as the administration of counteractive hormonic extracts, but by social patterning and behavior conditioning as

[4] Cf. C. S. Sherrington, *The Integrative Action of the Nervous System* (New York, 1906); also, W. B. Cannon, *Bodily Changes in Pain, Hunger, Fear and Rage* (New York, 1929).

well. Recent evidence seems to point rather conclusively to the fact that the state of endocrine balance of the human organism may be modified by the acquisition of new behavior processes and by exposure to altered social environments.[5]

(d) Inherent also within the human organism are certain intellectual capacities. These intellectual capacities depend upon the inherited facility with which certain neuro-muscular tracts may be innervated, and their functioning into ever widening tracts upon which our learned skills are based. Successful learning, a highly complex process, depends upon whether or not the organism possesses the physiological components required, whether the organism facilitates the co-ordination of such components into broader patterns, and finally, whether the organism is confronted with situations in the environment which will evoke the development of such integrated patterns. It is difficult at this stage to determine what are the precise physiological equivalents for the various aspects of the learning process. Psychologists such as L. L. Thurstone and others have attempted to study this question by the statistical method which is called "multiple factor analysis."[6] Thus far, they have shown that separate intellectual skills contain a great many common elements, such as memorative capacity, verbal capacity, enumerative capacity, and the like. The neurological complexes upon which these components are based have not been fully ascertained. The complexity of the physiological basis of learning can be seen in the estimate made by the physiologist Herrick that there are 9,200,000,000 neural terminals in the brain alone, which enter into innumerable combinations and permutations in conjunction with the automatic and muscular phases of the organic structure.[7]

There is an infinite variety of differences in the backgrounds which support the acquisition of certain skills. For the highly specialized and organized learning which is carried on in the present day, individuals must have the requisite physiological equipment and the organic propensity which directs their organization into a confluent whole. In addition, the environment must place before the individual those particular situations that elicit such learning capacities. The brain of an Einstein

[5] This entire question of the relationship between temperamental norms in society and the fundamental biological constitution is still an extremely significant area as yet unexplored. Although Margaret Mead, Ruth Benedict, Ruth Bunzel, Ralph Linton, Abram Kardiner, and others have sought to explain the basis for such characteristic social differences in temperament, the problem remains largely unsolved. Whether the treachery, deceit, and "paranoia" of the Dobuans and the Alorese, for example, are due to the cultural process or biologic racial differences is still an open question. Upon the social level, do given social and cultural conditions tend to induce hyperactivity of the endocrines, or does a certain prevalent endocrine condition lay the basis for characteristic social-emotional patterns?

[6] L. L. Thurstone, *The Vectors of the Mind* (Chicago, 1935).

[7] *Brains of Rats and Men* (Chicago, 1926).

would be wasted among the Hottentots since there is nothing in their culture to evoke such a capacity as his. Similarly, a potential poet among the share-croppers in the South may never learn to express himself because the unpermissive environment fails to elicit his abilities.

The totality of organic response. Although, for convenience, we have classified these biological traits into separate categories, they represent phases of unified organic activity. High intellectual ability, for example, is attained or impaired through its connections with the individual's other organic attributes. Thus, unless a high intellectual endowment, coupled with the environmental possibility of releasing it, is correlated with strong emotional drives to attain certain objectives, the potentialities of the organism may never be realized. Conversely, an individual possessing an intense organic drive toward success, actuated in part by his peculiar glandular predisposition, may yet founder because of intellectual limitations.

(4) THE EARLY ACCIDENTAL ADJUSTMENTS OF THE YOUNG CHILD

Despite the limitations that the physical constitution imposes upon the development of the human personality, the child is born into the world as a highly plastic organism or "sensorium." It may be helpful to review some of these conditions of child development in order to note the "accidental" ways in which the early functions of the human personality are achieved.

The child is born into a human society which possesses a culture. The adults around him, largely his immediate family, have already been, and are still being, shaped by the cultural forces of society. Moreover, their personalities are distinguished by certain peculiarities of temperament, disposition, and habit. The child is the "plastic sensory stuff" upon which these diverse forces will play. For the first few months of the child's life, his experiences are limited to what William James has so aptly described as the "big, buzzing, booming confusion" around him. All the child experiences at this stage are sensations of varying intensity following precipitately one after the other. Awareness, as we know it, does not exist for the young child. Awareness denotes the recognition of meaningful experiences and events in the environment and the capacity to respond to them. The infant during this early period is not even aware of the parts of his body. All he "knows," if we can use this term, is that sensations arise in his "feeling-zones" which automatically produce certain types of consequent behavior in the form of crying, wailing, whimpering, flailing about, or repose.

Endowed with a temperament, instinctual patterns, and an intellectual capacity peculiar to himself alone, the child achieves early adjustments to his environment in accordance with the ways in which the early outgoing releases of his biological tensions are responded to by the human "culture-bearers" in his environment. In the earliest stages of his development, cultural values are *expressed* differently by the human agents, and consequently, different individuals "fix" differing adjustment-techniques. Compare, for example, the behavior of the peasant mother who places her child to the breast whenever he cries and the "modern" mother who feeds her child according to rigid schedule. By virtue of the early fixing of routines in regard to child feeding, training, physical care, and sphincter control, the child experiences sensations of expectancy indicative of the tensions in his organism. In the case of the first child, crying immediately produces a highly passive and receptive state linked with tactual and gastronomic sensations and readily disposed to a cessation of crying, while in the case of the second child, such crying-activity denotes different anticipatory sensations leading to wholly different consequences.[8] Life for the very young child consists of a myriad of such accidental adjustments which, *unknown to him*, represent cultural values from the outside.

The accidental ways in which adjustments are made are conditioned by the peculiarities of the individuals who care for the child and by the cultural requirements which lay down the patterns to be followed. The cultural patterns, it should be observed, vary among social groups and the stratified levels of society. There is variation as well with respect to the latitude permitted the parent in exercising certain prerogatives. Thus, in our society, attitudes towards feeding habits and the development of sphincter control vary widely according to such factors as educational level and economic status. In illustration of inter-cultural variations, we may compare our scrupulous training of the child in the control of his bodily eliminations with the more permissive practice of the Chinese. Our attitudes towards this phase of the child's development are conditioned by our cultural conceptions of bodily hygiene and by such traditional injunctions as "cleanliness is next to godliness." Among the Chinese, who are not encumbered with compulsive attitudes towards cleanliness, toilet-training may be casual and mild.[9]

The cultural standards which vary from group to group are, without exception, of primary significance in the development of personality. The adjustment that the child makes in accordance with the characteristics of

[8] See, for example, Margaret Mead's pointed remarks in respect to the *Arapesh* in her *Male and Female* (New York, 1949), pp. 65–9.

[9] It is interesting to note in this respect that the Chinese garment for men, women, and children alike consists of loose trousers, separated in the crotch. This permits the young child to perform his bodily functions without interference from his elders.

his culture is exemplified in Kardiner's illustration of child-rearing practices among the Alorese of the Netherlands East Indies.[10] (Note how the cultural conditions, implied in the economic necessities and mode of family organization, determine the way in which the child's early adjustments are "fixed.")

After the descent from the house, breast feeding is supplemented by vegetable gruels and premasticated banana. The child is passed about from hand to hand. The young men seem more interested in the baby than the women; they have more time. The contacts of the child vary according to the location of the house. Fondling consists of rocking, joggling, mouthing or mock biting, but not kissing.

Before two weeks are over, the mother returns to work in the fields, for she is responsible for the vegetable crops, the mainstay of diet. She does not take the infant with her, but leaves him in the care of the father, older sibling, or grandmother. If birth takes place during the dry season, the mother has a chance to devote more time to the infant. But, for the greater part, the infant is fed by a surrogate, the regularity of the breast is interrupted, and premasticated food or gruel—from different people—is a poor substitute, judging from the fact that infants often spew this food out. When a man holds a child he is disturbed to find the child search for his breast. Sometimes other nursing mothers feed the baby, but there are no arrangements to make such practice regular or dependable.

Before he learns to walk, the child half-sits and cries in a shawl slung over one shoulder of his guardian. Generally a baby is not left alone to cry, or left on the ground to be annoyed by pigs, dogs, pig lice, etc. Late in the afternoon the mother returns and takes the child to feed and fondle. At this time the child suckles whenever restless. Women do not seem to enjoy breast feeding. At night the infant shares the mother's mat until he can crawl about, and continues to share the parental mat even after intercourse is resumed. This resumption takes place at a variable time, depending on the sexual opportunities of the husband. Most feminine complaints are about the haste of resumption, which makes more work for the woman.

The mother masturbates the child to keep him quiet, and the siblings do the same when they are his guardians. No effort is made to teach the child to talk. Sphincter control is disregarded in the pre-walking stage. Walking is not urged or encouraged; crawling is possible only when the child is not being carried about. They learn

[10] Kardiner, *The Psychological Frontiers of Society*, drawn from materials taken from *The People of Alor* by Cora Dubois (Minneapolis, 1944).

to stand erect by pulling themselves up on the leg of an adult. Anyone can aid in these unsystematic attempts.

As the toddler grows more sure-footed the carrying shawl loses importance except for long trips. It is discarded after the child is three. Then the child spends the day playing near the house under the casual supervision of an older sibling or an aged adult. Under these conditions, the mother being absent from eight in the morning until five in the afternoon, feeding is sporadic. During the day the child shifts for himself. He gets scraps from older children.

Feeding frustrations increase as the child grows. Weaning may be hastened by the mother's second pregnancy. She weans the child by pushing him away or slapping him. The mother will sometimes deliberately stimulate jealousy in a child by taking another infant to feed. Children often try to make sucking substitutes out of other things, such as toy balloons. But in spite of these feeding troubles, there is not much finger sucking, not more than in our society. Parents do not interfere, but rather encourage thumb sucking to keep the child quiet. In connection with this a teasing game is made of the finger sucking, whereby desire for food is stimulated, but not satisfied.

Toilet training is gradual; the mother takes the child to the privy and watches his performance. He is taught to use leaves for wiping but all are remiss in this, and the result is considerable irritation. If the child is first taken to the privy at nineteen months, he can be continent within two months. Between three and five they are all continent. No play with feces was observed. Constipation is uncommon.

Bladder control is taught later than anal control. Children from three to five urinate openly and adults treat it casually. There is little effort to control flatus. Bathing is extremely painful because of the cold water and the caustic medicines used on the skin ulcers. Childhood tantrums are most often connected with bathing, and these tantrums are often violent and long.

Sexual activities of childhood are confined to masturbation, started by the parents to quiet the child and continued by the child himself. This goes on freely and publicly. The child has the opportunity of observing parental coitus, and conversation about sex is not toned down in the presence of children. By the age of five children seem to know about intercourse and birth.

Children's sleep is much disturbed; a good deal of activity goes on at night, dancing, wandering in the village, narrating dreams and eating. Many of the dances last all night at which children of five are often present. Children take cat naps when they can, on the verandah or leaning against an adult. In other words, the sleep and rest of the child is a matter of small concern to parents.

Cries of distress are usually addressed to the mother. The word for "give" is early learned, and by five children have a good collection of imprecations, such as "Evil spirit, may you have smallpox." In angry moods the children are talkative, though generally they are shy and silent. There is no formal speech training, but ridicule is used as a corrective.

Children are sent on errands very early, and are sent off in a peremptory manner. There is no permissive, encouraging, nor even deliberate training; they learn by restrictive injunctions, shame, ridicule, and intimidation. They are not taught many avoidances or taboos. A boy often has his penis tugged, or fingers and arrows poked into his distended abdomen; if the child is irritated by this, he is greeted by cries: "Hit him. Kill him." The children do not have open fights, but slyly pinch and run.[11]

THE PERSISTENCE OF CERTAIN EARLY ADJUSTMENT-TECHNIQUES

Because of the intense and fundamental quality of the organic tension-states and imbalances which motivate the child to react in random and undirected ways, those reactions to the environment that succeed in appeasing his cravings are likely to become fixed and patterned. Sealed in with the child's early experiences are the ways in which he managed to obtain relief. As Gesell and Ilg have shown, the patterns of response that are fixed for children within our culture depend upon the culturally-determined routines we have acquired in handling children of different ages and also upon our powers to recognize the maturational levels of the organism appropriate for the fixing of certain habits.[12]

Certainly, the sensitive nature of the organism during the early period of the "feeling-states" will tend to "fix" patterns of neuro-muscular response in accordance with the satisfactions which the child has thereby obtained. As early as the first eighteen months of the child's life, significant basic habit-patterns have been laid down, largely as automatic forms of responding behavior. Only through the verbal ability he begins to develop thereafter does the child attain some awareness of himself and the social environment in which he functions. But by that time he has already embodied within himself many of the cultural values that have directed his growth and the *individuated habit-patterns* that reflect his

[11] Kardiner, *The Psychological Frontiers of Society*, pp. 130–3. Reprinted by permission of the Columbia University Press.

[12] Cf. *Infant and Child in the Culture of Today* (New York, 1943); and *The Child from Five to Ten* (New York, 1946).

reactions to his environment. As George H. Mead showed some years ago, it is through the spoken symbol that the child becomes aware of himself and the meaning of his behavior in relation to others. The mechanisms of this process are extremely complex and need not detain us here.[13]

The persistence of these early adjusted habit-techniques of the child is due primarily to (1) *the routine character of responses made by adults to young children* and (2) the *qualitative differences* in the responding behavior of young children. In his early contacts with the social world around him, the child is limited to the parent and later on to a few other intimate associates. These figures develop characteristic techniques of handling, feeding, and fondling the child, which reflect their own individuated attitudes and habit-patterns and the cultural standards which are their basis. Furthermore, the qualitative differences of the child's responses, reflecting different kinds of inner urgency and tension, will determine the degree to which certain routine handlings become fixed within his personality system. Such basic patterns of response-tendencies appear to continue as a "core" of the child's developing personality. There is nothing mystical or irrevocably deterministic in this conception. These early behavior-tendencies are essentially characteristic patterns of response which impart a "core of consistency" to the personality of the individual. Such primary, recognizable *determining* patterns appear to be laid down between the second and sixth years. The process takes place during these years because it is then that the child first becomes a verbalizing and self-initiating agent. It is during this period that his first limited freedoms are allowed and that he is exposed to a wider range of experience in the socializing process than that afforded by the personality of the mother.[14]

The child's activities have already been partially organized during the earlier amorphous stage of his prior adjustment- and feeling-states. These characteristic patterns of response are in no way fixed or unchangeable. They are primarily what the German psychologists have referred to as "determinierende Tendenzen," that is, *broad determining tendencies*. This "core of personality," expressed through these broad determining tendencies, we may call the *psychogenetic pattern* of the individual or, in its abbreviated form, the p.g.p.[15]

[13] See *Mind, Self and Society* (Chicago, 1934). An original statement of this view is contained in "A Behavioristic Account of the Significant Symbol," *Journal of Philosophy*, XIX (1922), 157–63. For an intensive analysis, see Herbert A. Bloch, *The Concept of our Changing Loyalties* (New York, 1934), pp. 197–212.

[14] See Gesell and Ilg, *Infant and Child in the Culture of Today*.

[15] It may be helpful at this point to clarify a disagreement among psychologists which has arisen concerning this view. Actually, within its broad outlines, the view of the p.g.p. does not differ radically from the dynamic conception of personality which Gordon W. Allport advances in his *Personality: A Psychological Interpretation* (New York, 1937). One point of contention which is raised, however, concerns the use of

THE STRUCTURE OF THE P.G.P.

The *psychogenetic pattern* of the personality consists of the habitual response-tendencies organized into a unified framework by means of which the basic needs and satisfactions of the personality are pursued and satisfied. This organized framework of the personality is characterized by a series of *needs* and by a series of *techniques* by which these needs have come to be served or satisfied. We refer to these component aspects of the p.g.p. as (1) the *need-phase* and (2) the *functional-phase*.

(1) *The need-phase of the p.g.p.* The needs of the *psychogenetic pattern* vary in character and degree from person to person. Although all human beings have in common certain organic needs, such as hunger and thirst, these needs have become associated with related ancillary ones. The needs of the psychogenetic structure are not the raw, biological needs of survival, but rather *derived* needs that are related to deeply implanted personality attributes. *Thus, they represent the organic needs that have become modified and channelized through the conditions of response set up by the environing adults.* Illustrations of this may be seen in the traits of possessiveness, indifference towards others, preoccupation with one's own problems, identification with others, and many other traits that have become identified with certain types of personalities. In view of the fact that individual behavior may be strongly motivated by the need incorporated within such traits, such distinctive attributes may be regarded as fundamental components of the "need-phase" of the personality. For the individual who has developed such needs, they are as much a part of the basic structure of personality as the more commonly recognized needs in terms of which we commonly define personality. Moreover, they arise largely in conjunction with the mode of satisfying the basic organic needs. Thus, the striving for security, prestige, or status constitutes a very definite need-element within various personalities. There are several such needs in all personalities, differing in multiplicity and number, the degree to which they function, the mode in which they operate, and the way in which they are organized.

---

the terms "persistence" and "consistency" of behavior-traits. Allport states, as do we, that the persistences in personality traits may be seen only as a form of historic continuity, or a matter of genetic development. The only basic difference in viewpoint which occurs centers about the question of the degree to which certain elements repeat themselves in different forms in the growth of personality. Allport contends that there is a "functional autonomy of motives," by which he implies that new motives may arise operating upon their own levels. We would concur, while adding that certain elements of past behavior patterns appear in the emergent forms of behavior. A knowledge of these elements, in their *modified integrated forms*, may be regarded as a persistence in trait composition which is helpful in the determination of human behavior.

Illustration (a): Child A: An energetic child who wails lustily for his food may or may not receive immediate attention. If the tendency is to give him attention because of his persistence in loud crying, he may acquire a basic "need-trait" of continuous effort to gain his end (surcease from inner tensions). By a process of growth, we may witness the following transformation:

Basic "need-trait"		*Adult Phase*
Continuous effort ⟶	aggressive-persistence ⟶	Tenacity, intense ambition, etc.

Illustration (b): Child B: Each need of this child is anticipated by environing adults so that a basic "need-trait" of being satisfied without effort on his own part is laid down. By a similar process of development, we may witness the following transformation:

Basic "need-trait"		*Adult Phase*
Need to be satisfied without effort ⟶	egoistic helplessness ⟶	Dependence upon others, egocentrism, etc.

(2) *The functional-phase of the p.g.p.* Closely related to the developed needs are the early acquired methods through which the child learns to satisfy them. This process of acquisition we refer to as the *functional-phase* of the p.g.p. The need-phase of the psychogenetic structure develops during the first two years of the child's growth; in American culture the functional-phase begins to disclose itself during the period of the child's early associations, from the second to the sixth years. Many mechanisms of satisfaction are entirely adventitious, depending largely upon the chance circumstances of the environment. Thus, the presence of other children, setting the stage for sibling rivalry, the parents' standards of proper child-behavior, and the avenues for early social expression which happen to be open, play determining roles in the establishment of mechanisms of adjustment.

The test of survival for many of these early adjustment-techniques is their functional effectiveness. If the adjustment works, whether developed by accident or design, it may tend to be retained. Thus, whining, crying, nagging, fighting, being "cute," and helping one's self become techniques of attaining satisfaction for the needs.

In appraising the structure of the psychogenetic pattern, needs and the functions by which they are satisfied must be analyzed separately. The accidental way in which functional needs may be developed may be shown by the following illustration.

A. M., an attractive child of four and one-half years, and the only girl in a family of two older brothers, was given considerable attention until the arrival of a new baby sister who immediately drew the admiring attention of all the family. There followed a number of attempts by the former "baby sister" to gain the exclusive attention which had been hers, ranging through peremptory demands, temper tantrums, and sulking. Upon one occasion, when the relatives were all foregathered, the child, freshly bathed and dressed in a starched new frock, and wearing a petulant scowl on her face, won the adulation of her relatives by "looking so cute." Without the child being fully aware of what "cuteness" meant, she gathered some conception of the effectiveness of the new technique. Whereas sulking, whining, and temper tantrums did not serve the purpose, "cuteness" did, and eventually became a recognized technique of gaining attention. The metamorphosis of such functional-phases of the psychogenetic structure is sometimes clearly discernible in the transformation of cuteness on the part of the young child, for example, to the coyness of the full-grown female.

Normal cultural determinants, varying in relation to class levels, help to produce approved and desired functional techniques, although individual differences in expression must continually be recognized. Thus, in courtship relations in certain societies, coyness is considered a desirable technique.

The conjunction of the need- and functional-phases in the psychogenetic structure. The psychogenetic structure consists of a number of interrelated needs and functions. The complexity of the structure can be seen in the fact that any acquired need may be associated with a large number of different functions. The possible functions that may arise in association with a single need may be illustrated by the following ex-

Illustration (a): Child A:

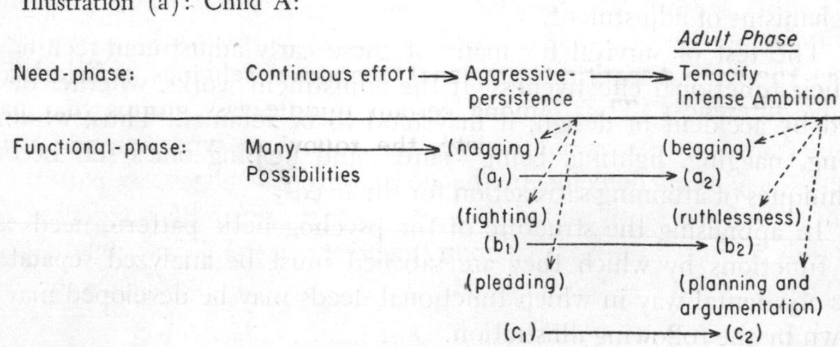

ample. The student should recall (1) that any number of combinations of functions are possible, (2) that transformations of patterns are achieved at advancing levels of maturity and growth for both the *needs and the functions*, and (3) that a given function may relate to more than one need.

To understand the functioning of the personality within social relationships, we must find out what function-aspects (or techniques) are serving *what* particular need or combinations of associated needs. Throughout, we must remember that these needs have become significant only through social and cultural processing. To interpret human relationships properly, we must be cognizant of another highly significant principle: *similar needs may manifest themselves in various functional techniques, and a particular functional technique may relate to different needs*. Thus, two different individuals may be motivated by a common need for prestige or status; while one attempts to satisfy this need by participating directly in the competitive activities of the group, attempting to excel, the other may attempt to draw attention to himself by various bizarre and unconventional activities. Both strive to satisfy the need for prestige but they employ different means. Similarly, two individuals may use the technique of avoidance, but whereas one individual employs it as a means of satisfying his need for retirement and seclusiveness, the other individual may employ it as a device to attract attention. Thus, individuals who may seem much alike in their outward behavior may be fundamentally different in their reasons for practicing certain behaviors; others, whose behaviors appear outwardly quite diverse, may be attempting to satisfy the same need.

Possible types of psychogenetic structure. Although it is difficult to classify personality structures precisely, it is possible nevertheless to detect certain broad patterns within given cultural systems. Such classifications are, at best, only suggestive; within the broad categorical limits imposed by such "types" there is highly variable individual behavior. Kardiner refers to such categories as "basic personality structures."[16] Such types differ within each society, and from society to society. The complexity of our modern social structure creates innumerable types, which reflect the wide disparities of regional, economic, religious, political, and family differences. Thus, among certain middle-class groups that have been studied in American society, the following types, among many others, have been detected in the developing psychogenetic patterns of children. As previously stated, these categories are simply suggestive and give only a limited perspective upon the great variety of functional aspects that may be related to specific needs.

[16] Kardiner, *The Psychological Frontiers of Society*, pp. 24 ff.

Possible Types of Psychogenetic Structure

Needs	*Possible Related Functional Aspects*
(a) Aggressive-persistence	Pugnacity, planning
(b) Egoistic-helplessness	Appeals for sympathy, weeping
(c) Apathetic-isolationism	Conforming to group demands
(d) Sporadic-aggression	Occasional pugnacity or co-operation

To the student familiar with modern psychological trends these broad classifications will resemble those of the extroverted, introverted, schizoid, and cyclothymic personalities which are so common in our time.

(5) THE P.G.P. AND THE GENERIC STATUS

The study of personality development through the family-mediated cultural processes enables us to discern the inter-personal and cultural factors that have shaped the biological materials of the human personality. It also provides us with an operational basis for the appraisal of the several techniques that the individual employs in meeting the conditions of the social environment. The sociologist is primarily concerned with how these personality processes condition the individual's conceptions of himself in relation to the social order, and how the social groups of which the individual is a part learn to react to this behavior. A simple illustration may make this clear. The biological mechanisms of the child have been conditioned by his social environment, but whether the result is good or bad will depend upon how the group regards the resultant behavior. A highly energetic child may be considered a boon in one family and a nuisance in another. For this reason, we sometimes say that the p.g.p. is organic and sub-cultural, i.e., *it represents the raw behavioral tendencies of the individual which have been shaped by his social environment* and upon which any number of cultural judgments may be placed.

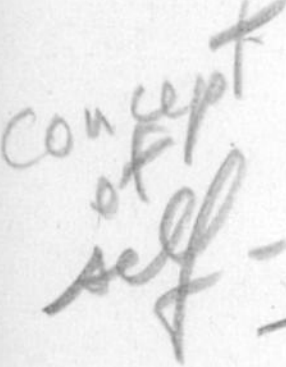

According to the social and cultural circumstances of the child's environment, he soon learns that other individuals regard his behavior as good or bad. The characteristic responses by which others react to his behavior soon give him some conception of how they regard him. This generalized conception he derives of himself and of how he appears to others we refer to as the *generic status.* The process whereby the child receives this conception of himself has been well described by Charles Horton Cooley and George H. Mead. Although the conception that the child forms is derived primarily from his parents and from his siblings, contacts with other persons also play a role. Verbal descriptions frequently play a part in making the child conscious of the "labels" that have been attached to him, but in the long run such descriptions become manifest by virtue of the more or less consistent attitudes and behavior-reactions of others.

The cultural setting of the family plays a predominant role in the perception by the child of his original generic status. For example, a highly energetic and active child may win the epithet of "bully" and "selfish child" in the home of a college professor. In a slum family, where the law of physical survival may still be uppermost, such a child may be regarded with favor as manly and self-sufficient. The designation of the child by a given generic status is extremely significant, from the social standpoint, because it narrows down the scope of his social objectives and, in the end, of his attainments as well. Thus, the "aggressive-persistent" child who wins the title of "bully" finds social meaning for the otherwise meaningless organic behavior-tendencies of his psychogenetic structure. The generic status circumscribes the range of his behavioral tendencies in view of (1) his growing conception of what bullies, selfish children, and so forth are supposed to do, and (2) the limitations imposed upon his behavior by the attitudes of others who regard him in this way.

The conferring of the generic status upon the child involves a process of *self-identification*. Until the behavior of others towards him suggests what their attitudes are, he has no true conception of the meaning of his behavior. In a metaphorical sense, the conferring of the generic status may be likened to the fixing of a mask upon the child's psyche; or, to put it a little differently, making the child aware of his status is a means of introducing the child to himself. He has no conception of himself other than through the reflected attitudes of others. The metaphor of the "psychological mask" we wear, covering the organized drives of the psychogenetic structure, is particularly striking when we recognize that our behavior towards others is conditioned by "how they appear" to us, or in terms of "the face or mask" that they reveal to us. In one sense, on the sociological level we recognize personalities only in terms of such "masks." It should be stressed that the generic status constitutes a complex picture of how the person has come to regard himself in all types of situations, with all the facets and nuances of meaning which such conceptions bear. Our self-conceptions are neither unambiguous nor unitary.[17]

[17] It is interesting to note that the derivation of the term "personality" comes from the Latin term for mask, *persona*. Many dramatists have given evidence of the way in which the generic status functions in human relations. Thus, Eugene O'Neill, in his *The Great God Brown*, has his characters appear on the stage wearing different types of masks. *They are known and reacted to in terms of their masks.* The Italian playwright and philosopher, Pirandello, has made the question of what he calls "the true self" the chief theme of his several dramatic and philosophic works. In his celebrated play, *As You Desire Me*, the heroine indicates that she is "what her lover conceives her to be."

(6) SELF-CONCEPTIONS AND PROCESSES OF DISORGANIZATION

As the individual matures and develops increasing social contacts, the generic conception of himself grows apace, becoming more complex and more extensive. *Breakdowns frequently occur when the individual's conception of himself differs from the conception which others have of him.* Consequently, individual pathologies frequently emerge in relation to specific groups. An individual's self-conception may find corroboration in some groups and rude contradiction in others.[18] Sample studies of maladjustments within given groups have found that the degree of personal maladjustment varies in relation to the group's willingness to accord a given generic status *which the individual identifies with himself*. Furthermore, it has been found that individuals hopelessly maladjusted in certain groups have been able to adjust effectively to others. Sometimes, a satisfactory readjustment may be made to the original group, provided the individual has succeeded in modifying his conception of himself and in identifying himself with the group's conception of him. To a certain degree, it might even be said that the hallucinated views which psychotics display are representative of extreme cleavages between the individual's view of himself and the group's conception of his behavior.

(7) THE GENERIC STATUS DETERMINES THE SOCIAL ROLES

Using the generic conception of himself which he has developed, the individual is called upon to participate in the activities of groups in his environment. The operation of the generic status in a given group determines its bearer's role within that group. An individual plays as many social roles as there are groups with which he identifies himself. The individual's generic status, in conjunction with the limitations imposed by the group situation, defines the specific role-behavior that emerges. Thus, the bully may become the leader of his gang, the town "bad boy," the "high-pressure" salesman or the "tough labor boss." The egoistic-helpless type, fitting into the generic status of the "nice quiet boy," may develop the behaviors of the "sissy," the "idealist," or the "profound, serious type." Note how the varying requirements of different cultural situations will affect the same generic status and psychogenetic pattern in

[18] Recent innovations and developments in psychotherapy recognize this principle. Increasingly, psychiatrists are discovering that individual maladjustments are matters of relationship to certain groups. Consequently, the methods of *group and social therapy* are coming increasingly to the fore. An aspect of this process, to be discussed later, can be seen in the effectiveness of *Alcoholics Anonymous* in curbing pathological drinking through close participation in highly integrated groups.

different ways, producing adjustments in certain cases and maladjustments in others.

(8) GROUP SITUATIONS ESTABLISH PATTERNS OF BEHAVIOR, OR "GESTALTEN," FOR THE DIFFERENT ROLES

Any situation to which the individual adjusts consists of a number of related parts. Thus, to be "a good boy at school" imposes requirements upon the personality which fulfill the several aspects of the adjustment—sitting quietly in one's seat, performing one's lessons faithfully, "not talking back to the teacher." These patterned arrangements of parts in a total social situation have been recognized for some time by the Gestalt psychologists.[19] The important thing for us to realize, however, is that these traits comprising a given situation are not pursued for themselves, *but largely as a means of fulfilling the requirements of the role-behavior.* Thus, the "profound and serious" boy avoids swearing, attempts to be neat in his appearance, and does the countless other things that are associated with that type of status not because these actions are initially significant or meaningful to him, but because *they are requirements for the fulfillment of the obligations imposed by his role.* Such traits are pursued not for themselves, but because they "express" the needs of a given psychogenetic pattern and self-conception.

(9) THE CONFIGURED ELEMENTS OF THE ROLES ESTABLISH OUR HABIT-PATTERNS

In the social growth of personality, the elements that comprise the roles establish the bases for the distinguishing habit-patterns of the individual. *Habits are tendencies to meet situations in particular ways in accordance with the roles the individual assumes.*[20] Such habit-systems tend to impart consistency to social behavior patterns. A given habit, therefore, must not be regarded as an isolated or discrete element of the personality but as an element related to a given role-complex of behavior. *The occasion which calls forth a given role necessarily calls forth appropriate actions as well.* Thus, the classroom situation elicits concentration upon the subject, quiet deportment, and the like, which manifest themselves as habitual behavior patterns whenever the conditions of such be-

[19] See K. Koffka, *Principles of Gestalt Psychology* (New York, 1935); W. Kohler, *Gestalt Psychology* (New York, 1929); M. Wertheimer, in W. D. Ellis (ed.), *A Sourcebook of Gestalt Psychology* (New York, 1938); and others.

[20] This view is substantially the same as the conception concerning habitual behavior laid down some time ago by John Dewey in his *Human Nature and Conduct* (New York, 1930), *Experience and Nature* (Chicago, 1925), and in several of his other works.

havior are presented. The habit-patterns that comprise our personalities, therefore, may be seen only in relation to the role-situations which manifest themselves in different forms of behavior, ranging through our economic, religious, political, and social life.

The Habit-Patterns That Comprise the Roles Determine Our Attitudes

Roles, through the complex habit-patterns that relate to them, determine attitudes. *Attitudes may be said to be the latent tendencies to respond to meaningful social experiences which have come to represent social values.* In short, a complex arrangement of habit-systems, arising from a series of role situations, causes the development of a general tendency to respond to situations in characteristic ways. Thus, a "pugnacious role" may manifest itself in tendencies towards "rough house" sports and direct action in politics; conversely, the "profound and serious" role may manifest itself in preferences for intellectual pursuits and in cautious political attitudes.

(10) THE ATTITUDES ESTABLISH THE BASIS FOR OUR WISH-PATTERNS

The attitudes we develop are composed of the networks of habits defining our roles. Such attitudes play a very important role in defining the objectives of our lives. It is our attitudes that give us our bearings as human beings in the endless drifts and crosscurrents of society. Without attitudes, there would be little direction or purpose in social life. Because our attitudes determine the broad pathways we seek, they likewise make it possible for us to determine the specific objectives we seek. Thus, our attitudes, somewhat modified by the circumstances of the environment, will determine for us what our specific wish-objectives will be.

Just as habits compose attitudes, attitudes, in turn, are narrowed down to certain specific focal points of human desire. The social setting and cultural environment invariably determine, as a *selective frame of reference,* what specific wish-objectives will materialize as a result of certain attitudes. Individuals showing a common attitude, but exposed to different social and cultural conditions, will express these attitudes in terms of different objectives. A favorable attitude towards competitive sports may lead to the wish, on the part of a slum boy, to become a Golden Gloves boxing champion; the upper middle-class boy, with the same favorable attitude towards contact sports, may manifest this attitude in the wish to be an All-American football player. A favorable attitude towards scholarly quiet, on the part of an Irish-American boy of the slums, may lead to the desire to become a priest; on the part of a boy from more comfortable economic circumstances, this same attitude may lead to the wish to be a writer or a college professor. What should be particularly noted is how the accidental conditions of a given environment will narrow the focus of the given attitude into a specific kind of wish.

Classification of social wishes. Many sociologists have attempted to indicate the nature of social life by positing the existence of specific wishes around which social individuals orient their lives. Among the several classifications that have been attempted, the most famous has been that of the "four wishes" of William I. Thomas and Florian Znaniecki. This classification was formulated in their classic *The Polish Peasant in Europe and America* and was also developed by Thomas in *The Unadjusted Girl.*[21] Such wish-patterns represent hypotheses by means of which the multi-faceted characteristics of human personalities may be simplified to facilitate the analysis of social patterns. They are not instincts, in the psychological sense; rather, they are socially conditioned patterns of behavior which appear to serve widespread and common needs. We may regard them as the goals of human personality, the partially fixed directive points toward which the human personality aspires in the organization of its social relationships. According to Thomas and Znaniecki, wish-patterns fall into four major categories: (a) the desire for new experience, (b) the desire for security, (c) the desire for response, and (d) the desire for recognition. As a means of implementing our analysis of social problems, in terms of social status, roles, habits, and attitudes, these wish-patterns may be extremely significant and helpful, providing we recognize the limitations of their scope and the diversity of human nature.

In the analysis of problems of personality and group adjustment, it is worthwhile to consider the consistencies involved in the fulfillment of social wishes. These consistencies frequently afford a significant clue as to the basic psychogenetic drives and the kinds of statuses and roles which have emerged in the social patterning of wishes. Moreover, the insistent drive to satisfy one type of wish at the expense of others indicates the type of imbalance which exists in personality and also the type of problem-situation which the overemphasis of a particular wish may produce. In the discussion of such problems as marital disorder, for example, it may be found that the woman who centers her whole life around her home, as a means of safeguarding her desire for security, has jeopardized other important phases of her marital relationship. Studies of delinquency, pathological drinking, sex excesses, and suicide frequently reveal similar processes of overemphasis.

[21] William I. Thomas and Florian Znaniecki, *The Polish Peasant in Europe and America* (New York, 1927); William I. Thomas, *The Unadjusted Girl* (Boston, 1923).

(11) THE SEX DRIVE AND THE PSYCHOGENETIC STRUCTURE

In our discussion of the processes of personality growth in relation to the social structure, we have thus far omitted any mention of the sex drives. The enormous importance attached to the Freudian view in many quarters is not subscribed to in our treatment. We would certainly not deny the significance of the sexual behavior of men and women in the development of social patterning and social behavior. Our view, however, is that the sex drive must be seen in relation to the entire psychogenetic structure of the personality as it has developed within a given cultural and social milieu. According to the sociological view of personality, *when the sex drive emerges, it impinges upon a psychogenetic organization that has already been firmly established.* The sex behavior of men and women, thus, becomes channelized according to the already existent network of roles, attitudes, and wishes. This is not to say that the contribution of Freud must be discarded. It means simply that Freud's view must be reworked with an eye to the sociological conditions attendant upon the development of personality. In fact, it is possible to reconcile many phases of the Freudian system with our theory of the psychogenetic structure of personality. (In the Appendix of this volume, a diagram indicates the ways in which many of the outstanding conceptions of the Freudian school may be utilized in conjunction with our theory of personality.) The sexual pathologies and the sex-directed influences upon the culture that exist in every society are patterned by the social processes.[22] Our analyses later on of various types of sexual disorders will bear out this point.

(12) PROBLEMS OF INDIVIDUAL AND SOCIAL PATHOLOGY AND PERSONALITY-SITUATIONAL DIFFICULTIES

On the basis of the sociological theory that we have developed, we should now be able to see the way in which the cultural and social processes have shaped the biological individual into a status- and role-oriented individual. Problems of individual and social breakdown should occur, therefore, whenever the intimate associations between role, status, and its corresponding situation is disturbed in such a way as to fail to meet the requirements of the total behavior of the situation. For example, if the social situation fails to elicit the proper role-fulfilling conditions implicit in the individual's behavior, or if the individual fails to fulfill the requirements of the social situation, *maladjustment to a greater or lesser*

[22] Cf. George P. Murdock, *Social Structure* (New York, 1949), Chaps. 9, 10, and 11.

degree will inhere within the total situation. Note that we refer to the entire situation as being maladjusted. Problems of pathology, in our view, whether individually or socially considered, arise out of a personality-situational context. The role of the individual has implications for specific situations which either fail to satisfy or fulfill the requirements of the individual's role behavior. It is the total context which must be seen, although we may fix our gaze, for purpose of analysis, upon certain phases of the personality or the social structure in order to apprehend the significant elements which have contributed to a situation of disorder. The point of view incorporated in our conception of personality and its relationship to the cultural and social situations which have produced it is summarized in the following principle:

Personality maladjustments and personality-situational changes arise because of the obstacles, impediments, and frustrations placed in the way of the psychogenetic drives, as these occur within the framework of normal sociological and cultural conditions expressed through the processes of social interaction.

SUMMARY[23]

(1) In the development of the individual life organization, the biological mechanisms of the organism are shaped by the cultural and social processes which are mediated through the family situation. (2) The individual, thus, is shaped by three important sets of conditions: (a) his biological constitution, (b) his personal-social relations, and (c) the cultural processes. (3) Each family establishes an *emotional atmosphere* in which the child is reared and which "refracts" the cultural values impinging upon family life. (4) The ways in which the child's needs for food and physical care are responded to by the environing adults mould the organism into a psychogenetic pattern (p.g.p.) which is characterized by a complex organization of needs (the need-phase) and an equally complex organization of means for their satisfaction (the functional-phase). (5) The manifestations of the child's behavior through the organization of the psychogenetic structure are labeled and reacted to by those in his surrounding groups, giving him a conception of himself called the "generic status." The generic status, a developing conception of the self, reflects the attitudes which others about the individual entertain towards him. (6) Personality difficulties may develop from the discrepancies arising between the individual's conception of himself and the conceptions which members of the groups in which he participates have of him. (7)

[23] A detailed structural outline of the development of personality within the framework of normative social and cultural conditions may be found in Appendix I, pp. 113–19.

The generic status determines the nature of the social roles which the individual pursues in the groups in which he has membership. (8) The social situation is composed of an organization of structured elements which make up the pattern of the situation to which the individual must adjust. These total patterned situations, or configurations, consist of diversified aspects which fulfill the conditions of the individual's role-behavior. (9) These aspects of the total situation establish the basis for the habit-systems comprising the person's life. Combinations of reinforced habits produce the broad behavioral tendencies to respond to certain meaningful social experiences, which are known as "attitudes." (10) The restrictive conditions of a given social environment narrow down the attitudes to specific wish-patterns, which are the focal objectives towards which human behavior is directed. (11) Sexual behavior impinges on the psychogenetic structure once it has been established, expressing itself through the existent network of roles, attitudes, habits, and wishes. (12) Problems of individual and social pathology arise in connection with the failure of the personality, through its roles, and the social situation to mutually fulfill the requirements implicit in each. Pathological processes must be seen in relation to such total personality-situational contexts.

The following diagram indicates the pattern of this developmental structure of the personality in relation to the social and cultural conditions which shape and process its growth.

Developmental Structure of the Individual Life Organization in Relation to Social Patterning

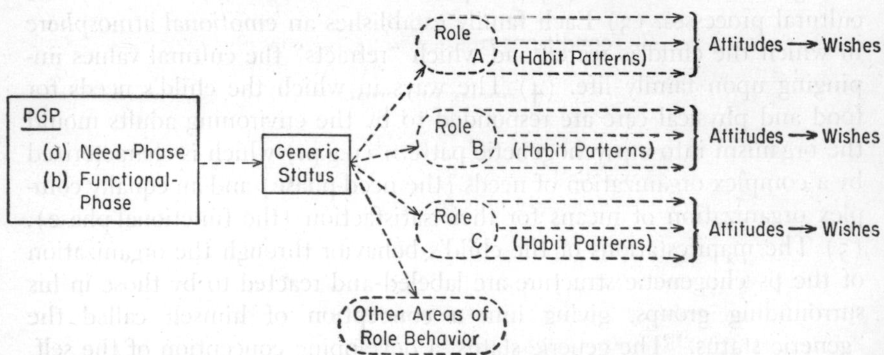

Note: **The broken lines surrounding the role situations signify the aspects that comprise the given situation. These aspects, as part of the total configuration, are specific behavior-practices which, in fulfilling the conditions of the role, establish the bases of the separate habit-systems which follow from them and lead to the attitudes.**

APPENDIX 1

A PSYCHO-SOCIOLOGICAL "SYSTEM" FOR UTILIZING THE CONCEPT OF THE SOCIAL INDIVIDUAL AS A PRIMARY DATUM

A. *The Concept of Social Interaction*

1. Definition of social interaction: *The reciprocal interplay of personalities within a given social environment*, keeping in mind the fact that this process is distinguished by the following characteristics, *viz.:*
   a. The unique background histories of the personalities involved (i.e., each individual trails his own special cloud of glory and disrepute behind him);
   b. The reciprocal effects upon personalities which this interaction produces;
   c. The anticipations and expectations which each interactive situation produces;
   d. The chief forms which interaction may take, i.e.:
      (1) Accommodation
      (2) Assimilation
      (3) Competition
      (4) Conflict
2. The "external" conditions under which interaction operates: The conditions imposed by culture.
   a. The meaning of culture: Its *pro*scriptive and its *pre*scriptive nature. Culture not only tells us
      (1) what we shall want, *but*
      (2) what we shall not want.
      Also, culture not only tells us
      (3) how we should attain the goal objects, *but*
      (4) how we should *not* proceed to go about obtaining them.
      Thus, in its effects upon the individual, culture consists of special incitements and encouragements, goadings and cajolings, discouragements and reproofs, etc.
   b. The *modes* or *techniques* through which these enjoinders and injunctions are imposed upon the individual consist of:
      (1) Physical coercion;
      (2) Verbal admonishment or encouragement;
      (3) Rewards, actual or potential;
      (4) Other expressive forms of approval and disapproval.
3. The unique function of the family in mediating the culture from without: the *emotional atmosphere* from the standpoint of the "deliverers of culture" (the "E.A.").

a. The "refraction" or "distortion" of the cultural values is dependent upon:
   (1) *The personality-characteristics* of the bearer of the cultural value (i.e., in the case of the child, the parent or other members of the family); and—
   (2) The attitude towards the given cultural value *entertained by these self-same human agents.*

b. The human agents surrounding the child comprise one set of factors contributing to the development and growth of his personality. The other "variables" arise from his biological endowment.

B. *The Biological Factors Contributing to the Growth of Personality*
   1. Simple organic reflex activities;
      a. The elementary "chained" reflexes.
   2. The *organic drives*
      a. Produced by "tension states" or internal imbalances actuated by bio-chemical stimulation to "chained" reflex activities.
      b. Very likely, they are "survival" mechanims primarily of the
         (1) *appetitive,* and
         (2) *defensive* or *protective types.*
   3. Inborn *temperamental predispositions*
      a. Associated, of course, with the glandular organization of the human organism.
   4. *Intellectual capacities.*

      Note: Although we have classified these into a set of pigeon-holes, we should note that these represent *phases* of total organic activity from the outset. E.g., if we presume a temperamental disposition marked by apathy, that should certainly reflect itself in the strength of certain organic drives and later on in the type of intellectual adjustments an individual makes.

      a. Endowed with varying intensities and qualitative differences of these endowed factors, the child achieves early *accidental adjustments* to his environment in keeping with the ways in which the early outgoing releases of his biological tensions were accorded response by the human "culture-bearers" in his environment.

         Note: In the earliest stages of his development, note how cultural values are *expressed* differently by the human agents and consequently, how they "fix" differing adjustment-techniques on the parts of different individuals. Compare, for example, the behavior of the peasant mother who places her child to the breast whenever he cries and the "modern mother" who feeds her child according to rigid schedule regardless of how much he cries. In the case of the first child, crying immediately produces anticipatory tactual and gastronomic sensations which, when forthcoming, lead to a cessation of crying while in the case of the second child such crying-activity leads to wholly different consequences. Life for the very young child consists of a myriad of such adjustments which, *unbeknownst to him,* represent cultural values from the outside.

C. *Certain adjustment-techniques, at the very earliest, appear to tend to persist:*
   1. This is based upon our presupposition that the sensitive afferent and efferent neural connections conform to a pattern when satisfactions are

afforded to organic imbalance. (Partial evidence: Semon, W. B. Cannon, et al.)

D. *These techniques tend to persist because of:*

1. The *routine adjustments* made by adults to young children,
2. The *qualitative differences* in response of young children—
   a. Basic patterns of response-tendencies are laid down for the child which inevitably appear to constitute a "core" of his personality. These are essentially characteristic patterns of response which impart a "core of consistency" to the personality of the individual. (Primary recognizable *determinative* patterns appear to be laid down between 2nd and 6th years. These are in no way to be construed as fixed or unchangeable patterns, but primarily "*determinierende Tendenzen.*" We would concur with Allport, at this point, in the view that they simply provide an historic nexus in the growth of personality but would certainly quarrel with his failure to recognize the causal significance of this condition. Allport, it appears, overlooks an important phase in the development of immanent causation and raises a "straw man." See his *Personality: A Psychological Interpretation*, New York, 1937, Chap. VII. *Vide:* Gesell, McGraw, Allport, et al.)
   b. We may call this "core of personality" the *psychogenetic pattern* of the individual. (Abbreviation: "p.g.p.")

E. *The structure of the "p.g.p."*

1. *The "need" phase:* Although organically derived, the need or needs acquired through early development (possibly, 2nd–6th years: see above) are the results of encounters with the environment. Thus, they represent the organic drives which have become modified and canalized through the conditions of response set up by the environing adults.

Illustration a. *Child A:* An energetic child who wails lustily for his food may or may not receive immediate attention. If the tendency is to give him attention because of his persistence in loud crying, he may acquire a basic "need-trait" of continuous effort to gain his end (or surcease from inner tensions). By a process of growth, we may witness the following transformation:

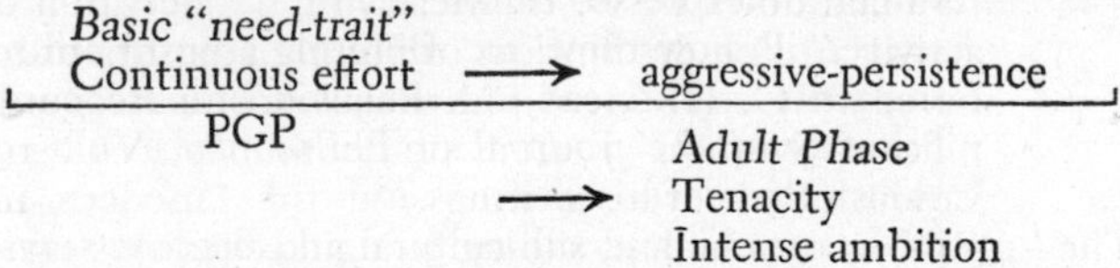

Illustration b. *Child B:* Each drive is anticipated so that a basic "need-trait" of being satisfied without effort on his own part is laid down. Similarly, by a process of development, we may witness the following transformation:

Basic "need-trait"
Need to be satisfied without effort ⟶ Egoistic, helplessness

PGP

Adult Phase
⟶ Dependence on others and conceit

2. *The "functional" phase:* Closely related to developed "needs" are the early acquired methods through which the child learns to satisfy the needs. (Fundamental to this entire structure, the sociologist should see the mechanism of the conditioned response.) E.g., whining, crying, nagging, fighting, being "cute," helping himself, etc., become techniques of attaining satisfaction for the needs.

Illustration a. *Child A:*

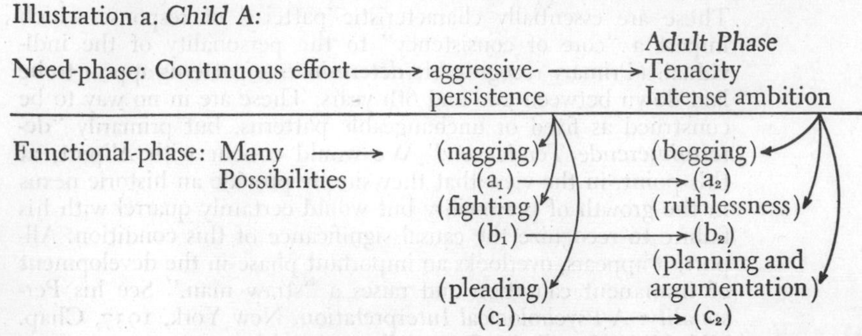

3. *Possible Types of Psychogenetic Structure*

Needs	*Possible Related Functional Aspects*
a. Aggressive-persistence	Pugnacity, planning
b. Egoistic-helplessness	Appeals for sympathy, weeping
c. Apathy-isolationism	Conforming to group demands
d. Sporadic-aggressive	Occasional pugnacity or co-operation

(1) Note how these are related to the conventional extrovert, introvert, schizoid, cyclothymic types.

(2) Note also that these represent behavioral tendencies which become socially significant only as they are "processed" into different types of socially and culturally recognized behavior.

Instead of the names employed, we might use the designations X, Y, Z, etc. They are premised upon movements towards and away from significant objects, fulfilling the suggested pattern laid down by G. H. Mead in his conception of "truncated activity." For description of this last point, the reader is referred to G. H. Mead, "A Behavioristic Account of the Significant Symbol," *Journal of Philosophy*, Vol. 19, 1922, and various others of his writings.

4. The "*p.g.p.*" is organic and sub-cultural and becomes crystallized, well defined, and *patterned* in relation to the GENERIC STATUS conferred upon it.

The "p.g.p." is primarily organically derived and is a unique physiologico-psychological mechanism, although the patterning has been accomplished in the primary groups. The term, "sub-cultural," taken from Folsom's usage in a different context appearing in the early edition of *The Family: Its Sociology and Social Psychiatry*, appears to suggest a valid interpretation of the essential character of this mechanism—"sub-cultural" since it expresses an early *socially developed* need not elaborated, as yet, into a *socially recognized* or conventional form.

F. *The generic status and the "p.g.p."*

1. The characteristic responses of the young child, as conditioned by the "p.g.p.," become conveniently labeled by the adults around him.

   Thus, the "aggressive-persistent" child (Type 1) wins the epithet of bully, fighter, cruel and selfish child, etc. [*Note:* This narrows down the range of the possibilities of his "p.g.p." in view of (1) The fact of his growing conception of what bullies, selfish children do, etc., and (2) Since the individuals who give him the epithet entertain attitudes toward him appropriate to bullies, fighters, etc.]

G. *The generic status becomes determinative of the roles he will play in social relationships.*

1. Given a certain generic status, the child will play certain roles in the various fields of social activity in keeping with this status. E.g., the bully will become the leader (perhaps) of his gang, the town "bad-boy," the "high-pressure" salesman, the "tough labor-boss," etc.

   The egoistic-helpless type may fit into the generic status of the "nice, quiet boy." His roles, then, the "sissy," the "idealist," the "profound, serious" type, etc.

H. *Culture creates patterns of behavior, or "Gestalten" for the different roles.*

1. Thus, the performance of a role predisposes to other activities; to-wit, the "profound and serious" boy must also be refined, neat in his appearance, considerate of others, must not swear, etc.

   Note: These traits, then, are not pursued for themselves but because fundamentally they "*express*" the need of the psychogenetic pattern.

I. *The roles lay down the bases for the habits that determine our lives.*

1. Habits, thus, are predisposing tendencies to meet certain situations in certain ways in accordance with the roles that are operative in certain situations. (Essentially John Dewey's conception of habits.)

   Illustration: The "quiet, refined, serious boy" may be expected to be bookish. His teachers may prefer him, encourage him to become a good student—in fact, set up certain conditions so that it becomes difficult not to be a conscientious student. Similar situations, later on, tend to elicit this appropriate behavior. Compare the deportment of the good student with that of the energetic, non-studious individual in the college library, the classroom, in respect to posture, sustained interest, time wasted in sharpening pencils, fidgeting, etc.

J. *The roles determine, through the complex habit-patterns that relate to them, the attitudes.*

1. The attitudes may be said to be the latent tendencies to respond to meaningful social experiences which have come to represent social values.

   Illustration: The pugnacious role may lead to favorable attitudes toward "rough-house" sports, capital punishment, direct action in politics, etc.

K. *The attitudes,* because of the limitations of the type of environment in which they operate, become focalized or narrowed down to certain *specific wishes.*

1. *Illustrations:*
   a. A favorable attitude towards competitive, bodily-contact sports may lead to the wish, on the part of the slum boy, to become a Golden Gloves boxing champion; on the part of the upper-middle-class boy, to become an All-American football player.
   b. A favorable attitude towards scholarly quiet, on the part of a slum Irish-American boy, may lead to the desire to become a priest. A boy in more fortunate circumstances with the same general favorable attitude, may express this in the desire to be a writer, a college professor, a researcher in some special field, etc.
2. The classification of wishes: W. I. Thomas
   a. New experience, security, response, recognition.
   Note: This is just one of many possible classifications.
   b. The intense desire to have one set of wishes satisfied at the expense of the others points inevitably to a basic and insistent psychogenetic need which is not being adequately satisfied.
   Thus, we have here, a clue to personality maladjustment. E.g., the woman who centers her whole life around her home in expressing an intense need for security.

L. *The emergence of the sex drive impinges upon the psychogenetic organization after it already has become firmly entrenched.*
1. The sex drive thus becomes canalized according to the already existent network of roles, attitudes, and wishes.
2. The Freudian contribution, thus, must be utilized in relation to the system we have set up.

M. *Illustration of how the Freudian contribution may be utilized within the socio-psychological framework.*
1. The three basic conceptions:
   a. The unconscious (relates to traumatic shock-effects upon the "p.g.p.").
   b. Repression (relates to the necessity to conform to the "p.g.p.").
   c. Transference (relates to the attitudes towards persons conditioned by role and status).
   Note: The translation of the chief Freudian concepts into the requirements of this framework has already been done, and beginning supporting evidence is to be found in the work of Abraham Kardiner, *The Individual and His Society,* and Karen Horney, *The Neurotic Personality of Our Time.* The following simply suggests how some of the major categories may be systematically transliterated into the sociological frame of reference.
   d. The unconscious wish: the unloading of energy in wrong channels manifesting itself in the form of neurotic symptoms.
2. *Repressions, resistance, transference.*
   a. ". . . everything in the mind that might lead to a psychic disturbance was once conscious and, becoming no longer consciously bearable, was driven into the unconscious." (The orthodox Freudian position.)
      (1) Hence, concept of free associations
         (a) Projection
         (b) Rationalization

(2) What is repressed?

(a) Depends upon the goal (wish) and the intellectual character ("p.g.p.") of the individual.

(b) Pleasure-pain principle.

(3) Degree of repression.

(a) The type of mental data.

(b) Reaction pattern of the personality.

(I.e., the nature of the organization of the individual's "p.g.p." from the standpoint of "need" phase and "functional" phase.)

b. Transference.

(1) Positive and negative.

(2) The dissolution of the transference experience.

(Accounted for on the basis of directed person-to-person relationships providing congruent or non-congruent effects in the operation of the "p.g.p.")

Note: This phase of the outline is simply suggestive. The manifold Freudian conceptions, including the Freudian dynamisms which are already operationally treated on the sociological level, as well as the conceptions of free association, mistakes, dream-manifestations, the complexes, the libido and the various other exhibits of the Freudian pantheon may likewise be interpreted on the operational socio-psychogenetic level. In fact, they are already rapidly becoming "respectable citizens" under the sociological reformative influence.

N. Personality maladjustments and personality-situational changes arise because of obstacles, impedimenta and frustrations placed in the way of the psychogenetic drives as these occur within the framework of normative sociological and cultural conditions expressed through the processes of social interaction.

CHAPTER SIX

THE FRAMEWORK OF INDIVIDUAL AND SOCIAL DISORGANIZATION

Fitting Our Concepts Into a Frame of Reference

ON THE basis of the theoretical materials which we have thus far discussed, we should now be able to assemble these concepts into some co-ordinated form to give a coherent framework by which we may gain insight into the problems of pathology. Although our emphasis at one time may be upon the individual or some phase of his personality, and at another time upon a particular aspect of the social processes or the social structure, these various facets of the human complex we call society are always bound together in definite and intricate ways.

By presenting these concepts in a unified and related form, showing the relative position of each in the total scheme of social change and problem analysis, we establish what we originally called a "frame of reference," or, in this specific instance, a framework of social disorganization. Earlier we proposed that our frame of reference be sufficiently inclusive to account for the following three considerations: (a) the conditions of social change, (b) the reciprocal relations between individual and social change, and (c) the way in which personality develops in the changing social structure. The chief value of such a frame of reference is that it enables us to see each part of a given problem in proper perspective. It reminds us that while we may be concentrating upon one aspect of the problem at any given time, there are other parts of the problem related to it which must also receive consideration. It serves to channel our analysis by indicating the directions in which our investigation and our curiosity should run. Finally, it assists us in assigning proper weight to the important factors which have contributed to the development of a given area of experience. It imposes discipline by forcing us to think in certain directed and systematic ways.

The Continual Interdependence of Individual and Society

A fundamental premise in all sociological thinking is that the individual and the social group are both aspects of the same process. No matter what the individual does, thinks, or says, his behavior expresses the social conditions that have produced him. Conversely, all group policies, objectives, and aspirations express the points of view of interacting members of the group. We can never study the individual apart from the group conditions that have produced him, no more than we can study the social conditions of life without taking into consideration the individual personalities whose interactions manifest themselves in the recognized procedures of social life.[1] For this reason, whenever we appraise any social problem, or any given aspect of the social situation, we must be cognizant of the related effects which such conditions must have upon the different individuals and groups who react to them.

This in no way implies that there always exists a "parallelism" between the conditions of the social structure and the conditions of the individual's *private* behavior. In our previous discussion, we showed that custom and habit are *not* identical. When we speak of the "related aspects" of individual and social life, we simply refer to the fact that the individual has an outward focus, in his behavior, upon the many groups that hedge in his life. His multiple memberships and the effects which they have individually exercised at different times in his career, preclude the possibility of complete and perfect identification with any single group. Any decision he makes as an individual must have some repercussions, however slight, upon the social groups of which he is a part. Conversely, alteration of group policy and objectives will affect not only his individual career but the manner and degree of his participation in the social groups in which he has membership. In our framework of personal and social disorganization, this duality of individual and society must always be kept in mind. Changes in the realm of one order must be viewed in the light of their possible effects upon the other.[2]

A final illustration may serve to clarify this continual interdependence between the individual and society. As we have seen, the growth of the personality involves the absorption by the individual of the cultural standards and procedures that guide the society and the social groups of which he is a part. This is a *unique* process for each individual, and involves, for each, a unique *degree of participation and identification* with the social groups that bear directly upon his life. John Doe may be a

[1] This view does not deny the position that human behavior may not be accounted for on cultural grounds. See Leslie A. White, "Culturological vs. Psychological Interpretations of Human Behavior," *American Sociological Review*, XII (Dec., 1947), 686–97. White affirms that "culturological" explanations may be sufficient for the interpretation of certain orders of problems, without the necessity of psychological explanation. He does admit, however, that to understand the function of an institution in the lives of men, "we must study their psychological reactions to it" (p. 698).

[2] A good statement of the nature of this continual interdependence of individual and society may be found in R. M. MacIver, *Society: A Textbook of Sociology* (New York, 1937), pp. 45–50.

member of the Masons, the Presbyterian Church, the Rotary, and the Board of Trustees of Siwash College. It is possible that others in his circle may find themselves members of the same groups. Moreover, each one of these individuals finds some facets of his personality satisfied by his participation in such memberships. Only through activity within the group may the needs and interests that society and culture have implanted within him be satisfied and fulfilled.

These needs have become indispensable parts of his nature. However, if any of these groups re-defines its purpose and objectives, his own personal life is altered to the same degree as the new orientation which he is willing to accept. The diverse loyalties which individuals bring to the groups in which they have membership are reflected in the differential responses they make to shifts in the group's policy. Thus, if old Siwash introduces a policy of optional chapel attendance, supplanting its earlier policy of obligatory attendance, John Doe (who fancies himself a "freethinker") may increase his annual donation to the endowment fund and look at his pastor with smug self-assurance. William Smith, on the other hand, may resign from the college board and accept in the Board of Vestry of his church the post which he had previously refused. At the same time, if the individual for some reason varies the pattern of his participation and identification, the group experiences the impact of such a change, whether in slight or marked degree. This reciprocal action must always be kept in the forefront of our thinking when we analyze the social and cultural processes in their effects upon human behavior.

The Behavior Sequence in Personal and Social Disorganization

With this injunction clearly in mind, we may review the process whereby individual and social change is brought about together with a description of how this change affects the development of social problems. We have recognized in our discussion of personality growth that the individual begins his life with certain organic needs. These needs are always processed by the society and culture as mediated by the family or primary group charged with the individual's rearing. As John Dollard has pointed out in his *Criteria for the Life History*, human needs may be recognized and expressed only through social patterns and cultural systems.[3] The

[3] John Dollard, *Criteria for the Life History* (New Haven, 1935), emphasizes the basic requirement of personality appraisal in stating as his fundamental criterion that "*organic motors of action must be viewed as socially relevant*" (p. 8 and passim). See also Leslie A. White, "Culturological vs. Psychological Interpretations of Human Behavior." The fundamental theoretical basis for this view has been admirably stated by Emile Durkheim, *The Rules of Sociological Method*, trans. by G. E. Simpson (Chicago, 1938), p. 104, and constitutes the essential premise of his oft-cited contribution, *De la Division du Travail Social* (Paris, 1893).

processing of these basic organic needs manifests itself in two separable, but related conditions: the individual life-organization of the personality and the structural conditions of the social organization. We have noted that these two separable structures continually reinforce and strengthen each other. Within the complex of the individual life-organization, with its "style of life" and its "consistencies," are implicit the several habits, attitudes, values, beliefs, and individuated reactions to customs and institutional usages. Implementing such personal usages, and inextricably interwoven with them, are the social practices, customs, folkways, and mores which comprise their own separate system of organization in the social structure. *It is within this area comprising personality and social structure that the latencies lie.* Within the personality structure, such latencies consist of those habits and customs that have oriented the individual to certain types of social situations. Within the social structure, they consist of those widespread social usages and group practices that have enabled the group to adjust to neighboring groups and the remaining elements that comprise the parts of the social structure.

The individual attitude implicit in the latency-structure always depends upon the native endowment of the individual and the type of social experience to which he has been exposed. *Corresponding to the individual attitudes descriptive of a given situation,* and historically derived from the physical environment and cultural attitudes, we have the social values of the social structure. In short, a given social attitude (seen in individual focus) corresponds to a given social value (viewed in the social dimension). From this standpoint, social values may be defined as the objective aspect of the individual attitude. Although this is apparent to the trained sociologist, it may be somewhat difficult for the beginning student to grasp. We may explain it by stating that a given attitude toward the Negro, for example, corresponds to a specific social value within the cultural milieu which may define Negroes as either inferior and indolent, or socially disenfranchised and capable and worthy of social improvement. We have learned that such social values, arising from a context of physical environment and culturally mediated attitudes, serve the important function of defining the group's conception of normalcy. In the last analysis, such conceptions of normalcy depend upon group consensus, or the way in which the group has learned to define the normality of situations.

Changes are always occurring either within the personality or the social environment. In the personality, changes may be induced by organic alterations within the human organism, or by psychological or sociocultural factors. In the social structure, changes may be brought about by a host of factors. Primary are those categorized as natural-environmental (which include various categories of organic change). We should list also changes in the group structure, cultural changes (such as those induced by the introduction of cultural innovations), and changes involved in the social processes. When such changes occur, either separately or simultaneously, the result may be further consolidation of the individual attitude and the group situation, or strain and conflict. If conflict situations arise, they reveal themselves in specific types of crisis-situations, the fundamental and underlying type being that of the *cumulative crisis.*

The Possible Emergents of Crisis-Situations

The outcomes of crisis-situations are limited in character. Either the individual may (1) choose to return to a previous norm of behavior which has been established or which has been regarded as acceptable or, (2) he may establish a novel form of behavior which eventually wins acceptance. Much acceptable social change and "progress" is established on this latter basis. The individual who rebels may have difficulty at first in winning adherents, and thus, for a time, may be considered eccentric or dangerous. But, eventually, if sufficient individuals subscribe to his point of view and share in what becomes a common form of behavior, a new norm is established and society has advanced another rung up the ladder of development and change. (3) There are some individuals, however, who, refusing to conform to the accepted norms, are equally lacking in the inclination, daring, imagination, ability, or opportunity to establish new norms of behavior. These are the individuals who strike out against the *status quo* and attempt to smash the current social situations. This type of response we call the *attack.* It constitutes the wide range of social disorders extending from delinquency and crime to those specific acts of antisocial behavior that contradict and deny the accepted mandates of society. (4) Some individuals, however, lack the capacity for such frontal assaults, and being deficient in the ability to devise the new or to return to the old, take refuge in *retreat* from the social order. Such *retreats* are of two orders. Either the individual may retreat "inwardly," seeking refuge in the delusional worlds that are characteristic of mental disorders, or he may flee outward in space, seeking in migration and mobility refuge from the harrowing tension which his inability to adjust has created. Such individuals, like the legendary Flying Dutchman, are the footloose personalities who seek a haven in every situation. (5) Finally there are the completely dispossessed, those for whom, in the words of the moving Negro spiritual, "there's no hidin' place down there." For such individuals there is no sanctuary. They can find no haven in their familiar pursuits, and lack the spirit to seek a place for themselves in a new world of their own making. Lacking in daring and the comforting sentiments of conformity, they are also incapable of impulsively "smashing the old situation" or of taking cover in a world of unreality. These are the "suicides" for whom the purposes of living have become stultified and for whom the social world has become devoid of meaning and value.

The Structure of Pathological Breakdown

The outcomes of the pathological process we have outlined fit into a logical structure. In the long run, those individuals who face the possibility of maladjustment to social situations are limited in the courses they may follow. They may return, they may seek, they may smash, they may flee, or they may destroy. The following schema is an attempt to depict the

The Framework of Personal and Social Disorganization *

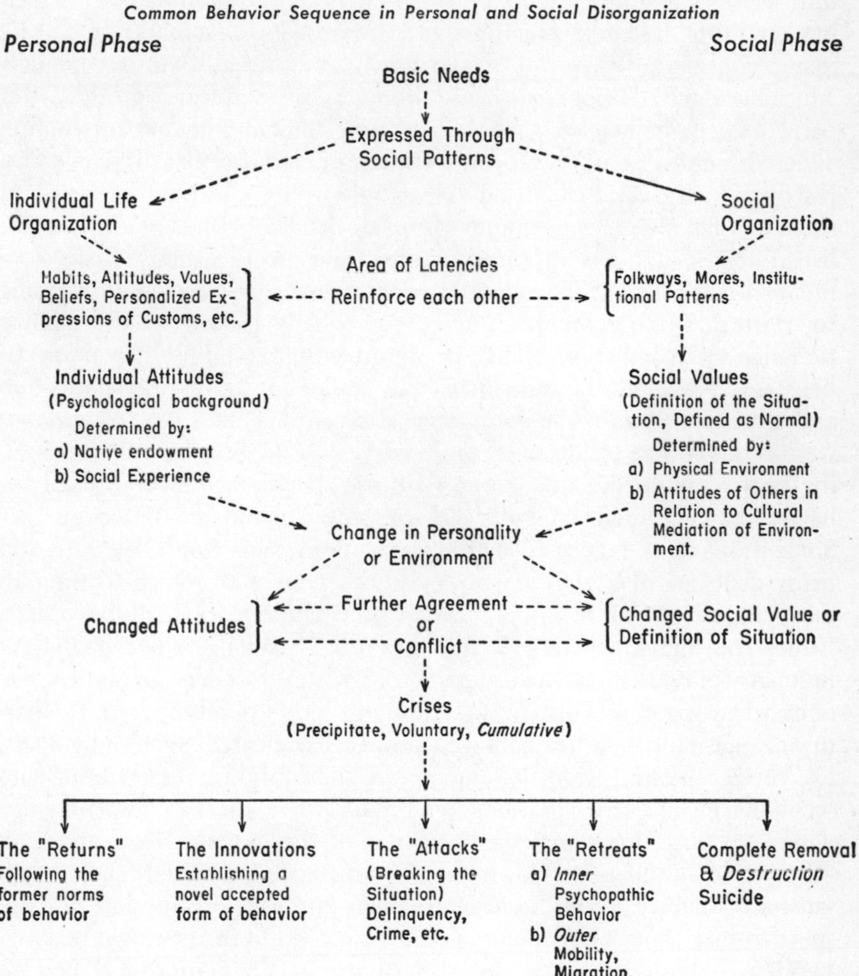

* See Appendix II, p. 127.

entire process, indicating the way in which the conjoined processes of social and personal growth develop, and the way in which the emergent social conditions may lead to further adjustment and integration, or to any of the less successful "problem solutions." In the case of each problem, a knowledge of (1) the attitude of the individual, (2) the given social situation that has developed in relation to it, and (3) the characteristic behavior-processes that have produced the individual should give us some understanding as to why a given outcome takes place.

APPENDIX 2

As a review exercise, the student should attempt to fill in the blank spaces corresponding to the conceptual parts of the framework of personal and social disorganization. At the same time, the student should be cognizant of the operational relationships existing among the several phases of this framework and how they contribute to the development of the five emergent processes of breakdown.

Common Behavior Sequence in Personal and Social Disorganization

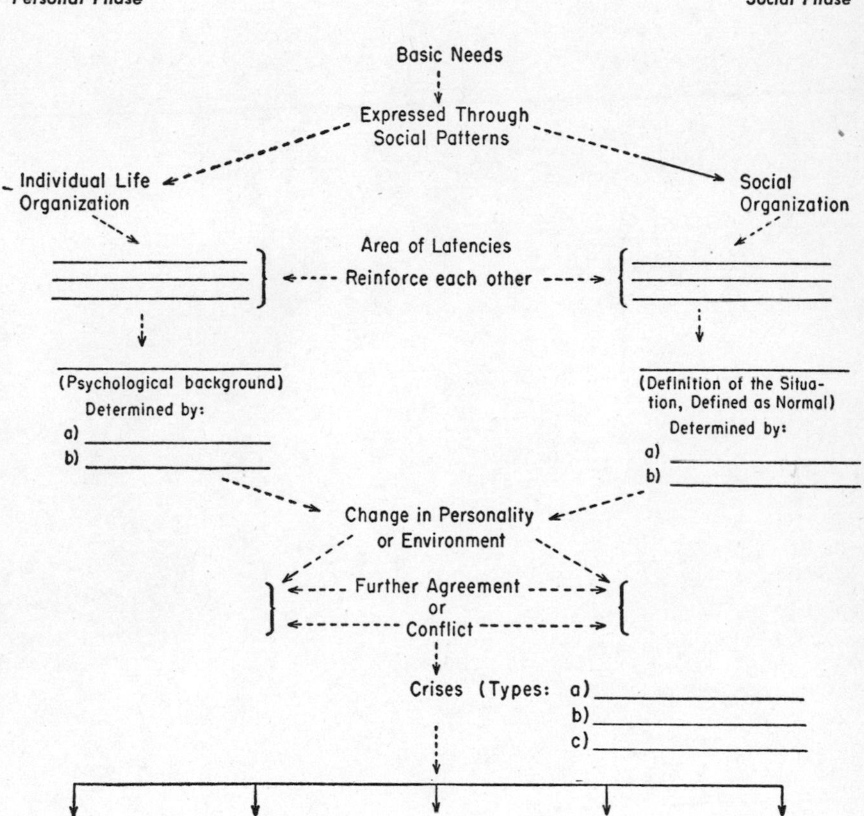

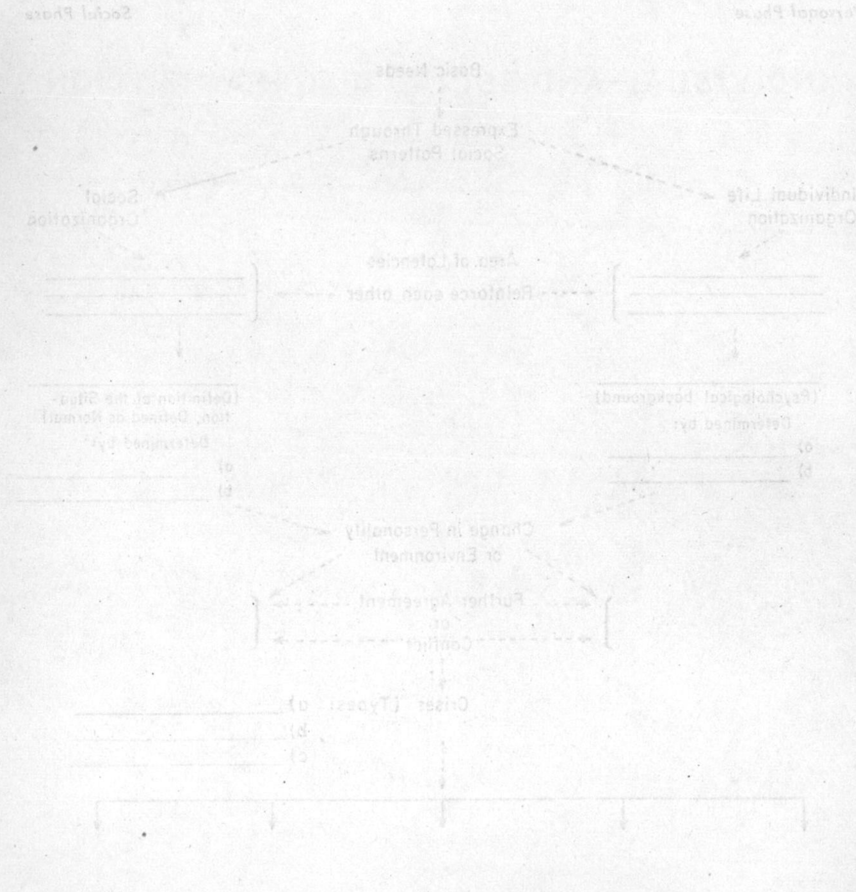

PART TWO

INDIVIDUAL AND SOCIAL DISORGANIZATION

CHAPTER SEVEN

ADOLESCENT TENSIONS AND THE CHANGING SOCIAL ORDER

The Case of Jennie

THE following case is presented not necessarily because of its typicalness, but because it suggests many of the problems that are found in cases of adolescent tension. It aims to provide some beginning understanding of how the attitudes within the latency-structure of the personality function in the development of human problems. The student will observe that there are a series of precipitate and voluntary crises which are provoked by the *cumulative* growth of tensions confronting the critical areas of the girl's social experience.

Jennie is a slender girl of eighteen, medium height, with light brown hair, blue eyes, and clear fair skin. Her manner is appealing, almost childish usually, but suddenly she will grow "frozen" and reticent. She has been known to the court since she was eleven; now she is about to be married. She is living with a small group of girls about her own age in a club. She has held four jobs in six months. She is an expert stenographer. The first time she left because the "surroundings were not refined." The next employer fired her after a few weeks because she was "so much on the defensive, suddenly shutting up and drawing into herself, as if she was afraid of everybody." Why she lost the third job was a mystery. The place was refined enough to suit her fastidious taste, she was punctual and thorough, there was no definite complaint. The director of the employment division hinted something about her "superior manner," but did not care to discuss it. . . . Her school record was unsatisfactory. Though of superior intelligence, she was twice expelled. "If a rule was laid down, it seemed she just had to break it." Her manner of "accepting" criticism angered her teachers: "She wants to stand out and be different from all the others." "She seems to derive satisfaction from hurting people's feelings." "She will never unburden herself in any way; it is as though she had utter contempt for us." She would leave the grounds whenever she felt like it, would fail to register in classes, and, when confronted, would stare at the teacher and refuse to open her mouth. She had no particular friendships with any of her school mates. Once she developed affection for a teacher, but later she said: "I was disappointed in her." She referred to her in her diary as "Feet of Clay."

She "ran every one down, so she could shine by comparison." She could never bear the least argument. A difference in opinion she could not tolerate; she acted as though "it was an effort on the part of the other person to frustrate her."

Negativism is her most frequent attitude. If she is invited to a theatre party, she refuses to go. If any one praises a dessert at dinner, she will not eat it. If someone suggests she is underweight, she proceeds to diet. Though unusually careful about her appearance, she plastered her face with rouge and mascara after hearing a lecture on the moderate use of cosmetics by business girls.

. . . . .

Jennie's father was a carpenter. He was born in New England of an old Catholic family. He married a woman fourteen years younger, a gay Southern girl, who ran away from her husband, leaving seven children, Jennie, aged five, being the youngest. She returned after an absence of several months, stayed a year, then deserted permanently, permitting her husband to divorce her, so she could "marry a man her own age."

Jennie remembers that her father was a morose, stubborn, grouchy man, refusing to talk for weeks at a time, then ending up with violent quarrels. Both parents were constantly criticizing each other, trying to get the children to side with one against the other.

. . . . .

After the parents separated, the children were sent to a friend's house to live. The father quarreled with the friend, and they were sent to an orphanage. When Jennie was eight, they were returned to the father. He took them to New England. . . . [The mother] reported them to the Children's Aid Society and relinquished her right to them for adoption. The father signed the papers too. Each of the seven was adopted into a different home. Jennie came to live in California. She says she does not remember her mother very well, but "didn't like her." Her father, however, she likes and all her day dreams are about the time she will go to live with him and go to college, and become a public speaker.[1]

[1] Taken from Miriam Van Waters, *Parents on Probation* (New York, 1931), pp. 176–81. Reprinted by permission of the *New Republic*.

We discern in the case of Jennie many elements that seem to be typical of the difficulties and tensions experienced by many adolescents within our kind of culture. The impulsiveness and impetuousness, the changeableness, the bridling at criticism (regardless of how well intended), the period of hero-worship, the day-dreaming, the "negativism" —all are characteristic of adolescent behavior in American life. Aside from these elements, however, it will be noticed that there are distinctive behavioral traits which appear to be characteristic only of Jennie and which obviously reflect the peculiarities of her neglected upbringing. These are seen most conspicuously in her desire to be a child, her sporadic reticence, her ultra-fastidiousness, her peculiar reaction to criticism (a common adolescent trait) as expressed by contempt and superiority, her avoidance of friendships, and her bizarre "negativism." Her "adolescent protest," while similar in many respects to the attitudes of others of her age-level, is nevertheless colored in good part by her peculiar upbringing. As a more extensive analysis of the case would reveal, there are a number of "consistencies" in her life-pattern, not contingent necessarily upon her attainment of the adolescent level.

In the complicated psychogenetic pattern of this girl, detailed analysis indicates a number of basic acquired "needs" and a number of specifically oriented functional traits. The youngest in a large family, she was exposed not only to the wrangling of her parents but also to the harrowing consequences of intense sibling-rivalry. Among other "socially processed" needs of Jennie are found intense desires for affection, status, and prestige. As they are intensified within the competitive community, these leave an indelible imprint upon the child's mind. The stigma of divorce within a religious community setting which condemns it, and the keen sense of the inadequacy and inferior status of her unstable family life reinforce her basic needs for security and affection. Although day-dreams of a glamorous and romantic nature are not unusual among adolescents, we are not surprised to find that this girl's fantasies revolve endlessly about her desire to go to college and to be a public speaker. We interpret this as a wish for a secure position of social prestige. Her haughty and often bizarre ways are manifestly attention-seeking devices calculated to obtain the satisfactions she so strongly craves and which her environment has denied her. With it are all the accompanying earmarks of childishness, indicating a strong need and desire for dependence in a person who was never afforded the opportunity of finding an adult status for herself in society. When she falls in love, for example, it is with a man considerably older than herself, who is indulgent towards her foibles and who possesses many of the "dream characteristics" she attributes to her father.

(1) TYPICALNESS OF ADOLESCENT PROBLEMS IN AMERICAN CULTURE

Not in all cultures are adolescent problems so acute and prevalent as in American life. The fact that we should have such widespread behavior disorders at the age of adolescence is an indication of certain dislocations within our institutional structure. Few cultures have been visited with such intense problems of maladjustment during the adolescent span. These problems, however, have not emerged with complete suddenness upon the American scene. From the middle of the nineteenth century onward, the intensification of the Industrial Revolution has been closely paced by the problems of adolescence which are its consequence.

It is difficult for Americans to realize that adolescent problems are so uncommon as to be virtually non-existent in certain areas of the world, particularly among primitives. We have become so inured to them as an inevitable accompaniment of the process of "growing up" that we find it difficult to accept the fact that to certain peoples such problems are highly unusual. When problems of adolescence do arise among these more fortunate peoples, they are likely to be regarded as indications of anti-social or pathological disturbances, rather than as "normal" accompaniments of maturing. That we should find this tranquil condition among primitives is not surprising, in view of the simplicity of their culture and the relative ease and speed with which adult status is attained. Margaret Mead has described the ease with which adult status is gained in the primitive communities of New Guinea and Samoa, unattended by the self-torments and "pushing and shoving contests" between parents and children so conspicuous in our own culture.[2]

To find that such problems are relatively infrequent in certain parts of Europe may also come as a surprise to many of us. This uneven distribution is indicative of the close association of adolescent-tensions with the peculiar institutions of education and child-rearing distinctive of the different cultures involved. In the "folk culture" of the peasants of middle Europe, even until the advent of the Second World War, the incidence of behavior-problems among young people of adolescent age was relatively low. Although France and particularly England (because of its extreme urbanization) do give evidences of certain forms of youthful disorder, the problem in these countries is not so extensive as in the United States and appears localized to the large urban centers. The same situation can be found in the Scandinavian countries, where the incidence of delinquent and disciplinary problems in school and in the family is at an extremely low level, in contrast with the United States. In the course of his investigation of certain folk high schools in Denmark during the summers of

[2] Cf. *Coming of Age in Samoa* (New York, 1927); and *Growing Up in New Guinea* (New York, 1930), by the same author.

1937 and 1938, the author had difficulty in making the teachers of these schools understand adequately the nature of the disciplinary problems that are found so frequently on the high school level in this country. Careful investigation of the records of three such schools over a ten-year period failed to reveal a single case of what we ordinarily term in this country a serious "behavior problem." In their classic *The Polish Peasant in Europe and America,* Thomas and Znaniecki showed how the integrated rural peasant communities of Poland prior to the First World War gave assurance to young people and defined for them their status in the community.[3] The demoralization that occurred among the young emigrants from these cultures in the mammoth industrial warrens of Chicago, Pittsburgh, St. Louis, and New York is not difficult to envisage.

It would appear that where adolescent problems manifest themselves in wide frequency and in a variety of different disorders, there is a close linkage with such sociological matters as cultural heterogeneity, degree of urbanization, extent of industrialization, rapid transitional phases of the cultural processes, and extensive mobility.

(2) INDICES OF ADOLESCENT PROBLEMS

We must recognize (in accordance with our framework of analysis) that the problems of adolescence manifest themselves in distinctive indices. Our previous discussion has indicated that adolescent disturbance is of greater significance in our society than elsewhere. Thus, the question is raised: What evidence indicates that such problems are indigenous to certain cultures and not characteristic of others? We find the answer in the study of comparative rates of behavioral breakdown among the youth of this country as contrasted with rates of breakdown elsewhere. This may be found, as suggested, in quantitative sociological indices as well as in literary-ideological indices. Among the individual indices of adolescent disorganization are to be found the impressively rising rates of delinquency and related disorders during the past three decades in this country. Although adequate comparative information is still difficult to obtain, and is highly suspect for the period prior to 1927 when the United States Children's Bureau first began to issue reports of greater scope and validity, the general secular trend affirms strongly the *continuity* of the problem and its sporadic rise since the beginning of the present century. Thus, Martin H. Neumeyer reports that "except for the decrease during 1944, and the decrease since 1945, the trend in juvenile delinquency, on the basis of cases disposed of by Juvenile Courts reporting to the United States Children's Bureau, was upward, with the main increases occurring during

[3] William I. Thomas and Florian Znaniecki, *The Polish Peasant in Europe and America* (New York, 1927), Vol. II, pp. 1171–6.

the early years of the war. For instance, 78 courts serving areas with populations of 100,000 or more reported an over-all increase of 64 per cent in cases handled from 1938 to 1943, the peak year. Boys' cases had increased 54 per cent and girls' cases 94 per cent."[4] Nor are these increasing rates of juvenile offenses concentrated wholly within the urban areas. Although it is true, as the criminologist E. H. Sutherland points out, that the number of serious offenses increases with the size of the community, the general mobility of the population and the spread of urban influence have involved gradual rises in rural juvenile offenses during the past three decades, especially for those rural regions which have increasingly become industrialized.[5]

Relative to tabooed forms of sexual experience, the Kinsey Report indicates that the highest incidence of premarital intercourse occurs in the late teens among nearly three-fourths (70.5 per cent) of the total population.[6] It is also significant to note in this respect that the percentage of extra-marital intercourse declines precipitately from the period of late adolescence to late maturity, from 70.5 per cent to 51.3 per cent between the ages of sixteen and fifty. Nevertheless, the percentage of highest frequency of extra-marital sex behavior falls within the late adolescent group of young males, from sixteen to twenty years of age, both from the standpoint of the total number of individuals involved and the incidence of such practices, which for this group attains a mean rate of 1.32 per week.[7]

Although girls are less often delinquent than boys, the increase in the rates of female offenders has been marked by a steadily increasing secular trend, particularly since the period of the First World War. Moreover, according to the Children's Bureau, girls' cases are concentrated in the same adolescent age periods as boys' cases, although the range of distribution of boys' cases seems to indicate a greater overlapping into the preadolescent group.[8] In addition to the concentration of these problems within the adolescent age groupings in the United States, we note as well an increasing concentration of mental pathologies and related behavior disorders.

Such individual indices may be supplemented by a wide variety of evidence suggestive of family and community breakdown as well. The extensive spread of Family Service Societies throughout the country testifies not only to the disorganization of the family but to the preoccupation with the problems of youth, as an examination of annual case-report loads

[4] *Juvenile Delinquency in Modern Society* (New York, 1949), pp. 47–8.

[5] *Principles of Criminology* (New York, 1939), pp. 44–5, 135–8.

[6] Alfred C. Kinsey, Wardel B. Pomeroy, and Clyde E. Martin, *Sexual Behavior in the Human Male* (New York, 1948), p. 238.

[7] Ibid., p. 250.

[8] Social Statistics, *The Child* (U. S. Children's Bureau, Washington), II, Nov., 1946.

makes extremely clear. In further testimony to the growing concern over the problem of our "wayward" youth, innumerable spontaneous community associations have arisen throughout the country such as the Community Co-ordinating Councils (which in Los Angeles alone number 88). There are also several types of specialized guidance agencies and clinics, associated with the schools or other local agencies, devoted to the problems of youth. Legislative enactments, such as the State Youth Authority Act in California and the New York State law establishing a Youth Commission to function in co-operation with other public agencies, have become increasingly common. The strong support of the American Law Institute for the passage of National and State Youth Authority Acts, framed according to the model statute which this body has devised, signifies the importance which we attach to this critical age group of our population.

Such quantitative and sociological evidence gives us only part of the picture, however. That Americans have been perennially concerned with the problems of adolescent youth can be seen in a great variety of literary-ideological evidences. Our speech is interlarded with the vernacular allusions we make to this turbulent age group, expressed in such terms as "shaver," "gawk," "moon-calf," "jelly bean" (a sectional usage in the South), and many others that have found root in our folklore and legends. Our literature and drama, both past and present, have devoted considerable attention to this problem. The beloved *Seventeen* of Booth Tarkington has become almost an American classic, while Americans of all ages have delighted in the antics of the heroes of America's genuine classics, Mark Twain's *Huckleberry Finn* and *Tom Sawyer*. The stage, too, has shared this American interest. Among others, we may cite Eugene O'Neill's *Ah Wilderness*, which deals with a crucial phase of the conflict between an adolescent son and his father.

(3) ADOLESCENT TENSIONS AND SOCIAL LATENCIES

The source of adolescent tensions in American life is to be found in the latent tendencies of the American social structure and not necessarily in the physiological changes occurring during adolescence. As Ruth Benedict has said, "not biological puberty but what adulthood means in that culture" conditions the significance of puberty.[9] Furthermore, "the clear physiological facts of adolescence . . . are first socially interpreted even where they are stressed." [10] Among all cultures we must draw the distinction between *biological maturity* and *sociological maturity*. *Biological maturity* refers to the development of the physical organism to its full procreative and other physiological capacities, while *sociological maturity*

[9] *Patterns of Culture* (New York, 1934), p. 23.
[10] Ibid., p. 23.

refers to the attribution by the group of those traits that endow the personality with adult social status. Sociological maturity involves the capacity of the individual to assume the social, economic, and political obligations that mature participation in the life of the community signifies.

Among primitive communities, the development of such an adult status is relatively easy to attain. The skills of hunting and the other types of physical skills involved in ritualistic participation frequently find a high level of achievement when the boy is relatively young. In a similar position during this period is the girl, who frequently enjoys greater dexterity and endurance than her mother, who is overburdened at an early age with continual childbearing and unrelenting toil. Thus, biological maturity and sociological maturity tend to coincide in primitive life.

The puberty ceremonials for young men and women in primitive society emphasize the fundamental adult skills and values which the given society holds paramount in the furtherance of its social life. A differential weighting, according to sex, in the emphasis on skills and social values comes conspicuously to the fore in puberty rites, indicating clearly what the group considers of chief importance in its own existence. Many communities neglect the puberty rites for girls, or hold them in a subordinate position, for the reason that the masculine virtues are considered to be the principal ones. Hence the focus on the male ritualistic ceremonials. Among the Northern Plains Indians, the chief virtue in social life was warfare, and consequently puberty ceremonials were reserved for males. These ceremonials stressed valor and feats of endurance. In Central Africa, where prestige is attained by marriage to females whose desirableness and beauty are characterized by extreme obesity, puberty ceremonials for young girls are associated with the "fattening houses," where the young maiden is sedulously fattened.

In our society, the trend has been toward the "prolongation of infancy." Public school education is mandatory in all states, and in many sections of the country the great majority of young people are expected to complete high school as well. The specialized occupations of modern life require the mastery of intricate skills which, for many of our young people, involve schooling into their late twenties. Physicians, lawyers, engineers, and other highly trained professionals frequently find themselves unable to assume the responsibilities of economic self-support and marriage until well beyond the onset of physiological maturity. *In the degree to which disparities exist between the attainment of biological and sociological maturity, adolescent problems multiply in scope and intensity.*

The dichotomy of biological and sociological maturity in American life indicates the functioning of social latencies. What was the nature of the early adjustments in American life which shaped the attitudes towards adolescence and which are now incompatible with present-day conditions? Among the several latencies that still persist in American life in the form of well-defined *social attitudes* and *values* may be found three primary conceptions: (1) the conceptions concerning early entrance into employment and the control of the parent over the employment of his children; (2) the vestiges of patriarchal control and its related patterns in family life; and (3) elements of the rigid code of sexual morality obtaining in family life, as manifested in part through the functioning of the "double standard" of sexual practice.

Against each one of these still-existent tendencies are counterpoised specific situations and conditions that conflict with them. Thus, opposed to the early entrance into industry of our nineteenth-century forebears, we find the contemporary process of prolonged education which postpones vocational placement until late in adolescence or the early twenties, and even beyond these age levels for persons trained in the professions. In view of the increasing percentage of young people attending college (approximately one out of every seven of college age before the Second World War), the disparity between the defined attitude and the concrete reality is likely to grow even more acute.[11]

In the place of the accepted subjection of the nineteenth-century child to the will of the father, there are now powerful sentiments in favor of individual initiative and freedom for young people. These have developed in part from our educational system itself; they have been intensified by the growth of mobility since the turn of the century.

Finally, in regard to the previous rigidity of our sexual mores, an unprecedented growth in sexual freedom and liberality has taken place, abetted by mobility (in which the automobile has played a key part), the growth of scientific knowledge in general and specific biological doctrines in particular, the associated widespread knowledge of contraception and its use, and the opportunities for unsupervised sexual companionship.

The configurations of secondary traits surrounding each one of these latent adjustment-areas have entered into deep conflict with our attitudes and social values, which contradict in countless ways the imposition of these new behaviors. The result is to leave us confused and unable to define the statuses which adolescent youth require in an adjusted social order. These latencies represent only a part of the total configuration of social patterns which function in respect to adolescent problems. We may see them in their contradictory form by means of the following summary.

[11] These figures have changed drastically since 1945. By 1949, approximately one out of every five young people of college age was attending some institution of learning above the high-school level. In New York State, for that year, the rate was approximately 12 per cent while in California, it attained the unprecedentedly high level of 30 per cent.

Some Latencies Operating in Adolescent Life

Nineteenth-Century Latencies (Persisting as elements in contemporary social attitudes and values)	*Contemporary Tendencies* *
1) Early entrance into vocations and employment.	1) Deferred entrance into employment brought about by prolonged compulsory schooling.
2) Patriarchal family control	2) Self-determination of youth, abetted by educational processes and modern mobility, etc.
3) Rigid sexual mores and the "double standard."	3) Increasing liberality and freedom in sexual matters, induced by mobility, modern science and biology, contraception, leisure, etc.

* In appraising latencies in relation to contemporary social tendencies, we should note whether they reinforce or contradict the contemporary social and cultural conditions, and in what specific respects.

The original tendencies in such latencies were integral parts of a balanced social order revolving about a stable agricultural economy whose principle social unit was the large, male-dominated kinship grouping. These fundamental agencies have tended to dissolve under the impact of modern industrial economy, although the ghosts of their attitudes still survive.

(4) SOCIAL STRUCTURE AND AGE-LEVEL STATUS

Within all societies, there exist what Professor Linton calls the *ascribed statuses* for the different age-levels, sexes, and ranks.[12] The term *ascribed statuses* refers to the expectations concerning behavior which are developed within the several structural groupings. Thus, according to the classic admonition of Saint Paul, the child is asked to put away childish things upon attaining a man's estate. The ascribed statuses comprise a number of socially approved *role-behaviors* which the individual is supposed to exercise in conjunction with his given status. In an integrated society, these "role-behaviors" are well-defined and the individual is able

[12] *The Study of Man* (New York, 1936), Chap. 8, esp. pp. 115 ff.

to practice them without undue strain. The statuses of the several age-groups and sexes frequently permit a number of "alternatives," as Linton puts it, which afford the individual a defined latitude of choice. Although there are occasional individuals among the primitives, such as the "contrary ones" of the Crazy Horse Societies of the Plains Indians, whose antics appear to contradict normal behavior patterns, they are not common and are usually given a status category of their own.

In general, personality tensions arise only if there is confusion concerning the definition of the status or if there are obstacles in the way of the individual's attaining his position. The confusion concerning the ascribed statuses to be conferred upon adolescents in American life is a reflection of the conflict between our latent attitudes and contemporary conditions. Thus, the individual is never sure of the degree of latitude he is to exercise in relation to the several "role-behaviors" incumbent on his status. In one breath, he is told to develop self-initiative and freedom, and in the next, he is peremptorily told that he must limit the range of this freedom. A good illustration can be seen in the encouragement given young people in their teens to engage with remarkable freedom in courtship practices as a forerunner to marriage, without their being provided with adequate safeguards for themselves and for society. Thus, under a condition which frequently encourages illicit sex relations, we condemn the outcome while approving the social process that creates it.

(5) INDIVIDUAL VARIATIONS OF ADOLESCENT DISORDERS

Whenever adolescent disorders occur on a large scale, incontrovertible evidence exists concerning the state of cultural disequilibrium and the status of the adolescent group. According to Kluckhohn and Murray: "In our society one may instance the constant pressure of the conflict between age-group standards and parental group standards upon youngsters and adolescents. This is without doubt a type conflict of our culture." [13]

There are, of course, individual variations in the expressions of such adolescent disorders. The individual patterning of adolescent disorders, which may manifest themselves in a wide variety of tensions ranging from simple obstreperousness to delinquency, may be sought only in the cumulative process of the individual's psychogenetic development. The basis of the adolescent disorder lies in the socio-psychological latencies or prior attitudes which are non-adjustive within some particular cultural or social framework. *In short, adolescent problems do not originate within the*

[13] Cf. Clyde Kluckhohn and Henry A. Murray, "Outline of a Conception of Personality," *Personality in Nature, Society and Culture*, edited by Kluckhohn and Murray (New York, 1949), p. 22.

period of adolescence. The measure of their seriousness and the form they take reflect the entire prior history of the individual. A popular misconception still exists that such disturbances have their specific origins at the time of puberty. Works such as G. Stanley Hall's volumes on *Adolescence,* which have shaped the thinking of prior generations concerning this problem, have been partially responsible for this false emphasis.[14] Actually these earlier works are themselves indicative of the cultural stress which has directed attention towards adolescence as a "universal problem" symptomatic of our civilization and age.

Whenever individual problems of adolescence occur, they indicate the conflict between the status-conceptions concerning youth and the attitude of the adolescent himself. Thus, in the case of Jennie, the attitudes she "inherited" from her past were a protest against the behavior expected of her by the adults with whom she came into contact.

(6) THE PHYSIOLOGY OF ADOLESCENCE: THE "ANXIETIES OF GROWTH"

The enormous physical changes in the human organism during puberty provoke disorders only to the extent that they are socially misinterpreted. This is not to deny that acute tensions are experienced by the individual in the attainment of full physical and sexual growth. We wish simply to indicate that the tensions manifest themselves in disorder only when the group fails to define adequately the nature of their outlets and fails to provide for their proper expression and understanding. In American life, the physical tensions attendant upon adolescent development have been considerable. Largely because they have been misinterpreted and misunderstood by the adolescent himself, or by his parents, these tensions have contributed to the development of anxieties. Such "anxieties of growth" are evidenced in the guilt-feelings of the young person who does not understand some of the perfectly normal experiences accompanying the development of his sexual life. Because such normal experiences are part of the process of growing up of all young people, and because they are so frequently misjudged by adults as well as by adolescents, we will examine briefly some of the principal psysiological conditions accompanying puberty.

(1) *Puberty and Intelligence.* The intellectual capacity of most individuals is firmly fixed by the time of puberty. In fact, the brain itself, unlike most of the other organs of the body, has already attained full size at this time. Good physical development frequently keeps pace with the intellectual development of the child, with the

[14] G. Stanley Hall, *Adolescence* (New York, 1904).

result that precocious children mature at an early age. The psychologist Terman, for example, in the study of gifted girls, discovered that almost one-half (48 per cent) attained puberty before the age of thirteen, as contrasted with groups of normal girls where approximately 25 per cent attained puberty before that age. We may conclude that, in general, the likelihood of early attainment of puberty is about twice as great among bright children as among normal or dull children. Thus, the parent of the bright child can anticipate an early onset of the problems of adolescence which are contingent on physiological development.

(2) *Age Levels.* Although it is extremely difficult to determine when active adolescence manifests itself, it is commonly assumed that girls of Anglo-Saxon background mature at an average age of thirteen and one-half years. In broad distributions, the variations may be from three to four years above and below this average. Sample studies of girls of Southern and Middle European background have indicated an average ranging from six months to a year lower than this estimate, with similar broad variations. Recent evidence, however, has appeared to contradict these findings. Statistical differences in the average ages of maturing for girls of different ethnic backgrounds fail in many cases to reveal such differentials.

It is generally agreed that boys mature about a year later, on the average, than do girls, and that the period of development is longer. It is currently suggested that the period of growth may be terminated for girls by the age of twenty, while it may extend to as high as twenty-five years for men.

(3) *The Secondary Sexual Characteristics.* Accompanying adolescent growth are a number of secondary sexual characteristics, such as the development of bodily hair, changes in voice, stature, shape, and other physical traits. For the boy, the growth of the beard may constitute a problem as, for example, when the "doting" parent who hates to see her child grow up discourages him from shaving. (It is significant to note here the origin of the term "shaver.") The vocal chords almost double in length during this period, with a corresponding enlargement of the larynx. Whereas the change in the pitch of the girl's voice is not so marked as that of the boy, her voice too becomes richer and more resonant. The boy frequently has a new and difficult vocal instrument to master; he never knows whether the tone he is about to produce will be a tremulous alto or a booming basso profundo and remains in considerable fear of provoking embarassment for himself. Occasions have been noted where parents showed concern over this perfectly natural phenomenon, even requesting, in one recorded instance, that the boy's tonsils be removed.

(4) *Changes in Size.* Dr. Nancy Bayley's recent studies at the University of Southern California on the rates of bodily growth have given us some interesting new perspectives on the prediction of bodily height and size.[15] Prior to the age of eleven, boys appear to be somewhat larger, on the average, than girls. At the age of eleven, both sexes appear to be approximately the same in weight and stature. Because of the earlier maturing of girls, however, at the age of twelve they begin to exceed boys in weight and height. This growth spurt does not ordinarily become common among boys until approximately the age of thirteen. After fourteen, boys begin to show marked differences in size from girls. The rates of growth are sporadic and irregular, often causing acute discomfort for the individuals and their families. Records indicate changes of as much as six inches in height and twenty to thirty pounds in weight within one year.

(5) *Disproportionate Bodily Growth.* Such rapid growth changes create further difficulty for many adolescents because of the highly disproportionate manner in which they occur. At a time when the young person is first becoming acutely self-conscious and aware of his appearance, he is confronted with the dilemmas of large feet and hands (a source of genuine embarrassment to the sensitive girl), which by the age of thirteen or fourteen have already attained full size. For families of insufficient means, the problem of keeping the young person in clothes—which he seems to outgrow overnight—is a considerable one, particularly in view of the young person's growing concern over his appearance. (A case is known to the writer of a child who was forced to sleep with his shoes on because of the rate at which he outgrew them!) Among other sources of embarrassment are the size of the nose (which reaches full size relatively early) and the enlarged skin pores. The sebaceous glands become hyperactive with the common result of clogged pores and a pimply, blemished skin condition known as "acne." The stomach enlarges considerably and the craving for food, as anyone who has lived with adolescents can testify, is perpetual and nothing short of phenomenal. Changes in shape become more pronounced, resulting in the characteristic contours of masculinity and femininity. Although obesity occurs, slenderness is the more typical condition of adolescence.

(6) *The Internal Structure.* The reproductive organs speedily attain full maturity which, in the case of the girl, creates an entire series of new problems of hygiene and psychological adaptation through the activation of the menses. The turbulent period of growth is essentially a matter of hyperactivity of all the glands associated with sexual

[15] "Size and Body Build of Adolescents in Relation to Rate of Skeletal Maturing," *Child Development* (1943), 14, 51–89.

maturation, with the result that the organism is in a highly charged state. An outer disclosure of this glandular change may be seen in the enlargement of the thyroid for girls, resulting in the fullness of the neck which loses its former "scrawny" appearance. In keeping with the general glandular tone, the sweat glands are active, resulting in damp hands and feet.

(7) *Vital Statistics of Adolescence.* Despite the precarious glandular state of the organism at this time, the resistance to disease is high. Mortality tables reveal that the smallest percentage of deaths from disease occurs between the ages of ten to fourteen. Incipient adult disorders, however, do manifest themselves as potential "danger-signals" in the form of anemia, nose-bleed, headache, nervousness, palpitations of the heart, and other symptoms. Although the death rate is low, the accident rate, as we would expect, is extremely high as a result of the characteristic recklessness of the age and the chafing under the control of adults.

These physical changes, manifesting themselves in novel inner impulsions and outer appearance, bring in their wake a whole series of "anxieties of growth." Conspicuous among such anxieties are the concerns experienced over one's appearance and the impression one is making upon others. Illustrative of such anxiety is the case of an unusually tall and slender girl of fifteen years who assumed a crouching position in order to diminish her stature.

(7) EMOTIONAL DEVELOPMENTS OF NORMAL ADOLESCENCE

Correlated with the development of the personality are certain emotional states appropriate to the enactment of the "role-behaviors" involved in the individual's changing status. The maturing of the individual proceeds upon physiological, intellectual, and emotional levels. Criteria in every culture indicate the expected patterns of growth upon each age level in respect to physical development, intellectual attainment, and emotional expression. During adolescence the individual redefines his status in terms of imminent adulthood. The struggle for the adult status manifests itself in a number of diffuse emotional efforts, aggravated by the underlying physiological conditions of glandular imbalance and change.

In attempting to win adult status in a highly competitive society, the individual must translate the physiologically "stirred up state of the organism" into patterns of effective social action. The ease with which these "stirred up states" of the organism arise is a direct result of the bodily changes which the adolescent is experiencing. These changes render him particularly susceptible to those circumstances of his environment that appear to deny or to fulfill for him the striving for status. W. B. Cannon, the eminent physiologist, has indicated that there is a fundamental physiological pattern for emotional states within the organism, regardless of the specific character of the emotion involved. Although such physiologically "stirred up states" may vary in intensity, their social functioning and the directions which they take are significant in the development of the individual into adulthood.

The precariousness of the emotional state during adolescence may be seen in the activities of a typical adolescent boy during a normal day. The hyperactive glandular development, coupled with the frustrations and annoyances associated with the new conception of the self as defined within our culture, produces one emotional outburst after another. Life for the adolescent becomes a never-ending series of major and minor emotional crises. The wear upon the organism is considerable. Much as his parents and teachers may disbelieve him, the adolescent, despite his sporadic furious outbursts of energy, is frequently as tired as he states. During anger, a common adolescent emotion, it is estimated that only fifteen per cent of the normal supply of digestive juices are secreted into the stomach.

> Even before breakfast, the adolescent boy has been subject to a number of violent rages. The disreputable garment, which his mother, despite his shrilling protests, has placed in the laundry, and his favorite necktie are not available. Breakfast is bolted, leading to complaints from the parent and recriminations from the young man. Rushing belatedly from the house, he finds that his girl, the current flame of his life, has grown tired of waiting, and has proceeded to school with his despised rival. Arriving late and breathless to his classroom, he becomes infuriated because the teacher calls upon him first to recite upon a lesson which he has only half prepared, if at all. From then on, he is precipitated from one crisis into another.

The criteria of "emotional maturity" are difficult to establish and vary from society to society and social group to social group. In general, emotional maturity consists in feeling and expressing those emotions which are appropriate to the existent situation, thus gaining adjustment for the individual. Appropriateness may be defined in terms of the standard conception of the situation.[16] In certain social orders, the patterning of emotional experience and expression in conjunction with an early acquired status may create difficulties for subsequent statuses. Thus, among the Comanche the young adult is expected to display emotions of rage and

[16] This problem of the social processing of the emotions has been largely neglected by sociologists and anthropologists who have dealt with it only indirectly in conjunction with the concepts of *status* and *role*.

jealousy in keeping with his honored status as warrior. As an old man who no longer fights, however, he must be inoffensive and quiet or be considered a malevolent person or even a dangerous sorcerer; yet all of his previous emotional training has ill prepared him for the role he must assume in old age.

Frankwood Williams has conceived of the emotional expression of adolescents in American society as moved by the striving for normal heterosexuality and the desire for emancipation from the home.[17] The emotional displays of adolescent protest may be offensive, he asserts, but the underlying condition is healthy and normal. On the basis of his interpretation of the grounds for these emotional processes, he formulates three criteria for emotional maturity: (1) the ability to respond to situations devoid of "infantile symbolic investments," that is, free of childish associations; (2) the ability to react to situations in terms of their necessities and realities and not in terms of inherent or acquired compulsions and fears; and (3) *the capacity to meet an unalterable situation with a minimum of emotional conflict.*

According to these criteria, few adults in American society can be said to have attained full emotional maturity in all respects. To illustrate this point, Williams cites a number of common "culture-types" who are unable to subject their emotional tendencies to the restraining conditions of socially approved and effective behavior. In his copious list of "emotionally immature" adults, he mentions among others: individuals who are incapable of living an adult sex life, frigid wives, men who must love many women briefly, parents embarrassed by the sex questions of their children, husbands more devoted to their mothers than to their wives, ministers "whose hearts bleed," husbands who are not understood by their wives, and executives who want what they want when they want it.[18]

(8) THE DEVELOPMENT OF THE MAJOR EMOTIONS IN AMERICAN CULTURE: LOVE, ANGER, FEAR

The specific occasions upon which love, anger, and fear may be experienced have been carefully defined by the culture. Critical observation reveals the several behavioral stages and the objectives that these separate emotions may take.

Love. In Western European culture, the patterns of sexuality and the emotions of love are a result of the peculiar conditions of family organization and of child care. During the earliest period of initial infantile development, the child's affections are turned inwardly upon himself, in the form of worship of his own body and its functions (an attitude which

[17] *Adolescence: Studies in Mental Hygiene* (New York, 1930), pp. 102 ff.
[18] Ibid., pp. 18, 19.

Freud calls *narcissism*), while at the same time it goes outward toward individuals who cater to his bodily needs. The initial love object outside the child is the mother or her substitute. The varying emphasis upon certain bodily functions and the mode of feeding and handling, lay the basis for the various types of fetishism and symbolism which appear in different cultures. The type of bodily care that is exercised in our culture, emphasizing the needs of hygienic cleanliness and the importance of sphincter control, places a premium upon certain types of bodily functions and relationships. Thus, the early emphasis upon routines and training, in stressing the anal-oral sensory tracts, causes these to be perceived as highly charged erogenous zones.[19]

The mother's control over the child through intensive and individualized care tends to develop acute dependencies coloring both the child's attitude (and especially the sensory-emotional basis for such attitudes) toward the mother, and the mother's conceptions of the child's needs. Personality structure in our culture, therefore, is considerably different from that among primitives, where early child-training may be socialized and distributed. In Western culture, this early dependency is inevitably followed by the trauma of rejection in some form, as signalized by the appearance of other siblings upon the scene, and the consequent maturing of the individual. The later status conceptions of childhood are not necessarily harmonious with the early dependence fostered by the mother-child relationship. Thus, the child's expression of his need for his mother is thwarted even long before the adolescent period by the fear of being considered a "mama's boy" or a "sissy." [20]

When the child leaves the highly limited environment of the mother's continuous care, his affectional tendencies become fixed on sub-

[19] The degree to which our time-sense in modern industrial society functions in respect to the attitude of parent to child constitutes an important feature of our child-rearing practices. It would be interesting to delineate the relationship between such fundamental concepts of our culture as emotional security and the need for routinized training. Certainly in primitive and folk cultures, the absence of such marked adherence to time-schedules, resulting in spontaneous and rhythmic organic responses, must result in profound differences in emotional and personality patterning.

[20] Class-structured differences are important to consider here. The use of the "wet-nurse" in aristocratic European culture imposes a formal relationship between parent and child. Among the English landed gentry, for example, the child may be nursed by the parent; the speedy rejection of the child after initial weaning constitutes the type of barrier which is reflected in the formal "mater" and "pater" relationship of the "well-bred" British child. The early age at which these English children leave home for boarding-school accentuates the formal relationship to their parents. The "stolidity" and impersonality of the British, if it actually exists, might prove to be a result of such child care.

The ambivalent attitude of concern towards the Negro and recurrent hostility as a culture pattern in our own South—particularly the ante-bellum South—might conceivably be attributable in part to the fact that the plantation wife, the aristocratic mistress of the household, relegated the care of her offspring to the Negro "mammy," who served as a surrogate mother.

stitute adults—schoolteachers, relatives, or other adults in the immediate environment. These adult-fixated processes continue until about the eighth or ninth year, when the individual's affections become attached to playmates of his own age and sex. In the sexual development of Western man, Freud regards this stage, which he calls "polymorphous perverse," as a period of latent homosexual development. This stage, referred to by one writer as the "yah-yah-yah" stage, is rather frequently marked during the late pre-adolescent period by intense hostility toward girls, particularly those of his own age. In earlier middle adolescence, he develops frequently shifting attachments to persons of the same age and the opposite sex. This is the period of violent and "soul-searing" crushes, which wane as rapidly as they blossom. The ultimate stage of this development appears to occur on the late adolescent and early adult levels, when affection is directed toward a person of the opposite sex for periods of relatively long duration. Regression may occur on any level in accordance with the social and cultural barriers created in the frustration of normative social expression. Luella Cole gives us a good picture of such regression in the following case: [21]

> Elaine was a thirty-two-year-old woman. She had been the youngest of three sisters. Her father died soon after her birth. The mother and the three girls then went to live with an aunt who was a missionary in India. At the mission there were two other white women, but no men. The girls were not allowed to play with native children. When Elaine was fifteen, she was sent to a boarding school in an eastern state. The rules there were strict; she saw no boys. . . . After two years she entered a women's college. At both boarding school and college she was conspicuous for her crushes. At one time she fell in love with her history teacher, spent several entire nights sitting outside the woman's door. . . . This affair lasted about six weeks, during which she lost over fifteen pounds. Later, she developed an equally intense crush on a senior girl. . . . They managed to spend the entire twenty-four hours of almost every day with each other. . . . Several other crushes followed. Finally, at the age of twenty-nine, she decided to get a Ph.D. in physics and matriculated at a large state university.
>
> There are few women majors in physics (her department) so she was for the first time in her life in classes with men. At first she treated them with utter scorn. . . . During her second graduate year a marked change took place and she became boy-crazy in the silliest possible fashion. She chased every man in the department. . . . Her behavior closely paralleled that of a thirteen-year-old girl

[21] *Psychology of Adolescence* (3rd ed., New York, 1948) pp. 109–11. Reprinted by permission of Rinehart & Company, Inc.

who has suddenly discovered that boys are nice instead of mean. . . . Then a new young man enrolled in the physics department to get an M.A. . . . There was a whirlwind love affair, followed by her elopement.

This woman remained in a homosexual stage of development, probably through environmental influences, until she was twenty-nine. Then she passed, in three years, through the early period of mixed scorn and attraction towards men and boys, through the boy-crazy phase, through a flowering of romantic love, and into a final adult adjustment.

Geoffrey Gorer, the British anthropologist, has shown that the development of affectional relations in American life is closely associated with the social processes of competition, a highly distinctive American cultural trait. The child is continually compared with others and affection is frequently bestowed as a reward for success in the competitive process. The result is that Americans tend to identify the two processes: to be loved is to be successful, and to be successful is to be loved. Gorer sees expressions of this in every phase of American life, especially in the peculiar American pattern of pre-courtship "dating," during adolescence, which he describes as follows: [22]

Because dating is so idiosyncratic of Americans, (though most Americans do not suspect this, believing like the rest of the world, that the behavior they are used to is "human nature") and because it employs the form—but not the content—of love-making, it has been the cause of innumerable and serious misunderstandings whenever young Americans have come in contact with foreigners of the opposite sex. An invitation to a date—a pleasant and mutually profitable evening to enhance each other's self-esteem and demonstrate one's skill in the game—is almost always interpreted by a non-American as an attempt at seduction. If it is indignantly repudiated, both parties are left angry and dissatisfied; if it is immediately acceded to, the American at least feels defrauded, as if one had set out for a hunt and the fox had insisted on sitting down in one's back yard.

What distinguishes the date from other conversation is a mixture of persiflage, flattery, wit, and love-making which was formerly called a "line," but which each generation dubs with a new name.

Most men are articulately self-conscious about their lines and can describe them with ease. . . . The object of the line is to entertain, amuse and captivate the girl, *but there is no deep emotional involvement* [italics ours]. It is a game of skill.

The girl's skill consists in parrying the line without discouraging

[22] *The American Character* (New York, 1947).

her partner or becoming emotionally involved herself. . . . To remain the winner, she must make the nicest discrimination between yielding and rigidity. . . .

. . . This period, roughly from twelve to twenty-five, is Youth—The Best Years of Our Lives—and is almost without *exaggeration* the *raison* d'être of living.

Anger. Causes and manifestations of anger, *as socially processed*, differ for the various age-levels. In young children anger is due primarily to *physical thwartings*; in adolescents anger is provoked by situations of a social nature, common among which are imagined slights to self-esteem. Among adults anger is frequently caused by interference with work or leisure, or by matters concerning social convictions, principles, beliefs, and procedures of behavior.[23]

The manifestations of anger also appear to follow prescribed forms. Among children, anger is expressed in rigidity, screaming, flailing about, kicking, and the like; adolescent responses tend to be vocal—although infantile temper tantrums may persist. Although adult responses assume the common form of verbal recrimination, women are known to weep and men to kick things.

Investigations have been conducted by T. H. Furfey and S. L. and L. C. Pressey to determine objective and measurable equivalents for the attainment of different age-levels of emotional response.[24] Such studies appear to support strongly the view that adolescent reactions of rage are precipitated largely by affronts to esteem. Luella Cole has listed some of the more typical reasons offered by adolescents of both sexes for their anger.[25] Among boys, such reasons as the following were common: "I was bawled out for talking in the library"; "a professor's daughter acted like she owned the place"; "I was to meet two friends at the theatre and they kept me waiting nearly an hour." Among girls: "somebody told me the boys were circulating an ugly snapshot of me"; "the hostess of our sorority gave me the poorest cut of meat"; "the professor explained every one else's paper but left out mine." The chief causes for anger among both sexes appeared to be indignities to the person, but this was more often true of girls (64 per cent) than of boys (36 per cent). Moreover, even in those situations where the sources of frustration were physical, the episodes themselves were closely associated with situations having to do with the appearance of the individual or the impression he made upon others. The differences in the duration of anger for young children and adolescents pointed also to

[23] Luella Cole, *Psychology of Adolescence*, p. 59.

[24] T. H. Furfey, "A Revised Scale for Determining Developmental Age in Boys," *Child Development*, II (1931); S. L. and L. C. Pressey, "Development of the Interest-Attitude Tests," *Journal of Applied Psychology*, XVII (1933), 1–16.

[25] Luella Cole, *Psychology of Adolescence*, pp. 58–62.

the increased attention which self-conceptions receive during adolescence. The rages of children were momentary and spontaneous, in 90 per cent of the cases lasting less than five minutes. Among adolescents, states of rage showed a high variability, ranging from periods of one minute to forty-eight hours. The rages of children may easily be deflected by directing their attention elsewhere, while the growing awareness of their status may cause the adolescent to "bear a grudge" for quite lengthy periods.

Fear. Fear, a destructive emotion, develops from a great variety of causes. From the few simple and diffuse fears of the infant, social conditioning can produce the most complicated patterns of fear response. Studies of fear responses of primitive peoples indicate the dominant focus which the value-systems of society exert in fear-producing situations. Adolescents in primitive communities are made aware of these predominant sources of fear during the *rites de passage* of puberty. These are occasions when they are literally "taught" what they must fear in the social and physical environment.

Within our own culture, the fears of the young child are produced by the physical occasions of violence, accidents, or natural phenomena of a destructive nature. Corresponding to the causes of the other emotional states, the adolescent's fears are essentially *social* in nature, while the adult's fears stem from practical sources, such as hazards to his security, or routines of his existence, employment, health, family, or friends. Interestingly enough, because of its primitive nature the emotion of fear does not result in such marked differences in behavior as are distinguishable in other emotional expressions.

Fear manifestations for the different age-levels are largely matters of degree, rather than of kind. Thus, while the child shows his fear by physical rigidity, scampering away, whimpering or "screaming to mother," the adolescent's reactions are a mild variation of the same reactions—walking rapidly away, chattering or whistling (instead of whimpering), and seeking the company of acquaintances. Because of this persistence of early fear responses in maturing habit-patterns, *the acquisition of patterned fear responses during adolescence is extremely significant.*

The association of fears with the conception of the adult self developed during the adolescent period very likely lays the basis for much of the pathological and psychoneurotic excess we discover in later adult life. The disparity between our actions and our professed beliefs concerning sex and other forms of adult behavior (revealed in one instance in our confused conceptions of the status of the adolescent in our society) encourages frustrations and fears from three sources: (1) the "sense of guilt" which many adolescents experience, (2) the failure to provide adequate outlets for normal aggressive tendencies, and (3) the sense of the "unknown" created by our ambiguous treatment of the adolescent.[26] In American life, the strong identification with the attitudes of the parent frequently leads to the disenchantment of adolescence when such attitudes are found to have no basis. If further evidence was needed to confirm this view, the studies of Hartshorne and May make this perfectly clear in exposing the illusory basis of the virtues we consistently inculcate in school and home by the time the child is in the fifth and sixth grades.[27] James West's study of an American community, *Plainville*, shows how deeply-implanted puritanical virtues may help produce the anguished self-doubts of many adolescents.[28] Little scope is afforded in adolescent rearing for the effective resolution of the many frustrations which the ordinary tensions of adolescence introduce. Failure to reconcile the previous status-conceptions of the child with the new impulses of adolescence leads to "unknown" and undefined modes of behavior which frequently strike terror in the heart and mind of the growing youth.[29]

(9) SYMPTOMS OF ADOLESCENT EMOTIONAL DISTURBANCE

Emotional disturbances among adolescents in American culture commonly take certain well-defined forms. Briefly, these are (1) projection, (2) compensation, (3) an excessive sense of superiority, (4) autism and fantasy, and (5) various forms of rationalization. The presence of these symptoms does not necessarily indicate a dangerous emotional problem, but their prevalence among adolescents in American life is symptomatic of the disturbed nature of this period. *All of these symptoms may be described as efforts to organize the adolescent personality upon a basis where special status and prestige may be accorded the individual.* This is their generic aspect. *Projection* represents the tendency to attribute to others one's own qualities or defects and the responsibilities for one's own deficiencies. The forms which projection takes in our society are particularly

[26] With respect to this latter point, Gardner Murphy emphasizes the "deviation from the familiar" which occurs during puberty, giving rise to "the unknown which terrifies." Cf. *Personality, a Biosocial Approach to Origins and Structure* (New York, 1947), p. 508.

[27] *Studies in Deceit* (New York, 1928).

[28] *Plainville, U.S.A.* (New York, 1945).

[29] The confused attitudes towards masturbation are an illustration of this. Traditionally, masturbation has been considered evil and harmful. The opposing viewpoints of modern medicine and psychiatry leave much to be desired, since their tolerant attitudes tend to be qualified in an ambiguous way. Thus, reference is made to the "inevitability" of masturbation; it is spoken of as "harmless when kept under control," its avoidance is recommended "where possible." Although our modern understanding has laid to rest the fantastic tabus which tradition concocted, we are far from the unanimity of opinion which would allay the fears of adolescents.

symptomatic of the relentless and competitive drives for higher status. Two forms of projection are commonly seen, one positive and the other negative. In one, the individual directly attributes his liabilities to another person (blaming the teacher for his failure to pass an examination, for example). In the other, the individual foists his own defects of personality and character upon someone else. *Compensation* is a common socially patterned "tension-reducing" device whereby the individual seeks to follow approved and esteemed social activities. This effort is intended to atone for his deficiencies in fields in which he fails to measure up to social standards to which he subscribes. By taking refuge in an unwarranted sense of *superiority*, some individuals succeed in salvaging their self-esteem. Resort to *fantasy* and *day-dreaming* is a common practice of the youth who finds no other channel through which he may establish himself as a respected personage. *Rationalization*, the invention of plausible and socially acceptable excuses for one's failures, becomes a camouflage for the inability to achieve a desired status.

(10) EMOTIONAL DEVIATIONS AMONG ADOLESCENTS

The sources of pathological disorder are always social and cultural in form, and psycho-social in origin. We would expect, therefore, in any culture, that the common manifestations of personality breakdown would reflect institutional disequilibria. Characteristic behavioral distortions and personality problems emerge in relation to the conceived and socially expected statuses of childhood, adolescence, adulthood, and old age. The truth of this in the American scene is becoming increasingly clear.

The conflicts about adolescent statuses are due to the ambiguities in delineating status objectives for young people and the frequent sharp disparities in orientation between the generations of parent and child. These conflicts and ambiguities stem from four complex variables in American culture: (1) the rate of social change, (2) the extent of complexity in the social structure, (3) the degree of integration in the culture, and (4) the velocity of movement within the society.

As Kingsley Davis has shown, the sources of conflicts may be localized in specific areas—the tendency in American life to pit the young and the old in competition against each other, cleavages between adult realism and youthful idealism, and the authoritarian position of the parent in our culture.[30] Unlike simple integrated societies, where role-behaviors of the young and old are complementary, in our society such role-behaviors are antagonistic. "If ours were a simple rural-stable society, mainly familistic, the emancipation from parental authority being gradual and marked by

[30] Kingsley Davis, "The Sociology of Parent-Youth Conflict," *American Sociological Review*, V (August, 1940), 523–35.

definite institutionalized steps, with no postponement of marriage, sex taboo, or open competition for status, parents and youth would not be in conflict."[31] This is yet another manifestation of the incompatibility between a highly mobile urban-industrial social system and our type of family structure.

The emotional difficulties experienced by adolescents, therefore, directly reflect either the obstacles placed in the way of status-achievement or, in succumbing to adult and parental pressure, protests against the cultural drives toward adulthood. This may be seen in the form which such emotional difficulties assume among adolescents. Emotional complaints of adolescents seem to revolve around five principal categories: (1) neurasthenia, (2) adolescent hysteria, (3) pathological fanaticism, (4) acute feelings of inferiority, and (5) psychopathic behavior. These designations are not in strict accord with the classifications employed in abnormal psychology; they are rather descriptive of the commonly envisaged emotional disturbances manifested by teen-agers. All of them represent in varying degree and character the inability or the unwillingness of the individual to confront the vicissitudes of an emerging adult status.

The *neurasthenic* suffers from nervous exhaustion engendered by the fears and worries encountered through his sense of inadequacy in assuming adult responsibilities. The frenzied emotional outbursts of *adolescent hysteria*, survivals of the temper tantrums of the child, may be regarded as frantic attempts by the individual to maintain or achieve a desired position. Such behavior betrays a lack of knowledge of the effective channels through which this may be accomplished. Hence, the futile and violent protests of undirected rage. The *pathological fanatic* strives desperately to maintain his status by means of a series of fixed ideas—the "idée fixe"—with which he identifies closely the well-being of his personality. Those who cast doubts upon such ideas are regarded as derogating his personality and are consequently treated with hostility and suspicion. The setbacks which many adolescents receive in their striving for adult status confirm their suspicion of their own inadequacy and lead to protracted and painful feelings of *inferiority*. These may develop even though the individual has genuine talents in abundance.[32] Finally, we have the adolescent personality type which, for want of a better term, we have described as the *psychopathic personality*. The psychopathic individual is one who refuses to accept the increasing responsibilities and the concomitant doubts of his adult status. The behavior of such individuals is distinguished by avoidance of duties and dependence upon others, "sponging" and parasitism,

[31] Kingsley Davis, "The Sociology of Parent-Youth Conflict," p. 535.

[32] This may account for the frequent loneliness which adolescents in our culture so often express and describe. Cf. Charlotte Bühler, *From Birth to Maturity* (London, 1936).

and the failure to meet normal obligations. These traits are symptomatic of a regressed state in personality development.

(11) ADOLESCENT INTERESTS REQUIRING ADJUSTMENT

In all cultures the attainment of adulthood involves identification with certain role-behaviors and ascribed statuses; the organization of institutional behavior, therefore, must be oriented in part toward those specific interests of youth which prepare them for adult social participation. In all cultures, we have learned, there are two necessary conditions involved in *sociological maturity*.[33] These conditions have largely to do with the development of culturally defined heterosexual impulses and the other adult activities prescribed by the regulations of the given society. In American culture, this means that the individual must be adjusted in relation to his *sexual, educational, vocational,* and broader *social-cultural* interests. This adjustment can be achieved only if education and family life prepare the individual realistically for the adult responsibilities which each one of these interests requires. Adequate sex education in the schools and the home, the establishment of educational standards that take into full account the realities of the social and political scene, the honest appraisal of the individual's vocational aptitudes and preparation, and the willingness to invite early and responsible participation in the social and cultural life of the community—all are of vital significance if we are to lessen the tensions of modern adolescence.

The commonly voiced complaint of youth—"Why wasn't I told?"—is an indication of our failure to give sufficient attention to these interests. If, in the long run, adolescent problems arise from the disparities between biological and sociological maturity, then the interests involved in the attainment of sociological maturity must be well-defined and noncontradictory. Such interests must be in accord with the realities which actually confront adolescents. They must be such as will accelerate the process of accomplishment and *understanding* relative to the limitations which concrete social conditions impose.

SUMMARY

(1) Adolescent problems reflect certain cultural disequilibria. The universality of these disequilibria within the American culture-pattern suggests the basic disorganization of many of our institutional forms. (2)

[33] For a commendable analysis of the social structural elements involved in "sociological maturity," and the prospects for their reconciliation within American culture, see Kingsley Davis, "Adolescence and Social Structure," *The Annals of the American Academy of Political and Social Science,* CCXXXVI (Nov., 1944), 8–15.

This universality is manifested through the various sociological indices of individual delinquency and family disorder, as well as through our ideologies and literature. (3) Conflicts about the status of adolescents emerge from latencies (former social adjustments relative to the patriarchal family, early employment, rigid sexual mores, and the like) which contradict contemporary trends. (4) In all societies, there are designated status-conceptions, with their appropriate role-behaviors, for the several age-levels and ranks of society. In American society, the status conceptions concerning adolescence are ill-defined and contradictory. (5) Individual problems of maladjustment during puberty, which may exist in *all* cultures, reflect the peculiar psychogenetic growth of the individual personality. (6) Fundamental to all adolescent tensions are the profound physiological changes, *which must be socially and culturally interpreted.* (7) Age-levels for distinctive emotional expressions may be discerned in all cultures in relation to the cultural conditions which have produced them. Our criteria of emotional maturity indicate that there are varied emotional "norms" which are ordinarily associated with adulthood as it is conceived of in different cultures. In American life, such criteria concern the necessity of the individual to attain normal heterosexuality and emancipation from the home. (8) The physiological changes of adolescence are particularly apparent in the development of the major emotions of love, anger, and fear, which are socially conditioned and culturally defined with respect to their forms and manifestations. (9) The prevalence of symptoms of emotional disturbance during adolescence gives testimony to the widespread nature of adolescent disorder. Such symptoms assume certain common patterns and forms. (10) Concrete evidence of emotional disturbances during puberty may be seen in the conspicuous forms of emotional deviation, such as neurasthenia, adolescent hysteria, pathological fanticism, acute feelings of inferiority, and psychopathic behavior. (11) The resolution of adolescent problems in any culture, and particularly in our own, necessitates the adjustment of specific interests within the framework of sociological maturity. These interests are primarily sexual, educational, vocational, and social-cultural.

CHAPTER EIGHT

DELINQUENT DISORDERS AND SOCIAL CHANGE

(1) "THE NATURAL HISTORY OF A DELINQUENT CAREER"[1]

THE classic case of Sydney Blotzman, which Clifford Shaw made the basis of an exhaustive study of delinquency, provides an excellent illustration of the many ways in which delinquency is related to community life. At the age of sixteen years and eight months, Sydney Blotzman was apprehended for rape, the culmination of a lengthy career of crime begun at the age of seven.

In appraising any case of delinquency, we must keep in mind the interrelated factors of community, family, and individual life organization which have combined to produce each criminal act. Moreover, the effect of delinquency upon community attitudes, through public opinion and the law, must be seen. Through the operation of these agencies the average citizen gains insight into the community's willingness to come to grips with the problem of crime. The machinery of criminal justice represents a case of "wheels within wheels," and the understanding of the actual functioning of the criminal process in its relation to the community and the courts gives some preliminary insight into causal processes and their relationship to the larger framework of social disorganization.

The public first learns of a crime through newspaper accounts, which, designed for reader interest, are frequently sensational.[2] The story, although built around the salient facts, is distorted in the mind of the reader by headlines, special emphases, and clichés.[3] Thus, the newspaper headlines, in calling attention to Blotzman's crime, stated: "MORON GANG LEADER CAUGHT, CONFESSES"; "SEEK TO PROVE

[1] Taken from Clifford Shaw's monograph of the same title (Chicago, The University of Chicago Press, 1931).

[2] See Helen MacGill Hughes, *News and the Human Interest Story* (Chicago, 1940), Chap. 9.

[3] An excellent account of how stereotyped conceptions are promoted through the press may be found in Walter Lippmann's *Public Opinion* (New York, 1929), especially Chaps. 1, 2, and 3.

CAPTIVE MORONS ATTACKED MANY"; "SCREAMS ROUT MORON; GANG FACES VICTIMS." Even editorial opinion, from which we expect more sober and objective judgment, reacted to the offense in the following way:

> What depraved youth needs is the example of condign punishment, not the judicial extenuation which substitutes the penitentiary for the rope or the law which regards a school farm as the punishment for an attempt at rape.
>
> . . . . .
>
> Crimes against women are the work of that sort of utter beast who can be controlled only by fear. Once let animals of that type imagine that the law is feeble to prevent or even to avenge such dastardly violence, and plenty of it will follow. . . .[4]

The public was given a stereotype focused on the dubious concept of "moron."

What are the actual facts of the case? Young Blotzman, far from being a moron, possessed an intelligence-quotient of 119, which places him in the category of "superior intelligence." The actual circumstances of the crime are first set forth in the deposition, the formal statement of charges which the arresting officers prepare for the court hearing. Even here, the statement is so prepared *as to further the probability of conviction.*[5] Thus, although such accounts come closer to the true nature of the facts, the evidence is presented to confirm the weight of testimony to be given in court. Thus, the formal deposition declares:

> About seven o'clock in the evening of September 16, Tony Recco, while driving his automobile in the city of Chicago, met the prosecuting witness, Margaret Milfords, at the age of twenty-one years, and invited her to take a ride in his automobile. She accepted and they drove around until about nine o'clock and then stopped the automobile on S—— Avenue, about fifty feet from the corner of L—— Street. There they stopped the car and remained seated in the front seat for about half an hour, conversing with each other. They had gone to school together and were well acquainted. While they were thus sitting in the automobile, the defendant and Blotzman walked by the car and then walked back and asked Recco if he had a cigarette, and he replied, "No." [The account then proceeds to outline in specific detail the various circumstances leading up to the actual commission of the crime.] [6]

[4] Shaw, *The Natural History of a Delinquent Career*, p. 5.

[5] Police officers, in order to make the charge "stick," are briefed in the use of stereotyped forms which slight the peculiarities of the individual case.

[6] Shaw, *The Natural History of a Delinquent Career*, pp. 5–6.

Clifford Shaw points out that "in accordance with accepted legal procedure attention was limited, throughout the apprehension, trial, and disposition of the case, to a consideration of evidence bearing strictly upon the question of the innocence or guilt of the defendant."[7]

What were the actual background circumstances of the case? Neither the court nor the arresting officers nor the public were ever made adequately aware of the series of preceding events in the lives of Blotzman and of his associates which led to their criminality. In the examination of the offender's official record of arrests and commitments, it is important to observe: (1) the frequency of offenses; (2) the types of offenses, and the ages at which they occurred; (3) whether the offenses were committed singly or in association with others; (4) the companions, if any, of the offenders; and (5) the action of the courts in treating the early offenses. Sydney Blotzman's official docket shows a total of no less than twenty-eight separate entries from the time he was seven until his final apprehension. These offenses began with running away from parental and custodial care as a young child, graduated into continual pilfering and shop-lifting, *frequently from the same premises*, during his pre-adolescent career, and culminated in the larceny of automobiles, holdups with a gun, and rape at the age of sixteen years, eight months. Conspicuous in the record is the fact of the court's repeatedly returning the child to the custodianship of a badly disorganized home and the failure to get at underlying causes. When Blotzman was charged with the larceny of automobiles at the age of fifteen years, elcven months—after eighteen previous offenses—the court was moved to say: "This boy, with his superior intelligence, ought to finish high school. *I don't think that he will do well at home.* [Italics ours.] He should be placed elsewhere and permitted to attend school. I will appoint a guardian with the right to place."[8] *Despite this, it is noteworthy that the boy was released to live at home,* at least temporarily. Blotzman's offenses were carried on at different periods of time with the same associates, as he graduated from one type of offense to another. The records of his associates are equally noteworthy, nonc of them having had less than seven counts on his record, with the average for each of his ten principal accomplices running to approximately fourteen offenses. These records, of course, do not include a vast number of "unofficial" offenses and those considerable illegal activities for which these boys were not apprehended.

The young offender's family background reveals conditions of poverty, domestic discord, and drunkenness as a constant accompaniment of his early childhood and adolescence. Of his father, forty-six years of age and

[7] Ibid., p. 7.
[8] Ibid., p. 10.

an emigrant from Poland at the age of sixteen, the social work record states:

> . . . a poor provider and inclined to shirk responsibility at the most crucial time. He is extremely impulsive, has a very bad temper, and an inordinate drinking habit. When he is intoxicated he is brutal to his wife and children. He has deserted many times, remaining away more than a year at times. He has been arrested for non-support, desertion, and beating his wife and children.[9]

The mother, forty-seven years of age and also a Polish immigrant, is pictured by the social work record as being

> a very good housekeeper, very much interested in her children and industrious. She has made every effort to provide for the needs of her children. She is rather timid, fearful, and nervous. Inclined to worry. Religious and abides by the traditions of [her faith].[10]

Despite the handicaps of such a home, Abe, the older brother, is conscientious and hard-working, and, unlike Sydney, in every sense decent and law-abiding.

The neighborhood in which Sydney grew up has been well described by another delinquent in this unrevised account:

> To begin with, the streets of Chicago in the naborhoods where I spent my early childhood were very poor and dirty like most of the slums are . . . In the naborhood there were Jews, polocks, and irish, mostly foreigners and a poor class of people that could hardly read or write but had a flock of "kids." . . . Many of them were supported by chairty societies like my people were.
>
> You can just about judge for yourself how the adults in the naborhood thought about delinquency. The way they looked at it was "let him steal if he wishes to, so long as its not from me but for me." Times were always poor in the naborhood and I and other children had to steal coal off the tracks of the railroad and sometimes break seals on the box cars to get fruit or whatever the cars contained. . . . The junk yard dealers bought stolen junk from boys and often encouraged boys to steal so they could buy the junk. They never asked any questions.[11]

Sydney Blotzman, vilified by society and branded as a "moron," in writing his own life history expressed himself with an eloquence scarcely

[9] Ibid., p. 42.
[10] Ibid., pp. 42–3.
[11] Ibid., p. 19.

to be matched by the trained college graduate. In beginning the account of his life, he says:

> In reviewing my life I now see, and in fact always knew without knowing how to avoid it, that it was a pointless, aimless, haphazard sort of existence. I failed miserably to understand life and how serious it was. The critical periods I bungled. The emotions I felt were the emotions of the hurt. And because I could not understand life I attributed my unhappiness to other people's thoughtlessness. Yet, I know that I my own self am the cause of all my troubles. *I know that I am a sore on the face of the earth.* Institutional life was only revengeful punishment. It offered no corrective, merely caused bitterness.[12]

The underlying consistencies in this boy's life are disclosed not only through his constant self-abasement—something which might have been patterned by his peculiar cultural environment—but by his persistent bravado and reckless escapades through which he sought to establish the esteem and group favor which were denied him in his own home.

(2) THE INDICES OF DELINQUENCY: ITS EXTENT

Criminologists have been hampered for years by the inadequacy of statistical information concerning juvenile delinquency and crime. There is no uniform reporting of statistical data on offenses and offenders, and most information concerning trends and the volume of delinquency is haphazard and based upon selected areas. Our current information is obtained from such sources as the *Uniform Crime Reports*, a semi-annual publication of the Federal Bureau of Investigation, and the supplement to the publication of the United States Children's Bureau, *The Child*, entitled *Social Statistics*. There are a number of other official publications dealing with special statistical characteristics of crime and delinquency, such as the *Judicial Criminal Statistics*, prepared by the Bureau of the Census, the annual census of prisoners in state and federal institutions, entitled *Prisoners in State and Federal Prisons and Reformatories*, and the annual report, *Federal Prisoners*, issued by the Federal Department of Justice. In addition there is a large volume of state publications, reports by local governments and counties, and separate court jurisdictions. The difficulty with all of these voluminous reports is that the data presented are *not comparable*, do not represent all of the sectional and jurisdictional administrations involved, fail to classify distinctions between the number of offenses and the number of offenders, and do not include adequate information concerning the offenses of children.

Despite these difficulties, it is possible to make some general esti-

[12] Ibid., p. 53.

mate concerning the volume of juvenile offenses and the general trends since the early 1920's. Such estimates seem to confirm the belief that the general volume of delinquency for both sexes has increased steadily although not precipitately since the period of the First World War. Fluctuations appear for such critical periods as the depression of 1929, although contradictory data exist as to how significant was the rise, if any, during this period and that of the recent war. Certainly, all the data show that there has been no decrease in the volume of delinquency, in actual numbers and percentage volumes, although the general, secular trend of increase may not be as appreciable as ordinarily imagined.

Lowell J. Carr's estimate, based upon reports made to the United States Children's Bureau, places the number of children passing through our courts before the war as approximately 1 percent of the total number of the country's 17 million children between the ages of ten to sixteen years inclusive.[13] This figure is confirmed by other studies which place the annual volume of juvenile offenders as falling between 170,000 to 200,000. Most recent studies have shown that the rate increased during the war. Martin H. Neumeyer's summary of data from various sources suggests that "from 1940 on the official and non-official reports indicated accelerated increases in delinquency, but the rates of increase varied by states and by counties.[14] The peak in the statistical volume of delinquency was reached in 1943, with trends in many parts of the country showing variable and gradual declines since that date. This appears to be a temporary phenomenon, however, with indications that the secular trend may again go upwards. Our general conclusion must be that there is no discernible decrease in the extent and volume of delinquency but rather certain signs which point to a continuing and gradual upward rise. The more recent tabulations of this data suggest the following inferences drawn by Neumeyer:

> Except for the decrease during 1944, and the decrease since 1945, the trend in juvenile delinquency, on the basis of cases disposed of by juvenile courts reporting to the United States Children's Bureau, was upward, with the main increases occurring during the early years of the war. For instance, 78 courts serving areas with populations of 100,000 or more reported an over-all increase of 64 per cent in cases handled from 1938 to 1943, the peak year. Boys' cases have increased 54 per cent and girls' cases 94 per cent. Since 1943, courts have reported a continuous decline in girls' cases disposed of, but the boys' cases registered an increase during 1945, after a decline during the preceding years.[15]

[13] *Delinquency Control* (1940), p. 37.
[14] *Juvenile Delinquency in Modern Society* (New York, 1949), p. 47.
[15] Neumeyer, *Juvenile Delinquency in Modern Society*, pp. 47–8.

Even with more accurate reporting of official data, it is difficult to determine with accuracy the great range of offenses and minor infractions which occur under the rubric of juvenile delinquency. An untold number of cases are handled through unofficial sources. The great majority of our cases concern children of fourteen years of age and over. Many of our courts and police jurisdictions are reluctant to expose young children to the ordeal of formal court procedure, and a great many agencies have sprung up to deal with juvenile misdemeanants on an unofficial basis. They function as referral agencies in seeing that the child is brought under the care of responsible private and semi-official facilities. This practice is common and if the total number of such cases were known, our annual figures for delinquency would be considerably in excess of 200,000.

(3) CULTURAL VALUES AND TYPES OF JUVENILE OFFENSES

Delinquent offenses, as well as criminal acts, are largely a matter of cultural definition. Thus, the nature of juvenile offenses and their variety and distribution reflect the opinions in different communities as to what may be regarded as an offense. The incidence of offenses and the frequencies of sex differences indicate the community's standards of values and the differences of the status of boys and girls. In general, reports to the United States Children's Bureau indicate that the primary offense among boys is stealing, followed by general acts of carelessness or mischief. Among girls the chief misdeeds are ungovernable behavior and sex offenses, in that order. Truancy, a common offense of both sexes, appears with greater frequency among girls than among boys. Thus unsupervised behavior looms as a more serious problem in the case of girls, frequently being associated with other malefactions, and is handled officially while boys' cases may be overlooked. Stealing, according to the 1945 Report of the Children's Bureau, appears first on the list of boys' offenses and fifth on that of girls' offenses. The ratio of offenses between the sexes shows a wide margin of difference, *more than four times as many boys as girls being apprehended for misconduct*, according to the reports of 1945 and 1946.[16] Although there is no adequate way of determining fluctuations of rates for sex groups over a period of time, the primacy of pilfering and acts of carelessness among boys, and sex offenses and ungovernable behavior among girls, appears well established. The fact that these sex-differentiated causal categories have consistently maintained their positions over a period of years illuminates American cultural values in their relation to differences in the role behavior of the sexes. The aver-

[16] *Social Statistics, The Child* (U. S. Children's Bureau, Washington, II, November, 1946), 11.

age American community is far more prone to deal officially with boys than with girls if stealing is involved, but is apt to be considerably less lenient toward girls if incipient or actual sexual offenses are concerned.

Reasons for Reference to Court in Boys' and in Girls' Cases Disposed of by 374 Courts: 1945 *

Reasons for reference to court	Juvenile Delinquency Cases					
	Number			Per Cent		
	Total	*Boys*	*Girls*	*Total*	*Boys*	*Girls*
Total Cases	122,851	101,240	21,611	...	...	...
Reasons for Reference Reported	111,939	92,671	19,268	100	100	100
Stealing	40,879	38,610	2,269	37	42	12
Act of carelessness or mischief	19,241	17,779	1,462	17	19	8
Traffic violation	9,852	9,659	193	9	10	1
Truancy	8,681	6,164	2,517	8	7	13
Running away	9,307	5,652	3,655	8	6	19
Being ungovernable	9,840	5,542	4,298	9	6	22
Sex offenses	5,990	2,579	3,411	5	3	18
Injury to person	3,224	2,828	396	3	3	2
Other reason	4,925	3,858	1,067	4	4	5
Reason for reference not reported	10,912	8,569	2,343	...	...	...

* *Social Statistics, The Child,* II, 11.

(4) MINORITY GROUPS AND DELINQUENCY

The number of children of foreign-born parents reported delinquent has dropped since the curtailment of immigration in 1924. Previously the native born child of immigrant parents, growing up in an area of cultural conflict, contributed considerably to the annual roll of juvenile offenders. Approximately two-fifths of the girls and one-half of the boys were of foreign born parentage in 1930. Today, the vast majority of offenders of both sexes, over 70 per cent, are native-born of native-born parents.

Decrease in delinquency appears to occur in direct proportion to the assimilation of minority groups. Today, delinquency occurs most frequently among the new "marginal groups." These are the groups making the transition from rural to urban areas, and they comprise much of the older American stock. Rural workers from the South and Southwest, in migrating to the large industrial areas of Detroit, Chicago, Los Angeles, and the Pacific Northwest, confront problems of adjustment similar to those faced by the older European immigrants. These sections of the population show an increasing amount of delinquency.

Among those groups feeling the impact of novel adjustments and increasing mobility is the large Negro population. On the labor market, the Negro might be considered the "new immigrant," used for the marginal trades and industries as unskilled or semi-skilled labor. Despite considerable evidence that discrimination is practiced on the part of law enforcement agencies in the apprehension of Negroes, the fact remains that by any standard, Negro rates of delinquency have mounted to startling proportions during the last two decades. *In view of the fact that crime and delinquency rates appear to be a function of cultural rejection, any barriers we place in the way of assimilation will tend to induce a continuing and increasing rate.* Although comprising 9.7 per cent of the total population, Negroes contribute 18 per cent to the total delinquency rate, or almost twice as much as their percentage composition in the population. In Los Angeles County, for example, 4.2 per cent of the juvenile population under eighteen was classified as Negro, according to a 1946 census, whereas 10.3 per cent of all delinquent court cases was Negro.[17] Compare this with the report of an even greater rise of delinquency among the Spanish-American section of our population. Whereas this juvenile group comprised 13.9 per cent of the child population in 1946, 34.9 per cent of all delinquents came from these minority categories during 1947, representing an estimated rise of 151 per cent over the population norm. Houston, Texas, a southern city with few foreign-born, but with large concentrations of Negroes and Latin-Americans, has much higher rates, as might be expected. Of 4,287 cases of delinquent children during 1939–1942, 1,115 were Negroes (almost 25 per cent) and 663 were classified as Latin-American.

The general pattern of discrimination toward the Negro in relation to his mode of living and the exercise of the law creates this situation to a considerable degree. Not only is the Negro subjected to marginal conditions of community life and community disorganization which would breed crime and delinquency in any group, but in addition the law makes short shrift of Negro offenders in many parts of the country. Whereas a white child may be released with a reprimand by the police authorities, a Negro child frequently has to suffer the full penalty for any offense which he may have committed. It is not uncommon for Negro children to be charged with offenses for which white children are not disturbed. The problem of Negro delinquency and crime may continue to be an ominous situation in the degree to which we are not prepared to grant equality to Negroes in social and political life.

(5) AGE-LEVELS AND DELINQUENCY

The ages at which delinquents are apprehended is largely a matter of legal definition and customary practice. In most states, the age of

[17] Neumeyer, *Juvenile Delinquency in Modern Society*, p. 30.

eighteen is defined as the dividing line between juvenile offenders and adult criminals. Some states, such as California, have raised the statutory age to twenty-one years, thus providing for offenders between eighteen and twenty-one a degree of latitude in the exercise of administrative procedure which does not exist under the regular criminal statutes. This trend is growing in many states. The importance of early rehabilitative procedures before the individual is remanded to adult penal custody is gaining wide support. Individualized treatment can best be accomplished when the individual is still young. The Model Youth Authority Act which the American Law Institute has prepared is designed to provide, at the discretion of the courts, greater scope for treatment until the age of twenty-one.

The chief frequency of ages of offenders clusters close to the legal separation between youthful and adult offenders. In those states where the juvenile courts have jurisdiction until the age of eighteen, one-third of the juvenile boys and two-fifths of the juvenile girls fall within the ages of sixteen and seventeen. Where the division occurs at sixteen, the largest percentages of juvenile offenders are distributed in the fourteen- and fifteen-year-old age groups. Delinquency thus emerges as a problem of early adolescence, for most delinquents have had records of resistance to social and familial control, as well as of more serious offenses, even before they pass through the official channels of the courts. The accompanying table will indicate the trends of age distribution for a recent sample year based upon the reports of 374 courts.

Ages of Boys and Girls When Referred to Court, in Cases Disposed of by 374 Courts: 1945 *

Age of Child When Referred to Court	Juvenile Delinquency Cases: Number			Per Cent		
	Total	*Boys*	*Girls*	*Total*	*Boys*	*Girls*
Total Cases	122,851	101,240	21,611	...	...	...
Age Reported	110,415	91,435	18,980	100	100	100
Under 10 years	4,175	3,763	409	4	4	2
10 yrs., under 12	8,032	7,311	721	7	8	4
12 yrs., under 14	18,362	15,558	2,804	17	17	15
14 yrs., under 16	40,872	32,645	8,227	37	36	43
16 yrs. and over	38,977	32,158	6,819	35	35	36
Age not reported	12,436	9,805	2,631	...	...	...

* *Social Statistics, The Child,* II, 11.

(6) RURAL-URBAN DIFFERENCES

Rural rates of delinquency and crime are far less than urban rates. However rural rates have been climbing steadily during the past two decades, and the rapid mobility of the population makes such comparisons somewhat untenable. Rates of offenses seem to occur in relation to the distance from cities of 100,000 or more in size. Although the chief concentration of offenses, both adult and juvenile, are in the larger urban areas, the next highest rates seem to fall in rural dependencies converging about these urban areas. The more industrialized the rural areas and such dependencies become, the greater is the tendency to commit offenses. However, for some types of offense of a serious personal nature such as rape, murder, and manslaughter, the rural rates are equally high and in certain instances, markedly higher.

In a recent Federal Bureau of Investigation report, whereas the increase in offenses in urban areas for 1946 as compared to 1945 was 7.4 per cent, the increase in rural areas for the same period was 14.1 per cent, almost twice as much.[18] With the increased industrialization of rural areas and the greater tendencies toward mobility, we may anticipate still further increases in the rural rates. Rural rates of delinquency seem to follow the secular trends for adult offenders. Some comparisons of urban and rural rates for general criminal offenses may be obtained from the following rates for leading crimes for the year 1947.

Urban and Rural Rates per 100,000 of the Population for Leading Criminal Offenses.*

	Offenses	Urban Areas (2,292 Cities: Total Population 68,280,062)	Rural Areas (Total Population: 36,519,339)
1)	Larceny	961.2	199.2
2)	Burglary	389.8	145.6
3)	Auto Theft	182.1	57.3
4)	Assault	72.2	36.6
5)	Robbery	59.6	19.2
6)	Rape	12.62	13.61
7)	Murder	6.12	6.36
8)	Manslaughter	4.28	4.52

* Derived from data appearing in *Uniform Crime Reports* (XVIII, 1947), 79, 106.

On the basis of such comparisons, we may estimate that the urban rate for criminal offenses in general is 3.5 times higher than the rural rate. Nevertheless, the 1947 report appears to confirm the view that rural rates for such offenses as rape, murder, and manslaughter are slightly higher than the overall rates for cities. In commitments to correctional institutions, urban rates are considerably higher. Our general conclusions must be that although delinquency is still closely associated with urban life, rural trends toward delinquency are increasing and are apt to continue to do so in the face of rapid modern industrial and social change.

[18] *Uniform Crime Reports* (XVIII, No. 2, 1947), p. 79.

(7) SEX AS A SELECTIVE FACTOR

Boys are apprehended for offenses approximately 4.5 times more frequently than are girls.[19] Because of role-behavior differences and the status distinctions accorded to adolescents in our culture, we expect girls to act differently than boys, surrounding their behavior with restrictions which act as barriers to delinquent activity. The years fourteen to sixteen show the greatest concentration of offenses for both girls and boys, with sixteen and over closely following. However, the percentages of offenders below the age of fourteen are higher for boys than for girls, indicating both our greater tendency to detect delinquencies among boys at an earlier age and the greater opportunity for delinquent behavior among boys.

Girls tend to conform more than do boys. In all cultures children learn early to discriminate between potential role-behaviors of the two sexes in relation to the division of labor, recreation, and social pursuits. The expression "Boys will be boys" shows acceptance of a certain degree of prankishness as a normal aspect of adolescent male behavior. The same behavior in the girl is regarded with suspicion, although we express a limited amount of tolerance in our attitudes towards the "tom-boy." Because of role restrictions, a girl's opportunity for engaging in the types of activity that we associate with delinquency are definitely inhibited.

Concern over feminine misbehavior in our culture revolves about the loss of parental control (inviting possible sexual and other forms of molestation), and incipient or actual forms of sexual laxity. For this reason, our courts are frequently moved to act only in cases where the family has actually lost its control over the young girl or in those cases where sexual lapses are definitely in evidence. Elio D. Monachesi has made a study of the personality traits of delinquents and non-delinquents by means of the Minnesota Multiphasic Personality Inventory.[20] The Minnesota Test attempts to determine the degree to which individuals differ from those who are clinically known to suffer emotional disturbances. Although not conclusive, Monachesi's results indicate a higher percentage of female delinquents suffering from such emotional disturbances than non-delinquent females and the sample groups of both delinquent and non-delinquent boys. These findings would tend to confirm our basic hypothesis. They suggest that delinquency among boys is induced largely by opportunities presented by the environment, while among girls, delinquencies are rather the results of emotional disturb-

[19] The Children's Bureau Reports for 1945 and 1946 show a ratio of 4.7 boys to 1 girl, and 4.4 boys to 1 girl, respectively. Cf. *Social Statistics, The Child* (U. S. Children's Bureau, Washington, II, November, 1946), 11.

[20] "Characteristics of Delinquents and Non-Delinquents," *The Journal of Criminal Law and Criminology* (XXXVIII, Jan.–Feb., 1948), 487–500.

ances. According to Monachesi, "the data presented . . . . suggest that delinquency in females is more often the expression of personal inadequacies rather than a manifestation of cultural imperatives." [21]

(8) PATTERNS OF CAUSATION IN DELINQUENCY

No single factors predispose the individual to delinquency. Virtually all of the studies of delinquency during the past three decades have emphasized the multiplicity of factors which contribute to the development of delinquent behavior. Statistical evidence bearing on environmental factors such as disorganized families, delinquency areas, bad housing, inadequate recreation, unfit companions, deficient supervision, inadequate schooling, and the like has been stressed. There has been the growing effort to find common patterns of behavior tendencies upon which an adequate theory of delinquency may be based. W. I. Thomas in his early studies of delinquent behavior indicated that the entire complex of environment and personality factors must be taken into consideration if we are to gain an understanding of delinquent activity.[22] Cyril Burt, in a pioneering study of delinquency, revealed as many as 170 different factors operating in an analysis of 197 cases, with at least 4 or 5 outstanding factors operating in each case.[23] Most of such studies have been vast statistical enterprises dealing with the records of as many as 4000 delinquents.[24] In view of the random selection of such cases and the failure to carry out scientific studies of comparable groups, the results have done no more than testify to the prevalence of certain statistical factors operating in the delinquent's environment. *But we have not learned why all individuals exposed to these conditions do not become criminals.* Such studies, while important in alerting public opinion to the conditions which breed delinquent disorder and in providing a basis for broad corrective policies, fail, nevertheless, in giving us an actual theory as to how delinquency is brought about.

(9) PROBLEMS OF CAUSATION

These *multiple factor theories* which stress the background factors of delinquency are deficient because: (1) they give little or no indication

[21] Ibid., p. 499.

[22] See *The Unadjusted Girl* (Boston, 1931); also, W. I. and Dorothy S. Thomas, *The Child in America* (New York, 1928), especially pp. 572–4.

[23] Cyril Burt, *The Young Delinquent* (New York, 1925).

[24] See William Healy and Augusta F. Bronner, *Delinquents and Criminals, Their Making and Unmaking* (New York, 1926); Sheldon and Eleanor T. Glueck, *1000 Juvenile Delinquents* (Cambridge, 1934), and by the same authors, *Later Criminal Careers* (New York, 1937) and *500 Criminal Careers* (New York, 1930); C. R. Shaw and H. D. McKay, "Social Factors in Juvenile Delinquency," National Commission on Law Observance and Enforcement, *Report on the Causes of Crime* (Washington, II, 1931).

as to the *primacy* of certain causal processes, (2) they fail to distinguish adequately between *efficient causes* and *sufficient causes* of delinquent behavior, and (3) they afford little insight into *the process of the combination of factors* entering into delinquency and crime. The gestalt theorists in psychology have long pointed out to us that the *combined* total of the factors of human experience is different from the sum of its parts. Whereas a potato consists of a certain amount of starch, sugar, water, and ash, the mere mixture of these separate physical components does not produce a potato. The creation of a potato involves the bio-chemical interaction of these several elements in a complicated organic growth-process. Similarly, the mere presence of bad housing, poor companions, inadequate schooling, and indifferent parents does not constitute a sufficient basis for delinquency. These factors must be interwoven in special ways if they are to produce delinquency.

(1) How do we assign *relative weights* in determining which factors are of most importance in the complex of interacting factors? It is obvious that the weights of the same type of factors differ radically from person to person, *even though all may be operative to a certain degree*. This is clearly demonstrated by Clifford Shaw in the following hypothetical case.

> X is in prison for burglary. On examination, it is found that he is also a "constitutionally inferior psychopathic personality" and an habitual alcoholic. Further inquiry discloses that X and his parents have been long in dire poverty and that they reside in the vilest tenement house in a "delinquency area." Has X's criminality been "caused" by his drunkenness, or have both the alcoholism and the misconduct been "caused" by his constitutional inadequacy, or did X's habitual imbibing of alcohol aggravate his original weak inhibitory capacity? Did X become a drunkard because he couldn't stand his family's miserable economic situation, or was the drunkenness the cause of that unhealthy economic status? All these behavioral sequences may have been in effect at different times in the life of X, as a series of vicious "action-reaction" mechanisms. But even aided by a close scrutiny of X's developmental history, it would be difficult to assign *primacy* to any of the factors involved.[25]

Multiple factor statistical studies, differing as they do because of the *unselected* and *non-comparable* basis of their findings, fail to give us an understanding of how such separate factors may be weighted. There is a tendency for the several factors involved in the causative complex of delinquency to react upon each other at different phases of the delin-

[25] "Housing and Delinquency," in J. M. Gries and James Ford, editors, *Housing and the Community-Home Repair and Remodeling* (The President's Conference on Home Building and Home Ownership, 1932), pp. 15–16.

quent's career in a "vicious circle." As Pauline V. Young states: "This presentation does not distinguish between symptoms and fundamental underlying causative factors, to say nothing of the lack of consideration of the role of the personal and social traits of the people who present these problems." [26] The following diagram of the "vicious circle" concept of multiple causation for a given case of delinquency will indicate the difficulty of adequate social diagnosis when such factors are conjointly presented. It will be noted that by moving *clockwise* or *counter-clockwise*

The "Vicious Circle" Concept of Causation *

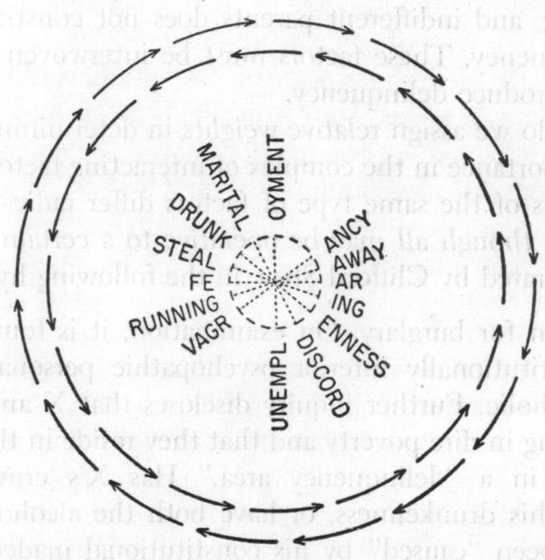

* Ibid., p. 119.

a reasonable sequence will appear in the pattern of misbehavior. For example, beginning with marital discord and moving clockwise, the factors may have resulted in unemployment, vagrancy, running away by a delinquent child, subsequent fear reactions, and stealing. In the reverse order, drunkenness of a parent, for example, may have induced stealing reactions on the part of the child, followed by a fear to return home, running away, and vagrancy as habitual modes of misconduct, eventuating in disorganized effects upon the family, such as unemployment and marital discord. In the same way, we may begin with *any* salient factor in the complex interaction of causation, and trace out innumerable reaction patterns in either direction.

[26] Pauline V. Young, *Social Treatment in Probation and Delinquency* (New York, 1937), p. 120. For an excellent treatment of this entire process of delinquent causation, upon which much of the above material is based, the reader is referred to Chap. 7, especially pp. 116–30, of the same book.

(2) Closely related to this matter of *primacy* in causal processes is the distinction to be drawn between *efficient* and *sufficient* causes. The presence of a great many social and personal factors in the life of the individual may be sufficient to account for the manifestation of delinquency. Such factors, however, in their profusion and complexity, will not necessarily indicate *why* the specific individual tends to react in delinquent fashion. Efficient factors of causation will indicate *why*, under specific conditions, a certain form of behavior, delinquent or otherwise, will ensue. We may know that certain general environmental conditions will be conducive to the development of criminality, but we have no certain knowledge in which individual cases delinquent behavior will inevitably follow. We may anticipate a higher percentage of misbehavior in "delinquency areas," but we can never be positive of the volume, or the character of the delinquency, or of the specific individuals who will practice delinquent actions. The determination of such specific factors will always depend upon an examination of the efficient factors of causation in the lives of predisposed individuals and groups.

One of the most devastating criticisms of this form of multiple factor analysis has been made by M. F. Ashley-Montagu.[27] The mere enumeration of the common factors found in a random sample of delinquents or criminals is not sufficient to determine causality of anti-social behavior. An examination of a random sample of so-called normal individuals often presents statistical evidence similar to the aberrational group. The examination of "normal" boys and girls from the same environment yields highly similar statistical findings. In neither case, therefore, can we infer the statistical factors of causation, normal or abnormal. Montagu illustrates this by an allusion to a random collection of cadavers in the dissecting room of a medical college. A statistical study of common factors of these cadavers might reveal that they fall within certain social groups, come from a common area of the city, were mostly manual laborers, had less than average I.Q.'s, and had limited educational advantages. Can we thus infer, according to Montagu, that these factors were *causal antecedents* of the situation in which they are now found? Many statistical studies of delinquency and crime come perilously close to drawing the same type of absurd conclusion. It is true that there *may* be a connection between such antecedent and subsequent states. Poverty and manual labor may be instrumental in the individual's becoming a subject for medical dissection. However, we must bear in mind the distinction between sufficient and efficient causes.

A knowledge of sufficient causes may indicate the general conditions under which an individual might break, without being able to predict this

[27] "The Biologist Looks at Crime," *The Annals of the American Academy of Political and Social Science* (CCXVII, 1942), 46–58.

result with certainty. Some criminologists, in accepting the broad base from which delinquency may spring, assert that certain crucial factors must be added to this complex to produce the expected result. Such "crucial" factors, themselves statistically determined, frequently comprise the basis of "semi-particularistic" theories. The criminologist Von Hentig, for example, has emphasized that the role of economic factors in the production of crime might be of primary significance when other conditions of the social environment are propitious.[28] His general position is stated as follows:

> Most of our criminals are milieu-made. They are law-abiding while the sun shines, economic life goes on undisturbed, and their ability of adjustment is not taxed excessively. When social storms are brewing, depressions set in, prices tumble, and the army of unemployed swells, the average law-abiding individual yields to extreme pressure and becomes a lawbreaker.[29]

In the same way, other salient factors may be defined as the catalytic agents precipitating underlying delinquent and criminal patterns.

(3) Attempts to determine whether certain combinations of factors are more conducive to delinquency than others show that the possible combinations are endless. They depend upon the compilation of vast quantities of statistical evidence, which do not produce the certainty of competent theories of causation. The result is a series of sociological "permutations and combinations" of associated conditions without the certainty of causal significance. This fact has been ably illustrated by Dr. William Healy in an analysis of certain common factors in the backgrounds, mentalities, and offenses of delinquents.[30] Thus, delinquent *A* may have emerged from a combination of defective heredity, bad companions, and broken home. He occupies a place in the feebleminded and psychoneurotic category, and has committed petty thievery. Delinquent *B* was conditioned by a combination of defective heredity, broken home, and poor parental control. His personality type is that of unstable adolescent and his eventual misconduct may be vagrancy or sex assault. Common and differing elements combine in various ways to produce similar or differing personality types whose anti-social behavior manifestations may be similar or different. The following chart, drawn from Dr. Healy's findings, will make this more apparent. Thus, any combination of factors *on any level* may produce any type of effects.

[28] *Crime: Causes and Conditions* (New York, 1947). See particularly pp. 7–14 and Chap. 10.

[29] Ibid., p. 11.

[30] *The Individual Delinquent* (Boston, 1915), pp. 164–5.

Combinations of Factors Entering into Differential Delinquent Behavior *

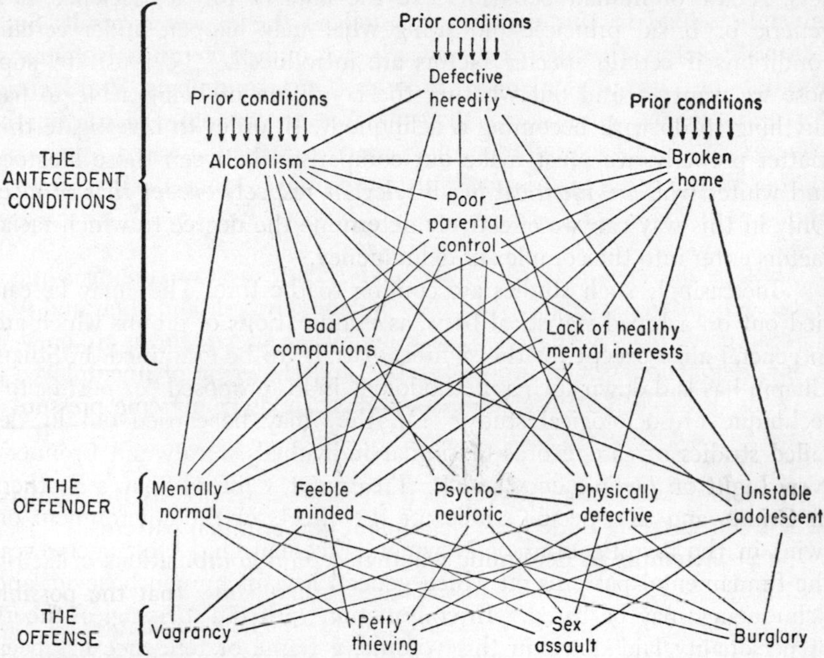

* William Healy, *The Individual Delinquent* (Boston, 1915), pp. 164–5. Reproduced by permission of William Healy.

Clearly it is a fallacy to attempt to understand the process of causation by classifying delinquents as to background, mentality, or offense.

(10) A CAUSAL THEORY OF DELINQUENCY AND CRIME

An adequate theory of the causation of delinquency is possible however, on the basis of materials developed thus far in this book, and it is to such an integrated hypothesis that we will now turn.

Previous studies of delinquency and crime have been important in enlarging our insights, but they have failed in the formulation of explicit assumptions and in the development of adequate comparisons between so-called "normal" individuals and delinquent individuals. Scientific theories of human behavior may be developed under conditions which permit common characteristics to be appraised in the light of unique distinguishing factors. A satisfactory theory of delinquency would tell us the con-

ditions under which a bad home or poverty is likely to induce delinquent acts. A law of human behavior, like the laws of physical science, is a *generic* or broad principle indicating what may happen under certain conditions if certain specific factors are introduced.[31] To illustrate, suppose we want to find out whether the condition of being a Negro has anything to do with becoming a delinquent. In order to investigate this matter properly, we must make our comparison between those Negroes and whites *who are identical in all relevant respects except that of race.* Only in this way can we effectively determine the degree to which racial factors enter into the complex of delinquency.

Increasingly such studies are coming to the fore. They may be carried out on a broad statistical basis, as examinations of groups which are in general alike except for the significant traits to be examined. F. Stuart Chapin has laid down such a methodology in his proposed "*ex post facto*" technique of sociological study.[32] Or, they may be carried out by detailed studies of case-records of similar individuals. Healy and Bronner's *New Light on Delinquency and Its Treatment*, Clifford Shaw's *Brothers in Crime*, and the specific studies of the effects of the environment on twins in the investigations of Newman, Freeman, and Holzinger reveal the fundamental patterns on which general laws of human behavior and delinquency may be based.[33] In conjunction with the sociological theory of personality laid down in this volume, a frame of reference has been established whereby an adequate theory of delinquency causation may be projected.

One of the most effective techniques for getting at the underlying causal processes in delinquent behavior is the "dual case recording" technique of Healy and Bronner. Under this system of study, twins and siblings from the same family are subjected to exhaustive examination

[31] The emphasis we are making bears some resemblance to the distinction which J. F. Brown makes between "genotypic" and "phenotypic" description. The "genotype" refers to a basic dynamic principle which may be used to account for seemingly different but statistically common experiences. The "phenotype" is a form of statistical "class-theory," that is, it searches for explanations within the statistical data themselves. The latter approach gives highly limited explanations and is being superseded by the genotypic forms of interpretation, which are basic to all modern science. Cf. J. F. Brown, *Psychology and the Social Order* (New York, 1936), Chap. 2, especially pp. 33–4.

[32] *Experimental Design in Sociological Research* (New York, 1947), see especially Chaps. 1 and 2.

[33] Healy and Bronner, *New Light on Delinquency and Its Treatment* (New Haven, 1936); Clifford Shaw, Henry D. McKay, James F. McDonald, *et al.*, *Brothers in Crime* (Chicago, 1938). For general studies of the effects of environment on twins, see W. E. Blatz, *The Five Sisters* (New York, 1938); H. H. Newman, F. N. Freeman, and K. Holzinger, *Twins: A Study of Heredity and Environment* (Chicago, 1937); M. McGraw, *Growth: A Study of Johnny and Jimmy* (New York, 1935). For specific studies dealing with delinquent patterns in the development of twins, see Johannes Lange, *Crime and Destiny*, trans. by Charlotte Haldane (New York, 1930); A. J. Rosanoff *et al.*, "Criminality and Delinquency in Twins," *Journal of Criminal Law and Criminology* (XXIV, 1934), 929.

at each stage of genetic development. In making such "point for point" comparisons, the unique environmental elements which may have predisposed the individual to crime and delinquency become strikingly apparent. Healy and Bronner show in the case of a set of six-year-old twins, one of whom had already become a confirmed delinquent, that the individual patterns of growth were marked by developmental differences not immediately discernible to the untrained observer.[34] The following abridged and summarized case of two brothers in the same family will give some indication of the effectiveness of such comparisons.

Case of the Laner Brothers

Father fifty, mechanic, good earner. Mother fifty, motherly, very good manager and housekeeper. Parents of mixed ancestry, came from eastern Canadian province. Both healthy, strong characters, high standards, religious, and thrifty; happy marriage, forging ahead, intent on children having best possible education. Own their home. All boys in magazine distributing business under charge of eldest who organized it. Extraordinarily fine ambitious family with much good feeling among them. Four children; two eldest boys preparing for college, one younger than George regarded as very promising and somewhat favored on that account. All children big, strong, good looking.

George—b. 1915	Donald—b. 1914
One year ago stole fancy skates. More recently, forged and cashed a check found in office when delivering magazines; also, later opened envelopes in another office and took money. Bought play things, mostly.	Always honest, though knew about theft of skates and kept silent.
. . .	. . .
Normal developmental history. Long nursing. Always seemed healthy, but fatigues more easily than brothers. Overweight for three or four years. Craving for sweets.	Normal developmental history. Long nursing. Always healthy. Careful eater.
. . .	. . .
Normal height. Fifty lbs. overweight, high pitched voice, retarded sexual development. (The brothers are all in early	Big, strong, stout within normal limits. Good features. Wears glasses.

[34] Healy and Bronner, *New Light on Delinquency*, pp. 95–8. Reprinted by permission of Yale University Press.

GEORGE—b. 1915	DONALD—b. 1914
puberty.) Underwent thorough endocrine study, diagnosed as hypopituitary. Defective vision, no glasses.	
. . .	. . .
I.Q. 108 (later 116). Very rapid, alert worker. Pleasantly responsive.	I.Q. 99. Very serious worker. Especially good in mechanical tests.
. . .	. . .
First year high school, poor marks, well liked.	Second year high school, taking technical course, doing very well.
. . .	. . .
Personality: Active but tires easily, impulsive, changeable, pleasure-loving, talkative, carefree, frank, even-tempered. He differs from his brothers in these respects. Worked in brother's business since nine, little time for companionship.	Personality: Active, steady, quiet, planful, reserved, inarticulate, ambitious; studies hard. Worked in brother's business since ten, little time for companionship.

Interpretations: For two or three years, mainly on account of his endocrine disorder, George has felt inadequate to meet high ambitions of family who have tried to spur him on. Has felt different and isolated in family circle. Attempted to get substitute satisfaction through stealing money in order to buy young boyish possessions, which according to family standards were silly and useless. . . . Felt thwarted in normal desires and impulses: fond of sports but no time to indulge. Worked outside school for years; didn't have same privileges as other boys. As Christmas approached, he anticipated he wouldn't have much. Revengeful display of impulsive aggressiveness: he would get things anyhow. . . . Felt strongly discriminated against; younger brother, "a popular hero" was favored. Discouraged at this fact. Hostile attitude for a time; knocked his brother about. Then followed floundering aggressive impulses to get compensatory satisfactions through gaining his own pleasures.[35]

In appraising such cases, similarities as well as differences in psychogenetic adjustments to the social environment may be weighted and gauged according to critical behavioral tendencies. Distinctive factors of development are *precipitated* through the comparative process and may be made the basis for comprehensive analysis of the total personality development.

[35] Ibid., pp. 137–8.

(a) *The emergence of the "hidden motive" in such comparative studies.* The analyses of such comparative studies indicate the "hidden motives" which underlie a good deal of the delinquent's behavior. These hidden motives disclose the different ways in which delinquents perceive certain common experiences. We are likely to erroneously identify a common experience with a common motive. Studies of truancy, for example, reveal a great variety of reasons for such activity. Some children absent themselves from school because they are inordinately bored with their classroom exercises, others because of fear of the teachers, and still others because of their desire to embarrass their parents. All such motives reveal the less obvious facets of the personality yet constitute a primary basis for delinquent activities and behavior. In one case of reported theft from an individual's business, the guilt was finally traced to a seemingly well-adjusted and "model" son who stole from his father in order to embarrass and frustrate him. The boy never spent the money, but hid it in his shoe. Resenting his father's continual quarrels with the mother over money matters, the boy took this form of revenge, touching upon a particularly sensitive area of the father's personality. The hidden motive reveals the essential reason for the person's misbehavior while shedding light upon his peculiar mode of life-organization. In the case of Herman, later to be discussed, his stealing from the high school locker room included compacts and other trivial trinkets which he gave away as a means of winning esteem from his associates. The variety of motivations to delinquent behavior is endless.

The operation of human motives through the wish-patterns of new experience, security, response, and recognition is clearly shown by W. I. Thomas.[36] Common forms of aberrational behavior are used to satisfy different kinds of wishes, while different forms of overt misbehavior conceal common wish-patterns. Thus, according to Thomas, "the vagabond, the adventurer, the spendthrift, the bohemian are dominated by the desire for new experience, but so are the inventor and the scientist; adventures with women and a tendency to domesticity are both expressions of the desire for response; vain ostentation and creative artistic work both are designed to provoke recognition; avarice and business enterprise are actuated by the desire for security." [37]

(b) *The Causal Pattern of Delinquency and Crime.* The following psychogenetic schema, adapted in part from Healy and Bronner, uses an organized frame of reference to show the causal sequence in the type of behavior problems we have been discussing.[38] If the frame of reference is utilized effectively, it will suggest the form which different "hidden

[36] *The Unadjusted Girl*, Chap. 1.

[37] Ibid., p. 38.

[38] Healy and Bronner, *New Light on Delinquency*, pp. 4–5. Reprinted by permission of Yale University Press.

motives" may take, and will illustrate why poor playmates may figure prominently in one case while inadequate family conditions may be significant in another.

We have learned that the organization of the psychogenetic pattern through the mediation by the family of the social and cultural environment produces certain patterned needs and procedures for their fulfillment. Within certain social milieus, the satisfaction of such basic needs becomes increasingly difficult. The organization of the many-faceted environmental influences upon the child, ranging from poverty to intense

A Suggested Schema for the Causal Pattern of Delinquency and Crime

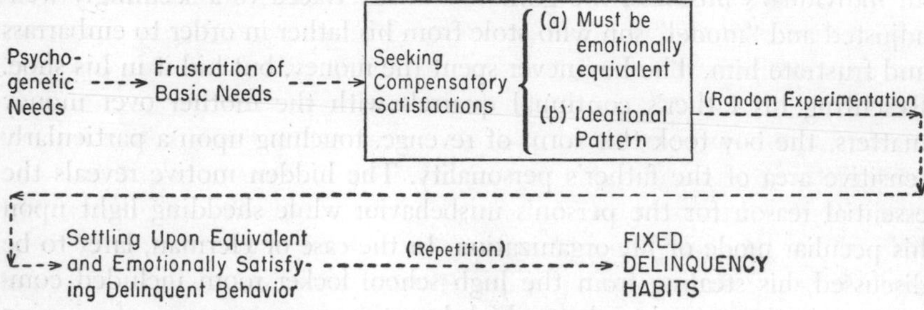

sibling rivalry, may militate in their total effects against the normal expressions of the psychogenetic needs. An investigation of the basis of the psychogenetic pattern and the nature of the immediate environment frequently discloses which of the factors are of *crucial* significance in weighing against the normative expression of such wishes. In one case it may be the neglect by the mother, through conditions created by poverty, while in another it may be the sense of rejection and resentment invoked by the competition for parental affection among the children of the family. In all cases, the organization of the family structure must be carefully observed in order to determine the extent to which environmental factors (overcrowding in the home, general conditions of poverty, delinquency areas, etc.) affect the functioning of the psychogenetic pattern.

The failure to find normal expressions of satisfaction leads to an exploration for other channels of fulfillment. This is the point where the *nature of the environment* plays an extremely important role. This process of seeking compensatory satisfactions is always accompanied by two conditions, viz., (a) the *emotional equivalence* of the substitutive outlet; and (b) the *ideational patterns* present in the immediate environment. The mode of satisfaction, if it is to be consistently pursued, must be equivalent to the emotional experience of which the individual has been deprived. It should be noted that we speak of *equivalence* and not *identity* in the nature of the emotional reaction. A child who craves the esteem of his parent may find a substitute in the esteem of a teacher or an older companion. For a child who searches for imaginative adventure, reading a geography lesson is not likely to provide equivalent satisfaction. The young girl who has recently undergone some vivid and highly exciting amorous adventures is likely to be unresponsive to participation in the local Youth Home Makers' Circle. Emotional payments do not necessarily have to be in the same coin, but they must be of equivalent worth. This gives the delinquent a wide area in which he may operate. The craving for adventure may be satisfied by pilfering from a deserted house, or by membership in a boys' athletic club, hiking group, or secret society.

Every neighborhood abounds in suggestive stimulational outlets which may provide emotional equivalents. Those suggestive outlets comprise the basis for the *ideational patterns.* By *ideational patterns,* we mean those suggestive environmental outlets or channels whereby the child may find solutions for the frustrations of his personality cravings. If the social milieu abounds in illicit or anti-social environmental outlets, the possibilities for delinquent and anti-social behavior are so much greater. The individual does not necessarily seek with deliberate intention such illicit outlets. They are simply ready-at-hand, affording an egress from an acutely disturbing or emotionally unsatisfying situation. Children from better-class homes do not become delinquents as frequently as slum children. This is not because they do not suffer any liabilities or frustrations, but because the environments in which they are reared do not provide as many suggestive stimuli of an anti-social nature.[39]

The experimental period of seeking substitutive outlets is marked by a high degree of emotional instability and impulsiveness. Studies of delinquents and pre-delinquents show the high rate of emotional disturbances existing among such children. Healy and Bronner, for example, show that out of 143 cases studied in one sample, 131 suffered from some type of emotional disturbance, approximately 92 per cent. Furthermore, of those suffering from emotional difficulties, those who did not engage in delinquent activities were largely forestalled either because they suffered physical handicaps or because opportunities did not present themselves.[40] Cyril Burt reports that approximately 85 per cent of the delinquents whom he studied suffered from some form of "acquired or inherent"

[39] It is instructive to note, however, that recent reports of private agencies and institutions dealing with delinquent children indicate a rising percentage of delinquencies among children from better-class homes. These delinquencies, it is further reported, are less of the normative type, being more frequently actuated by psycho-neurotic tendencies and acute emotional disturbances. Cf., for example, *Annual Report,* Hawthorne-Cedar Knolls School (Westchester County, New York, July 30th, 1949).

[40] Healy and Bronner, *New Light on Delinquency,* pp. 87, 122.

emotional defect.[41] The impulsive nature and changeable character of delinquents is well known. This is due to their high *suggestibility* which arises out of the circumstances of their psychogenetic neglect. A common psychological condition associated with frustration is the suggestibility to which even the best adjusted of individuals fall prey.

The adventitious and random activities discovered during the period of initial unadjustment frequently result in the discovery of satisfactory modes of behavior. The individual is likely to engage in these *irrespective of how they are defined by the community. This is the normal aspect of delinquency*. As the psychiatrist Karl Menninger has put it, *delinquency represents a normal response to an abnormal situation*. Habits of behavior which are emotionally satisfying soon settle into a routine. Should this behavior be delinquent, its repetition soon leads to the fixation of delinquent conduct as an habitual mode of response to the environment. The net result of the investigation of numerous delinquents and their case-histories suggests that effective normal adjustment can best be accomplished during the suggestible stage of random experimentation. Once the habit of delinquency is firmly established, the problem of readjusting and reorganizing the objectives of the personality becomes greater in direct proportion to the profoundity of the emotional satisfaction and its duration as an integrated habit-pattern. Studies of normally adjusted individuals coming from the adverse family and community conditions of the slums illustrate the highly accidental manner of their normal adjustments and give credence to the oft-repeated phrase "there but for the grace of God go I."

(11) FORMAL AND INFORMAL SUGGESTIVE OUTLETS IN THE ENVIRONMENT

There abound in the traditions and legends of all peoples the great folk heroes, vagabonds, robbers, and other romantic characters who have enriched and stimulated the imagination of youth. Tales of the exploits of the James Brothers, Robin Hood and his colorful band, Wild Bill Hickok have contributed to the imaginative processes of the young. The patterned ways in which delinquencies occur in various cultures suggest the manner in which traditional accounts leave their impress upon anti-social activities. Finnish delinquents, for example, perform a higher percentage of their unlawful acts with long knives than do delinquents elsewhere because of the deep impression their great legendary folk hero, a famous knife-wielder, has made on the youthful imagination. Negro delinquencies are frequently associated with the brandishing of razors, a prac-

[41] Cyril Burt, *The Young Delinquent* (New York, 1925), p. 541.

tice arising out of the peculiar historical pattern surrounding the use of this weapon among Negroes. The exploits of white delinquents in our society reflect the characteristics of traditions handed down by generations of anti-social groups and gangs.

The spontaneous play-groups and gangs of children provide ample stimulus for the performance of illegal activities. In delinquency areas there exists a continuous source of motivation to socially proscribed behavior in the persons of local heroes, the "big-shots" whose prestige, manners, dress, and conspicuous leisure afford a continual spur to the youthful imagination. Although the associations with which the pre-delinquent and the young delinquent identify themselves are informal in character, the developmental process of such contacts tends, to a degree, to become institutionalized and formal in structure. Although there are no formal "schools for crime," in the technical sense, gangs and "ganging activities" do assume organized forms of expression, involving quasi-formal indoctrination of tradition and practice. Recent studies of delinquent associations stress the formal organizational patterns which such delinquent activities can take. In Harlem, youthful gangs have a well-organized leadership and membership function, in which training, indoctrination, and planning comprise significant elements. Adult gangs, on the other hand, frequently assume a highly organized structure with well-established differences of rank, specialization of function, subservience to a code, and defined responsibilities.

Among the suggestive stimuli of an informal character which play a part in the development of delinquent attitudes, such agencies as the moving pictures, the radio, and the comic books must be taken into account. The studies of Blumer, Hauser, and Forman have attempted to determine the effects of the moving pictures upon our youth.[42] A knowledge of the causal process which we have outlined, with the facts of suggestibility clearly kept in mind, should indicate what might be the role of the moving picture in the development of delinquency. Despite the rationalizations of such youthful offenders as the notorious "Two Gun" Crowley of the thirties, moving pictures do not, in a direct sense, *make* criminals. The impulsive and highly suggestible state of mind of pre-delinquent youth, however, is amenable to the stimulus which such moving pictures may convey. There must already exist a *latent tendency* or *predisposition* to delinquent activity if the moving picture is to have any effect. Moving pictures may very definitely suggest techniques of *crime and delinquency* to the suggestible child and the practicing delin-

[42] See Herbert Blumer, *Movies and Conduct* (New York, 1933); H. Blumer and P. M. Hauser, *The Movies, Delinquency, and Crime* (New York, 1933); H. J. Forman, *Our Movie Made Children* (New York, 1933).

quent. Delinquent children have frequently affirmed that their knowledge of a type of crime was gained directly from a moving picture. Although research upon the effects of such imaginatively provocative media as the radio and the comic books have as yet been quite meagre, the results of such studies should substantiate the findings that have been made in the field of the movies. The clue to an understanding of such stimuli lies in the suggestible state of mind of young people during periods when the psychogenetic needs of the personality fail to find adequate outlet.

(12) A SUGGESTED CLINICAL PROCEDURE FOR THE DIAGNOSIS OF DELINQUENT BEHAVIOR

In view of the fact that delinquency represents a total response of the organism to the environment, it might be helpful to inject a view which is becoming increasingly important in the medical diagnosis of disease. The new emphasis in psychosomatic medicine stresses the need to regard diseases, illness, and personality manifestations as forms of total adaptation to the environment.[43] Our recent discussion would suggest that this procedure represents more than an analogy and may, in fact, constitute a bona fide methodology for the analysis of delinquent behavior. The logical sequence of analysis in bodily and behavioral disorders would be fundamentally and substantially the same.[44]

A Diagnostic Procedure for the Analysis of Delinquent Acts

	Medical Diagnostic Procedure	*Diagnosis of Behavior Problems in Human Relations*
(A) Symptom	Fever	Delinquent Activity
(B) Etiology (Cause)	Specific and Related Microbic Infection	Special and General Nature of Maladjustments Inducing Social and Emotional Disturbances
(C) Recommended Treatment	Application of Medical Specific and Course of Treatment to Remove Source of Infection	Application of Therapeutic and Social Case Procedure to Remove Source of Disturbance, or Finding Normative Outlet for Disturbed Emotional Behavior

[43] Cf. James L. Halliday, *Psychosocial Medicine* (New York, 1948), Chap. 1.
[44] Cf. Healy and Bronner, *New Light on Delinquency*, p. 207.

	Medical Diagnostic Procedure	*Diagnosis of Behavior Problems in Human Relations*
(D) Prognosis	Estimated Chance for Recovery on Basis of Treatment Procedure and Bodily Condition of the Individual	Possibility of Successful Treatment with View toward Protracted Custodial Care, Removal from Accustomed Environment, Change in Family Situation, etc.

SUMMARY

(1) The analysis of case-records of delinquents indicates the multiplicity of factors, individual and social, which enter into the formation of delinquent attitudes. We are impressed with the fact that the underlying causal complex producing delinquencies is unknown or misunderstood by the public in general, which receives its impressions from the press and through the formal accounts of courtroom procedure. Moreover, this fundamental causal pattern in many instances eludes the attention of the special legal agencies charged with the handling of delinquents. Case records of delinquents reveal the long prior record of delinquencies, bad associations, characteristic types of offenses, and the widespread failure of responsible public agencies to take effective corrective action during the early stages of the delinquent's career. (2) Keeping in mind W. I. Thomas' injunction concerning statistical data in respect to delinquency —"Statistics in themselves are nothing more than the symptoms of causal processes"—the lack of uniformity and universality in the reporting of criminal activities renders it extremely difficult to gain an adequate and comprehensive picture of American delinquency.[45] Nevertheless, certain facts concerning volume and trends may be readily ascertained. During the past three decades, the evidence appears conclusive that there has been no substantial percentage decrease in the annual volume of delinquency. On the contrary, the evidence appears to point to a continuing secular rise, although not as appreciable as popularly believed. Prior to the recent war, the annual volume of delinquency fell within the range of 170,000 to 200,000 offenders per year, with a peak of offenses occurring in 1943. Since that date there has been a decline, although there is little reason to believe that the underlying upward secular trend has been altered. (3) Statistical studies disclose that the principal offenses for boys are stealing and general acts of carelessness, while for girls misbehaviors assumed the form chiefly of ungovernable behavior and sex offenses. (4) The rates of delinquency are associated with marginal and unassimilated

[45] *The Unadjusted Girl* (Boston, 1931), Preface, p. 6.

groups, the former immigrant groups in this country giving way to recent rural migrants to the city, other mobile and economically marginal groups, and the Negro population. It is stated as a general sociological axiom that delinquency is a function of marginality. (5) In view of the age differentiations existing in the several states dividing adult from juvenile offenders, as established by law, the most common age-levels at which delinquent offenders appear before our courts are affected by these dividing lines. Nevertheless, the age-classification with the highest frequency for juvenile offenders is the fourteen to sixteen year old category, with the sixteen years and older category following. (6) Urban rates are approximately 3.5 times as high as rural rates for the majority of the more common criminal offenses, although rural rates have shown a steady rise. Distinctions between the categories of rural and urban are hard to maintain in the face of the extreme mobility of the population, the spread of industrialization into rural areas, and sectional differences. (7) Because of the different cultural expectancies in the role-behaviors of boys and girls, the male delinquency rate is approximately 4.5 times as high as the female rate: there are differences in the nature of offenses as well. (8) Statistical indices, while pointing to crucial population factors, provide us with no adequate theory of crime and delinquency causation. (9) Because of the non-comparable nature of such data and the neglect of adequate "control groups," multiple factor theories tend to stress the invariant relationship between adverse environmental circumstances, such as poor housing, inadequate schooling, faulty parental control, etc., and delinquency. (A) The complex of the totality of factors entering into delinquency makes it difficult to assign *primacy* to particular factors. This is in keeping with the "vicious circle" pattern of crime, and suggests the *sufficient* basis upon which delinquent patterns may be established. (B) Competent theories of causation of crime and delinquency, as well as of all human behavior, must distinguish between the *efficient* and the *sufficient* bases of human action. (10) The causal pattern of delinquency herein described indicates the necessity for adequate substitutive emotional response for deprivations experienced in psychogenetic growth within certain social environments. Moreover, it reveals the "accidental" manner in which delinquent adjustments are made, and the function of suggestibility in relation to the social environment. (11) Such a theory as we have proposed is suggestive not only because of its comprehensive inclusion of both individual *and* social factors, but because it establishes a frame of reference whereby related statistical studies and the influence of a great variety of specific factors, such as the moving pictures, may be properly integrated. (12) Utilizing such a causal frame of reference enables us to employ a procedure for diagnosing behavioral difficulties which is analogous and comparable to procedures effectively used in medicine.

CHAPTER NINE

CONTEMPORARY FACTORS IN DELINQUENCY

(1) THE SOCIOLOGICAL PATTERN OF DELINQUENCY

THE social factors in the development of delinquency must be viewed within an organized frame of reference. Otherwise they remain isolated, specific factors which, while *possibly* applying to a given sample group of delinquents, do little to aid our fundamental understanding of delinquent problems. The causal frame of reference which we seek to apply in this volume provides us with a vantage point from which we can appraise the significance of the countless statistical and related studies which have been conducted in the field of delinquency during the past three decades.

The *sociological pattern of delinquency* consists of the combination of factors within an organized framework of individual and social disorganization *by which discrete and separate causal conditions within the social situation may be evaluated.* Gough has recently shown that the roles played by individuals provide nuclear points wherein such sociological and psychological variables may be integrated in our understanding of the effects of separate conditions.[1] This is similar to our previous suggestion that the socius, the concept of the social individual as a psychogenetically developed role-playing individual, should occupy the central place in our analysis of social problems.[2] In viewing this sociological pattern consisting of separate social factors which impinge upon the life of the individual, we enjoy a *selective focus* for judging the significant results of the innumerable separate studies that have been made.

To appreciate this point, we have only to consider how contradictory many of our statistical findings are. The investigator may have begun with some particular assumptions of his own and with frames of reference different from those employed by others. Let us consider, for illustration, the contradictory evidence presented in studies of the effects of broken homes or of poverty upon delinquency. The results of such studies are disparate largely for two reasons: (1) the causative condition itself is a complex

[1] H. A. Gough, "A Sociological Theory of Psychopathy," *American Journal of Sociology*, LIII (March, 1948), 359–66.

[2] Herbert A. Bloch, "A Synthetic View of the Social Individual," *American Sociological Review*, VIII (Oct., 1943), 499–512.

entity which must be subdivided and re-defined; (2) the groups of individuals that are studied are erroneously considered *homogeneous* because they have been "defined" as delinquents or criminals. A condition such as a "broken home" or poverty is a highly variable entity, each manifestation of which differs in degree, form, and structure. Furthermore, individuals exposed to such conditions are highly unlike in their responses. Hence, in evaluating studies made of the social and physical factors in delinquency, the careful student will ask: (1) What is the nature of the factor that the investigator is studying? and (2) What is the composition of the group being investigated in relation to this factor? These considerations will assist us in evaluating the findings and in discerning the frequent contradictions of such studies.

(2) DELINQUENCY AS A "FAMILY" PROBLEM

Judges and public officials, in commenting upon the extent and gravity of delinquency, frequently fulminate against "the family" as the unit chiefly responsible for the waywardness of youth. If by this they mean that the family is the fundamental agency for the inculcation of attitudes which, under certain conditions, may eventuate in delinquent patterns of behavior, there can be little doubt about the judgment. Such judgments, however, tell us very little. The behavior of all of us represents to a considerable degree the attitudes that our families have implanted within us. Families themselves are patterned by the social and cultural forces to which they are subjected. In a broad sense, all problems, delinquent as well as non-delinquent, are "family" problems. Certain types of family situations, however, are more conducive to delinquent behavior than others. Such families are of numerous types and are characterized by various kinds of *faulty human relationships*. These conditions of disorganization are not restricted to broken homes, that is, homes in which death, divorce, separation, or desertion by one or both parents has occurred. In fact, as will be pointed out shortly, broken homes are not nearly so significant in delinquency as disorganized homes.

According to Coulter, disorganized homes may be classified into five principal categories: "(1) homes with criminal patterns; (2) homes in which there are unsatisfactory personal relations because of domination, favoritism, nonsolicitude, overseverity, neglect, jealousy, a stepparent, or other interfering relatives; (3) homes in which one parent has a physical or mental disability; (4) homes socially or morally maladjusted because of differences in race, religion, conventions and standards, or an immoral situation; (5) homes under economic pressures—unemployment, low income, homes in which mothers work out." [3]

[3] Charles W. Coulter, "Family Disorganization as a Causal Factor in Delinquency and Crime," *Federal Probation*, XII (September, 1948), 13–17.

The role of the home with criminal patterns is not difficult to picture. Clifford Shaw's study of *Brothers in Crime* shows in detail the demoralizing effects which the criminal activity of one or more members of the family has upon the remaining members.[4] In such homes the criminality of all siblings is by no means inevitable, but the percentage of youthful offenders who have come from this background is high. Thus, "in Burt's classical study of vice and crime in England he found five times as many delinquents from homes in which crime was present as in noncriminally-patterned homes. The Gluecks found that 84.8 per cent of the reformatory population of Massachusetts came from homes with other criminal members, and 86.7 per cent of all juvenile delinquents studied came from such homes. The New York Crime Commission in its study of truancy found that 83 per cent of those later charged with felonies had come from homes with criminal records. . . . Crime breeds crime. Criminal homes breed criminals."[5]

Homes with unsatisfactory personal relationships, whether the result of over-domination, neglect, or quarrelling by the parents, make it difficult for the child to find normal satisfaction for the fundamental acquired drives of his personality. Participation in compensatory activities, frequently of an anti-social nature, is virtually unavoidable in such environments. The home in which the parent is a chronic invalid, or has a serious physical disability, or suffers from a mental disorder may present the simulacrum of an organized home without its actual substance. The disability frequently impairs the ability of the parent to assume his normal responsibility toward the child. Morally maladjusted homes in which there are differences of belief or custom, or indifference to accepted moral practice, leave the child confused and unable to integrate the various facets of his personality. Economically under-privileged homes create problems only in so far as the conditions of poverty preclude the normal development of personality. Employment of children without adequate supervision, absence from the home of the employed mother, loss of status of the father, and similar considerations stand as critical factors in many poor homes.

In all of these homes, where failure occurs it is due to the loss of effective primary controls. These controls, exercised by adults, range from tolerance and genuine parental affection to severe coercion. In Burt's famous study of English delinquents, defective discipline was found 6.9 times more frequently in homes of delinquents than in the homes of non-delinquents.[6] It was four times more important than poverty in the production of delinquency. Confirmation of this fact has been demonstrated repeatedly. The Gluecks noted that the homes of 70 per cent of the de-

[4] Clifford Shaw *et al.*, *Brothers in Crime* (Chicago, 1938).
[5] Coulter, "Family Disorganization," p. 15.
[6] Cyril Burt, *The Young Delinquent* (New York, 1925).

linquents they surveyed were marked by "unsound disciplinary methods."[7] Coulter draws the following conclusion:

> The American home, so far as it fails, does so not through design or malignance, but through neglect, ignorance, and unwillingness to take the responsibility for directing its children. In a few cases is the discipline vicious or criminal. In most cases it is inadequate and inconsistent. Our problem of delinquency is basically a problem of educating, directing, training, advising with and safeguarding parents, and of impressing upon them their continued responsibility. Give us better, more informed and responsible parents and we will guarantee a reduction of the problem of delinquency and crime.[8]

Furthermore, in their recent compendium, *Unraveling Juvenile Delinquency*, based upon ten years of continuous research in which 500 delinquents were compared with 500 non-delinquents, the Gluecks show that "the paternal and maternal families of the delinquents were to a greater extent characterized by mental retardation, emotional disturbance, drunkenness, and criminality."[9] This was clearly evidenced despite the fact that both delinquents and non-delinquents stemmed from backgrounds highly similar in respect to size of families, economic circumstances, limited education of parents, and the presence of serious physical ailments in family groups. So impressive are the data gathered by the Gluecks concerning the influence of "under-the-roof" culture upon delinquency, that they conclude that a study of cultural influences is inadequate if limited to comparison of the external and crude factors comprising the neighborhood or residential area.[10]

(3) HEREDITARY ASPECTS AND CRIMINO-BIOLOGY

Despite the advances in criminological and delinquency research since the beginning of this century, the belief still persists that delinquent behavior is partially to be explained by the transmission of hereditary traits. On the grounds of this belief, frequent attempts have been made to link delinquent behavior with the biological constitution of the individual. The mere presence of delinquency within the same family and its reappearance in successive generations has for some investigators constituted evidence of biological continuity. Most of these investigators have been remiss in too rarely considering the environmental influences.

When, in 1869, Francis Galton, the father of modern eugenics, pub-

[7] Sheldon and Eleanor T. Glueck, *One Thousand Juvenile Delinquents* (Cambridge, 1934), p. 82.

[8] Coulter, "Family Disorganization," p. 17.

[9] Sheldon and Eleanor Glueck, *Unraveling Juvenile Delinquency* (New York, 1950), p. 107.

[10] Ibid., p. 116.

lished his famous study on hereditary genius, considerable interest was aroused as to whether man's qualities were determined by his germ plasm. In retrospect, we find Galton's famous investigation to have arrived at the comforting conclusion that if one's grandfather was a peer of the realm and one's father a member of the Board of Governors of the Bank of England, the chances were more than reasonably good that the individual would not find himself on a bread-line or behind prison bars. A long series of studies have followed, designed to demonstrate the connection between adverse social circumstances and degenerative biological antecedents. Notable among these have been the famous studies of the Jukes and the Kallikaks. Dugdale's study of the 1200 descendants of the Jukes family, who yielded no less than 140 criminals, of whom 7 were murderers, 60 were thieves, and 50 were prostitutes during the short span of their illustrious career of seventy-three years, at a cost to the state of New York of approximately $1,300,000, was for a long time thought to represent ample evidence that criminality is transmitted through defective biological stock.[11] Dugdale's neglect of the conspicuous evidence of degenerative social factors soon became apparent, however. This fault was presumably corrected in the study of an equally corrupt family line, the Kallikaks. Goddard sought to make allowance for the methodological failure of the Dugdale study by establishing a "control" through the comparison of the legitimate and illegitimate issue in the same family.[12] The legitimate Kallikak line produced a high percentage of illustrious citizens in public and private life, whereas the illegitimate line, resulting from the putative *mésalliance* of one, "Martin Kallikak," and a nameless barmaid, produced a sizable quota of felons, alcoholics, and prostitutes among its 480 descendants. Aside from the unproven assumption concerning the union of Kallikak and an unknown girl—there is no certain knowledge of the original paternity of this line—no valid scientific controls were established to separate environmental influences from biological determinants.

The social practices that are termed "delinquent" and "criminal" are, we recognize, different from culture to culture, and from period to period. They represent complex adjustments made by the total organism to the environment, adjustments which, by cultural definition, are regarded as anti-social. Inasmuch as we regard them as *acquired* behavior practices, we cannot believe that they may be biologically transmitted from one generation to another. Nevertheless, physical structure *is* transmitted by biological inheritance, although the functional possibilities in behavior of such structures are endless, as Professor Hankins has shown.[13] The ques-

[11] Richard L. Dugdale, *The Jukes* (New York, 1877); see also Arthur H. Estabrook, *The Jukes in 1915* (Washington, 1916).

[12] Henry H. Goddard, *The Kallikak Family* (New York, 1912).

[13] Cf. F. H. Hankins, "Organic Plasticity vs. Organic Responsiveness," *Publications of the American Sociological Society*, XXII (1928), 44–7, 49–50.

tion is not whether criminal traits are inherited but, as Nathaniel Cantor has put it, "do some individuals come into the world with inferior organic constitutions which predispose them towards criminal behavior, especially if they are brought up in unfavorable surroundings?" [14]

If we look at the problem in this way, the entire field opens up in new directions. As the psychiatrist Kretschmer has tried to show, certain connections exist between physical constitution and temperamental disposition.[15] It is reasonable to expect that physical components of the body, such as the glandular organization, in conditioning temperament, may eventually have an impact upon certain behavior processes. Charles Goring, an English investigator, sought to demonstrate the limited manner in which environment affects certain behavioral characteristics of delinquents by showing that even when siblings are removed from a given family, criminal characteristics common to the family asserted themselves in the separated individuals.[16] Here again, however, we find a neglect of those social conditions that determined the extent to which temperament and acquired attitudes could exercise their influence upon anti-social behavior processes.

More positive proof of the existence of hereditary factors in the development of criminality was claimed by Rosanoff, Handy, and Rosanoff in their study of 340 pairs of twins.[17] Their conclusions purport to demonstrate "the existence of either pre-germinal or germinal causative factors in adult criminality." Again, the evidence may be accepted only if we take care to consider the constitutional factors *as conditioned by the cultural and social environment*. In the same sense, Schlapp's findings that over one-third of the 20,000 prison inmates he examined were glandularly unbalanced must be viewed within the overall sociological pattern and *not as biologically determinative except in this restricted sense*.[18] In any consideration of the role of constitutional factors in behavior, the sociological pattern must always occupy first place in our frame of reference.

That correlations may eventually be established between such specific bodily characteristics as blood classifications, skin capillaries, and other distinguishing constitutional earmarks is a possibility; likewise the claimed findings of Doctors Levy and Braunstein that differences exist in the spinal fluid of criminals and non-criminals may be established.[19] However, whether such differences exist because of similarities of bodily types and

[14] Nathaniel Cantor, *Crime and Society* (New York, 1939), pp. 40–1.

[15] Ernst Kretschmer, *Körperbau und Charakter* (1921).

[16] *The English Convict* (London, 1913).

[17] "Criminality and Delinquency in Twins," *Journal of Criminal Law and Criminology* (1934), 929.

[18] Max A. Schlapp and Edward H. Smith, *The New Criminology* (New York, 1928).

[19] John P. McCaffrey, "The Disease Theory of Crime," *Commonweal*, XXVII (March, 1938), 509–11; see also Cantor, *Crime and Society*, p. 41.

temperamental characteristics for sections of the population as a whole, criminal and non-criminal, and whether they result from certain experiences in the environment, sexual lapses for example, has never been conclusively shown.

Despite the general view that delinquency and crime are behavioral traits of the personality and must be regarded in this light, the neo-Lombrosian pursuit of distinguishing physical characteristics still goes forward. Until Earnest A. Hooton's recent study, it was believed that we had laid to rest forever the ghost of physiological determinism.[20] The Harvard anthropometrist has examined a series of 10,953 male prisoners in two widely separated states, comparing their detailed anthropometric measurements and distinguishing physical characteristics with a "comparable" sample of 909 white civilians and 1,067 Negroid subjects drawn from a diverse sample of Nashville firemen, frequenters of public bath houses, patients at the Massachusetts General Hospital, and the Massachusetts militia. In addition to his confirmation of previously claimed discoveries that prisoners were slighter in build and less heavy than comparable groups in the general population, Hooton claims to have discovered that "the American criminal" is marked by such distinguishing features as thinner beards and bodily hair, eye-folds, sloping and low foreheads, high narrow nasal roots and bridges, a roll helix to the ear, a marked over-bite, and similar characteristics.

What can we say about such findings? Von Hentig's caustic strictures upon these findings appear well taken.[21] In the first place, crime is a *social* phenomenon. Behavior traits are not biologically transmitted; only the physical traits of the organic structure may be transmitted by heredity. We have no way of knowing how such physical factors play a part in producing crime and delinquency and if, in fact, in the event that they exist at all as general traits, whether they are not resultants rather than causes. Secondly, the sampling procedure leaves much open to question, both as to the composition of the samples and their disparities in size.[22] The assumption is that the residue of delinquency and criminality determined by groups of prisoners found in our state institutions provides us with an adequate cross-section of the criminal population. Anyone who has attempted to utilize in research such statistical data as an index of American crime and delinquency knows how tenuous is such an assumption. Hooton assumes that there may be an American criminal type. Can

[20] Earnest A. Hooton, *The American Criminal* (Cambridge, 1939).

[21] Hans Von Hentig, *Crime: Causes and Conditions* (New York, 1947), Chap. VIII, esp. pp. 191–3.

[22] See T. J. McCormick's review of Hooton's work in the *American Sociological Review*, V (April, 1940), 252–4; also the reviews by E. H. Sutherland, *Journal of Criminal Law and Criminology*, XXIX (March–April, 1939), 911–14, and E. B. Reuter, *The American Sociological Review*, XLV (July, 1939), 123–6.

we classify the highly variegated individuals, with different backgrounds and committed to our jails and state and federal institutions for different offenses—ranging from minor derelictions to serious and highly varied major infractions—as falling within a common criminal class? Finally, the multifarious generality of the population against whom criminal characteristics are drawn is so variable that the calibre of Hooton's "law-abiding" samples bears only a very rough approximation to the common characteristics of the criminal population. We are moved to paraphrase the oft-cited admonition: any resemblances existing between Hooton's samples, *homos criminalus*, and *"the law-abiding citizen"* are purely coincidental. *In summary, physical determinants may only be considered to be relative to the behavioral propensities to which they give rise, as these are shaped and defined by the socio-cultural environment.*

(4) THE BROKEN HOME

We have already distinguished between the broken home and the disorganized family. Most of the research literature on the subject fails to distinguish adequately between these two sets of conditions. The broken home refers specifically to that type of home marked by the absence, through death, divorce, separation, or desertion, of one or both of the parents. Occasionally, such a home may be considered "broken" in the absence of one of the other important and integrally related adult members, such as an older brother or sister or other relative. Broken homes do not of themselves necessarily produce family disorganization, although they frequently constitute a vital factor.

Without a certain amount of evaluation of the psychological atmosphere created by the broken home and the character of the individuals who are affected, it is virtually impossible to draw definite conclusions concerning this environmental factor. Shideler, for example, estimated in an early study that from 40 to 70 per cent of delinquents come from broken homes, as compared with 25 per cent in the normal population who came from such homes. This figure finds some verification in the findings of Healy and Bronner in their study of 4,000 delinquents in Boston and Chicago.[23] They estimated that approximately 50 per cent of the delinquents they studied came from such broken homes. They discovered further that this factor was particularly significant in the case of the delinquent girl. Many studies, in fact, concur in the finding that broken homes constitute a more serious handicap for the girl than for the boy. Studies by Mabel Elliott of the Sleighton Farm girls in Darlington, Pennsylvania, and by Hazel Ormsbee, indicate the prevalence of broken homes

[23] William Healy and Augusta F. Bronner, *Delinquents and Criminals, Their Making and Unmaking* (New York, 1926), pp. 121–5.

among female delinquents.[24] In a recent study of 220 Negro and white truants of both sexes appearing before the municipal court in Philadelphia, Reinemann discovered that in almost two-thirds of the cases (65 per cent), broken home conditions prevailed.[25]

Until the findings of Shaw and McKay were published, the significance of the broken home as a factor in producing delinquency was widely accepted. The careful work of these investigators, however, leads us to reappraise the importance of this factor.[26] Guided by the considerations of the heterogeneity of the delinquent group, they discovered that broken homes were significant only in relation to specific categories of delinquents. When they assessed the overall picture, without taking into account the differential characteristics of specific groups, they did find a positive correlation coefficient between broken homes and delinquency; but it was of negligible and insubstantial proportions. For children of ten years of age and under, however, the problem of broken homes became increasingly significant. Racial differences were also noted: a higher percentage of delinquent Negro children came from broken homes than similar groups of whites, regardless of national origin. In general, they concluded that broken homes do not create an inevitable factor in delinquency unless complicated by other conditions, such as bad companions, poor neighborhood, low economic status, and the like.

The trend in these investigations enables us to draw certain general inferences. (1) Not *any* broken home will produce delinquency—only those homes marked by related deleterious conditions. (2) Harmful effects upon the child will depend largely upon which of the parents is removed from the scene and the general structural characteristics of the home. (3) Girls are likely to be more affected by the loss of a parent, apparently, than boys. (4) The age at which the effects of such disintegration are experienced is likely to affect the behavior of the child. Male children at the age of ten show adverse effects in greater proportion than do any other age groups. In general, the effects are more serious for children below ten and less serious for those above this age.

In view of what we have already learned concerning the dependence of young children upon the family and the nature of the developing psychogenetic needs within American family life prior to the age of adolescence, as well as the different status conceptions associated with boys and girls in American society, these general statistical findings should

[24] Mabel A. Elliott, *Correctional Education and the Delinquent Girl* (Harrisburg, Penn. 1929), pp. 26–7; Hazel Grant Ormsbee, *The Young Unemployed Girl* (New York, 1927), pp. 58–60.

[25] J. O. Reinemann, "The Truant Before the Court," *Federal Probation*, XII (Sept., 1948), 8–12.

[26] "Social Factors in Juvenile Delinquency," *Report on the Causes of Crime*, National Commission on Law Observance and Enforcement, II (1931), 266.

come as no surprise. In general, they seem to support the broad assumptions of our frame of reference. Before puberty, within limited spheres of behavior, the child relies much more heavily upon the parent for his fundamental satisfactions. When adolescence has been reached, the individual, having availed himself of a wider margin of freedom, has frequently made adequate extra-familial adjustments to the environment. These adjustments of the older individual represent, in a sense, a continuation of the parents' direction; the young child, on the other hand, must adjust to his environment without the aid or guidance of the trusted parent. In the case of the girl, the more stringent supervision may serve as a check on delinquency until such time as these controls are shattered by death or desertion in the family.

(5) THE MORAL ATMOSPHERE OF THE HOME

When we speak of the broken home or the disorganized family, what we are primarily concerned with is the emotional atmosphere or the "moral condition" of the home. This intangible factor is much more difficult to get at than specific statistical factors. It has to do with those human relationships which have in some way adversely affected the child's psychogenetic development and those specific attributes of the behavior of the environing adults which in some way make it difficult for the child to adjust normally.

An adverse emotional atmosphere is not necessarily confined solely to such easily recognizable and obviously unsavory conditions as drunkenness, crime, marital discord, and open immorality. Harmful emotional atmospheres may be of a more subtle character, as when they reduce the child's sense of his own worth and induce feelings of not being wanted. This latter condition, incidentally, may be found even in the so-called "better homes."

Some attempts have been made to measure this factor of the "moral status" of the home, or what we prefer to call the "emotional atmosphere." These studies look for specific factors of corruptive malfunctioning, such as the conditions of crime, alcoholism, neglect, and marital infidelity, which are the earmarks of emotional discord and confusion. It must be borne in mind that different investigators use the term "immorality" in diverse ways, with the result that the studies of family immorality rarely ever cover the same ground.

Obvious instances of family immorality may be seen in those cases where the parent actually corrupts the young child either through neglect or through actual incitement to delinquency and crime. The atmosphere of such a home may be recognized in the letter which the sister of a young delinquent sent to him during his stay at a well-known boys' reformatory. It follows in its original form.[27]

Dear Stanley I am writing you a letter. Ma is not going to buy you a box of candy because pa did not give ma the pay. pa hit ma and ma went to the St. Anthonys hospital. Ma had a cracked rib the doctor said. The other week he hit ma fast. He said that he is going to kill ma and he hit rosie when she came he grabed her by the hair and chased her out. Pa comes drunk every day he calls ma names he curses at ma. Ma did not say a word to him ma has to close herself up in the dining room.

From Marie

Good by

Equally revealing of the nature of such a home is the account which the social worker gives of the indifference of the stepmother toward the boy's stealing.[28]

Visited at the home of Mrs. K. [Stanley's stepmother] today to warn her against letting the children steal. Told her that complaints had come to our attention about her children stealing from the freight cars. She acknowledged the charge, and only said she could not help it. Said that Stanley went with older boys, who stole and that he should be sent away to an institution. *She acknowledged that she used the stolen goods, and didn't seem to be greatly concerned about the thefts*. . . . [Italics ours.]

The degenerative atmosphere of this same home can be seen from the viewpoint of the boy, who says:[29]

The stepmother also made us (brother, sister and myself) do all the hard work in the house. And then she would beat us if we complained. That is what embittered me against her and her children. I developed a hatred against her that still lasts; a hatred that was so burning that when she would look into my eyes she would read it there, and in that way she knew my feelings. . . . My stepmother sent me out with William (my stepbrother) to pick rags and bottles in the alleys. She said that would pay for my board and make me more useful than fretting and sulking at home. I did not mind that in the least. In fact, I enjoyed it, because I was at least out of the old lady's reach. . . . One day my stepmother told William to take me to the railroad yard to break into boxcars. . . . After a year of break-

[27] Clifford R. Shaw, *The Jack-Roller* (Chicago, 1930), pp. 42–3. Reprinted by permission of Clifford R. Shaw.

[28] Ibid., p. 43. Reprinted by permission of Clifford R. Shaw.

[29] Ibid., pp. 50–3. Reprinted by permission of Clifford R. Shaw.

ing into box cars and stealing from stores, my stepmother realized that she could send me to the market to steal vegetables for her.

Studies of the breakdown of a family in its effects upon children can best be accomplished when specific and selected factors are isolated for examination. This can be done, as will be illustrated in relation to our subsequent discussion of the disorganized family, if we recognize that family life is distinguished by certain structural aspects that are indispensable for effective child guidance. Although the term "immoral," broadly used, does not provide us with scientific information of unquestionable accuracy, it does nevertheless afford some insight into the characteristic effects of disorganized homes. The incidence of delinquency in the immoral home will vary with the breadth of the investigator's definition of the term itself. Thus, Mabel Elliott discovered that 56 per cent of the delinquent girls she studied at the Sleighton Farm came from homes which would readily be defined as "immoral" in a general sense. On the other hand, the Healy and Bronner study of 4,000 delinquents yielded an incidence of only 21 per cent.[30] Here the term was used in a more restricted sense, denoting homes whose members were alcoholic, or were engaged in practices legally defined as immoral, or were possessors of criminal records. If we include in our criteria of immoral homes the various malfunctionings characteristic of the broken home and the disorganized family, the scope of our results would be commensurate with the incidence of delinquency itself.

Where homes fail because of reprehensible moral conditions, this is due *fundamentally* to two conditions. (1) They may neglect to exercise properly those *permissive* functions in regard to child rearing with which the family is charged by society; or (2) they may misapply the *restrictive* functions that all families must exercise. In either case, there is a departure from culturally defined primary controls. From the standpoint of family control, each family must be adjudged on the basis of the permissive and restrictive functions it exercises. The consent granted the child to engage in activities that are normally considered detrimental to his welfare represents a form of moral abuse. Conversely, the restrictions placed upon the child's normal pursuit of his acquired needs may likewise represent a failure of the family to maintain normal primary controls. The operation of primary controls will often vary according to class. Within the framework of American society, the possibilities for collapse are considerably greater for economically under-privileged families than for middle-class and upper middle-class families. However, the possibility of failure in the exercise of primary controls among middle-class families is still considerable and is growing steadily, as is attested by rising delinquency figures for such

[30] Healy and Bronner, *Delinquents and Criminals*, pp. 126–7.

groups. *The emotional atmosphere of the slum home may directly incite towards delinquency, whereas the atmosphere of the better-favored home may conduce towards delinquency by indirect means.*

(6) ECONOMIC STATUS AND DELINQUENCY

The recent studies of poverty in relation to delinquency, as contrasted with the earlier investigations by Booth, Rowntree, and Hunter, indicate a decreasing importance of this factor in the production of delinquency.[31] This is in part due to the rising standards of living for the population as a whole. During the early part of this century, it was readily apparent that poverty and delinquency were positively and closely associated. This does not mean, however, that conditions of poverty no longer breed crime and delinquency. It means simply that while economic conditions have improved, rates of delinquency are still high and are becoming more widely dispersed among the general population. In short, the improvements in our economic life during the past three decades, bringing in their wake steadier and more widespread employment, social security, higher wage standards, aid to dependent children, and increased social benefits, have not produced the decline in delinquency that might reasonably have been expected. Instead, other factors are becoming increasingly instrumental in producing youthful disorders.

Adverse economic conditions nevertheless still appear to be potent contributory stimuli to delinquency. Wealth and economic status function *relatively* as limiting conditions in producing delinquency. The highest incidence of delinquency is always induced among the marginal economic groups. As these groups contract in size, the relative incidence appears to shrink accordingly. In 1912, before the advent of the improved economic conditions largely brought about by legislative advances since 1930, Sophonisba P. Breckenridge and Edith Abbott in their investigation of delinquents appearing before the Cook County Court in Illinois discovered that over 75 per cent came from homes denominated as "very poor" or "poor." [32]

It must not be forgotten, however, that a large section of the population during this period lived on a relatively low economic level and yet only a small percentage of this group produced delinquent children. In fact, as late as 1929 the Brookings Institution Report of that year stated that approximately 20 per cent of our families had incomes of less than

[31] Charles Booth, *Life and Labour of the People in London* (New York, 1892–7), Vol. I; Benjamin S. Rowntree, *Poverty, A Study of Town Life* (New York, 1902); Robert Hunter, *Poverty* (New York, 1904). These early classical investigations showed the extensive demoralization associated with poverty, of which delinquency and crime were conspicuous phases.

[32] *The Delinquent Child and the Home* (New York, 1912), p. 72.

$1,000 a year. The disparity in income levels during the decade prior to 1929 may be seen in the fact that approximately one-half of the total national income went to about one-seventh of the population. This condition grew worse during the depression when, according to the Report of the National Economic Resources Committee, approximately one out of every four families in the United States had an income of $500 per year or less. The delinquency rate is not correlated in direct ratio to the changing economic circumstances of our population. Improved economic conditions affect the locus of delinquency rather than the overall and percentage rates. The Healy and Bronner study seems to give some substance to this view in reporting that about 27 per cent of their cases were associated with inferior economic circumstances.[33] Of this number, 22 per cent were listed as coming from backgrounds which might be termed as poverty conditions, and 5 per cent from surroundings recognized as destitute. Studies of institutional inmates invariably show a high percentage whose parents are laborers or engaged in unskilled employments. High percentages also reveal the part which the full time employment of the mother away from home may play in producing delinquency. When we recall, however, that a considerable volume of our institutional inmates are Negroes and that Negroes, as a class, comprise the largest section of the population falling into such unskilled categories, it is not surprising to find this incidence among institutional inmates.

Low economic status is not a direct cause of delinquency, although it is frequently an important associated factor when found in conjunction with certain other specific types of conditions. Hans Von Hentig makes much of this factor as a "sufficient" basis for crime when the threshhold of resistance is effectively lowered.[34] It is interesting to note in this connection that his peculiar doctrine of *temptation* in relation to criminal activity—that when economic conditions are sufficiently disadvantageous, the resistance to crime of many individuals will break—applies to no particular class. According to this view, the changing economic status of the individual may provide an incentive to crime when the pressure of the situation becomes sufficiently acute.

Poverty and low economic standards, therefore, although important concomitants, are not indispensable characteristics of delinquency. To be "poor but honest" is the rule rather than the exception. Again, we must view poverty from the standpoint of those separate conditions it creates which disorganize the family process, particularly in their effects upon the child. Conditions of early child employment which, under certain aspects, are very likely to demoralize the child, or conditions of overcrowding in

[33] Healy and Bronner, *Delinquents and Criminals*, p. 263.
[34] *Crime: Causes and Conditions* (New York, 1947), pp. 225–6.

the home, or conditions which render it extremely difficult for the family to discharge its primary responsibilities of supervision, and other related factors in the *complex* of poverty, may have a direct bearing upon the waywardness of children. This again testifies to the importance of breaking down such a broad concept as poverty into its functional and related behavioral components. *It is the separate behavioral components operating within a given situation which must be assessed in relation to any problem.*

The Components of Poverty

If we examine such a component as child employment, we find that delinquency occurs four times more frequently among employed children than among unemployed, a fact disclosed by the Federal Children's Bureau as early as 1911. Of 188 girls committed between the ages of fourteen and seventeen to Sleighton Farm, 162 had been wage earners prior to commitment. Further investigation of delinquency among employed children suggests that it is brought about by the *loss of primary parental control* and *the tendency of the child to assume adult standards for which he is unprepared.* Many of the employments in which children find themselves bring them into association with conditions that are emotionally unhealthful. The desire to emulate the adults with whom this employment brings them into contact may likewise prove a dangerous factor. The employment itself may be carried on under harmful conditions, presenting pitfalls to the immature person. Common employments of children are street employments, such as selling newspapers, shining shoes, and the like. These preoccupy the child at an age when he is particularly in need of supervision and when he is especially impressionable. Such employments, taking the child far afield from his own neighborhood at an early age, may have highly disastrous consequences.

Conditions of poverty invariably bring in their wake the harrowing conditions of overcrowding and loss of privacy. These factors may be seen to be directly related to the incidence of delinquency. In parts of Harlem where the *hot bed system* prevails (sleeping in shifts because of the shortage of space and beds), as many as fourteen people living in three small rooms is not uncommon. Lack of opportunity to observe the simplest amenities which middle-class families take so readily for granted, such as bathing and dressing in private, is a recognized commonplace among such families. The important integrating function of the family dinner hour is completely lacking in such homes. The failure to maintain supervisory controls over the child, either through inability or indifference, is a common prelude to truancy, the recurring symptom of all delinquent and predelinquent problems.

(7) HEALTH AND PHYSICAL DEVELOPMENT OF DELINQUENTS

General surveys of the health and physical characteristics of delinquents indicate that the physical disabilities from which they suffer are due primarily to poverty and parental neglect rather than to heredity, although certain exceptional instances must be noted. Today, it is considered obligatory to give the delinquent child entering an institution a very careful medical examination and to follow up as carefully as possible any defects which such examinations may reveal. It is extremely difficult to establish genuine statistical differences between the incidence of certain physical defects among the criminal and delinquent populations and selected samples from the normal population, although a great many statistical studies do reveal certain percentage differences.[35] The inference which many investigators make is that the delinquent population is to a small degree distinguished from the non-delinquent population by poor health and physical abnormalities.

If such facts are to be significant we must distinguish between three sets of factors: (1) differential health characteristics; (2) actual physical differences in size, weight, physical handicaps and stigmata; and (3) biological factors that differentiate delinquent individuals from non-delinquent types. Very few studies have been conducted on an adequate basis to distinguish between these three sets of physical factors and their possible interconnections.

(1) Morbidity rates do appear somewhat higher among delinquents than among non-delinquents. This factor is largely due to physical neglect and poverty, as well as to inadequate medical care (the cost may be prohibitive to the marginal family) and malnutrition. Malnutrition may be a result not alone of poverty, but of indifference as to the child's diet. Wealthy children, as well as the poverty-stricken, have frequently been found to suffer from various forms of undernourishment, although the rate, of course, is much higher among the economically under-privileged. Thurston, for example, has shown that the rate of malnutrition is considerably higher among children from delinquency areas than for children living outside of such areas.[36] The difference he finds of 42 per cent for the delinquency areas in New York City as contrasted with 19 per cent for the general population appears substantial, although whether this represents a definitive difference for the population as a whole may not as yet be fully established.

Although the majority of findings have seemed to support the view that delinquents suffer from poorer health more than non-delinquents, the

[35] Cf. Edwin H. Sutherland, *Principles of Criminology* (Philadelphia, 1947), Chap. 6.

[36] Henry W. Thurston, *Concerning Juvenile Delinquency* (New York, 1942), p. 26.

most recent evidence compiled by the Gluecks disputes this claim rather sharply. In their matched study of 500 delinquents and 500 non-delinquents, they conclude that very little, if any, difference exists between the physical condition of the two groups as a whole.[37] In view of the recency of their evidence and the particular area (Boston) where the study was conducted, it should be noted that factors of physical health are variable conditions in relation to time, place, and ethnic background.

(2) The evidence about differences in size and weight is ambiguous and somewhat confusing. Complicating the picture is the recent evidence of the Cleveland pediatrician, Dr. Norman C. Wetzel, who, by means of an axillary grid-chart, has demonstrated that normal growth patterns of children (seven hereditary types, according to Wetzel) may be distorted by glandular and emotional disturbances. Upon the basis of such findings, therefore, and the assumption that serious emotional disturbances often accompany delinquent misbehavior, delinquent disorders should be characterized by differences in growth and size with some regularity. The recency of the "Wetzel-grid" findings in relation to emotional disturbances, however, has not as yet permitted specific studies to be made upon differences in size and weight of delinquents. It is dubious that the standard studies upon weight and size of delinquents performed thus far have any genuine scientific validity. Healy and Bronner, for example, like John B. Slawson, note that delinquent boys may be inclined to be either somewhat taller and stronger than normal children or else conspicuously smaller.[38] In either event, such facts might conceivably contribute to the formation of delinquent patterns. The superior strength and size of certain boys may be instrumental in making them outstanding in their exploits and thus leaders among delinquents. On the other hand, a diminutive stature may have both a psychological effect on the individual, predisposing him to certain types of misbehavior, and may also be considered of value in the accomplishing of certain delinquent exploits. When the young Sydney Blotzman began his career at the age of seven, his slight stature and his diminutive height proved a decided asset to himself and his comrades in their escapades, a fact which he himself comments upon. As the psychologist Alfred Adler has pointed out, the psychological compensation for smallness in stature may be considerable; it may not be entirely fortuitous that some of the world's greatest military leaders, from Hannibal and Napoleon to General Pershing, were men of short stature.[39]

The most striking evidence compiled thus far concerning defini-

[37] Sheldon and Eleanor Glueck, *Unraveling Juvenile Delinquency*, Chap. XIV.

[38] John B. Slawson, *The Delinquent Boy* (Boston, 1926), Chap. 5.

[39] See Alfred Adler, "A Study of Organ Inferiority and Its Psychical Compensation," *Nervous and Mental Disease Monograph*, 1917, Series No. 24; also, by the same author, *The Practise and Theory of Individual Psychology*, trans. by P. Radin (New York, 1925).

tive differences in bodily build for delinquents as compared with non-delinquents is advanced by the Gluecks. Utilizing the findings of Dr. Carl C. Seltzer, Harvard University anthropologist, their study of 500 delinquents and 500 non-delinquents in the Boston area reveals that, absolutely and relatively, the delinquents are mesomorphic in constitution (muscular), containing a much higher proportion of all mesomorphic types than the non-delinquents and a far lower proportion of ectomorphs (linear, thin types). Ectomorphs, endomorphs (round, plump types), and balanced types, they find, are decidedly subordinate among the delinquents. The control group of non-delinquents, it was found, contained no extreme predominance of any bodily type, although substantial numbers of ectomorphs and mesomorphs were found, with the former predominating.[40] Although probably of some significance for this particular study and suggestive for future research, it is too soon yet to say whether such differences constitute genuine critical factors separating delinquents and non-delinquents in relation to such contingent conditions as differential family structure, ethnic factors, neighborhood and surrounding areas, cultural determinants, and the like.

The facts concerning stature and weight of delinquent girls appear far more conclusive. Healy and Bronner discovered that about 70 per cent of the delinquent girls they examined were above the average weight and height norms for girls from the general population, a fact which appears to be borne out by other studies. This is significant for a number of reasons. In the first place, it indicates sexual precocity for such girls, facilitating their exposure to various illicit activities. Secondly, the earlier maturation of such girls renders it far more difficult to maintain them under adequate family and school control. In view of the fact that delinquent girls involved in sexual offenses are also frequently marked by low intelligence, the combination of factors is such that delinquency, under stipulated circumstances, would appear to be the expected outcome rather than the unusual occurrence. We must note, however, that early physical maturation is also frequently associated with high intelligence and that girls of high intelligence rarely become sexual delinquents in the accepted sense. The explanation is probably to be sought in the fact that for those girls who *do mature early*, under conditions of an adverse environment and marked by *low intelligence*, the predisposing characteristics may be sufficient to induce delinquency.

Burt showed that approximately 70 per cent of the delinquents he studied suffered from various physical defects, although most of them were not serious.[41] Recent studies of American delinquents, while still showing a relatively high percentage of such defects, largely induced by neglect, do

[40] Sheldon and Eleanor Glueck, *Unraveling Juvenile Delinquency*, Chapter XV.
[41] Burt, *The Young Delinquent*, pp. 238–40.

not indicate a volume as high as that disclosed in the Burt study. Even Burt's findings suggested that the large majority of the delinquents he studied were quite normal and free of serious disease. With the general improvement in medical care for all sections of the population, the incidence of physical defects among pre-delinquent and delinquent children should show a proportionate decrease. Resultant effects which are still manifested, such as carious teeth, latent infections due to neglected injuries, and the like, will reveal the indifference of parental concern within the entire delinquent setting rather than the crucial significance of physical differences.

Physical stigmata, such as a repulsive appearance, deafness, or poor vision, may produce psychological effects conducive towards delinquency. Adler's conception of "organic inferiority" might well apply to certain delinquent types, particularly to the child who feels himself rejected because of his ugliness or ungainliness. The psychiatrist Karl Menninger has aptly stated that some of the best correctives for certain types of behavior problems might come from the hands of the plastic surgeon rather than from the clinical psychologist and psychiatrist. The State of Illinois, which has been in the forefront in attempting to bring about rehabilitation of state institution inmates by means of plastic surgery, has released some impressive figures. By 1947, of the 376 convicts released from Illinois' Stateville Penitentiary after plastic surgery had been performed, less than 1 per cent got into further difficulty as contrasted with the ordinary rate of parole violations of 17 per cent.[42] The case of John W. Glaefke in the State of Ohio is interesting in this respect.[43] Rejected by members of his own family and his associates as a child, he left school in the tenth grade, seeking employment in back rooms, basements, and dark quarters where he could not easily be seen. He was arrested for stealing at the age of twenty-three; upon his release he was drafted into the army where his ugliness increased his resentment and bitterness towards society. Upon his discharge from the army, he again was arrested for stealing. This time a sympathetic judge sought to obtain for him the plastic surgery which he thought might be effective in deterring his anti-social tendencies. Today, this young man, steadily employed and learning to make friends for the first time in his life, appears well on the road towards rehabilitation. Dr. Royal Grossman, in commenting upon his case, has stated: "[His] appearance was a factor in his maladjustment. . . . He reacted in the only way he knew how. It's like hauling off and punching the wall when you are frustrated." Cautiously, however, the psychiatrist added: "If he lives by

[42] What should also be noted in such cases, however, is the fact that the special attention given to such individuals may serve an important therapeutic function as great as, and possibly greater than, the beneficial results imputed to plastic surgery.

[43] *Time* Magazine, April 11, 1949, p. 69.

society's conventions and laws for ten years I'll know we have accomplished something." There is little doubt but that in certain cases such facial surgery can be of instrumental value in ameliorating the person's emotional and social outlook.

(3) Biological factors, other than the physical defects alluded to, may play a predisposing role towards the formation of delinquent patterns. The precise way in which this may be brought about is still largely unknown. The functioning of such factors, however, may only be understood in relation to the formation of the person's entire set of reactive patterns as these have been shaped by the environment. The Wetzel physical growth studies within the past five years, for example, illustrate the way in which emotional behavior, whether functionally or organically derived, may have an effect upon such physical characteristics as size and weight. As previously indicated in our discussion of hereditary factors, the possibilities of various biological structures are endless.

The types of biological characteristics discussed in relation to delinquency, therefore, are primarily symptomatic of disturbed emotional states which *may or may not* be the accompaniment of delinquency. Hirsch, for example, has discovered that 32 per cent of the delinquents he studied suffered from enuresis (bed-wetting) as compared with 26.1 per cent in the non-delinquent population.[44] Enuresis is frequently associated with deep-seated emotional disturbances among children. Endocrine disorders, which are closely associated with emotional states, may be induced by the environment as well as by innate factors and, in any event, do not necessarily imply delinquent behavior. We have difficulty in assessing the effects of endocrine dysfunctioning upon bodily states; such effects may be direct in producing injurious emotional states (such as hyperadrenalism) or they may have specific physical effects (such as hyperpituitarism in excessive growth or the development of bodily fat) from which compensatory psychological results may take place. Moreover, as we have continually reiterated, a given emotional state, regardless of how derived, does not necessarily lead to delinquent behavior. The total sociological pattern conducive to delinquent behavior must always be present.

Nevertheless, Rowe, in studying the behavior of seventeen-year-old children suffering from endocrine malfunctioning, found that of those actually suffering from specific endocrine disorders, 18.3 per cent gave evidence of behavioral disorders of a more or less serious nature as contrasted with 13 per cent who did not.[45] This difference is not sufficiently large to enable us to state with certainty that endocrine disorders may constitute a predisposing factor, although it is suggestive. In respect to specific dam-

[44] Nathaniel Hirsch, *Dynamic Causes of Juvenile Crime* (Cambridge, 1937), p. 103.

[45] A. W. Rowe, "A Possible Endocrine Factor in the Behavior Problems of the Young," *American Journal of Orthopsychiatry*, I (1931), 451–75.

age to the brain tissue, however, the evidence is somewhat different. George M. Thompson, in making a detailed neurological study of 500 juvenile delinquents, discovered that over 60 per cent gave indication of actual damage to the brain.[46] Such injuries might have been incurred in a number of ways, although the examination results seem to point to considerable evidence of birth and post-natal traumas.

Our general conclusions concerning the effect of physical disabilities and considerations of health upon delinquency patterns are that physical patterns do not create delinquency any more than they create other forms of specific behavioral malfunctioning. That they play a contributory role is, of course, not to be gainsaid. The part which such factors play is highly variable, depending in general upon the entire organic constitution, the psychological aptitudes and capabilities towards adjustment, and the social environment. Moreover, many of the emotional states and their physical correlatives discovered in conjunction with delinquency are the emotional and physiological by-products of the entire social setting within which delinquency thrives—adverse family conditions, poor housing, poverty, and childhood employment.

(8) MENTAL COMPONENTS IN DELINQUENCY

Emotional instability. When we consider emotional instability and the other disturbed emotional states accompanying delinquency, we can be more definite. In agreement with our causal conception of the formation of delinquent attitudes, we would expect to find in most delinquents evidence of disturbed emotional states. Most investigators, particularly the more recent ones, do in fact find that emotional difficulties occur frequently among delinquents. The recent Boston area study by the Gluecks, for example, based upon extended use of the Rorschach Test, show that the delinquents studied exceed significantly the non-delinquents in such traits as assertiveness, defiance, resentfulness, and ambivalent attitudes towards authority. The results also show greater traits of sadism and impulsiveness than for non-delinquents.[47] Nevertheless, it is significant to note that in the comparison of both groups for diagnosed neurotic trends, the delinquents fare better than their non-delinquent controls, the results showing neuroticism among 24.6 per cent of the delinquents as compared with 35.8 per cent of all the non-delinquents.[48] This high percentage among the "controls" produces considerable doubt as to the representativeness of this sample.

[46] "Psychiatric Factors Influencing Learning," *The Journal of Nervous and Mental Diseases*, CI (April, 1945).

[47] Sheldon and Eleanor Glueck, *Unraveling Juvenile Delinquency*, Chaps. XVIII and XIX.

[48] Ibid., p. 240.

Delinquency is accompanied and abetted by the development of several types of emotional instability, which may occur as forerunners to acts of delinquency, or which may materialize as a chronic accompanying condition of delinquent states. Since very few cases of psychosis and neurosis occur before the age of fifteen, it is understandable that the incidence of such disturbances is rare among juvenile delinquents. However, we do find present discernible incipient symptoms which, in due course of time, may develop into recognizable adult forms of mental aberration. Thus, despite the fact that mental disease among juvenile offenders is conspicuous in its absence—a fact that is true for the juvenile population as a whole—the rate of psychotic disorders is relatively high among the adult criminal population. This may be accounted for on two bases: (1) the distorted emotional state accompanying many forms of delinquency may degenerate into the full-blown adult psychosis, the accelerating factor being the process of time; and (2) the original emotional state of the delinquent may become worsened as he furthers his delinquent and criminal career. The emotional stress accompanying asocial and anti-social activities may be all that is required to topple an already precarious emotional balance.

On the basis of our general causal hypothesis, we would expect a larger percentage of cases of emotional instability among the delinquent population than among the non-delinquent. Healy and Bronner confirm this expectation very clearly in their analysis of delinquent and non-delinquent siblings of the same families. Of the 143 delinquents studied, 91.6 per cent (131 cases) afford substantial evidence of emotional malfunctioning. Thus, 53 cases gave evidence of feelings of rejection, being unloved, and insecurity; 45 gave evidence of being thwarted in self-expression; 62 showed symptoms of inadequacy and feelings of inferiority; 43 displayed patterns of broad emotional disturbance relating to family disharmony; and 43 were marked by manifestations of sibling jealousy and rivalry.[49] In further confirmation of our thesis are the facts concerning the emotional characteristics of the non-delinquent "controls" within the same family. Why, we may ask, did these children fail to show the same types of emotional behavior as did their siblings? And in cases where the emotional behavior was the same, why did they not develop delinquent patterns? The findings of Healy and Bronner provide a substantial answer to this problem. The results of this carefully detailed investigation show that such non-delinquents (1) developed different types of emotional patterns because of accidents of birth and rearing; or (2) were fortunately able to develop adequate normative "emotional equivalents" in connection with crisis-situations; or (3) were in some cases, because of bodily

[49] William Healy and Augusta F. Bronner, *New Light Upon Delinquency and Its Treatment* (New Haven, 1936), p. 49.

defects, physically unable to develop delinquent traits; or (4) lacked the opportunities presented to the delinquents.[50]

One aspect of these findings seems to afford ample demonstration of the efficacy of our hypothesis: the manner in which the various forms of emotional strain are related to the fundamental patterns of wish-formation suggested by W. I. Thomas and incorporated within our causal framework. Virtually all of the frustrating emotional states may be visualized as being directly related to the wish patterns of new experience, security, response, and recognition. The following diagram demonstrates these relationships and interconnections.

Emotional States Occurring in Conjunction with Delinquent Behavior (Healy and Bronner)**

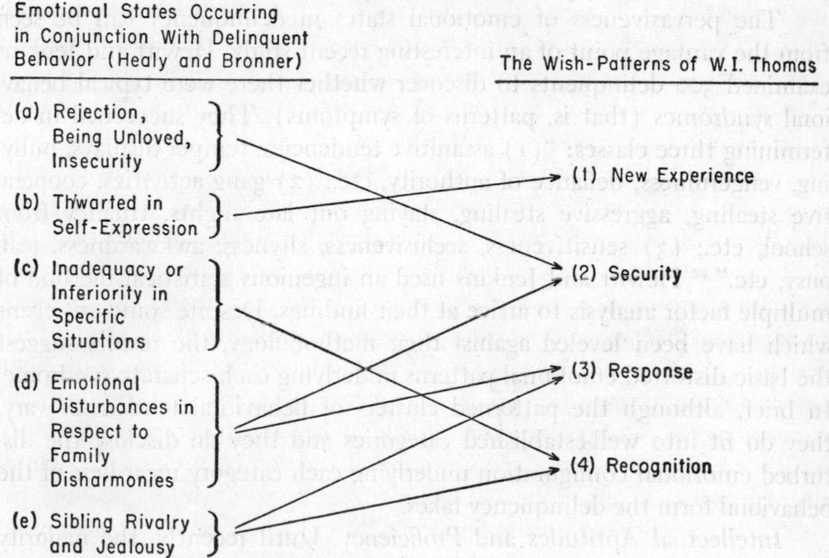

* Adapted from the principal categories of emotional disturbance found among the 143 delinquents studied by Healy and Bronner. See *New Light on Delinquency and Its Treatment*, pp. 49, 128.

Virtually all workers in the field of delinquency are struck by the marked emotional characteristics of their charges. Burt has indicated that these emotional characteristics are the most outstanding traits of delinquency. About one-half (48.1 per cent) of the delinquents of both sexes he studied were found to suffer from innate emotional difficulties, while approximately 85 per cent were emotionally disturbed if acquired disorders

[50] Ibid., pp. 87–9.

were considered.[51] Similar conclusions have been drawn by Eleanor and Sheldon Glueck, John Slawson, L. J. Carr, and others.[52]

An emotional disturbance is a pervasive symptom and can frequently be readily recognized, although not so readily diagnosed. It is symptomatic of the total malfunctioning of the organism, regardless of the specific factor or set of factors that brought it about. Consequently, the appearance of emotional disorder among the majority of the delinquents we examine is not surprising. Unlike other specific factors, such as particular aspects of the environment or the biological organism, disturbed emotional states are the accompanying conditions brought about by maladaptation, irrespective of the specific internal or external factor. For this reason, studies vary considerably in their appraisal of the extent of the operation of specific bodily or environmental conditions, but they do display a remarkable unanimity about the vitality of the emotional factors.

The pervasiveness of emotional states in delinquency can be seen from the vantage point of an interesting recent study. Hewitt and Jenkins examined 500 delinquents to discover whether there were typical behavioral *syndromes* (that is, patterns of symptoms). They succeeded in determining three classes: "(1) assaultive tendencies, temper displays, bullying, vengefulness, defiance of authority, etc.; (2) gang activities, cooperative stealing, aggressive stealing, staying out late nights, truancy from school, etc.; (3) sensitiveness, seclusiveness, shyness, awkwardness, jealousy, etc." [53] Hewitt and Jenkins used an ingenious statistical method of multiple factor analysis to arrive at their findings. Despite some criticisms which have been leveled against their methodology, the results suggest the basic distorted emotional patterns underlying each separate syndrome. In brief, although the patterned clusters of behavioral tendencies vary, they do fit into well-established categories and they do disclose the disturbed emotional configuration underlying each category regardless of the behavioral form the delinquency takes.

Intellectual Aptitudes and Proficiency. Until recently, the majority of studies were in remarkable agreement as to the high incidence of subnormal intelligence among delinquents. *This agreement was all the more striking in view of the fact that criminals, as a body, were shown to compare favorably with the general population.* Thus, Healy and Bronner in their comprehensive study of delinquency in 1926 discovered that only 63 per cent of the large group they examined were of normal intelligence.[54]

[51] Burt, *The Young Delinquent*, pp. 491–2, 541.

[52] Sheldon and Eleanor T. Glueck, *One Thousand Juvenile Delinquents* (Cambridge, 1934), pp. 102–06; John Slawson, *The Delinquent Boy* (Boston, 1926), pp. 223 *et seq.*; Lowell J. Carr, *Delinquency Control* (New York, 1950), pp. 140–8.

[53] Lester E. Hewitt and Richard L. Jenkins, *Fundamental Patterns of Maladjustment: The Dynamics of Their Origin* (Springfield, Ill., 1947), p. 26.

[54] Healy and Bronner, *Delinquents and Criminals*, pp. 151, 274.

Upon a comparative basis, they estimated that delinquency was likely to occur five to ten times more frequently among the feebleminded than among the normally endowed population. Goddard seemed to imply that feeblemindedness and low intelligence were direct incitements towards delinquency.[55] These findings concerning feeblemindedness, low intelligence, and delinquency appeared even more pronounced among females.

With the exception of female sex delinquents, many of the recent studies seem to indicate that the intelligence levels of the delinquent population do not differ greatly from those of control groups drawn from the same levels of the general population. Dr. David B. Rotman, on the basis of prolonged investigations of the intellectual and psychological aptitudes of delinquents appearing before the Chicago courts, derides strongly the notion that any mental differences exist between delinquents and non-delinquents. He points out that the percentages of low-grade intelligence and feeblemindedness he finds among such delinquents ranges from about 2 to 5 per cent, which is about the same as is expected among the non-delinquent population.[56] Although his investigations do not relate specifically to delinquents, Sutherland points out that among both criminals and delinquents the incidence of feeblemindedness has decreased from over 50 per cent to approximately 20 per cent. This conclusion is based on the test findings of 350 reports, comparing the period 1910–1914 with the period 1925–1928.[57] Metfessel and Lovell, in examining the voluminous literature on intelligence and crime, come to the general conclusion that deficient intelligence is not nearly so serious a causal factor as it was heretofore considered.[58] They do contend, however, that the majority of studies places the delinquent in the dull normal class.

In the recent Glueck study, although the factors of intelligence were "controlled" so that disparities in average levels of intelligence between delinquents and non-delinquents could not be gauged, it was determined nevertheless that the delinquents in the study averaged less in verbal intelligence than did the non-delinquents, while the two groups resembled each other closely in performance intelligence.[59] Of greater significance perhaps, however, is the finding that "the differences between delinquents and non-delinquents are concerned with intellectual tendencies that are interwoven with emotional dynamics"—a conclusion which supports the general contention that delinquency is closely associated with disturbed emotional states, rather than with mental defects.[60]

[55] Henry H. Goddard, *Juvenile Delinquency* (New York, 1921), p. 22.
[56] David B. Rotman, *Federal Probation*, XI, 3 (September, 1947).
[57] Sutherland, *Principles of Criminology*, pp. 104–05.
[58] Milton Metfessel and Constant Lovell, "Recent Literature on Individual Correlates of Crime," *Psychological Bulletin*, XXXIX (March, 1942), 148.
[59] Sheldon and Eleanor Glueck, *Unraveling Juvenile Delinquency*, p. 207.
[60] Ibid., p. 214.

How are we to account for the new conclusions that low intelligence is not so important a factor in delinquency as was previously maintained? On the basis of logical inference, such changes in the intellectual composition of our delinquent population might be sought on the following grounds: (1) an actual change in the character of our delinquent population may have taken place since the time of the early studies; (2) the changed results may reflect improvement in our testing techniques and instruments and in the method of administering such tests; (3) the general improvement in the levels of schooling for the country as a whole may manifest itself in the higher levels of test results for delinquents as well as non-delinquents; and (4) improved methods of scientific study may have enabled us to procure more adequate representative samples of the delinquent and non-delinquent groups than were obtained in the past. In assessing each of these possibilities, we are led to conclude that all may be operating in various degrees. Certainly, the character of the delinquent population has changed since the early decades of the century; the delinquent son of the immigrant has given way to various other types of marginal groups in the population. Our testing techniques have been constantly improved as have the clinical diagnoses we now make of individual delinquents.

Although the majority of juvenile offenders may fall within the dull normal and normal groups, sex offenders fall more frequently into subnormal and feebleminded categories than do others. Other types of offense as well appear to be correlated with low intelligence. As Jacob and Rosamond Goldberg have shown, for example, mental retardation and intellectual deficiency still operate as significant factors in sex delinquency among girls.[61] We should bear in mind that such factors may not be thought of as constituting the *prime* causes of deficiency. In general, low intelligence and mental subnormality do not constitute the principal causes of delinquency any more than do the other factors previously mentioned. *In every case, the factor of low intelligence must be seen in relation to the entire situational and psychological complex productive of anti-social tendencies.*

We will now consider how it may be possible that the intelligence of the adult criminal population is higher than that of the delinquent groups in the United States. Dr. Herman A. Adler estimated, on the basis of his survey of Illinois prisoners, that their intelligence was generally higher than that of selected samples of troops in the peace-time United States Army after the First World War.[62] Such samples are usually not

[61] Jacob A. and Rosamond W. Goldberg, *Girls in the City Streets* (New York, 1935).

[62] Herman M. Adler and Myrtle R. Worthington, "The Scope of the Problem of Delinquency and Crime as Related to Mental Deficiency," *Journal of Psycho-Asthenics*, XXX (1925), 47–57.

adequately representative of soldiers themselves, and certainly not representative of comparable groups in the civilian population. There appears to be reasonable evidence, nevertheless, that adult offenders possess a higher level of intelligence than do their juvenile counterparts. The reasons for such a disparity prove to be rather significant. It would seem that, except for sexual offenses, the more common forms of criminality require at least average intelligence for successful practice and for evasion of the law. The dull youthful offender is likely to be weeded out quickly and apprehended as a juvenile. In addition, certain psychological traits, such as suggestibility, are more closely related to low intelligence, with the result that corrective measures may be more effectively applied. The larger percentage of juvenile offenders of low intelligence who are apprehended during the earlier periods of their careers are more likely to be institutionalized and given custodial care if they give evidence of such abnormality. The net result probably is that a residue is produced of the relatively more advanced and intellectually proficient to continue their careers as adults.

(9) THE ECOLOGICAL DISTRIBUTION OF DELINQUENCY

Ecological studies in sociology deal with the spatial distribution of various segments of the population within a given area. The term itself is derived from the field of zoology and deals with the natural patterns of adaptation and distribution of the indigenous flora and fauna within a given territory. In its sociological usage, the concept has developed considerable significance. Ecological studies are concerned with the ways in which the population naturally distributes itself over a given area, and with how the given environment, natural and man-made, conditions the groups settled within it.

In the field of problem studies (i.e., delinquency, crime, poverty, mental disease, etc.) a number of significant relationships have been discovered between the incidence of such problems and the areas within which they happen to be localized. Members of the sociology department of the University of Chicago have conducted a number of important studies showing the relationship between the development of certain "natural" areas in the city and the development of certain orders of social problems. Under the leadership of Professors Park and Burgess, a conceptual scheme has been developed to show how the natural growth of urban areas in the United States, pictured in the idealized form of a series of concentric circles, has been associated with such distinctive factors as the price of real estate, rentals, land use, family types, and social disorders.[63] A number of revisions of the fundamental applications of this concept have been recently made, both in respect to its generalized use as an instrument of field research and in its specific application to certain urban areas. Nevertheless, general relationships have been thoroughly established between land-use, commercial speculation with respect to changing land-use, deteriorating community areas, and problem rates.[64]

Ecological studies invariably show the relationship between the proximity of deteriorated community areas of poor housing and social disorganization, and urban centers of industry and transportation. These disorganized areas are marked not only by poor housing and inadequate civic facilities, but by certain indigenous characteristics as well. Among these are the "invasion" by commercial interests, both specialized and indiscriminate land use, ethnic enclaves (areas of foreign settlement and Negro quarters, such as "Little Italy," Harlem, the ghetto), and other peculiar forms of urban breakdown. Such areas are "zones in transition," that is, areas characterized by a lack of stability and continually undergoing change through the encroachment of outside interests, frequently commercial and industrial. Poor housing is a conspicuous earmark of such areas. Within their confines thrive the problems of mobility, families on relief, delinquency, crime, sexual disorders, desertion, homelessness, and the like.

Clifford Shaw and his several associates have named such urban areas "delinquency areas" and have shown in detail the high rates of delinquency which flourish there.[65] By means of various techniques of sampling rates for these problem areas and the remaining zones of the city, they have shown the existence of a *gradient*—a declining rate of delinquency extending from the center of the urban area to its periphery. Although the concept of the gradient does not apply to all American cities, the highest rates of delinquency are invariably found in such "zones of transition." Moreover, such rates are correlated with other high indices of disorganization, such as family desertion, unemployment, morbidity, broken homes, inadequate play-space, and overcrowdedness.

[63] See Robert E. Park, Ernest W. Burgess, and Roderick D. McKenzie, *The City* (Chicago, 1925), and particularly "The Ecological Approach to the Study of the Human Community," by McKenzie in this volume. See also R. D. McKenzie, *The Metropolitan Community* (New York, 1933), pp. 8–83, and "The Rise of Metropolitan Communities," *Recent Social Trends in the United States* (New York, 1933), Vol. 1, pp. 443–96, by the same author.

[64] For a comprehensive critique of the entire ecological concept in its sociological usage, see Milla A. Alihan, *Social Ecology* (New York, 1938), especially pp. 11–49, 136–81, and 204–41. For the limitations of the concept as applied to particularized urban areas, see Maurice R. Davie, "The Pattern of Urban Growth," in G. P. Murdock, ed., *Studies in the Science of Society* (New Haven, 1937).

[65] *Delinquency Areas* (Chicago, 1929).

The detailed findings of the urban ecological studies represent the physical aspects of the types of community decadence existing in such areas. Delinquency areas in themselves do not produce delinquency, although this is a common inference which many civic leaders draw. Delinquency areas foster youthful misbehavior because of the character of the resident families and the nature of the circumstances that have brought them into these areas and because of the opportunities they provide for illicit activity. Individuals who are forced to settle in such sections are already affected by the causal mechanisms productive of disorder; the disorganized nature of the community serves merely to intensify such latent capacities. If we are to understand adequately the function of delinquency areas, we must recognize the psychological and social disabilities that such areas create, as well as the psychological, cultural, economic, and social circumstances that have affected the individuals forced to live within them.

Social base maps. An effective research instrument by means of which the delinquency area may be surveyed is the *social base map.* The social base map is in effect a "three-dimensional" sociological map. In addition to showing the ordinary physical characteristics of the area that is being surveyed, it gives a clear picture of the disorganizing agencies that flourish there. It provides some basis for determining the character of the social problems that may arise as well as those that may be anticipated. Such a highly detailed graphical protrayal of a well-known delinquency area in the East Harlem section of New York City was prepared by Professor Frederic M. Thrasher of New York University and his staff.[66] The development of such an instrument provides a comprehensive portrayal of the deteriorated conditions of such communities, and demonstrates the effective use to which social base maps may be employed as a basis for community organization and planning.

An examination of the data contained within the map reveals clearly the character of some of the deteriorating forces in the area. Selecting almost any block in the middle of the district, it will be noticed that there are a great many commercial establishments, small businesses, stores, and taverns. There is little evidence of concentrated residential housing, and in the few sections where this may be observed, the extent of overcrowding is considerable. Originally, this area was settled principally by immigrants of Jewish extraction, Irish-Americans, and Germans. Survivals of these former groups remain. However, the area has been invaded since 1914 by an influx of Italian-Americans who have given the neighborhood its present predominant character. This wave of settlement was followed by a heavy influx of Puerto Ricans, which continues to the present. The

[66] Cf. *Social Base Map, Local Neighborhoods, New York City, 1931* (New York University), prepared under the direction of Frederic M. Thrasher.

eastern section of the area is bounded by one of the largest wholesale produce markets in the city, a district which teems with activity in the early hours of the morning when the rest of the city sleeps. It will also be noted that a large modern recreation center, swimming pool, and outdoor playground have been established close to the heart of this market district. Although originally somewhat effective in curbing the rising incidence of delinquency in this area of the city, the successive invasions of other groups into the area, with the resultant culture conflicts which this has induced, as well as the disorganizing effects of the depression of the Thirties, the recent war, and the egregious overcrowding in the tenements of the area, have together conduced to sustain this zone as one of the highest delinquency areas in New York City.

(10) THE SCHOOLS AND DELINQUENCY

The schools have a special responsibility with respect to delinquency, although the degree of this responsibility has been overestimated by non-professional authorities. By the time the child reaches school a great many of his fundamental behavior patterns have already been formed. In addition, despite the fact that the school has the child under its control during a great period of the average day, the school program and its general facilities are inadequate to deal with incipient and active behavior disorders, even if they are recognized. Moreover, formal educational procedures are handicapped in the degree to which they may affect the transformation of personality characteristics. Effective educational procedures, if they are to correct behavioral difficulties as well as to educate minds, must be closely integrated with conditions of family life and the household. We know, of course, that the school has little control over the extramural life of its members. For these reasons, the chief effectiveness of the school in curbing delinquency may lie only in those fields where incipient disorders may be recognized and referred to the proper source for treatment, or in such matters as engaging the child's interest so that frustrations and attendant problems may be dealt with. In these latter respects, the school has been only partially successful. The competitors of the school for the child's attention are powerful. The degree to which the school should supplement such agencies as the home, the play-group, and the neighborhood are not generally agreed upon, even among educators themselves. As one experienced public school administrator has put it: "What a school does is determined by what a school believes its function to be." [67]

The problem of the schools in relation to delinquency resolves itself

[67] Sampson G. Smith, "The Schools and Delinquency," *1948 Yearbook*, National Probation and Parole Association (New York), p. 3.

into two major parts. (1) If the school is to be charged with the responsibility of dealing with problems of personality development, of which delinquent behavior is one, what are the physical conditions and instrumentalities required in order to attain this objective? (2) If schools now contribute toward delinquency, in what degree may this responsibility at the present time be assessed?

(1) The consensus today appears to favor maintaining the school's responsibility. In order to suggest the enormous disparity between opinion and action, we need cite only the conditions of extreme overcrowding existing today in the nation's schools. At the National Conference on Prevention and Control of Juvenile Delinquency held in Washington, D. C., in 1946, the general findings suggested strongly that overcrowding in our schools, underpaid teachers, and limitations of the teaching program contribute materially to the incidence of youthful behavior problems. Ratios of 50 to 60 pupils per teacher were cited as being neither unusual nor uncommon.

(2) Delinquent children tend to lose interest in school at an early age and manifest behavioral difficulties which the schools are frequently in a position to check. The chief problem with which the school authorities come to grips is truancy, and it is largely through *truancy corrective programs* that the schools have expended their chief efforts in curbing delinquency. The dissatisfaction of delinquent children with school appears to be concentrated mainly in the upper elementary and the early high school grades. This observation may be examined in relation to our discoveries concerning the problems of early adolescence. Kvaraceus discovered that more than half of the delinquents referred to the Passaic Children's Bureau came from the junior and middle high school grades.[68] This in itself is significant as an index as to where a considerable source of our problem lies. Healy and Bronner have revealed that approximately four out of ten of the delinquents they investigated manifested an intense dislike towards school, while the Gluecks showed that approximately 25 per cent gave evidence of a similar sentiment.[69] The fact that so many delinquents leave school at the first opportunity for employment is an indication not only of possible economic difficulties at home, but also of the attitudes which many of them manifest towards school activity.

Areas in which the schools fail. As our schools are presently constituted, they may contribute toward delinquency by promoting in the classroom certain problems that may create an additional incitement toward delinquent behavior. Thus, subjection to a regimen that the child finds

[68] William C. Kvaraceus, *Juvenile Delinquency and the School* (New York, 1945).

[69] Healy and Bronner, *New Light on Delinquency and Its Treatment*, p. 62; Sheldon and Eleanor T. Glueck, *One Thousand Juvenile Delinquents*, and by the same authors, *500 Criminal Careers* (New York, 1930).

distasteful and frustrating, inability to participate freely with other children in learning and extra-curricular activities—these and many other factors may play their roles in hastening the process towards delinquency. These are positive elements in the creation of delinquency. The school may fail in negative ways as well. By its failure to uncover the sources of the child's emotional difficulties and to take reasonable corrective action through community and family channels, the school may be held partially responsible for juvenile misbehavior.

No significant action may be taken by the school without the effective co-operation of associated agencies in the community.[70] Comprehensive guidance services within the school conducted in conjunction with a curriculum suited to the individual child, a competent visiting teachers service, and a well-planned counseling program with outreaches in the community are all indispensable features of a successful plan. The development of such a program will frequently require the assistance of the state. The New York State Youth Commission, for example, has recently inaugurated an extensive program to enable the schools to sift out those children with incipient behavior problems and to make special arrangements for their treatment. Its activities are supplemented by local recreational programs and child guidance services. This state agency, through its local bureaus, attempts through the local schools and community facilities to detect and to deter such problems before they manifest themselves in the more serious forms of delinquency and other behavior problems.[71] In the lack of provision for many of these facilities in most modern communities, even in the more progressive areas, the "failure of the schools," if it can properly be accounted as such, will continue, and the responsibility for such failure must be lodged with the larger community where it most significantly and rightly belongs.

(11) RECREATION AND DELINQUENCY

Recreation is often considered to be the best device for the curbing of delinquency. Recreational programs are frequently launched by high-minded and enthusiastic citizens' committees in the belief that they constitute a panacea for delinquency. From the sociological standpoint, this view is a delusion. Although recreation may play a very important part in

[70] Cf. Sampson G. Smith, "The Schools and Delinquency," especially p. 8.

[71] Since 1949, this program has been attempted primarily in major urban delinquency areas, notably in New York City. Special referral and diagnostic agencies have been established, working in co-ordination with the schools. These agencies, in turn, contract for the actual treatment of disturbed children with several outstanding case-work organizations. For a comprehensive analysis of the methods employed by schools and case-work agencies for the discovery, diagnosis, treatment, and prevention of deviant behavior trends in children, see Lowell J. Carr, *Delinquency Control* (New York, 1950), Chap. 12.

either the development or the curbing of delinquency, recreation in itself is rarely a directly instrumental factor. Considerable difficulty lies in properly evaluating the function which recreation may play as a positive or negative force largely because many of the statistical studies falsely attribute to this factor a highly significant deterrent role. Conspicuous in such studies, frequently, is a rather remarkable disregard for the operation of other factors. *Recreation as an influence in the development of personality is effective only when integrated and co-ordinated with the manifold other phases of the individual's personality and environment.* Chamber of Commerce brochures and Council of Social Agencies' bulletins, generously interlarded though they are with impressive statistics, frequently overlook this elementary fact.[72]

Very few cogent studies have been made of the actual effects which recreation may exercise in the development of personality patterns. Effective studies, however, have been developed on the effects of selected types of recreation upon delinquent and non-delinquent children from delinquency areas. Such studies have been designed to determine whether recreation, when sufficient in scope and supervision, may serve as a deterrent to delinquency. An elaborate program was launched by the Chicago Recreation Commission under the chairmanship of Ernest W. Burgess. Four well-defined "delinquency areas" and one control area were examined to determine the extent of participation of delinquent children in recreational programs and the variation of recreational preferences of delinquent and non-delinquent children.[73] A total of 15,217 boys and 7,939 girls were examined during the course of the survey.

Although the study revealed that the delinquents who attended the recreational projects committed fewer delinquencies than delinquents who did not participate, *it was also shown that delinquents spent more time in recreational projects than non-delinquents.* Further, for those who attended recreational projects and became delinquent, it was shown that they did not participate as freely in supervised activities. Of the non-delinquents studied, 1.7 per cent of those who participated in supervised recreation became delinquent as compared with 5.1 per cent who did not participate. "The proportion of non-delinquents not in recreation who became delinquent was three times as high as the rate for non-delinquents in recreation." [74] Of considerable further interest are the conclusions con-

[72] As an indication of this, the report of the New York State Youth Commission, issued on April 23, 1949, may be cited. After illustrating in this report the fact that the anticipated post-war increase in delinquency did not take place, largely because the re-emergence of stabilizing factors in the home and community prevented it, the report goes on to suggest that its own program has been instrumental in crushing this rise, without adequately weighing such inhibitory factors.

[73] Ethel Shanas, *Recreation and Delinquency*, Chicago Recreation Commission (Chicago, 1942).

[74] Ibid., p. 241.

cerning the types of activities preferred by delinquents and non-delinquents. Delinquents who attended the recreation centers preferred unsupervised recreation, active competitive sports, and the moving pictures; moreover, they moved more frequently than non-delinquents from one recreation center to another. This latter factor in particular suggests the perennial restlessness of the delinquent.

As Sullenger's study has shown, the accessibility of playgrounds and recreational areas may have a good deal to do with reducing delinquency.[75] His study in Omaha shows that over 90 per cent of the delinquents lived at a distance of one-half mile or more from the nearest play area. In consequence, he estimates that probably 55 per cent of the delinquency might have been eliminated, provided convenient and properly spaced recreation areas had been introduced. The voluminous five-volume report on recreation carried on in Chicago during the depression years, under the editorship of Arthur J. Todd, although conducted under the special circumstances of a depression period, testifies further to the fact that a paucity of adequate, supervised recreation and playground space is likely to foster delinquency.[76]

Although helpful, these surveys do not indicate the specific relationships that exist between behavioral patterns and types of recreation. Thurston has indicated that 75 per cent of the delinquents he studied in Cleveland fell into their delinquent ways because of the habitual misuse of their leisure time.[77] This appears to be the most obvious of tautologies: *delinquents become so because they use their leisure time for delinquent activities.* However, it does suggest that if uncontrolled recreational opportunities of an anti-social nature exist within a given area, without the counterbalancing controls which supervised recreation may introduce, the tendencies toward delinquency are much greater. Of this there can be no doubt. However, a recreational program may be truly efficacious only if it (1) studies the effects of recreation upon the developing personalities of the young people for whom it is intended, and (2) *if it is carefully integrated with other agencies of social control operating within the delinquent's environment.* The recognition of this fact is becoming increasingly known to social workers, who are employing with promising success the combined techniques of *group work* and *individual case work.*[78]

These conclusions have been amply demonstrated by Frederic M. Thrasher. In an elaborate study of the functioning of the Boys' Club in an acutely disorganized area in New York City, he discovered that not

[75] Thomas E. Sullenger, *Social Determinants of Juvenile Delinquency* (Columbia, Mo., 1929).

[76] *Chicago Recreation Survey,* Vols. 1–5 (1937–40).

[77] H. W. Thurston, *Delinquency and Spare Time,* The Cleveland Recreational Survey (Cleveland, 1918), pp. 105–18.

[78] See Grace L. Coyle, ed., *Studies in Group Behavior* (New York, 1937).

only did this organization fail to make effective inroads upon the rate of delinquency during four years of operation, but the incidence of delinquency was higher among members than among non-members.[79] This was not necessarily a reflection upon the organization or its program; it represented primarily the inability of one such agency to deal *by itself* with a problem of long standing. Thrasher's conclusion is clear in its exposition of the need for a concerted attack by many agencies to achieve a common goal.

Where recreation programs appear to have been most successful, they have been organized as phases of a wider program for community development. Here is a field in which schools and other interested agencies may profitably combine their efforts. The pattern set by the Berkeley Co-ordinating Council in California, and widely employed in that state and elsewhere, provides an illustration. The Council brings together every interested public and private agency in the community. Through the careful planning of its separate sections, the needs of individuals *and* groups are considered in relation to recreation, housing, education, family problems, and relief. The development of many recreational programs represents a growth of concern for the child by other specialized agencies. Recreational programs have been devised by municipal police departments and their associated agencies, such as the Juvenile Aid Bureau in New York City. The Police Athletic League of that city has for many years conducted a successful program of competitive sports for children from delinquency areas, providing leadership, equipment, and facilities. All of these activities can serve as partial deterrents to delinquency, provided the program is sufficiently extensive to cover all necessary areas, is well planned and directed, is continuous and not sporadic, has sufficient and adequately trained personnel, and is conducted in conjunction with a broader program of community rehabilitation.

(12) THE GANG AS A RECREATIONAL AND EDUCATIONAL AGENCY

Prominent in all studies of delinquent behavior is the youthful offender's association with a gang. The gangs are natural and spontaneous play groupings which serve an important role in the development of the delinquent's behavior and personality. Gang activities of boys are expressions of natural gregarious patterns found among all pre-adolescent and adolescent groups in all areas of society. As such, they may exercise a very salutary influence upon the boy's behavior. In his famous study of 1,313 boys' gangs, Frederic M. Thrasher shows that the gang process goes

[79] "The Boys' Club and Juvenile Delinquency," *The American Journal of Sociology*, XLII (July, 1936), 66–80.

through specific stages, beginning with spontaneous and random primary contacts and developing into a closely-knit group, characterized by well-defined structure, objectives, and leadership.[80] The structural development of the gang into an organized unit is precipitated by conflict and by sharp hostility to outsiders. It eventually develops a high level of *esprit*, its own traditions and usages, and a physical locus in which it operates. In a highly realistic novel of gang life among adolescent boys in the Brownsville section of Brooklyn, Irving Shulman shows how the *Amboy Dukes* provided the most important center of the boy's life away from home and how powerfully such a group called upon his deepest loyalties.[81] The gang fulfills two important requirements of the delinquent boy. It provides (1) an ever ready source of entertainment, recreation, and imaginative challenge; and (2) the elementary training and skills required for successful predatory and unlawful activity. Thus, it is both a recreational and an educational influence.

The great majority of the delinquencies for which male offenders are apprehended are executed in conjunction with gangs or paired associations arising from gangs. Healy and Bronner have shown that 62 per cent of the delinquents they studied carried on their activities with companions.[82] While youthful gangs differ in degree of organization and structure from the adult gangs of criminals, they nevertheless resemble them closely in many details. Although gangs appear to be an inevitable aspect of life in the disorganized areas of American cities, their numbers and forms have been somewhat altered during the past two decades as a result of the mobility affecting the life of the city. The Federal Bureau of Investigation in 1948 estimated a rise in the number of gangs appearing in American cities after a decline in a sixteen-year cycle. Whether this finding is valid or not may not be determined at the present time. However, it is a fact that many boys' gangs have been undergoing transformation during the recent war years. They appear to have developed stricter discipline and more formal structures.

In many cities, gang activity among youths in their late teens begins to assume a more formal structure as they form their so-called "cellar clubs." Occupying untenanted stores and basements, such clubs, commonly known as social and athletic clubs, maintain a formal organization and a program of regular activities which frequently serve as a mask for their illicit purposes. Sydney Blotzman, for example, in the company of his companions in crime, William Paddock, William Leggett, and George Gerard, was associated with a club known as the Burns Athletic Club.

[80] *The Gang* (Chicago, 1927). For a description of the stages in development, see p. 57.

[81] Irving Shulman, *The Amboy Dukes* (New York, 1947).

[82] Healy and Bronner, *Delinquents and Criminals*, p. 179.

Frank Goldfarb, the fictional delinquent in *The Amboy Dukes*, discovers that his "cellar club" is a convenient headquarters for the sexual and other types of misconduct in which the gang engages.

The police and juvenile social work agencies have attempted to curb or control such clubs. Although it is difficult to curb them outright, they may be placed under effective guidance and control. During the depression the Henry Street Settlement in New York City sent out its trained workers to provide adequate programs and guidance for such groups. Eventually they were combined into neighborhood leagues and councils with activity programs directed towards community betterment. In 1948, after eighteen months of research into gang problems, the Welfare Council of New York City sponsored a similar program in Harlem, while more recently, the New York City Youth Commission launched similar projects in the delinquency areas of Manhattan and Brooklyn. A special committee of the Welfare Council, investigating the rehabilitative possibilities present in boys' gangs, stressed the following points:

(1) Street clubs, or gangs, represent a "natural tendency" on the part of adolescents which are not peculiar to any social strata and, therefore, have constructive potentialities.

(2) The degree of violence indulged in by gangs has increased because of the glorification of commando tactics during the war, because of the intensification of racial prejudices indulged by Fascist propaganda, and because of the disruption by the war of normal family life.

(3) Existing agencies are not equipped to cope with this problem.

(4) Punitive measures have not worked in the past and they can never effect a solution.

(5) Gangs will accept adult leadership if they are approached in the proper manner; simply making park and playground facilities available is insufficient.

(6) A personal approach on a long-range basis (at least three years) is necessary.

When properly redirected, the patterning of delinquent groups may provide a valuable foothold for improvement and readjustment. We are learning more and more that the sense of participation in the gang is important for the individual's self-esteem and for the development of a sense of social normalcy. This sense of social normalcy may be directed into useful and constructive channels or into destructive activities that may eventually bring about the disintegration of the personality. Psychotherapy may frequently be best accomplished through the agency of the groups with which the individual is identified. The writer was able to participate in the transformation of such a delinquent group, capitalizing upon the latent idealism and the craving for excitement and adventure. The group abandoned its hoodlumism and became a highly idealistic boys' fraternity, replete with ritual, ceremony, and a positive program for community improvement. The channeling of the activities of such groups may take any number of socially constructive forms.

(13) DELINQUENCY AND CULTURE CONFLICT

Culture conflict produces the dual problem of *cultural hybridism* and *marginality*; the individual falls between two sets of cultural standards and values which impose a strain upon the integrated pattern of his personality. One of the reasons for the high rate of delinquency and crime in the United States is our vast cultural heterogeneity. The early high delinquency rates of the children of immigrants and today's high rates for Negroes and rural-urban migrants afford evidence of the importance of this factor. The wider the divergence of cultural standards from the dominant ones existing in the particular American community, and the greater the obstacles placed in the way of cultural reconciliation, the greater is the possibility of individual personality conflict, delinquency, and crime.

This problem is not restricted to American communities. Primitive communities and colonial areas subjected to the enormous impact of Westernization have shown similar widespread demoralization.[83] In American life, however, culture-conflict has always produced its conspicuous by-product of acute pathological states and delinquency. Thorsten Sellin, in pointing up the relationship between culture conflict and crime, has indicated the vast areas which still remain in this field for further study.[84]

The operations of culture-conflict in the production of delinquency may be viewed under the following categories. (1) Culture-conflict always produces areas of community demoralization and declining social controls which make it easier for the child to acquire delinquent patterns of behavior by incitement, imitation, and the learning process itself.[85] (2) Culture conflict creates barriers in the individual family between members of different generations, accentuated by language, idiomatic, and value differences, inducing (among other results) the breakdown of parental authority. (3) The inability to identify one's self with both cultures leads to confusion about guiding standards. This confusion is deepened by the strain to achieve the superficial values of the dominant culture. Homes in which culture-conflict takes place are frequently marked by contempt of the children for the parents, who are identified

[83] Cf. R. Kennedy, "The Colonial Crisis and the Future," in Ralph Linton, ed., *The Science of Man in the World Crisis* (New York, 1945).

[84] *Culture Conflicts and Crime* (New York, 1938).

[85] See Sutherland, *Principles of Criminology*, pp. 6, 77–80.

with an "inferior" cultural group. There is an acute desire for those who are between two cultures to become a part of the dominant culture. Geoffrey Gorer suggests that a broad base for lawlessness has been established throughout the entire range of American culture because successive generations have rejected the status of parental authority, which is identified with an inferior culture.[86]

As demonstration of how misdemeanors may arise in culture-conflict environments, we may consider the types of problems presented by the school situation. In the school, the child is encouraged to adhere to standards of behavior that may be alien to his family. We may take the case of the child who is asked to bring his toothbrush to school for an oral hygiene demonstration. Should the child be a member of a subgroup that does not practice toothbrushing, he may steal to obtain money for a toothbrush so as not to be embarrassed before his classmates. Pauline V. Young's study of the Russian Molokan children in Los Angeles indicates the degree of demoralization which may ensue particularly among the very young when the standards of subgroups and majority groups are highly disparate.[87] Here the incidence of delinquency was highest among members of the younger age-groups, who were born into dual and conflicting culture patterns. The older age-groups, born abroad and already closely identified with their culture, had a delinquency rate of only 5 per cent, as compared with the rate of 78.3 per cent for the nine to nineteen-year-old age-group. Recent studies of Negro children show the frustration which results from the operation of dual cultural processes and the aggressive tendencies which such processes tend to engender.[88] Culture-conflict makes difficult the development of an integrating center around which normal community life may revolve; it will inevitably figure in the development of personality disorders and juvenile crime.

(14) THE CONTROL OF DELINQUENCY

Our primary concern in the study of social pathology is discovering the factors that produce a given problem. Because the problem of delinquency is so extensive and has aroused so much public interest, however, it will be helpful to review briefly the procedures that have been developed for the care and treatment of delinquents. Many present programs have arisen as a direct result of inquiries into the causation of delinquency. The failure or success of these programs may serve as indications of how

86 *The American People: A Study in National Character* (New York, 1948).
87 *Pilgrims of Russiantown* (Chicago, 1932).
88 Cf. Hortense Powdermaker, "The Channelling of Negro Aggression by the Cultural Process," and Bingham Dai, "Some Problems of Personality Development Among Negro Children," in C. Kluckhohn and H. A. Murray, eds., *Personality in Nature, Society, and Culture* (New York, 1948).

accurate our researches have been.[89] In any event, no program of delinquency control and prevention may be successful unless it is based upon sound factual and theoretical evidence concerning causal processes. *Delinquency control, at the very outset, depends upon the adequacy of research and research methods.*

Delinquency control may be conceived of as encompassing two broad fields: (1) the custodial care and treatment of those already apprehended for delinquency; and (2) the development of procedures for the control of incipient delinquents and former offenders. Our two emphases, thus, are *treatment* and *prevention*. Although modern correctional reform movements date back at least to the work of the celebrated English penal reformer of the eighteenth century, John Howard, the development of adequate correctional and custodial methods for the care of delinquent children has been relatively slow. The first separation of juvenile offenders from adult offenders in penal institutions took place in New York in 1824. Philadelphia followed in 1826. The first state institution devoted specifically to juvenile offenders was not established until 1847, in Massachusetts. These early divisions in penal care, however, were not much more than token procedures. Despite the fact that the term "reformatory" was subsequently to be applied to these separate institutions, they remained prisons in every sense. During the nineteenth century, however, particularly the latter half, a number of movements sprang up designed to bring about the genuine reforms in our penal institutions which the term "reformatory" was supposed to signify.

Custodial and related treatment. The interest in juvenile reform during the latter part of the nineteenth century resulted, in 1899, in the creation of the first juvenile court, established in Cook County, Illinois. Despite certain previous beginnings in this separate court handling of juveniles in Switzerland and England, the juvenile court has been predominantly an American institution. At the present time, it is estimated that there are some 3,000 juvenile courts in the United States, the majority of them under county and municipal jurisdiction. Not all of them retain separate judges, the rural counties frequently depending upon the same official to preside at both juvenile and adult courts. In accordance

[89] W. I. Thomas and others maintained some time ago that the experiments in social reform and social work procedures may constitute a *laboratory* in which theoretical conceptions and research results may be tested. Just as the sociologist has come to depend upon comparative studies of social organization in anthropology, so may the results obtained from the application of various legislative programs, institutional reforms, and community procedures enable him to gauge the validity of his research and theoretical insights. For an able presentation of a similar view, see R. M. MacIver, *The Contribution of Sociology to Social Work* (New York, 1931). See also Ada E. Sheffield, *Social Insight in Case Situations* (New York, 1937), pp. 257–66; and, more recently, Olive M. Stone, "Social Case Work and the Social Sciences," *American Sociological Review*, XV (Feb., 1950), 66–73.

with the provisions of the "Standard Juvenile Court Act," whose revised draft was prepared in 1943 by the National Probation Association, such courts employ informal procedures in dealing with the young offender and are usually permitted discretionary powers ordinarily not allowed in the regular criminal courts. Such courts, in accordance with the varying statutes of the separate state jurisdictions, differ in the age groups of the individuals they handle, some states, as California, having jurisdiction over offenders up to twenty-one years of age, while the majority exercise jurisdiction over offenders up to the age of eighteen.[90]

Today, our chief institutions for the custodial care of delinquent children are the public training schools. In 1944, there were approximately 166 schools of this character under public auspices in this country; 115 were under the jurisdiction of the state or federal governments, and 51 were county or municipal training centers. In general, although such institutions are commonly employed, the trend is away from such forms of supervisory care. If custodial care is considered essential, the models that are being increasingly employed are the private and quasi-public institutions based upon the cottage-system. Under the cottage-system, relatively small groups of children live in separate unit-dwellings, under the general supervision of "house parents."[91] These are exemplified by such institutions as the George Junior Republic, Boys' Town, The Children's Village at Dobbs Ferry, and The Hawthorne-Cedar Knolls School at Hawthorne, New York. Such institutions attempt to deal with offenders on the basis of classification of personality. Trained supervisors handle small groups, and case-work and psychiatric treatment are provided when necessary. Vocational training related to the needs of the individual is made available and good follow-up work is undertaken after release. That these agencies are not always able to live up to their objectives is due largely to the inadequacy of staff and facilities.

Foster home placement has been found to be particularly effective in dealing with delinquents. Although the Gluecks noted a high rate of recidivism for foster home placement cases, Healy and his associates have shown a remarkable degree of success in rehabilitating such offenders *where the homes are carefully selected and counseled and protracted case-work treatment is provided.*[92] Of 501 such children studied, 75 per

[90] The Federal Juvenile Court Act, passed in 1938, has jurisdiction over offenders seventeen years of age and under, and prohibits a sentence of life imprisonment or death for juvenile offenders under federal jurisdiction.

[91] Although seemingly an ideal procedure for the administration of institutionalized children, such programs are frequently inadequate in operation, largely because of the size of the groups in the separate cottages (45 to 50 not being uncommon), lack of professionally trained "house parents," and the heavy additional duties imposed upon cottage supervisors.

[92] W. Healy, A. F. Bronner, E. M. H. Baylor, J. P. Murphy, *Reconstructing Behavior in Youth* (New York, 1929), Chap. 24.

cent had been recidivists and 65 per cent had had court records. Nevertheless, 90 per cent of those with normal mentality and 70 per cent of those with defective mentality made successful adjustments. Of those with abnormal personalities, however, only 45 per cent succeeded.

Preventive measures. The development of preventive measures has usually been accomplished through organized community action of several varieties and through legislative efforts. The American Law Institute, recognizing the predominance of youthful offenders appearing before our courts, created in 1940 a Model Youth Correction Authority Act with wide scope and powers.[93] Thus far, only five states, California, Minnesota, Wisconsin, Texas, and Massachusetts, have developed such Youth Correction Authorities. The success of this program may be seen by the fact that Governor Earl Warren of California in 1944, three years after its establishment, called a special meeting of the legislature to establish a similar Authority for adult offenders.

The Authorities have complete control over the child from commitment to final replacement in society. This program thus undertakes intensive work in three fields: (1) diagnosis and careful classification of each offender; (2) carefully sustained treatment in relation to diagnostic findings; and (3) re-establishment in society. To accomplish these objectives, each child is committed to the custody of the Authority, not to a specific institution which may or may not be suitable to his needs. The Authority maintains a special reception center where, for a period of from four to eight weeks, the child is carefully studied and tested by a team composed of a pediatrician, psychiatrist, clinical psychologist, social investigator, special supervisors, and teachers. After this period of observation, the disposition may take any number of forms, from probation or foster-home care to special schools for the mentally defective. The program for the child is then sustained on an individualized basis, in so far as this is possible, with the objective kept continuously in mind of the child's eventual restoration to society. If the child requires special custodial care, this program is carried on in conjunction with the parole or supervising officer who, at every stage of treatment, prepares the groundwork in the community for the child's eventual release to society. Notable in the operation of this program is the employment of special teams of experts who, upon call from the community, make intensive investigation of the local community's resources with a view towards delinquency and crime prevention. By 1947, 22 of California's 58 counties had been surveyed upon invitation by local authorities; as a result, 18 new recreational

[93] Cf. John R. Ellingston, "Protecting Our Children From Criminal Careers," Federal Probation, XII (Sept., 1948), 34–7. According to Ellingston, "minors commit over half of all auto thefts, a third of all robberies, burglaries, and other thefts, one in five, rapes; one in seven, murders." (Ibid., p. 34.)

commissions, 22 juvenile bureaus, 18 new detention homes, and 64 community councils were established.

Nevertheless, in a recent evaluation of the Youth Authority program by Bertram M. Beck of the Bureau of Public Affairs of the Community Service Society (October, 1951), in those states where the act is operating, the program was judged not to be "an outstanding success." The primary reasons were declared to be the reluctance of the courts to abandon their powers of judicial control over the delinquent to the established authorities, and the failure to incorporate the treatment of delinquents within a general program embracing all neglected and dependent children.

Although a Youth Correction Authority has not been established in New York State, a development somewhat similar to this program was established in 1945 for youthful male offenders, 16 to 21 years of age, at the Reception Center maintained by the Department of Correction in Elmira, New York.[94] Supplementing such programs for actual juvenile offenders have been the preventive plans of State Youth Commissions. The New York State Youth Commission, an independent agency operating under the executive branch of the state government and established at the close of the last war, is designed to assist schools and communities in detecting and counteracting incipient and actual behavior problems which may eventuate in delinquent and other serious forms of disorder. The broad statutory mandate given to this Commission permits it to carry on research, public education through visual and other means, and assist in the establishment of local recreation commissions and guidance programs in the schools through monetary grants. The mandate is a recognition of both the variable sources of disorder in each community and the unwillingness to recognize the need of a systematic and programmatic formula for the curbing of youthful disorder.

Although it is too soon to appraise such a program, its weaknesses seem to lie in its emphasis upon the more spectacular and seemingly demonstrable aspects of youthful behavior disorders, with an undue reliance upon the ready-made instruments of recreation and a neglect of the application of organized community programs based upon valid research findings. Such programs, unlike the attempted scientific procedure found in California, frequently beguile the public into believing that more is actually being accomplished than the results of the program actually warrant.

If the objectives of Lowell Carr's adequate summarization of the validated principles of delinquency control are to be carried out, planning and research must be co-ordinated on every level of community life, with

[94] Cf. Glenn M. Kendall, "The New York State Reception Center," *Federal Probation*, XII (Sept., 1948), 42–7.

realistic implementation designed to test effectively such procedures in practice.[95]

SUMMARY

(1) In the previous chapter we examined the causal process through which behavior problems and delinquent disorders are brought about. The development of such problems will take place only if there is a particular configuration of community and environmental circumstances operating in conjunction with a particular personality. This configuration of circumstances provides the basis for what we have termed "the sociological pattern of delinquency." If we determine the relevant causal process, we are in a position to understand and appraise statistical studies of the specific factors contributing to delinquency. (2) Always a crucial factor is the individual's family. The broken and physically disorganized families are not necessarily most conducive to delinquency; families foremost in the causation of delinquency are those which present serious malfunctions in human relationships affecting the child. Except for those households where actual criminality exists, the physical setting of the family simply provides the occasion for such malfunctioning to occur more readily. (3) With respect to the hereditary aspects of criminality, certain organic factors may, within a limited range, dispose the individual to behavioral difficulty. Delinquent behavior is a form of social activity variously defined as such in time and place by different cultural groups. Transmitted biological determinants may affect only the structural aspects of the organism. The behavioral possibilities, delinquent as well as non-delinquent, are always conditioned by the peculiar eliciting circumstances of the social and cultural environment. (4) In view of the fact that the physical conditions of the home can provide no more than the basis for the malfunctioning within the family which may affect the child, we should recognize the variation in effects produced by the broken home. As we might expect, such homes are mostly harmful to younger children, and apparently constitute a greater danger for adolescent girls than for boys. The nature of the broken home, whether it has been brought about by death, divorce, or separation, and the question of *which* of the parents is removed from the household, will also be important in determining the effects of the environment upon the behavior of children. (5) Thus, the "emotional atmosphere" or the moral status of the home is a fundamental factor in the eliciting of youthful misbehavior. The home may directly encourage the child to engage in delinquent acts or it may function negatively by preventing the child from enjoying the

[95] Lowell Juillard Carr, *Delinquency Control* (New York, 1950), Part 5 and especially Chap. 25.

conditions of normal development. Studies concerning the "moral status" of the home differ in the attributes that they select as denoting low moral status, with the result that conclusions are variable. However, there is little ambiguity concerning the harmful effect of homes whose low moral status is manifested in faulty human relationships and indifference to the child's development. (6) In view of the generally improved living standards of the population as a whole, the incidence of poverty in relation to delinquency is not as high as it once was. Although inferior economic status does not directly bring about delinquency, it creates conditions, such as early employment, overcrowding in the home, and lack of supervision, which may be conducive to youthful disorders. (7) The health and physical development of delinquents afford further illustration of our fundamental hypothesis concerning the sociological pattern. Youthful offenders as a class tend to show physical disabilities that are evidence of parental neglect and poverty rather than of distinct organic differences. While female sex delinquents are larger and heavier than members of comparable age groups in the population (because of their early sexual precocity), delinquent boys do not invariably appear heavier or taller. There is some indication presented by a recent study of a selected group, however, that male delinquents may tend to fall more generally in the mesomorphic (muscular) category. (8) With respect to the mental characteristics of delinquents, most studies emphasize the marked emotional disturbance of delinquent subjects, again confirming our fundamental hypothesis. Recent studies of youthful male offenders have tended to find them of an intelligence roughly comparable to that of children drawn from the same social and economic circumstances, or only slightly inferior. The intelligence of female sex delinquents is generally found to be low. (9) A high proportion of delinquents come from the so-called "delinquency areas" which are fundamentally zones of transition, bordering upon the industrial and transportation centers of the city. Such delinquency areas, however, while facilitating the acquisition of delinquent habits through the opportunities afforded by the environment, are not the direct causal factors of delinquency. Such delinquency areas provide the physical setting in which disorganized families and individuals concentrate. The primary atmosphere of such families, compelled to settle in such communities, may exercise its corruptive effects upon children and neighborhoods, irrespective of the augmenting factors of the disorganized community. (10) The school's role in the formation of delinquency is created largely by its failure to detect and to take appropriate action about incipient behavior disorders in the classroom, and by its inability to adapt the curriculum and classroom procedure to the needs of the predelinquent. The function of the school in dealing with delinquency, upon which not all educators agree, may be effective only if closely co-ordinated with other community agencies and the family. The scope of the school's program must be considerably enlarged to include such new objectives. (11) Undirected and unsupervised recreation is frequently regarded as a factor contributing to the delinquent process. Delinquency has been described as the habitual misuse of leisure time. Recreation as "the nostrum of the citizens' committees," in order to be truly effective, must be co-ordinated with a broad and intensive community program embracing the family and other phases of the delinquent's career. (12) The spontaneous and natural groupings of children into gangs play an important part in the personality development of the growing child. These activities represent the natural outgrowths of youthful associative tendencies. Gangs may exercise a recreational and an informal educative influence upon the child in giving him an early acquaintance with anti-social practices. The group solidarity of the gang may also, under proper guidance and direction, be used as a positive influence toward normal social participation. (13) Delinquency thrives in areas of cultural conflict. Cultural conflict as a phase of social disorganization and personal demoralization is most acute when the differences between cultures are wide and when the individual is not well integrated within either of the conflicting culture patterns. (14) On the basis of our increasing knowledge of the causal factors producing delinquency, procedures may be devised to control and eliminate such youthful disorders. Delinquency control refers to the adequate treatment, custodial and otherwise, of delinquents already apprehended, and to preventive measures. Programs of delinquency control will not be effective unless they are based upon sound and scientifically conceived research findings, and unless they are systematically applied to the numerous aspects of the total sociological pattern contributing to delinquency.

CHAPTER TEN

THE ANALYSIS OF A CASE DOCUMENT

(1) THE ANALYSIS OF THE HUMAN DOCUMENT

ONE of the most valuable sources of social data concerning the development of human problems is the human document itself. We may obtain our information about the individual from an autobiographical or biographical account, or from one of the more formal procedures of case observation and recording. Adequate materials are most effectively obtained when both methods are combined. This does not mean that the best type of information for the interpretation of human problems comes from individual life history records or from personal case histories; the technique of individual case analysis is simply one of the many methods that the student of human relationships employs to understand human motives and human relationships. Sociologists in general are far more likely to employ one of the other accredited methods in the analysis of human problems—various quantitative-statistical techniques, sociometric devices of various kinds, ecological approaches, or survey methods.[1]

The individual case history, adequately analyzed, may prove exceedingly helpful in understanding human problems. Frequently, it makes more vivid many points of view contained within the broader statistical and community studies. In this way, much of our understanding of processes of causation may be enriched and developed. Statistical surveys frequently can be combined successfully with case record analyses to give a more complete understanding of comprehensive problems. Furthermore, a considerable portion of our material, whether used statistically or ecologically, is derived in part from personal contacts with various individuals who provide us with aspects of material ordinarily contained in case records.

[1] For a good recent account of such methods, see Stuart Chase, *The Proper Study of Mankind* (New York, 1948). Also, F. Stuart Chapin's carefully detailed and ingenious control techniques, described in his *Experimental Designs in Sociological Research* (New York, 1948), indicate the increasing precision and scientific comparability developed in more recent quantitative approaches. For a general elementary survey of sociological techniques of analysis and research, see Pauline V. Young's handbook, *Scientific Social Surveys and Research* (second edition, New York, 1949).

The case method, purely as a pedogogical device, should provide the student with an understanding of the intricate ways in which the factors of the socio-cultural environment affect the individual's behavior and social relationships. Since we are concerned primarily with giving the student some awareness of the ways in which human problems are brought into being through social patterns, an analysis of the case document of a "typical" delinquent should prove enlightening.

As sociologists, our concern with the case record is not exactly the same as that of the psychologist, although at several points the two interests may overlap. Our principal concern is to indicate the way in which the socio-cultural factors operate, to see how the structure and organization of the family within a given social order may shape the actions of its members. Dollard has indicated the difficulties involved in making scientific sense out of biographical and human material.[2] In the criteria which he has developed for the study of the human document, he continually emphasizes the importance of seeing the total human being as part of a continuing cultural process and a family situation. Even the organic motors of action (as we have observed in the last chapter) must always be seen in relation to processes of social action. Dollard characterizes this entire undertaking as a "deliberate attempt to define the growth of a person in a cultural milieu and to make theoretical sense out of it." He summarizes what he believes to be the inclusive criteria by which the entire life history of the individual may be analyzed.[3] He brings together the criteria of social conditions and cultural milieu to provide a comprehensive and detailed sociological framework within which the personality functions.

1. The subject must be viewed as a specimen in a cultural series.
2. The organic motors of action ascribed must be socially relevant.
3. The peculiar role of the family group in transmitting the culture must be recognized.
4. The specific method of elaboration of organic materials into social behavior must be shown.
5. The continuous related character of experience from childhood through adulthood must be stressed.
6. The "social situation" must be carefully and continuously specified as a factor.
7. The life-history material itself must be organized and conceptualized.

[2] John Dollard, *Criteria for the Life History* (New Haven, 1935).
[3] Ibid., p. 8 and *passim*.

(2) THE SOCIAL FACTORS IN THE LIFE HISTORY AND CASE RECORD

Autobiographical accounts, such as those employed by Clifford Shaw in his studies of delinquent behavior, may be extremely helpful in facilitating our understanding of the growth of human behavior and human motivation. They have little value, however, unless carefully checked and corroborated by factual accounts and case records drawn outside the individual's own story. The individual's own account of his life history must, of necessity, be distorted in the light of his psychological values and motivations. As a record of his attitudes, values, and his general conception of his behavior, it may prove of undoubted value when correlated with factual checks.

Since our primary task is to illustrate the way in which social factors exert a determining influence upon the life of the individual, the data we must consider are the immediate factors in the individual's social situation and the cultural milieu. In terms of the general framework we have employed in this book, we classify these factors in four major categories: (1) social considerations and cultural milieu surrounding the individual and his family, operating in the form of restraints and positive urges; (2) the considerations of the family environment in so far as it operates as a mediating influence upon the individual; (3) the consequent effects upon the child and his developmental patterns; (4) the total developmental pattern of the individual as it is affected in its genetic growth within the broader patterns of the community and the society.[4]

(3) FALLACIES IN THE HUMAN DOCUMENT

Since human documents depend primarily upon observations of the behavior of others or upon the recollections and observations of the subject himself, we would expect to find them replete with error. This is unfortunately the case, despite the best safeguards we may take. We may attempt to overcome these errors by adequate authentication, that is, by corroborating through other reported accounts and by checking with factual evidences wherever possible. To a certain degree, every human record contains a number of unwarranted human judgments. Just as the ethnologist, however, frequently has to call upon a native informant in order to gain information about the primitive people he is studying, so we frequently employ the observations of others in order to gain an in-

[4] See Chap. V, "Personality and the Changing Social Processes." For a detailed statement of the socio-cultural configurations that control the development of the individual—what Abram Kardiner calls the "key integrational systems"—see Abram Kardiner, *The Psychological Frontiers of Society* (New York, 1948), p. 26 and *passim.*

sight into human problems. The fallacies committed by even reliable witnesses in reporting what they have observed are notorious.

The necessity of developing techniques for authentic observation of human behavior is now widely recognized. In a number of instances, social scientists have conducted observations within carefully defined frameworks and under carefully controlled scientific conditions. Such conditions of laboratory control are, however, difficult to establish in most normal human behavior situations. Furthermore, our interest in a problem, such as delinquency, is frequently aroused after a significant amount of time has passed.[5] Therefore, we must frequently rely upon information based on past events. Nevertheless, some corroboration may be attained. The facts we obtain by carefully checking formal records and the confirmation or denial of data we receive in the reports of others enable us to sift out the reality of the situation from the misconceptions and illusions.

In every human document we deal with, we must be on our guard to determine whether the fact as reported is true or whether it is a figment of somebody's fancy. If it is not a genuine "fact," it may still be important as representative of an attitude of the subject himself, or of the informant. We must carefully distinguish between "facts of record" and facts that may serve as keys to attitudes. While both may be significant, they must be assessed and weighed differently, as different kinds of facts.

(4) PRELIMINARY STEPS IN THE INTERPRETATION OF HUMAN BEHAVIOR AS REVEALED BY A CASE RECORD

Although it is not our purpose in this book to provide training in the scientific methods of case analysis, it is important for the student nevertheless to learn how to deal with different kinds of facts as they impinge upon the lives of human beings and human situations in the "problem-areas" of society. Case methods may proceed from specific standpoints, involving the approaches of special psychological schools or sociological viewpoints, or they may be eclectic, bringing together under one point of view the diverse insights of several methods and approaches.[6] Much case investigation today is eclectic.

Case approaches, however, may begin from another point of view.

[5] Much of the logic employed by social scientists in their analysis of case records is *retrospective*, the analysis taking place *after* the event has occurred. This contrasts with *projective* logic, which is an analysis of anticipated or expected events. See Herbert A. Bloch, *The Concept of Our Changing Loyalties* (New York, 1934) in the section entitled "The Interpretive Difficulty," Chap. 12.

[6] Case techniques may also be applied to social areas and groups. In fact, the purposive and deliberate attempt to study any given unique instance, whether it concerns a single human being, a community, an institution or a social area, may be considered an application of the case method.

Instead of assuming the particular doctrinaire approach of a given theoretical school, they may be systematically organized so that a consistency in logical interpretation is possible. Thus, the approach may be systematic and organized so as to synchronize the several aspects of the case into a conceptual whole. This is the basis that Dollard, for example, employs in the development of his several criteria. Such an interpretive approach does not uphold the views of any single psychological or sociological school. This approach simply stipulates that the facts of the case, as revealed by the record, must be ordered and organized to indicate the relatedness of the entire structure. In such an organized approach, the different facts of the record are examined from the standpoint of how they contribute to the growing development of the problem and how they either support or deny the sociological validity ordinarily accorded to facts of this nature.

In approaching the diverse data of the average case record, the first step is to arrange our materials so that we can see relationships and possible conceptual patterns. Regardless of the type of case approach employed, all analyses appear to conform in general to some such broad organizational pattern as herein described. Invariably, the organization of the case record includes: (1) some *basic point of view or framework* within which the case is examined; (2) some basis of *classification* by which the various kinds of facts may be organized and analyzed; (3) interpretation of a cross-sectional or genetic nature indicating the degree to which certain inferences concerning the case are proven or disproven; and (4) general indications as to specific types of information which are still lacking or which may be necessary in order to confirm stated hypotheses. It is common, as well, to indicate the prognosis for rehabilitation and the procedures to effect it.

(5) PRELIMINARY INDICATIONS

Before setting up a procedure for analyzing a case of delinquency, or any other social problem, it is important to take note of the following considerations:

(1) The procedure itself establishes a framework within which the case is to be analyzed.

(2) The procedure sets up or implies a basis for *classification* which must be rigorously followed. One of the most arduous tasks in all case analysis, as, in fact, in all science, is to classify one's data. In a sense, the most fundamental feature of any scientific endeavor is its system of classification. Until facts are placed systematically in order, it is impossible to make comparisons, check the authenticity of data, and make adequate generalizations. In all cases, the types of categories we employ for our

classification will depend upon the nature of the framework for analysis that we have devised.

(3) *We must distinguish between genuine facts and data reported as facts.* When such distinctions cannot be carefully drawn, we are obliged to make certain assumptions in our analysis. Such assumptions should be carefully stipulated. The conclusions we draw may come very close to those accorded by the genuine facts of the case. Whenever we are confronted by uncertainty as to factual data, however, we must express this uncertainty clearly by stating that *if* these facts are true, then certain guarded inferences may be drawn. Ambiguities in factual information may have the healthy effect of making us scientifically skeptical about our case and, moreover, may lead us to follow other clues suggestive of factual information which may actually confirm our findings.

(4) We must exercise extreme caution to infer from the facts only as much as the facts themselves will allow. All too frequently, under the influence of the trend of our interpretation, we "read into the facts" more than may be permitted. Imaginative insight is helpful in any scientific enterprise if it respects the limitations of factual evidence.

(5) The organization of the case frequently brings to light a distinctive pattern of symptoms. These patterns of behavior-symptoms and activities, or syndromes, are highly indicative of the fundamental causal process in operation. They are frequently incorporated within the title of the case in order to assist us in visualizing the framework within which we are operating. This will be noted in the procedural outline which follows.

(6) In accordance with our stress on the importance of the family as a mediating influence within the cultural setting, we will consider the structural organization of the family. Discussion of the family structure enables us to see at the outset the way in which the cultural influences of the environment will distort and emphasize certain phases of the social environment.

(7) The family as a unit, therefore, affects the lives of each one of its members in terms of its own *internal interaction.* It is likewise affected as a unit by the broader circumstances of the environment. These two patterns of influence should be carefully portrayed.

(8) On the basis of our previous classification and observation of such interactive factors, we are now in a position to understand the process of causal interpretation. Not until the facts have been seen and sifted, and not until the character of the interaction within and outside the family has been duly examined, may we truly apprehend the functioning of the causal sequences. This type of causal analysis will disclose the organization of the psychogenetic structure which has resulted from the operation of the previously mentioned factors, and *will at the same time*

reveal the way in which the cultural environment provides the occasion for the functioning of certain role behaviors.

(9) The conflicts that the case presents are usually reflected in the dramatic episodes of crisis, cumulative, precipitate, and voluntary. These episodes signify the alteration of structural components in the environment and indicate the degree of tension and social participation experienced by the individual. Such crisis-situations epitomize the conflicts within the entire situation. They may be most effectively appraised in relation to the total psychogenetic structure.

(10) The prognosis and recommendations which follow at the conclusion of a case are extremely helpful from the standpoint of revealing how the case itself may be resolved. The validity of our causal hypothesis, in the last resort, may only be sustained in the light of how adequately the subject "lives up" to the prognosis.

With these precautions established, we propose now to (I) suggest a procedure of analysis, (II) present a case of delinquency that is notably "typical," and (III) illustrate an application of the procedure to the case.

(6) A SUGGESTED OUTLINE FOR CASE ANALYSIS

Incorporating the suggestions that have just been made and utilizing the frame of reference employed in our analysis thus far, the following outline summarizes the important steps to be used in organizing and analyzing the "raw data" of a given problem.

Directions and Procedures for the Analysis of Case-Problems

Some basic principles to be observed:

1) Be sure to follow the rules as specifically directed;
2) Divide your data into categories as suggested;
3) Be concise in your statements of fact;
4) *Distinguish between authenticated facts and the unauthenticated information provided by reports and informants.*

General Axioms:

Success in any form of analysis can be obtained only if:

1) Precision in expression is employed;
2) No more is inferred from the facts than the facts themselves will allow.

Part A: Complete descriptive title.

1) This title constitutes a tentative working hypothesis for evaluating the data of the case.
2) Include within the title all of the outstanding features of the case.
3) This type of title summarizes the important characteris-

tics of the given problem. It provides an elementary and simple frame of reference suggesting the form of analysis employed.

Illustration: "Case of J. S., involving *continuous* petty thievery, *induced* by a highly repressive family situation, *producing* acute inferiority feelings, and *resulting* in attempts to gain prestige." *Note* the key words: "involving," "induced," "producing," "resulting." Similar forms may be employed to indicate the predominant syndromes of traits distinguishing the behavioral complex of the case.

Part B: *Compilation of "vital statistics" relevant to the case.*

1) Age; I.Q., schooling; delinquency or problem record; etc.
2) Father and mother: ages; schooling; profession; income; etc.
3) Residence, present and past.
4) Siblings (brothers and sisters): ages in descending order; other facts concerning them, such as schooling, illnesses, delinquency records, etc.
5) Nationality, ethnic and religious background, etc.

Part C: *Family organization.*

Short descriptive paragraph (factual and objective) of the organization of the family, including such items as dominant members, patriarchal or matriarchal characteristics, member-roles, and attitudes of other members towards parents and towards each other.

(Examples: Does the father rule with an iron hand? Is corporal punishment administered? Are both parents employed? Is there preferential treatment of siblings by either or both parents?)

Part D: *Factors in adjustment and conflict between family and community.*

1) Economic status of the family;
2) Health problems of the family;
3) Sex problems;
4) Cultural factors (church membership, lodges, social clubs, educational interests, if any, etc.).

Part E: *Factors in adjustment and conflict within the family.*

1) (a) Relationship to father;
   (b) Relationship to mother;
   (c) Relationship to siblings.

2)* *Psychogenetic development within the socio-cultural setting of the family and community:* characteristic types of emotional traits and temperamental factors developed; types of emotional needs and securities acquired within the particular community and associational milieu; *the structure of the p.g.p., particularly in the light of the structure of the status and role configurations in the social environment of the delinquent.*

Part F: Precipitating, cumulative, and voluntary factors of conflict. Enumerate under separate headings the crisis-situations which have produced the deviations in the subject's behavior.

Part G: Brief summary of the case.

Part H: Prognosis.

On the basis of the diagnostic procedure as outlined in the concluding section of Chapter VIII, indicate the conditions under which you believe the subject may be enabled to make a satisfactory adjustment. (Examples: Indefinite custodial care? Type and character? Removal from family environment? Special educational and therapeutic program?)

II. Case of Herman

The following represents a summary of materials in one case record gathered over a period of years from many sources. It is not presented systematically. Part of the function of interpretation involves putting the material in order so that we may draw adequate inferences and conclusions from the case. It will be noted that there are many contradictions in the observations of different individuals in contact with the case. The evidence presented by many observers, trained as well as non-professional, includes a great many random observations and casual impressions that have to be evaluated in terms of the entire case record. Unfortunately, except in the relatively few instances of systematic studies made by specialized social work agencies and child study institutes, case records are generally drawn together in this loose manner.

Problem: A long series of petty pilferings from stores, school lockers, and his own family, beginning when he was fifteen years of age. Recently, in conjunction with a companion his own age, he was arrested for stealing a car in which they were

* This is the most important analytical feature of any case. Considerable attention should be devoted, upon the basis of the authenticated facts available, to developing the "logical" structure of the case. This "logical structure" (including the p.g.p.) should indicate the basic needs developed in early childhood, the socio-cultural configuration and conditions for the establishment of such needs, and the way in which these needs *express themselves* in the diverse social roles and activities comprising the subject's behavior.

> taking a "joy ride." His childhood has been characterized by continuous misbehavior at home and ungovernable conduct, particularly towards certain members of his family.

Report as it appears in the Child Guidance Clinic files, March, 1946

Herman: born 1930; high school, grade 10B; race, white; religion, Catholic.

Offenses: Thefts from his father's change carrier. First time one year ago. Took gum from the A. & P. Took candy and fountain pen from Five and Ten. Found compact and cigarette case, sold it for thirty-five cents and bought "eats" (candy).

Findings: The father and mother were born in the U. S. They are both about forty years of age and reported to be psychoneurotic. The father has been employed as a bus driver for eighteen years. Earns about fifty-five dollars a week. Mother says she suffered from epilepsy when a child.

Herman is the oldest of three children. The other two children are girls. The older girl is in her first year of high school, and the younger is in grade 5A. The family report that both girls are making satisfactory scholastic progress. The family history as regards disease has no particular bearing on the problem of Herman as presented to us.

Herman is getting about eleven hours of sleep per day. He goes to bed about 8:30 P.M. and arises about 7:00 A.M. His sleep is apparently restful except during occasional nervous spells. He weighs about 123 pounds. (Average for his height is about 133 pounds.) He is about 5 feet 8 inches in height and well built for an adolescent boy.

Herman, though only sixteen when first seen, had been smoking for the past three years. For the past few months he has been stealing and lying to get cigarettes. He has also stolen from a Five and Ten Cent Store and an A. & P. Store. He always has an excuse for all his failures. He has an imaginative mind which leads him into wild schemes for making money. He keeps company with boys of questionable character. He does not get along well with his sisters. There is a constant nagging and teasing between them. Had female companion last year, but was not "silly about girls."

When first seen, the boy was smoking one pack of cigarettes a day. Within a week's time he had reduced his smoking to about four cigarettes a week. This was accomplished by discussing the problem of excessive smoking with him. No promises of breaking the habit were exacted from him. However, the serious conditions which might result from such practice were discussed with him in a friendly way.

The material side of the home is about average. It is comfortably furnished and is neat and clean. It is a first-floor apartment in a three-family house. The boy is well cared for. His meals are well-regulated and the food which is supplied is of the proper kind. The boy is given an allowance of a dollar a week. Fifty cents is deposited as a Christmas Fund, twenty-five cents is used for church contributions, and twenty-five cents he spends as he sees fit. He goes to the movies once a week. Aside from participation in an orchestra rehearsal once a week, and a visit to his mother's people on Sunday, his recreation is somewhat limited.

The father is an impulsive man, loud of voice, aggressive, and domineering. There is considerable friction between the father and son. The father tries to give one the impression he has stinted the boy on nothing that is good for him. The boy, although now sixteen years of age, goes to bed around 8:30 P.M. each night. The father has to arise early in the morning; therefore, the whole family retires in order that he may not be disturbed. The father finds fault whether or not the boy studies. He seems to have no faith or confidence in the boy and the youth senses this.

Statement from the Case Investigator's Report

"I made a visit to the home recently. The mother was first contacted. She is rather a timid and retiring person. She realizes the existing turmoil between the son and the father and she enters into the fray with caution. Fortunately she is rather soft voiced and her understanding of the boy is on a much higher plane than that of the father. She is open to discussion and is co-operative in accepting suggestions made in the case. On the other hand, the father instead of working out the strained relations which exist with the boy upbraids him in a loud voice, all the while wildly gesticulating.

"During my visit, the topic of conversation was the lack of musical ability which the boy displayed. The father insisted that the boy played by ear and would really never make a violinist, which instrument the boy plays. Having some acquaintance with the violin myself, I asked the boy to play a selection for me. Very willingly he did so. The selection was played by note and quite well rendered. The father was quite perturbed when I expressed my view that the boy had played by note. The father immediately made the boy play a second selection and eventually a third, trying to show the boy could not in any way master the instrument. Fortunately, the boy acquitted himself efficiently.

"Still not convinced of the boy's ability, the father waded through the rack of music and placed before the boy a showy selection quite filled with the finer techniques of music. For the minute the boy was embarrassed. Sensing the situation, I asked Herman to play the selection, paying more attention to notes and their place on the finger board, omitting the value of time and rhythm. He did a good piece of work. I congratulated him. The father quite chagrined at his own attitude covered up by saying, 'You see, he plays all right because you are here looking at him!' No credit was given the boy for the ability he may have.

"The boy has been reprimanded lately for visiting a candy and cigarette store. The younger sister (ten years of age) burst into the house during a recent visit and began a long story about having seen Herman in the candy store with a number of friends. Assuming the attitude of the good Samaritan, she entered the store and before all of Herman's friends informed him she was going to "tell Mama." Other humiliating remarks were made. This report was made to mother before Herman arrived from school. When Herman did come in, his mother began to ask all kinds of questions and created some embarassing situations.

"The boy has experienced the life of the average school boy. He received his elementary training in a private school. His work was of a fair grade. His behavior of clowning attracted attention and he felt it was best to change to public school.

"From the summary of the findings there is no question but that Herman has ability to do work of more than average calibre."

This is merely the preliminary statement found in the copious case record. Following his initial offenses of petty pilfering and disorderliness, Herman graduated into a series of more serious offenses, culminating in the theft of an automobile with an older companion. Because of limitations of space, it is not possible to include the detailed reports, clinical findings, and personal interviews appearing in the entire case record. In the complete handling of the case are included reports from several of Herman's teachers at different times in his career; case records from the reformatory (to which he was committed) and from a special neuropsychiatric clinic; interviews with doctors, psychiatrists, and his former parish priest; and early child guidance clinic findings. We will proceed to an analysis of the case in which many of these reports and findings appear.

III. Classification, Analysis, and Interpretation

In accordance with the previous outline for the organization and classification of our materials, we may now proceed to analyze the case of Herman. Despite differences of interpretation regarding some factors of his background, and despite the uncertainty concerning some of the factual evidence, it is possible to ascertain some of the arrangements of traits, elicited by his peculiar family and social situation, that appear to predispose him to anti-social and delinquent acts.

The fact that his father is an impulsive and domineering individual, and his mother a weak and retiring person, is not sufficient to account for the formation of his behavior deficiencies. Nor are his physiological weaknesses, if any are present, sufficient to account for his difficulties. The responsible factors are the structure of the family, the relationships of the father and mother to each other and to their children, Herman's constitutional characteristics, and the peculiar structure of his lower middle-class environment. It is these that have predisposed him to the kinds of difficulty in which he finds himself.

Part A: Complete descriptive title.

Case of Herman, involving periodic petty thievery, induced by a family situation which is highly repressive and unresponsive, producing inadequacies in personality and inferiority feelings, resulting in a desire for prestige, attention, recognition, and response.

Part B: Vital statistics.

1) Age: Sixteen years (when first observed by Child Guidance Clinic); present age, eighteen years.

I.Q.: Appears above average (according to most of the observers).

Schooling: Highest grade, 10B (High School; received his elementary training in a private (parochial) school where his work was of a fair grade. Due to his "clowning" behavior, was transferred to public school.

(a) Quality of work: average.

(b) Synopsis of teachers' reports:

(i) General attitude is that Herman does not study enough.

(ii) Most teachers feel that he could do better work.

(iii) All plans of improvement were followed for a time and then dropped.

(iv) Work improves with encouragement.

(v) Subject tries to draw attention to himself.

(vi) Co-operates sporadically and wishes to make restitution.

Delinquency record: The subject took money from his father's change carrier for the first time one year prior to reporting of case. Took gum from the A. & P. Took candy and fountain pen from Five and Ten. Found a compact and cigarette case, sold them for thirty-five cents, and bought candy with the money. He has been smoking for the past three years, and for the past few months has been seen stealing and lying in order to get cigarettes. He keeps company with boys of questionable character. Lost his job in a pocketbook factory because of his "kiddishness," after working there nearly a year. After this, he went to a farm school for about a month where he met a certain Jim, a much older boy with a criminal record. Both stole a car and were apprehended when they were found speeding on the wrong side of road in heavy traffic. There are also two more warrants against the subject for stealing other cars. He was admitted to the penitentiary from the reformatory.

Related problem record: During his entire high school career, he was in frequent difficulties as a result of stealing from the school, from churches, and from various doctors and professional men in the neighborhood.

Nationality: Born in the U. S.

Race: White.

Religion: Catholic.

Residence: Home is a first floor apartment in a three-family house. It is comfortably furnished and is neat and clean. Herman has always lived there except for periods when he was at the farm school and reformatory.

Constitutional factors:

(a) *Birth and early childhood:*

- (i) Premature birth, seven months after conception.
- (ii) Instrument birth, in incubator for one and one-half months.
- (iii) Infant and early childhood development: extremely fat infant; bottle fed; late in walking, talking; fall at two years, head injury, but no immediate serious consequences.

(b) *Pre-adolescent growth:*

- (i) Measles, only reported childhood disease.
- (ii) Severe temper tantrums.
- (iii) Always more or less "nervous."
- (iv) Frequent headaches.
- (v) Glasses at eleven years.

(vi) Alleged "nervous breakdown" at age of twelve years.

(c) *Recent developments:*

(i) 5 feet, 8 inches tall, well proportioned.

(ii) Eleven hours sleep per night.

(iii) Well regulated meals, proper diet.

(iv) Smoking: had been smoking for three years previous to first observation, as much as one package per day; reduced to four cigarettes per week upon counsel.

(v) Does not drink or use drugs.

(vi) Greatly concerned about his health.

(vii) Suffers from periods of depression.

2) *Parents:*

	Father	*Mother*
(a) Ages:	Approximately forty.	Approximately forty.
(b) Schooling:	No information, (reputed by Dr. Adolph to have been "village idiot").	No information.
(c) Nationality:	Born in U. S.	Born in U. S.
(d) Religion:	Catholic.	Catholic.
(e) Race:	White.	White.
(f) Health:	Reputed psychoneurotic.	Possible epilepsy as child.
(g) Occupation:	Bus driver.	Housewife.
(h) Income:	Fifty-five dollars per week.	None.

3) *Siblings:* Two sisters, ages fourteen and ten years. The older sister is in her first year of high school, the other sister is in grade 5A. Both girls, according to a family report, are making satisfactory scholastic progress. Health is apparently normal, and there is no delinquency record for the sisters.

Part C: Family organization.

1) *Characteristics of family members:*

(a) Father

(i) Strict disciplinarian.

(ii) Believes in corporal punishment.

(iii) Domineering, aggressive, loud-voiced, impulsive.
(iv) Wants things his way.

(b) Mother
(i) Timid and retiring.
(ii) Soft-voiced.
(iii) Open to discussion and usually ready to co-operate.

(c) Siblings
(i) "Nagging" type.
(ii) Average intelligence.

(d) Herman
(i) Nervous.
(ii) Quick tempered and argumentative.
(iii) Imaginative mind.
(iv) Shrewd, intelligent.
(v) Realizes his faults.
(vi) Co-operative to a certain extent.
(vii) Blames others for his failures.

2) *Family organization*

Herman is not close to either of his parents. His relationship with his father is strained and the two of them are in continual conflict. The father has no faith in the boy and this the boy realizes, with the result that he has little incentive to work at school or to practice on the violin. What work the boy does is never praised, but is continually criticized. At times, when the father was approached and asked to co-operate and change his attitude toward the boy, he did respond for a while. However, when results were not immediately forthcoming, he reverted to the old type of treatment. It seems that the father is seriously afraid of sacrificing any of his authority or prestige to any member of the family.

From the data given, it is assumed that the mother understands Herman better than does the father. However, she seldom interferes in the relations between father and son. She probably has the same fear of incurring the wrath of her husband as do the children. She is apparently concerned about Herman and uses her two daughters to obtain information about his activities. This procedure creates misunderstanding on Herman's part, and results in a breach between mother and son. The concern of the mother in this case does more harm than good because she is ignorant of the proper way in which to channel her help. She has proven co-operative and willing to do what she can to help Herman.

Herman's two sisters are apparently well adjusted to the parents but are in constant conflict with Herman himself. Their role as "spies" for the mother is understandably irritating to the boy. Added to this is the fact that both sisters are younger and probably receive a good part of the attention Herman had been receiving before they were born. This feeling of resentment colors his attitude toward them and, although he may not understand it, inhibits his understanding of them and their relationship to him as an older brother.

Part D: Factors in adjustment and conflict between family and community.

1) *Economic status:* The family income is about fifty-five dollars a week. The home is about average (comfortably furnished, neat and clean). Herman receives an allowance of a dollar a week, out of which he has twenty-five cents to spend as he sees fit. Fifty cents is deposited in Christmas fund and twenty-five cents is used for church contributions.

2) *Health problems of the family:* The family history with regard to disease has no particular bearing on Herman's problem. The father has been reported to be psychoneurotic. Mother states that she suffered from epilepsy when a child. There seems to be no evidence of epilepsy or mental deterioration in Herman. Herman claims that at the age of twelve he had a nervous breakdown with a vague feeling of fear at its onset. (The facts and circumstances surrounding this episode are highly conflicting as reported by different people.) Says he lived in a world of his own for two years. Only childhood disease was measles at the age of six months. He suffered frequently from headaches and began to wear glasses at the age of eleven.

3) *Sex problems:* Subject stated he had normal sexual desires but had always inhibited them because of his religious scruples. He occasionally took girls out to socials, but did not associate with girls to any great extent.

4) *Cultural factors:* Family professes the Catholic faith. Apparently the family is not especially "club-minded." Herman never belonged to any clubs or organizations other than to participate in an orchestra rehearsal once a week.

His reading was confined largely to Western adventure and detective magazines. His participation in sports has been limited to basketball. He went to the movies once a week. Aside from his orchestra participation and a visit to his mother's people on Sundays, his recreation is limited. The subject plays the violin quite well, but the father gives him no credit for the ability he may have. Educational interests are not reported.

Part E: Factors in adjustment and conflict within the family.

1) (a) *Relationship to father:* There is considerable friction between father and son. The father finds fault whether the boy studies or not. He seems to have no faith or confidence in the boy, who senses the situation. When sixteen years of age, the subject went to bed around 8:30 P.M. each night. The father has to arise early in the morning; therefore, the whole family retires early in order that he may not be disturbed. It is hardly proper to expect a boy of Herman's age to sleep approximately eleven hours a night. All of the members of the family are completely dominated by the father, and Herman especially is repressed to an excessive degree. The father, as a result of his "village idiot" status in early childhood, may have developed a feeling of inferiority, which he resolves by making himself the supreme figure in his own home. Thus, he does not want any other member of the family to gain more praise or prestige than he does. Perhaps he feels that Herman, by playing the violin well, would detract from his own status and so will not help or encourage him. Instead, he expresses his feelings in a loud, aggressive voice and manner and in corporal punishment. The subject is not particularly close to either parent, having had a defensive dislike for both for a number of years.

(b) *Relationship to mother:* The mother is also repressed by the father. She is not as severe as the father, nor as aggressive with the boy. She recognizes the turmoil between the son and the father, and she enters into the fray with caution. Her understanding of the boy is on a much higher plane than that of the father. Still, she apparently trusts her daughters more or shows her concern. She listens to their tales about Herman, and then asks him all sorts of questions, creating embarrassing situations when outsiders are present. There is little evidence of constructive guidance from either of the parents. Both parents seem to be more conscious of appearances and the opinions of others than of the dangers and implications of the internal conflict in their own home. The mother is, however, a good housekeeper, keeps the home neat and clean, and prepares well-planned meals.

(c) *Relationship to siblings:* Herman is the oldest of three children. The other two children are girls. The girls are making satisfactory scholastic progress according to the report of the family. According to reports, Herman apparently lags in his school work and seems lazy and disinterested, yet quite capable of the work. There is no evidence of aggression or friction between either parent and the girls. The girls feel the tension between the father and Herman, and appear to take the father's side. The younger sister often assumes the attitude of the "good Samaritan" and tattles on Herman, as when he visited the candy store once, when he was not supposed to. The general relationship is one of friction.

2) *Psychogenetic development*

Herman was of premature birth, an instrument baby; he remained in an incubator for a month and a half. These facts may have had a significant effect upon his immediate development. In the first place, there is the possibility of injury to the nervous system as a result of traumatic shock, and secondly, the attitudes of his parents toward him were undoubtedly affected by the circumstances of his birth. Special care and concern by both parents, but particularly by the mother, were probably given him because of the abnormal conditions enumerated above. A significant clue in this respect is shown by his delayed walking and talking. The fact that he did not begin to really talk until he was two and one-half years old, and didn't begin walking until he was "about two," may not only have caused the parents consternation; it suggests as well the administration of considerable care on the part of the mother. The verbal and ambulatory behavior of the child represents functional adaptation to his environment. If he is continually served and his wishes anticipated, such functional adaptations may not be elicited. Hence, the child may appear "retarded." Thus, there are two possibilities concerning these early circumstances: (1) either Herman represented a case of delayed maturational development, indicating a possible organic deficiency; or (2) the child was excessively cared for as a consequence of the parent's concern. Evidence in support of the latter possibility may be seen in the fact that the child was extremely fat. Fully as important, however, is the fact that the parents now feel their child is not quite normal and requires special attention.

The older sister was born when Herman was about two years of age, a critical period in his life. This birth naturally drew from Herman some share of the attention to which he had become accustomed. (The period around the age of two is a highly critical one in any child's life, for it is at this period that the child's self-conceptions begin to form. He begins to *recognize* and to *identify himself* with the attitudes of his parents towards him.) The jealousy and rivalry he entertains especially towards this older sister may be accounted for in part by the initial and continuing frustrations her presence creates for him. The report states that as a child the subject had severe and continual temper tantrums *arising shortly after this period* (the second year). These were not only protests against the divided care of his environment, but *functional* devices for gaining attention and recognition. The father, dull, aggressive, domineering, and impulsive, in punishing him severely for these tantrums, laid the basis for Herman's nervous temperament and the intense dislike of the son for his parent.

Four years later, the youngest child was born. Herman was about six years of age at this time. This meant one more person with whom the parents' attention had to be shared. The father, by this time, having lost all patience with the boy, regarded him as "bad." Corporal punishment was still inflicted liberally. At the age of eleven, the subject began to wear glasses because of frequent headaches. These may be the result of his highly nervous state, the head injury he is reported to have received at the age of two, or a combination of both sets of circumstances.

While in its material aspect the home is comfortable and average lower middle-class, it is emotionally unstable and is extremely repressive. The whole family operates in accordance with the father's schedule and wishes. The subject seems to be thrust into playing a series of special roles as a result of his external environment. He may feel he is a martyr to his father, that he need not excel in school because he gets little or no credit when he tries. His imaginative mind leads him to indulge in daydreams of the "suffering hero" and "identification" types. He is treated as a bad boy at home and by many of his teachers, with the result that he begins to play the part and romanticizes himself as a spectacular failure. The general conception which he has attained of himself manifests itself in a number of different roles which *reflect the conditions, values, needs, and circumstances of the separate social situations* in which he finds himself. These roles establish the basis for certain habit patterns and attitudinal traits which may be summarized in the following diagram. (The student should note that the circumstances of these separate situations vary from culture to culture, and from environment to environment.) In the typical lower middle-class environment of Herman's upbringing, they manifest themselves as follows:

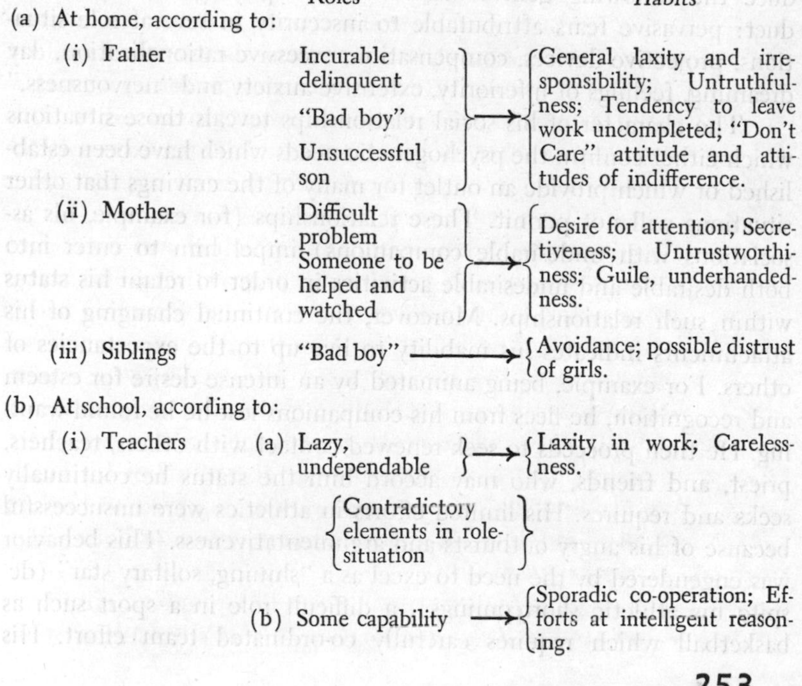

	Roles	*Habits*
(a) At home, according to:		
(i) Father	Incurable delinquent "Bad boy" Unsuccessful son	→ General laxity and irresponsibility; Untruthfulness; Tendency to leave work uncompleted; "Don't Care" attitude and attitudes of indifference.
(ii) Mother	Difficult problem Someone to be helped and watched	→ Desire for attention; Secretiveness; Untrustworthiness; Guile, underhandedness.
(iii) Siblings	"Bad boy"	→ Avoidance; possible distrust of girls.
(b) At school, according to:		
(i) Teachers	(a) Lazy, undependable	→ Laxity in work; Carelessness.
	Contradictory elements in role-situation	
	(b) Some capability	→ Sporadic co-operation; Efforts at intelligent reasoning.

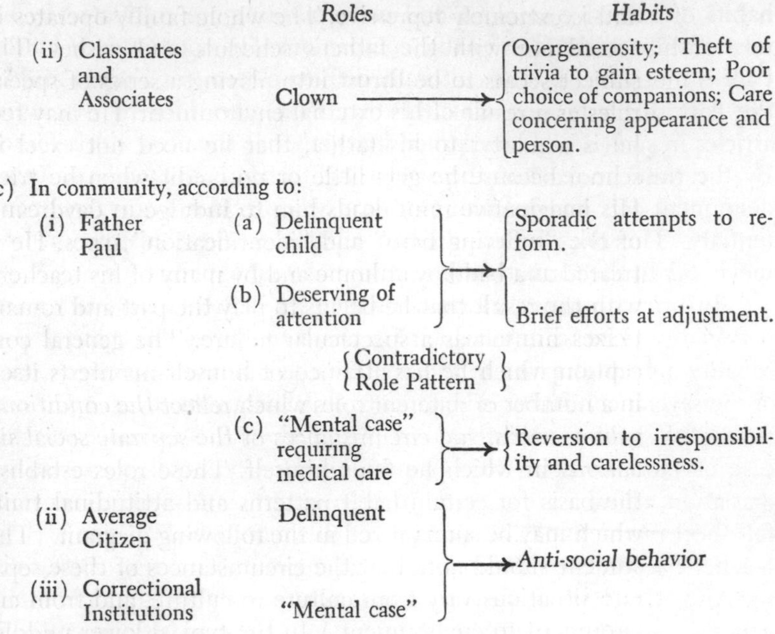

Attitudes: The combination of the several habit-patterns in this case, clustering together and reinforcing each other, tends to produce the following generalized attitudes typifying Herman's conduct: pervasive fears attributable to insecurity in several role situations, projective devices, compensation, excessive rationalization, day dreaming, feelings of inferiority, extensive anxiety and "nervousness."

The character of his social relationships reveals those situations which either confirm the psychogenetic needs which have been established or which provide an outlet for many of the cravings that other situations will not permit. These relationships (for example, his associations with undesirable companions) impel him to enter into both desirable and undesirable activities in order to retain his status within such relationships. Moreover, the continual changing of his attachments indicates his inability to live up to the expectancies of others. For example, being animated by an intense desire for esteem and recognition, he flees from his companions lest he be found wanting. He then proceeds to seek renewed contact with others, teachers, priest, and friends, who may accord him the status he continually seeks and requires. His limited efforts in athletics were unsuccessful because of his angry outbursts and argumentativeness. This behavior was engendered by the need to excel as a "shining, solitary star" (despite his athletic shortcomings), a difficult role in a sport such as basketball which requires carefully co-ordinated team effort. His habits of excessive smoking and petty pilfering are cultivated by his relationships with questionable companions. His contact with Father Paul is motivated by the culturally defined esteem for a priest and by the flattering attention which Father Paul gives him by discussing articles in such a highly regarded newspaper as the *New York Times*. By the time he reached the age of eighteen, his thievery and other delinquent acts had led him to a farm school, reformatory, and penitentiary. The roles he acquired in relation to these institutions led inevitably to the formation of certain undesirable habits.

In brief summary, Herman might be classified as an inadequate personality. The features which are characteristic of this type of personality are: dominance of momentary and immediate interests, lack of perseverance, faulty adjustment, shiftlessness, and an incessant stream of short-lived enthusiasms. All of these are evidenced in the case of Herman. This type of person may often, as a means of ingratiation, show a great desire to help others, but appears always to fall short of the mark. An example of this may be seen in the biology teacher's report that Herman seemed anxious to help but never did so. Also, this type of person, is not infrequently of superior intelligence.

Part F: Crisis factors of conflict.

The crises in Herman's case are essentially cumulative. The case materials are not sufficiently detailed to give us a good picture of a number of the precipitating events and voluntary crises which undoubtedly did occur. However, if we examine the case carefully, there appears a definite pattern of small precipitating factors that did contribute to the concluding series of maladjustments.

1) Among the earliest crises is the birth of Herman's older sister, occurring at a time when the overzealous care of the mother had created a bond of intense dependence.
2) Another crisis may be supposed to occur at the time Herman retires from the private parochial school and transfers to public school. This crisis must be seen in conjunction with the immediate precipitating factors which were associated with this event.
3) The alleged "nervous breakdown" at the age of twelve may indicate another critical situation, marked by certain volitional elements. This episode may also have been influenced by his desire to stay away from his associates and to isolate himself for a period of time.
4) The "depression periods" to which Father Paul refers may be seen as forms of crises whose total impact conduce towards a major behavioral development.

5) Herman's first act of petty thievery might be thought of as constituting a major precipitating crisis. The situation in which it resulted may have induced strong feelings of gratification through the discovery of a way of gaining the recognition of his group.
6) The final major theft which brought Herman into the limelight contributed one of the last precipitating factors, up to the time the case study was made. Depending on how the situation was handled, an opportunity was provided for Herman to continue his anti-social regression or to work his way out and make an approach to the problem of adjustment.

The critical situations mentioned above are only suggestive of a great many which a complete and detailed unraveling of the case would disclose. Such factors must be viewed as phases of the general cumulative effect which the development of Herman's personality has invoked.

Part G: Brief summarization.

The case of Herman appears to be that of an irresponsible personality, produced by various emotional upsets, tensions, and conflicts created by possible traumatic injury, an unfavorable environment, and family relationships. Resultant acts of petty thievery, delinquent activities, and major offenses appear to be the consequence of an attempt to gain status and to overcome feelings of personality inadequacy.

Part H: Prognosis.

Any prognosis must be based upon (1) an inventory of the subject's present psychological assets and liabilities, (2) his culturally defined roles and the possibilities of their fulfillment, and (3) the available opportunities to place him in a social environment that may elicit the development of positive adaptive measures. Among the positive traits that may elicit satisfactory normal adjustment may be listed such factors as his better-than-average intelligence, his identification with an interested religious group, his desire to be thought well of, his proficiency and interest in the violin, and his concern about his person. Against these, however, must be listed such adverse items as his entrenched habits of carelessness and indifference, the emotional satisfactions he derives from his nefarious escapades, an unsatisfactory family environment, his pathological desire to gain attention, his impetuousness and irresponsibility, and his intense dislike of his father. On the basis of such an evaluation, the general prognosis for effective adjustment is only fair. However, if adequate and sustained supervision from the outside is given the home, or if Herman can be removed to a different type of environment such as might be provided by a good home, there is a reasonable chance that this boy may make a satisfactory adjustment.

SUMMARY

In this chapter we have presented a method for the analysis of a problem of social disorder. The purpose of this presentation was to show how, in an actual case, the several factors of the social and cultural environment, the community, the family, and the individual, combine to produce a given pattern of behavior malfunctioning. (1) The analysis of human documentary materials is *not* a principal method of sociological research. If anything, it is largely an auxiliary method, designed to shed further light upon special aspects of the more commonly employed quantitative-statistical, sociometric, ecological, and survey methods. Biographical, autobiographical, and formal case record data, however, do enable us to observe the functioning of socio-cultural and family factors within the life of the individual vividly and highly realistically, particularly from the standpoint of the operation of human motives and attitudes. Human documentary materials, as Dollard has pointed out, must always be seen in relation to the changing cultural stream, the family situation, and the social relevance of organic factors. (2) Case record materials, therefore, will always reveal the operation of broad social factors in the life of the individual, as well as those immediate social situations that activate his behavior. (3) Because case record materials depend upon the observations of others and upon a person's own self-evaluation, it is to be expected that they will contain a great many inaccuracies of fact and judgment. It is important, therefore, for the investigator to distinguish between genuine "facts of record," i.e., facts concerning the life of the individual about which there is reasonable certainty, and *opinions* concerning such facts. Both types may be important, but they must nevertheless be appraised as different kinds of "facts." (4) In examining a case history, we do not propose a point of view based upon the restricted theoretical position of a given psychological or sociological school. Instead, we suggest a dynamic method of organization, i.e., a framework of analysis, within which the case may be studied. (5) Our method of organization stresses a framework that includes consideration of physiological tendencies, family structure, relationships within the family, and the relationship of the family to outer cultural and social factors. In addition, it emphasizes adequate classification of data, interpretation of data within the limitations of factual evidence, and the inferences and further findings which are required in order to gain comprehensive insight into the case. (6) Upon the basis of the foregoing considerations, a systematic outline for the analysis of an actual case of delinquency has been provided and applied.

CHAPTER ELEVEN

SOCIAL CHANGE AND NEW PERSPECTIVES UPON CRIME

(1) CULTURAL CHANGE AND CRIME

INDIVIDUALS who do not conform to the mores and social institutions are not necessarily criminals. The distinction between crime and other forms of non-conforming behavior rests on legal definition. An act may be heinous, repulsive, and socially reprehensible, but unless it is defined as criminal by the laws in the statute books, it may not be considered a crime. Thus, the non-conforming individual does not become a "criminal" until he is apprehended for committing an act that is a defined breach of the law.

There is, therefore, no such thing as a *crime* in the absolute sense. On the contrary, in all organized societies specific acts are defined as crimes according to the criminal statutes of such societies. Definitions as to what is a crime differ greatly from culture to culture and at different times in history. Indeed, *the nature of the offenses considered as criminal, and their general extent, always afford some index of the institutional structure and stability of a society.* During the Middle Ages, when the Church was supreme, the most important offenses were heresy and such related misdemeanors as witchcraft. It is estimated that about a quarter of a million persons were put to death for witchcraft between the fifteenth and the eighteenth centuries. As late as the seventeenth century, stealing a sheep was considered a capital offense in England. Under the aegis of a strongly centralized royal rule and a powerful landed aristocracy, the chief offenses in Norman England were theft, rape, murder, arson, robbery, breach of the peace, counterfeiting, concealment of a treasure trove, and treason. According to Cantor, by the middle of the seventeenth century, the list had grown to about thirty statutory felonies.[1] In the dictatorial states of this present century treasonable activities have been considered the most important offenses. The significance of such acts may be seen in the widely publicized treason trials of modern Russia and the other Communist-dominated countries.

[1] Nathaniel F. Cantor, *Crime and Society* (New York, 1939), pp. 344–5.

The development of legal concepts is in direct accord with the major theoretical framework of our book. The social conception of what constitutes an offense against society rests upon changing "definitions of the situation" and changing standards of normalcy. The only difference, in so far as the legal definition of crime is concerned, exists in the fact that the law is the *formal* vehicle through which anti-social activities are defined. The scope and dimension of definitions of criminal activities will change always in relation to the changing consensus of the members of society. A recent evidence can be seen in the growing awareness that there are certain types of criminal activities now recognized as "white-collar" crimes, activities which in the past did not bear the same onus as the traditional types of offenses to which society had become accustomed.

(2) AMERICANS AS LAW BREAKERS

The heterogeneity of American social life has tended to produce an enormous area in which violations of the law may occur. The extensiveness of culture-conflict and strain in the United States has brought about attempts to reconcile such divergence through the ready-made formulae of the law, with the result that Americans are probably the most "over-legislated" people in the world. It has been estimated that there are about two million laws on our statute books, the great majority of which are obsolete and not observed.

Because of the complexity of our social structure, the opportunities for breaking the law are widely expanded. The result has been a casualness in the attitude towards the law, particularly as it functions in respect to certain areas of American society. Petty offenses (misdemeanors) flourish in this type of environment, and it is the rare individual who at some time or other has not knowingly or unwittingly found himself disregarding the law. Differences in the statutory requirements of the several states have made it almost inevitable that certain types of offenses of a more serious nature shall occur as well. In addition, confusion exists because of the difficulties involved in defining precisely those occasions when a breach of the law has actually occurred. There is a great marginal area in which the outwardly respectable citizen may operate in violation of the spirit of the statutory code while apparently conforming to its letter. Because they avail themselves of the opportunities which the character of the law affords, Americans have frequently been called the most lawless people in the world. This observation is in part confirmed by the enormous amount of litigation which annually passes through our courts.

In response to a questionnaire given to 340 college juniors and seniors by the author during the period 1943–8, approximately 91 per cent admitted to having knowingly committed offenses against the law, both misdemeanors and felonies. Women students were as glaringly delinquent in this respect as men, although the volume of major offenses (felonies) which they admitted to having committed was somewhat smaller than that for men. For the women, 77.1 per cent of the offenses committed were misdemeanors and 22.9 per cent felonies, as compared with 73.5 per cent of misdemeanors and 26.5 per cent of felonies for the men. The differences obtained may have been due to greater candor on the part of the men, better recollection of certain youthful episodes, or actual differences in the character of the offenses which had taken place. Study of a controlled sample of a small group of professional and upper middle-class individuals produced results highly similar to the results obtained for college students. This group was asked whether they considered themselves lawbreakers at the time the offenses were committed and whether they considered such activities illegal in retrospect. Of the women, 18 per cent considered themselves violators at the time of the occurrence, while an additional 20 per cent considered their activities to have been illegal in retrospect. Of the men, 30 per cent were apparently aware of their illegal activity at the time the offenses were committed, while an additional 35 per cent, upon subsequent consideration, considered their activities to have been illicit.

It is striking to note how small was the percentage of those who considered their activities as lawless even when the illegality of their activity was pointed out to them. The explanation is probably to be found in the fact that Americans have been accustomed to a certain amount of evasion of the law. They apparently have no special concern for certain types of illegal activity of a minor variety, provided they are not caught and provided that these events occur during childhood. Such features of American life as the lawlessness of the prohibition era, with its widespread passive acceptance by the American people, the traditional lawlessness of the frontier, the veneration of the outlaw James Brothers and the Daltons, and the knowledge of corruption in civic life, may have contributed to this attitude. This condition is all the more significant in view of the serious nature of some of the offenses that were reported in the above-mentioned survey. Among the felonious activities admitted to were such major offenses as various kinds of stealing, house breaking, felonious assault, forgery, and sex offenses.

(3) THE CRIMINAL AND HIS VICTIM

In an interesting and novel investigation of criminal behavior in its relation to society, the criminologist, von Hentig, has studied the emergence of criminal acts in their relation to the character of the victims and certain predisposing social situations.[2] The study of criminal acts from von Hentig's standpoint is significant for (1) dealing with each criminal act in relation to the total field-structured situation, (2) delineating the importance of cultural factors, and (3) taking account of the discrete nature of individual maladjustment.

The character of the predisposing social situation and the personality of the victim, *as developed within a given culture*, are relevant to the development of crime. For example, a recent wave of Pyramid Clubs, made popular by the American interest in "getting something for nothing" and "getting rich quick," invited a series of crimes in the home by smoothing the way for the entry of strangers. We may speak of "crime-proneness" among certain sections of the American people after the concept of "accident-proneness" employed by psychoanalysts and actuaries.

Thus, as von Hentig says: "Often victims seem to be born. Often they are society made. Sometimes the most valuable qualities render us easy victims; in a sense the victim shapes and molds the criminal." The cultural definitions of roles in certain situations and the character of the social values promoted will combine to yield repetitions of certain kinds of offenses, occurring with some regularity among certain age groups, sexes, and at stipulated times. Wealthy widows, imbued with the desire to find a husband, congregate in resort areas and provide ready bait and opportunity for fraudulent males, bigamists, and murderers. This type of crime is peculiar to such cultures as ours, where approximately 80 per cent of death benefits is passed on to widows, and where the importance of leisure and the necessity of acquiring status through marriage are emphasized.

Situational analyses point up the strict periodicity which most crimes follow. Thus, 45 per cent of all homicides occur between six P.M. and midnight; most burglars are arrested between two and four o'clock in the morning; crimes of violence and the serious sex crimes culminate on Saturday, Sunday, and "blue" Monday. Similarly, it is revealed that most women commit suicide on Sunday, most men on Monday; burglary tends to increase from Friday night on; Saturday night criminality "is obviously caused largely by alcoholic and other excesses," while Sunday is the day of family catastrophes, for reasons which a knowledge of American culture patterns should readily make apparent.

(4) THE ADULT OFFENDER AND THE JUVENILE DELINQUENT

In view of the fact that "crime" consists of criminal acts of many kinds as defined by legislative statutes, it is impossible to speak of "the

[2] *The Criminal and His Victim* (New Haven, 1948).

criminal" or the "adult offender" as constituting a simple, specific type. Abandoning the concept of the "criminal type," we note that those who get into difficulty with the law tend to fall into certain broad classes. In general, these are: (1) the casual offender, (2) the occasional criminal, (3) the episodic criminal, (4) the white-collar criminal, (5) the habitual criminal, and (6) the professional criminal.[3] Except for the last two categories, these groups consist of individuals who find themselves running afoul of the law only when under mental stress and certain other provocations.

The *casual offender* is one who, not necessarily wilfully, commits any of the numerous misdemeanors which abound in our statute books. Traffic and parking violations, disorderly and boisterous conduct, and similar offenses characterize this type of offender. None of these actions may of course be considered serious.

The *occasional criminal* is not a criminal in the usual sense. Unlike the habitual offender, he does not justify his offense. He does not regard himself as a criminal in any sense of the word. He identifies himself closely with the conventional law-abiding world but regards his crime as a misadventure and an unfortunate source of embarrassment and trouble. Such criminal activity may be the "hit and run" automobile accident. Such crime is usually the result of fear, panic, and the stress of the moment, rather than any calculated attempt to violate the law.

The *episodic criminal*, described by Ploscowe and Cavan, is one who, although normally law-abiding and conventional, is impelled under great emotional stress to commit a crime, usually one of a serious nature.[4] An instance of this is the *crime passionel*, frequently committed by an individual who has been perfectly normal until goaded by what appears to him as an intolerable situation. Certainly such an individual is not endowed with any habitual criminal tendencies and, except for the peculiar circumstances of the crime, might have lived out his days as a socially conforming individual.

The *white-collar criminal* operates within the penumbra of the law, as previously described. Sharing the general contempt of the public towards lawless elements, he nevertheless manages to evade the law in furthering his economic position. His questionable activity is usually carried on in conjunction with perfectly legitimate business enterprise. The proprietor of a famous chain of well-appointed restaurants who managed to defraud the government of almost three million dollars in income taxes represents such a type of white-collar criminal. The high-placed military officer who managed to secure important contracts for military supplies

[3] See Ruth Shonle Cavan, *Criminology* (New York, 1948), pp. 22–4.

[4] Morris Ploscowe, *Crime and the Criminal Law* (The National Law Library, II, 1939), pp. 6–18.

during the last war, contrary to official regulations, is another illustration of the white-collar criminal. It appears that such persons, regardless of the seriousness of the charges against them, may not be considered criminals in the sense of being identified with lawless and criminal elements as distinctive antisocial groups.

The *habitual criminal* is one who ordinarily experiences no hesitancy in repeating his crimes. Usually he has a lengthy record of arrests and convictions. Although crime may not be his chief occupation, the circumstances of his life are such that he feels no strong inhibitions about committing offenses when it suits his purpose.

Lastly, we have the *professional criminal* who, because of training, general psychological orientation, and background, devotes his career to criminal activity, just as lawful elements in the population devote their lives to more conventional professional and vocational pursuits. The character of such professional criminal activities are highly variable, extending from the skillful operation of the confidence man to the practices of the burglar and the pickpocket. Closely allied to the professional criminal career are the various types of organized crime.

In addition to the common types of illicit activity described so far, Cavan refers to the *mentally abnormal* and *non-malicious criminal.*[5] A certain percentage of offenders, particularly those apprehended for crimes of violence and sex offenses, are pathological individuals, whose mental abnormalities express themselves in criminal form. The mentally abnormal offender is an individual who suffers from a serious psychopathological or psychotic state that makes it impossible for him to achieve a normal social adjustment. Non-malicious criminals are those who have no specific antisocial animus, but who, because of private conviction or social belief, refuse to accept some of the dictates of conventional society. Members of religious sects, whose beliefs concerning compulsory school attendance for their children, swearing official oaths of fealty, or marital arrangements differ from those held by the larger social order, occasionally find themselves in difficulty with the law. To term such individuals "criminal" is highly misleading. However, in view of the fact that they do not conform to the legislative will of the public and are thus vulnerable to court action, they may be classified as a special group of offenders. The recent fundamentalist group of the Mormon Church who defied the federal ban on plural marriages and the Jehovah's Witnesses who refused to register for the draft during the last war are instances of this type of "socially conscious" offender.

Of all the types described so far, the most significant are the habitual and professional offenders, for the reason that they represent an actual lawless group in society, a "society within a society." The relationship

[5] Cavan, *Criminology*, pp. 30–2.

between these groups and the heavy incidence of repeated juvenile delinquencies described in the previous chapters is particularly significant. The habitual and professional groups are composed of individuals whose long records of previous offenses and juvenile misbehaviors have been directly instrumental in molding them for a life of crime. These individuals represent the failure of our courts, police, and society to deal effectively with the delinquent at a time when the conditions for producing desirable results are most propitious. To a considerable degree, the habitual and professional offender is the juvenile delinquent "grown up." Because of the failure of our courts to develop effective procedures for the care of delinquents during the dangerous adolescent age and the inability of our reform institutions to successfully "reform," the habitual and professional classes of offenders develop into organized groups within society with objectives, values, and "definitions of the situation" peculiar to their own purposes.

(5) A "STATISTICAL PROFILE" OF THE "TYPICAL" OFFENDER

Although recognizing that there are no "typical criminals," we may nevertheless determine certain common trends from the statistical information concerning prisoners in the United States. It should first be noted that prisoners do not represent the entire criminal population of the country. At any given time, only a small percentage of those who actually commit crimes eventually find themselves in prison. Of the more serious offenses, which the Federal Bureau of Investigation classifies as Class I crimes (larceny, burglary, assault, automobile theft, robbery, homicide, and rape), only 3 to 4 per cent of the total reported to the police eventuate in imprisonment for the offenders.[6] Not only do a great many who commit serious offenses manage to escape apprehension by the police, but a very sizable number of cases are dropped or otherwise disposed of because of insufficiency of convicting evidence. As for the minor, or Class II, offenses, the defendants are frequently fined, given short sentences in local jails, placed under local surveillance, or, on occasion, dismissed, even when found guilty. The result is that if we try to gauge the criminal population on the basis of the character, type, and number of inmates in state and federal penitentiaries, we may at best gain only a partial perspective. One popular estimate is that there are approximately 500,000 arrests per year, which represent about one-fifth of the actual number of offenses committed.

More recent estimates, however, based upon the figures of the *Uniform Crime Reports* released by the Federal Bureau of Investigation for

[6] C. C. Van Vechten, "Differential Criminal Case Mortality in Selected Jurisdictions," *American Sociological Review,* VII (1942) 833–9.

1949, provide a more precise account of the extent of crime in the United States and *the relatively small percentage of offenders who finally are convicted and penalized for their offenses.* Annual police activity is considerable in this country, resulting in a yearly reported total of arrests of approximately 14,500,000 for 1,654 American cities. It should be noted that this figure does not include data for the country as a whole. Basing our estimate on such a total reported volume of arrests, we may infer that approximately 1,700,000 major offenses occur in the areas reporting. Of this number, however, only 220,000 (12.9 per cent) result in arrests for serious offenses. When we further recognize that the annual prison population in the United States in federal and state penitentiaries is 78,000, we may further infer that only 4.6 per cent of the serious crimes result in custodial punishment. In speaking of criminals, therefore, we must recognize that those presently serving time in penal institutions represent only a small fraction of the large number of legal offenders of various types and categories.

In view of the high rate of recidivism among the prison population, however, the prison population does afford some insight into the general characteristics of the professional and habitual criminal population. While bearing in mind the insufficiency of statistical evidence concerning crime and delinquency discussed in the previous chapters, and the variability and noncomparability of many of our sources, municipal, state, and federal, we may attempt nevertheless to gain a generalized picture of some of the outstanding traits and practices of prisoners. This voluminous statistical material may be reduced to a "statistical profile." This statistical profile, based upon current official compilations, may serve to indicate the statistical probabilities of certain features of the total criminal population, both in and out of prison. These statistical probabilities do *not* represent either certainties or even overwhelming probabilities, but simply *tendencies.* Upon this basis, we find that the "typical" offender in our prisons appears to be characterized by the following traits:

1) *Conviction:* First conviction occurred very likely between the ages of nineteen and twenty.
2) *Age at Time of Incarceration:* Probably twenty-six and one-half years.
3) *Marital Status:* Is unmarried or, if married, separated from his wife.
4) *Family Background:* Has a greater chance of coming from a broken than an unbroken home.
5) *Associational Activity:* Is inclined to live by himself.
6) *Place of Offense:* May commit his offense away from home, probably in a city of 100,000 or more in size, unless he is a rural

offender. These are more inclined to commit their offenses in the smaller cities.

7) *Type of Offense:* His offense is most apt to be one against property, with larcenies first, followed by burglaries and automobile thefts, in that order.

8) *Intelligence:* Is apt to be of normal, or possibly slightly below normal, intelligence.

9) *Education:* Has had some elementary school education, with less probability of high school training.

10) *Mental Traits:* May show a proneness to emotional instability and various pathological states.

11) *Developmental Background:* Has very likely had a difficult and "poorly controlled" adolescent period.

This profile represents the condensation of an enormous amount of frequently contradictory statistical material. It does, however, provide us with a fairly adequate picture of some of the outstanding characteristics of our criminal population. Let us now examine some of its characteristics further.

The youthfulness of our offenders. Crime is largely an activity of youth. Youths under twenty-one still comprise the larger percentages of prisoners committed to correctional institutions in most of the states. If we examine the data for the past two decades, we still find the highest incidence of commitments for single age-categories are for offenders approximately nineteen years of age. From the standpoint of age-categories, however, the twenty-one to twenty-four-year age-group constantly yields the highest rate of commitments. The rate declines precipitously thereafter for each successive four-year group.[7]

The youthfulness of our offenders can be still more strikingly shown by the annual arrest and fingerprint reports of the Federal Bureau of Investigation. For 1945, for example, 21 per cent of 543,852 persons arrested and fingerprinted were under 21 years of age, as compared with 14.6 per cent in the 21–4 year age classification. During 1947, the volume of arrests for those under 21 years of age fell to 16.1 per cent of all arrests. In 1946 and 1947, for the first time since 1938, the highest frequency for any single age category was 21 years of age. Nevertheless, during the peak year of the war, the age of the highest number of arrests fell to the astounding level of 17 years.

Age of prisoners. Data from the Bureau of the Census on *Prisoners in State and Federal Prisons and Reformatories* show that the highest modal classes of such prisoners are the 21–4 and the 25–9 year old age-

[7] *Uniform Crime Reports,* Vol. XVI, No. 2, pp. 112–18; also, *Uniform Crime Reports,* Vol. XVII, No. 2, 1946; Annual Bulletin, Vol. XVIII, No. 2, 1947.

groups. From 1926 to 1930, the median age for male and female prisoners was 26.5 years and 25 years, respectively. By 1937, the median had changed to 27.9 years for men and 28.9 for women.[8] The war years, however, have once more reversed the trend, so that the present median age hovers close to 26.5 years for men and slightly less for women.

Marital status. The fact of the youthfulness of such a large percentage of our offenders indicates why so many of them are unmarried. In 1937, according to Elliott and Merrill, more than one-half (51.2 per cent) of prison and reformatory inmates were unmarried as compared with 41.9 per cent who were married and 6.9 per cent who were widowed or divorced.[9] Citing a previous study of 1923, they point out that the divorced group as a whole yielded three times as many prisoners as the single group and that widowed males yielded six times as many prisoners as married males.[10] The percentage of unmarried female prisoners was considerably less, the 1937 report indicating that slightly less than 25 per cent fell into the single category. The percentage of divorces among female prisoners was substantially higher than that among male prisoners, suggesting that marital discord is a more potent disorganizing factor for women offenders than for men.

The conditions concerning marital status have altered somewhat during recent years, possibly as a result of the increasing youthfulness of our prison population. In 1943, 52.8 per cent of male prisoners were single as compared with 29.7 per cent of the total number of female inmates.[11] With respect to divorce, the percentages for both male and female offenders are high as compared with the total population. The recent report shows that 5.1 per cent of the men and 8.4 per cent of the women were divorced as compared with an overall rate for the general population in 1940 of approximately 1.5 per cent. When it is realized that divorce rates in general are lower for teen-age categories and for groups in their early twenties, the difference appears even more acute, in view of the large percentage of offenders who fall into these youthful categories. Marriage has been shown by the Gluecks to be a stabilizing factor in some careers which might otherwise have become or continued delinquent.[12] The relatively high percentage of divorced persons among the criminal population suggests the possibility that divorce may be an accompanying causal condition of crime. At the very least, the high rate of divorce may be interpreted

[8] Cf. Elliott and Merrill, *Social Disorganization* (New York, 1941), pp. 162–3.

[9] Ibid., p. 181.

[10] Ibid. Original citation taken from *The Prisoners' Antecedents*, Bureau of the Census (Washington, 1929), p. 23.

[11] *Prisoners in State and Federal Prisons and Reformatories*, 1943, U. S. Bureau of the Census (Washington, 1946), p. 27.

[12] Sheldon and Eleanor T. Glueck. Cf. the case of Armand in *Five Hundred Criminal Careers* (New York, 1930), pp. 63–4.

as a further manifestation of personality disorganization. The significance of divorce in relation to criminality may be seen in E. H. Sutherland's conclusion that divorced persons have the highest proportional commitment rate.[13]

Family background. Among habitual criminals, the percentage of broken homes is quite high. In their study of five hundred and ten male prisoners at the Massachusetts State Reformatory, the Gluecks discovered that 60 per cent came from homes where one or both parents were absent because of death, desertion, or divorce.[14] They revealed further that a very high percentage (60 per cent) of broken homes were caused by the death of either or both parents. While it is perhaps not valid to generalize too widely on the basis of the Gluecks' study it may be said that the frequency of broken homes among this portion of the population is significantly high.

Residence of offenders. In view of the considerably heavier concentration of offenses in urban areas as compared with rural areas, it is significant to note that a large percentage of the offenses occurring in urban areas are committed by non-residents. The mobility of the professional criminal is a natural consequence of the occupational hazards of his profession. The rate of non-residence for criminals appears to be directly proportionate to the increased size of the community.

The Uniform Crime Reports for 1940 show that the greatest frequency of thefts, robbery, and homicide occur in cities of 100,000 or more in population, while rape is most frequent in cities of 250,000 or more. Crimes against the person, such as aggravated assaults, appear to be most frequent in cities of 50,000 to 100,000 in population.[15] The comparative ease and impunity with which laws may be broken in urban areas would tend to foster a higher rate of crime.

Types of offenses. Among the more serious offenses, crimes against property are still by far the most common. Larceny, burglary, automobile theft, and robbery, in the order given, outweigh all other forms of serious malefactions, comprising almost 95 per cent of all major offenses, as compared with approximately 5 per cent covering personal assault. The preponderance of minor offenses over serious offenses can be seen in the fact that for 1946 the rate of traffic and motor vehicle violations was 10,514.5 per 100,000 of the population as contrasted with the rate of

[13] Cf. E. H. Sutherland, *Principles of Criminology* (fourth edition, Chicago, 1947), p. 170. In the significant twenty to twenty-four year age bracket, for example, "divorced males . . . have a rate of commitment 6.2 times as high as single males of the same age, while divorced females of that age have a rate 10.4 times as high as single females and 9.3 times as high as married females of the same age." (Pp. 170–1.)

[14] Glueck and Glueck, *Five Hundred Criminal Careers*, p. 117.

[15] *Uniform Crime Reports for the United States and Its Possessions*, U. S. Department of Justice (Washington, 1940), Vol. X, p. 4.

*Nature of Offenses and Rates per 100,000 of the Population for Serious and Less Serious Offenses.**

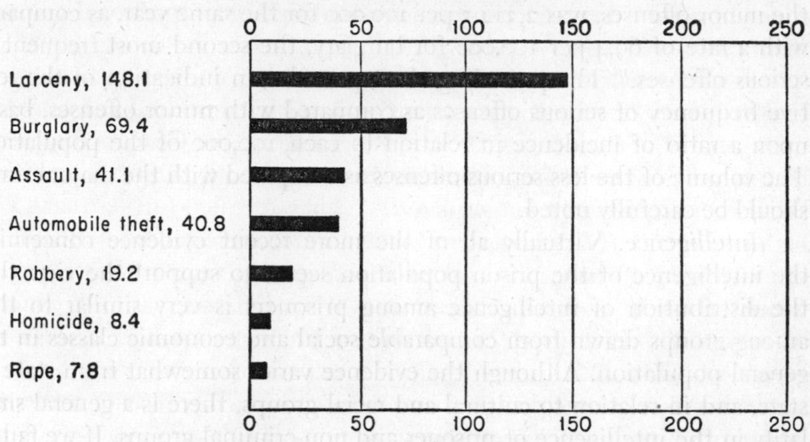

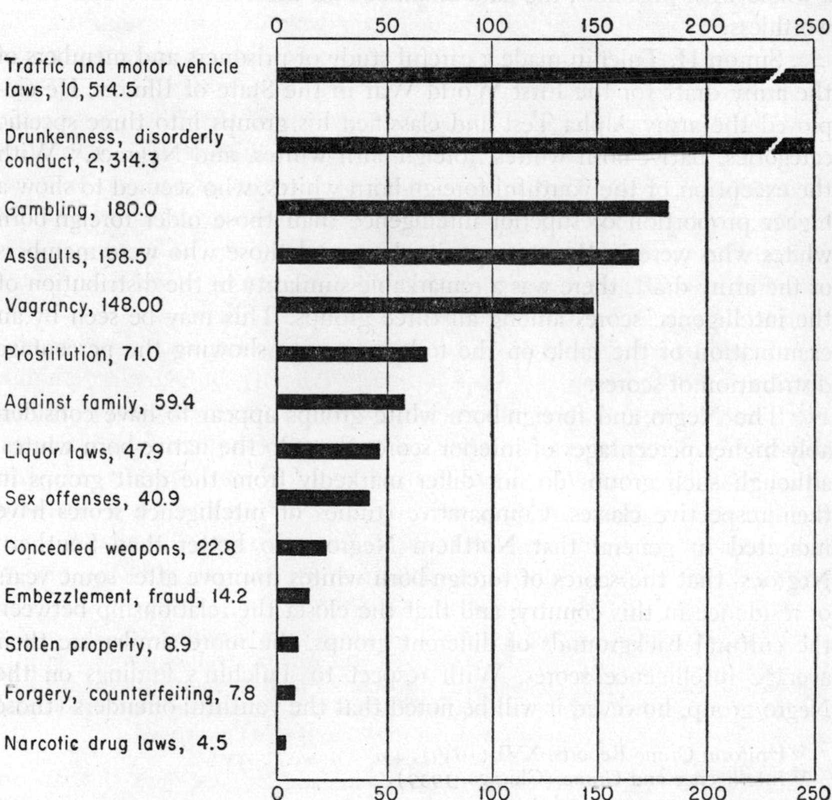

* Cavan, *Criminology*, p. 44, based upon data taken from *Uniform Crime Reports*, XVI (1946), 43. Reprinted by permission of Thomas Y. Crowell Company.

148.1 per 100,000 for larceny, the most common of all serious crimes. The rate of drunkenness and disorderly conduct, the second most frequent of the minor offenses, was 2,314.3 per 100,000 for the same year, as compared with a rate of 69.4 per 100,000 for burglary, the second most frequent of serious offenses.[16] The preceding chart provides an indication of the relative frequency of serious offenses as compared with minor offenses, based upon a ratio of incidence in relation to each 100,000 of the population. The volume of the less serious offenses as compared with the major crimes should be carefully noted.

Intelligence. Virtually all of the more recent evidence concerning the intelligence of the prison population seems to support the view that the distribution of intelligence among prisoners is very similar to that among groups drawn from *comparable* social and economic classes in the general population. Although the evidence varies somewhat from state to state, and in relation to cultural and racial groups, there is a general similarity in the intelligence of prisoner and non-criminal groups. If we fail to make comparisons in this way, and attempt to compare the population as a whole with prisoners, the data obtained and the conclusions derived are worthless.

Simon H. Tulchin made a careful study of prisoners and members of the army draft for the First World War in the State of Illinois. He employed the army Alpha Test and classified his groups into three specific categories, native-born whites, foreign-born whites, and Negroes.[17] With the exception of the youthful foreign-born whites, who seemed to show a higher proportion of superior intelligence than those older foreign-born whites who were in the state penitentiary and those who were members of the army draft, there was a remarkable similarity in the distribution of the intelligence scores among all three groups. This may be seen by an examination of the table on the following page showing the percentage distribution of scores.

The Negro and foreign-born white groups appear to have considerably higher percentages of inferior scores than do the native-born whites, although such groups do not differ markedly from the draft groups in their respective classes. Comparative studies of intelligence scores have indicated in general that Northern Negroes do better than Southern Negroes; that the scores of foreign-born whites improve after some years of residence in this country; and that the closer the relationship between the cultural backgrounds of different groups, the more similar are their average intelligence scores. With respect to Tulchin's findings on the Negro group, however, it will be noted that the youthful offenders (those

[16] *Uniform Crime Reports*, XVI (1946), 43.

[17] *Intelligence and Crime* (Chicago, 1939).

Comparison of Scores on the Army Alpha Intelligence Tests for Penitentiary and Reformatory Inmates, and Members of the Draft for the First World War, for Illinois *

	Inferior Scores 0–25	*Average Scores 25–104*	*Superior Scores 105–212*	*Number of Cases*
Native-born whites				
Illinois State Penitentiary	9.2	73.9	16.9	3,199
Illinois State Reformatory	9.5	75.2	15.3	3,646
Illinois Army Draft	10.3	73.6	16.1	2,102
Foreign-born whites				
Illinois State Penitentiary	44.6	47.6	7.8	1,011
Illinois State Reformatory	25.3	64.6	10.1	336
Illinois Army Draft	44.2	50.3	5.5	728
Negroes				
Illinois State Penitentiary	41.6	56.2	2.2	1,302
Illinois State Reformatory	36.8	59.9	3.3	766
Illinois Army Draft	43.1	53.1	3.8	1,139

* *Intelligence and Crime*, pp. 19 ff. (Period covered was from 1920–6.)

in the reformatory group) had a higher average of intelligence than the older members in thc penitentiary and draft groups. This may be accounted for in part by the fact that youthful offenders may have had more schooling in the North than the older Negro groups.

Murchison's data, covering extended comparative studies of intelligence scores of prisoners and non-prisoners in several states, are largely in agreement with these findings.[18] He has shown that in some states the intelligence scores for prisoners have been higher than for comparable cultural groups among drafted army men, while in other states average prison scores were much the same or somewhat lower. We should be aware of the fact that such selected studies do not always take into account the large mass of minor and specialized offenders, such as the notably feebleminded and mentally deficient, or those arrested for habitual drunkenness, vagrancy, and prostitution. The intelligence scores of these persons would very likely alter the results indicated by Tulchin and Murchison. On the other hand, if we include in the criminal population the increasingly large number of white-collar criminals, a large percentage of whom manage to evade detection, the total results again might conceivably be quite different from those presented in the better organized comparative studies.

Our conclusion (after discounting the special considerations involved in the types of intelligence and mental defects reprcsented by the random mass of derelicts, minor offenders, and special groups like the white-collar criminal) is that the habitual and professional offenders, by and large,

[18] Carl Murchison, *Criminal Intelligence* (Worcester, 1926).

tend to reveal the same distribution of intelligence as that found in the general public.

Education. As we might expect on the basis of the distribution of intelligence and the nature of the offenses committed, a great mass of prisoners have not proceeded beyond the elementary grades while relatively small percentages have had the benefits of high school or college training. The volume of illiteracy is quite great. Hooton's well known anthropological study, covering almost 12 per cent of the total prison population, revealed that 10.16 per cent might be classified as illiterate, as compared with an illiteracy rate of about 7 per cent for the entire population.[19] Earlier studies show that about two-thirds of this country's prisoners had had some elementary school training, while about 15 per cent attended high school and slightly more than 3 per cent, college.[20]

The character of the education received by the prisoner before detention has little bearing upon the nature of his offense, except in the case of certain types of specialized crime, such as embezzling and possibly fraud, where a certain degree of education might be helpful in executing the crime. In the case of embezzlement, 22.5 per cent of those convicted had received some college training, and in the case of fraud, 16.6 per cent.

Mental traits. Although it is extremely difficult to classify properly abnormal emotional states, the numerous studies that have been made suggest strongly that criminals as a group have a considerably higher percentage of abnormalities than do comparable groups in the population. However, as Professor Cantor has stated: "The differences in the results of psychiatric investigators, as in the case of intelligence testers, is due, in part, to the different standards employed as an index of mental abnormality as well as the different classifications employed. Such terms as 'abnormality,' 'psychopathic personality,' 'psychoneurotic,' and 'psychotic' are loosely defined. They mean different things to different investigators."[21] Moreover, differences in standards of evaluation may result in sizable differences in the claimed percentages of emotional deviation existing in different prison populations.[22] Nevertheless, the majority of studies suggest that high proportions of emotional disturbance exist among prisoners. Dr. Bernard Glueck's study at Sing Sing Prison in 1916 classified 608

[19] E. A. Hooton, *The American Criminal* (Cambridge, 1939), Vol. IX, p. 71.

[20] *The Prisoners' Antecedents* (U. S. Bureau of the Census, Washington, 1929), p. 21.

[21] Nathaniel F. Cantor, *Crime, Criminals, and Criminal Justice* (New York, 1932), p. 48.

[22] In a study made by Thompson (*Mental Hygiene*, XXII, 1936, 529), for example, as Professor Cantor points out, he uses an age eleven standard as his basis for the classification of mental defectives, as compared with Dr. Bernard Glueck's standard of age twelve in the study of Sing Sing inmates. This difference of one year eliminates 58 per cent of those listed by Glueck as defective.

admissions of which 12 per cent were listed as mentally diseased and 19 per cent as constitutionally inferior. An additional 28 per cent were listed as mentally deficient.[23] The National Committe for Mental Hygiene, in its summarization of findings for different areas of the United States, reported that 70.6 per cent of 3,451 Texas prisoners, 69 per cent of 781 New York City juvenile court cases, and 46 per cent of 1,000 Boston municipal court cases were found to be abnormal.[24] However, a later study by the Psychiatric Clinic of the Court of General Sessions in New York City for the years 1932–5 does not support these findings. In this report, only 1.5 per cent of those examined were found to be psychotic and only 2.4 per cent defective.[25]

Even if the authenticity of some of these data is questionable because of the failure to arrive at precise diagnoses of those who were examined, the general impression of most investigators is that large numbers of criminals are emotionally unstable. On the basis of more recent and detailed clinical tests, it appears likely that this impression may be validated. Although, as Cantor stipulated, the general conclusion testifying to the high rate of emotional instability among prisoners "is far from being 100 per cent reliable . . . neither is it altogether speculative, nor mere opinion and without any significance." [26] Anyone who has studied and spent time with delinquents and adult offenders cannot help detecting their emotional tension.

Developmental background. Fingerprint records for 1945 on file with the Identification Division of the Federal Bureau of Investigation show that 55.2 per cent of the males and 34 per cent of the females had prior records before their apprehension.[27] As has already been noted in our discussion of juvenile offenders, the records clearly indicate the great repetition of offenses characteristic of youthful offenders. Of the 1,000 juvenile delinquents studied by the Gluecks, 63.5 per cent had been arrested one or more times prior to the study.[28] These official records do not include the unofficial contacts with the law and offenses for which the individual has not been apprehended; they exceed by far the number of official arrests. Such records suggest the difficulties in adjustment and the critical situations in the backgrounds of these offenders.

[23] *First Annual Report of the Psychiatric Clinic in Collaboration with Sing Sing Prison, for the Nine Months Ending April 30, 1917,* National Committee for Mental Hygiene, 1917; see also, "A Study of 608 Admissions to Sing Sing Prison," *Mental Hygiene* (Jan. 1918), 92 ff.

[24] "Mental Hygiene and Delinquency," *Mental Hygiene,* Bulletin No. I, 1925, No. 3.

[25] Thompson, "Some New Aspects of the Psychiatric Approach to Crime," *Mental Hygiene,* XXII (1936), 529.

[26] Cantor, *Crime, Criminals and Criminal Justice,* p. 49.

[27] *Uniform Crime Reports,* XVI (No. 2), pp. 112–18.

[28] Glueck and Glueck, *One Thousand Juvenile Delinquents,* pp. 96–7.

(6) THE PROFESSIONAL CRIMINAL AS A SOCIAL TYPE

Despite the individual differences among adult criminals, there is a basic framework, with its own rationale, that identifies criminal behavior in much the same way as occupations and family statuses identify middle-class men and women with conventional middle-class culture. This framework consists of broad behavioral principles of a social nature (what Freud might have called the criminal's "superego"), within which the criminal's life operates and in relation to which it takes on value and meaning. What the public rarely realizes is that the professional criminal has a *modus operandi* and a *modus vivendi* of his own, sanctioned and supported by the underworld society which is his substitute for conventional and normal associations. The criminal is not devoid of ethics and loyalties, nor is he intrinsically anti-social. Social patterning exists for the criminal as it does for the public at large, with the difference that the criminal associates himself with a special world that has its own loyalties, values, ethics, sacrifices, and inhibitions.

According to Tannenbaum, the fundamental framework within which the criminal operates is distinguished by the following five characteristics: (1) the logic of crime, (2) the "psychosis" of the warrior, (3) professional insight, (4) pride and confidence in his associations and activities, and (5) the view of life as a "racket." [29]

The criminal's frame of reference: his rationale. All of us seek justification for our activities on the basis of socially acceptable rationalizations. The criminal employs rationalizations too, geared to the special values of "normalcy" acceptable to the criminal world. They constitute the *rationale* of his existence, the "ideological" frame of reference which satisfies his criminal purposes and needs. To the criminal, granting his own assumptions, distorted as they may appear from our standpoint, his own activities appear meaningful and logical. The "logic" of this existence is seen in the types of values and prestige considerations that he venerates. Thus, he recognizes class distinctions and differences in caste as we do. Prison life is marked by class barriers, and even caste distinctions, which frequently are more extreme than those we recognize on the outside. "Big shots" consort with their own kind, the petty sneak thief finds his own level, the fraudulent "bucket shop" manipulator and the embezzler may meet upon common ground, while all regard with the same undisguised contempt the malefactor on the lowest rung of the ladder, the sexual offender and rapist. An ex-convict has declared that "there is no more caste in the heart of India than in an American penitentiary."

As part of the "logic of crime," considerable respect is shown towards the property rights of other offenders. In fact, in the desperate drive to-

[29] Frank Tannenbaum, *Crime and the Community* (New York, 1938), pp. 174–94.

ward security and in the need to safeguard himself in his constant war against society, the criminal frequently develops a respectful attitude toward the property rights of his associates which may have more integrity than the attitudes of the non-criminal population. Since stolen goods must be handled through his own agents, in a world where legal protection is not afforded, a criminal's bond may actually be as good as his word inasmuch as no security exists other than that provided by his reliance upon his companions in crime. The venerable ex-burglar, who writes under the pseudonym of Jack Black, states:

> Respect for property in the underworld is as deep as it is in the upperworld. The fact that it is upperworld property which is involved makes no difference, for when property is transferred from the upperworld to the underworld, it becomes sacred again.
>
> The burglar who shoots his partner for holding out a lady's watch goes up in the social scale of the underworld. Like the clubman who perjures himself to save a lady's reputation, he has done the right thing in the sight of his fellows. Each is a gentleman according to the code.[30]

The "logic of crime" presupposes its own code of justice, and criminals have long been known for the maintenance of their own "criminal code." The antiquity of phases of this code are astounding. Not only have certain methods of theft, burglary, and robbery been long known to criminals, dating back to the Roman World and passed on to their European successors over the centuries, but the rationalizations, justifications, and punitive ethics have likewise been preserved through the centuries. The close-knit bonds of secrecy and silence, and the willingness to protect their own members at considerable sacrifice to self, expressed in the virtriolic contempt toward the "stoolie" or "stool pigeon," are well known to law enforcement officials. Indeed, police departments have on occasion passively accepted the administration of underworld justice as an instrument whereby their own burdens might be lessened. An instance of this is the laissez-faire policy followed in the handling of many gang murders in Chicago during the prohibition era of the Capone-Torrio Gang. Such justice can be swift and summary, and may even be promoted through its own organized social instruments, as in the case of the notorious Murder, Incorporated of a scant decade ago. Thus, the *New York Times* of December 9, 1930, describes the killing of Nick Luciano, a petty racketeer, who failed in his "ethical" obligations to his associates:

[30] Cited from Frank Tannenbaum, *Crime and the Community*, quoting from Jack Black, "A Burglar Looks at Laws and Codes," *Harper's Magazine*, CLX (Feb., 1930), 306.

> Nick Luciano was shot to death at four o'clock yesterday morning in Pete LaBella's grimy restaurant at 165 Elizabeth Street. The men who had waited patiently for seven years to "get" Luciano made a thorough job of it. They put more than twenty bullets into him.
>
> Nick Luciano was the youth who, seven years ago, turned State's evidence against his five accomplices in the West End bank robbery in Brooklyn, in which two bank messengers were shot dead. When the State was finished, John Farina, Joe Diamond and Morris Diamond had died in the electric chair, Anthony Pantano was sent to state's prison for life and George Desaro was doomed to spend the remainder of his days in solitary in a dungeon in Italy.
>
> From that time Nick—they called him "Cheeks," because of a long white scar that spread from the right side of his neck to his face—was marked, and he knew it.

Honor, truth, loyalty, and justice are relative, and the criminal well understands the nature of their relative significance in his own life.

Argot. The language behavior of criminals indicates the social logic of their existence and the close-knit order of certain phases of their society. The development of argots and specialized vernacular usages not only affords the sociologist an insight into the mental functioning of groups, but also indicates the degree to which they have developed structures and standards of their own. This applies to many other deviant groups besides criminals. The degree of elaboration of such language forms and their divergence from the main usages of the society, by virtue of specialized allusions, inflections, and suggestive devices, is indicative of the deviation of such groups from the larger society. Argots frequently illustrate the presence of minor "societies" within a society. Thus, anthropologists have shown that among certain Polynesian groups dialects and special verbal usages distinguish various class and caste groups, each existing within a social world of its own as well as within the total social order.[31] Among certain African tribes, the women maintain a separate dialect from the men, enabling them to sustain a peculiar cultural existence of their own. Within our own society, language barriers exist not only among the various foreign language groups of the country, but among other segments of society who, partly through their own peculiar methods of communication, maintain a restricted culture of their own. Paul G.

[31] As among the Polynesian Tonga, for example, where class distinctions are excessively developed. Cf. E. W. Gifford, "Tongan Society," Bernice P. Bishop Museum, Bulletin No. 61, pp. 120–1. Similar distinctions are found among the Dobu (cf. R. F. Fortune, *Sorcerers of Dobu*, New York, pp. 13–14), and among the Javanese, where as many as five vocabularies are employed in connection with the system of social ranking (cf. R. Kennedy, *The Ethnology of the Greater Sunda Islands*, pp. 706–08). For a good summary of such language behavior differentials, see W. I. Thomas, *Primitive Behavior* (New York, 1937), pp. 81–7.

Cressey has alluded to such "private worlds" in his reference to taxi-dance hall jargon, which serves to exclude the outsider.[32]

An illustration of the specialized jargon of the criminal may be found in the following statement:

> I think I'll go out on a whiz in the hole this afternoon and if I get myself a good frame I'll get in a sting or two. It would help some if I had a good stall or fanner, but you can't have everything. Perhaps I will get a lush, or find a moll to buzz.
>
> (*Translation:* I think I'll go out on a pickpocket job in the subway this afternoon, and if I get myself a good spot, I'll be able to pick a pocket or two. It would help some if I had a good man to distract my victim or one to locate his wallet for me, but you can't have everything. Perhaps I'll find a sleeping person or a drunk to work on, or be able to find a woman whose purse I can pick.)

The following is a limited glossary of terms used by pickpockets.

whiz	a pickpocket job
to stall	to distract the victim or jostle him
moll buzzer	a female pickpocket
moll buzzing	stealing from a woman
lush	a sleeping person or drunk
dip	a pickpocket
softie	a victim for a pickpocket
stagger man	one who feigns drunkenness to distract softie
fanner	one who locates wallet for a pickpocket
poke, oakus, leather	a wallet
come-down	a victim who grasps the pickpocket's hand
breech-bridge	a side pocket
frame	an ideal spot for picking a pocket
to sting	to pick a pocket
duke	hand
scratch	loose bills
shorts	trolleys or busses
reefing	bringing up pocket lining with fingers
fronting	blocking victim's passage
fuzz	a pickpocket detective
rumble	thief noticed by victim; fear of apprehension or detection
sneeze	an arrest
hole	a subway
Fagin	one who trains others to be pickpockets

[32] *The Taxi-Dance Hall* (Chicago, 1932).

The criminal's "psychosis." Since the criminal is always at war with society, he feels he has ample reason to fear it. This fear takes the form of intense feelings of distrust, hostility, and suspicion towards anyone who is not associated with him in the world of his nefarious enterprises. As Tannenbaum puts it, in his quotation from an unpublished prison record, "The criminal hates society because he fears it." [33] This fear is translated into a malignant distrust even of those from whom he might expect the greatest show of loyalty—his wife, his sweetheart, or his friend. Conversely, his greatest loyalty and trust is placed in those who are associated with him in his life of crime, and particularly in those on whom he is forced to depend in carrying out his unlawful operations. The intense hatred he frequently feels toward society is concentrated in the direction of those agents who symbolize for him the punitive measures of conventional society. One of the earliest attitudes inculcated by the gang is that of hatred towards the police and the agents of the law.

> From the time I started to hang around with the older guys in the neighborhood, I learned to look at the police as my sworn enemies. All the guys in the bunch looked at them that way. . . . [The] older guys knew all about the police, their ways, the third degree, and how to elude the police.
>
> . . . So the police and the criminal are on two sides of the fence. If one doesn't get the other, the other will get him. The criminal is to be caught and the police are to be avoided, escaped from, or bought off. It's natural for enmity to grow up between them. I knew from the time I was young not to trust the police, but to keep out of his clutches. That's the way all the guys in the bunch felt.[34]

Conspicuous in this attitude is the deep-dyed cynicism and skepticism which the hardened criminal experiences. This is part of the configuration of hostile attitudes which has actually given the criminal a systematized point of reference around which his vitriolic hatreds of normal society may converge.

Professional insight. The criminal's activity may be divided into three phases: (1) the planning of criminal acts; (2) the performance of these acts and the related activities that such performance involves, such as the disposal of stolen property; and (3) the evasion of detection and prosecution. This last is accomplished by various procedures, ranging from secreting himself from normal society to engaging legal protection. Since all of these activities are carried on under the general aura of fear and hostility which surrounds the criminal's life, the activities in which he

[33] Tannenbaum, *Crime and the Community*, p. 179.

[34] C. R. Shaw and H. D. McKay, "Social Factors in Juvenile Delinquency," *National Commission on Law Observance and Enforcement*, Washington, II (1931), 242, 243.

engages become emotionally heightened and give added point to his professional competence and success. Just as in conventional life the "long arm of the job" is always with us, as the Lynds have put it, so for the criminal this "occupational complex" is a never-ending part of his daily life. Unlike the normal citizen, the criminal can never escape the consequences of his job. So habituated does he become to the continual planning, connivance, and execution of the activities in which he engages, that his awareness of professional problems is extremely high. The world about him is viewed in terms of its vulnerability to his predatory leanings and the possibilities of escape it affords. Jack Black puts it very clearly when he says: "I thought in terms of theft. Houses were built to be robbed, citizens were to be robbed. . . . That was the atmosphere I breathed." [35]

Professional skill and competence. Success in many criminal occupations requires not only daring but a considerable degree of occupational skill. The pride that the criminal experiences is for work well done and for the ability to live up to the code of his confederates. The skill of the professional thief requires a certain amount of individual dexterity together with the ability to co-ordinate his activities with others, as in the common teams of two and three pickpockets. A "blue-print of operations," or "job analysis sheet," for successful team operation has been described by one young adept as follows:

> If the victim hasn't a pocketbook in his pants pocket or a roll of money, whenever the occasion may be, if it is on a train or at a convention, and a man looks prosperous enough, you would know that he had money some place. So it is then that they try what is known as an "insider," meaning that the man has his wallet in his inside coat pocket. This work, to take a "poke" from the inside pocket is altogether different. The "wire" (the actual pickpocket) has to be facing the victim. . . . The "stall" is directly behind the "mark" in the position otherwise occupied by the "wire." The "duke" man is standing behind the "wire," bracing him with his body, if it is on a subway or a car or train, and a newspaper or coat shades his hand while working. He can unbutton three buttons on a "mark's" coat and reach in and take a man's pocketbook from inside his coat or even vest. The same thing goes for a stud or diamond pin. I myself and several others that I have talked to find an "insider" as easy, if not easier, than a "prat poke" [i.e., wallet in rear trousers pocket] if the man will stand for a "throw." . . .
>
> Among pickpockets they always stay spread out, no matter where you may be. On a train, you stand by yourself, never "connecting."

[35] Jack Black, *You Can't Win* (New York, 1926), p. 241.

Working in the city, you never "connect," never stand talking to each other. While standing on a corner waiting for a street car to pull up, one of the mob sees a "dick." Then we have what is known as a "works office." He reaches up and pulls with his right hand on the lapel of his coat—gets one of his companion's eyes, and then does this. That signifies that there is "heat." The other fellow passes that to the third, and so on, and when the car pulls up, you get on that "natural"— that is, you don't work.[36]

Many criminal operations have become highly specialized and technical. Various kinds of confidence frauds require careful planning by members of a criminal group in laying the basis for plausible misrepresentation. Execution of these frauds requires intimate knowledge of certain forms of business activity. Success in these operations involves an extreme nicety of timing.

The professional criminal takes pride not only in his professional competence but in the exploits and virtues which his sub-culture extols. He becomes a "man of distinction," as well as a "man of character," by his ability to withstand successfully the police, by his ability to dupe his enemies and "cheat the law," and by the tenacity and courage he displays in safeguarding the interests of his associates. The sanctuary afforded by his own group is all the more desirable and heartwarming because it is the only sanctuary he knows. Continually harassed by the fear of detection, the pleasures he derives from following the code is all the more keen because it is so closely related to his own preservation and safety. Thus, homage and tribute are frequently lavished upon the individual who can live up to the rules of the game. The loyalty to his associates and his associates' loyalty to him become the criminal's greatest security. John Landesco, in his investigation of crime in Chicago, describes the adulation and loyalty accorded a young gangster who was seriously wounded in the course of an exchange of gunfire with the police:

> At the hospital he received the best medical attention. . . . The boy endured the treatment with great patience and (his) arm was saved from amputation finally. During the hospitalization period, which extended over months, he had a constant flow of visitors with gifts of fruit and cigarettes. . . . (He) had three or four different radio sets in his room. They arranged to avoid taking him to the House of Correction hospital by having deputy sheriffs on alternating watches, whose salary they paid to the county. With an especially constructed frame supporting the arm, he was taken to a court and

[36] Shaw and McKay, "Social Factors in Juvenile Delinquency," p. 238; see also E. H. Sutherland, *The Professional Thief* (Chicago, 1937).

> bail bond was set at over twenty thousand dollars. The bail bond was arranged in cash. The hours during hospitalization were passed in fleet conversation about "jobs" and "raps" and gossip about gang friends. As soon as he became a little better, the boys would bring up his girl friends who were admirers of the young gangster.[37]

The attitudes towards disloyalty among criminals are at least as well patterned as the attitudes towards loyalty. The hatred felt by criminals for the informer or "rat" is comparable to our own hatred of traitors during times of war. A confessed felon Danny Ahearn tells us in his own account: "A rat deserves to be dead. He deserves to be in the dirt, buried face down, so if he ever comes to life again he will go deeper and deeper." [38]

Life as a racket. Daniel Crawford, in an early anthropological prospectus, spoke of the difficulty of "thinking black," that is, identifying ourselves with the attitudes and values of different cultural groups. Warped by the distorted circumstances of his living, the professional criminal has great difficulty believing in the honesty of the average citizen and the average public official. The basic tenet in his philosophy is that "everybody has his price." Although this is an extreme view, there is much in our society that has given the criminal a basis for this conviction. American life in the past has frequently been rife with corruption, as Lincoln Steffens has shown in his classic *Shame of the Cities*. It is a fact that many of the activities in which the criminal engages may be pursued successfully only with the connivance of the police. In the celebrated report of the Wickersham Commission on law observance and enforcement, the following observation was made:

> The investigators were repeatedly told—not by sensation mongers but by observers of high position and ability, long experience and unquestioned disinterestedness—that the courts know that some of the prosecutors are crooked, and the prosecutors know that some of the courts are crooked, and the police are equally well informed as to them.[39]

(7) THE RACKET AS A FORM OF ORGANIZED AMERICAN CRIME

Cultures may reveal themselves in the nature of the lawlessness and non-conforming behavior they condemn. Civilized societies appear to breed their own types of crime and criminals. Thus, the racket is a pecul-

[37] John Landesco, *Organized Crime in Chicago* (Illinois Crime Survey, Chicago, 1929), pp. 1055–6.

[38] Danny Ahearn, *How to Commit a Murder* (New York, 1930), p. 28.

[39] Z. Chafee, W. H. Pollak, and C. S. Stern, *Report on Lawlessness in Law Enforcement* (National Commission on Law Observance and Law Enforcement, Washington, No. 11, 1931), pp. 86–7.

iarly American institution, while the *apache* is as distinctive of Paris as is the *nervi* of the Marseilles dock areas. Black market operations have thrived particularly in post-war Europe where the scarcity of food has been severe.

During this century, organized crime in the United States has largely taken the form of the racket. The racket is organized extortion from either legitimate or illegitimate enterprises. It may assume all or any one of three forms. (1) Under the threat of damage to person and property, shopkeepers, small merchants, and business men are ordered to pay regularly sums of money for their "protection." (2) Merchants operating in the marginal areas of economic activity where competition is extreme and unscrupulous are compelled to join an organization which fixes prices. The organization takes a percentage of profits for its service, which may extend to "protection" of the character discussed in (1). (3) Illicit activities, such as gambling, bootlegging, black market operations, and prostitution may be organized into syndicates, operated on a regular business or quasi-business basis, whenever public demand is sufficient. Rackets of the third category particularly make themselves felt in conventional society. An indication of the extensiveness of such operations may be seen in the recent disclosures of the California Commission on Organized Crime concerning slot and gambling machines. Their yearly intake, according to the report of March, 1949, attained a total of approximately $2,000,000,000.

What are the conditions in American life that have fostered the racket? We may mention first the cultural diversity of this country which has led to the sanctioning of operations which the law disallows, as in the case of bootlegging and gambling. Further, the intense competition in business life, particularly as manifested in certain phases of retail trade in our large cities, has led to the development of price-fixing policies similar to those of big business. The character of the trades in which the racket flourishes is frequently an indication of depressed and unscrupulously competitive conditions. The New York City Police Department Report of 1931 stated that rackets existed in the flower, syrup, soda, and millinery trades. Following the pattern of legitimate monopolistic control, rackets frequently move from area to area and city to city in order to broaden the scope of their operations.

(8) WHITE-COLLAR CRIMINALITY: A NEW DIMENSION

Although we ordinarily regard crime as an activity of underworld elements, we are becoming increasingly aware of the extent of criminal activities among "respectable" groups of the population. The general increase of illegal activity among the business and professional classes has been graphically portrayed by the criminologist, E. H. Sutherland.[40] For the year 1943, Barnes and Teeters estimate that the total cost of white-collar crime to the American people was approximately $40,000,000,000. This sum may be compared with the toll of $400,000,000 exacted in the same year by the commonplace and readily recognized crimes of robbery, burglary, and thievery.[41] The operations in which such personages as Ivar Krueger, Richard F. Whitney, Philip Musica, Albert B. Fall, and Harry F. Sinclair have figured are vast as compared with the minor operations of the ordinary criminal. Thus, Sutherland speaks of the embezzlement by an executive of a chain grocery store which in one year involved a loss of $600,000. This is six times as great as the total amount of the losses incurred through five hundred thefts from the same chain during the same period. He also makes note of the fact that although public enemies one to six managed to obtain $130,000 by robbery and burglary in 1938, Ivar Krueger's peculations reached the vast sum of $250,000,000, a sum two thousand times as great.

While flourishing particularly in the area of big business, white-collar criminality occurs frequently in the various professions. Even the medical profession, long recognized as probably the most ethical of all modern professions, is far from exempt. Aside from illegal operations and abortions, such practices as fee-splitting, recommendation of unnecessary treatment, connivance for the sale of certain pharmaceuticals, dubious service as consultants and technical experts, and the protection of professional colleagues by refusal to divulge information, are not uncommon. In February 1948, the Massachusetts Courts imposed damages of $15,000 upon two physicians for negligence in a case resulting in death. The charge was made by the husband of the deceased that the physicians involved supported each other's false diagnosis.[42]

Opportunities for evasion of the law are especially well known to members of the legal profession, who frequently avail themselves of this special knowledge.[43] In 1946 a controversy developed over the right of a Justice of the Federal Supreme Court to sit in a case in which his former law partner was presenting the brief. United States Senators in 1946 were

[40] "White Collar Criminality," *American Sociological Review*, V (Feb., 1940), 1–12; see also, Edwin H. Sutherland, *Principles of Criminology* (New York, 1947, 4th ed.), pp. 36–43, 175–6, 182–3, 587–8, and his *White Collar Crime* (New York, 1949).

[41] H. E. Barnes and N. K. Teeters, *New Horizons in Criminology* (New York, 1943).

[42] This decision in the case of *Rines vs. Beth Israel Hospital* has been set aside and is slated for a rehearing before the Massachusetts Supreme Court. See *Time Magazine*, March 8, 1948, p. 89.

[43] The implications of this point have been ably presented by R. M. MacIver in his *Society: A Textbook of Sociology* (New York, 1937), where he considers the law from the standpoint of its special institutional character.

charged with utilizing their private information gained in committee hearings on cotton production to speculate in the cotton futures market.

The recent war brought to light a spate of illegal evasions of the wartime restrictions on essential items. Even under the strongest of patriotic appeals, many American business men and consumers evaded the law in procuring and distributing basic and scarce items. The Office of Price Administration, while carefully stipulating the costs to be charged for various products, was unable to control the innumerable devious procedures for changing prices. Thus, in order to obtain certain materials, heavy charges were added for the "cost of packaging," which raised the total price far in excess of what was authorized. In order to purchase an automobile during the period of shortage, the consumer was obliged to accept numerous accessories, whether he wanted them or not, for which exorbitant prices were charged. Thus, the letter of the law was dubiously maintained, while the spirit was absolutely destroyed.[44]

Our general causal hypothesis concerning criminality and other forms of deviational behavior helps to explain the development of white-collar crime. This hypothesis is in general agreement with the explanation of "differential association" employed by E. H. Sutherland.[45] According to Sutherland, there tends to be a systematic inculcation of certain attitudes and behavior patterns in relation to specific groups afforded by the culturally diverse opportunities extant in American culture. Criminal behavior is learned behavior, according to Sutherland, the same as any other form of behavior. This behavior, learned in interaction with other persons within intimate personal groups, takes criminal patterns because they have outweighed anti-criminal patterns.[46]

White-collar offenses may be encouraged through the incorporation of certain cultural values and attitudes in the individual's life-pattern, abetted by the character of his social participation in certain groups where such practices take place. Our own causal principles suggest that the individual's needs arise in relation to certain groups with which he identifies himself. In relation to the compelling dictates of the needs of his psychogenetic pattern, he will embrace certain activities which in part may contain elements of such illicit behavior. The absorption of such elements within his personality in the form of attitudes and wishes may culminate in the eventual practice of illegal activities, white collar or otherwise. Thus, the dishonest fee-splitting physician does not necessarily begin by being dishonest. He may accept the practice of calling in outside consultation as a legitimate part of his professional privileges which, in time, may degenerate into an outright practice of fee-splitting itself.

[44] Cf. Marshall Clinard, "Criminological Theories of Violations of Wartime Regulations," *American Sociological Review*, XI (June, 1946), 258–70.

[45] Edwin H. Sutherland, *Principles of Criminology* (4th ed.), pp. 6–8.

[46] Ibid., p. 6.

(9) THE LEGAL PROCESS AND CRIME

Specificity of the legal process. The vast institutional legal structure which we have developed in respect to crime is an interesting reflection upon American culture. Although a crime does not become such until it is specifically defined by the legal statutes as an abridgement of the social mores, the law is extremely specific about both the *nature* of the offense committed and the *type of punishment* that is meted out. We may compare a primitive community with a modern community in this respect by observing the operation of institutional behavior in regard to an act of stealing. Among certain primitives, such as the Tshagga in Africa, such behavior is so unusual that the community rarely knows what action should take place. If, however, a violation occurs among certain primitive peoples, the ambiguity of the *mos* or the folkway makes it difficult to establish whether the offense has *actually* been committed, precisely *who* is guilty, and what form of redress, if any, shall be considered sufficient. The eventual punishment, if it occurs at all, may depend upon the social temper of the moment, the prestige of the individuals involved, and the changing attitude about the putative offense. Compare such tenuousness in operation with an episode of housebreaking in a modern community.

An individual loiters across the street from a certain household. He may or may not be intent upon breaking into the building he is examining. Thus far, there is no basis for legal prosecution. Eventually, he crosses the street and puts his foot upon the lawn. The moment he puts his foot deliberately upon the lawn, he is liable to prosecution on the minor charge of trespassing, for which the penalty may be negligible. However, he draws close to the building and peers through the window. This, too, may be construed as a misdemeanor, a slight offense, with the added circumstance that he may be charged with "suspicion of felonious behavior." During the next few minutes, he opens the window and puts one leg across the window sill. Within a matter of seconds, in its specificity, the law may now define such action as "breaking or entering," i.e., housebreaking with an attempt to commit burglary. He enters the building, rendering himself more liable to the full charge of housebreaking, and picks up an object or a number of objects within the building. By the addition of a few more moments in time, he has committed an act of burglary, in addition to the previous succession of offenses of trespassing and housebreaking. In passing through the door, he is suddenly accosted by the householder, and either accidentally or deliberately, jostles him so that the householder falls down. He has now added to his offenses by commission of the serious felony of assault. In the event that he has been successful in his marauding and is found an hour later on the

Main Street with the stolen property under his arm, he may claim that he was unaware of its source and has simply been holding it for some unidentified stranger. In the event that the actual episode of his stealing may not be proven, he may simply be charged with a lesser offense of being the recipient or being in custody of stolen property.

The important aspect of this entire account is that the law is so *specific* that the *same individual*, apprehended at different intervals during this entire process, must be charged with specific events *for each one of which the punishment varies according to the law.*

The criminal act as defined by law. A criminal act consists of two parts: (1) the *intent*, or intention, to commit a certain offense; and (2) the *actual* event or occurrence of the act itself. Both phases must be proven in order to indicate the commission of an actual criminal occurrence. It is not enough to have committed the misdeed, the courts must be convinced that there was a bona fide intention to commit it, as well. A person is just as dead whether he is killed by the accidental dropping of a weight out of a tall building or whether an individual has wilfully crushed his skull with a paper weight. The first occurrence is not a crime, however, while the latter is. In addition to proving intent, offenses against the law are broadly classified into *misdemeanors* and *felonies*. Misdemeanors are the relatively minor offenses, punishable by imprisonment in a local jail for a period not exceeding one year, by fine, or both. Vagrancy, disorderly conduct, public loitering and begging, and a whole host of other such minor offenses, may fit into this category. Felonies constitute the more serious offenses of burglary, robbery, theft, personal assault, arson, and rape, which are punishable by imprisonment in a state or federal penitentiary for a period in excess of one year.

The laws of the several states vary widely in their definition of misdemeanors and felonies. An act constituting a misdemeanor in one state may constitute a felony in another, and vice versa. Moreover, a new category has arisen during the past few decades, especially since the lawlessness of the 1920's, known as the *technical felonies*. Many states, in their efforts to curb recidivism, or repetition of offenses, and the continual lawlessness of certain known offenders, have passed laws which make the repetition of certain offenses "technical felonies," requiring the courts in such cases to impose arbitrarily high sentences or life sentences. In this connection, the entire problem of recidivism must be reviewed.

The definition of a technical felony varies in different states. In general, there are technical felonies which might be considered acts of *specific recidivism* and others which might be termed *general* recidivism. Thus, in some states, technical felonies may not occur unless an individual has been convicted for the *same kind of offense* a certain number of times, usually three times. *General recidivism* in respect to technical felonies refers to the repetition of any three felonies, not necessarily the same offenses. In general, present court jurisdictions in the United States, dependent upon separate state enactments, may recognize *technical felonies* of different kinds, involving different punishments (mandatory or otherwise) for the following types of repeated offenses: (1) three convictions for the same type of felony, establishing a mandatory life sentence in certain states; (2) three convictions for any type of major felony; and (3) three or more convictions for specific misdemeanors. The last eventuality has been conceived as a basis for deterring and possibly correcting certain habitual minor offenders, such as drunkards and certain derelicts, who throng our lower courts.

The general reaction by the courts to the attempts to curb crime by means of "technical felonies" has been one of sustained opposition. This opposition has usually been more acute in those cases where the imposition of mandatory sentences has been required of the judge, giving him little or no discretionary powers. The reasons for the opposition are largely threefold: (1) It removes from the judge the proper exercise of his judicial authority, frequently making him a "rubber stamp" agent for the mandatory provision of the law; (2) it sets aside "due process of the law," guaranteed by the constitution, whereby every individual must be tried on the basis of the actual merits of a given case; and (3) it emphasizes the punitive aspects of the law at the expense of its rehabilitative function.

The judicial process and the courts. In the course of apprehension and possible eventual conviction, the offender proceeds through certain fundamental legal steps guaranteed by our constitution. (1) The first step is the *preliminary hearing.* Within twenty-four hours after apprehension by the police, an alleged offender must be brought before the magistrate's court, or court of first instance, for a hearing. This hearing is *not* a trial, although the accused may be defended by counsel. The purpose of the hearing is twofold: (a) to determine whether or not an offense, as charged, has been committed; and (b) whether or not there exists reasonable evidence that the person as charged has been guilty of the given offense. The right to a magistrate's hearing is a constitutional guarantee and applies to misdemeanors as well as to felonies. However, it is frequently practiced in the breach by our police. Individuals are frequently locked up and then released illegally, without having been afforded the opportunity of the magistrate's hearing.

(2) If the preliminary hearing results in reasonable suspicion for the detention of the alleged offender for further hearing and trial, then the magistrate may order that the individual be kept in jail until he may appear before the grand jury, or he may release him upon the posting of

bail, set by the court, until the meeting of the grand jury before which he must appear. Each contingency presents its own set of problems.

(A) The posting of bail is one of the most anomalous features of our judicial process. It means in effect that in order to guarantee that the individual will not flee the jurisdiction of the court before he comes to trial or a grand jury hearing, he must place with the court a certain sum of money or a guarantee to pay such a sum, which is forfeited in the event of his disappearance. Usually bonds, or promissory notes to pay, are posted with the court for the defendant by a professional bondsman who charges certain fees for this service. Aside from the fact that the inability to file such a bond represents a form of discrimination against the impecunious defendant, the posting of bail bonds, frequently at extortionate rates, has produced a very unsavory racket of its own.

Although rates have been fixed by law, in most cases, the opportunity for circumventing such provisions by various means is readily available. Special service charges are sometimes added, and "private arrangements" are not infrequently made between the defendant-client and the bondsman. Moreover, employees of the court may work in close conjunction with the bondsman in order to procure his business, and fee-splitting of a decidedly unwholesome nature takes place. Upon occasion, courts themselves have shown preference for certain bail bondsmen. Moreover, courts have been known to impose bail where there really was no basis for such action since substantial guarantees were on hand for the return of the defendant on the specified date for his trial or hearing. Moreover, bail bondsmen themselves, operating in different courts, frequently pledge the same piece of property as security over and over again, actually reaping a large return from property which is worthless or which cannot be redeemed. This malodorous phase of our court procedure has been well described by Samuel Seabury whose investigations revealed the following:

> Independent bondsmen often offer real estate as security. In many cases, however, they have in the property an equity far below the amount which they have pledged. There may be liens against the property. The bondsmen may have pledged the value of the property many times over.[47]

The character of certain bondsmen and their operations have been described by Raymond B. Moley in the case of one such individual whose earnings during one year were about $33,000, based upon real estate holdings valued at $24,100 against a mortgage of $31,500, and for which he had issued bonds for $67,295.[48] Other investigations, such as the Missouri

[47] *First Judicial Department Investigation of the Magistrates' Courts, New York State, Final Report of Samuel Seabury, Referee* (New York, March 28, 1932), p. 104.
[48] *Our Criminal Courts* (New York, 1930), pp. 46–7.

Crime Survey of 1926, reveal a common pattern in many of our courts concerning the abuse of the bail privilege.

(B) In the event that bail is not granted or the defendant is not otherwise temporarily released, he is detained in the local jail until such time as the grand jury makes a disposition of his case. Our jails are very likely the worst phase of our entire penal system. There are approximately three thousand county jails in the United States and an estimated ten thousand local lockups and detention pens, if we include municipal and other local custodial jails as well. The Federal government, because it frequently houses Federal law violators temporarily in local jails, has reserved the right to inspect and rate such local jails through the Bureau of Prisons of the Federal Department of Justice. Based upon a one hundred point rating scale, 97.5 per cent of 3,097 jails examined had ratings of under 60 per cent, while only five jails, or 0.1 per cent, had ratings of 80 to 89 per cent in 1946. No jail was rated over 90 per cent. It must be remembered that not all of the individuals held in jail will be proven guilty or *will even be held for trial* after hearing by the grand jury. Approximately one-third of the inmates of our jails are not convicted for their charged felonies and crimes.

An individual held for a grand jury hearing may remain in jail for a period of months awaiting such a hearing, only to be dismissed when his case comes up for investigation. Investigations by federal inspectors reveal a common pattern of abuses which may be summarized as follows:

(1) Sheriffs of local jails are elected officials, frequently completely unsuited by training and background for their task of custodial care, and in many cases shockingly ignorant of their duties and the character of the inmates of their jails. It is not uncommon for certain of such officials to accept the conclusion that all of their inmates are felons, whether convicted or not.

(2) A great many jails are still operated on a fee system whereby a set sum is assigned to the sheriff for each inmate under his care. It is to his interest, therefore, to cut down on food and maintenance to the utmost and pocket the rest as his own income.

(3) Jails still function in many communities as "catch-alls" for all kinds of offenders, the young and innocent, as well as the hardened felon of both sexes. Frequently, over-night derelicts, drunks, and street-walkers find themselves in the same company with juvenile offenders and hardened criminals. Although the Federal Bureau of Prisons has set as one of its minimum standards the absolute segregation of different types of offenders, many of our rural jails and lockups still fail to observe this indispensable basic rule. Not only does this opportunity for intimate association between the habitual offender and the young delinquent carry its own implicit threat, but the possibilities of immorality and license are ex-

treme. In the disclosures by Austin H. MacCormick of the conditions in the cell-blocks at Welfare Island in New York City in 1933, before the municipal custodial system was reorganized under the LaGuardia Administration, the presence of the illicit sale of drugs and liquors, and other flagrant forms of immorality, was demonstrated on a large scale.

(4) Standards of cleanliness in the general maintenance of quarters and the preparation of food have been strongly condemned by the Federal Bureau.

(5) One of the most condemnatory features of the jail system is the frequent permission given to prisoners for their own self-administration. While high-sounding in principle, this is frequently nothing but a device to pass responsibility on to those inmates most able to preserve order, usually the most vicious and corrupted of the prisoners. The prisoners themselves practice extortion on each other and especially upon the new inmates through the vicious practice of the "kangaroo courts." These are mock tribunals in which inmates are tried for supposed "offenses" and in which tribute is exacted from newcomers in the form of cash, food, service, and cigarettes.

Such kangaroo courts have been particularly common in the states of the Pacific Northwest. Of such jails, one veteran inspector has stated: "With few exceptions, kangaroo courts are allowed even in the bigger and supposedly better run jails. Jailors and sheriffs either approve of kangaroo courts or offer a flimsy alibi." In respect to one large western jail, he said: "A kangaroo court is permitted to fine and search all prisoners. The jail officials had even typed up the kangaroo court rules. The 'judge' of the court is in jail on a charge of killing two persons with a butcher knife." During Christmas, 1944, a dull-witted sixteen-year-old boy was picked up in Seattle for wearing an army uniform. His death at the hands of a kangaroo court twenty-three days later has been described by a youthful eye-witness: "I saw them tie Emberg, with his bare feet in the air, against the bars of the cell. He was resting on the back of his neck. Then they put lighted cigarettes against his bare feet and between his toes. He screamed, but the jailors paid no attention."

The grand jury and final disposition. The grand jury is a selected panel of local citizens, appointed by the court, which meets periodically in order to determine whether an individual accused of a felony shall be held for trial. The process of arraignment whereby the individual is given a formal hearing before such a body is designed to determine whether he shall or shall not be indicted for the offense as charged. The indictment itself refers to the formal declaration and charges by the court, after such a hearing has taken place, that the individual shall be held for trial upon such charges. The determination as to whether such an indictment shall be made depends upon the decision of the grand jury. This body may return a "true bill," or a statement declaring that the individual must be held for trial, or "no bill," which indicates that the grounds for such charges appear legally baseless and that the individual shall be released herewith from any further charges or detention. It should be noted that the grand jury hearing, as in the case of the preliminary hearing, does *not* constitute a trial. As in the preliminary hearing, however, the accused has the right to defense of counsel and may produce witnesses in his behalf.

Although the grand jury system contains a fundamental right guaranteed by Amendment V of the Federal Constitution, it is in effect frequently a repetition of much that has transpired upon the occasion of the preliminary hearing. Its sole advantages appear to lie in the fact that the accused is given an opportunity to be heard by a panel of disinterested citizens and a lengthier period is afforded in which evidence in his support may be gathered by his counsel. For the person who is released through the authorization of a "no bill," it has meant unwarranted incarceration in a local jail or the posting of a bond, and the indignities which such accusations naturally involve.

A considerable percentage of those brought before the grand jury, even for serious charges, are released without further trial or legal proceedings. In view of these facts, the grand jury process was abandoned in Great Britain in 1934 and has been superseded in approximately half of the states of this country. Instead, many of our states now authorize the use of the "information," which is a formal statement and petition made before the courts by the official prosecutor, for a direct proceeding to trial without the intervening steps of the grand jury hearing. There is much to commend the "information" as a legal step in place of the expensive and delayed use of the grand jury process. Actually, most of the legal work in our courts is carried on behind the scenes. The prosecutor is usually well aware of how good the chances for conviction are on the basis of the stipulated charges. The grand jury, despite its pretensions towards disinterestedness and impartiality, frequently does little more than endorse the recommendations of the county or district attorney. When this occurs, the only result obtained has been a delay, costly to the authorities and the accused person, in the final administration of justice.

On the basis of the grand jury indictment or the "information," the accused now becomes a bona fide defendant in respect to a given crime, and may either be returned to jail or released upon bail, pending the date set for his actual trial. Frequently, the charges returned in the actual indictment represent those counts upon which the prosecuting attorney is reasonably certain that he may obtain a conviction. Prior to the grand jury hearings and subsequent to them, it is not uncommon for the prosecutor and defense attorney to get together to "agree" upon a basis for the grand jury hearing and trial. Our court records confirm this in part by the high ratio of defendants who, upon final trial and sentence, are convicted on lesser offenses than originally charged. In New York City in 1926, for example, for each one hundred defendants charged with felonies, eighty-one were convicted on lesser charges. In Chicago, the ratio was seventy-five convicted on lesser charges for each one hundred felony cases tried.[49] This latter fact itself points significantly to an ominous aspect of the judicial process. The "bargaining" and "collusion" which take place as a means of altering convictions is a far cry from the principles of our legal institutional framework, which have as their premise the belief that an individual must stand trial for an offense as committed and charged.

The reasons for this difficulty are not difficult to apprehend in American life. The district or county attorney's office is frequently a stepping stone to further political advancement. The success with which he discharges his office, manifested on the bare record of the number of successful convictions which he obtains, is frequently a basis for further consideration for higher political office. The chief concern, therefore, is not in the essential justice of the given situation but the probability of success in gaining a certain number of convictions. Although the county and prosecuting attorney's office is frequently envisaged, both in law and practice, as an instrument whereby true justice may be served, such ends may be subverted in the interests of the political realities of a given situation. For this reason, increasing agitation has been apparent in many legal quarters for the establishment of a new office, that of public defender, whose function it will be to see that the genuine administration of justice is preserved rather than the compromises inherent in the dictates of political expedience. Since it does not appear feasible to combine this function with the present public prosecutor's office, the new trend is to recognize the desirability of this function as a completely separate public enterprise.

The eventual disposition of the case after trial imposes upon the judge the responsibility of determining sentence on the basis of the law.[50] Although the individual may be granted a trial for a rehearing of his case or may be granted the right of petition on the basis of new evidence or a faulty trial, the eventual disposition carries the accused, if the indictment has been confirmed by the final verdict, to either a state or federal penitentiary, or suspension of sentence in the form of probation. He is returned to the jail to remain there until surrendered to the authority of the warden of the assigned penal institution or to the custody of the probation officer. Increasingly, in many of our states, the tendency has been to fix a

[49] *Report on Prosecution* (National Commission on Law Observance and Enforcement, 1931), p. 186.

[50] For a discussion of new trends in respect to the judicial function—the determination of guilt and the imposition of sentence—see Herbert A. Bloch, "Social Change and the Delinquent Personality" (concluding section), *1949 Yearbook* (National Probation and Parole Association, New York).

minimum and maximum sentence with a view towards the prisoner's eventual rehabilitation. Our present criminal codes are contradictory in their emphasis of punitive *and* rehabilitative measures.[51] Recognizing this diversity and representing an *inherent contradiction* in the growth of our scientific psycho-medical technologies and our legal framework, most modern legislation attempts to meet the problem by affording the court some latitude in the imposition of the minor and maximum sentence.[52] The basic minimum sentence may be conceived of as a punitive and observational procedure whereby the prisoner, in indicating his potentialities for release under the supervision of parole, may be placed once more in society before the expiration of the upper limits of his sentence, provided he displays his worthiness and fitness for such controlled freedom.[53]

SUMMARY

(1) We have seen in this chapter that crime does not consist of any non-conforming behavior whatsoever, but of that type which is defined by law as criminal. Consequently, crime varies according to the changing definitions developed by society. (2) The peculiar character of American crime and its relatively high rates reflect some of the basic attitudes and latent tendencies in the American culture pattern. The great diversity of American culture has permitted the growth of a degree of casualness toward the law and a wide margin of illicit behavior existing on the fringes of the law. The vast complexities of the American cultural system have resulted in the large-scale attempt to impose social control by legislative means, with the result that Americans may be the most over-legislated people in the world and, at the same time, the most lawless. (3) The peculiar social situations and cultural definitions existing in American life have laid the groundwork for the elicitation of special types of crime by the social environment and by the character of the victims. Periodic occurrences of certain types of crime and among special classes of the population are to be expected. (4) Although Americans are likely to regard crime as a special propensity of the habitual or professional offender, it must be recognized that a large volume of crimes are committed annually by casual, occasional, episodic, white-collar, mentally abnormal, and non-

[51] Cf. Mabel A. Elliott, *Conflicting Penal Theories in Statutory Criminal Law*, Chicago, 1931.

[52] Probably the best recent example of this may be found in the passage of the Sexual Offenders Law (Senate No. 3372) in New York State on March 15, 1950, in which considerable latitude is afforded the courts in the disposition of the cases of such special offenders. The detention of such offenders, ranging up to permanent imprisonment, is almost wholly contingent upon the offender's capacity for rehabilitation, provision for which is made under the law.

[53] For a good review of the legal process in relation to crime, see Nathaniel F. Cantor, *Crime and Society* (New York, 1939), chaps. IV–VII.

malicious offenders as well. (5) It is the confirmed criminal, however, who develops a special social framework of his own, differing from that of normal society. Such habitual offenders show patterned statistical similarities relative to conviction, penal experience, marital status, family background, place and type of offense, intelligence, and developmental background. (6) The deviant character of the criminal offender's existence as a member of a "society within a society" is evidenced in the rational structures he develops toward the life of crime and his cynicism concerning the normal and conventional motives of others. (7) The racket has arisen as a characteristic organized and institutionalized form of American crime. The racket has thrived in this country largely because of the cultural disunity previously mentioned, the unscrupulous competition in marginal economic activity, and the demand among certain sections of the public for services and commodities banned by law. (8) White-collar crime far outweighs the cost of ordinary crime. While more frequent in the realm of business, it may be found in varied professional activities as well. (9) The legal institutions concerning crime reflect the close relation to American culture. The extreme specificity with which the law operates, as contrasted with the functions of social customs and folkways, creates many special problems concerning the control and deterrence of crime. The special problems concerning the preliminary hearing, the use of bail, the jail system, the grand jury hearings, the prosecutor's office, and the final disposition of a case reflect the lag between our growing conception of the nature of crime and its control, and the ofttimes archaic means by which we attempt to serve the ends of justice and the protection of the public.

CHAPTER TWELVE

SOCIAL CHANGE AND THE CRIMINAL

(1) THE PRIORITY OF THE SOCIOLOGICAL FRAME OF REFERENCE

SOME phases of criminal activity should be clarified before we turn to other aspects of social pathology. In this chapter we will discuss underlying psychological patterns in their relation to cultural configurations, the nature of variations in the types and rates of crime, the role of economic factors, and some new developments in penal philosophy and practice.

Both *natural* factors, such as climatic and seasonal conditions, as well as isolated *institutional* factors, such as economic conditions, must always be studied within the sociological manifold. The sociological manifold in this volume consists of the structural relationships of the cultural, institutional, and social factors which, in their interrelated effects, condition the needs of the individual through the medium of the family organization. It consists, furthermore, of the projection of the socially created and defined needs upon the social structure and the channels that are afforded by the immediate social environment for their expression.

To illustrate this viewpoint, we may consider studies dealing with seasonal variations in crime rates. If we find in modern European countries that the rate for crimes against property is highest during the winter months, there can be no immediate inference that the colder weather is directly instrumental in bringing about these crimes. In communities, for example, where employment rates are higher in the winter than in summer, or where, because of the cultural patterns, the winter months are employed for supported leisure-time programs, it is possible that crime rates would not increase. The month of the year, the character and rate of employment, the extensiveness of the social welfare system, and other such factors impinge directly upon the seasonal factor, conditioning the rate of crime. Yet, many analysts have studied such factors as climatic conditions (among others) as if they operated in isolation from the cultural pattern. In learning to utilize the sociological frame of reference, therefore, we must learn to assess such studies in terms of these interacting cultural and social factors. With this *caveat* established, let us proceed to examine some of the conspicuous remaining environmental, institutional, and psychological factors that may play a part in producing crime.

(2) THE PSYCHOPATHOLOGY OF CRIME

In our previous discussion, we showed that some evidence exists pointing to the conclusion that a relatively high frequency of abnormal emotional states may exist among the criminal population.[1] This high correlation should not properly be interpreted as proof that mental unbalance is a direct cause of crime. If we *did* accept this causal hypothesis, it would be incumbent on us to show why the large numbers of mentally disturbed persons in the population at large do not commit crimes. As an additional argument against such an hypothesis, we may cite the fact that there is certainly no "criminal psychosis" in the clinical sense, although a certain percentage of clinically verifiable psychotic states may result in certain types of crime, particularly crimes of violence and crimes of the episodic variety.

Clinically diagnosed pathological states and crime. The principal problem to be discussed here is what percentage of those in our population who are identified as psychotic actually commit crimes as a result of their psychotic states. Most states segregate carefully those prisoners who are found to be suffering from some type of psychotic condition. This segregation may be based upon the time of the commission of a certain offense. For example, in New York State, two institutions are maintained, one for the detention of the criminally insane and one for those identified as insane criminals. The distinction is based on whether the individual was adjudged psychotic before the commission of the offense, or whether the mental degeneration occurred after the individual was apprehended and convicted for his crime. In many states, the study of the records of male psychotic patients in general mental hospitals indicates a relatively high percentage who have had prior prison and criminal records. Thus, in the State of Michigan, a study of 1,262 male psychotic patients at the Eloise State Hospital in 1938 revealed that approximately 25 per cent either had previous criminal records or gave evidence of attempts to commit crimes.[2] Of the 25 per cent, the greater number, 21.1 per cent, had previous criminal records, leaving only 4 per cent who had made attempts. However, of the total number studied, 1,262, only 15.6 per cent had committed a crime after the onset of the disease. We are led to the conclusion that we can be certain of a direct relation between abnormal emotional states and criminality only in the case of the 15.6 per cent mentioned.

[1] See pp. 272–3.

[2] M. H. Erickson, "Criminality in a Group of Male Psychiatric Patients," *Mental Hygiene*, XXII (1938), 459–76.

One of the best organized studies of the relationship between specific psychotic states and crime has been done by H. W. Dunham in the State of Illinois.[3] His findings concern the relationship between schizophrenia and crime and the percentage of crimes committed by psychotics domiciled in the general mental hospitals of Illinois. His general conclusion appears to be that schizophrenics are more likely to commit crimes than are other types of psychotics, although these crimes are largely of a non-serious nature. For his study, Dunham reviewed the cases of 870 youthful schizophrenics committed from Chicago to the general state hospitals from the years 1922 to 1934. A relatively high percentage of these youthful patients had previous criminal records, although the majority of these offenses were of a minor character. Further, he discovered that the seclusive catatonic type of schizophrenic yielded a lower percentage of offenses than the aggressive and suspicious paranoid type. That a relationship exists between certain forms of this abnormality and the commission of offenses was further demonstrated by the fact that 11 per cent of the catatonics and 15 per cent of the paranoids committed their offenses after they had been released from hospital custodial care.

On the basis of these and similar studies, we present the following conclusions: (1) A higher percentage of mental abnormality exists among the criminal population than among the non-criminal groups of the population. (2) A certain percentage of crime is committed by individuals who suffer from serious psychotic states, although very likely no more than 25 per cent of the psychotic population are responsible for such crimes. (3) With the exception of those individuals with seriously disturbed genuine paranoid states, such offenders do not commit many crimes of a serious nature. (4) Schizophrenics are apparently responsible for the larger share of these crimes, although the crimes which they commit are principally of a minor nature. (5) Where serious crimes do occur among schizophrenics, they are likely to take the form of personal assault, theft, and murder. Acts of violence among this group appear to be most frequently confined to the individual's own family. (6) The severe emotional states, especially those of paranoia, may manifest themselves in sporadic and episodic crimes of violence. The most serious crimes are committed by psychotics of this category, although the total percentage of crimes committed by this group is relatively small. (7) There is certainly no specifically criminal syndrome in psychotic states, although psychotic states may manifest themselves in certain forms of crime.

Psychiatric and psychoanalytic theories concerning crime. Although it is impossible to link the commission of all crimes to basic emotional disturbances, the fact remains nevertheless that criminal activity is frequently

[3] H. W. Dunham, "The Schizophrene and Criminal Behavior," *American Sociological Review*, IV (June, 1939), 352–61.

associated with various types of emotional tension. If we accept the supposition that in the development of incipient stages of crime the individual is driven by the desire to satisfy basic, culturally denied needs, the emotional states converging upon these needs and their satisfaction must be said to comprise an important part of the criminal process. For this reason, the psychiatric view can be of signal importance, when comprehended within a sociological frame of reference. This is *not* to say that the basis of criminal activity lies in pathological or emotionally disturbed states.

Approaching this problem from the standpoint of the unique emotional state of the individual, the psychiatrist has on occasion been able to give us some penetrating insights into the nature of specific types of crime. Kleptomania, pyromania, juvenile recidivism, crimes of violence, and crimes involving sexual disorders—all of these have received skillful interpretation in studies by psychiatrists. In the forefront of such studies, although not wholly accepted by a great many psychiatrists, have been the views of the psychoanalysts.

The psychoanalytical view of crime. The Freudian view is premised largely on the assumption that human activity in general is motivated by unconscious impulses. According to this view, the human mind may be supposed to contain three broad areas: the *id*, or the unconscious, instinctual, and amoral cravings of man; the *ego*, or the organized personality which acts as a restraint upon the social demands of the community and the instinctual cravings of the *id;* and the *superego*, or the social mandates and controls of the group and the community as they have been integrated by the personality. All human beings maintain a precarious balance among the conflicting claims and demands of these three divergent sections of the personality. Another important aspect of the Freudian system is the emphasis on the attachment of the son to the mother and the daughter to the father. These attachments are primarily sexual in nature, although it should be understood that the conception of this sexual attachment is extremely broad in character.

Although the theory is extremely complex, the crux of its meaning may be reduced to the following terms. In the normal course of psychological development, the young male child passes through a period of rivalry with the father for the mother's affection. In time, he is enabled to find substitutive emotional outlets for his attachment to the mother through association with girls and eventually through marriage. In some cases, this normal sequence of events is thwarted, with the result that the desire for the mother's affection may become extremely acute and protracted. Prompted by the insistent urgings of the *id*, which runs counter to the moral dictates of the *superego*, the boy develops acute anxiety and guilt feelings about his attachment to the mother and his hostility toward the father. This guilt may be relieved only by seeking punishment. Thus, according to psychoanalytical view, some persons under the weight of the intolerable guilt-feelings, will deliberately commit crimes in order to expiate the sinful attitudes held toward the parents.

This is a highly simplified condensation of an extremely subtle and complex view, which the peculiar Freudian terminology does not always help to clarify. An illustration of the application of this view is provided in the interpretation by Dr. Frederic Wertham of the violent murder committed by a young Italian boy upon his mother.[4]

Gino, a young Italian boy, murdered his mother by stabbing her with a bread knife thirty-two times. The strange thing about this brutal matricide was the apparent absence of motive and the fact that the young murderer had no previous delinquent or criminal record. Moreover, the boy himself appeared to have no remorse, and in fact expressed himself upon occasion as happy that the deed had been committed. The courts ruled that young Gino was insane and he was committed to a special institution for the criminally insane.

During the course of his incarceration at this institution, he was given an intensive psychoanalytical and psychiatric investigation, in which the following causal processes were disclosed. Gino was the oldest child in the family and strongly attached to the mother. Upon the occasion of his father's death, while he was still a young boy, Gino attempted to perform the father's role in the family by exercising some of his authority towards the mother and younger children, and attempting unsuccessfully to operate a small bakery which was the family's business. His mother turned to a married man and subsequently other male companions which infuriated the boy. Believing that the mother had dishonored the family and the father's name, he dramatically swore vengeance at the father's grave and frequently contemplated the prospect of murdering the mother.

During the period of his adolescence when he should ordinarily have been attempting to find companionship with young girls of his own age, he brooded darkly over his mother's behavior and developed an intense repugnance to the entire idea of sexual relations. His attitude towards his mother was sharply ambivalent, divided between his desire to destroy her and his desire to protect her. For a period of five years, he was torn by these attitudes of intense conflict. In an attempt to free himself from the bondage of the mother, he attempted to have sexual intimacies with young women but was strongly inhibited by the attachment to the mother, which had come to signify the uncleanliness and evil of all sexual relationships. Finally, in one great

[4] Dark Legend: *A Study in Murder* (New York, 1941).

outburst of emotional fury, he killed her, attempting in this way to free himself from the restraining influence which her existence and presence imposed upon his deeply troubled conscience.

In a later volume of studies, Wertham attempts to show how crimes are fostered by the twisted pathological states of certain disordered minds.[5] In this work he does not depend entirely on the psychoanalytic viewpoint and takes some account of the social background. Yet his analysis still points to the emotional distortions in primary personal relationships as a basis for criminal violence. Thus, Robert Irwin, the talented young sculptor and student at a theological seminary, who committed three murders in one night during the spring of 1937, is regarded as having committed these murders because "the decent part of his character—his superego—was out of commission." Martin Lavin, an habitual criminal who feigned "insanity" after a murder and was subsequently dismissed from an institution to perpetrate further crimes, is regarded as suffering from certain types of dangerous compulsive mechanisms. Madeline, a mother who murdered her two children when she discovered that her husband was a homosexual, is regarded as having suffered from a catathymic crisis, i.e., "the aberration of reasoning under the impact of emotional complexes" which caused the outbreak of violence.

Certain kinds of offenses seem to stem from profound emotional disturbances and personality maladjustments. These emotional difficulties, manifesting themselves in such criminal activities as kleptomania and pyromania may be particularly susceptible of psychiatric interpretation and treatment. In such cases, the basic cause of the offense appears to lie in pathological and neurotic compulsions, whose outer forms are the illicit behaviors. Pyromaniacs are frequently seriously disturbed psychotic persons whose crimes are intimately associated with compulsions related to delusions of status, repressed aggressions, recessiveness, and acute anxiety symptoms. Their offenses are definitely to be classified as pathological in origin and within the psychiatric orbit.

Kleptomania, too, may be viewed as an abnormal obsessional crime in which the criminal activity is symptomatic of emotional disturbance and personality maladjustment. The primary mechanisms at work in such cases are psychoneurotic compulsions developed as a means of escaping inner conflict. Thus, the child may steal as a means of overcoming his feelings of insecurity or guilt or as an expression of aggression. The following case, which came to the attention of a well-known psychiatric social case-work agency in New York City, gives some indication of the causal patterns operating in such situations.

[5] Frederic Wertham, *The Show of Violence* (New York, 1949).

A young adolescent boy, strongly attached to his mother, was suspected of stealing money from the till of the small neighborhood stationery and candy store which his family operated. Sums of money disappeared regularly, and there was no indication of who was responsible. The family, although not wealthy, provided amply for the needs of the children and there was little apparent basis for theft by the children. Upon discovering that the oldest boy had developed a limp, his shoes were examined. It was revealed that the stolen money had been secreted in the heel of his left shoe.

Investigation revealed that there was intense antagonism between husband and wife which had been concealed from the neighbors. The source of this continual strife had to do with money and the family income. The child had witnessed a particularly brutal assault by the father upon the mother which had a profound emotional and terrifying effect upon him. At first, used as a pawn by both parents in their bitter struggle, he found himself drawn alternately to one or the other. The parents' preoccupation with their own problem resulted in a growing feeling of rejection by the boy, manifested in recurrent phases of intense affection and hostility toward both parents, which finally culminated in the traumatic episode described above. Fear and hostility toward the father led to ambitious and sadistic schemes for his punishment and undoing. Shortly after this episode, the youth became subject to a number of compulsive actions of a minor sort, directed principally toward the father, such as disturbing the stock in the store and muttering oaths, imprecations, and prayers. Finally, the stealing resulted and continued over a period of months. The money stolen served no financial benefit to the child. It is noteworthy that the thefts touched on the major source of the family difficulty and were directed at the father's most vulnerable point.

General psychiatric views. The general psychiatric views on the causation of crime are eclectic and disinclined to favor any single approach. While they stress the emotional origins of personality maladjustment which motivate criminal and delinquent activity, they also take increasing cognizance of the role of the social and family environments. Because of the organic and medical orientation of psychiatry, emphasis has frequently been placed upon the individual clinical and organic factors at the expense of the relevant behavioral and interactive processes. Recent research, however, is making plain the necessity of combining the individual, case-centered approach with examination of the socio-cultural factors in the background of each case.

Fundamentally, criminal activity is a form of behavior resulting from the conjunction at a given moment in time of a peculiarly disposed personality and a peculiarly organized configuration of social circumstances. The way in which these factors combine at a given moment in the history of the personality-situational equation determines whether or not a crime will take place. The emotional volatility characteristic of emotionally disturbed and maladjusted individuals makes them susceptible to abandoning social inhibitions and embarking on criminal activity.

(3) SEASONAL AND CLIMATIC VARIATIONS IN CRIME

Earlier students of crime, such as Lombroso and Ferri, attempted to show specific relationships between crime rates, types of crime, and geographical and climatic factors. Their findings, based primarily on data drawn from Italy, France, and, later, Germany, purported to show that climatic conditions had a direct bearing upon the character and amount of crime. Studies based on nineteenth century statistics appear to show that crimes against the person are relatively high in frequency in warmer climates while crimes against property are comparatively low. These studies, most of which were undertaken before the recent development of psycho-sociological and cultural views on the causation of crime, attempted to show that temperature had a direct bearing on certain faculties of the human organism. Thus, it was thought that irritability and interpersonal conflict were more likely to occur in warm than in cool regions. Although it is conceivable that temperature changes may have an effect on the body and subsequently, its behavior, recent evidence seems to point to the conclusion that such effects are always mediated by economic conditions, cultural factors, psychological processes, and the like. Anthropological studies of primitive communities in equatorial regions give no evidence of increased irritability during the warmer seasons of the year. However, reports from various parts of the world affected by periodic changes in the amounts of humidity and subject to precipitate increases of temperature, such as the monsoon and sirocco belts, suggest that psychological changes, emotional volatility, and fatigue are more common there. These regions would therefore appear to have more favorable psychological atmosphere for the creation of inter-personal tension and conflict than more temperate regions. There is little conclusive evidence, however, concerning the effects of such conditions upon the crime rates.

Closely related to these climatic studies are the investigations of seasonal variations of crime rates. In general, on the basis of evidence collected thus far, crimes against the person are likely to be more frequent during the warmer months and crimes against property during the cooler months. This is partly confirmed by European statistics on the general climatic variations in crime, which appear to show higher rates of personal assault in southern Italy and southern France, with an increased number of property crimes in the northern sections of these countries. This is not universally confirmed, however. Compilations of nineteenth-century data, for example, show that in Germany crime rates appear to vary from east to west rather than from north to south, with the higher rates appearing in the east.[6]

In general, there appears to be more crime against the person in the summer than in the winter, with the frequency of crimes against property just the reverse; Ferri's study of crime rates in France and Italy appears to support this. Using the work of A. Lacassagne and other French students who developed calendar sequences for crime rates, he showed that with the exception of infanticide, which yielded the highest rates in January, February, March, and April, respectively, and patricide, committed most frequently in January and October, crimes against the person did occur with greater frequency in the summer months. Homicide and assault achieved their highest rates in July, rapes upon adults in June, and rapes upon children during May, July, and August. Property crimes, while not so marked in variation, tended to be most numerous in December and January.[7]

If these variations in rates of crime exist as reported, the explanations should not be difficult to find. Instead of searching for physiological bases for crime, it is more reasonable to assume that the summer months afford a much greater opportunity for outdoor personal contacts. These contacts, in turn, provide increased opportunity for personal antagonisms and the commission of sex offenses. A high infanticide rate, occurring during the winter months, may point significantly to the attempt to do away with illegitimate offspring conceived during the spring and summer months. The high patricide rate may be understood in relation to the high level of intra-family friction resulting from the economic stress and limited scope for movement during winter months. Higher rates of crime against property during cold weather would appear to result from seasonal unemployment and the other economic difficulties that coincide with this period of the year. Studies of the economic aspects of the business cycle and seasonal variations in industry, when such conditions are unrelieved by adequate relief and welfare measures, would seem to support this conclusion.

Other early studies, such as Dexter's investigation of the effect of the weather upon crime in New York City and Denver, are of little merit because of the dubious nature of the data he employs and the unqualified nature of the inferences he draws.[8] His conclusions that the number of ar-

[6] See Mayo-Smith, *Statistics and Sociology* (New York, 1904), pp. 270–1.

[7] Ibid. See also, A. Lacassagne, "Marche de la Criminalité en France de 1825 à 1880," *Revue Scientifique* (May 28th, 1881), 674–84, cited in Maurice Parmalee, *Criminology* (New York, 1918), pp. 69–70.

[8] Dexter, *Weather Influences* (New York, 1904), p. 266.

rests increased with rises in the temperature and with the falling of the barometer, and that assaults are correlated with low humidity, and similar conclusions relative to wind velocity and fair and cloudy days, are of little worth because of the complete neglect of interposing socio-psychological and cultural conditions. To explain a low rate of assault as due to the debilitating effects of high humidity represents a naïve neglect of the complex factors that enter into human behavior. It can be just as readily argued that high humidity develops feelings of perverseness and hence causes men to commit assaults.

(4) CRIME, UNEMPLOYMENT, AND THE BUSINESS CYCLE

The numerous studies of crime in relation to poverty, unemployment, and depressed economic conditions reveal the shortcomings of those theories that fail to include well-organized and carefully defined frames of reference. For example, the term "unemployment" used in the generic sense is not very helpful from a diagnostic standpoint in view of the multiplicity of the conditions that it covers. The state of being unemployed may signify many different things, depending on its duration, whether the affected persons are given relief and public assistance, which member or members of the family are unemployed, the effects upon remaining members of the family, and the opportunities for substitutive employment. These, and a host of other factors in relation to a particular community and a particular individual, must be taken into account if we are to obtain an adequate picture of the effects of unemployment and poverty upon crime. The public attitude in relation to unemployment is important, for example, in defining the status of the individual. In a class-structured society, determined largely by economic considerations, unemployment may be identified in the public mind with anti-social behavior. Thus, Eli Ginzberg, in reference to the predominant cultural and economic drives of an era, has stated the following: [9]

> During the unprecedented expansion of the United States in the early twentieth century, a man, if willing to work, had little reason to be unemployed. Hence the public came to look upon the unemployed in much the same light as the hobo, the alcoholic, the criminal.
>
> After the stock market collapse in the fall of 1929, however, the ranks of the unemployed were swelled, not by thousands but by millions. Even the most hidebound conservative began to realize that there was more to unemployment than the economic or moral failings of the individual.

[9] Eli Ginzberg, *The Unemployed* (New York, 1943), p. 35.

The general conception that the unemployed were largely responsible for their own plight and hence to be considered morally and socially reprehensible, was sustained until the present century.

Within our present economically oriented civilization, where the life of the average wage-earning family is directly affected by the loss of employment of its breadwinners, the psychological consequences of loss of employment may be considerable. Among these consequences may be the lowering of the threshold of social inhibitions, which renders the individual more prone to criminality. Dr. James L. Halliday has found that the percentage of those suffering from psychological disabilities because of unemployment tends to rise with the prolongation of the period of unemployment.[10]

> [The percentage rates] suggest that after falling out of work there is a short period of a sense of release [a holiday freedom]; gradually anxiety and depression set in with a loss of mental equilibrium; finally after several years adaptation takes place to a new and debased level of life, lacking hope as well as fear of the future. *As far as delinquency goes there is a danger zone between six months and two years of unemployment.* [Italics ours.]

Most studies appear to agree that prolonged unemployment tends to bring about an increase in crimes against property and minor infractions of the law, although the findings are inconclusive in relation to crimes against the person. (With respect to these latter offenses, the more recent studies appear to indicate a slight increase or no increase at all.) Although there is an important relation between unemployment and the rate of crime, it cannot be said that crime is *directly* caused by unemployment, or any other type of economic condition.

The most pronounced economic-deterministic view of criminality was held by the Dutch criminologist Bonger. In examining the effects of economic adversity on rates of crimes against property, he found an inverse correlation between the price of wheat in England, Wales, and France, and the rate of thefts in these countries. By correlating the price of rye in Germany, the equivalent basic agricultural commodity in that country, he found that a similar set of conditions prevailed.[11] These inverse ratios support the conclusion that as prices rose, indicating periods of increasing prosperity, crime rates decreased. Even Bonger, however, recognized that the incentive to crime is not produced by economic privation alone. He indicated that the desire to maintain a standard of living or to emulate the standards of others may be a relevant factor.

[10] *Men Without Work, A Report to the Pilgrim Trust* (Cambridge, 1938), pp. 136–7.

[11] William A. Bonger, *Criminality and Economic Conditions* (Boston, 1916), pp. 564–71.

One of the best organized studies of the relationship between the business cycle and crime rates, and a pioneer in its field, is the celebrated investigation by Dorothy S. Thomas of the business cycle in England for the years 1857–1913, exclusive of the years 1880–2.[12] In view of the fact that this study for many years constituted a basis for a number of similar studies made elsewhere, it will be helpful to examine briefly some of its statistical shortcomings.

Such studies as Thomas's attempt to find correlations between the entire span of years, with its various minor cycles, and the total development of crime rates. Single correlation coefficients of this sort are rarely useful unless they are evaluated and computed in relation to specific periods within the long-range span of years. The fluctuations within the cycle and their direct, intermediate, and remote effects upon the crime rate, must be taken into consideration. Furthermore, the balancing of correlation coefficients in terms of long-range secular trends and other modifying factors and variables must be carefully reviewed if we are to understand the functioning of the business cycle in relation to crime. The real clue to the effects of economic conditions upon crime can frequently be best assessed in terms of sudden fluctuations of crime rates, both upward and downward, in relation to the long-range trend.

In Thomas's study, a composite price index was employed as a basis for the measurement of economic prosperity. This price index was correlated with prosecution rates per 100,000 of the population for the years covered by the business cycle. In general, her results showed a slight correlation between certain types of crime and business conditions, although these indexes were not high and showed irregular variations for certain parts of the period studied. When the crime rate and the business cycle were related simultaneously, the highest correlation was found between violent crimes against property and business conditions, an inverse coefficient of $-.44 \pm .11$ being yielded.[13]

This would indicate that as business conditions worsen there is a

[12] *Social Aspects of the Business Cycle* (New York, 1925).

[13] The following rule-of-thumb for interpreting correlation coefficients is suggested. A correlation of 1.00 signifies perfect correlation or relationship, never actually attained in statistical research. Coefficients greater than .70 indicate high correlation, coefficients greater than .40 and less than .70 indicate substantial correlation, and coefficients greater than .20 and less than .40 indicate low correlation. Coefficients less than .20 represent negligible correlation. The plus signs and minus signs preceding correlation coefficients indicate positive and negative (inverse) correlations respectively. A minus sign does not indicate an *absence* of relationship, as is so frequently believed. Negative correlations indicate an inverse relationship, i.e., as the numerical index of one set of factors or conditions goes up, the index of the other set of related variables tends to go down. The plus-and-minus figures following correlation coefficients are known as *standard errors.* They indicate the degree of reliability with which the coefficient may be accepted. In general, the smaller the standard error in relation to the correlation coefficient, the more reliable, statistically, is the coefficient of correlation.

greater likelihood of this type of crime. For property crimes without violence, a coefficient of correlation for the entire period of $-.25 \pm .13$ was found, indicating that although the tendency for such crimes to occur during depressed conditions was present, it was not as high as for the previous type of offense. Interestingly enough, when the attempt was made to correlate crimes against the person (i.e., murder, manslaughter, assault, and intimidation) with business conditions, it was found that a low positive correlation existed, unlike the negative correlation found in the previous property offenses. This would indicate a very slight tendency for crimes against the person to occur during periods of prosperity. Other positive correlations were found to exist in the case of drunkenness ($+.33 \pm .14$) and prostitution ($+.22 \pm .13$). Our conclusion would be that both drunkenness and prostitution appear to increase during periods of improving business conditions. However, in the case of prostitution, when specific periods within the long-range span of years were studied, the correlation became negative, which indicated that variables other than economic conditions were effective in producing this type of offense.

In order to study the delayed effect of business conditions upon crime, correlations were sought upon the basis of a lag of one year in the crime rates. Although the correlation coefficents were not as high, the differences were not sufficiently marked, especially in the case of property crimes, to indicate any substantial changes in the conclusions of this study.

Although somewhat different indexes for crime rates and business conditions were used, similar studies have been carried on in this country. On the basis of data from Rhode Island and Massachusetts, substantially the same results were found. Phelps's study of Rhode Island data for the years 1898–1926 showed a relatively high correlation of +.33 for crimes against property and families on relief.[14] In a later study, using unemployment figures as a basis, Winslow found that the highest correlations existed between property crimes (such as burglary, breaking and entering, and larceny) and unemployment, as compared with other types of offenses. He discovered a relatively high correlation for vagrancy as well, an offense which inevitably increases during periods of depression.[15]

The depression of 1929. With the great depression of 1929, the entire character of our economic system was transformed. This transformation produced new conceptions of individual responsibility in relation to public welfare and relief. The studies of the character of the American depression in its effects upon crime are inconclusive and unintegrated, although certain broad trends are discernible. These trends are particularly

[14] H. A. Phelps, "Cycle of Crime," *Journal of Criminal Law and Criminology* (1929), 107–21.

[15] E. A. Winslow, "Relationship Between Employment and Crime Fluctuations as Shown by Massachusetts Statistics," *Report on Causes of Crime* (National Commission on Law Observance and Enforcement, Washington, 1931), 310–11.

significant in so far as they indicate that the changing conceptions of social responsibility very definitely had an effect on rates of crime. In general, these studies show that there was a tendency for property offenses to increase with the early years of the depression, culminating in 1932. There was a steady decrease and falling off in the rates of property offenses after this period. The physical crimes of violence, homicide, rape, and assault, do not seem to show this same increase.[16]

The inferences to be drawn are that as the various public relief agencies got under way the character of family and community life was strengthened to withstand the pressures of economic adversity. With the prolongation of the depression, the reluctance on the part of the American public to accept such forms of assistance apparently weakened, and a new form of adaptation took place. In assessing the depression years of 1930 to 1934 as compared with the preceding five-year period in relation to juvenile delinquency, J. B. Maller discovered that, for the metropolitan area of New York, major crimes in general tended to decline while minor offenses tended to increase.[17] These findings are not generally supported for the country as a whole in an investigation by George B. Vold for the years 1929 to 1934.[18] In fact, Vold's findings appear to reverse a great many of the previous studies. In the United States, after the peak year of 1932, the crime indexes appear to show a gradual decrease. According to Vold, there was no commensurate increase in crime in relation to the widespread nature and extreme duration of the depression. Furthermore, he concludes that, unlike the earlier studies, the depression brought about no sudden or great increase of crimes against property. His net conclusion seems to be that the depression brought about no general transformation in American behavior habits conducive to crime.

Rural crime and depression. Very few studies have been conducted concerning the rural offender in general and, specifically, concerning the effect of economic conditions upon rural crime rates. There is reason to believe that the character of rural offenses and their rates may be changing, partially as a result of the depression.[19] In order to determine the effect of economic depression upon a highly stable rural area, the author studied the cases of 159 offenders indicted before the county courts for the period 1927–9 and 356 offenders indicated between the years 1938–

[16] See Thorsten Sellin, *Research Memorandum on Crime in the Depression* (Social Science Research Council, New York, 1937), for a comprehensive survey and analysis of the studies made during this period.

[17] "Juvenile Delinquency in New York City: A Summary of a Comprehensive Report," *Journal of Psychology*, III (Jan., 1937), 1–25.

[18] "The Amount and Nature of Crime," *American Journal of Sociology*, 40 (May, 1935), 796–803.

[19] Cf. Marshall Clinard, "Rural Criminal Offenders," *The American Journal of Sociology*, L (July, 1944), 38.

41.[20] In view of the stationary character of the population of the area, it was concluded that the changes noted were largely attributable to changing economic circumstances brought about by the entire depression trend. Although some increase in the overall crime rate was noted, especially for such property offenses as burglary and forgery, the most conspicuous changes appear to occur in the character of the offenders. Open-country, farm, and village youths were not so vitally affected as the lower middle-class, white-collar youths who inhabited the intermediate, primary service, shopping and trading centers. The increases noted seemed to fall predominantly among this group. The findings indicated that the greater the proximity to the farm and small village community, the less prone was the population to delinquency and crime. Further, it was seen that the largest incidence of offenses occurred within the twenty-one to twenty-nine year old age-group, as contrasted with the more youthful offender class arising before the depression. Finally, among the small town group, the increasing rates of recidivism suggest the development of an habitual offender class in such rural areas which was relatively uncommon before the depression. Although sufficient studies are not available for comparison, it is possible that the depression has altered the character of rural crime.

Conclusions. Despite the confusing array of different studies, there seems to be a general agreement that economic privation and economic adversity do play a limited part in producing a certain amount of delinquency and crime. Reasoning that prolonged and widespread economic crisis must inevitably weaken the inhibitions of certain sections of the population, Von Hentig has developed his doctrine of *temptation*, resulting from adverse economic conditions, as a causal factor in relation to crime.[21] He quotes the ancient Hebraic proverb: "Not the mouse, but the hole is the thief." Basing his argument on the surveys of rising German crime rates during the post-war era of the First World War, he concludes: "Human beings are not made to resist thunderbolts. . . . We must acknowledge similar configurations of our cultural life when extreme want, extreme provocation, or extreme frustration wrings an unlawful act from an otherwise law-abiding individual. . . . Most of our criminals are milieu-made. They are law-abiding while the sun shines, economic life goes on undisturbed, and their ability of adjustment is not taxed excessively. When social storms are brewing, depressions set in; prices tumble, and the army of unemployed swells, the average law-abiding individual yields to extreme pressure and becomes a law-breaker."[22] Although this state-

[20] H. A. Bloch, "Economic Depression as a Factor in Rural Crime," *Journal of Criminal Law and Criminology*, XL (Nov.–Dec., 1949), 458–70.

[21] Hans von Hentig, *Crime: Causes and Conditions* (New York, 1947), p. 225.

[22] Ibid., p. 11.

ment is extreme, we may recognize some truth in it as it bears on certain kinds of individuals.

Our general conclusion must remain that depressed economic conditions may bring about a certain small increase in crimes committed for economic gain. There appears to be little evidence that crimes against the person show a significant measurable rise. Moreover, it appears likely that with change in public attitudes concerning relief and welfare, the effects of depressions can be largely ameliorated. In view of the fact that fluctuations in crime rates, both economic and personal, appear during depressed stages of the business cycle irrespective of corrective measures taken, it is evident that economic conditions constitute only a limited causal factor in the commission of crime. Any community may break if the stress is strong enough and produce more than its quota of crime. Whether it succumbs to economic pressure or is vulnerable on other grounds depends on the social and cultural configurations that characterize the community at a given time in its history.

(5) INCREASING KNOWLEDGE OF CRIME DETERMINANTS AND PENAL PHILOSOPHY

To a considerable degree, the knowledge concerning the treatment and classification of criminals, and the public attitudes developed accordingly, may be said to reflect an important aspect of the ideology of the entire culture.[23] The underlying attitudes toward the poverty-stricken, the disenfranchised, the marginal groups, the strangers, and the prisoners of a society afford a significant insight into the prevailing culture-mentality, its standards and its values.

Since the early work of Lombroso and his associates during the latter part of the nineteenth century, enormous strides have been made toward the fuller comprehension of the factors that lead to crime. The development of human knowledge, however, is not always paced by the development of corresponding programs of action. If it is to be acted upon, a new conception, regardless of its objective validity, must in some way be congenial to the prevailing system of values. The resistance to new ideas, as the history of science has shown, is often prolonged and bitter. If the new conception runs counter to fundamental mores and deeply entrenched institutional values, the nature of the opposition will be particularly bitter.

Although basic modifications in penal philosophy have been developed since the work of Lombroso, the formulation of adequate procedures for treatment of the offenders has not kept pace. Our increasing insights into the problem of how to eradicate crime have not met with adequate response for three major reasons: (1) The large mass of the public and its

[23] Cf. Lewis E. Lawes, *Twenty Thousand Years in Sing Sing* (New York, 1932).

legislative representatives are still ignorant of the advances made in the field of the social sciences. (2) There is an unwillingness to "experiment" with new methods. This is due particularly to the punitive attitude that persists among the public, in the courts, and elsewhere in the administration of criminal justice. (3) Responsible agencies fail to implement accepted principles with comprehensive programs of action. To illustrate the last point, adequate probation and parole work may not be undertaken unless the community is willing to underwrite the expense of well-trained officials in sufficient quantity to do the job that has been approved by law. The result has been a kind of "cultural lag" in our legislature, courts, prisons, and reformatories in the acceptance, application, and promotion of the new findings in criminology.

The indeterminate sentence and the new methods of classification. Two emphases have been apparent in penological thought since the beginning of the present century: (a) the prevention of crime and (b) the potentialities for reform of the apprehended offender. In addition to sporadic community efforts, the result of this new trend has manifested itself in revised court procedures and reform in our reformatories and prisons. On the assumption, largely psychiatric in origin, that crime represents abnormal behavior tendencies it has seemed to some reasonable that jail and prison sentences should be administered with an eye to the rehabilitation of the offender. The argument is frequently advanced that crime is nothing but a kind of "mental illness"; since it is foolhardy to sentence a sick patient to the hospital for a stipulated period of years, it is equally baseless to sentence an offender to an institution except as a measure of reformation, treatment, and cure. The length of his incarceration (as in the case of the contagiously sick person) would depend upon the duration of his "illness" and the evidence he gives of making an adjustment to society as a "normal person." The shortcomings of this argument are (1) we still lack precise knowledge concerning the causation of crime, and (2) the signs of "moral" reformation are not as readily visible as are the signs of physical reformation that medical examiners make use of. Too many inaccurate diagnoses would result in considerable danger to the community.

Since the end of the nineteenth century there has been an increasing recourse to the "indeterminate sentence," which is based fundamentally on the above philosophy. At the discretion of the courts in many of our states, a minimum sentence, usually of one year, may be set. In addition, an undetermined upper limit, or, more commonly, a specific upper limit, is set. Within this period, the prisoner may, theoretically, be released if he is considered a "good risk." The entire procedure thus rests on the belief that the prisoner, under adequate guidance, may in time display possibilities of reform warranting his release from custody.

According to the procedure of the indeterminate sentence, administration depends on the psychological potentialities of the offender and not on the nature of the offense, although in most jurisdictions the nature of the offense still plays the major role in controlling the judge's disposition of the case. The criminal codes in all states are still largely oriented about the traditional conception of the commission of a culpable offense and the intent behind it. The confusion in the law about the responsibility of the offender is apparent in the frequent wranglings in our courts that are occasioned by the testimony of expert alienists on the "sanity" of defendants.

The indeterminate sentence represents a new principle in the law. Its limits are set in theory by the requirements of the protection of the public from further molestation by the offender and of the ability of the offender to make an effective return to society as a normal individual. Just as the criminal code has been steadily rewritten so that youthful malefactors in some states are classified as *types* of offenders, rather than according to the nature of their offenses, so we are likely to witness a slow transformation of the law concerning adult offenders.

Prisons and correctional institutions are also feeling the effect of this development. Special institutions for special kinds of offenders, based on their age, psychological constitutions, and social qualities, and the careful classification of offenders upon entry into the penal system are becoming common. The earlier penal philosophy classified criminals according to the nature of their felonies, despite the diverse factors of causation that entered into each unique offense. The increasing recognition that certain kinds of legal transgressions, such as various sex crimes, are based on psychopathologies is causing medical and therapeutic care to supplant and to supplement forms of custodial care in many of our institutions. Recognizing that these offenses have a pathological basis and may not be adjudged on the same ground as other felonies, the New York State Legislature in 1948, impelled by a special message from Governor Thomas E. Dewey, mandated a special committee to make a study of this type of crime, with powers to recommend special treatment for such offenders.[24] Massachusetts, Pennsylvania, California, and other states have instituted similar investigations with a view toward modifying the law.

The classification of offenders along the lines indicated has already resulted in the establishment of classification centers in many of our states. In California, for example, a number of these centers have been established for the purpose of early intensive investigation of different kinds of offenders. The effort is made to insure proper penal placement

[24] The investigations of this committee resulted in the passage of the Sexual Offenders Law in March 1950, which gives the courts extremely wide latitude in the disposition of such cases, according to reformative capacities of the offenders.

and eventual social reform and return to society. In New York State, the Elmira Reception Center, housed in a separate wing of one of the state's oldest reformatories, and staffed by psychiatrists, clinical psychologists, and professional educators, has been in operation since 1945. According to the director of this center, which deals primarily with youthful offenders from sixteen to twenty-one years of age, its primary functions are: (1) careful study of offenders by a competent professional staff, (2) segregation based on scientific methods, (3) treatment based on careful study of the individual inmate, (4) a sound orientation program for all inmates, (5) improvement of institutional programs based on study of the inmates, and (6) the development of research concerning the causes and treatment of delinquency.[25]

If the indeterminate sentence is to become an effective instrument of penal reform and penal rehabilitation, it will be only through careful classification methods and improvement in the scope, objectives, and administration of custodial care. The trend toward improvement of educational standards in our institutions and the character of custodial care, from sheer protective custody to a form of genuine guidance, has been belated and slow. The last three decades, however, have been marked by a certain amount of progress. The movement to supplant the old-time politically appointed wardens by competent and well-trained penal administrators, many of them psychiatrists or trained in the social sciences and psychiatric care, has grown. This movement is most marked, perhaps, in New York, Massachusetts, Connecticut, Pennsylvania, Illinois, Wisconsin, Minnesota, and California. An institution, despite the legal framework within which it operates, may reflect the point of view and the penal attitudes of its administration.[26]

Even the well-trained administrator, however, is helpless if his staff is inadequate. In 1935, Governor Lehman of New York called a conference in Albany on *Crime, the Criminal, and Society*. There it was observed that, unless the standards of prison personnel were sufficiently raised, the best designed plans and the most highly qualified administrations would in the long run prove ineffective. For this reason, the conference urged that minimal educational standards be established for the custodial staff of the prisons and reformatories of the state. It was further recommended that members of the staff be specialists in teaching and guidance so that programs of re-education and rehabilitation could be developed as an integral phase of the entire penal process. Although segregation and detention, as punitive and protective measures, still con-

[25] Cf. Glenn M. Kendall, "The New York State Reception Center," *Federal Probation*, XII (Sept., 1948), 42–7.

[26] See Victor F. Nelson, *Prison Days and Nights* (Boston, 1933), pp. 51–72 and *passim*.

stitute the major concern of most penal systems, the growth of the larger view—of the prison and the reformatory as temporary detention centers for the redemption of those offenders who are capable of reform—is being slowly implemented as the result of our increasing knowledge.

Probation. In keeping with the new penal philosophy, the procedures of probation have become widely established in courts throughout the country. Probation is the procedure whereby, on the occasion of his conviction by the court, the offender receives a conditional suspended sentence. He is released by the court under the supervision of an appointed probation officer for a given period of time. The objective of good probationary care is to provide effective guidance and supervision in a normal community environment, based upon principles of social case work and sound diagnosis of the probationer's personality. During the period of this supervision, he has regular contact with this official and is subject to a series of rules and regulations circumscribing and controlling his behavior. In accordance with the conditional nature of the particular suspended sentence, any infraction of the rules deemed serious by the probationary supervisor may result in the offender's return to the jurisdiction of the court and consequent sentencing to a penal institution.

Probation services in our states have been organized in both the juvenile and the adult courts. They are designed primarily to assist the first offender, to spare him the blemish of a prison or a reformatory record and the adverse effect on his personality which prison life may produce. Although the procedures for adults and juveniles have much in common, they are usually most commonly employed and most intensively pursued for child offenders. In most states, preliminary investigations of the indicted individual must be made by the probation officer before the case actually comes to trial. It has become fairly common for the courts to exercise the option of appointing volunteer and temporary probation officers, as well, from the ranks of responsible and competent citizens who are willing to assume the responsibility. Frequently, officials of case-work agencies and private children's institutions may be called upon to serve in this capacity, usually in conjunction with their responsibilities as heads of private institutions with which the child may be placed. As with other phases of a well-regulated penal system, however, probation services can be best accomplished only through the functioning of well-trained and professional probation officers.

Probationary care of convicted offenders, if properly administered, can be an effective method for the treatment of delinquents and criminals. Not only is it realistic in that it attempts at the outset to train the individual for living and working in the normal community, instead of exposing him to the degenerative atmosphere of the average prison, but it may be conducted at considerable saving to the taxpayer. When probationers fail, they usually do so because they are poor risks in the first place, and second, because the officials who supervise them are frequently poorly equipped for the task. The shortcomings of probation officers may be summarized as follows: (1) They are still, for the greater part, inadequately qualified in training and experience for their positions; (2) their case-loads in most instances are far too heavy to enable them to give the individual care which each case requires; (3) they are frequently overburdened with additional duties which make it difficult for them to carry on properly their duties in behalf of probationers; and (4) they frequently lack understanding and training in the proper use of community resources.

After the preliminary investigation has been presented to the court the remainder of the supervision many probation officers conduct is largely perfunctory and nominal. Yet, probation, to be a significant instrument in the redemption of offenders, must be based on sound case-work principles. Effective case-work, psychiatric and otherwise, involves concentrated application to each individual case by highly trained workers. Very few graduate schools of social work even today give the type of specialized training which this kind of guidance demands.

Parole. Parole is that penal procedure whereby the convicted offender, after having spent a certain amount of time in prison, is released under the supervision of specially designated parole officers. Probation involves custodial supervision for convicted persons who are *not* sentenced to prison; parole is a conditional, supervised release granted after the person has already served part of his sentence.

In order to safeguard the interests of the community, parole boards are likely to be extremely stringent in the granting of parole. Contrary to popular opinion, the large majority of offenders who apply for parole, or who automatically are brought up for consideration, are *not* granted this privilege. In 1937, over 70 per cent of those whose cases were considered during the first nine months by the New York State Board of Parole were rejected. In 1947, 55.7 per cent of those who were eligible for a hearing were rejected.[27] Because of the great care exercised in selection, the percentage of those who make good during the period of parole supervision is quite high. In 1946, for example, in a study made by the New York Board of Parole of paroled prisoners supervised for a five year period, 88 per cent were found to have not been convicted of new crimes.[28] In recent reports by the Federal Board of Parole, it is estimated that about 90 per cent of federal parolees make good during the period of parole. Although promising, figures are not as high in several other states, and the

[27] *Eighteenth Annual Report of the Division of Parole,* January 1, 1947 to December 31, 1947, New York State, p. 8.

[28] *Seventeenth Annual Report of the Division of Parole,* January 1, 1946 to December 31, 1946, New York State, p. 157.

percentages in general are not as high for the post-parole period after supervision has been removed.[29]

The attitudes of the released offender may be quite different from those of the convicted offender who has never been in prison. For this reason, modern methods of parole emphasize the need for preliminary preparation (beginning as early as the first day of entering into prison) for the prisoner's eventual release, as well as the guarantee of employment and a place for him in the community, upon his return. Under the leadership of Frederick B. Moran, chairman of the New York State Board of Parole and an experienced social worker, an attempt has been made to put into action this fundamental parole procedure. To this end, an interesting experiment has been developed since 1937 in Wallkill State Prison in New York through the institution of the so-called "service units." Through these service units, the inmate has direct and continuous access to an agency within the prison which assists him in planning for his eventual release on the basis of his vocational, educational, and general needs. The parole officer, to whom he will eventually be assigned, operates in close conjunction with the "service unit" during the period preparatory to release, and the prisoner is released only when adequate assurance exists as to employment and acceptance in his native community or other community of settlement. By the development of such comprehensive case-work methods, parole techniques may become increasingly effective as instruments of rehabilitation and reformation.

(6) MODERN PENAL TRENDS AND OBJECTIVES

In the foreword to the Gluecks' study of five hundred and ten offenders, Dr. Richard C. Cabot, in referring to the habitual type of offender, says: "Either he must be prevented (if any one can do it), or he must be kept indefinitely in confinement, or he must be turned loose—as he is now—to continue his life of crime until he gets tired of it." [30] The general trends in research during the past two decades have shown the general directions which must be taken in regard to the three eventualities mentioned by Dr. Cabot if the problem of crime prevention is to be solved. Recent findings about crime and the changing social situation have indicated that criminal activity does not consist of unitary acts performed by certain types of individuals. Rather, it is a kind of behavior, induced by a particular set of circumstances in the environment, which society has termed criminal. *Criminal conduct represents a kind of adaptive response to the environment*. Those whom we call criminals either have developed

[29] *Five Hundred Criminal Careers* (New York, 1930), pp. 184–5.
[30] Glueck and Glueck, *Five Hundred Criminal Careers* (New York, 1930), p. xiii.

their practices through "differential associations" (that is, by indentifying themselves with certain groups whose activities and general orientations are anti-social) or have become temporarily disposed toward the commission of illegal acts under special circumstances of emotional stress, need, or pathological deficiency. Our knowledge of the criminal process, as Ruth Cavan has indicated, suggests the following principles for dealing with crime and crime prevention: [31]

(1) Since criminal behavior is a response to special social contacts or frustrations, it may be prevented from developing by removal of criminal patterns of conduct on the one hand and of frustrating situations on the other. . . .

(2) Since criminal habits are learned, they may be modified or replaced by law-abiding habits through a process of retraining. . . .

(3) Since the successful treatment of criminals is rehabilitative, there is little need for punishment unless it is incorporated into a general and integrated program of rehabilitation.

(4) Since crime results from various motives and criminals are not all of the same personality type, individualized treatment is necessary.

In keeping with these principles, the attack upon crime involves a multiple approach. It requires the integration of community resources and a broadening of the scope of both the judicial process and penal administration. The current ideology is based on principles of rehabilitation and an increasing acceptance of the naturalistic view that the individual's failures are determined by forces not entirely within his own control. The effects of this ideology, present and anticipated, are threefold.

In the first place, the trend is undoubtedly toward continued use of our prisons, penitentiaries, and reformatories as centers of correction. This corrective function will be advanced by the collaboration of outside community resources through such programs as parole. Eventually, the conception of the law as a punitive instrument will be modified.

Secondly, the function of the courts will also undergo continuing transformation. If the courts are to function in the reclamation process, they must recognize the division of their responsibility: (a) the determination of guilt and (b) the imposition of penalties. No one will deny the right of the judge to serve as arbiter in the determination of guilt under the present penal codes. If the reformative interest is to be served, however, it must be recognized that the matter of imposing penalties involves

[31] Ruth S. Cavan, *Criminology* (New York, 1948), p. 665.

a completely different kind of process, for which most judges are entirely unsuited. Legal training cannot make a person adequate to the task of formulating the difficult decisions upon which successful rehabilitation may be based. This is a matter for social diagnosis by experts, rather than for decision by law, although it is the law that must determine the limitations within which such a diagnosis will operate. For this reason, the criminal courts may come in time to depend on the services of panels of experts, consisting of psychiatrists, clinical psychologists, sociologists, educators, and social case-workers, to assist them in the sentencing procedure. Indeed, some recommendations go so far as to urge that the sentencing procedure be taken out of the judge's hands completely and placed under the authority of such panels. That these recommendations have a very considerable basis in reality may be seen in the fact that the Youth Correction Authority Act, drafted by the American Law Institute, and already in practice in California, Minnesota, Wisconsin, Texas, and Massachusetts, places convicted youthful offenders under twenty-one years of age under the jurisdiction of the State Youth Authority, with wide discretionary responsibility for diagnosis, treatment, and re-establishment in the community.[32]

Thirdly, the growing recognition of the responsibility of the local community must be noted. The voluntary efforts by interested and sympathetic public-minded citizens, while helpful, are largely ineffective in the long run unless supplemented by state assistance on a legal basis. The experience of the teams of diagnostic experts sent out to make intensive studies of local communities with specific recommendations for the improvement of local conditions, operating under the California Youth Authority Act, is an indication of the kind of effective approach required in many cases. The findings of such community surveys are of little value, however, unless the resources of the community are successfully integrated and co-ordinated in a unified effort to meet the problem of local crime. If maladjusted and delinquent behavior represents an adaptation to a *determining* set of victimizing circumstances, then adjusted and non-criminal behavior may be obtained by "entrapping" the impulses of the delinquent and criminal within the matrix of socially beneficial conditions. In the verse from a well-known Gilbert and Sullivan operetta, "When a felon's not engaged in his employment, nor pursuing his nefarious little plans, his capacity for innocent enjoyment is just as great as any honest man's." The task of the community is to create a set of conditions that will meet his capacity for "innocent enjoyment" and, in the

[32] In this connection, see H. A. Bloch, "Social Change and the Delinquent Personality," (*Current Approaches to Delinquency*), 1949 *Yearbook* (National Probation and Parole Association, New York), pp. 231–48.

inimitable verse of Gilbert, keep him "a-basking in the sun" and not "a-jumping on his mother."

SUMMARY

In the comprehensive survey of crime which we have undertaken, we have attempted to show the primacy of the sociological frame of reference. (1) The separate factors that are studied in relation to crime must always be viewed in the particular social setting. (2) Although a basis exists for the belief that modern cultural life produces a higher rate of psychoneurotic and psychotic disorders, such pathological states are responsible for only a limited amount of crime. The large bulk of crime is caused by individuals of normal mentality, although such factors as emotional stress and differential personality growth must always be considered in studying the individual offender. Psychoanalytical and psychiatric interpretations have been most successful when they have sought to determine the basis for specific types of "abnormal crimes" and when they have taken into account the sociological and cultural factors. (3) Seasonal and climatic variations in crime are affected by the social, cultural, and economic needs affecting the behavior of individuals during the different seasons of the year and under varying climatic conditions. The evidence in studies seeking to find relationships between climatic and seasonal conditions and crime is highly insubstantial and inconclusive. When such relationships are found—as between property crimes and cooler climates, and crimes against the person and warmer regions and seasons—the basis for such relationships is to be sought in the socio-cultural opportunities manifesting themselves within different physical, climatic, and seasonal settings. (4) Changing conditions of economic life and the variations of the business cycle seem to have affected both crime rates and the character of crime. Recent studies of the depression of 1929, unlike earlier investigations, disclose that crime rates did not rise appreciably as a result of depressed economic conditions. The effects of economic depressions upon the more stable rural areas, however, may have produced changes in the character and type of crime in such regions. (5) The increasing knowledge of the determinants of crime has had an effect on penal philosophy and practice. This knowledge, as is the case with all social innovations, encounters resistance in the degree to which it is uncongenial to the values of the culture. Nevertheless, the growth of the indeterminate sentence, parole, and probation services attests to the increasing acceptance of the new deterministic theories of crime, with their modern emphasis on rehabilitation rather than on punishment. The degree of resistance to the new theories is exemplified by the fact that the new procedures they entail, because of lack of adequate implementation in action, are frequently little more than "legislative gestures." (6) Finally, the new drifts in penal philosophy are becoming discernible in the modification of penal institutions as centers for rehabilitation and reform, the insistence on change in judicial procedures, and emphasis on the responsibility of the community for the development of integrated and coordinated programs in conjunction with the state.

CHAPTER THIRTEEN

SEXUAL PATHOLOGIES AND THE SOCIAL ORDER

(1) THE UNIVERSALITY OF SEXUAL CODES*

CODES of sexual behavior are found in all societies; even in primitive societies unrestricted sexual expression is extremely rare if not nonexistent. To be sure, the sexual codes of other cultures may be so unlike our own that we may regard them as "abnormal"; in so viewing them, however, we are examining another culture not by its norms but by our own values.

What we regard as the "normal" behavior of men and women in their relations to each other and in respect to their attitudes towards themselves is largely a reflection of traditional values which have been deeply and early implanted within the personality by training and social conditioning. Equipped with these "normal" outlooks, we are inclined to regard as abnormal or pathological such practices as the "sexual hospitality" of the Eskimo, who extends the sexual favors of his wife to a visiting guest, or the tacit approval given to freedom in premarital sex relations among the Samoans. Nevertheless, irrespective of the differences in patterning of sexual behavior from society to society and the common but erroneous notion that such differences are representative of instinctive mechanisms rather than cultural conditioning, all societies have developed their own codes for the regulation of sexual conduct.

(2) SOCIOLOGY, NOT BIOLOGY, EXPLAINS SEXUAL CODES AND BEHAVIORS

Biological differences, of course, generally determine sexual behavior; yet, the traditional functions of men and women are only partially, and sometimes to a very limited extent, determined by differences in physiological structure and physical capacity. In Western culture men generally till the soil, build the house, and provide for the family; but in many primitive communities such activities remain largely the duties of women while the men live in comparative ease.

* Numbers of the subheads in this chapter refer to the summary at the end of Chapter XIV.

Men behave like men and women like women because society has taught them how to do so and has come to expect such behavior from them. Different modes of behavior and attitudes are inculcated in individuals from the time they are children; they comprise not only a part of the training procedures and techniques to which children are exposed, but are part of the entire emotional and social atmosphere in which they pass their lives as human beings. The play-habits of children and their imitation of adults embody the differing social conceptions of the roles and characteristics of men and women. The early childhood play of the girl with dolls and simulated households tasks, and the interest of the boy in the masculine activities of his father, reflect the deeply ingrained attitudes which each society tends to foster in its children.

Because such different functions carry with them certain attitudes, expectancies, and emotional involvements, by the time the child has reached adulthood, the differences appear to be a fundamental and almost "innate" part of the organism. However such differences do not necessarily arise from differences in the instinctual mechanisms of men and women. The great variety of differences we observe in the attitudes and emotional behavior of men and women are created out of the social expectancies which have been developed during the period of their early training.

Although it has been recognized for some time that these differences may be fostered by the environment, only recently has scientific confirmation of this view come from the anthropologist. Recent studies of Mead, Malinowski, and Benedict document the observation that the behaviors suitable for men and for women are culturally determined. Of the three South Pacific groups studied by Mead, the Arapesh appear to produce a like form of behavior for both sexes. The male is quiet, gentle, docile, and entirely "lady-like." The Mundugumor, however, appear to foster in both sexes a bellicose, truculent, "bully-ish" type of behavior that reminds us of certain forms of ideal masculine behavior in our own society. Among the Tchambuli the men are reared according to a standard of behavior that is similar to what we would expect of women in our society, while the women appear to be decidedly "masculine," by our standards, in their attitudes and emotional displays.[1]

The historical past of each of these separate sexual traditions gave rise to the formation of ideal "sex types." Very few men and very few

[1] That certain deeply rooted psychological differences may exist, as emphasized particularly by the Freudian school of psychology, is not denied. Cf. F. Lundberg and M. F. Farnham, *Modern Woman: The Lost Sex* (New York, 1947), Chaps. 6–9. However, the greater number of secondary psychological characteristics, by which we most frequently characterize and identify such differences between the sexes, are created primarily out of conditions of social contact and the social processes. Cf. Mead, *Male and Female* (New York, 1949), pp. 128–43.

women in any society can conform completely to all features of these "ideal types." In all societies, some women will tend, on occasion, to display masculine behavior, while some men will display feminine behavior. Psychologically speaking, sexual behavior may be portrayed as extended along a spectrum, with deviation from the ideal norms which each society fosters.[2]

The "ideal types" developed in each society, however, are significant not only because they represent the desired objectives towards which all men and women should aspire, but because they represent, as well, the judgments and attitudes which the sexes have developed toward each other and toward society in general. As society changes, the ideal statuses and roles of men and women change likewise. Actually, there are "styles in women" as there are styles in manners, clothes, and houses.

The position of women, particularly in Western society, has constituted a vital index of the state of culture of that society and the types of judgments which have been made historically upon many of its important values. In general, despite the periodic attempts in Western history to elevate the status of women to a position of equality with men, the predominant tendency nurtured in European and American history has been to promote the ascendancy and supremacy of men. In Western culture, until recently, women have had a secondary position in society, a position which has provided the basis for many of our confused attitudes today. The role, status, and psychological complexitics of woman were considered to be the results of her inner constitution.

Sexual codes, a matter of sociological status. We have learned that the structure of every society depends upon the conceived expectancies of different groups and individuals as they reveal themselves in more or less uniform behavior tendencies. Furthermore, these behavior tendencies are culturally patterned. The conceptions which individuals have of their own functions in society and their notions of the functions of others fit into a general pattern of statuses. *These statuses are the traditionally and socially developed positions which individuals maintain with respect to certain conventional social patterns, and their psychological conditions arise out of the accompanying expectancies individuals develop in relation to such statuses.* A minister, for example, has a specific status in our social organization. We expect of him certain types of behavior relative to a personal code of ethics, position in the community, attitudes toward his parishioners, and the kind of pronouncements he is expected to deliver on Sundays. Our conception of his status is quite distinct from our conception of the status of the habitué of the corner tavern and the betting fraternity in the back room of the local news shop. In the case of other status-positions, particularly in respect to the prestige-rankings which such

[2] Margaret Mead, *Male and Female*, pp. 132–6.

positions enjoy, culturally specified conditions denote the range and permissive limitations which such behavior should take. In a status such as that of the industrial or business tycoon, the banker, the local physician or lawyer, occupational and other social attributes combine to determine the area in which the prescribed behavior of the individual shall function. Thus, it might be possible for the local tycoon, with a bland yet dangerous ignorance, to hold forth on any number of different issues, frequently far removed from the definitions prescribed by the status, and have his judgments relative to religious issues, political views, and the morality of youth, listened to with a great deal of respect. The minister, however, who ventures afield from his judgments on religious and parish matters, to give opinions on economic, political, and social issues, may not only find his views unacceptable but his very status in the community strongly threatened. The latitude with which an individual may, in his expression, move from the circumscribed limits of his defined status frequently denotes the degree to which certain values are maintained within the culture, and reveals a good deal about the character of the culture itself.

Sex behavior is largely dependent on status-definition. These status definitions change in relation to age. The status definitions for both sexes may be quite similar at one stage, only to diverge widely as the individual matures and achieves adulthood. Such social definitions, denoting the differences in sexual behavior, spring largely from economic, political, social, and cultural considerations. In a highly competitive society, where economic privilege and property are handed down through the female line, and where property rights are largely in female hands, the position of women is likely to be quite high. In a militaristic caste society, however, where the prowess of the warrior is necessary for the preservation of the group, male virtues are highly exalted, while women may be prized only for their capacity to produce strong male offspring (as in the case of the Spartans).

The roles of men and women are always conditioned by considerations of prestige as they reflect the dominant cultural notions of a given society. As societies are modified in structure and form, the cultural values show the new directions in which the society is facing. Through modifications of status, prestige values change, and alterations occur in the relative positions of men and women. However, here as in all phases of the social fabric, dislocations are likely to occur. Although changing conditions may seem to foster the development of new statuses for men and women, "cultural lags" may still exist, as evidenced by the reluctance with which these new values are accepted. Consequently, despite important new privileges which may be accorded to women, the public attitudes toward their status may reflect an earlier period in the growth of the society.[3] In any event, the status of the sexes always gives an important indication of the structure of the society and an effective insight into the way in which the cultural values of the group are organized.

Linton, in his analysis of status and role, regards sex status as one of the basic structural components of the social order, ranking along with age and family relationships. Such statuses, determined by biological considerations and accidents of birth, are culturally *given* and constitute "ascribed statuses." These are contrasted with the "achieved statuses" which, within the limitations imposed by the culture, the individual may attain by technical skill and other proficiencies. Despite the general significance accorded to the various types of ascribed status, such as membership in certain social units and class and caste, he appears to hold these in general to be secondary to the cultural roles reflecting the biological considerations just mentioned.[4]

(3) HISTORICAL FACTORS IN CONTEMPORARY SEXUAL MORALITY

Statuses not only provide the basic structural elements around which the society is organized but also represent the nodal points of resistance to the factors of social change. During periods of rapid social transition, the basic attitudes involved in accepting the traditional conceptions of the roles in society frequently contradict the emergent new definitions which spring up as a result of such change. (During the contemporary period, the definitions concerning sexual functions and prerogatives are frequently highly contradictory.) In general, the problems concerning status during a period of social change arise from three primary sources: (1) there may be conflicts in attitude and definition concerning the nature of the status in question; (2) difficulties may be created as a result of the inability and unwillingness of masses of individuals to identify themselves with the given status; and (3) emergent definitions of status, accepted in certain social areas and by certain social groups, may be incompatible with traditional conceptions, creating contradictions throughout the entire culture pattern.

At the present time, all three of these modes seem to be present in relation to the role of women in modern society. The failure to integrate the conception of woman's status not only brings about a high incidence of personality conflict and personality disorder, particularly among

[3] To a certain degree, this is the position in which modern Western women find themselves to-day.

[4] Cf. Ralph Linton, *The Study of Man* (New York, 1936), Chap. 8, pp. 126–7.

women, but at the same time disorients a great many other important aspects of social life. Marred family life, sexual difficulties within and outside the family, and strain in the relationship of parents to children are all aspects of the disorganizing effects which this inability to determine the integrated status of women in modern society has produced. Although the modern definition of men's sexual role is also not free of ambiguity, the central place of woman in the family and her primary function of child-rearing and nurture makes this dilemma of the contemporary period a problem peculiarly of "the modern woman."

The traditional factors determining the status of modern women in society are themselves highly contradictory. They are representative of the development of different phases in the history of Western culture. Historically considered, the major social forces which have played an instrumental role in fashioning our prevalent conceptions concerning sexual behavior are the following: (1) the ascetic ideal of the Christian Church, particularly in its early development; (2) the romantic movement and its subsequent historical effects; (3) the Industrial Revolution; (4) the rising movement of political individualism; and (5) modern developments in science, particularly those of the nineteenth century, and recent perspectives in the field of biology.

(1) To a certain degree, we have never fully escaped the strong ascetic ideals of the early Church fathers. The strictures upon sexual freedom and license by St. Paul, Augustine, Tertullian, and others are extremely emphatic and severe. The early Church, springing into prominence during a period of vast sexual license and extravagance, was strongly impelled to denounce a set of conditions which were at such variance with its ideals. Despite changing attitudes towards sexual morality in Western history, the condemnation of sexual behavior, tolerated only in marriage, has become and still remains an important basis of our present morality.

(2) Contradicting this emphasis, and rising in partial reaction to it, has been the development of the romantic movement. Manifested at first in the peculiar cult of the Virgin, an attempt to idealize the Holy Mother at the expense of the other sacred figures of the Trinity, and banned by the Church, a number of movements arose which had as their chief objective the glorification of woman. Abetted by the medieval chivalric code, the movement was further advanced by the humanism of the Renaissance. The post-Renaissance period and the Reformation succeeded in modifying the concept upon a more realistic basis. The recognition of the importance of personal response and satisfaction in sexual relations, supplanting the attitude that sexual relations were (for women) a social rite and obligation, began to win increasing adherence. Finally, encouraged and facilitated by the commercial, industrial, and political develop-

ments of the eighteenth and nineteenth centuries, the romantic movement has found a peculiar expression in modern American life, where sex relations are regarded in terms of personal response rather than in terms of social obligation.

(3) The Industrial Revolution, promoting the impersonality of social relations, and giving rise to women's employment, placed the relationship of the sexes in still a new form. No longer the chattels of men as far as their economic rights were concerned, women were moved to express their new-found freedom in the direction of political emancipation and the various women's rights movements.

(4) Stirred into being during the eighteenth century "age of enlightenment," the political individualism of the nineteenth century was far-reaching in its effect. Although women's political emancipation was considerably retarded as compared with the growing enfranchisement of men, and still is, the concept of individual rights and liberties affected many phases of social life other than the political.

(5) These historic forces, running counter to the early ascetic ideal, appear to have won confirmation for individual rights through the accomplishments of nineteenth-century science, particularly in the field of biology. The disintegration of former theological views was promoted by the new biological and naturalistic emphasis in human relations, abetted by the work of Darwin and Freud, and publicized through the writings of the so-called sexologists, Kraft-Ebbing, Havelock Ellis, and others.

(4) RECENT SECONDARY INFLUENCES AFFECTING MODERN SEXUALITY

A number of immediate influences upon the conception of individual responsibility have arisen out of the conditions of our modern industrial and commercial environment. These immediate influences can be summarized under the following headings: (1) mobility; (2) anonymity; (3) cultural individualization; and (4) scientific discoveries, particularly as they (a) encourage the development of leisure in the household, and (b) foster ideologies contradictory to older theological conceptions. These emergent forces have added to the complexities of our modern sexual attitudes, intensifying the contradictions in attitude which the historical process has produced.

The efficiency and speed of modern communication have produced high levels of mobility. Among the earliest effects of this mobility has been the continuing concentration of vast numbers of the population in our large cities, to live in close physical proximity and yet impersonally. Mobility has weakened the bonds which hold the family together and has created a number of incidental by-products in the form of special psychological characteristics modifying still further our attitudes toward sex, family life, and general morality. These associated alterations in attitude may be seen in the readiness with which change itself is accepted, and, what is probably even more basic, they manifest themselves in the weakening of our primary ties to geographical location and group. For centuries past, these basic linkages to place and group—what Carleton Hayes, the historian, has referred to in another connection as "localism"—were instrumental in both integrating and providing an emotional basis for personality. Such integrating factors of the personality have been considerably dissipated.

Closely associated with this mobility have been the factors of anonymity and impersonality, which migration and mobility inevitably induce. This anonymity is found primarily in our large cities and particularly in those areas where young people live and congregate. It is relatively easy for individuals, separated from their home ties, to develop relationships which ordinarily would not be permissible in their own communities.

A third important phase of our contemporary society is the acute degree of individualization it promotes. This individualization is not only a phase of our political life but constitutes, in effect, a phase of every aspect of our social living. It is encouraged by our competitive economic practice and is supported by our traditional belief in the relatively unrestricted rights of the individual in commerce and industry. Such values have crept into our vast educational and cultural enterprises as well, placing a high premium upon individual values in a great variety of activities. From the very outset, young people are encouraged to "be themselves" and to think and act for themselves. Despite enormous pressures to conform, individualization is as much a part of our cultural life as the very atmosphere which we breathe. Through the encouragement of the cultural setting favoring individuality, hedonistic values are attached to matters of personal response and personal satisfaction. One of the significant consequences is that an unusually high premium is placed upon the rights of the individual to find free expression in those matters which are associated with his person, and upon the satisfactions to be derived from personal privilege and pleasure.

Finally, as the last contemporary factor which has affected significantly our sex morality, we have the enormous impact of scientific discoveries, which have created leisure for the masses of the population on an unprecedented scale. The effects of modern science upon our contemporary sexuality may be seen in two principal respects. In the first place, many modern women have been freed from the previous drudgeries which accompanied the life of the wife and housekeeper. Modern time-saving devices have created a historically unique class of "leisure-ridden" women who find themselves unable to put to effective use the time which the benefits of science have produced. Modern science has also made it possible to rid men and women of many of their former fears concerning the sex act. Not only have individual horizons been enlarged by the scientific view, but advances in medical science have freed human beings for the first time from the responsibilities of child-rearing which, heretofore, had always been regarded as the natural consequence of the sex act. The universality of knowledge concerning the use of contraceptive devices and the ease with which they may be obtained have tended to place a value upon the sex act itself. The fear of conceiving is no longer an important deterrent to sexual activity.

(5) TREND TOWARD A SINGLE STANDARD

With the beginning of the nineteenth century, the trend toward a single standard of sexual behavior was already clearly marked. The theory of the single standard of morality admits of no essential differences in the sexual practices of men and women. In the past, when differences in sexual standards for men and women were accepted with an air of realistic resignation, despite the ideal of continence for both sexes preached by the church, it was universally recognized that sex indulgence for a woman could not be condoned. Since the period of medieval culture, various kinds of rationalizations were produced, attesting to the necessity of sexual gratification for men, even when sexual practices were not officially condoned. The nineteenth century witnessed a liberalization in the thinking of men and women concerning distinctions in sexual activity. With the growth of women's movements for the emancipation and liberation of their sex in political and social matters, there followed a less resistant attitude toward sex indulgence on the part of women. Helped along by the fact that the sex act need no more bring about the consequences of child-birth, and the diminution of fears which this knowledge induced, the belief became current in certain quarters that both men and women had a "right" to sex activity, provided that certain essential legal and social obligations were not destroyed.

It is interesting to note in this respect that, with the development toward a single standard of sex practice, considerable stress has been laid on the necessity of full emotional satisfaction in sex life as well as in other phases of personality development. Nevertheless, little distinction has been drawn as to the differing psychological involvements and problems created for men and women by this affirmation of identical sexual privileges. In fact, the sexual needs of men and women, even relative to such matters as periodicity and frequency of the sex act, were frequently considered to be quite similar. Other than for the fact of their anatomical differences, men and women were regarded as identical elements in the sexual equation, a fact which the proponents of liberal sexual attitudes believe was obscured by the superstitious beliefs of the past, and which the new age of scientific liberalism is supposed to have brought once more to light.

This failure to distinguish adequately between the differing psychological and emotional needs of men and women with respect to the sex act Lundberg and Farnham regard as constituting a fundamental source of tension in contemporary society.[5] They make it clear that the nature of the sex act, regardless of whether or not children are produced, will always of necessity be quite different for men and women from the standpoint of emotional involvements and social consequences. Farnham seems to believe that a great many of the social and psychological difficulties which modern women suffer may be attributed, in considerable degree, to this failure to distinguish between the character of sexual participation for men and women. The complex organism of the woman, *irrespective of the sexual mores which may be prevailing,* seems to require a different type of sexual orientation, based upon her uniquely constituted needs. According to Lundberg and Farnham, we are living in a revolutionary period where our sexual standards are quite chaotic, particularly in regard to the effects they produce upon the personalities of modern women. Disorganization in personal relationships occurs as a consequence of this confused notion of the single standard.[6]

Nevertheless, the single standard of sexual practice, although a matter of public discussion and recognition, has never been widely adopted in American culture.[7] Public interest in the single standard betokens an increased tolerance and liberalism about the entire problem of sexual practice, part of which is reflected in a more liberal attitude toward the sexual practices of women. However, even to-day, the public attitude in general still remains largely condemnatory as far as the uncommitted sexual acts of women are concerned.

The "new morality." The modern point of view about sexual practice is sometimes regarded as constituting a "new morality." According to this doctrine, sexuality becomes an end in itself. Among virtually all past societies, sexuality was never divorced from the conception of social responsibility. To a certain degree, the modern age has destroyed this conception. Reduced frequently to an inadequately defined social aspect in the total related complex of the personality, the sex act frequently be-

[5] Cf. Lundberg and Farnham, *Modern Woman,* Chaps. 6, 7, and 11.

[6] Ibid., Chap. 8.

[7] With respect to our institutionalized sexual practices, the single standard may be seen to operate as a *latent* function in American culture rather than as a manifest function, although for certain ultra-liberal groups, its operation might be considered *manifest.*

comes extremely elemental and dehumanized. Thus, to a certain degree, the modern sex interest has become a morbid and clinical, rather than a positive and integrating, factor of the human personality. In well-integrated cultures, sexual activity is a phase of the entirety of human living. As such, and because it is never fully divorced from the important concerns of human life expressed through family relationships and social obligations, the patterned sexual behavior of many previous cultures was vital and invigorating, rather than destructive and katabolic; permissive, rather than proscriptive; holistic, rather than fragmentary and isolated.

Since the turn of the present century, a number of explicit attitudes have been formulated in relation to sexual practice. Called by various names and dignified as the new "philosophies of love," they have been unanimous in their criticism of the conventional morality, even though they have differed as to the means by which this morality could be successfully modified. Such publicists and writers as Ellen Key, Laura and Bertrand Russell, Elsie Clews Parsons, Judge Lindsey, and others have, in the recent past, been vociferous in demanding a new appraisal of conventional sexual morality. Although these expressions have frequently been closely associated with particular cultish groups, they have gradually spread into many other areas of society. They are not so important from the standpoint of the influence which they have exercised as they are from the fact that they are symptomatic of the changes which characterize our modern views in relation to sexual matters.

Ellen Key, for example, refers to the "ethical obtuseness of the times" in our readiness to condemn too complacently the so-called sex misbehavior of the young. As do so many others who share her views, she indicates that an adequate sexual life must proceed in relation to the emotional development of the individual. Therefore, postponement in marriage because of economic conditions is a situation to be condemned and deplored. Young couples should be encouraged to marry as soon as emotionally ready. Not overlooking the importance of social maturity as well, she recommends that marriage in the case of women take place at approximately twenty years of age, while in the case of men she recommends the age of twenty-five years. Although not anarchistic in her attitude toward sexual life, she holds that "love" (by which she means the full psycho-sexual attachment and involvement of individuals to each other), instead of legality, should be the condition of sex expression.[8]

According to the Russells premarital chastity may be considered a dubious virtue and sex freedom in marriage should not be wholly condemned. In fact, the one important limitation on the free execution of the sex act, according to the early writings of this pair, should be the recognition of the responsibility for children produced in marriage. Pro-

[8] Cf. Ellen Key, *Love and Marriage* (New York, 1911).

vided the children are adequately cared for, no immediate danger is seen arising from free sexual activity outside of marriage. Bertrand Russell does warn that the social obligations in marriage must be upheld, but if sexual attraction has decayed, he does indicate that some latitude and freedom in sexual relations outside of marriage should be countenanced.

Concrete formulation and expression of these attitudes in legal form was recommended by Elsie Clews Parsons, who shocked her generation, in 1906, by her advocacy of "trial marriage." [9] According to this view, marriage should be entered into with the idea of permanence if it proves satisfactory, but if not, latitude was to be permitted in the law so that marriage could be broken off without the necessity of resorting to a great amount of difficult legal machinery. A provision was established to the effect that a certain period of time would be allowed for the young couple to make this momentous decision and choice. Judge Ben Lindsey, whose experience in the domestic relations courts of Denver, Colorado, apparently convinced him of the failure of modern sexual morality, suggested twenty years later the institution of the "companionate marriage." [10] The chief difference between the conceptions of Parsons and Lindsey is that, in the case of the former, the marriage would be considered on a trial basis until it was proven that it could prosper and succeed, while in the case of the latter, the marriage relationship itself was to be regarded for the initial period as a genuine legal wedlock, while a means of separation was provided should the marriage fail.

Both the Parsons conception of "trial marriage" and the Lindsey conception of "companionate marriage" agree in that (a) the marriage bond is sacred and should not be broken unless it is completely unavoidable; (b) the bearing of children should be postponed until it is known more or less definitely that the marriage will be permanent; and (c) that after a limited period of time, ranging from two to five years, if the marriage proves unsatisfactory, the marriage may be terminated without recourse to lengthy and difficult court litigation. The problem of children complicates the issue in each case, even though both Parsons and Lindsey recommend that child-bearing be avoided until the marriage has a substantial basis for permanence. However, the presence of children should help preserve the marital bond, although this condition is not deemed to be absolutely essential.[11]

[9] Cf. *The Family* (New York, 1906).

[10] Cf. Ben B. Lindsey and Wainright Evans, *The Companionate Marriage* (New York, 1927).

[11] For a full discussion of these views, in their various emphases and colorations, see Ira S. Wile, ed., *The Sex Life of the Unmarried Adult* (New York, 1934); Dorothy D. Bromley and Florence H. Britten, *Youth and Sex* (New York, 1938); Freda Kirchway, ed., *Our Changing Morality* (New York, 1924); Ben B. Lindsey and Wainright Evans, *The Revolt of Modern Youth* (New York, 1925); and Bertrand Russell, *Marriage and Morals* (New York, 1929).

These attitudes and opinions, which were particularly rife during the turbulent period of the "roaring twenties," reflect the attitudes of a considerable portion of the American public even at the present time. Such views, which Maurice Bigelow aptly calls a precursor of "sexual shopping," are representative of the cleavages which still exist in the acceptance of a universal sex morality and of the public attitude toward the alleged laxity of our sexual codes.[12]

In speaking of a "new morality," however, it must always be kept in mind that standards are highly variable in a complex, class-structured society. Differences in the acceptance of certain new ideas and their practice exist in relation to such background factors as education, family status, economic position, cultural determinants, and areas of residence. The degree to which college students and the college-trained, for example, have been affected by such new ideologies is difficult to determine. (The recent Kinsey report, despite its methodological shortcomings, may enable us to gain some perspective upon differences in class practice.) [13]

Bromley and Britten, in a questionnaire study of 1,364 students from fifteen representative colleges, supplemented by a limited number of personal interviews, provide some basis for the belief that our changing morality has made important inroads in the sexual behavior of the student population. Basing their discussion on data drawn from the period immediately preceding the Second World War, they estimate that one-half of the men, and approximately one-quarter of the women juniors and seniors, had premarital sexual intercourse.[14]

J. K. Folsom has attempted to summarize the new point of view implicit in the behavioral practices in modern sex relations of certain social classes. The values which the "new code" appears to stress are as follows: (1) the moral "rightness" of sex relationships if there is evidence of mutual love and exclusiveness, irrespective of the bonds of formal marriage; (2) the importance and necessity of the sex experience in itself, regardless of its reproductive function; (3) the recognition that sexual feeling is not wrong, although some merit is still seen in the capacity of the female to draw the line at intercourse; (4) the increasing acceptance of a single standard of morality, although differences in motives between men and women are recognized, and males still hesitate to approve of the "aggressive" female; (5) the belief that, whereas lifelong monogamy is an ideal arrangement, it should not be considered a "moral obligation" if love fails; (6) the removal of former taboos upon sex as a topic of conversation, although some restrictions still exist with respect to the dis-

[12] See Maurice Bigelow, "Youth and Morals," *Journal of Social Hygiene*, XIV (Jan., 1928), 1–5.

[13] Alfred C. Kinsey, Wardell B. Pomeroy, and Clyde E. Martin, *Sexual Behavior in the Human Male* (Philadelphia, 1948).

[14] *Youth and Sex*, pp. 41–3.

closure of personal experiences; (7) the belief that romantic and sexual love is primarily a monopoly of youth and is "indecent" in the case of older persons.[15] It is extremely difficult to formulate in concrete terms such a complex ideology, and considerable doubt may still remain as to its extensiveness and acceptance. Nevertheless, evidence may be found to indicate that such a point of view is shared by many groups of the population, although they may not always act in accordance with these opinions. Furthermore, the enunciation of these views is sharply counter to the traditional morality sustained by precept, if not always by behavior, as recently as a few generations ago.

Whether the traditional morality may be maintained at all, in the face of the vast impersonalities of human relationships brought about by recent economic, industrial, and social changes, is questioned by Floyd Dell. Sexual patterns, according to this writer, generated in a unique social milieu of patriarchal familism, handicraft economy, isolation, and agricultural settlement, are ill-adapted to the requirements of a highly technical "machine-age." [16] There is little doubt that the increase of sexual difficulties and the breakdown of the American family argue strongly that new orientations are required, if modern sexuality is to become an integral phase of social living.[17] Certainly, whether or not a basis exists for the "new morality," the dysfunctioning of much of our modern sex life is attributable, in the words of the hero of Odets' *Rocket to the Moon*, to the fact that "[sex] no longer is a part of the totality of human life," but is frequently fragmentary and consequently "dehumanized."

(6) THE FACTS OF CHANGE IN SEXUAL ATTITUDES AND PRACTICE

Although the publicizing of the "new morality" suggests that fundamental changes have taken place in our sexual attitudes and behavior, have we a substantial basis for the belief that such changes have actually taken place? Does our behavior differ radically from the sexual practices of our forebears, despite the assurance of the traditional moralist that it does? These questions are extremely difficult to answer, and until recently, in fact, we had a very negligible basis upon which any answers might be attempted. The recent Kinsey, and Hohman and Schaffner, reports, despite

[15] J. K. Folsom, *The Family*, pp. 408–09.

[16] *Love in the Machine Age* (New York, 1930).

[17] The development of certain opposing views on this issue can be found in J. K. Folsom, *The Family and Democratic Society*, (New York, 1943), pp. 234–51; and in his earlier edition, *The Family: Its Sociology and Social Psychiatry* (New York, 1934), pp. 561–5. See also C. C. Zimmerman and M. E. Frampton, *Family and Society* (New York, 1935), as well as Zimmerman's later *Family and Civilization* (New York, 1947), and *The Family of Tomorrow* (New York, 1949).

their shortcomings, may enable us to gain a partial perspective upon these questions.

Because of the intimate nature of the information required, and the reluctance of most persons to divulge such information even to trained investigators, an adequate knowledge of contemporary sexual life is extremely difficult to attain. Furthermore, even if valid contemporary information may be obtained, we have virtually no adequate data concerning sexual behavior in the last century for comparison. Although a considerable number of studies on the question of contemporary sexual practice have been made during the last three decades, most of them have been deficient on grounds alluded to in our previous discussion concerning criminal statistics and the sociological frame of reference. Quantitative studies of sexual behavior are frequently limited in character, based upon insubstantial and unverifiable evidence, and reflective of special biases of the investigator. In appraising the results of such studies, therefore, we must always be aware of the critical factors involved in their limited and unrepresentative samples, the limited frames of reference from which they operate, the purposes (frequently unscientific) for which they were undertaken, the passage of time which may invalidate the data for contemporary reference, and similar methodological shortcomings.

Prior to the present decade, much of our information was gained from two celebrated studies, the work of Katherine B. Davis on the sex life of 2,200 women, and the research on marriage in a selected professional group conducted by G. V. Hamilton.[18] According to Davis, who used large samples of both married and unmarried women of better than average social standing and education, variations existed in the percentages of those who admitted to having engaged in premarital sexual intercourse. Of 1,000 married women, all of whom were college graduates, and whose average age was thirty-nine years at the time the study was conducted (1920), 7.1 per cent claimed to have engaged in sex behavior before marriage. Of 1,064 unmarried college graduate women, whose average age was thirty-seven years, 12.7 per cent admitted to having had sex experiences. The relative maturity of both of these groups and the factor of memory must be taken into consideration in appraising these results. For women of lower economic, educational, and social status, the percentages appear to be much higher. The Gluecks, for example, report that of 254 married women admitted to the Massachusetts State Reformatory, 74.1 per cent had engaged in extramarital sexual experiences, while of the entire 500 studied, all but 1.8 per cent had at some time had similar experiences.[19] Hamilton's results, derived from a special group of women

[18] Cf. Katherine B. Davis, *Sex Factors in the Life of Twenty-two Hundred Women* (New York, 1929); G. V. Hamilton, *A Research in Marriage* (New York, 1929).

[19] Sheldon and Eleanor Glueck, *Five Hundred Delinquent Women*, (New York, 1934), pp. 88–9.

married to professional men and representing a peculiar cultural background and unconventional standards, revealed that 35 per cent of the 100 subjects studied in 1927 admitted to premarital sexual relations. Because of the unusual nature of this group, it is doubtful as to whether these results might be considered representative of the general population.

On the other hand, Hamilton discovered that of the 100 married, college-educated, and urban men he studied, 54 per cent admitted to premarital sexual experiences. Peck and Wells, dealing with a more normal group of recent college graduates, disclosed that 35 per cent, in their first study, and 37 per cent, in a later study, claimed to have engaged in such sexual practices.[20] In view of the more representative samples in these latter studies, the results may be more typical, although the differences in the average ages of the two groups must be taken into consideration. In a study made by Hughes of a limited sample of representative college undergraduates, 27 per cent gave evidence of sexual experiences. The summarization of these earlier studies may be seen in the following tabulation.

PERCENTAGES OF MEN AND WOMEN FROM SELECTED STUDIES WHO ADMITTED TO HAVING HAD PREMARITAL SEXUAL RELATIONSHIPS *

Women	*Per Cent*
Katherine B. Davis: 1000 normal, married women of respectable standing and super-average education, average age 39, about 1920	7.1
Davis: 1064 unmarried women, all college graduates of five years or more standing, average age 37, about 1920	12.7
Hamilton: 100 married, urban, educated women, 1927	35.0
Men	
Hamilton: 100 married, urban, educated men, 1927	54.0
Hughes: 26 representative college undergraduates	27.0
Peck and Wells: 100 college graduate men, median age 23 (first study)	35.0
Peck and Wells: similar group (second study)	37.0

* Reproduced by permission from *The Family: Its Sociology and Social Psychiatry* by J. K. Folsom, published by John Wiley & Sons, Inc., 1934, p. 398.

As a commentary upon contemporary sexual morality, it is instructive to note the percentages of men and women who admitted to having engaged in premarital sexual intercourse with individuals to whom they later became married. Although not necessarily a support of the traditional morality in these matters, if the percentages are relatively high, it may indicate, nevertheless, a less drastic modification of our sexual mo-

[20] M. W. Peck and F. L. Wells, "On the Psycho-Sexuality of College Graduate Men," *Mental Hygiene*, VII (1923), 697–714; also "Further Studies in the Psycho-Sexuality of College Graduate Men," *Mental Hygiene*, IX (1925), 502–20.

rality. Of the 54 per cent of the men who had premarital sex experience in the Hamilton study, only 10 per cent had such experiences with women who later became their wives, while in the case of the women in the study, 20 per cent claimed such experiences. Female reluctance to engage in random sex experience may be seen in the fact that the frequency of illicit sex experience is approximately twice as high for men. The figures for premarital and extramarital sex experience change quite drastically, particularly in the case of the women. Of the men, 59 per cent admit to such experiences (indicating no significant fundamental change from their premarital experiences), while in the case of the women, 47 per cent concede that they have indulged in such behavior. For this group, we may infer that the tendency toward such sex behavior has been weakened in the case of women after marriage.

In the summary by O. L. Harvey of studies made up until 1932, the evidence seems to be that 15 per cent of women and 35 per cent of men of superior intellectual and social status admit to having engaged in premarital sex experiences.[21] Of particular significance in his compilation is the fact that the amount of socially unsanctioned sex behavior, estimated on the basis of frequency of coitus, is relatively small as compared with sexual indulgence within marriage.

In relation to the important problem of whether our sexual morality has *actually changed*, it has been extremely difficult to gain accurate information. In the case of the Hamilton study, with its limited frame of reference, using birth-dates as a basis of division for comparison, it was found that of the oldest group in the sample, 20 per cent of the men and 55 per cent of the women claimed never to have had any form of illicit sexual experiences, as compared with the youngest age group in which 49 per cent of the men and 40 per cent of the women made similar claims.[22] On this basis, there would appear to have been a decrease in such sex relations among men and an increase among women. However, the student must be cautioned against accepting too readily the findings of this limited study.

Finally, with respect to the connection between premarital and extramarital sex indulgence, the Hamilton study shows a high correlation between the frequency of such practices before and after marriage for men, while in the case of women, no such correlation could be found. One possible inference to be drawn is that virtuousness before marriage, in the case of the women in the study, affords no indication of necessary virtuousness after marriage, with the converse of the proposition also being true. Relative to changing attitudes on questions of morality, 69

[21] O. L. Harvey, "Some Statistics Derived From Recent Questionnaire Studies Relative to Human Sexual Behavior," *Journal of Social Psychology*, III (1932), 97–100.
[22] Hamilton, *A Research in Marriage*.

per cent of the men and 55 per cent of the women stated that adultery may be justified under certain special circumstances, while 16 per cent of the men and 13 per cent of the women indicated that adultery required no justification whatsoever. If these results could be said to be truly representative, then the case for the collapse of our traditional morality could be said to be closed indeed!

Recent studies. While a number of specialized studies concerning sexual behavior for certain specific sub-groups of the population have been conducted during the past two decades (such as William F. Whyte's observations of the sexual codes of the male slum-dweller), very few adequate large-scale studies of the population in general have been made, with the exception of the famous report by Kinsey, Pomeroy, and Martin.[23] Since this study purports to give a realistic and truly scientific picture of the contemporary sexual behavior of American males and has been widely publicized, it should be given extended analysis. Monumental in scope, the entire study, dealing with the various sociological, psychological, and physiological aspects of sex in relation to childhood, adolescence, and old age for both men and women, is expected to eventually comprise the results of 100,000 case studies. The first volume, dealing specifically with the sexual behavior of the American male, is based upon intensive interviews of each subject covering 300 to 500 items. In the words of Kinsey, the first released volume is "a report on what people do, which raises no question of what they should do."

According to the tabulated results, Kinsey and his associates have estimated that 85 per cent of the total male population in the United States engage or have engaged in premarital sexual intercourse. Nearly 70 per cent of this group have engaged in relations with prostitutes, while between 30 per cent and 45 per cent are involved in extramarital sex relations. Particularly outstanding has been the revelation concerning homosexual practice. According to the investigators, 37 per cent of the male population studied had engaged in homosexual experience, the highest rate occurring among single males between the ages of thirty-six and forty years. One of the most conspicuous features of the report is its disclosure of the fact that there is no general standard of sexual behavior for all males in the population. Differences are based upon educational, economic, religious, and other cultural factors. The key index in the existence of such differences seems to depend upon variations in levels of educational attainment. Thus, it was found that 98 per cent of males whose education terminated at the grade school level have intercourse before marriage, while 84 per cent of males at the high school level and 67 per cent of those of college background experienced premarital coitus.

[23] A. C. Kinsey, W. B. Pomeroy, and C. E. Martin, *Sexual Behavior in the Human Male* (Philadelphia, 1948).

In general, petting and amorous play seem to be more common among the high school and college groups, and highest among the college-trained, while among the males of lower educational levels, there is more sexual intercourse and less petting. According to Kinsey, attitudes have sprung up corresponding to these differences in behavior. The upper educational levels, corresponding roughly to the economic middle-class groups, express the belief that the lower levels lack "ideals" and "principles." The lower levels feel that the upper-class groups are artificial in their sex expression, and worse, attempt to foist their "standards of morality" upon the total population. According to Kinsey, "legends about the immorality of the lower level are matched by legends about the perversions of the upper levels."

The highest incidence of premarital sexual indulgence falls, as we would expect, during the late adolescence and the teens, between the ages of sixteen and twenty. Almost three-fourths (70.5 per cent) of the total male population is involved according to Kinsey, with the highest rate of indulgence also falling within this age group. Differences in sexual practice appear to exist as well with respect to religious affiliation. The least promiscuous appear to be members of the orthodox Jewish faith, with devout Catholics and Protestants following in close order, as compared with the more active transgressors among the non-devout Catholics, Protestants, and Jews. However, in no case, are such differences as marked or acute as the differences reflecting the distinctions in general social and educational levels.

While the Kinsey Report may be the most thorough study we have had thus far concerning sexual behavior in the United States, it has been justifiably criticized on a number of significant technical grounds.[24] According to Wallin, "The phenomenal sale of the Report is well known. It is highly regrettable that only a negligible fraction of its readers will recognize its limitations."[25] The criticisms appear to center on three principal shortcomings: (1) the unrepresentative nature and inadequacy of the samples employed, despite their size and claims of representativeness; (2) Kinsey's ingenuous and disdainful dismissal of psychological and sociological conditions as unrelated to the purely objective and scientific nature of his investigations; and (3) the gross limitations of the interview techniques of obtaining information.[26]

[24] One of the most thorough critiques may be found in Paul Wallin, "An Appraisal of Some Methodological Aspects of the Kinsey Report," *American Sociological Review*, XIV (April, 1949) 197–210. See also the critical summary of A. R. Hobbs and R. D. Lambert reported in the *New York Times*, "Science in Review," March 6, 1949, Section E, p. 9. For an acidulous commentary, see Geoffrey Gorer, "Justification by Numbers," *The American Scholar*, XVII (1948), 250–86.

[25] Wallin, "An Appraisal of the Kinsey Report," p. 210.

[26] Thus, Standen, in his caustic criticisms of the popular veneration of science and the scientific method *Science Is a Sacred Cow* (New York, 1950), has aptly criti-

Space does not permit the full discussion of these limitations, but some few indications may be given to illustrate these shortcomings. In the case of the criticisms concerning the deficiencies of the samples—one of the major faults of the study—it has been shown that although those in the population who are twenty years of age and over constitute 75 per cent of the total population, they comprise only 20 per cent of the sample employed. Sample after sample has been shown to be deficient on such grounds. Secondly, Kinsey's naive comparison of human behavior with other forms of mammalian behavior on the single basis of sexual "outlets" apparently takes no account of the differences between the socialized behavior of human beings and the instinctual behavior patterns of other animals. Finally, in relation to the interview techniques employed by Kinsey, which he has upheld as superior to previous questionnaire techniques of other studies, the difficulties of obtaining accurate and authentic information by this process are well known to expert users of such methods.[27] This is particularly true in the case of deriving such intimate information as that of a sexual nature, unsubstantiated by reliable empirical checks, and inadequately tested by subsequent proof at different intervals of time.

How much, then, of this celebrated report may we accept? According to Wallin, "In general it might be said that the evidence warrants acceptance of the findings that *in the samples studied* there are differences in regard to various sexual outlets among educational levels, age groups, religious groups, occupational groups, and rural-urban groups. . . . [Only] the findings for the younger age groups of urban, Protestant, college level males can be generalized from the samples to the universe."[28]

On the basis of a comparison with other studies, we conclude that the facts concerning the college-trained group may be accepted as substantially verified. In view of the known differences which may be said to operate with respect to the lower educational and social levels, the larger percentages of socially unsanctioned sex behavior for such groups may be said to be suggestive and probable.

Although publication of the data on women has not as yet been

---

cized the generalizations concerning Kinsey's work by stating that they represent the results of statements "*by 5300 men who were willing to talk.*"

[27] The "unscientific credulity" with which Kinsey has accepted this method, without further corroboration through external proof, is attested by his naive reliance upon the method of "looking (his subjects) straight in the eye and asking questions of them in rapid-fire order." The limited check upon the authenticity of his replies gained by resubmitting a small sub-sample to examination upon the same items some 37.5 months later testifies not to the accuracy of the data but to the corroboration of reported evidence which may have been biased by factors of memory and recollection in the first place. Cf. Albert Ellis, "Questionnaire *versus* Interview Methods in the Study of Human Love Relationships," *American Sociological Review*, XII (1947), 541–53.

[28] Wallin, "An Appraisal of the Kinsey Report," p. 210.

made by Kinsey, there are a number of preliminary indications of the study which should afford some suggestion as to what may be forthcoming. Despite the fact that the sample of women upon which the findings will be based is estimated to be about twice as large as that employed in the study of male behavior, there is no way of determining at this point whether the data are fully representative.

From the standpoint of class differentials based upon levels of educational attainment, the behavioral patterns of women appear to parallel fairly closely the behavioral practices of the men studied. In general, the higher the level of education, the greater the number of inhibitions among women toward unrestricted sexual activity. This does not appear to hold for various types of related amorous practice, such as petting and variations in sex play. Nevertheless, the degree of premarital and postmarital sexual freedom among women may be considerably higher than that disclosed in the earlier Davis and Hamilton studies, although less sexual freedom exists among women than among men. The amount of extramarital experience among women should prove to be a good deal less than among men, although even here the divergence between principle and practice will very likely prove uncomfortably wide. Nevertheless, Dr. Kinsey implies that the difference in sexual behavior between the unmarried woman of today and her sister of an earlier day may be more apparent than real, being considerably less than ordinarily expected.

Although the published study on men revealed that the peak of sexual activity for the male occurs during the teens and tends to decline after the mid-twenties, woman's sexual peak is apparently reached in the late twenties, remaining at a relatively high level for a period of five to six years thereafter. Of particular interest is the confirmation that of college-trained women, possibly as many as one-third never attain orgasm. One of the controversial features of the report, which appears to contradict earlier evidence, is the expectation that the figures on homosexuality for women may be higher than those for men.

Without the fanfare attending the release of the Kinsey investigations, the recently released study by L. B. Hohman and B. Schaffner of 4,600 unmarried men between the ages of twenty-one and twenty-eight inducted into the Army during the recent war appears to give us a comparable set of conclusions.[29] According to these findings, 79.4 per cent of the men studied admitted to sex experiences. In keeping with the conclusions of the Kinsey study, the rate of virginity among unmarried males rose in relation to educational and economic status. Higher economic status was not as significant a correlate as higher education. In the case of religious differentiation, there is disagreement with the Kinsey Report.

[29] "The Sex Lives of Unmarried Men," *American Journal of Sociology*, LII (May, 1947), 501–08.

The highest rate of virginity occurred among the Protestant group, followed by the Catholic and Jewish groups, in that order. Of particular import as an indication of changes in sexual attitudes was the claim of 71 per cent of the men that they had sexual relations with "nice" girls, i.e., girls whom, by definition, they would have no objections to marrying and whom they would be willing to introduce to their parents. The general conclusions appear to support the reliability of these results, in view of the fact that sexual behavior is based upon habitual patterns and are more modifiable in frequency than in character. The conclusion by Hohman and Schaffner that, at this rate, "intercourse with future spouses before marriage will become universal by 1950 or 1955" is, however, unwarranted. However, both this and the Kinsey studies make it clear that the divergence between our "ideal" traditional sexual morality and actual practice is so great as to constitute a basic anomaly and contradiction in the entire sequence of activities concerned with sex behavior throughout our culture. In view of the profound hold which the traditional sexual morality exercises upon the cultural patterns of Western man, the fundamental conflicts produced must inevitably bring about an extensive range of personality and social tensions converging about the sex interest. Nowhere more than in the realm of modern sex relations are our concepts concerning "normality" and "abnormality" seen to be more confused and chaotic. "In no other field of science," says Kinsey, "have scientists been satisfied to accept the biologic notions of ancient jurists and theologians, or the analyses made by the mystics of two or three thousand years ago."

(7) PSYCHO-SEXUAL LATENCIES AND CONFLICTING SEXUAL STANDARDS

The fact remains that despite changes in our codes of sexual practice, our traditional sexual behavior is strongly entrenched in our culture. The Judaeo-Christian sexual ethic has remained the primary basis upon which the patterning of social attitudes with respect to the sexual behavior of men and women, both inside and outside of the family, is established. This traditional code, however, has been one of the least resilient of all the institutionalized patterns governing behavior in Western society. The orthodox sexual code was a natural resultant arising from former conditions of rural and pastoral life and a patriarchal kinship system. During earlier periods, the advent of many offspring did not constitute the type of problem which such a condition introduces today. Under the consanguineal family arrangements of the past, the care of offspring, both legitimate and illegitimate, was the responsibility of large kinship groups. Illegitimacy was a problem induced primarily by the necessity of safeguarding the rightful transmission of property. It differed from the contemporary conception, in which the dilemmas of economic support and sexual fidelity have become joint and paramount concerns. Even the problem of an excessively large birth rate and the economic burdens which this constituted for the individual family were not crucial in the pre-Malthusian, pre-industrial era, where the high infant mortality rate tended to preserve the equilibrium of family life and family sexual relationships.

Our modern industrial life has transformed the basis of previous sexual attitudes. The emphasis on individuality in modern culture, its anonymity and impersonality, and the stress on the necessity of preserving and maintaining higher standards of living, have removed the former social implications of the sexual impulse from their roots in the family structure. Increasingly, sexual behavior has become a private matter.

In the past, even the most transitory sexual dalliance incurred specific social responsibilities with respect to the offspring of such unions. In well-structured societies, the clearly defined conceptions of women, family status, and the status of the child, invested sexual behavior with profound social and moral values and restrictions, affecting every phase of personality and social attitudes. This may be compared with the situation in our contemporary society, where social opportunities for the unrestricted mingling of the sexes are freely created by our mode of social organization and where the consequences of sexual contacts do not incur the same heavy social risks and penalties as previously existed. Our modern knowledge of contraceptives and the change in character of our family organization from the large self-sustaining unit to the small, restricted, conjugal unit, has freed the volatile compulsions of the sexual drive.

These contrasting points of view have been brought sharply to the fore, recently, in the challenge raised by the Yale anthropologist, G. P. Murdock, concerning the results of his findings among 250 primitive societies.[30] On the basis of the elaborate cross-cultural index compiled at Yale University, Murdock has shown that of 250 societies studied, 70 per cent permit certain degrees of sexual experimentation before marriage. As a result of these extensive comparisons, he has concluded that "there is nothing in man's social experience to indicate that the ideal of premarital chastity has any scientific value." Although stating that "the sexual laxity among our own youth is admittedly an unlovely phenomenon from an esthetic point of view," Murdock apparently sees no grounds for regarding it as socially dangerous. Moreover, with the advent of contraception and the scientific mastery of venereal infection, Murdock anticipates that our sexual laxity will remain, since these former fears, "the principal props of the older morality," have been removed.

While recognizing the need for some social control, Murdock says

[30] Cf. *Proceedings of the American Social Hygiene Association*, Thirty-seventh Annual Meeting, New York, February, 1950.

certain advantages are to be gained in relaxing our present institutionalized controls: (1) the removal of guilt-feelings, hence less psychoneurosis; (2) the acknowledgement of the need for approved outlet when sexual vigor is at its peak; (3) facilitation of the development of normal heterosexual habits; (4) aid in adequate comprehension of the sex role in human relationships ("Relief from sexual frustration is a very inadequate motive for marriage"); and (5) aid in the prevention of marriage of individuals who are sexually incompatible.

This acknowledgement of sexual freedom before marriage by a recognized scientist has met with a speedy and explosive rejoinder. For religion, the Reverend William J. Gibbons of the National Catholic Rural Life Conference has stated that such unrestricted behavior is a prelude to moral anarchy and a denial of the function of reason in man's social life. "Man," stated Father Gibbons, "is a moral being. . . . Man's reason, properly used, can still tell him what *ought* to be, even if his concrete behavior falls short of the ideal."[31] Implying that the need for stable married life in the tradition of Western culture is indispensable to the preservation of contemporary society, he warned that the encouragement of the young to succumb to uncontrolled sexual desire will make it increasingly difficult for them, if not impossible, to fit into a pattern of traditional family life.

A highly effective response to the implicit anarchy of the Murdock statement which simply constitutes, from one standpoint, an acknowledgement of what may be an existent fact has come from Luther E. Woodward of the New York State Department of Hygiene. Woodward has answered Professor Murdock on the very sociological and anthropological grounds with which he should have been conversant and which he apparently has overlooked. Sexual patterns, argues Woodward, may not be transplanted from one culture to another, irrespective of their extensiveness in certain cultures, but must be part of the functioning unity of a given social order. The sex patterns of the Trobriand Islanders may fit into their social order, and yet be quite unsuited to the complex needs developed in our highly diversified social life. To think differently is to court disaster. Thus, according to Woodward: "From his findings that 70 per cent of the cultures he studied have no taboo against premarital promiscuity, Professor Murdock jumps to the conclusion that the taboo is out of place in this culture. This is not a scientific conclusion on his part. You can't transplant the sex habits of the inhabitants of Truk and the Samoa Islands into Christian industrial America unless you transplant the meaning those sex habits have there."[32]

Even the more conservative and orthodox elements of the popula-

[31] *Time*, February 13, 1950, p. 57.
[32] *Time*, February 13, 1950, p. 58.

tion may be giving evidence of the confusion in our current sexual mores. In the degree to which such groups (representing the last stronghold against the rising trend of the times) succumb to the pressures introducing changes in attitude and practice, the full force of any change in institutionalized behavior can be seen. Such groups, naturally, are the very last to be affected by the full impact of a social trend from the standpoint of their acknowledgement and acceptance of its reality in principle and in practice.

Some token of the degree to which our sexual mores may have broken down may be seen in the studies of Porterfield and Salley of a particularly conservative group of college students and college-trained men and women.[33] The investigators used a sample of 285 men and 328 women, heavily weighted with members of the ministry, ministers' wives, and other sub-groups tending to be representative of the more orthodox views in relation to sexual behavior. Their findings present a picture of unchastity among the men which involves one out of every five of those who have entered the vocation of the ministry; three out of five student naval recruits (V-12 students) before they entered active naval service; nearly two out of five of the male members of the church; and nearly three out of four non-church men. Although the ratios for the women involved in the study are not nearly as high, particularly with respect to those women who are identified with church groups, one out of five of the non-church members reported evidence of premarital intercourse.[34]

The conclusions of this study are quite striking in so far as the "factual arrays strongly suggest that, even in the groups which we have every right to assume are most conservative . . . there is much sexual experimentation, followed by careers that society respects and honors." [35] Further, in final token of the nature of the breakdown which we may presently be witnessing, they assert: "First, the older universals of the sex mores are breaking down and are being replaced by numerous alternatives in the current sexual folkways, with the result that control over sex behavior is much relaxed. Second, in the light of this change, it is becoming increasingly difficult to define sex delinquency and perhaps meaningless to try to do so, except in certain types of behavior involving cruelty and exploitation." [36]

The acceptance of a well-established, traditional ideology produces serious conflicts in the degree to which contemporary behavioral practices diverge from such established codes. In addition to the high incidence of personal difficulty resulting from adjustments of sexual behavior to

[33] A. L. Porterfield and H. Ellison Salley, "Current Folkways of Sexual Behavior," *The American Journal of Sociology*, LII (Nov., 1946), 209–16.

[34] Ibid., p. 213.

[35] Ibid., p. 215.

[36] Ibid., p. 216.

the varying and contradictory codes of the day, and the psycho-sexual tensions induced by the enormous growth of psychoneurotic anxieties and guilt feelings, this so-called liberation of the sex impulse has had a strong impact upon many agencies and institutions of social life. When sexual behavior has well-defined linkages to many phases of social existence in a well integrated society, the consequences of sexual activity are provided for through stipulated social arrangements which have become acceptable to a given society.

In our own society, there are no clear-cut, patterned arrangements through which the consequences of many phases of sexual activity may be equitably handled so as to preserve social balance and equilibrium. The result has been confusion in the handling of such problems as illegitimacy, abortion, contraception, and venereal disease. In the absence of well-defined and agreed upon social policies in such matters, the consequences of poorly defined sexual behavior loom up in the form of serious social problems and social dislocations. Such problems as abortion, illegitimacy, contraception, and venereal disease are not only symptomatic of the breakdown of our sexual morality, but represent serious problems in themselves because of their specific social effects. In our failure to deal with them as emblematic of a profound disturbance in our social relations, and in our inability to appraise them adequately in terms of their serious social consequences, we encounter the grave risk of undermining the social patterns to which they relate. Our handling of these problems is another evidence of the common failure to dissociate causes from symptoms.

Against the broad background of change in sexual and social attitudes which we have described, and which has created the occasions and conditions of these problems, we shall discuss abortion, illegitimacy, contraception, and venereal disease in our contemporary society.*

* Summary for this chapter will be found at the end of Chapter XIV.

CHAPTER FOURTEEN

CULTURAL DRIFTS AND SEXUAL PATHOLOGIES

(8) ABORTION

ABORTION is an extremely ancient practice. According to Carr-Saunders, the population expert, abortions have been performed for many centuries among preliterate and ancient peoples. Ethnological reports and historical records of the past indicate how extensively it has been practiced. Probably in no culture, however, has the pressure against its practice been as great as in our own. To the present day, the sentiment against abortion is still extremely strong in most parts of the Western world.

It is difficult to estimate how widespread the practice of abortion really is, because of the clandestine manner in which it is carried on. Most published estimates include the great number of spontaneous abortions or miscarriages, and those performed legally as a means of safeguarding the mother's life. However, the number of self-induced abortions and those performed illegally by professional abortionists is extremely high. If known, they would augment considerably the figures published in the official estimates.

Abortion rates are highly variable, differing from country to country, for different sections of the same country, and for urban and rural areas. One of the highest rates before the Second World War was in Germany, where the estimate placed the volume at approximately 600,000 to 800,000 a year, a figure which is three times as high as the estimated rates before the First World War. The rate of abortion was approximately two-thirds the annual birth rate.[1]

In this country, the rate of abortions is still enormously high. One conservative estimate puts the figure at a minimum of 680,000 per year, while the more common estimates place the figure at 1,000,000 or more, or approximately one half the number of births.[2] The estimate holds, contrary to the popular impression, that approximately nine-tenths of

[1] C. Tietze, "German Population Movements, and Some Comparisons With Those of Other Countries," *Eugenics Review*, XXI (1930), 265–9.

[2] Cf. Meyer F. Nimkoff, *Marriage and the Family* (Cambridge, 1947), pp. 555–6; and Willystine Goodsell, *Problems of the Family* (New York, 1930), p. 368.

these abortions are performed upon married women.[3] It seems likely that at least one-half of all illegitimate pregnancies are prematurely interrupted, a minimum of at least 70,000 per year. According to Nimkoff, the rate for all abortions is high and probably rising. That the abortion index may exceed the birth rate on occasion has been shown by one Cincinnati study where, between 1918 and 1932, the rate of increase of abortions exceeded the percentage rise of the birth rate. Of induced abortions, it is probable that about three-fifths are illegal.[4]

Evidence varies as to whether abortion is a class problem, the rates differing for different socio-economic groups.[5] Certain European studies seem to indicate that abortion has been restricted in the past to working-class groups and upper middle-class urban dwellers. The First Birth Rate Commission in Great Britain, for example, discovered a greater tendency among women of the lower economic and urban working classes to practice abortion, while those of superior economic status tended to prevent births by contraceptive measures. Sufficient studies of large enough samples covering stratified groups have not been made in this country to give us an adequate picture of group differences. However, the practice of induced abortions appears to be more prevalent among the lower economic classes than among others. Yet Katherine B. Davis discovered that one out of nine of 826 married women college graduates had had one or more abortions performed.[6] No significant differences were discovered in the rates of induced abortions for wives of manual workers and for wives of white-collar workers, although some differences were noted on the basis of religion. Catholic women tended to have relatively fewer abortions than non-Catholic, although, on the basis of absolute numbers, the differences are not so great particularly in view of the greater fertility of Catholic women. The rate of illegal abortions among Jewish women was lower in general than for gentile women. Of particular significance is the fact that the rate of illegal abortions goes up in relation to the number of children in the family, showing a volume of 5 per cent in the case of first pregnancies and increasing to over 50 per cent of all pregnancies after the fifth child.[7]

[3] Frederick I. Taussig, *Abortion, Spontaneous and Induced* (St. Louis, 1936), p. 26.

[4] Max Handman, "Abortion," *Encyclopaedia of the Social Sciences*, Vol. 1, p. 373.

[5] Nimkoff questions this, indicating that "abortion (unlike illegitimacy) is not a class problem, in the sense of being preponderant in a particular socio-economic group, although it occurs more frequently in the lower-income groups than in the higher." Nimkoff, *Marriage and the Family*, p. 556.

[6] "A Study of the Sex Life of the Normal Married Woman," *Journal of Social Hygiene*, IX (March, 1923), 129–46, cited in Nimkoff, *Marriage and the Family*, p. 557.

[7] R. K. Stix and F. W. Notestein, *Controlled Fertility* (Baltimore, 1940), p. 83.

Legality and social results. Artificially induced abortions are illegal in all states unless authorized by a physician as necessary to save the mother's life or safeguard her health. In fact, the statutes are so severe that in most states even to attempt to assist a women to procure an abortion or to become a party to the commission of the act constitutes a serious infraction of the law. In addition, because of the traditional attitude of the medical profession and because of the general fear which the law has induced, physicians themselves are frequently reluctant to recommend abortion except in cases where the woman's life is seriously jeopardized. The result has been an institutionalized "racket," existing particularly on the borders of respectable medical practice. The unpleasant psychological aspects of abortion are frequently more ruinous to the women who visit the abortionist than the physical effects. The number of midwives, unlicensed nurses, and other unqualified persons who ply this profession, particularly in our large cities, is reported to be fairly large. An additional large number of women attempt to abort by sundry mechanical and pharmaceutical means, as any experienced social worker can attest.

Ideological opposition. Today all Western countries with the exception of Sweden forbid the practice of abortion except under stipulated medical conditions. The most unequivocal and uncompromising opposition still comes from the Roman Catholic Church. In his famous *Encyclical on Christian Marriage* in 1930, Pope Pius XI lashed out severely against abortion as one of the practices that he felt were inimical to the Christian law as defined by the Roman Catholic Church. According to this position, abortion is not permissible even when a physician advises it for medical reasons.

Until its abolition in 1936, the Russians were most liberal in permitting abortions under legal auspices. Under the Russian system, established in 1920, any pregnant woman could have an abortion performed, provided the pregnancy was not advanced beyond two and one-half months and provided it was not a first pregnancy.[8] The operation had to be performed by registered hospital physicians, hospitalization was required for three days, and a period of recuperation of two weeks was made mandatory. The demand for abortions grew so excessive within a short period of time, however, that existent hospital facilities and medical services were heavily taxed. This led to a revision of the law in 1924. The new law imposed an elastic fee, ranging from fifty cents to twenty dollars, depending on the economic circumstances of the individuals involved. This measure did little to curtail the rate of abortion, as is indicated by the statistics for Leningrad. These showed a rise of abortions from 21 per 100 births in

[8] This latter requirement was waived in the event that the woman's health was jeopardized.

1924 to 139 per 100 births in 1928, or two-fifths more abortions than births. Rural rates, as elsewhere, were considerably lower than urban rates, about one-half the urban rates in Russia. During the period from 1924 to 1936, 90 per cent of the cases applying for abortion were accepted. Because they felt the need to safeguard the birth rate, the Russians abandoned the policy in 1936. It was officially stated that the continuance of this policy on abortions was not in the best interests of the people.

We may not generalize directly from the Russian experience, however. The removal of legal restrictions does not necessarily mean that the volume of abortions will increase to enormous proportions. In fact, depending on the cultural conditions and sexual practices of a people, there is reason to believe that the removal of barriers, although possibly precipitating an immediate increase, will not produce a rising incidence over a period of years.[9] Sweden, despite a falling birth rate, still maintains a policy of official abortions, and there has been no appreciable and alarming rise since the introduction of the policy. Social behavior in relation to sex is conditioned by deep-seated social and cultural attitudes; there is no reason to believe that change in official policy will bring about increases in activities formerly banned by law.

Of considerable concern is the high percentage of fatalities arising from abortion. Margaret Sanger, who utilized this fact in support of her earlier arguments for contraception, estimated that one out of every four fatalities occurring among women in childbirth or pregnancy was due to abortion. Recent evidence seems to indicate that abortions may be responsible for as many as 30 to 35 per cent of all maternal deaths from all causes, accounting for about 3000 to 4000 deaths among pregnant women each year.[10]

As our discussion has shown, the spread of the practice of abortion continues despite strong governmental controls, powerful religious opposition, and physical and psychological ill-effects. There seems to be little evidence in existent socio-cultural trends for the belief that the trend will be reversed or stopped within the foreseeable future, despite the continuance of official policies of stringent suppression.

The reasons for the persistence of high abortion rates may be understood in connection with the general process of a steadily declining birth rate. In the background are the significant factors of the small modern urbanized family, intent on maintaining or achieving a rising standard of living, the necessity of postponing child-bearing for many married couples, the lack of adequate sexual controls and knowledge among many of

[9] What frequently occurs is that many abortions come out into the open, figuring as part of the official statistics from which they were previously concealed. Thus, no actual increase in the *real* rate occurs.

[10] H. L. Dunn, "Frequency of Abortion: Its Effect on Maternal Mortality Rates," *Vital Statistics-Special Reports,* XV (July, 1942), 443.

the unmarried, and the "cultural lag" in the dissemination and practice of contraceptive techniques.

(9) ILLEGITIMACY

Although virtually all cultures have had serious reservations concerning childbirth apart from marriage, among early cultures and among contemporary nonliterate ones illegitimacy has never constituted as serious a problem as it does among the Western countries. Because of their conceptions of unilineal descent and the consanguineal structure of primitive family organization, children born out of wedlock could readily be absorbed into the social structure of most primitive communities. Moreover the social tolerance of pre-marital sexual relations and the earlier age of marriage may both play a part in forestalling high rates of illegitimacy. According to Malinowski, in his study of the Trobriand Islanders, unmarried mothers were responsible for only about 1 per cent of all births in this society, a vastly smaller percentage than is found in modern Western countries.[11] In view of the fact that conception is difficult until two years after the onset of the initial menstrual flow, as Nimkoff has suggested, the percentage of births among such primitive communities may be definitely curtailed until close to the time that marriage ordinarily takes place.[12]

In Western European society, the strictures against illegitimacy have been unusually severe. According to medieval law, it was expressly forbidden to search out the father of the child. The early English common law stipulated that the illegitimate child could have no legal status of relationship to either the father or the mother. This disability endured until the Elizabethan period when the local magistrates were empowered to enforce support of illegitimate children by the father, if his identity could be established. This legal provision has continued in British and American law to the present time.

Anglo-Saxon law and illegitimacy. Because of the necessity in Anglo-American culture to identify the child with a specific type of family, support, and inheritance system, the law dealing with the status of illegitimate children has been extremely severe. Although some liberalization in the care and legal status of such children has taken place during the present century, the legal burdens and disabilities under which the child and the unmarried mother suffer are still extremely harsh. Three fundamental legal principles have come to be observed in the majority of states, tracing their origin directly to the English common law, in connection with the legal status of illegitimate children: (1) offspring of marriages declared null and void may nevertheless be declared of legitimate status; (2) mar-

[11] Bronislaw Malinowski, *The Sexual Life of Savages* (New York, 1929).
[12] Nimkoff, *Marriage and the Family*, p. 550.

riage subsequent to the birth of a child may establish the legitimacy of the child in all but four states; and (3) certain restricted rights of support and inheritance may accrue to the illegitimate child under prescribed legal limitations. Some states, such as California, have attempted to liberalize illegitimacy statutes by permitting the father, if he is already married and his wife consents, to declare the child's legitimate status and to bring him into his home. This resembles the procedure followed in most states whereby both parents, if subsequently married, or one of the parents, may formally adopt the child and legitimize his status.

Our laws have not progressed far in the matter of safeguarding the illegitimate child's rights, except with respect to the provision of minimal support. The ancient legal definition of the illegitimate child as *filius nullius*, a child without normal claims upon the family, is still, to a degree, in effect. In a survey of existent paternity laws made by the U. S. Department of Labor in 1938 it was found that (1) most of our present state laws are completely unadapted to modern social conditions, being incompatible with the increasing socialized and "informal" procedures utilized in our domestic relations courts; (2) legal provisions by the states do not go far beyond compelling the father, if he can be discovered, to assist in the child's support, utilizing punishment where necessary; and (3) the laws assume too readily that the father of the child is able to pay the stipulated sum for his support and that he will be able to continue to do so during the years.[13] Short of adoption, the law does little to protect the illegitimate child's legal status.

In contrast to the discrepancy which our laws show in theory and contemporary needs, the Norwegian legislative body, the *Storting*, passed in January, 1915, what is probably the most liberal legislation concerning the status of the illegitimate child.[14] Beginning with the reasonable assumption that any transgression of the parents is no responsibility of the child, the law has gone to remarkable lengths in assuring the child a legal status comparable to that of the child born in wedlock. Under the Norwegian code, frequently referred to as the Castberg Law, there are the following five provisions: (1) The mother is compelled to name the father, although the alleged father has the right to contest this charge in the courts within four weeks time. (2) Adequate steps are taken to administer the law. (3) The burden of proof is on the alleged father in cases of disputed paternity. (4) The father pays all expenses incurred in the child's upbringing until his sixteenth birthday. He also pays all medical and hospital expenses of the mother for a period of at least three months prior to the child's birth. (5) There is a guarantee of the right of the

[13] *Paternity Laws*, U. S. Department of Labor, Childrens' Bureau, Chart #16, 1938, p. 22.

[14] Cf. *Norwegian Laws Concerning Illegitimate Children*, U. S. Department of Labor, Childrens' Bureau, Publication #31, 1918.

child to be his father's heir. He may take either the mother's or father's name, after establishment of paternity.[15] Under the older Norwegian laws, only 40 per cent of the fathers of illegitimate children had been named. Under the new law, this number has been doubled, and in 75 per cent of the cases, parentage was admitted by the father without contest of the claim in the courts.

Unlike this liberal Norwegian law, the chief concern of the American courts has been to determine paternity primarily as a matter of gaining assistance in the child's support. The determination of paternity, however, is no easy matter. Aside from the physical difficulties involved, legal action may not be instituted in a vast number of cases because of the refusal of the mother to institute such proceedings or even to co-operate with interested social agencies. However, the Federal Social Security Act makes no distinction as to the status of the child in the allocation of its benefits, eligibility for assistance being based wholly upon the child's needs. In respect to the determination of paternity by the courts some advances have been made by the use of the Landsteiner blood-grouping tests and the use of the Rh-factor determinant. Under the original blood-grouping test, developed by Doctor Karl Landsteiner, if the claimed father does not fall within one of the standardized blood-types of the child, A-B or M-N, paternity is disproven. However, falling within one of the common blood-types of the child does not necessarily establish parenthood. All that the Landsteiner test can do is to indicate in approximately 30 per cent of the cases that an individual is *not* the father. For this reason, American courts are reluctant to admit the use of the test and in no case where a common blood-type is established is it valid unless corroborated by considerable other evidence. Recently, however, the Rh-factor test, discovered by Doctors Landsteiner and Wiener, has done much to reduce the odds of determining paternity. Although this test will also not conclusively demonstrate paternity in all cases, according to Doctor Wiener, by the combined use of the Landsteiner and the Rh-factor tests, the percentage of chances to disprove parenthood is about 55 per cent.[16] However, despite these efforts to improve paternity proceedings by the use of modern scientific techniques, the chief recourse is through the testimony of the mother and the putative father, as well as corroborative witnesses—a procedure frequently involving lengthy and difficult litigation in our courts and frequently involving hardships upon the child and mother.

[15] Cf. Christian T. Jonassen, "A Comparative Study of the Status of the Illegitimate Child in the United States and Norway," *The Alpha Kappa Delta Quarterly*, XVIII (Jan., 1948), 4–9.

[16] Justice Panken of the Kings County, New York, Family Court accepted as evidence for the first time the findings of the Rh-factor test in July 1947, in a case involving disputed parentage, thereby establishing a precedent in American courts for the use of the combined Landsteiner and Rh-tests.

The extent of illegitimacy. Illegitimacy rates show fluctuations in time and place. The rates for American whites are not as high as the general European or South American rates. It is generally believed, however, that rates in this country have risen since the First World War. In 1914 and 1915, rates for the white population were approximately 15 per 1000 births and rose to approximately 19 per 1000 births by 1931. The rates for the Negro population, are much higher, the rate in 1930 being 148 per 1000. The combined Negro and white rate for the entire population in the same year was 35 per 1000 births.[17] Differences in rates between the colored and white populations are primarily due to differences in cultural and socio-economic standards. Although urban Negro rates tend to be higher than comparable white rates in our cities, they diminish progressively the farther removed such Negro groups are from the rural folk culture. In general, Negro rates of illegitimacy are from 5 to 10 times as high as white rates. In parts of the rural South, 10 to 20 per cent of Negro children are born out of wedlock.[18]

Although data on illegitimacy are more readily available than data on other types of sexual irregularity, due to the fact of compulsory birth registrations, such figures, too, are unreliable and do not show the extent of the problem. Data in the past have given the impression of a lower rate of illegitimacy than was actually the case. According to recent census data, the illegitimacy rate in 1927 was reported as 28 per 1000 total live births as contrasted with an overall rate of 40.5 in 1940.[19] However, in the interests of the child, some states today do not require that illegitimate births be registered as such. By January 1st, 1944, ten states did not require such registration: California, Colorado, Connecticut, Maryland, Massachusetts, Nebraska, New Hampshire, New Mexico, New York, and Wyoming.

Variations in rates in this country may be seen by a comparison of urban rates. New York City with a rate of 11 to 12 per 1000 has one of the lowest rates in the country, as compared to rates of 44 per 1000 in Boston, 42 per 1000 in Pittsburgh, 45 per 1000 in St. Paul, 56 per 1000 in Denver, and 95 per 1000 in Kansas City. The high rates in such places as Kansas City, however, are not due to any special intrinsic factors present in the Kansas City area but are due to the fact that certain areas have developed special facilities for the care of unmarried mothers and their offspring, upon which they have commercialized. In Kansas City, a number of private hospitals and institutions have been established which cater

[17] *Statistical Abstract of the United States*, Department of Commerce (U. S. Government Printing Office, Washington, 1933), p. 86.

[18] E. Franklin Frazier, "An Analysis of Statistics on Negro Illegitimacy in the United States," *Social Forces*, XI (Dec., 1932), 249–57.

[19] *Vital Statistics of the United States, 1940* (U. S. Government Printing Office, Washington, 1942).

to the needs of unmarried mothers and which assume responsibility for the care of their offspring, even going to such lengths as advertising in widely outlying rural areas. Naturally, such an "industry" will tend to produce a concentration of such cases within a given geographical section. The relatively low rate in New York City may not be due to a greater range of sexual control in such a metropolitan district but is largely attributable to the greater ease with which abortions may be obtained in such an area, and a greater knowledge of the use of contraception and the ease with which such information may be obtained.

As high as the American rates may appear to be, they are considerably lower than European and Latin-American rates.[20] Illegitimacy rates as high as 100 to 200 per 1000 births have been reported for Hungary, Austria, Germany, Denmark, and Sweden. It should be noted that though these countries differ in religious, economic, social, and cultural conditions, the rates are nevertheless uniformly high. This is primarily due to the fact that different cultural conditions prevail in these countries relative to certain forms of sexual practice, and to the fact that the peasant cultures in these areas approve of the principle of testing fertility before marriage. Many births appearing as illegitimate are eventually legitimized by the subsequent marriage of the partners concerned. Because of these cultural conditions, the rates will continue to be high in many such areas. In Sweden, for example, the illegitimacy rate has invariably been high, accounting for approximately one-seventh of all births during the last two decades.[21] In England and Wales, too, the rates are extremely high. Between 1939 and 1943, an average of approximately 80,000 illegitimate births were reported. These constituted about one-third of all first maternities and one-eighth of all maternities registered during that period.[22] The percentage of illegitimate births in relation to first pregnancies is invariably found to be higher than the percentages for subsequent pregnancies in all Western areas.

Latin-American rates are even higher than European rates. Rates ranging from 200 to 700 per 1000 are found in different parts of South and Central America. In certain parts of rural Mexico and the remote hinterlands, rates of illegitimacy in excess of rates for normal births are sometimes found. It must be remembered, however, that in many cultures illegitimacy does not necessarily bear the same stigma as in our culture. In many parts of the world simple folk cultures still prevail where certain types of sexual union are not regarded as illicit in our sense and where the legal requirements for the registration of marriage have not

[20] Frank H. Hankins, "Illegitimacy," *Encyclopaedia of the Social Sciences*, Vol. 7, p. 579.

[21] Alva Myrdal, "A Program for Family Security in Sweden," *International Labour Review*, XXX (June, 1939), 723–63.

[22] David R. Mace, *The Outlook for Marriage* (London, 1944), p. 4.

been enforced in the light of various types of customary arrangements.

The existence of these high rates of illegitimacy in all parts of the Western world indicates how difficult it would be to enforce the contemporary codes of sexuality. These rates mount still higher during periods of extreme social stress and social breakdown. While American troops were quartered in Great Britain during the recent war, an estimated 22,500 illegitimate births occurred, of which 550 were the result of sexual unions with Negro troops.[23] The uneven ratio of the sexes which war and other social disasters produce tends still further to accentuate this problem because of the difficulties in contracting normal marriages. In view of the rising trend towards greater freedom in sexual behavior, the various socio-economic barriers placed in the way of marriage, and the legal and social difficulties that defeat the proper development of abortion and contraceptive procedures, there is little reason to believe that the trends in illegitimacy rates will reveal any sharp decrease or modification of their present directions.

The development of social policy. In the light of these considerations, it is evident that treatment of the problem of illegitimacy requires a completely new orientation. With respect to the child, a certain degree of minimum protection must be afforded which our present laws do not allow. The illegitimate child should not be burdened with a stigma and with disabilities for acts he did not commit. Moreover, unless we take further steps in the development of stringent methods of control over illicit sexual behavior, which appears unlikely in the face of contemporary conditions, the problem of the approach to the parents involved in such unions will require careful reconsideration. The punitive aspect of the law, which still appears prominent, has not proven a satisfactory means for conserving the interests of the community and the individuals concerned.

Individual psychological and sociological characteristics must be carefully considered. Whereas until very recently the unmarried mother was of a low economic and social level, we now find increasingly that the parents of illegitimate children are of all classes. The former solution of the problem, the separation of the mother and the child, has been found to be harmful to both and has produced a great many physical and psychological difficulties. The relatively high incidence of fatalities among illegitimate children may be partially attributed to this policy of separation. The modern procedure involves social case work diagnosis and treatment in which each case is handled individually in order to insure the best potential development of the mother and child.[24] It is frequently found that the best solution is to maintain the child and mother together and to help

[23] *Special News Despatch*, Foreign Service News, Feb. 10, 1949.

[24] Cf. Ruth F. Brenner, *Case Work Service for Unmarried Mothers, New York* (Family Welfare Association of America, New York, 1941).

them make an adjustment to the environment in which they must live. The former harsh procedure of the forced marriage, the "shot gun" wedding, so-called, has most often proven destructive to the personalities of all individuals concerned in such relationships. Not only do forced marriages lack a substantial basis for permanence and the establishment of a wholesome family atmosphere, but the children are frequently crucified in such unions. The solution for the present must lie in the development of physical protection for the child and mother, with the cost shared by the father. Provisions must be made for the adjustment of each case in accordance with the peculiar circumstances involved.

(10) CONTRACEPTION

Historical development. The history of birth control and the use of contraception is extremely ancient. As far back as 1850 B.C. recorded knowledge of the use of contraception has been found, incorporated within the ancient *Kahun Papyrus* of the Egyptians. Knowledge of birth control methods was well known among the Greeks and the Romans, and various primitive peoples have shown great ingenuity in the development of contraceptive devices.[25] During the medieval period, the strongly censorious attitude of the Church did much to curtail the knowledge and use of such devices, although evidence exists that such practices were known and continued to be employed.

The modern movement began during the early nineteenth century as a reaction to the spread of the Malthusian doctrines of the period. In fact, the birth control movement as a powerful social trend actually began as a counter-movement to the economic and social pressures of the early industrial revolution, auspiciously introduced in its population aspects through the celebrated *Essay on Population* by Malthus in 1798. Early opposition took the form of strenuous objections to the dire pronouncements of this doctrine, which held that the misery of the poor could only be diminished by voluntary curtailment of the birth rate through continence and postponement of marriage. The first important leader of these neo-Malthusians was an English workingman, Francis Place, who, in 1823, distributed a leaflet in which he set forth his "indications" or reasons for the necessity of popular birth control. There ensued immediately a series of violent and bitter denunciations of this point of view, based almost wholly upon religious and traditional moralistic arguments, even though some of the great reform leaders of the period, Robert Owen, Jeremy Bentham, and John Stuart Mill, were inclined to regard with favor the spread of such information.

In 1832, an American physician, Doctor Charles Knowlton, published

[25] Norman E. Himes, *The Medical History of Contraception* (Baltimore 1936).

a tract on the subject in Boston, entitled *The Fruits of Philosophy*. This celebrated document became the periodic focus of vitriolic controversy for almost half a century, culminating finally in the famous trial in 1878 of Charles Bradlaugh and Mrs. Annie Besant in England. Bradlaugh and Mrs. Besant were prosecuted amidst considerable notoriety for distributing this pamphlet and although the court decision was equivocal, they were given a full acquittal a few years later. The enormous publicity given to the trial and the consequent widespread knowledge of the literature upon which it was based is thought to have had a tremendous effect upon the subsequent knowledge of birth control for the masses and its results. The steady decline of the birth rate since 1880 in England and in western Europe is believed to be in part the result of the widespread notoriety which this trial, as a *cause célèbre*, received.

By 1878, the first birth control clinic was established in Amsterdam. The scene soon shifted to America and the opposition here, largely under the auspices of Anthony Comstock of the New York Society for the Suppression of Vice, was so acute and prolonged that even now the entire subject is still obscured by controversy in many quarters. It is interesting to note that the form of the opposition was almost entirely on traditional moralistic grounds, as contrasted with the specific arguments of birth control advocates who based their points of view almost wholly upon social necessity. This basis for the controversy, ironically enough, still persists until the present time.

In 1873, through the efforts of Comstock and his cohorts, a federal law was passed in this country which made it illegal to transmit information and materials concerning contraception and devices through the mails. Despite efforts of the early Birth Control League in this country to countermand this proscription by attempted legislation and to establish a legal basis for the dissemination of birth control information and materials through accredited medical channels, no substantial progress was made until 1917 when a federal court ruling produced a dramatic change in the entire picture. In that year, Judge Crane of the Federal Courts, in passing upon the arrest of Margaret Sanger who was jailed for thirty days for opening a birth control clinic in New York, ruled that such information may be dispensed by a legally practicing physician as a means of preventing disease. The clause concerning "the prevention of disease" has come to be broadly interpreted as giving the physician the right to give such information whenever it is deemed that the social and economic aspects of the case may produce problems conducive to the undermining of health. The result has been that despite the many legal restrictions which still exist in respect to the indiscriminate giving of such information, the majority of our states now permit the dispensing of such information by physicians under varying degrees of restriction.

The liberalization of public attitudes in relation to the dispensation of contraceptive information, thus, has been brought about by broader interpretation of existent laws rather than by actual modifications of the law. In thirty-one of our states, physicians may now give such information; in eleven others, such information may be given but not published; while in two others (New York and Minnesota) such information can be given by a physician only as a means of curing and preventing disease. The chief opposition has been lodged primarily in Mississippi, Massachusetts, and Connecticut. In the state of Connecticut, it is not only illegal to distribute such information, but a criminal offense to practice contraception. Upon appeal to the United States Supreme Court in 1947, testing the validity of a Connecticut Supreme Court decision of 1879 which held that "complete abstinence" was an adequate alternative to contraceptive devices, our highest federal court refused to hear the case upon jurisdictional grounds. In 1938 and 1939, both the Massachusetts and the Connecticut Supreme Courts ordered the closing of birth control clinics in their respective states. However, since 1930, a number of states—notably Wisconsin, Colorado, Delaware, Idaho, Montana, and Oregon—broadened their provisions for the distribution of such information, permitting certified pharmacists as well as physicians to dispense contraceptive information and materials.

Of particular interest has been the growing acceptance of the dissemination of birth control information through public health clinics. As of January 1st, 1946, seven states (Alabama, North Carolina, South Carolina, Virginia, Florida, Texas, and Mississippi) permitted the use of their public health facilities for the distribution of birth control information and devices, as public health measures. In addition, many local and county public health services, of which the Los Angeles County Clinic may particularly be cited, have established facilities for such services as a part of their regular program of work, particularly in conjunction with their venereal disease and tuberculosis control programs. The case of South Carolina is particularly notable. In 1935, South Carolina had the highest maternal mortality rate in the country, 96 deaths of mothers for each 10,000 live births. By 1940, this rate had been reduced to 66 deaths per 10,000 live births, a decrease of 30 per cent in the space of five years, even though the enabling legislation was not authorized until 1938.

A survey of the historical development of the contraceptive movement in this country indicates that the progress has been uneven, and that although growing favor has been won in the acceptance and distribution of such information, the opposition is still bitter and powerful in some quarters, despite the enormous growth of contraception among all sections of the population. Unlike the ready access to such information which has become universal in certain European countries, such as Sweden, the barriers existing in the United States have resulted in an inequity of practice among different levels of the population. In Sweden, despite a falling birth rate, information has been made generally available to all members of the public upon the basis that such a procedure is in keeping with democratic practice and as a means of safeguarding the quality of the population as well as the quantity.

Public attitudes and opposition. The chief opposition to birth control methods has come from the Roman Catholic Church. The opposition of the Church has been unequivocal and clear. The official position of this body has been definitively formulated by Pope Pius XI in the *Encyclical on Christian Marriage* of 1930.

> When we consider the great excellence of chaste wedlock, venerable brethren, it appears all the more regrettable that, particularly in our day, we should witness this divine institution often scorned and on every side degraded. . . .
>
> First consideration is due to the offspring, which many have the boldness to call the disagreeable burden of matrimony and which they say is to be carefully avoided by married people, not through virtuous continence (which Christian law permits in matrimony when both parties consent), but by frustrating the marriage act. Some justify this criminal abuse on the ground that they are weary of children and wish to gratify their desires without their consequent burden. Others say that they cannot, on the one hand, remain continent nor, on the other, can they have children because of the difficulties, whether on the part of the mother or because of family circumstances.
>
> But no reason, however grave, may be put forward by which anything intrinsically against nature may become conformable to nature and morally good. Since, therefore, the conjugal act is destined primarily by nature for the begetting of children, those who in exercising it deliberately frustrate its natural power and purpose, sin against nature and commit a deed which is shameful and intrinsically vicious. . . .

During the early part of the century, the opposition of various church groups, particularly the more orthodox religious bodies, assumed a position closely parallel to that of the Roman Catholic Church. However, in varying degrees, virtually all of our large denominational groups have begun to move away from this position in the face of an almost irresistible tide. In 1929, at the celebrated Lambeth Conference, the House of Bishops of the Church of England approved the use of contraception if kept within the bounds of the Christian principles of that church. Similarly, the Presbyterian General Assembly in this country, upon the recommendation of its *Special Committee on Marriage, Divorce, and Remarriage*, approved the same kind of action in the same year. Highly significant has been the action taken by the *Committee on Marriage and the Home* of the Federal Council of Churches of Christ in America, our largest interdenominational Protestant group in America, which, by a large majority, approved contraceptive use in 1931. The Central Conference of American Rabbis, the organization of the Reformed Jewish Congregations in America, took a similar step in 1929. Lately, however, modification of these positions has been taken by some church bodies. Although not repudiating its earlier stand, the *Committee on Marriage and the Home* of the Federal Council of Churches on January 15, 1946, expressing some concern over possible deleterious effects through unbridled use of contraception, recommended that people of good health, physical and mental, and of "good principles," should have their full quota of children. This does not necessarily mean a surrender of its former position, but a realization of the potentialities which unrestricted use of contraception may entail.

The issues between the Catholic Church and the proponents of birth control have been sharply drawn upon purely moralistic grounds. This has been well expressed by various spokesmen of the Church, although it should be kept in mind that the assumptions upon which these arguments are based are not held by large groups of the population and are not necessarily valid in light of modern conceptions of marriage and sexual union. For example, Patrick J. Ward, in writing upon the Catholic position has stated:

> Those who support artificial birth restrictions and who hold that the gratification of sexual appetite is the central purpose in marital life are simply adhering to the view that the human being is primarily governed by his animal appetites rather than by his intellect. It is safe to assume that these persons do not truly understand the unselfish, spiritual love which is peculiar to human creatures.[26]

Further, he states that "since this is the universal moral law, it applies with equal force to Catholic and non-Catholic." Non-Catholics might resent this on two grounds: (1) as impugning their own moral and ethical principles, particularly in respect to their own conceptions of modern Christian marriage; and (2) because of the imputed right to impose a dogma upon groups not associated with the Catholic Church.

The basic population principles which are involved in the entire birth control controversy are not unrecognized by the Catholic Church. In fact, aside from continence, which it recognizes as a valid principle of birth control, provided that both partners in the marriage are agreeable, the church has condoned the use of the so-called "safe period" or

[26] "The Catholics and Birth Control," *New Republic*, 59 (May 29, 1929), 35–7.

"rhythm system" as a means of circumventing births. This method, based upon the research of Herman Knaus and K. Ogino, has shown that there are cycles of fertility dependent upon the woman's period of ovulation.[27] Relative immunity from conception may be obtained during the weeks preceding and following the woman's menstrual period. Although research evidence has shown that a significant degree of infertility may be present during the week preceding the menstrual period, evidence is highly contradictory concerning the immunity from pregnancy during the week following this period.[28] Because of the differences in regularity of the menstrual cycle for many women, and related physical and psychological difficulties, the method is not a complete safeguard for all individuals, although it may have effectiveness in curtailing the birth rate of a group. The fact that the Church recognizes this as a method, however, is significant. Although no evidence is immediately available that this may constitute an "opening wedge" whereby the Church may alter its policy in line with other groups, the question may at least be raised as to whether this is not tantamount to the limited recognition of birth control. In view of the fact that the Church has come to recognize *intent* in the matter of prevention of births, the argument now seems to revolve around the conception of *means*. Even upon the basis of ethical and moral grounds, there are those who believe that the Church has weakened its position in view of the fact that moral purposes may be destroyed by virtue of the intentions with which an object is pursued, regardless of the techniques, methods and procedures which may be employed in the accomplishment of such ends. Certainly, upon the basis of the declining birth rate for both Catholic and non-Catholic women since the early part of the century, whereas the absolute birth rate of Catholic women is still higher than for non-Catholic, the percentage decrease of the Catholic rate has been greater than that for non-Catholics and is steadily growing.[29]

Studies on changing attitudes towards contraception show an increasing and widespread acceptance of its use among all classes of the population and among the different religious groups. Using a representative sample of 100,000 voters in all states, a Gallup Poll in 1936 revealed that 70 per cent of this large group approved the legalization of birth control measures. More significant, an analysis and survey organized in 1938

[27] Cf. Eric M. Matsner, "The Safe Period," *Birth Control Review*, January, 1935.

[28] Cf. S. Fleck, E. F. Snedeker and J. Rock, "The Contraceptive Safe Period," *New England Journal of Medicine*, 223 (1940), 1005–09. Dr. R. L. Dickinson, whose work has been reviewed by Matsner (ibid.), states that there is a "safe period" for every woman, but it is highly variable. Further, that there is no time during the menstrual cycle when conception has not taken place among certain women. Although the week preceding the menstrual flow is a period of relatively low risk, the days directly following menstruation are periods of extreme fertility for certain women.

[29] Cf. S. A. Stouffer, "Trends in the Fertility of Catholics and Non-Catholics," *American Journal of Sociology*, XLI (Sept. 1935), 143–66.

by the *Ladies' Home Journal* showed that 79 per cent of the women questioned were in favor of birth control. Of this group, 51 per cent of the Catholic women questioned sanctioned contraceptive measures as compared with 84 per cent of the Protestant women. A later study by Henry F. Pringle, reported in the *Ladies' Home Journal* of August, 1943, showed that 84.9 per cent of the women surveyed, between the ages of 20 and 35, endorsed the position that birth control should be available to all married women. Of the Catholic women queried, 69 per cent gave approval of the same view.

Although evidence varies as to the frequency of use of birth control clinics by Catholics and non-Catholics, studies of attendance figures indicate that participation by Catholic women may be relatively high. An earlier report by Himes on the distribution of clients at a New York City clinic in 1930 revealed that the patronage was about equally divided among Catholics, Protestants, and Jews, the bulk of whom, as suggested by the earnings of the husbands, were from the lower middle-class, white-collar groups.[30] This is not in accord with findings disclosed shortly thereafter of attendance at a private birth control clinic in New York City during 1931 and 1932 where the figures showed that about one-sixth of the women attending were Catholic.[31] Although most of the studies show a higher percentage of use of contraception among Protestants and Jews, in a study by Riley and White it was shown that about two-fifths of the Catholics surveyed employed means other than abstinence, while only a quarter reported not using any form of birth control.[32]

Social Results and Policy. Some token of the increase of contraceptive facilities may be gathered from the fact that the number of public and free clinics has grown appreciably during the past two decades. In 1930, there were reported to be 81 such clinics in the United States; in 1933, 140 clinical centers; while by the end of 1944, there were a reported 783 birth control centers.[33] In 1939, the American Birth Control League combined its forces with the Birth Control Clinical Research Bureau to organize the *Planned Parenthood Federation of America*, which has spread its facilities for the distribution of information and services throughout the country.

The spread of these clinics and the enlarged program of the *Planned Parenthood Federation* have done much to equalize the use of planned birth control procedures. However, there are still wide discrepancies in

[30] Norman E. Himes, "Birth Control in Historical and Clinical Perspective," *Annals of the American Academy of Political and Social Science*, 160 (1932), 49–65.

[31] R. K. Stix and S. W. Notestein, *Controlled Fertility* (Baltimore, 1940), p. 11.

[32] J. W. Riley and M. White, "The Use of Various Methods of Contraception," *American Sociological Review*, 5 (Dec., 1940), 890–904.

[33] Cf. *The Directory of Planned Parenthood Services* (Planned Parenthood Federation of America, Inc., New York City, 1945).

the use and knowledge of such devices among the various sections of the population. In general, there appears to be a positive correlation between the non-use of contraception and low economic status. Rural areas seem to lag behind urban centers in contraceptive practice. Associated with such correlations are the factors of lack of knowledge, due in part to absence of established public clinical facilities, the expense involved in the purchase of materials, and the inadequacy of proper sanitary facilities. The use of contraceptive devices by the Negro population, because of their inferior economic and educational status, falls far behind the extensiveness of practice among white groups, although the differences are not so great when comparable white groups are considered. Pearl, for example, discovered that of 2,000 maternity hospital cases he studied, whereas 36 per cent of the white women reported using contraception, only 15 per cent of the Negro women made such a report.[34] In respect to those classes with superior social and educational advantages, Katherine Davis showed that of the 1,000 college-trained women she studied, all but 79 approved of its use, with 730 actually employing contraceptive means, while the Lynds, in their study of *Middletown*, revealed the almost universal practice of contraception among the business class, with less than half the working class showing such use.[35] In general, thus, the use of contraception appears to increase in relation to educational and economic status, and the size of the community.

In respect to age levels, contraception appears to be more widely practiced among the young than among the older age groups of the population. The rate of usage is higher for those under 35 years of age than for those between 35 and 45 years. That this may indicate a greater incentive to sexual immorality among the young is a direct possibility. V. F. Calverton, for example, has attempted to show that in certain urban areas, about one-half who purchase contraceptive devices are unmarried.[36]

Aside from the general inferences we may draw concerning the continuous decline of the birth rate since 1880, specific studies have shown the serious curtailment of the birth rate which efficacious use of contraception brings about. There can be little question concerning the effectiveness of modern contrivances and devices. Some indication of their effectiveness may be gleaned from the fact that for women who have had one pregnancy and who do not practice contraception, the records indicate 86 to 105 pregnancies per 100 woman-years of exposure to sexual relations. The evidence shows that this rate may be decreased to a rate of 27 to 40 upon the same basis of calculation by the use of contraception, based upon

[34] Raymond F. Pearl, "Contraception and Fertility in Two Thousand Women," *Human Biology*, 4 (1939), 363–407.

[35] Katherine B. Davis, *Sex Factors in the Life of Twenty Two Hundred Women* (New York, 1929); R. S. and H. M. Lynd, *Middletown* (New York, 1929), p. 123.

[36] V. F. Calverton, *The Bankruptcy of Marriage* (New York, 1928), p. 141.

studies made of clinic patrons.[37] For women of college education, a rate of 31 was reduced to 6 unplanned pregnancies per 100 woman-years of sexual exposure.[38] Genuine alarm has been expressed by some of the advocates of birth control, as well as their opponents, concerning dysgenic effects upon the standards of the population where contraceptive practices are widely introduced, particularly in view of their greater use among the better-educated and the socially better-placed. This fear has likewise prompted the argument for increased democratization of birth control practice.

One of the results of the widespread use of contraception may be its possible effects upon the sex ratio of the population. In the long run, in a society which tends to be masculine-dominated such as our own, the effect would be to produce a preponderance of males over females. This is due to the fact that the normal ratio of conceptions indicates a rate of 110 males to 100 females. However, due to the greater fatality of male fetuses, the actual rate is approximately 105 males to every 100 females. Actual studies reveal that the ratio may be higher than the normal expectation rate and even higher than the conception rate—as high as 112 to 100 in certain instances.[39] The fact that the ratio has been as high as 117.4 in the case of last children indicates the results which contraception may have produced. In view of the preference of many married pairs for male children as well as families of limited size, child-bearing is frequently curtailed after a male child has been born.

Prospects. Contemporary social trends, for good or for bad, are increasingly shaping the development of the contraceptive movement as an instrument of social policy. This means that the basis upon which it is being advanced is quite counter, and frequently diametrically opposed, to the points of view put forward by the antagonists of birth control. This may be seen by the type of arguments offered by the proponents of democratized contraceptive services as contrasted with the traditional moral arguments advanced by the adversaries of birth control programs. Actually, *the two points of view begin with separate premises and relate to two separate frames of reference.* The character of the arguments offered by birth control advocates may be seen in the following justifications, virtually all of which would be inadmissible to the moral and orthodox view. Thus, it is argued that contraception is needed because: (1) it serves to prevent transmissible diseases and defects; (2) it reduces maternal

[37] Cf. G. W. Beebe and C. J. Gamble, "The Effect of Contraception Upon Human Fertility," *Human Biology*, 10 (1938), 372–87; R. K. Stix, "The Medical Aspects of Variations in Fertility," *American Journal of Obstetrics and Gynecology*, 35 (1938), 571–80.

[38] L. Dewees and G. W. Beebe, "Contraception in Private Practice," *Journal of American Medical Association*, 110 (1938), 1169–72.

[39] Cf. S. Winston, "Birth Control and the Sex Ratio at Birth," *American Journal of Sociology*, 38 (Sept., 1932), 225–31, cited in Nimkoff, *Marriage and the Family*, p. 567.

mortality because of the undue susceptibility of certain women to puerperal disorders; (3) it makes possible adequate "spacing" between births, thus safeguarding mother and child; (4) in the event that a defective child is born, the parents may voluntarily reduce the further risk of producing such children; (5) it provides an opportunity for a young married couple to establish economic and personal adjustment before becoming burdened with children by "honeymoon pregnancies"; (6) it safeguards the interests of the family in the event of financial inability to support other children; and (7) it makes it possible to plan for the improvement of the quality of the population.

In the face of (a) the altered composition of the population today, (b) the desire to maintain a rising standard of living, (c) the different status of children in an urban-dominated civilization, and (d) the high premium placed upon individual values, social security, and the qualitative improvement of the population, it seems doubtful that the trends towards voluntary parenthood and increased contraceptive use will diminish. However, it is conceivable that a precipitately declining birth rate, and changes in the political and social structure, may produce modification of the existent ideology which favors this development. We have seen how dictatorial societies, such as the former Nazi State and the present Communist regime in Russia, have served to counteract the trend towards wider use of contraceptive measures. Even in our own democratic society, we have seen how certain religious bodies, after having gone on record as favoring judicious use of contraception, have shown concern over the failure of those who are economically and socially sufficient to reproduce themselves adequately. Although some critics of the modern democratic social order have indicated that birth control and modern eugenics programs are class-favored doctrines which are unwarranted if the economic level is improved for the masses of the population, the fact remains that the basis for the small family among all classes has become well-rooted in the contemporary social structure.[40] In the last resort, the ultimate decision in the development of further movements of this character will depend upon the changing conceptions of human worth and dignity, as these are reflected by changing ideological considerations fostered by the inevitable characteristics of social, cultural, and economic change.

SUMMARY

(1) In the last two chapters, our discussion of contemporary sexuality has emphasized the fact that sexual codes are universal, although highly variable, reflecting the different cultural and social conditions of a given

[40] Cf. H. J. Muller, "The Dominance of Economics over Eugenics," *Proceedings of Third International Congress of Eugenics* (New York, August 1932).

society. (2) Sexual codes are primarily a matter of sociological rather than biological interpretation. In human society, the sexual instinct becomes a highly organized and structured outlet, developed and channelized in accordance with the structural organization of each society.[41] In contemporary Western society, this has been illustrated in the way in which contemporary sexual mores have been conditioned by certain long-range historical and immediate social factors. Such factors do not necessarily reinforce each other, but frequently are contradictory. (3) Our contemporary sexual codes reflect the complex and contradictory nature of the social forces which have shaped our attitudes. Prominent in the development of our sexual outlook and practice have been (a) the ascetic ideal of the Christian Church; (b) the romantic movement; (c) the Industrial Revolution; (d) the development of political individualism; and (e) the trend of scientific development, particularly in respect to discoveries in the field of biology. (4) Immediate and more recent factors which have played a part in shaping our sexual morality have been (a) the anonymity and impersonality of current social relationships, considerably induced by (b) modern mobility, (c) increasing ideological emphasis upon individualization, and (d) technical discoveries which have produced extensive leisure in the household and which have altered various phases of personal relationships. (5) The liberation of the individual, engendered by these recent factors, has laid the basis for a trend towards a single standard in sexual behavior and the emergence of a "new morality." This "new morality," nevertheless, is not entirely in accord with the facts of human preference, ideology, and practice. (6) Although it is difficult to determine the precise degree to which current sexual behavior differs from that of the past, recent studies, such as the Kinsey report, the Hohman and Schaffner survey, and the Porterfield and Salley studies, despite their shortcomings, afford some basis for our conclusions that current sexual behavior has become increasingly liberalized for both sexes. (7) Despite the fact that our contemporary codes of sexual behavior may have become altered and will continue to reflect the drifts of social change, the deeply entrenched attitudes concerning sex behavior, reflecting religious, moral, and traditional evaluative considerations, still function as a counterpoise to extremes in sexual behavior, creating rifts and dichotomies in our social structure. Against this background, the problems of abortion, illegitimacy, and contraception have taken important new dimensions. (8) As an indication of the type of conflict created, the practice of abortion, despite its extensive and rising rate, is subject to stringent legal penalties virtually universal in Western codes of law. Such problems as abortion and illegitimacy fluctuate in relation to special characteristics of the social structure and the cultural traditions of the social order. (9) Because of the nature

[41] Cf. George P. Murdock, *Social Structure* (New York, 1949), Chaps. 9, 10, and 11.

of the family structure and marriage in Western culture, particularly exemplified in Anglo-Saxon law and American social development, the strictures against illegitimacy have been extremely severe. Modifications of existent law have been relatively slow in this country and have taken the form largely of providing economic support for the child. Establishment of paternity by the courts has been undertaken primarily as a measure of receiving contributory assistance in the support of the child. Because of the differences in traditional folk-cultures, rates of illegitimate births have been conspicuously higher in European and Latin-American countries. The Norwegian Castberg Law represents one of the few attempts to equalize the strain in the social structure created by this problem, by reorienting the law in respect to the actual problems created by the illegitimate birth rate. (10) The enormous growth of contraception, particularly since 1880, illustrates the effects of modern biological discoveries and the alterations in social structure brought about by the industrial revolution. A social policy of birth control was originally formulated into a positive program by the neo-Malthusians. The spread of contraceptive practices has varied in accordance with differences in educational, economic, social, and religious factors, and in relation to the degree with which public information has been made generally available. The chief opposition has come from the Roman Catholic Church and other religious bodies, although most religious groups have now abandoned their original opposition in keeping with specific stipulations and requirements. In view of the trends in the contemporary social structure, it is not likely that the social practice of contraception on an increasingly wide scale will be abridged in the immediate future, although modifications may result as a consequence of changes in the social drift.

CHAPTER FIFTEEN

PROBLEMS OF THE SEX OFFENDER

(1) SOCIO-CULTURAL CHANGE AND THE INDIVIDUAL SEX PATHOLOGIES*

IN THE previous chapters, we considered the broad trends of contemporary sexuality in the modern Western world, as well as some of the underlying socio-cultural causal patterns that have contributed to their development. In this chapter, we shall examine some of the specific sexual abnormalities and pathologics that manifest themselves as accompaniments of the broad sociological process thus far described.

Breakdowns of the sexual mores and the drift of changing opinion concerning sexual morality affect individuals in our class-structured society in different ways. Thus, the ease with which sexual unions may be accomplished and the casual disregard of the conventional sexual proprieties may result in a cavalicr attitude concerning the sacredness of the marital vow and the tolerance of a certain amount of infidelity in marriage among the middle class and the upper economic groups. Among the relatively unprivileged groups, on the other hand, the incentives to sexual license may take a number of unchecked, unrestrained, or disapproved forms. *From a theoretical standpoint, the specific pathologies of sex will reflect specific class, status, and personality differentials.*

Moreover, cataclysmic changes brought about by revolutions, wars, or prolonged economic depressions produce vast dislocations in socially stratified sexual attitudes. These dislocations reflect the basic changes that have taken place in the social structure, and may be adequately understood only when viewed in relation to the shifting social scene. In the light of these considerations, we will analyze the delinquent girl, the unmarried mother, prostitution (and its related problem of venereal disease), and homosexuality.

* Numbers of the subheads in this chapter refer to the summary at the end of Chapter XVI.

(2) INDIVIDUAL SEX PATHOLOGIES: THE DELINQUENT GIRL

In discussing the problem of delinquency among women, it is significant to note the relatively high percentage of women who are apprehended for various types of sexual offenses. However, it must be borne in mind that the numbers of female offenders, both adult and juvenile, are relatively small as compared with the volume of arrests and commitments for male offenders. Of female offenders, however, the majority—possibly as many as 80 to 90 per cent—are remanded before the courts or are institutionalized for acts of a sexual or near-sexual nature.[1]

If men were held equally culpable with women in the commission of sex offenses, the disparity in the numbers of male and female sex offenders would be considerably different. Thus, it is important to note at the outset of our discussion that the cultural attitudes toward sexual offenses are quite different for male and for female transgressors. Except for rape and other forms of physical sexual assault, and except for the limited responsibility imposed by the courts on fathers of illegitimate children, the law is never as severe toward men as it is toward women. One of the most acute paradoxes in the modern attitude toward sexual behavior consists in the failure to recognize joint culpability in the commission of sex offenses, despite the fact that masculine responsibility is prior and fundamentally instrumental. As Elliott and Merrill have put it: "We cannot 'save' the girls without 'saving' the boys."[2]

The expectation that those female delinquents who have not yet committed sexual offenses will eventually engage in some form of illicit sexuality has colored the attitudes of our courts of law. Here, then, is a partial explanation for the fact that statistical tabulations of offenses committed by girls show such high frequencies for such offenses as ungovernability and running away. When a boy is found to be ungovernable or when he runs away the problem does not appear so serious to law enforcement agencies. Thus, the statistical differences that we discover may be more reflective of differential law enforcement than of actual offenses committed.

The volume of female delinquency. For the reasons discussed in our chapters on juvenile delinquency, it is significant to note that the volume of female offenders does not become large until the age of adolescence is reached. In the case of both male and female juvenile offenders most misbehavior is concentrated between the ages of fourteen to seventeen

[1] Cf. *Uniform Crime Reports for the United States and Its Possessions,* XVI (1945); also "Juvenile Court Statistics, 1943," *Social Statistics,* Supplement to *The Child,* U. S. Children's Bureau, Washington, IX (June, 1945), 16.

[2] Mabel A. Elliott and Francis T. Merrill, *Social Disorganization* (rev. ed., New York, 1941), p. 213.

years, with the category of seventeen to twenty-one years of age closely following. Among boys there is a more pronounced spread of delinquent behavior in the pre-adolescent age-groups than among girls. Thus, in 1943, in cases appearing before our juvenile courts, 4 per cent of the boys and 2 per cent of the girls were under ten years of age; the ten- to eleven-year-old category comprised 9 per cent for the boys and 4 per cent for the girls. In the twelve- to thirteen-year-old category the distribution was 18 per cent for the boys and 15 per cent for the girls, while in the fourteen- to fifteen-year-old category the distribution was 35 per cent and 43 per cent for boys and girls, respectively.[3]

It is significant to compare the overall volume of male and female violations. In 1945, the fingerprint records of the arrest reports made to the Federal Bureau of Investigation showed a total volume of 459,709 male arrests as compared with 84,144 female arrests; in percentages, 84.5 per cent for male offenders as compared with 15.5 per cent for women.[4] In 1946, according to the same source, the percentage volume of female arrests had dropped to 10.7 per cent. The ratio of *adult* male arrests to female arrests for all ages, as reported in 1945 by the F.B.I., is 5.5 to 1, as compared with a ratio for juvenile offenders in the same year of 4.7 to 1.[5]

For the crucial years of adolescence, thus, there are approximately four to five male offenders for each female offender. The recent overall trends appear to support the continuance of this ratio, although differences appear for different sections of the country. Thus, in Passaic, New Jersey, in a report made in 1944, 74 per cent of all juvenile offenders were male and 26 per cent were female.[6] In Chicago, during the years 1929 to 1935, juvenile delinquents were 79.8 per cent boys and 20.1 per cent girls.[7] In Houston, Texas, a highly unique area, the volume differences were 61.9 per cent and 38.1 per cent for male and female juvenile offenders respectively.[8]

More revealing, however, are the ratios for male and female delinquencies and offenses at specific age levels. The student should observe that, beginning with the category below ten years of age, the preponderance of male over female delinquencies and offenses decreases until the

[3] "Juvenile Court Statistics, 1943," *Social Statistics*, Supplement to Volume XIV, No. 12, June 1945, *The Child*, U. S. Department of Labor, Children's Bureau, Government Printing Office, p. 16.

[4] *Uniform Crime Reports, 1945*, XVI (1946).

[5] *Social Statistics, 1944 and 1945*, Supplement to Volume II, *The Child*, November 1946, U. S. Department of Labor, Children's Bureau, p. 9.

[6] W. C. Kvaraceus, "Chronological Ages of 761 Delinquents at Time of Initial Apprehension," *Journal of Criminal Law and Criminology*, XXXV (1944), 166–8.

[7] Ernest R. Mowrer, *Disorganization, Personal and Social* (New York, 1942), p. 581.

[8] *The Houston Delinquent in His Community Setting* (Council of Social Agencies, Houston, Texas, 1945), p. 2.

ages of advancing adolescence. These statistics indicate the significant concentration of female offenses in this critical age group. A series of progressively decreasing ratios until the early adult years are also reported. Thus, for the category below ten years of age, the ratio of male to female delinquents is 8.9 to 1; for the ten- to eleven-year-old category, the ratio is 9.9 to 1; for the twelve- to thirteen-year-old group, 5.0 to 1; for the fourteen- to fifteen-year-old category, 4.1 to 1.[9] The ratios of male to female offenders that are based on reports made to the Federal Bureau of Investigation are somewhat different. This is because the various state jurisdictions do not define the ages of juveniles alike, and because certain serious offenses of young girls are tried in the adult courts. In 1945, the F.B.I. arrest reports revealed a ratio of 9.6 to 1 for the age of sixteen years, 9.2 to 1 for the age of seventeen, and 3.8 to 1 for the age of eighteen. Reports on the arrests for the next six successive age years indicated a variability in male-female ratios ranging between 2.6 and 3.2 to 1.[10] It appears evident from these figures that as girls approach the adolescent period and the immediate post-adolescent years, the number of female offenders, although still smaller than the number of male offenders, increases significantly, until, in the twenties, females comprise from one-fourth to one-third of the entire offender group.

The nature of female delinquencies. As revealing as the concentration of female offenders in the adolescent and post-adolescent categories appears to be, even more significant is the distribution of the most commonly listed offenses for girls. This distribution is the more revealing when comparison is made with typical male offenses. In the report of the juvenile courts to the Children's Bureau, nearly six out of ten referrals of girls related to the invariant trilogy of *ungovernability, running away,* and *sex offenses.* The major offenses among boys were stealing, acts of carelessness or mischief, and traffic violations.[11] In 1945, 18 per cent of juvenile female offenders were apprehended for sexual misbehavior, 22 per cent for ungovernability, and 19 per cent for running away. In the same year, these offenses constituted 3 per cent, 6 per cent, and 6 per cent, respectively, of all offenses committed by boys.[12] If we accept the veiwpoint that ungovernability and running away among girls are actually or potentially related to sexual delinquency, we must conclude that 59 per cent of all female offenses have to do directly or indirectly with sex. For 1943, the juvenile court figures show a total of 61 per cent for the three signal offenses of girls as compared with 14 per cent for the same offenses among boys, while an earlier breakdown in 1931 in New York City indicated a

[9] "Juvenile Court Statistics, 1943," p. 16.
[10] *Uniform Crime Reports,* XVI (1946), 114–16.
[11] *Social Statistics, 1944 and 1945,* p. 11.
[12] Ibid.

total percentage of 71.7 per cent for the same offenses for girls, with the listed offense of ungovernability contributing 48.4 per cent to this total figure.[13] From the vantage point of frequency of offenses in relation to sex, the F.B.I. figures for 1945 show a male to female ratio of offenses of 9.3 for stealing, 8.2 for drunkenness and driving while drunk, 7.3 for assault and homicide, and 10.1 for gambling. However, for such offenses as disorderly conduct, vagrancy, and all types of sex offenses, the ratios are considerably less, 3.4, 2.4, and 1.5, respectively.[14] We may conclude from the statistics on female delinquency that illicit sexual behavior is a major problem in this category of offenders.

(3) A STATISTICAL PROFILE OF THE DELINQUENT GIRL

There is a remarkable uniformity in the various statistical disclosures concerning the delinquent girl.

In general, the delinquent girl comes from a broken home or a home of low moral status; she is emotionally unstable because of inherent or acquired defects; she comes from a poverty-stricken background and has begun work at an early age; she is of low mentality and of limited education; she is a member of a large family, frequently of five or more children. Although exceptions to this statistical portrayal exist, of course, a heavy concentration of factors in respect to these characteristics appears in many of the statistical compilations.

In a series of studies made of delinquent and non-delinquent girls and boys in Wisconsin, Massachusetts, Spokane, and Indianapolis, it was found that more delinquent girls than boys came from homes broken by the death of one or both parents, or by divorce or separation.[15] For girls, the percentage of broken homes caused by death ranged from 30.9 per cent in Spokane, Washington, to 40.0 per cent in the State of Wisconsin, while for boys in the same areas, the range was from 16.4 per cent to 26.6 per cent. For homes divided by divorce or separation, the girls' cases again show the highest incidence, ranging from 22.6 per cent to 37.2 per cent, as compared with from 10.8 per cent to 23.2 per cent for male delinquents. Although we recognize, on the basis of the earlier Shaw and McKay study, that broken homes vary in their effects according to whether the break-up

[13] Cf. *Preventing Crime*, Sheldon and Eleanor T. Glueck, editors (New York 1936), p. 224.

[14] *Uniform Crime Reports*, XVI (1946), 113.

[15] Cf. M. G. Caldwell, "Home Conditions of Institutional Delinquents," *Social Forces*, VIII (1929–1930), 390; H. A. Weeks, "Male and Female Broken Home Rates by Types of Delinquency," *American Sociological Review*, V (1940), 603; Sheldon and Eleanor T. Glueck, *Five Hundred Delinquent Women* (New York, 1934), p. 451; and E. M. Bushong, "Family Estrangement and Juvenile Delinquency," *Social Forces*, V (1926), 79–83.

is due to divorce, separation, or death, and according to the ages of the persons involved when the break-up occurs, there seems to be little doubt but that girls suffer more from such disorganized home conditions than do boys.[16] H. A. Weeks, for example, showed that 68.1 per cent of the girl delinquents studied in Spokane, Washington, came from broken homes, as compared with 39.6 per cent of the boys.[17] Although Weeks discovered that for both sexes ungovernability, running away, and truancy are related to broken homes—misbehavior that may have less serious consequences for boys than for girls, as has already been pointed out—the evidence discloses a greater number of sex crimes among girls than among boys coming from broken homes.

Of considerable importance to the problem, too, are the disclosures of faulty home relationships in the backgrounds of delinquent girls. Of the delinquent women studied by the Gluecks, only 10 per cent came from unbroken homes and from homes where salutary personal relationships existed.[18] Defining as unsatisfactory background factors the following three conditions—broken homes, contacts with social agencies, and "social defective tendencies" (i.e., presence in the family of alcoholism, epilepsy, mental defectiveness, sexual irregularity, etc.)—Catherine Lumpkin found in a study of Wisconsin Correctional School girls that only 10 per cent came from homes that had none of these defects, while 36 per cent came from backgrounds where all three existed.[19]

The role of inadequate homes and other environmental factors in the lives of delinquent girls has been graphically portrayed by the Gluecks in their study of *Five Hundred Delinquent Women* who had served sentences in the Massachusetts Reformatory.[20] Their findings show that during adolescence, 44.3 per cent of their subjects lived in poor neighborhoods, and that 87 per cent had had unwholesome companions, such as street-walkers, "drunks," "pickups," and the like.[21]

In a comprehensive study made of 203 delinquent girls committed to the Sleighton Farm in Darlington, Pennsylvania, Mabel Elliott shows the high incidence of disorganizing factors entering into the lives of such girls, corroborating many of the previous studies mentioned.[22] More than half

[16] Clifford R. Shaw and Henry D. McKay, "Social Factors in Juvenile Delinquency," National Commission on Law Observance and Enforcement, *Report on the Causes of Crime*, No. 13, Washington, II (1931), p. 266.

[17] *Male and Female Broken Home Rates*, pp. 601–09.

[18] Sheldon and Eleanor T. Glueck, *Five Hundred Delinquent Women*, p. 454.

[19] "Factors in the Commitment of Correctional School Girls in Wisconsin," *American Journal of Sociology*, XXXVII (1931), 225–9.

[20] *Five Hundred Delinquent Women.*

[21] Ibid., pp. 69, 85.

[22] Mabel A. Elliott, *Correctional Education and the Delinquent Girl*, Department of Welfare, Commonwealth of Pennsylvania (Harrisburg, Pennsylvania, 1929).

(103) of these girls came from broken homes, with specific indications of lack of supervision and related economic handicaps. In almost one-third of the broken homes from which these girls came, the mothers had to seek employment away from the home, thus depriving the young girl of supervision. Even more impressive are the data showing the extent of immorality in the home. While Elliott's findings show that 56.3 per cent of the girls she studied came from homes where immorality was clearly evident, the indications are that the percentage would have been even greater had all the facts been available. Coupled with the disabilities thus far described are the corrosive elements of continous poverty. More than half (57.6 per cent) of these girls came from homes where the breadwinners were semi-skilled and unskilled laborers, and over 60 per cent were members of families in which there were five or more children. The dangers of early unsupervised employment away from home are clearly revealed by these facts.

The limited intellectual capacity of delinquent girls is shown in the high percentage of those who were classified as "morons" (41.5 per cent). Only a little more than one-fourth of those tested were found to be of "normal" intelligence. The limited intelligence of the greater number of these girls and the urgent necessity, in many cases, to help supplement the meagre family income accounted for the fact that the majority of these girls did not proceed beyond the fifth grade at school.

(4) THE CAREER OF THE DELINQUENT GIRL

The steps by which the young girl is inducted into delinquent activity, and the ease with which habituation to sex experience may occur at an early age, is well shown in the following case taken from Cavan: [23]

> (1) As a child, she lived in a two-room basement apartment with her parents and four brothers and sisters. The back yard was used by a junk man and elevator tracks ran overhead. After starting school she made friends first with a girl called Bunny, then with another girl called Peaches. Either in the company of these girls or alone she engaged in many unsupervised activities of a doubtful nature.
>
> (2) She collected junk and sold it, picked up coal along the tracks, and sometimes seized the chance to "snitch" a bottle of milk or a loaf of bread. When a gang of boys upset a pushcart she grabbed some of the fruit that rolled off. She begged in railroad stations and became truant from school. By the age of eight she had learned not to

[23] Ruth Shonle Cavan, *Criminology* (New York, 1948), pp. 127–8. Reprinted by permission of Thomas Y. Crowell Company.

beg too often in one station, and to conceal her address if questioned by the police.

(3) With her two friends, Bunny and Peaches, she began to go to stores in the main business section of the city where she lived, and was taught by these girls to steal small articles, possibly for personal use. She stole a string of beads—the first thing of the kind she had ever had. She also stole small articles of clothing, either to wear or to sell. She learned how to hide these things in her clothing and also to avoid the floorwalker or store detective. When she was twelve she and one of her friends began to have sexual relations with boys. At this time she also began to drink and to stay out half the night.

(4) Her mother objected to the late hours she was keeping, but was unable to control her. Later, she influenced her mother to move to a better apartment and provided her with better clothing and food, which were accepted.

(5) With one of her friends, she associated with various men, from whom the two girls demanded and received money for sexual relations. She met a man, named Darcy, who had an apartment, and stayed with him for three weeks. When she and her friends got into trouble, they turned to Darcy. He was a member of a group that had favorable connections and could "fix things." However, he was sent to prison for two years. The girl's parents objected strenuously to her activities and she left home. She was then fourteen years of age, and prostitution had made her independent financially. She rented three rooms in another neighborhood, not telling her mother where she was. Bunny joined her and the two girls began to work in a combination speakeasy and brothel. She had various adventures—wild automobile rides, drunken episodes, and sexual experiences. The gang she associated with carried guns. At last, "it didn't seem as if we were getting anywhere," and she returned home and re-entered school. But she persisted in her night life, and school was of little interest in comparison.

(6) She continued to associate with her two girl companions and quickly encountered several male criminals who planned crimes in the presence of the girls. Although the girls did not participate in these crimes, they spent much of their time in the men's apartments. Finally, this girl was discovered at home by the truant officer, was found to be suffering from venereal disease, and was arrested and sentenced to the state girls training school. Although the detective tried to get her to tell with whom she had been going and where the gang's hangouts were, she refused, as she was proud to follow the criminal code of silence. She was sixteen at this time.

Although unquestionably, the greater numbers of sexually delinquent girls come from family and environmental conditions of poverty, privation, and seriously impaired surroundings emotionally, the general ecological setting in which these girls live affords further incitement and occasion for the encouragement of such illicit activities. As in the case of the career of the delinquent boy, envisaged in the causal behavioral patterns of the psychogenetic pattern and the "ideational patterns" of the environment, the encouragement towards delinquent sexual acts frequently abounds in disorganized areas, as E. Franklin Frazier has so graphically shown in the studies made of Negro delinquent girls.[24] As Frazier puts it: "One needs only to read the description of one of the neighborhoods in which illegitimacy flourishes to see to what extent the environment in which these women live influences their sex behavior." [25] He cites the description given by an unmarried mother, just fourteen years of age, of the building in which her cousin lived and in which she met her "beaux." [26]

> That building where my cousin lives at now is terrible. I remember one time they shot crap from one o'clock at night on up till in the morning. . . . Some of them women in that building was ahustling. You know, they sell themselves. . . . Men used to go up there all the time. . . . I remember one time all the girls and boys were out there in front of [the] house and [one of the female residents] sent for us all to go inside, she couldn't make no money out there with all of us around. Police used to go up there and raid the place all the time.

Stimulation to sexual behavior occurs frequently even in the early play groups in such areas. Thus, according to Frazier: "We often find in the life-histories of the unmarried mothers that their first interest in sexual knowledge has been aroused by the play groups in these disorganized areas. Consequently, their attitudes toward sex as well as their behavior reflect the attitudes of the groups in which sexual knowledge gives them status." [27] Although these descriptions refer to sub-marginal Negro groups of disenfranchised status, the similarities to the environmental conditions affecting the early developmental patterns of young white girls are quite striking.

[24] E. Franklin Frazier, *The Negro Family in the United States* (Chicago, 1939), pp. 349–57. Cf. also, *The Negro Family in Chicago* (Chicago, 1932), by the same author.

[25] *The Negro Family in the United States*, p. 350.

[26] Ibid.

[27] Ibid., p. 351.

Sexual problems of the young middle-class girl. The habitual female delinquent is largely a product of extreme environmental stress; nevertheless, trends towards ungovernability and loss of parental control, with the ominous possibility of sexual transgression, may appear among those individuals and families of relatively superior and privileged environments. Such cases do not ordinarily reach our courts nor the more widely used social agencies. The wayward girl of a middle-class home is usually protected before she gets into serious difficulty. Frequently, she is sent away to private schools and institutions, or, if she does get "into trouble," the situation is "hushed up" and protective steps, medical and otherwise, are taken to "save her reputation." Faulty psychological conditioning may occur in many better-established families and communities and lay the basis for loss of parental control and potential sexual misbehavior. Such conditions may exist in family situations whose outward physical circumstances would appear to deny such a possibility. Thus, Pauline V. Young, in describing the case of Marilyn Smith, states that the "rather high economic level of the Smith family is not uncommon in private or public child welfare cases, but the problems presented by the family and the girl are not vastly different from the problems presented in homes on any economic level." [28] In this case, although the physical conditions of the home were considerably higher than average, the psychological disabilities under which the girl labored impelled her to escape parental custody, providing the occasion for possible sexual entanglements. Although no definite principle may be formulated, we may state that the maladjustment of the young adolescent girl, irrespective of her class affiliation, frequently places her in situations where she is amenable to sexual exploitation. An illustration of this pattern is provided in the detailed study which Pauline Young makes of the casc of sixteen-year-old Marilyn Smith, excerpts of which are briefly described below.[29] It should be noted in this case how the general psychological atmosphere and the circumstances of parental rejection, sibling position, and the fact that the subject was the only girl in a family of boys helped to induce the given problem despite the superior economic and social status of this family.

In our culture, the sibling position and the sex of the offspring have been shown to bear a relationship to the development of delinquency, and in certain instances, to sexual delinquency. This would not necessarily tend to be the case in other cultures—folk-cultures, for example—where the large number of children and the co-operative demands made upon

[28] Pauline V. Young, *Social Treatment in Probation and Delinquency* (New York, 1937), pp. 33–4.

[29] Ibid., pp. 33–43, 133–4, 296–315, and *passim*. By permission from *Social Treatment in Probation and Delinquency* by P. V. Young. Copyright, 1937. McGraw-Hill Book Company, Inc.

them would hinder the development of anti-social patterns. In our type of class-structured society, the order of birth, when related to the sex distribution of siblings, has been shown to be of statistical significance in juvenile delinquency. Under certain conditions, older brothers and older sisters tend to have higher delinquency rates than younger brothers and sisters. Moreover, the tendency toward delinquency is greater in the case of only sisters than in the case of sisters all of whose other siblings are girls.

Problem complex and nature of problem. According to the mother's statement, Marilyn has been defiant, and unresponsive to discipline. She stays out after midnight, absenting herself from home and school, and chooses "a rather rough crowd of boys and girls to run around with." Three months ago, she found a job working week ends in a drive-in sandwich shop. She met a Catholic man fifteen years her senior, "became infatuated with him, and the trouble started then." He has partial paralysis of the left leg. He is the brother of a girl co-worker at the shop. When the parents objected to her keeping company with "this cripple," Marilyn left home. Her defiance is of long standing. "She is stubborn, but she comes by it honestly—from her father's side of the family. . . . She is unfeeling, hard, and hard to deal with. Mind you, she wants to marry this cripple."

Family background and relationships. Dr. and Mrs. Smith are American born of American white parentage, nominally of Methodist faith. (Dr. Smith is a well-known physician in his home town, which is of about 60,000 population and located about forty-five miles from Los Angeles.) Dr. Smith is Mrs. Smith's second husband. Her first husband, an older brother of the doctor, died in a railroad accident when their first child was four years of age, and the second was three. "The fact that Dr. Smith is the stepfather of the two oldest boys has never made any difference to any member of the family. The children have never been conscious of any differences and don't even remember their own father."

Mrs. Smith states that her parents moved several times from California to the middle west. . . . There were times when the ten children of her family had very little food for several days in succession. . . . Nothing disturbed her until she was a girl in high school and craved pretty clothes which her mother could not supply. She believes that she has perhaps paid too much attention to Marilyn's wardrobe because of an "unsatisfied desire carried over from childhood. But do you believe she [Marilyn] appreciates it? She is careless and even ungrateful for the finest clothes she gets."

. . . . .

Marilyn is the only survivor of a set of triplets. Her only sister died at birth and her brother died a few days later. She has, however, four brothers, three older and one younger than herself. Mrs. Smith states that Marilyn, being the only girl in the family, received considerable attention from parents, grandmother, and friends, which did not cease when the last baby was born. "She early acquired a sense of her own importance and expected the family to cater to her whims. As soon as that trait was recognized, Marilyn was made to feel and take her place as any child in a large family, but she resented this bitterly. She was over-sensitive to reprimand, but continued to get under the skin of everybody. This had to stop and we quit paying attention to her. She was then about eight years of age."

"She has been rather seclusive, withdrawing, and even secretive." . . . She does not get along well with her brothers, has never participated in their games and play. . . .

"As a young child Marilyn was devoted to her mother, but disliked her mother's constant preoccupation with relatives and guests," says Dr. Smith. Mrs. Smith spent considerable time "chauffeuring the child to dancing lessons, music lessons, French lessons," but she was always "on the rush either to entertain at home or to keep an engagement with friends."

There has always been "a close and friendly bond between the two older brothers because of their ages." Ever since the birth of Charles (the youngest child), they have regarded him as "the mascot" and paid considerable attention to him. . . .

Dr. and Mrs. Smith are seemingly unusually devoted to each other. . . .

The excerpts taken from this detailed case study should provide some indication of its salient factors, psychological, social, and intra-familial. Pauline Young gives an excellent summarization of the case, from the standpoint of the "presenting situations," the complex of basic problems and contributory factors. She suggests a causal pattern closely allied to an analysis of the psychogenetic factors. In her analysis, she discusses the positive and negative factors in the case that might facilitate and impede corrective procedures, and draws up a prognosis.[80]

Summary of Tentative Social Diagnosis of the Case of Marilyn Smith

Presenting situations: Running away, truancy, emotional attachment to a man nearly twice her age.

The complex of basic problems and their contributing factors: Social isolation of and lack of common interests between parents and

[80] Ibid., pp. 133–4.

girl. Girl craves companionship and response but both parents are preoccupied with own interests. Lack of parents' participation in girl's recreation. High degree of native intelligence, wide reading, and numerous social contacts contribute to girl's maturity, which is not recognized by parents. Parental protection and overindulgence of girl as a young child and later inconsistent discipline, which provoked confusion and impulsive behavior. Lack of girl's participation in family affairs causes further estrangement and social isolation. Lack of ethical standards of conduct of friends and relatives, also:

Religious hybridism and lack of religious affiliation.

Lack of challenging activities in school.

Unwholesome employment.

Precipitating incidents or crises: Newly found economic freedom. Meeting a man who showed interest and attachment.

Assets upon which to build:

Girl's craving for affection.

Devotion of parents to girl and to each other, as well as to the rest of the family.

Intelligence and good health of entire family.

Girl's wholesome interests and desire for career.

Girl's cautious attitude toward sex matters.

Parents' high ambitions for girl.

Four well-adjusted and devoted sons.

A feeling of accomplishment and success in ability to raise the sons.

Happy and harmonious home background of both parents.

Liabilities operating against successful plan of treatment: Parent-child conflicts are of long standing and are deeply colored emotionally, extending into many phases of Marilyn's and her parents' relationships.

Mother's popularity with a wide circle of friends and relatives cannot easily be set aside in favor of closer relationships with daughter.

Girl's transference of affection to an interested and satisfying male.

Lack of early training in assumption of duties and responsibilities.

Mother's conviction that Marilyn's traits of selfishness, isolation, and individuality are unchangeable and innate.

Parents' lack of understanding of basic problems in girl's behavior; overemphasis on symptomatic behavior.

Ready access to and easy success in blind-alley occupation that provides many stimulating but promiscuous contacts.

Prognosis: It may be argued that, in view of the fact that the emotional conflicts are of long standing and are deeply rooted, in almost every relationship between the girl, her parents, and brothers, and every phase of her life, such as work, recreation, religion, choice of mate, social attitudes and values, the prognosis is only fair. On the other hand, the devotion of the parents to the girl and the girl's craving for parental attachment, her intelligence, wholesome interests, and happy and harmonious home background are all strong indicators of a favorable outcome of the case.

(5) THE CAUSAL PATTERN OF SEXUAL DELINQUENCY

The statistical profile of the delinquent girl and the previous discussion should have suggested in part the basic elements that appear to form the predominant phases of the causal syndrome leading to sexual delinquency. Although we recognize the emotional maladjustment that may arise in middle- and upper-class homes, predisposing the young girl to certain types of premature and early sexual experiences, the environment as such does not tend to incite the type of sexual demoralization that occurs among the underprivileged family groups, irrespective of the occasional promiscuity to which upper-class sexual behavior may lead.

Examination of the data seems to suggest very strongly that pronounced and habitual sexual delinquency or laxity, as defined by custom and law, is closely associated with two sets of factors: (a) familial-environmental and (b) certain distinctive personality characteristics.

Familial-environmental conditions. Although familial-environmental conditions differ, two types of circumstances are frequently found: (1) low economic status and (2) amoral conditions in the household. The bulk of studies of sexual delinquency and prostitution since the beginning of the century emphasize that the families of the individuals investigated were dependent on very low earnings.[31]

A state of amorality is frequently to be found closely allied to these depressed economic conditions abetted and fostered by the migratory and mobile patterns of living such families often follow. The term "amoral" refers to those persons who do not share the culturally prevalent concep-

[31] Cf. Mabel R. Fernald, Mary H. S. Hayes, and Almena Dawley, *A Study of Women Delinquents in New York State* (New York, 1920); Abraham Flexner, *Prostitution in Europe* (New York, 1914); George J. Kneeland, *Commercialized Prostitution in New York City* (New York, 1913); Walter C. Reckless, *Vice in Chicago* (Chicago, 1933); *The Social Evil in Chicago* (Vice Commission of Chicago, Chicago, 1911).

tions of sexual virtue and chastity. The child of the lower class family frequently receives no awareness of such cultural standards—significant in view of the great stress our culture places on morality. W. I. Thomas, in presenting the views of Commenge, the French student of prostitution in Paris, states that "some delinquent girls can never be said to have fallen, because they have never risen to the standards expected of them." [32] He quotes from Commenge: "No sentiment, no calculation, pushes them into a man's arms. They let themselves go without reflexion and without motive, in an almost animal manner, from indifference and without pleasure." [33] A vivid illustration of amorality is found in the descriptive account of her own childhood given by a former prostitute, known by the colorful name of Box-Car Bertha: [34]

> . . . I have always known strange people, vagrants, hoboes, both males and females. I don't remember when I didn't know about wanderers, prostitutes. . . . My first playhouse was a box-car. Conductors in freight yards used to let me ride in their cabooses. Before I was twelve I had ridden in a box-car to the next division and back.
>
> Police and pinches, jails, bughouses, and joints seemed to have always been a part of my life. When I knew that a man was stealing, or a woman hustling, or some poor girl going nutty, or that a guy was on the lam, or learned that a pimp was living with four women—*it all seemed natural to me, an attitude given me by my mother, to whom nothing was ever terrible, vulgar, or nasty. Our family never had any hard luck, because nothing seemed hard luck to it, nor was it ever disgraced for there was nothing which it would acknowledge as disgrace.* [Italics ours.] When my mother changed her "husband," I simply took it for granted. When I was pinched for the first time for riding in a box-car, it didn't seem unusual to me. Many of the men and women I knew had been arrested for the same thing. In my world somebody was always getting arrested. My mother was arrested when I was a baby because she wouldn't marry my father. As I grew up, if we missed a meal or two now and then, or a half-dozen meals, it wasn't anything to get excited about. All my life I have lived with hungry and lonely people.
>
> My mother wasn't what the world would call a good woman. . . . The man whom I called "father" was the foreman of the gang laying the tracks of the Northwestern. I was the oldest of mother's four children. Each of us had a different father.

[32] *The Unadjusted Girl* (Boston, 1931), pp. 98–9.
[33] Ibid., p. 99.
[34] *Sister of the Road: the Autobiography of Box-Car Bertha*, as told to Dr. Ben L. Reitman (New York, 1937), pp. 7–8.

Frazier has described the amoral backgrounds common among many of the sexually delinquent girls and young unmarried mothers who have migrated to Harlem, New York.[35]

> . . . You want to know my early childhood. Well, it was hell. My mother never loved me and I never loved her. I never had a father and—I mean he never married my mother and her father never married her mother. . . . We girls used to mess around a hell of a lot. I guess I was around twelve when I really found out what it was all about. My mother said I had a white liver. I guess I have too. What the hell! She was a hell of a mother. Hell, when I was fourteen she tried to sick an old guy on me just because he had a good farm. Sure I [had sexual relations with] him a couple of times. . . . I was fifteen when the kid [her acknowledged illegitimate child] was born. . . .

Personality conditions. As we have learned, conditions of the environment, regardless of how adverse, do not necessarily or automatically impel an individual to anti-social behavior patterns of a sexual or delinquent nature. The possibilities of unfavorable "differential association" are, of course, more abundant in such deficient environments and may produce various types of personal pathologies. However, the peculiar organization of the personality itself must always be taken into consideration when we attempt to trace the effects on the individual.

The question always arises as to whether certain specific types of delinquent and anti-social acts may be linked to specific personality configurations. Linkages of this sort have been discerned in certain psychopathologies, and in certain specific types of socially acquired disorders such as alcoholism. While it is difficult to ascertain the personality characteristics that are associated with ordinary delinquencies and criminal acts, there is reason to believe that it may be possible to achieve this understanding in the case of sexual disorders.

The intelligence of the habitual female sex offender tends to be low,[36] and in general is lower than the average intelligence of property offenders among women.[37] Katherine Davis, for example, found, on the basis of the Binet-Simon test, that 29.8 per cent of the sexually delinquent inmates at Bedford Reformatory in New York were mentally deficient. Fernald, in a later study, showed that for the diversified groups of female sex offenders she studied, the average intelligence was lower than for compara-

[35] *The Negro Family in the United States*, pp. 287–8.

[36] Cf. for example, Jacob and Rosamond Goldberg, *Girls in the City Streets* (New York, 1935); also, the supplementary study made by Katherine Davis on Bedford Reformatory inmates for the famous Kneeland Report, *Commercialized Prostitution in New York City* (New York, 1913), p. 188; also, Fernald, Hayes, and Dawley, *op. cit.*, p. 431.

[37] Fernald, Hayes, and Dawley, *A Study of Women Delinquents in New York State*, pp. 478, 612.

ble male groups, and decidedly lower in the case of the Bedford and other institutionalized groups.[38] As Gillin has stated: "Over and over again case studies show a large number of girls who are mentally deficient. These girls are physically mature but mentally and emotionally retarded; because of their defective intelligence they do not have the foresight to understand the dangers inherent in social situations with men. They possess the impulses of the adult, but not the ordinary inhibitions. Consequently, they are more likely to fall into prostitution than girls with greater intelligence." [39]

Low intelligence and adverse economic conditions are not sufficient to account for the motivations and impulses that drive the young girl toward sexual delinquency, important factors though they may be. In most cases of sexual delinquency the organization of the psychogenetic pattern is such that, in the face of certain frustrations to acquired needs *in a given kind of social order and on a given social level, the sex impulse is used as an instrument whereby fundamental needs are satisfied* and a state of tension balance is established. W. I. Thomas has illustrated this principle in his analysis of the case histories of three thousand delinquent girls. He showed how the impediments to normative wish-striving—for new experience, security, response, and recognition—may become significant critical elements in motivating the girl toward sexual delinquency.[40]

According to Thomas and others, there is no overwhelming sexual desire (except possibly in exceptional cases) which drives a girl into delinquency. On the contrary, the girl's sex constitutes her *means*, her "capital," as Thomas puts it, through which she may attain satisfaction of certain ends. If the girl were bright, or if she had great imaginative vision, or if the environment offered her opportunities for "sublimating" the frustrations to which she is exposed, the available alternatives would reduce the probability of her becoming sexually delinquent. But such girls, denied, in a great many cases, the ordinary restraints that normal intelligence provides, and denied, by their environment and their native capacities, any possibility of broader fulfillment of their desires, find themselves with no other recourse than to barter upon their desirability as sex-objects. Thomas amplifies this view in his detailed investigation of specific cases: [41]

> The beginning of delinquency in girls is usually an impulse to get amusement, adventure, pretty clothes, favorable notice, distinction, freedom in the larger world, which presents so many allurements and

[38] Davis, *Commercialized Prostitution in New York*, p. 188; Fernald *et al.*, *A Study of Women Delinquents in New York State*, pp. 420, 423.

[39] J. L. Gillin, *Social Pathology* (3rd ed., New York, 1946), p. 342.

[40] See Thomas, *The Unadjusted Girl*, particularly Chaps. 3 and 4.

[41] Ibid., p. 109.

comparisons. The cases which I have examined [about 3000] show that sexual passion does not play an important role, for the girls have usually become "wild" before the development of sexual desire, and their casual sexual relations do not usually awaken sex feeling. *Their sex is used as a condition of the realization of other wishes.* [Italics ours.] It is their capital. In the cases cited below Mary . . . begins by stealing to satisfy her desire for pretty clothes and "good times," then has sexual relations for the same purpose. Kate . . . begins as a vagabond and sells her body just as she does occasional work or borrows money, in order to support herself on her vagabonding tours, sexual intercourse being only a means by which freedom from school work is secured. In the case of Stella . . . the sexual element is part of a joy ride, probably not the first one. Marien . . . treats sexual life as a condition of her "high life," including restaurants, moving pictures, hotels, and showy clothes. Helen . . . said, "I always wanted good clothes." To the young girl of this class sexual intercourse is something submitted to with some reluctance and embarrassment and something she is glad to be over with.

Although the grim reality and sordid nature of their existence may soon become apparent to delinquent girls, their easy, emotional suggestibility is frequently stimulated by shallow, romantic notions. Moving pictures, television, and pulpwood thrillers all contribute materials for the fantasies in which these girls become absorbed. Thus, among Negro delinquent girls, "although the majority have never gone beyond the eighth grade, they are often influenced in their attitudes towards sex by the printed page. As a rule the literature with which they are acquainted is restricted to such magazines as *True Stories* and *True Confessions*. Significantly enough, one girl recounted in her life-history a story from one of these magazines that centered about the romantic career of an unmarried mother." [42]

Despite the seeming validity of the view that disorganized personalities of the type we have described may utilize their sex as a means of wish fulfillment, there is no complete unanimity on this point. Despite ostensible support to this view in their analysis of sex offenders, Elliott and Merrill appear to take a strongly arbitrary and somewhat diametric summarizing viewpoint.[43] In drawing their conclusions, they state: "In the final analysis, however, an important reason for most sex delinquency is sex impulse, arguments to the contrary notwithstanding. Despite all the rationalized explanations of illicit sex experience—and the so-called

[42] Cf. E. Franklin Frazier, *The Negro Family in the United States*, p. 353; see also, Ruth Reed, *The Illegitimate Family in New York City* (New York, 1934), pp. 132–3; and E. Franklin Frazier, *The Negro Family in Chicago* (Chicago, 1932), p. 272.

[43] Elliott and Merrill, *Social Disorganization* (rev. ed., New York, 1941), p. 209.

sexual passivity of women—it must be remembered that yielding to sexual advances is a natural female reaction." [44]

In relation to the sex impulse, all societies have appeared to place an inordinate pressure upon its suppression in certain phases and its opportunity for unrestrained exercise. These strong social pressures and mechanisms have resulted in a wide variety of attitudes concerning the occasions and the opportunities when sexual expression may be exercised. Not all hungry men and women steal; in fact, the vast majority do not. Similarly, irrespective of the compulsions of the sex drive, men and women have learned to inhibit this drive under carefully controlled stipulations and conditions, and have imputed to its expression a framework of ideological values, meanings, and purposes. To a certain degree, even the most unregenerate of sexual delinquents is aware of the meaning of this controlling and supervening sociological structure. Consequently, any deviation from these profoundly rooted norms involves an awareness of the meaning of such transgressions and a motivation wholly supplementary to the raw, basic urge of sex itself.

Some dominant motivations in sex aberrations. Although the motivations controlling anti-social sex behavior may be devious and complex, as the Freudians have so well shown, Thomas' analysis, based on his concept of the "four wishes," is highly suggestive. Not all of the wish-patterns of Thomas, however, appear to have the same significance. In the last analysis made of wayward girls, the motivational force of the wishes for new experience and recognition appears to manifest itself with conspicuous regularity. In our highly competitive culture, the spirit of self-advancement continues to be powerful, and the gratifications associated with positions of high status are amply portrayed for the masses of the population through the popular entertainment media. In such an environment, the incentives toward status advancement and the persistent excitement of glamorous living are enormous. It follows that the interests in attractive clothes, good times, and the prospects of an "enchanted world" would be particularly powerful in those environments that are conspicuous for their sordidness and grinding monotony. If this view is valid, we should expect that sex delinquents would come from those professions and occupations where the opportunities for varied experience and status are limited. The statistical evidence seems to support this supposition, inasmuch as large numbers of sex delinquents and prostitutes come from occupations where high status and changing experiences are denied.

A study by Fernald, Hayes, and Dawley, for example, found that the most frequent occupations of sex delinquents were domestic service, factory employment, and work in stores, in that order.[45] In the Davis

[44] Ibid.
[45] *A Study of Women Delinquents in New York State*, p. 402.

study, the high percentages of waitresses and others whose occupations bring them into frequent and casual contact with men of all types should be noted. In a statistical analysis of almost a thousand delinquent women, Kneeland found that servants and waitresses accounted for 28.7 per cent of all occupations reported, followed by factory operatives (11.06 per cent), dressmakers (10.04 per cent), saleswomen (6.02 per cent), seam-

A Suggested Structure for the Causal Pattern of Sexual Delinquency

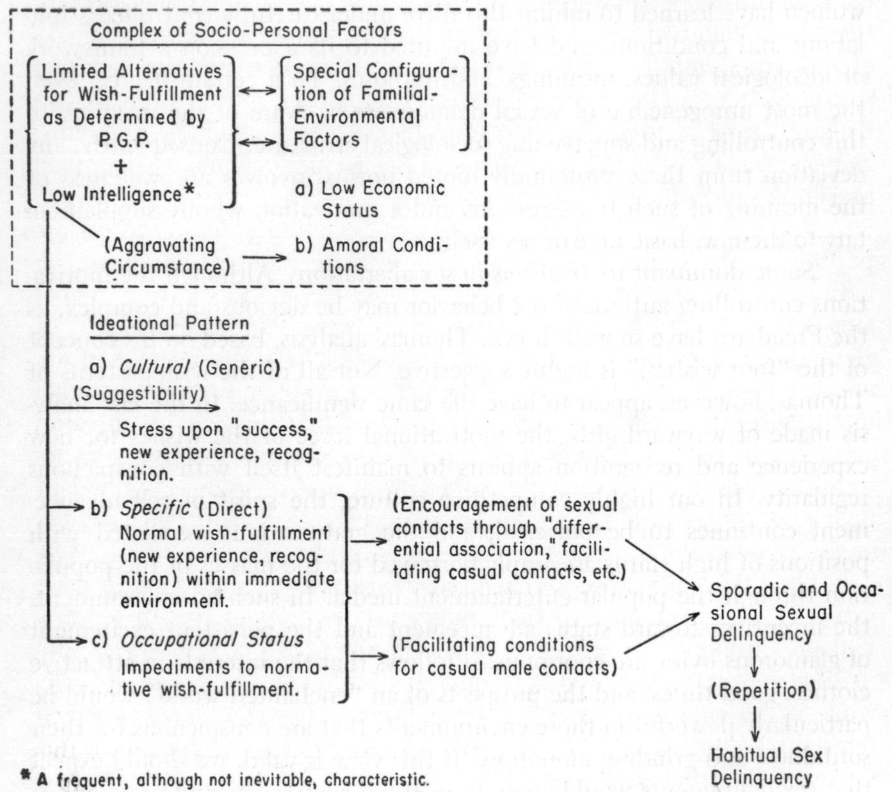

stresses (4.8 per cent), and laundresses (4.5 per cent).[46] For many years, these vocations were held in low esteem. Earnings were low and the regimen was monotonous. Particularly significant is the high incidence of delinquent women who were in domestic employment, as many studies have revealed. In this country, for many years, domestics have been accorded especially low status.

A suggested *structure for the causal pattern of sexual delinquency*. In

[46] *Commercialized Prostitution in New York City*, p. 176.

summarization of the suggested elements which in their combination may contribute to the pattern of sexual delinquency and waywardness, the schema shown on the previous page is suggested. It appears to describe the causal process in a great number of cases.

(6) THE UNMARRIED MOTHER

Closely related to the problem of female sexual delinquency is the special problem of the unmarried mother. Not all mothers of illegitimate children are to be considered habitual sexual delinquents, however. Although the habitual sexual delinquent does, of course, encounter the risks of unmarried motherhood, many unmarried mothers are not habitual sexual offenders. The statistical profile of unmarried mothers reveals two striking sets of factors: (1) their resemblance—occupationally, mentally, and emotionally—to the large mass of sexual delinquents as described previously; and (2) their extreme youth.

Nimkoff reports that in every 100 cases of unmarried mothers appearing on the records of a city agency dealing with this problem, 37 have been domestic servants, 13 have been waitresses, and 15 were school girls. The rest, according to the same source, were composed primarily of clerks, telephone operators, and factory workers.[47] Moreover, studies of unmarried mothers reveal that a high percentage of them are of subnormal intelligence. It should be recognized, of course, that this conclusion varies according to the group studied and to the period when the given studies were conducted. For example, with the increase in illegitimacy attendant upon the disorganized conditions brought about by war, the percentages of girls of normal intelligence increase considerably.

The vast majority of unwed mothers, as revealed in all studies, are extremely youthful, most of them under twenty years of age. In an early Federal Children's Bureau study made in 1923, 48 per cent of the unmarried mothers studied were found to be under twenty years of age, while 17 per cent were below eighteen. These percentages have remained remarkably consistent over the years. Thus, in 1942, the Bureau of the Census found that 46 per cent of the unmarried mothers reported to the Bureau were from fifteen to nineteen years of age. The youthfulness of most of our unmarried mothers is revealed by still another index, the frequency of illegitimate births for age-level classifications under nineteen, as compared with legitimate births. In view of prevailing legal and customary restraints in our states concerning marriages of girls below sixteen, the ratio of illegitimate to legitimate births is extremely high in the more youthful categories and decreases sharply for girls over the age of nineteen.

[47] Cf. Meyer F. Nimkoff, *Marriage and the Family* (Boston, 1947), p. 551; also C. Mathews, "Case Work with Unmarried Mothers," *The Family*, XIII (October, 1932), 185–90.

Thus, the ratio of illegitimate births to each thousand total births, by age of the mother, attains the astounding index of 649.4 for the age level of ten to fourteen, 120.8 for the fifteen to nineteen year old group, and then drops precipitously to 29.9 for the next category, twenty to twenty-four years. The decline is sharp after this age, attaining its lowest level of 7.4 for the age-category of forty to forty-four years of age.[48]

Studies of unmarried mothers reveal that they are generally of five types: (1) mentally subnormal girls who, through ignorance and pressure, have readily succumbed to sexual advances; (2) young and unprotected girls who, through lack of knowledge and force, have been victimized; (3) habitual sex offenders to whom pregnancy has become one of the unfortunate hazards of their activity; (4) older girls of good reputation who have been betrayed, frequently in anticipation of their marriage; and (5) a relatively small group of "emancipated" women who have assumed the risk and burden of pregnancy as a concomitant of their unconventional careers. The statistics reveal graphically, however, that the greatest number come from the ranks of the subnormal, emotionally deficient, and youthful sex delinquent categories.

In the study of social pathology, unmarried motherhood constitutes a particularly arresting problem for analysis. By utilizing the means-end scheme of analysis employed by Talcott Parsons in his *The Structure of Social Action*, considerable light is shed upon the basis for unmarried motherhood and the entire conception of marriage in American society.[49]

The procedures whereby ends are attained in all societies are largely contingent upon the status-positions of the individuals involved. Thus, the status conferred by marriage provides the right to have sexual relations. Sexual relations constitute a legitimate means within the formal marriage contract, although the end-result may not always, under the present conditions of our mores, consist in the production of children. The sexuality of the girl who becomes an unmarried mother, on the other hand, has usually been employed as a means for the attainment of end-objects considerably different from those defined within the marital contract. The condemnatory and conflicting attitude towards the unmarried mother in modern society arises from the fact that the unmarried mother has preempted a status which ordinarily is ascribed only to married women. *Thus, the sex act itself is not so strongly condemned as the result*

[48] *Births, Stillbirths, and Infant Mortality* (U. S. Bureau of the Census, Washington, 1929), p. 15.

[49] For a complete statement of this significant view in contemporary sociology, which bases its analysis upon social structure, see Talcott Parsons, *The Structure of Social Action* (New York, 1937), especially Chap. 9. Also, by the same author, "The Social Structure of the Family," Chap. 10 in Ruth N. Anshen (ed.), *The Family: Its Function and Destiny* (New York, 1949). For a succinct condensation of the means-end view, see Kingsley Davis, *Human Society* (New York, 1949), Chap. 5, "The Elements of Social Action."

of the "mistake." The unmarried mother represents an anomaly in modern society which, while not officially approving sexual incontinence, nevertheless permits it tacitly. On the other hand, it condemns the unanticipated consequences of premarital sexuality for which no legitimate status has been provided by the social order.

The social disapproval of unmarried motherhood may be viewed from another standpoint. Human objects may be pursued for themselves or simply as a means for the attainment of ulterior objectives. Thus, men and women marry each other, ideally, because of their interest in each other as persons. Human beings may also be utilized as instrumentalities or means for the attainment of other satisfactions. The use of another person as an instrument places the relationship within a utilitarian or economic category. Thus, because the sexual appetite, of men especially, is continual, and the opportunities for its gratification are limited for many individuals, there is a constant demand for persons to gratify this one sector of human need.

The young girl who has become an "unmarried mother" is often little more than a depersonalized agent in an essentially utilitarian proceeding. The attitude and proprietary rights of the love-object who becomes a wife are paramount. In the case of the temporary paramour or sex-agent, the attitude and proprietary rights are not essential. In the one case (the conventional love-relationship in marriage), the exclusive proprietary rights over the person and the progeny which results are bolstered by the institutional patterns of the social order. In the second case, no proprietary rights are involved, and the woman, thus, becomes the accidental and sole custodian of any issue which may result from her sexual *mésalliances*. The condemnation of the unmarried mother (and, relatedly, of her illegitimate child) arise primarily because *she is purely an instrumentality* of sex gratification while her child is an anomaly for whom, in the distribution of social values, society has provided no place. An economic "good" is an instrumentality and *not* an end in itself. In the eyes of society, a transgressing female who becomes the unmarried mother has attempted to usurp a status-position which rightfully, *by definition of society*, does not belong to her. She represents, in Kingsley Davis' terminology, a "form of property" for whom no one is prepared to make a claim and in whom no one is prepared to exercise a "proprietary interest." [50]

The Negro unmarried mother. The problem of unmarried motherhood among Negroes presents all the aspects of the problem as it appears

[50] Unlike other forms of sex relationships of the conventionally approved variety, in which jealousy is provoked, the unmarried mother incites the emotion of resentment in view of the fact that she has exercised a *right* (reserved only for married women in our culture) for which society has failed to provide a commensurate *obligation*. For an excellent treatment of a like problem, see Kingsley Davis, *Human Society*, Chap. 7, entitled "Jealousy and Sexual Property: An Illustration."

among white girls, aggravated by the added factors of more depressed socio-economic conditions, migration, and exploitation of a subordinate race. Thus, according to Frazier, the problem among Negroes presents "all the factors involved in the general problem: poverty, ignorance, the absence of family traditions and community controls, and finally the sexual exploitation of the subordinate race by the dominant race." [51] The greater prevalence of disorganized socio-economic and cultural conditions existing among Negroes results in an incidence of illegitimate births five to ten times as high as among white groups. There are, nevertheless, certain unique aspects of the problem among this group, which Frazier calls the "outlawed motherhood" of the Negro girl.

Despite the expectation that the Negro girl might be more readily exploited by white males, the fact is that there are relatively few white fathers of colored illegitimate offspring. In a study made in New York City, Dr. Reed discovered that among 962 cases for which data had been collected by the Health Department, only eighteen instances of race crossing had been detected.[52] Of these cases, fifteen were those of Negro women whose children had white fathers, while the reverse was true in the three remaining instances. According to Frazier, further studies in Chicago support this finding.

Migration and the anonymity afforded by city life are factors significantly related to unmarried motherhood among both Negroes and whites. Of importance, too, is the fact that large numbers of unwed Negro mothers had been migrants for some time and had traversed large distances—from the South or from the West Indies, in many cases—and had been in the city for periods of less than five years before they became the mothers of illegitimate children. In New York City, approximately three-fourths of the Negro unwed mothers born in the South had been in the city less than five years, while in Chicago the number was over one-half.[53] As in the case of the white unmarried mothers, the concentration of cases appears to follow an ecological patterning, the greatest incidence occurring in the most disorganized settlements. The problem is ably summarized by Professor Frazier, who states: [54]

> Our analysis of Negro illegitimacy has revealed that it is a problem almost entirely of the naïve and ignorant peasant folk who are newcomers to the city. Occasionally, a girl with some education and a good family background will be found among the cases in the social agencies. But among Negroes, as among whites, when women and girls who have the advantage of education and economic security and

[51] Frazier, *The Negro Family in the United States*, p. 343.
[52] Ruth Reed, *The Illegitimate Family* (New York, 1934), p. 170.
[53] Cf. Frazier, *The Negro Family in the United States*, p. 348.
[54] Ibid., pp. 356–7. Reprinted by permission of the University of Chicago Press.

the protection of family become pregnant as a result of extra-marital sex relations, they are generally shielded both from the censure of society and from the scrutiny of social agencies. It is, of course, different with the great mass of simple peasant folk who are without these economic and cultural resources. During the course of their migration to the city, family ties are broken, and the restraints which once held in check immoral sex conduct lose their force. However, in some cases where the rural folkways concerning unmarried motherhood are in conflict with the legal requirements of the city, the persistence of these folkways in the urban environment will create social problems. Illegitimacy, like other forms of family disorganization, tends to become segregated in the poorer sections of the Negro community located in the slum areas of our cities.

(7) THE UNMARRIED FATHER

Although ample literature exists concerning the unmarried mother and the several factors relating to her condition, very few adequate studies have been made of the unmarried father. Some significant evidence exists in reference to rural-urban and cultural differences. In general, the unmarried father is youthful, although a few years older than the unwed mother. In urban areas, a large percentage of these men are unskilled or semiskilled workers, with low earning capacity, coming from the disorganized sections of the city. A significant percentage comes from the rooming house areas, a fact that signifies their migratory and anonymous background. The larger percentage by far, however, emerges from conditions closely resembling those of the unmarried mother.[55]

Despite the disorganizing influences of slum areas, certain cultural prohibitions and restraints appear to exist with respect to sexual promiscuity. Slum-dwellers of Italian, Polish, Irish, and Jewish background, for example, tend to exploit sexually other groups rather than their own. *In view of the cultural patterning of marital ties to young people of their own background*, young women outside the group are far more likely to become the objects of sexual exploitation. This appears to confirm our hypothesis of the preceding section concerning unmarried mothers. Within a common cultural group, the young woman may be regarded as a potential wife and mother. The girl in the "out-group" may then become a ready target for sexual exploitation.

There are certain exceptions to this principle. In the first place, it does not apply to Negroes in the same degree as it applies to other groups because of the presence of powerful caste barriers and racial prejudice.

[55] Cf. *The Unmarried Father* (Proceedings of the National Conference of Social Work, Grand Rapids, Michigan, May 1940, prepared by Youth Consultation Service, Newark, N. J.).

Nevertheless, the frequency of illicit sex relations may be fairly high in certain urban areas. Promiscuous sex relations between members of different races assume more commonly an economic character, enabling the Negro girl, for example, to protect herself from the consequences of unmarried motherhood. Here the element of exploitation of the innocent is lacking. Although evidence is not available as to the exploitation of the colored girl within her own group, it appears reasonable to expect that the economically and culturally privileged male Negro would tend to exploit the lower-class colored girl, following the same pattern that exists among white groups.

Among white groups, aside from the cross-cultural sexual exploitation of demoralized girls, the occasional philandering of the middle- and upper-class male among girls of lower economic and social strata produces a quota of illicit offspring. Girls of the upper classes do not ordinarily become the targets of sexual exploitation by members of their own class.

The author, in observing the nature of sexual exploitation in selected rural areas, has found that the urban and rural patterns are somewhat different. Because of the primary contacts in these communities and their relative cultural homogeneity, sexual exclusiveness does not operate in the same degree. Unmarried mothers frequently come from the same class, occupational, and cultural group as the fathers. The critical factors appear to be those of opportunity and the barriers of marital ineligibility on the basis of age, as is the case in the peasant and folk cultures of northern and central Europe. Even in the rural areas of this country, however, where an upper class tradition or similar class distinctions exist, "seignorial rights" are not entirely unknown and may be manifested in the sexual exploitation of girls of lower socio-economic groups or of different cultural groups.

(8) PROSTITUTION AND THE INDIVIDUAL PROSTITUTE

Prostitution, long recognized as the world's most "ancient profession," has existed in some degree in all civilized communities. The prostitute must be distinguished from the habitual sexual offender, whose promiscuity may be intermittent and is carried on as a phase of her generally demoralized outlook upon life. The prostitute is a person, according to Dr. G. Paul-Boncour, who "traffics with his or her body, habitually or occasionally." Abraham Flexner, in his broad study of European conditions of prostitution before the First World War, defines prostitution more widely as a "sexual relationship characterized by barter, promiscuity, and emotional indifference." [56] These definitions incorporate several important features.

[56] *Prostitution in Europe* (New York, 1914), p. 11.

In the first place, the sexual relationship of prostitution is characterized by an element of habituation which may be absent in other forms of sexual delinquency. Secondly, it invariably involves the element of hire, whether for a conventional fee or for some other form of payment, such as "good times," gifts, or the assurance of companionship. Thirdly, although commonly regarded as a profession of women, prostitution may be practiced by men as well. Finally, "trafficking with one's body" has a broad connotation, covering a wide series of relationships in which the individual uses his body for profit, homosexual or otherwise.

A striking characteristic of prostitution as a social phenomenon is that, despite the violent attitudes that have often been held against it, it appears to have flourished throughout human history. In fact, so widespread has been its practice that it has frequently been justified by scholars and civic leaders alike as a necessary evil, if not an outright good.

Like the generality of sexual offenders, prostitutes are recruited from socially disadvantageous environments of poverty, low economic and cultural standards, and lack of family controls. They too are characterized by a high incidence of subnormal intelligence and emotional instability. The habitual sex offender accepts prostitution as a normal course of employment, while recognizing the stigma that society places upon her activity. It is rarely that a girl deliberately enters upon such a profession. The processes that operate to produce this extreme type of sexual delinquency resemble those of differential association, which we found of key significance in the development of general delinquent careers. At some time in her career, the young girl finds herself in association with others whose delinquent behavior serves as a suggestible model. Unlike the occasional sex offender, whose sexual misbehavior is an accompaniment of the pursuit of masculine favor and companionship, the prostitute recognizes her activity as proper to her vocation.

Prostitutes are the most demoralized of offenders. In common with other practitioners of anti-social behavior, the prostitute suffers from a peculiar psychological disability because of her awareness of the extreme stigma attached to her position. Yet her position is in a sense the worst, because of the contempt in which her profession is held by persons of all walks of life. The ordinary criminal may find a minimal social solidarity and approval for his actions among people of his own kind. To the prostitute, even this is denied. The delinquent slum boy may anticipate the possibility of some day becoming a "big shot" in the criminal world; but the prostitute cannot look forward to any advancement.

The female sex offender recognizes her status as a prostitute only after the adverse conditions of her social environment have closed off any possibility of escape. This observation is supported by the differential that exists between the average age of the first sexual offense, as acknowledged by prostitutes, and the average age when the individual acknowledges that she is a prostitute by profession. Thus, Fernald, Hayes, and Dawley discovered that the average age for entering prostitution of the girls in their study was 20.68 years, while the average age of the first acknowledged sex offense was 18.46 years.[57]

The acceptance and belated recognition by a young girl that she is a confirmed prostitute is described in the following excerpt from a case-study done by the author.

> I had lots of jobs and lots of good times. After a while it seemed that I had more good times than jobs. The first time I got into trouble with a man, I was working in a factory. I didn't show up for three days and was fired. However, I soon got another job. One of the fellows I went with, after I got started, was going to marry me, but it never came off. It's hard to remember now, but after a while it got too hard to get up in the morning and go to work. I always thought that one of these days I'd get a regular job and go home. One of my old girl friends settled down and married. She's got two kids now. She was always begging me to quit and go home to my folks. I kept on postponing it too long, I guess. One afternoon, I walked past the tavern on my corner and the boys shouted at me. I realized what I was then and didn't care very much.

As far as can be determined, entering upon a career of prostitution does not necessarily constitute a form of mental abnormality. In view of the low-paying occupations from which these girls come—waitresses, barmaids, tavern attendants and the like—it is not a difficult transition in either income or status. Moreover, although coercive "white slavery" may have existed before the First World War, there is doubt as to whether it exists today. On the contrary, young girls enter into prostitution because an opportunity is afforded them to make their living thereby, and because the barriers to illicit sexuality were destroyed by early promiscuity and exposure to sexually demoralized conditions.*

[57] *A Study of Women Delinquents in New York State* (New York, 1920).
* Summary for this chapter will be found at the end of Chapter Sixteen.

CHAPTER SIXTEEN

SPECIAL PROBLEMS OF SEXUAL DISORDERS

(9) THE SOCIOLOGICAL PATTERN OF PROSTITUTION

THE persistence of prostitution as a social phenomenon must be rooted in the nature of our social organization. Aside from the crucial social conditions and the specific psychological disabilities that make it possible for certain women to follow prostitution as a profession, there must be certain aspects of the social system that function in such a way as to make prostitution possible. As we have seen, sexuality may be employed as a means for obtaining non-sexual ends or gratifications. The urgency and prevalence of sexual needs, in conjunction with the inability of the social structure to provide for some individuals adequate outlets for the satisfaction of these needs, appear to make a certain degree of prostitution inevitable in most cultures. Where, as in the case of certain primitive communities, sexual freedom is permissible to all individuals on certain occasions, the drives towards sexual exploitation may not arise or may be entirely unknown.[1]

Kingsley Davis has discussed how the patterning of statuses in Western culture leads inevitably to a degree of prostitution.[2] In most societies, the arrangement of statuses accords to men positions of greater prestige and power than women enjoy. The result is that women, because of their generally subordinate position, are forced to use sexual means in order to gain influence. Consequently, sexual devices and artifices are utilized as a means of promoting a great variety of social interests. In our male-dominated society, it is not only the young lady, well-bred or otherwise, who uses her sex as a means of enticing males and bending them to her will. Business houses and charitable organizations frequently employ sexual "lures" in order to achieve their special purposes. According to Davis, even the respectable and conventional agencies of social life will resort to sexual influences as a means of gaining their ends. The portrayal of attractive

[1] Cf. Margaret Mead, *Coming of Age in Samoa* (New York, 1928), particularly Chaps. 6 and 7; also, Bronislaw Malinowski, *Sexual Life of Savages* (New York, 1929), Chap. 7.

[2] Kingsley Davis, "The Sociology of Prostitution," *American Sociological Review*, II (Oct., 1937), 745–56.

women in advertising and the sale of kisses are representative of the more innocuous types of sexual exploitation. The employment of sexual themes in an extensive series of human relationships in which direct sexual gratification is not involved sheds light on the exploitative character of sexual relationships in Western society. Prostitution, then, may be understood as an extreme expression of a common tendency.

Certain individuals, both male and female, are inevitably excluded from the possibility of achieving sexual gratification because of their undesirability. As Davis puts it: "All men are not born handsome, nor all women beautiful. Instead, there is a perfect gradation from extremely attractive to extremely unattractive, with an unfavorable balance of the old and ugly. This being the case, the persons at the wrong end of the scale must, and inevitably will, use extraneous means to obtain gratification."[3] The result will be, therefore, a constant residue of prostitution in Western society, in accordance with the preferential nature of our sexual attachments, as the following excerpt shows.[4]

> Even if present trends continue, there is no likelihood that sex freedom will ever displace prostitution. Not only will there always be a set of reproductive institutions which place a check upon sexual liberty, a system of social dominance which gives a motive for selling sexual favors, and a scale of attractiveness which created the need for buying these favors, for prostitution is, in the last analysis, economical. Enabling a small number of women to take care of the needs of a large number of men, it is the most convenient sexual outlet for an army, and for the legions of strangers, perverts, and physically repulsive in our midst. It performs a function, apparently, which no other institution fully performs.

That the practical and "hard-boiled" administrators of vice suppression are ultimately forced to the same conclusions can be seen in the statement of Reckless, who says:[5]

> In summary, one may say that most of the work of public or private agencies, dealing with the problem of prostitution, is suppressive. Very few persons, nowadays, actively believe that what the Vice Commission recommended and hoped for, namely, complete destruction of the traffic, is possible. The Committee of Fifteen today does not believe that vice can be harried out of Chicago and kept out. It conceives its own task well done if it can keep the business of vice at a minimum or keep it from growing.

The differential in the sex ratio also plays a part in this equation,

[3] "The Sociology of Prostitution," p. 754.
[4] Ibid., p. 755.
[5] Walter C. Reckless, *Vice in Chicago* (Chicago, 1933), p. 268.

especially within given areas. Where males seriously outnumber females, or females outnumber males, circumstances are propitious for the spread of prostitution or other forms of sexual exploitation. A recent estimate by the Twentieth Century Fund predicts that women in the United States will outnumber men by about 700,000 in 1960. While such a condition would diminish the possibility of men exploiting women, the reverse situation, exploitation of men by women, might conceivably come into effect.

(10) EXTENT OF PROSTITUTION AND VARYING RATES

There seems to be considerable evidence that the incidence of prostitution in many parts of the Western world is diminishing. Such a decrease is due in large part to the increasing liberality of the sexual mores. The moralist, because of this fact, is placed in an unenviable dilemma. On the one hand, he may regard with approval the decrease of prostitution in many civilized areas of the world, including the United States. He must deplore, on the other hand, the very agency that brings the decrease about.

The extent of prostitution may be gauged by the vast amounts of money spent for its support. Studies of prostitution in the early part of this century all showed the enormous profits that prostitution gained for its entrepreneurs. Thus Flexner, in his celebrated study of *Prostitution in Europe*, estimated that the annual cost of commercialized prostitution in Germany before the First World War ranged from $75,000,000 to $125,000,000, an estimate which appeared highly conservative to many American critics. For the city of Chicago, during the same period, the Vice Commission estimated annual total profits of $5,400,000 gained from prostitution exclusive of additional receipts for liquor and sundry items, which brought the total to over $15,000,000. The decade preceding the First World War was a period of intense investigation and muck-raking concerning civic corruption, and similar surveys in Philadelphia and Syracuse in 1913 revealed annual costs of $6,250,400 and $750,000 respectively.[6] Kneeland, in his famous survey, recognizing the difficulty of making an adequate appraisal of the cost of prostitution in a city the size of New York, made an estimate of the paid receipts in thirty parlor houses in that city.[7] He found that the total annual income of these thirty houses solely for the services of the prostitutes was over $2,000,000. If additional charges were taken into account, including such items as liquor, room

[6] Cf. *The Social Evil in Chicago* (Report of the Vice Commission of Chicago, 1911), pp. 113–15; *Report of the Vice Commission of Philadelphia* (Philadelphia, 1913), p. 15; and *The Social Evil in Syracuse* (Report of the Syracuse Vice Commission, 1913), p. 21.

[7] George J. Kneeland, *Commercialized Prostitution in New York City* (New York, 1913), p. 130.

rentals, and meals, the total income may have been more than five times this amount.

Estimates of numbers of prostitutes are quite variable. Even in those European cities where prostitutes are registered and held under police and health department surveillance, it is difficult to obtain an adequate appraisal of their numbers. Flexner's early study regarded as far too low an estimate of 20,000 prostitutes in Paris at that time. Another estimate at about the same period gave the figure of 120,000, six times as large. Other surveys during the same decade, all conservative and of highly dubious accuracy, gave estimates of 8,000 prostitutes in London, 30,000 in Vienna, 17,000 in Glasgow, 5,000 in Rome, and 7,000 in Amsterdam. In 1913, there were an estimated 330,000 prostitutes in the entire German Empire, as reported in the same Flexner study.[8] In Japan, where the *Yoshiwara*, a legalized area in Tokyo devoted to prostitution, flourished for many years before the recent war, an estimated 48,000 women catered to approximately 22,000,000 male patrons annually.

In the United States, accurate reports on the extent of prostitution are even more difficult to obtain because of the generally clandestine conditions under which prostitution exists. The various vice commissions functioning in many of our large cities during the first two decades of the present century made numerous estimates of the scope of the problem. The figures in general appear to have been lower than the estimates made for European cities of like size. In 1913, Kneeland's study of New York revealed that there were an estimated 15,000 professional prostitutes in that city. The Chicago Commission in 1911 reported an estimated 5,000 prostitutes in the mid-Western metropolis, while the Philadelphia Commission gave a number of 3,311. Estimates for the country as a whole have ranged from 200,000 to 500,000. The so-called "official" estimates are based largely on official police and clinical reports and records, and do not take into account the large numbers of shifting, footloose women who make up the larger part of this surreptitious trade.

Gillin points out that since commercial prostitution requires from fifteen to twenty men for the support of one woman, the extension of the problem into the larger community is of considerable significance.[9]

Although commercial prostitution is primarily a feature of urban life, its spread into smaller industrialized communities, and even into several rural areas, has been quite rapid. The decentralization of industry into small communities and rural areas and the disorganization brought about by the recent war have resulted in the appearance of commercialized prostitution in areas where it had previously been relatively unknown.

Prostitution, both in this country and in Europe, seems to have fol-

[8] *Prostitution in Europe*, pp. 25–8.

[9] Cf. John L. Gillin, *Social Pathology* (3rd ed., New York, 1946), pp. 336–7.

lowed a series of growths and declines since the end of the nineteenth century. This has been particularly true of the organized prostitution that has been undertaken on a large scale as part of the vice racket and other related forms of illicit traffic. Both wars of this century, abetted by the widespread condoning of illegal activities during the prohibition period of the roaring twenties, have encouraged the growth of large-scale vice syndicates. It is to be noted, however, that vice syndicates with organized prostitution as an important phase of their operations wane in power during periods of stability and during periods following wars and other forms of socio-economic stress. Thus, a recrudescence of syndicated vice appeared during the recent war, but since 1943 there has been a decline of organized vice. Although prostitution and vice as "big business" may show a decrease, there is no conclusive evidence that the incidence of prostitution itself is showing any marked decline.[10]

The Patrons of Prostitution

Generally speaking, the patrons of prostitutes are the very young and those individuals who come from disorganized areas. These latter are persons who themselves experience various types of personal demoralization, disabilities, or frustrations. As Reckless, May, and Hall have shown, a large percentage of the men who visit prostitutes are the footloose and unattached who come from the cheap rooming house and hotel districts of the large cities. In Chicago, it was found that the distribution of (a) persons who died of venereal disease, (b) persons who were victims of paralysis, and (c) persons who were arrested in vice raids, coincided with the locations of the highly mobile areas of the city and with the location of the sections characterized by an absence of family life.[11] A certain percentage of the patronage consists of youths of middle-class families who are out "on a fling" and the sensation-seeking business executive and convention-attending middle-aged individuals who seek the abandon of youth. The bulk of the habituees of prostitution, however, come from the youthful, unattached migrant males of the cities. These persons generally follow semi-skilled manual or clerical occupations and are lacking in strong family ties.

That the pattern of prostitution and sexual promiscuity may be changing is indicated by another interesting sign. The tourist camps and motels that flourish in the vicinity of smaller cities provide convenient locations for illicit sexual activity. This development points directly to a type of sexual indulgence practiced by the middle and upper economic groups who do not ordinarily patronize prostitutes. In Dallas, Texas,

[10] Cf. M. H. Hall, *Prostitution in the Modern World* (New York, 1936), pp. 76–7.

[11] Cf. R. Faris and H. W. Dunham, *Mental Disorders in Urban Areas* (Chicago, 1939), p. 126.

Elbert Hooker conducted an investigation based on the automobile licenses of 100 cars that were seen in such tourist camps, whose owners and users were putatively employing the premises for illicit sexual purposes. The distribution of the owners of these cars was found to be city-wide, suggesting participation by a variety of classes.[12]

Classes of prostitutes. The fact that prostitution appears to function as an economic utility results in the creation of several categories of prostitutes suggestive of class-levels involved. While the bulk of prostitutes and patrons come from the lower economic groups, there is also a "class-clientele" and a corresponding category of prostitutes to serve them. Dr. Ben L. Reitman has discerned at least eleven categories of prostitutes on the basis of the study of a great many cases.[13] It should be noted that although the classes in which these women fall suggest differences in their ages, they correspond primarily to the cultural and economic levels of the patrons who patronize these types of women. According to Reitman, these classes include: (1) the "juvenile" prostitutes, ranging in age from 10 to 15 years, who often appear in juvenile courts; (2) the "potential" prostitutes, whose services may be on a voluntary as well as a financial basis; (3) the "amateur" prostitutes—scornfully called the "amateur girls" by the hardened prostitutes—who may live at home and supplement their incomes by prostitution; (4) the "young professionals" who have recently entered the profession; (5) the "old professionals," habituees of brothels, and "old hands" at the game; (6) the "field workers," or street-walkers, who solicit men on the street and take them to their rooms; (7) the "bats," the aged and decrepit derelicts who cater to the lowest male element and who are frequently ill and narcotic-ridden; (8) the "gold-diggers" or "boulevard women," who maintain themselves in fine residential hotels in which they entertain their clients; (9) the "kept women," who supplement their incomes by contacts with other men; (10) the "loose" married women, who supplement their incomes by extra-marital affairs; and (11) the "call girls" who, through the offices of hotel proprietors and others, arrange assignations discreetly with out-of-town visitors and special clients.

The recent growth of a discreet form of "glamorized" prostitution, restricted in its operations and flourishing in the central hotel districts of our large cities, was disclosed during the spring and summer of 1949 in Hollywood, where this practice hovered on the fringes of the moving picture industry. The outright candor with which this trade was carried on is illustrated by the fact that the female entrepreneur of a well-known "party-girl" agency was able to insert discreet advertisements in a Holly-

[12] "The Urban Tourist Camp," *Studies in Sociology* (Southern Methodist University, Dallas, Texas), Vol. I.

[13] *The Second Oldest Profession* (New York, 1931), Chap. 1.

wood periodical devoted to listing the services of business and professional specialists.

Prostitution as a Business Enterprise

The high costs of prostitution do not figure in physical and psychological terms alone. As in all illicit activity for which there is a continual demand, the sums paid for protection are extremely high, ranging from the small fees paid to the corner policeman to the large sums of "protection" money extorted by political "higher-ups" and public officials. Very few illegal enterprises, however, support such an enormous number of intermediaries as prostitution, all of whom demand their share of the profit made by the individual prostitute. The parasitic superstructure constitutes one of the most unsavory aspects of this tragic profession. From the small procurer or "pimp" who maintains a few girls in his service to the "madame" who runs a large house and the extensive syndicates which traffic in various forms of vice, the parasitic claims upon the earnings of the prostitutes are extremely heavy. In addition to these claimants, there are numerous other individuals—"steerers," taxi-drivers, messengers, and personal attendants—all of whom demand a part of the receipts.

Significant among the economic charges which this profession bears are the high rental fees for their premises which landlords and disreputable hotel proprietors impose. Lohman has shown that the real estate owner, frequently delegating the responsibility of his property to a renting agent, is either oblivious or indifferent to the purposes for which his premises are employed.[14] Not only tolerance but actual approval of the use of their property for illicit purposes has been shown by renting agents and proprietors. It is to the renting agent's advantage to keep his premises in occupancy at the highest fees he may be able to obtain and with the least responsibility for the financial costs involved in their upkeep. According to Lohman, one agent made the following statement:

> I know this district as good as anybody. I ought to after thirty years. The bank gives us all their property to manage in this district, buildings they hold in trust and others their clients have them take care of. I'll tell you why we get their business—it's because they get the best returns. I know who to rent to. Give me a *hooker* all the time. She pays regular and she pays good. You never have to wait for the rent. There's only one thing can beat her and that's a bookie. I get three times as much out of that property as it's worth. The bank don't ask questions and neither do I. I just bring in the rents.

[14] Joseph D. Lohman, "A Note on Vice and the Local Community," *Bulletin of the Society for Social Research*, Chicago (Dec., 1938).

The owner's attitude is frequently not much different. On the commonly held and morally dubious assumption that if his property were not used for this purpose, someone else's would be, one proprietor openly expressed his emphatic preference for such tenants:

> I'd rather rent to the street-walkers any day. I'd hate to have to invest any money in the property, which I'd have to do in order that respectable people would live there. . . . I didn't even have to fix the broken windows but once, they patched them themselves. . . . Nobody's going to tell me what I can do with my property.

Means of Control

When an illicit profession based upon institutionalized demands becomes so firmly rooted in the social structure, reaching into the political, economic, and social life of the community, it becomes extremely difficult to curb it or to extirpate it. This, at least, has been the experience of the United States.

Since, in its practical aspects, the curbing of prostitution depends upon the efforts of the police, success in this attempt may be attained only with the full and earnest co-operation of our municipal and local police departments. If prostitution flourishes in any area, it may do so only with either the active or tacit connivance of the police. This does not mean, of course, that police officials must be held solely responsible for the existence of prostitution in our large cities and urban areas. It suggests simply that any legal procedure devised will be effective only in the degree to which the agencies of the law exert their capacities to carry out its provisions. Where the legal procedures have been successful, it is in part because an honest police department and a forthright public prosecutor's office have been conscientious and zealous in their duties. Where the laws have failed, it has frequently been because the execution of the law has not received the best efforts of the police and the district attorney.

The efforts to curb prostitution during this century have taken two forms, the development of adequate legislation and the periodic purging and strengthening of police departments. Among the most common legal procedures developed in this country have been laws designed to curb the use of property for sexually immoral purposes by placing the responsibility for its misuse upon the landlord, and to advance the surveillance and tighten the penalties for the offense of procuring, rather than for prostitution itself. Private and semi-public organizations, too, have contributed their efforts to the control of this social problem. There follow brief statements concerning the steps that have been taken by the various interested agencies, legislative, police, and educational.

(a) In regard to the first procedure, the first Injunction and Abatement Act was passed in 1909 in Iowa. This law became the prototype for a whole series of similar laws that have been passed since that time. In their essence, these laws state that legal action may be instituted by any citizen against any individual who permits his property to be used for immoral purposes. The owner of property must undertake a direct responsibility to see that his property is employed solely for legitimate purposes.

(b) Some municipalities have tried to restrict prostitution to quasi-legal "red-light" districts as a supervisory and health measure, confining their prosecution to sexual offenses committed outside of segregated areas. Military officials, particularly during times of war, have felt that this is the only way to effectively handle the problem in population centers near army camps. This procedure, aside from its tacit defeatism, has been singularly ineffectual. Where it has been attempted, it has invariably been found that the amount of prostitution outside of the segregated districts has been as great or greater than that occurring within the supervised area. It almost goes without saying as well that such pseudo-legal procedures tend to elicit and encourage corruption of law-enforcement officials.

(c) Periodic efforts have been made by Citizens' Committees, such as the Committee of Fourteen in New York, The Committee of Fifteen in Chicago, the Philadelphia Vice Commission, and the Syracuse Vice Commission, frequently as phases of more widespread political reform, to focus attention upon the problem and to remove dishonest and recalcitrant elements from the police departments and prosecutors' offices. Such civic-minded groups have frequently been aided in their efforts by the American Social Hygiene Association or its affiliated agencies, such as the New York Bureau of Social Hygiene, as a means of improving legislation and developing preventive and therapeutic measures for delinquent girls and prostitutes. Arising from the efforts of such groups, various municipal agencies have been created to deal with the problems of the wayward girl or the hardened offender. The difficulty with such campaigns has been their sporadic nature and their lack of sustained organized effort. While performing an excellent function in disclosing socially unhealthful conditions, they have frequently failed because a sustained organizational, legislative, and enforcement program has not been developed.

(d) Frequently emerging from such periodic investigations has been the creation of special agencies and enlarged facilities in the public prosecutor's office and the police vice squads. The former Crime Prevention Bureau in New York City, now the Juvenile Aid Bureau, is a police agency with a unique therapeutic, referral, and social case-work function. Philadelphia, Chicago, Cleveland, and many other major cities in the

United States have developed similar agencies with related functions. The chief function of such bureaus is to carry out preventive and rehabilitative work with young offenders, frequently in association with broad educational and recreational programs. Because of the police authority vested in this kind of work, these agencies may prove extremely effective, particularly for their referral function. They recognized increasingly the social case-work treatment required for the rehabilitation of incipient and active sexual delinquents, and the many community ramifications which such therapeutic procedures ultimately involve.

(e) Control has also been sought through educational procedures. Too often, educational programs, particularly when conducted in public institutions and schools, emphasize the more frightening aspects of repression. The enlightened programs and literature of the American Social Hygiene Association have done much during the past twenty-five years to lay the basis for sound education and control, and have played an instrumental role in the dissemination of scientific information. Such national bodies as the American Mental Hygiene Association have also assisted in this process.

(f) Remarkable claims have been made in the past by the Russians for great success in ridding Moscow and other large urban, industrial areas of the blight of prostitution. As with many other claims of social advance made by the Russians, it is difficult to establish verification on the basis of authentic statistical information and other forms of proof. The Russians have established the so-called *prophylactoria*, centers for the rehabilitation—physical, emotional, and vocational—of prostitutes. An educational program has been developed for the patrons of prostitution and the public at large on sexual matters. Because of the vast coercive powers inherent in police states, the Russians have been able to exercise extreme pressure against Communist Party members and others. By such procedures the Russians claim to have eradicated prostitution in Moscow and other major cities. These claims must be taken with some reservation, however. Reports of foreign journalists and other visitors in Russia since 1932 have noted the presence in Moscow and elsewhere of the so-called "valuta" girls, women who exchange sexual favors for money. With the growing Puritanism in sex matters and the tightening of family controls developed since the recent war, it seems possible that prostitution in Russia may become as formidable a problem as it has elsewhere.

(11) VENEREAL DISEASE

For many centuries, the dread legacy of sexual promiscuity has been venereal disease. There are four types of venereal disease that may arise from infected sexual sources: (a) syphilis, (b) gonorrhea, (c) chancroid, and (d) tropical bubo. Of these, the first two have been particularly virulent and disastrous in their effects in Western history, while chancroid has also accounted for a large number of physical infections. The chief danger has invariably come from syphilis, known as the "great deceiver" by the medical profession, because of the ease with which the *spirochaeta pallida* may invade the human organism when once infection begins, attacking nerve tissue, skeletal structure, and the vital organs of the body. Gonorrhea, a less insidious disease, and, because of their bodily structure, of greater danger to women than to men, has also produced its annual heavy toll in Western society. Even today, as much as twenty-five per cent of all blindness may be due to gonorrheal infections, and possibly as many as one-half of all known cases of sterility.

Directly prior to the recent war, significant strides forward had been taken in the combat of this scourge, which for centuries had undermined the mental and physical capacities of men and women in Western culture. Under the vigorous leadership of Doctor Thomas Parran, former U. S. Surgeon-General, a campaign to bring the disease out into the open for cure and treatment was steadfastly waged for the decade prior to Pearl Harbor. The discovery of the use of sulfanilamide derivatives and penicillin, accelerated by their recent war-time success, is writing a new chapter in the struggle against these age-long enemies of mankind.

The prevalence of venereal disease. The widespread existence today of venereal disease, despite the development of knowledge since the early part of the century of how to combat it, is an indication of how society still resists dissociating the disease from its traditional *moralistic* and *censorious* definitions. That this attitude of resistance is breaking down, and that there is an increasing awareness of the fact that venereal diseases must be regarded as any other form of combatable infectious disorders, affords an index of the weakening of views we have previously held on sexuality morality.

Before the Second World War, the combined venereal disease rate of syphilis and gonorrhea for males, on the basis of those being actually treated at any given time, was approximately ten for each thousand males in the population. The female rate was a little less than one-half the male rate, an average of 4.86 per thousand in 1930. Although the overall gonorrhea rate is generally higher than the rate for syphilis—two to three times for specific periods in certain areas before the recent war—the rates vary for men and women. While men contract gonorrhea at a greater rate than women, the effects upon woman of this dread disease are far more serious because of their bodily structure. Men, on the other hand, appear to be more seriously impaired by syphilis. With respect to both syphilis and gonorrhea, the male rate exceeds the female.[15] The probability of infection before marriage was greater for men than for women, indicating that a great percentage of married women innocently contracted venereal disease after marriage.

The *expectation* rates for the contraction of venereal disease before the recent war revealed a much more ominous picture. The reports of the U. S. Surgeon-General showed that 95 per thousand males and 62 per thousand females could expect to contract syphilis before the age of twenty-five. On the basis of these expectancy rates, Dr. Parran revealed that syphilis struck one out of every ten adults in the United States, with approximately one-half of the infections falling within the youthful category of twenty to thirty years.[16] During the period 1935–40 there were approximately six men infected for every four women. The rates were four times as high in urban areas as rural, and, because of lower preventive, health, and social standards, the rates were nearly six times as high for Negroes as for whites in our population. Further indication of the extent of syphilis in the United States can be found in the fact that even today, the greatest single *organic* factor in producing mental disorders in this country is syphilis, causing the dread disorder of *paresis*. A large percentage of hospital beds in may state and federal mental hospitals, accounting for approximately ten per cent of first admissions to state hospitals, are occupied by paretic patients, those rendered insane by syphilitic infections.

As high as these rates appear to be, they are not as high as rates in several European countries. Before the First World War, and in the decade following, investigations of the incidence of venereal disease among the male population aged fifteen to fifty in leading German cities suggested an expectation rate for gonorrhea of approximately 88 per cent. The syphilis expectation rate, not quite as high, indicated that one man out of every five in this age category had had or was suffering from syphilis.[17]

The reality of these statistics became apparent to the United States Army units stationed in Europe during the period of occupation following the recent war. In certain districts of occupied Bavaria a year after V-E Day, the combined syphilis and gonorrhea rates among American

[15] In 1930, according to reports from the U. S. Surgeon-General's Office, the rates of gonorrhea for each thousand of the population was 4.88 for males and 1.78 for females. For syphilis, the rates were 4.77 and 3.08 respectively.

[16] Thomas Parran, *Shadows on the Land* (New York, 1937), pp. 60 f.

[17] The pre-1914 Flexner Report revealed the same findings for Germany at that time. In his citing of one authority (Blaschka), it was shown that 45 per cent of merchants and clerks in Berlin, between the ages of eighteen and twenty-eight had suffered from syphilis. Also, one out of every five men from the same group had had gonorrhea twice, while in Breslau, 77 per cent had had syphilis and 100 per cent had had gonorrhea twice. Cf. Flexner, *Prostitution in Europe*, pp. 367–8.

troops were as high as 300 per 1000. In one district in which the writer assisted in the establishment of venereal disease control clinics for civilians, the American troop rate reached a figure of 343 per 1000. An unofficial survey of selected detachments, including Negro batallions in the French port of Marseilles in December, 1945, showed record-breaking figures of 700 infections per 1000 men. The upheaval of war and the movements of vast numbers of displaced persons throughout Europe have produced a legacy of venereal disease, the full measure of which we cannot assess as yet. Some indication of the ravages yet to follow may be seen in the report of Dr. Evan W. Thomas of the World Health Organization. He found in a personal survey conducted during the spring of 1949, that 50 per cent of the school children in Bosnia, Yugoslavia, suffered from secondary syphilis. Even in Denmark, where the problem of venereal disease had been negligible before the war, due to stable population conditions and effective control, the rate rose to 20 per 10,000 during the period of the Nazi occupation.

Wars have inevitably spread the scourage of syphilis and gonorrhea. Yet, before the recent war, the United States Army had made a very creditable attack upon the problem among its own personnel. From a high rate of 103 per 1000 before 1914, the Army medical authorities, through their efforts in prophylaxis and education, had reduced the rate to 48 per 1000 by 1930, and to less than 10 per 1000, lower than the average civilian rate, by the time of the recent world conflict. The Chamberlin-Kahn Act passed during the First World War, setting up public health clinics for the treatment of venereal diseases in virtually all states, achieved a good deal in curtailing venereal disease. In May, 1941, the May Act was passed by Congress, giving the military and naval authorities considerable scope in curbing prostitution in areas adjacent to military and naval establishments. The powers incorporated within this act were so broad that military commanders could exercise enormous authority even over areas at some distance from military installations. These measures, coupled with education in prophylaxis, did much at the outset of the war to cut down rates of syphilis and gonorrhea among military and naval personnel. However, a general slackening of control occurred after the termination of hostilities in Europe and in the Pacific, with the result that the rates grew to unprecedented dimensions.

The final battle with syphilis. It is possible that we may have reached the final act in the drama of mankind to overcome the scourges of syphilis and gonorrhea. During February 1949, the United States Public Health Service, in commenting upon the successful outcome of rapid treatment methods by means of penicillin, reported that it had "watched skeptically, hopefully, scarcely daring to believe the evidence." In the case of gonorrhea, a single intramuscular injection of 300,000 units of penicillin is so lethal that a cure rate of 92 to 98 per cent for men and women, whether in acute or chronic gonococcal infections, is now certain. From the medical standpoint, when adequately treated, gonorrhea may actually be considered neither "as uncomfortable or as serious as a head cold." By the same token, because of the ease of cure, the incidence of this common venereal disease is probably rising once more, through the rapidity and multiplicity of infections. Although also promising, the use of rapid penicillin treatment in the case of syphilis does not yield the same high curative results. In January 1948, Dr. Joseph Earle Moore of the United States Public Health Service and the Johns Hopkins University Venereal Disease Research Center, Baltimore, brought the research findings up to date with the following significant facts: (1) in the case of *early syphilis*, up to three years after treatment, penicillin seems to have been very effective in 90 per cent of the cases treated, if by cure is meant "freedom from relapse and prolonged negative blood and spinal fluid tests." (2) In the case of *pre-natal syphilis*, penicillin is "spectacularly and nearly completely successful" in the prevention and cure of infection in the unborn child by treatment of the pregnant syphilitic woman, regardless of the period of pregnancy in which it is given. (3) In respect to *infantile congenital syphilis*, penicillin has done a little to reduce the mortality rate in this condition which still remains at about 10 to 15 per cent. In babies who survive, however, the death rate is substantially lower than in adults who acquire the disease. (4) For those suffering from *late syphilis*, "nothing can be said of the eventual outcome, since years of post-treatment observation are necessary to determine the point." In February 1949, however, Dr. Leonard Scheele, Surgeon-General of the United States Public Health Service, was able to say: "We are no longer fighting a defensive battle. . . . We have been able to take the offensive." In substantiation of this optimistic note, during 1947 and 1948, the number of new cases reported dropped 20 per cent, even though, as a result of a concerted educational program, there were 30 per cent more clinical examinations. Even more promising has been the precipitate decrease in the number of deaths from syphilis. Deaths from syphilis dropped from about 21,000 in 1938 to 13,000 in 1948, while the numbers of civilian cases reported dropped from 480,140 to 338,141 during the same period.

That we can eradicate syphilis today with the aid of penicillin is almost a foregone conclusion. Even without this new drug, considerable success has been achieved elsewhere, notably in Sweden, through *epidemiological control*, and in pre-war England, extensive services were made available to the public. The two techniques provide an illuminating comparison of the results that may be achieved. In Sweden, syphilis has become virtually extinct through *epidemiological control*, i.e., tracing out all sources of infection and subsequent contact. Under the Swedish law, it is mandatory for physicians and patients to report the victims of venereal disease. The sources of infection are then sought out and medical controls are established to prevent further contact and infection, as is done with other infectious disorders. Although great success has been achieved in overcoming syphilis by this means, before the advent of penicillin, the same could not be said for the problem of gonorrhea in Sweden and elsewhere. In England, where, after the First World War, an extensive educational and public treatment campaign was instituted, the rate of syphilis was reduced by one-half after ten years, although the gonorrhea rate still remained extremely high.

Armed with modern drugs and with modern techniques of propaganda, the U. S. Public Health Service inaugurated a nation-wide campaign in July, 1949, to strike the first of a series of death blows to syphilis and gonorrhea. The anti-venereal disease campaign, assisted in its propaganda work by the Communications Materials Center of Columbia University, planned to extend its operations to more than three hundred cities in twenty-eight states. With the aid of slogans painted on sidewalks, billboard advertising, radio songs and announcements, television dramatizations, and even of juke-boxes in corner taverns, the Public Health Service hoped to reach 96,500,000 persons and the estimated 2,000,000 unreported victims of syphilis in the United States. Within ten years' time, it is possible that we may have achieved almost as enviable a record as has Scandinavia. However, because of the size and heterogeneity of this country, it is doubtful whether we will be able to attain the virtual extinction of syphilis as has Sweden.

Because of the lack of penicillin resources in other parts of the globe, the immediate world picture is not so promising. However, the World Health Organization of the United Nations is conducting a vast international survey of conditions, with the view of determining the possibility of establishing such rapid treatment centers as are employed in this country.

(12) HOMOSEXUALITY

A sociological analysis of homosexuality presents some extremely interesting problems, particularly in the light of the concepts we have thus far presented. While our culture regards homosexuality as an acute abnormality and visits it with the contempt and opprobrium that extreme deviation in sexual behavior generally draws, other cultures have taken much more tolerant attitudes. Viewed as a proper subject for abnormal clinical evaluation in our culture, Ruth Benedict points out that "the adjustments that (our) society demands of (homosexuals) would strain any man's vitality, and the consequences of this conflict we identify with their homosexuality."[18]

A number of societies have accorded the sexual invert acceptance in the social order, and in some instances have awarded him a position of honorable distinction. We do not have to look to the primitives alone for examples of this. Periclean Athens, long regarded with extreme veneration for its contributions to the development of Western civilization, regarded with considerable pride some of its most notable citizens who were homosexuals. As Ruth Benedict states: "Plato's *Republic* is . . . the most convincing statement of the honorable estate of homosexuality."[19] Among the Romans, particularly during the latter days of the Empire, homosexuality was widespread and, if not officially condoned, was tacitly accepted as a common practice among members of patrician society. The institution of the *berdache*, as the French refer to it, is widely known among primitives. Unlike ourselves, among whom the very suspicion of homosexuality is frequently sufficient to render it difficult, if not impossible, for the individual to make normal adjustments in his social life, primitives have condemned homosexuals only when they have been unable to comply with the other mandates of society. In Siberia, the *berdaches* were regarded as having a special status involving certain rights and distinctions; they were generally believed to be possessed of unusual supernatural powers. Although not accorded the same high prestige among the Indian tribes of North America, sexual inverts were, nevertheless, unmolested and, on occasion, granted unique privileges. One of the best known and respected members of the Zunis of a generation ago, according to Benedict, was such a "man-woman." Among the warlike Plains Indians, the institution of the *berdache* showed a remarkable development. Among the Dakota, for example, it was considered very high praise when a woman's household possessions were said to be "as fine as those of a *berdache*."

The sociological problem centering on homosexuality appears to present a dual aspect: (1) the socio-cultural conditions that determine why some cultures accept homosexuality as a normal pattern while others reject it; and (2) the reasons for the occurrence of homosexuality in the face of its strenuous suppression in societies such as ours, and the reasons for its increase in such societies during periods of social disintegration and rapid change.

(1) The cultivation of sexual inversion as a social norm seems to follow in those societies that show excessive male dominance and where, because of preferred institutionalized values and structure, a certain de-

[18] Ruth Benedict, *Patterns of Culture* (New York, 1934), p. 245.

[19] Ibid., p. 243.

gree of sexual segregation takes place. It is not uncommon to find homosexual practices socially accepted in social orders that are highly militaristic. This may come about not only because the activities of war remove men from women for long periods of time, but also because in societies of this sort woman's status and her accomplishments are often poorly regarded. Typifying such a derogatory attitude is Demosthenes' classic statement concerning the Greek gentleman's attitude toward women: "We maintain our wives to bear us legitimate heirs, our concubines to serve our persons, and our mistresses to afford us pleasure." The emergence of such norms in a modern, complex social structure was seen in the prevalence and acceptance of homosexuality among German stormtroopers and members of the former Nazi Elite Corps and S. S. detachments. In fact, the execution of Captain Ernst Roehm, the organizer of the S. S. troops and a notorious homosexual, was occasioned in part by his open aberration and his alleged encouragement of these practices among his personnel.

A detailed analysis of the sociological basis for "normative" sexuality requires investigation of the organizational patterns of the family. When a rigid and extreme patriarchal family structure, such as is typical of some parts of modern Germany, is exposed to rapid social change that is inimical to it, one of the consequences appears to be a relatively high degree of sexual abnormality of various types, including homosexuality.[20]

(2) Despite the denunciation of sexual deviation and the punishment visited upon sexual inverts in Western culture, sizable numbers of homosexuals are to be found in all European countries and the United States at all times. The incidence of homosexuality appears to rise during periods of social change and breakdown. This is very likely due, first, to the fact that, with the relaxation of social controls, more aberrant individuals will come forward. Second, the unsettled character of such periods induces an interest in "sexual experimentation" because of the instability of traditional sexual standards. It is significant to note that at the time of the decline of the Roman Empire, and in the periods of the Renaissance and the Reformation, as well as in the contemporary period, the incidence of various forms of sexual deviation appears to have risen sharply.

Homosexuality is not especially a class phenomenon, although there is evidence that upper class groups, particularly intellectuals, writers, and

[20] Although the data are not conclusive, the rates of homosexuality in Germany since the beginning of the century, and especially in the decade following the First World War, seem to have been much higher than in other European countries. The relationship of this symptom to other forms of breakdown, when viewed in conjunction with the peculiar pattern of the German family during the period of rapid social change and disintegration, may provide a fruitful clue in the analysis of some of the attitudes that facilitated the rise of the Nazi Party.

artists, produce greater numbers than do other classes of the population.[21] The wide publicity given to the sexual aberrations of famous artistic personalities such as Oscar Wilde and Tschaikowsky, may serve to exaggerate estimates of the extent of the problem among this class, however. Nevertheless, the percentage of sexual deviants among outstanding writers, poets, musicians, and actors appears to be quite high.

Prevalence. Because of the nature of its suppression, it is difficult to ascertain precisely the extent of homosexuality. The recent Kinsey Report is causing considerable revision of early estimates. According to a popular estimate, approximately 2 per cent of the population possess constitutional characteristics producing homosexuality, while possibly as many as 4 or 5 per cent in addition give evidence of latent or acquired homosexuality.[22] The Kinsey estimate states that as many as 37 per cent of the males investigated participated in some form of homosexual activity. This statistic is not to be construed as an estimate of the number of active homosexuals in the population, although it stands as evidence that there is a larger number of latent homosexuals than was previously thought. What Kinsey refers to as homosexual behavior, in many cases, appears to apply to various forms of adolescent sexual behavior that occur quite commonly in boys' groups, without necessarily resulting in the development of genuine homosexuals.[23] In the light of recent evidence, it is likely that our general estimates may have to be revised upward rather than downward. The estimate that 5 to 8 per cent of the population are homosexuals, constitutional and otherwise, may be found too low.

Causal patterns. The biological doctrine accounting for homosexuality states that sex is determined by a specific chromosome, the X-chromosome. Whereas the male germ cell contains both, an X and a Y chromosome, the female cell (determining the neutral female physiological structure) contains only the X-chromosome. The structure of the sex chromosome is a complex entity with the result that the developed glandular structure may produce predominant "internal" characteristics of the opposite sex. In view of the structural complexity of the genetic constituents, the physical determination of sex is never a simple, unitary

[21] The class character of homosexuality is partially attested to by Kinsey and his collaborators in their work, *Sex Behavior of the Human Male* (Philadelphia, 1948).

[22] Homosexuality should not be confused with hermaphroditism, the state in which the sex organs of both sexes are present in a single individual. True hermaphroditism is extremely rare, only about thirty authenticated cases appearing in medical history. The constitutional homosexual, while presenting the external features of a given sex, is physiologically conditioned by a unique glandular structure that predisposes him to prefer sexual relations with members of his own sex.

[23] The preliminary unpublished data of Kinsey's researches on women suggest that among women early isolated homosexual experiences may result in constant homosexuality at a later date. This contrasts with the observation that among males, such early practices do not necessarily eventuate in chronic homosexuality.

process. To a certain degree, therefore, certain latent physiological elements of the opposite sex are present in all organisms, and sex is largely a matter of degree.

This explanation appears to provide a substantial physiological basis for the Freudian and various socio-psychological hypotheses that emphasize the bi-sexual character of all human beings. As Margaret Mead has shown in a number of her works, human societies tend to elicit the desired masculine and feminine traits, temperamental and social.[24] Under the impact of certain culturally derived personal-social relationships, particularly as manifested in the early training of children, the tendency may be to elicit behavior-responses proper to the opposite sex. Thus, an only male child in a family of girls, particularly if his latent constitutional structure predisposes him in that direction, may tend to develop characteristics of the opposite sex. The Freudian view suggests that this may be developed in part as a result of excessive anal and oral eroticism, which is in turn the consequence of certain forms of early childhood care. That a degree of bi-sexuality exists in all normal human beings is evidenced in the results of tests that have been devised to determine degrees of bisexuality—the Terman-Miles Masculinity-Feminity Test, for example.

Types of homosexual personalities and practices. Aside from certain common characteristics that are the result of social repression, homosexual personalities are as heterogeneous as the personalities of the balance of the population. However, depending on the character of the social situation and their personalities, homosexuals generally fall into three categories: (1) those who, irrespective of opportunities for heterosexual association, resort only to homosexual activity; (2) those whose behavior may vary from homosexual to heterosexual forms, depending on circumstances; and (3) those who accept homosexual relations only in the absence of opportunities for heterosexual relations. The last condition is especially common in one-sex groups, such as prisons, camps, military establishments, boys' or girls' schools, and the like. In one sense, only the first type of behavior can be said truly to constitute homosexual behavior of a consistent form.

Not only does the behavior vary, but the roles enacted may differ as well. Homosexual roles may be of the (1) active, or male type; (2) passive, or female type; or (3) mixed, where the individual may assume one or the other role. The last type seems to be the most common. As an interesting reflection of male dominance in our culture, we note that the passive type of homosexuality seems to be the most condemned even among homosexuals themselves.[25]

[24] Cf. Margaret Mead, *Sex and Temperament in Three Primitive Societies* (New York, 1935); also her more recent work, *Male and Female* (New York, 1949).
[25] Cf. Aaron J. Rosanoff, *Manual of Psychiatry* (New York, 1927), pp. 202–03.

Social patterning, status, and rank. It has previously been observed that repression of anti-social behavior brings about a considerable degree of solidarity among the repressed groups. The degree of integration of such groups follows in part from the severity of the out-group's disapproval. The grouping process, thus, provides a type of safeguard for the preservation of emotional normalcy. In effect, this means that complete emotional breakdown does not take place insofar as the individual is afforded some sanctuary in groups that condone or support his behavior. The coherence of these groups is often betokened by the development of unique social patterns and a distinctive vocabulary.[26] The elaborate terminology of homosexuals, coupled with the fact that many of their terms have been adopted by the larger cultural group, provides testimony of the extensiveness and the solidarity of homosexual groups in the population—"societies" within the larger social structure.

The abhorrence with which conventional society regards homosexuals causes the majority of them to live in constant fear of detection. This fear is particularly acute in the case of latent homosexuals, who discover their deviation belatedly, and in the case of those who attempt to suppress their feelings and live like normal individuals. Such individuals are constantly threatened with social ostracism, blackmail, economic ruin, and legal prosecution.[27] The painful subterfuges they must employ and the corrupting effect upon their mentality were portrayed to the author by a homosexual male, a professional man of standing in a small community, married and seemingly devoted to his wife, and the father of two children. Men of this sort live a particularly tragic existence, as Charles Jackson points out so well in his sensitive novel on the subject, *The Fall of Valor*. For John Grandin, the strange and belated disquiet he suffered in approaching middle age "interrupted his work, interfered with his attentions to his family and to family duties, left his mind far from rest. Working of an evening in his study—or even of an afternoon in broad daylight—he would lift his head, his senses all aware, and catch himself in the act of expressing the baffling thought: When will the blow fall?"

A heavy concentration of homosexuals exists in those occupations that are usually reserved for women or are associated with women's interests. Thus, a great many homosexuals are found in the fields of dress

[26] As in the case of criminal groups, the nature and extent of the vocabulary frequently affords a valuable key to the nature of the group and the degree of its integration.

[27] The reputed 183 homosexuals in the State Department, disclosed by the investigation of the U. S. Senate in its loyalty probe of employees in federal services during the spring of 1950, were considered "politically" dangerous because of the ease with which they could be blackmailed.

designing and dressmaking, cosmetics, hairdressing, millinery, and related occupations. Because aesthetic interests have been associated with feminine interests in our culture, a great many homosexuals are found in the arts. On the lower occupational levels, many homosexuals find employment as bathhouse attendants, masseurs, male nurses, and prison guards, for the sake of opportunities for contact and voyeurism.

The fact that a relatively high percentage of homosexuals are of better than average intelligence suggests that, possibly, superior family environments tend to foster sexual inversion. This superior intelligence might also account for the relatively high number who enter artistic and professional fields.

The U. S. Army released a report in June, 1947, on homosexuals in the armed services during the recent war.[28] Although efforts were made during the preliminary physical and mental examinations to weed out men of this category, a great many nevertheless managed to elude detection. The study of the U. S. Army medical authorities provides interesting data concerning those homosexuals who entered the army: (1) They topped the average soldier in intelligence, education, and personnel rating; at least 10 per cent were college graduates. More than 50 per cent had finished high school and only a small handful were illiterate. (2) Including all ages, there were more whites than Negroes in this group. (3) Most of them came from cities rather than rural areas. (4) Although the majority had no family history of mental or nervous disease, many came from homes broken by divorce or separation.[29] (5) In many instances, the man had been brought up as a girl or as the only son in a family of girls. (6) About half assumed a "feminine" role, the other half a "masculine" role. (7) The majority were unmarried or had made a failure of marriage. (8) As a whole, these men were law-abiding and hard-working, and, despite unstable and hysterical temperaments, performed admirably as office workers. Many tried to be good soldiers.

The dilemma of homosexuality. Homosexuality in our culture remains a psychopathological disorder and a concern for psychiatrists. Despite this fact, attempts are made to reconstitute known homosexuals on the basis of normative patterns, even when it is recognized that their problems require specialized and psychiatric care. This is seen both in

[28] This report was based in part on the study of L. H. Loeser, "Sexual Psychopaths in the Military Services," *American Journal of Psychiatry*, CII (July, 1945) 92–101. For a comprehensive digest of the problem of homosexuality in the U. S. Armed Services, see William C. Menninger, *Psychiatry in a Troubled World* (New York, 1948), Chap. 16, pp. 222–31.

[29] This is an interesting point for further investigation. It suggests a lack of opportunity for identification with the male parent, maternal rejection (evidenced by the need for stabilizing feminine care), and the tendency toward dependence and passivism.

our criminal courts, where sexual offenses are still classified as penal infractions,[30] and in the general counsel we offer those who suffer from such disabilities. The common belief, for example, that marriage will help to solve the homosexual's problems is an illustration of this short-sightedness. It results often in tragic consequences not only to the individual himself, but to the members of his family. An illustration of this kind of catastrophe is portrayed in the following case.[31]

> Up to the time of his marriage at the age of thirty-three years the patient had had but little sexual experience and that was uninspiring and otherwise unsatisfactory. He was moody, somewhat seclusive, yet felt lonesome, and finally made up his mind to marry, mainly for companionship.
>
> This caused matters to become worse instead of better. At the end of three years of rather tempestuous domestic life it happened that a relative of the wife's died and she had to take a trip to the East to secure her share of the inheritance. It was thought that she would have to remain away at least six months. Both were pleased with the prospect of a temporary separation.
>
> About two weeks after the wife's departure the patient became acquainted with a young man. The latter was homosexual, but the patient was not aware of that fact. The young man soon "fell violently in love" with the patient, but did not reveal the sexual nature of his attachment. The patient, on his part, found his new friend most interesting and congenial and readily accepted the suggestion that they go to live together in an apartment. . . .
>
> [Upon the wife's return], the domestic situation quickly became worse than ever and in less than a month the patient decided to make a clean breast of the whole matter to his wife, in order that she, too, might understand what was at the bottom of their troubles and perhaps cooperate in devising some solution.
>
> She took it "in the wrong spirit," became enraged, said this was the last straw, that she would not tolerate such outrageous and degenerate conduct, and threatened to take the whole matter into the criminal courts.
>
> With much difficulty the patient succeeded in getting her to join in an agreement to bury the past and continue to live "normally"

[30] In New York State, this has been partially modified by the passage of the Sexual Offenders Law (Senate No. 3372) on March 15, 1950. This law alters the normal conception of sexual offenses under the penal code, bringing them under the conjoined control of the Department of Mental Hygiene. It is based partly on an intensive two-year study of 102 sexual offenders at Sing Sing Prison, conducted under the direction of the psychiatrist, Dr. David Abrahamsen.

[31] Reprinted by permission from *Manual of Psychiatry and Mental Hygiene* by A. J. Rosanoff, published by John Wiley & Sons, Inc., 1938, pp. 205–06.

without ever again referring to what had happened. But he found he had undertaken a contract which he could not fulfill. Normal marital life proved no longer possible for him. He grew depressed, could not sleep, had scarcely any appetite, lost weight, and thoughts of suicide kept running through his mind.

(13) THE CONTROL OF SEXUAL ABNORMALITY

For the most part, our courts have failed to comprehend and control sexual abnormality. The prevalent attitudes are survivals of previous ethico-sociological beliefs concerning the "sinfulness" of man. Despite tendencies toward an enlightened point of view in regard to conventional types of offenders and offenses, the attitudes of most judges remain extremely atavistic in their emphasis on condemnation.

Periodic waves of sexual offenses have aroused public opinion in favor of more concerted action. Since the close of the recent war, a series of sexual offenses involving sexual inverts and psychopathic persons have had the effect of bringing the public to appraise the problem on a new basis. There has been some recognition of the ineffectualness of the conventional method of treating the sex offender as an ordinary law-breaker. The traditional procedures failed to bring about any corrective results; in many instances, they have proven harmful in exposing the invert and other offenders to the destructive influences of the prison environment. The celebrated Heirens case in Chicago, and a series of similar tragic episodes in Pennsylvania, New York, and Massachusetts, involving assault and homicide upon young children, have finally motivated several state legislatures to reconsider the status of the abnormal sexual offender under the law.

The Elmira Reception Center of the New York State Department of Correction has attempted for some time to provide special psychiatric examinations and treatment for such offenders, and to maintain them separately. The difficulty has been that no specialized institutions have thus far been established for the treatment of these cases. During the spring of 1948, Governor Thomas E. Dewey of New York mandated a special investigations committee to make a study of this problem. Other states have now followed suit. Senator Desmond of the New York legislature prepared a bill for the 1950 session of this body recommending that the jurisdiction over sex offenders be removed from the normal routine of the courts. The bill recommended further that special facilities be established for the segregation and treatment of these offenders in accordance with modern psychotherapeutic procedures. This bill has now been enacted into law.

A number of specific courses of action are required to cope with the problem of sex offenses. (1) In cooperation with the public schools system, adequate sex education should be provided, both as a means of improving public understanding and as a means of assisting in the early recognition of a culturally-oriented disability. (2) In view of the fact that sexual deviations may frequently be noted at an early age, public provision for early clinical diagnosis and treatment should be established in conjunction with both public and private agencies. (3) In view of our modern understanding of the causal processes involved in sexual deviation our legal structure must be sufficiently broadened to enable the courts to (a) provide adequate psychiatric diagnosis, (b) provide disposition of cases in accordance with psychiatric recommendations whenever feasible, (c) remand cases to institutions, public and private, where medical and psychotherapeutic treatment may be intensively pursued, and (d) provide strict segregation of offenders through psychiatric facilities, separate detention centers, or both.

SUMMARY

The conception of cultural normalcy in a given society determines the nature of its sexual standards and the general views of heterosexual reality. The patterning of male and female roles, and the impact of socio-cultural change upon institutional patterns, bring about different types of sexual pathology. (1) Such problems as prostitution, sexual promiscuity, homosexuality, and perversion emerge in a class-structured society during periods of change in accordance with the interests and cultural levels of the different stratified groups of the social order. The prevalent conceptions of sexual propriety differ in their effects and in their attitudinal manifestations in accordance with such stratified differences. (2) The fact that sexual delinquency is an offense primarily of women, and the fact of its relatively heavy incidence among young girls of lower economic and cultural levels, are indications of our ambivalent cultural emphasis in sexual morality. Although the percentage of female offenders is relatively small as compared with the total volume of male offenders, the majority of female offenders appear in our courts for sexual offenses or offenses of a related character.[32] The ratio of male to female offenders appears to diminish toward the middle adolescent and early adult years. (3) Although sexual problems make their appearance on various cultural levels, the heaviest incidence occurs within the ranks of the marginal and depressed groups. Thus, the "statistical profile" of the

[32] The Federal Childrens' Bureau, in fact, estimates that 80 to 90 per cent of young girls in correctional and custodial institutions are committed because of sex offenses, although official designations of their offenses may appear different. Cf. *Children in the Courts*, U. S. Department of Labor, Childrens' Bureau Publication No. 235 (Washington, 1937), p. 46.

delinquent girl reveals a background of broken homes, homes of low moral character, emotional instability, poverty-stricken surroundings, low mentality, limited education, and families of large size. Particularly significant is the high rate of broken homes. (4) The career of the delinquent girl may be seen to follow steps similar to those of the delinquent boy. For both, the principle of differential association applies. Adverse surroundings and bad companions play their roles in conducing towards sexual delinquency of the young girl. (5) An analysis of the careers of sexually delinquent girls reveals that sex is a means whereby deprivations caused by the environment may be satisfied. Thus, the causal pattern of female sexual delinquency revolves about certain familial-environmental factors, such as low economic status and amoral conditions of the household, and certain unique personality characteristics (also related to the environment), such as wishes for new experience and recognition. (6) The condition of unmarried motherhood is not a phenomenon restricted to the lower classes. The resemblance—occupational, mental, and emotional—of unmarried mothers to sexual delinquents is marked. Also of significance is the extreme youth of the unmarried mothers in our society. (7) The unmarried father presents a background similar in many respects to that of his unmarried consort. The practice of cross-cultural sexual exploitation, i.e., seeking sexual favors outside one's own cultural group, provides an interesting commentary on contemporary sexual mores and the social structure. (8) The process of habituation may subtly transform the sexual delinquent into the professional prostitute. In the history of Western culture, prostitution has varied in its manifestations and extent, and in the degree of approval granted to it. Increasing relaxation of our sexual mores has very likely resulted in a diminution of syndicated prostitution, although no conclusive evidence may be adduced to indicate a decline in occasional or random prostitution. (9) In view of the manifold ramifications of prostitution in the life of the community and its frequent alliance with unscrupulous business interests and law enforcement agencies, it has proven extremely difficult to suppress in American society. (10) In fact, because of the dominance of male roles over female roles in Western society, and the competitive nature of the social order, sexual exploitation appears to exist in some form on all social levels, producing a social atmosphere conducive to prostitution. (11) Venereal disease has traditionally appeared as the invariable and inevitable concomitant of sexual promiscuity. The difficulties our culture sets in the way of relieving sexual outlooks from traditional moral censure has made it difficult to separate the medical problem, with its social consequences, from the moral issues involved. The recent remarkable discoveries of new drugs for the treatment of syphilis and gonorrhea, and the growth of a scientific-secular ideology, augur well for the virtual elimination of these scourges within the foreseeable future. (12) The emergence of the problems of homosexuality and perversion is always related to certain cultural stresses and social strains. The basis for the acceptance of sexual deviants in certain cultures has been presented, as well as the reasons for their sporadic increase and decrease in frequency. The sociological factors of most significance in the development of homosexuality are (a) those types of social structures that foster male segregation, (b) the pre-eminence of masculine values, and (c) the rigid and impermeable type of patriarchal family organization. (13) The control of sexual deviants requires their separation from the traditional penological and judicial process. Segregation, detention, and psychiatric care should be provided for such cases.

CHAPTER SEVENTEEN

LEISURE AND THE PERSONAL VICES

(1) LEISURE AND THE SOCIAL STRUCTURE

THE problems created by what we have called, for lack of a better term, the personal vices, must be studied, like all other social problems, in relation to the field in which they occur. And the field most closely related to the personal vices is that of leisure and recreation. Drinking may not only constitute a problem for certain individuals and groups in the population, but in its emergence as a problem *it reflects the prevalence of certain widespread recreational standards as well as the social atmosphere of much of our leisure and recreation.* Because drinking has become an integral part of our recreational life in America, affecting different classes in different ways, the problem of its pathological effects may not be dissociated from the recreational pattern itself.

Leisure plays a very significant role in a highly complex, impersonal, and changing society. As Seldon D. Bacon has pointed out, the multiplicity of restraints and frustrations which such a society presents translates our leisure into those relatively infrequent occasions where freedom and spontaneity in inter-personal relationships are possible.[1] In any society, the use to which leisure time is put provides an index of (1) the predominant end-values and objectives of the society, and (2) *the strains and characteristic distortions to which the culture is exposed.*

In the history of Western culture, the amount of time available for leisure and recreation has in itself frequently constituted a significant index of the status of the individual in society, provided the individual fulfills his primary vocational and family obligations. The proper performance of these obligations frees the individual, in the words of Irwin Edman, for "unhurried pleasurable living among one's native enthusiasms." *The necessary pre-condition for leisure in society and the enjoyment of its use, therefore, depends upon the removal of those barriers which the performance of social obligations imposes upon the individual.*

[1] Cf. Seldon D. Bacon, "Alcohol and Complex Society," *Alcohol, Science and Society* (New Haven; *Quarterly Journal of Studies on Alcohol*, 1945), pp. 179–94.

(2) SOCIAL VALUES AND RECREATION

Some of the basic values of the culture are to be found in its recreational patterns, although these values manifest themselves in devious and complex ways. Competition, the desire for novel experiences, and many other elements find their way into our recreational activities. Such elements, produced by the mobile, technological, and other *nonrecreational phases of our social life*, become inculcated within the basic attitudinal structures of society and ultimately find release through recreational outlets.

In reflecting certain nonrecreational value concepts the prestige factor plays an important part in developing recreational and leisure-time outlooks. Although the kind of recreation of elite groups frequently precludes the possibility of their ready adoption throughout the social order (the "exclusiveness" of the recreation having a distinct virtue of its own), other classes in time attempt to emulate them. This does not apply solely to the acquisition of novel recreational skills or practices, but relates as well to the several prestige-factors that become associated with various forms of recreation. "To be seen in the right places" (because of the pleasurable distinctions it brings) becomes just as important a part of the recreational pattern as the recreation itself. As Thorstein Veblen has shown in *The Theory of the Leisure Class*, the traits formerly distinctive of an elite class in Western culture, such as "conspicuous consumption," "ostentatious display," and "pecuniary emulation" also become characteristic of other classes in the culture.[2]

Recreational patterns frequently disclose (a) the peculiar cultural interests of different stratified groups in society, and (b) the peculiar stresses and tensions to which such groups are exposed. This is nowhere better illustrated than in the class differences in recreation in American society.[3]

(3) GROUP INTERESTS, RECREATIONAL PATTERNS, AND LEISURE

(a) Education, economic position, family size, and physical location and character of the home all play a part in producing different recreational activities of different groups. Although not necessarily typical of the wealthy classes in American life, and certainly not restricted to them, aesthetic, literary, and intellectual interests are likely to arise with greater statistical frequency in those groups that have enjoyed special educational

[2] Thorstein Veblen, *The Theory of the Leisure Class* (New York, 1917).

[3] Even sexual dalliance, if regarded as a form of recreational activity, conforms to different class standards, as the Kinsey Report has shown.

privileges. Further, the possibility of certain leisure-time pursuits, such as golf, will depend largely upon the financial ability to become a member of a country club, the matter of transportation, community pressure and atmosphere, and the place of residence. Moreover, recreation and leisure-time activity, both inside and outside of the home, are frequently a reflection of the size of the family itself.

(b) There is, however, another and deeply revealing way in which class differences in recreation are exposed. *In any culture, those significant activities, both productive and non-productive, that the group has come to regard as constituting the basic orientations and social instrumentalities in the culture are frequently pursued as ends in themselves.* This is ordinarily a highly restrictive class affair, but in the pursuit of such activities it becomes increasingly difficult to dissociate such practices from recreational activities themselves. We see this to a certain degree in our own culture where the practice of a man's profession may become so important to him, aside from its practical and pecuniary considerations, that it becomes an avocation as well as a vocation. Such activities, however, are largely restricted to specialized classes and to those professional occupations or callings where the individual enjoys some leadership functions or a number of discretionary privileges.

American culture reveals its culture-oriented recreational drives in a characteristic way—by means of the heavy emphasis it places upon business activity. Not only has business activity become a form of recreation for many American men, but the pervasive character of American business has invaded many areas of social activity which we would ordinarily call recreational. As the Lynds point out, members of the business class in Middletown rather significantly refer to their activities in plant and office as the "business game" although it is decidedly not customary for working-class members to refer to their manner of gaining a livelihood as the "factory game."[4]

In addition, in American life recreational activities are frequently carried on as a means of promoting one's business interests. Thus, golfing, membership in certain clubs, the frequenting of certain bars, night-clubs, and restaurants, for example, may not be engaged in solely for the pleasure to be derived from such participation, but largely as a means of promoting or abetting one's interests. Even the wives and children of businessmen are not exempt from this process and are affected by this overlapping of functions. The selection of friends and bridge-playing teas for the housewife, as well as dancing-classes and camps for children may, under the guise of pleasurable occupations, be motivated by the more sober considerations of consolidating one's position or, in the words of

[4] Robert S. and Helen M. Lynd, *Middletown in Transition* (New York, 1937), pp. 242–5.

the novelist Marquand, by the necessity for "sweetening one's contacts." [5] For the working classes in Middletown, recreation has a much more direct and uncomplicated function. For the workingman, "leisure assumes a simple, direct, and important place in your scheme of things: *it's* when you *live*, and you get all of it you can—here, now, and all the time."

This difference in the class-structured attitudes towards leisure is probably nowhere more effectively portrayed than in the different attitudes towards car-ownership entertained by the two classes in Middletown.[6]

> Only by understanding this different focus upon leisure of the lives of those living north and south of the tracks can one appreciate the tenacity with which the workingman clings to his automobile. If the automobile is by now a habit with the business class, a comfortable, convenient, pleasant addition to the paraphernalia of living, it represents far more than this to the working class; for to the latter it gives the status which his job increasingly denies, and, more than any other possession or facility to which he has access, it symbolizes living, having a good time, the thing that keeps you working. And again, only by understanding how these two groups weigh the importance of work and leisure can one understand the exasperation of the businessman over the workingman's frequent preference for his car rather than for the slow, painful process of saving for the future.

(c) In any consideration of leisure, we must be concerned with the enormous changes brought about by modern technological processes which have made it possible for large masses of the population, particularly women, children, and old-age groups, to be freed from the drudgery of ordinary toil. The complex dilemma of the modern middle-class woman who, relieved from the burdensome duties of her household, finds herself without adequate fulfillment of herself and with little effective function for the community, presents an acute and, in some cases, a tragic problem. The increasing number of old-age individuals in the population, brought about by a combination of circumstances involving a declining birth rate, improved medical care, and greater productivity in industry, have created a new problem for the utilization of such groups in the social order and in the consideration of how the leisure, for which they are ill-prepared, may be employed.

(d) The impersonality of our contemporary social order makes it difficult to secure normal release through primary and spontaneous relationships. This, in part, has resulted in vast commercialized enterprises

[5] In fact, this is the basic philosophy incorporated within Marquand's novel, *Point of No Return* (New York, 1949).

[6] R. S. and H. M. Lynd, *Middletown in Transition*, p. 245. Reprinted by permission of Harcourt, Brace and Company, Inc.

in the field of recreation which have capitalized upon the need for the rhythmic freeing of bodily and psychological tensions induced by the social order. As a token of this phenomenal increase, the growth of the moving picture industry to its present place as one of the ten major industries in the United States, with an estimated number of paid weekly admissions of over 100,000,000, provides an adequate example. Standardization of recreation, in the form of radio and television, has become a necessity in this type of culture.

(e) If leisure and its unprecedented growth have assumed special proportions and significance in our culture, it must be recognized that in this vary matter of growth, special strains upon individuals are induced in a complex social order. Simply by virtue of the fact that the other individual's leisure impinges directly upon one's own, a series of special problems are created. As Professor Jacks has put it:

> Thanks to the telephone, motor-car, and such like inventions, our neighbors have it in their power to turn our leisure into a series of interruptions, and the more leisure they have the more active do they become in destroying ours. Nor are we less active in destroying theirs. We spend a great deal of our leisure in mutual botheration. In whatever conditions you place a man, the use he can make of his leisure will always be limited by the use that other people are making of theirs.[7]

(4) CHANGES IN PERSPECTIVE UPON THE ALCOHOLIC PROBLEM[8]

In any analysis of alcoholism in America, the roseate days of the Prohibition Era and the lusty, roaring twenties must be regarded as significant and interesting symptoms. It appears obvious that America's present-day drinking habits are not the result of the Prohibition fiasco and the era of the "speakeasy" (although these have undoubtedly contributed their share to the intensified drinking pattern which is characteristic of our own day), but are deeply rooted in the entire complex of American culture and civilization. More recently, the growth of the problem and the contemporary focus of interest in alcoholism have assumed some significant new dimensions.

(1) In the first place, through the enlivened interest of the universities and such groups as Alcoholics Anonymous, we are becoming aware of the enormous number of genial imbibers, euphemistically called "social drinkers." By skillfully devised propaganda and through an aroused

[7] Cited in G. A. Lundberg, M. Komarovsky, and M. A. McInerny, *Leisure: A Suburban Study* (New York, 1934), pp. 6–8.

[8] For a full discussion of this problem, see Herbert A. Bloch, "Alcohol and American Recreational Life," *The American Scholar*, XVIII (Winter, 1948–9), 54–66.

public interest, excursions and alarums are being raised because of the continual potential yield of excessive pathological drinkers which the large number of "social drinkers" are presumably producing.

(2) Of equal interest, and designed to shock the American mentality to even great depression, is *the current emphasis upon such pathological drinkers as representing symptomatic disorders of a psychotic or psychoneurotic type.* No longer is John Barleycorn a moral problem, a reprehensible degenerate and an object of scorn or pity. Instead, he is now a sick man—a very sick man. The celebrated target of the pulpits now becomes a matter of scientific concern and analytical vivisection to the psychiatrist, the sociologist, the physiologist, and the doctor. This transition from moral dubiety to a sociologically rooted problem has been fashioned by the growth of the scientific attitude and the general impersonality induced by a highly mobile and urbanized civilization. Once the problem is changed from its constraining moral dimensions to a problem of the laboratory, it undergoes a corresponding transition in mass education, public enlightenment, and propagandist disclosure.

(5) ESTIMATED EXTENT OF PROBLEM

According to the estimates made by the Yale University Laboratory of Applied Physiology and the disclosures of the Alcoholics Anonymous group, there are at least 44 million social drinkers in the United States, and possibly as many as 50 million—figures, incidentally, which provide us with a comfortable margin of choice and which would be extremely difficult to confirm.[9] Of this minimal number, it is further presumed that approximately 2,400,000 may be classified as alcoholics, i.e., those for whom drinking constitutes an indispensable part of daily living. Of this latter group, it is further estimated that no less than one-quarter (about 600,000) may be regarded as confirmed alcoholics, constituting a serious public health problem. This latter group is comprised of those whose excessive drinking is related as cause or effect to various types of psychopathological disorders sufficiently serious to require concerted and prolonged therapeutic care. The dimensions of the problem may be further confirmed in the view suggested by its comparison with traditional public health problems such as cancer, which numbers approximately 500,000 active patients, and tuberculosis, which still claims about 700,000 victims.

(6) THE DISTINCTIVE PATTERN OF AMERICAN DRINKING

Aside from the claims made by the groups mentioned above, the fact that Americans drink both uniquely and excessively can be clearly

[9] Cf. Benson Y. Landis, "Some Economic Aspects of Inebriety," *Alcohol, Science, and Society* (New Haven, 1945), p. 201.

shown. American drinking habits, incorporated within an entire complex of customs, attitudes, beliefs, and values, which we may call the American drinking pattern, contain elements peculiar to American culture, reflecting specifically characteristic traits in the broader pattern of American recreation. Traditionally, in European cultures, aside from past dietetic necessity, drinking has been a phase of deeply rooted, stable, and integrated social and recreational patterns. Among Europeans, drinking may remain a satisfying social practice rather than a vice or social problem, largely because it remains an element within otherwise integrated and participating recreational practices. To separate drinking from the well-established social and recreational procedures of which it has traditionally been a part, and to focus attention upon it as an isolated element apart from the social amenities of group recreation, renders it a problem and not a spontaneous social act. With Europeans, for example, drinking has traditionally been a phase of the occasion of the group's coming together; with Americans, conversely, coming together has all too frequently provided the occasion for drinking. In that distinction, and its historical evolution, appears to lie one of the salient factors in the more disturbing features of our drinking habits.

But do Americans actually drink differently, and if so, in what respects are their drinking habits unique and distinct? Various types of evidence may be produced to indicate rather specifically that Americans *do* drink differently from other people, and with far greater zeal. Such evidence, which we are shortly to examine, not only corroborates what is largely well known, but serves as a sympton of the profoundly disturbed patterns characteristic of American use of leisure and the peculiar American penchant for "having a good time."

To appraise this problem adequately requires careful examination of two kinds of indices or symptomatic data. (1) In the first place, it is illuminating to observe the peculiarly distinctive physical manifestations of the problem, distinguishing these from institutional drinking patterns elsewhere, which reveal themselves in such phenomena as (a) the volume and the types of consumption of alcoholic beverages in this country, and (b) those specific problems of social disorder, such as public drunkenness and disorderly conduct, which are disclosed by our police records.

(2) But perhaps of even greater importance, as a testimonial to the distorted relationship existing between excessive drinking and the peculiar American ideology concerning recreation, are the characteristic drinking customs of Homo Americanus in the relative absence of socially considered restraint (the salubrious folk sanctions and disapprovals marking group customs elsewhere being conspicuously absent), and the distinguishing temper of American convivial occasions and drinking bouts. Also enlightening are the typically American attitudes toward mixed

drinking on different class levels, which suggest rather clearly the emotional and psychological atmosphere in which the average American pursues his frenzied bent toward leisure-time activity.

Volume of drinking. The per capita consumption of alcoholic beverages in this country appears to have risen steadily since the end of the last century. By 1910, the per capita consumption in liters of absolute alcohol was claimed to have risen already to 6.89 as compared with an index of 4.30 for the period 1880–90.[10] According to published estimates of the Department of Commerce, as reported by Benson Y. Landis, the total amount spent for alcoholic beverages by the people of the United States in 1934 was $2,003,000,000; that for 1940, $3,595,000,000; and for 1943, $6,083,000,000. Keeping in mind the fact that "during the same period the national income increased rapidly" (as did the rate of taxation), Landis further reports that "these . . . expenditures . . . have apparently been equal to between 4 and 5 per cent of the total income of all the people in the years 1934–43. In 1940, the estimated expenditure for alcoholic beverages was slightly less than 5 per cent of the total income of all the people from all sources. For the (entire population) the expenditure . . . was the equivalent of about 27 dollars plus, per capita. For the approximately 44 million users of alcoholic beverages, it was an average of about 81 dollars per person."[11]

It can be argued, of course, that any increase in per capita consumption represents a general increase in consumers' normal standards of living, but even accepting this, the fundamental implication of such an increase is not necessarily challenged. Conditions which promote the consumption of alcoholic beverages elsewhere, such as conditions arising out of dietary needs or traditional mealtime use, have never presented themselves as extended practices in American life. Americans may have taken to drink because they were unhappy, or for countless other reasons, but rarely because their diet necessitated it.

Types of liquors consumed. Likewise testifying to the particularism of American drinking habits is the relatively high percentage of beverages of concentrated alcoholic content, whiskey and gin, for example, consumed in vast quantities as contrasted with less potent liquors, such as beer and wines. Americans have long been known as drinkers of the so-called "hard liquors," in striking contrast to the regularized, daily mealtime drinking of many Europeans who consume primarily beers and wines.

Consider, for example, the cocktail, a peculiarly American concoction, developed apparently to make palatable drinks which ordinarily might not be considered potable. This use of adulterants has itself ini-

[10] Haven Emerson, *Alcohol, Its Effects on Men* (New York, 1936), p. 95.
[11] Benson Y. Landis, "Some Economic Aspects of Inebriety," p. 214.

tiated a series of practices, both in relation to the type of drinks served and that peculiar American efflorescence known as the "cocktail party," which Americans, by dint of exuberance and social contagion, have given to the world as a distinct cultural contribution. Significant to note in this respect are the class and status characteristics of such occasions, relating them rather specifically to certain forms of middle-class and upper middle-class society.

Police arrests and drunkenness. Annual police reports show a high percentage of arrests for public drunkenness and the minor related offense of disorderly conduct. Within the last two decades, in the state of Massachusetts, for example, a sample year indicates that out of a total of 187,560 arrests, 93,151—or almost one-half—were on charges of drunkenness. Samples of several states indicate ranges of anywhere from 30 to 50 per cent for similar classifications of offenses. Such figures would very likely be even higher if minor disorders of this type in rural areas were adequately reported.

Socio-Psychological Aspects of American Drinking

Psychological manifestations of American drinking are even more pertinent in revealing the peculiarities of the American recreational temperament. Recognizing that American drinking practices differ in relation to differing social, educational, cultural, and economic levels, a common pattern may nonetheless be detected. American speed of drinking and timing provide a case in point. Among the French, for example, it is not uncommon that the amount of liquor consumed during the course of an ordinary evening's entertainment is relatively small, typified perhaps by the French boulevardier who sits all evening at his sidewalk cafe with his solitary glass of aperitif before him. Americans often drink in the spirit of attaining that pleasant state of aftermath or euphoria with as great celerity as possible, as manifested in the peculiar American folkway of enjoining the late-comer to "catch-up."

(7) DRINKING BY THE SEXES IN COMMON

Associated with the manner in which Americans drink is the related problem of drinking by the sexes in company. The nature of ritual, ceremonial, and recreation, among both primitive and modern cultures, is reflected in the degree to which women, children, and the several age-groupings of a society are permitted to participate in the social practice itself. Whether women are excluded or admitted into such social practices not only gives meaning and relevance to the social pattern itself, but often cogently expresses deeply entrenched and venerated social values.

It is significant to note, therefore, that drinking by the sexes in the same group is a relatively recent development in American social evolution. The ethos of America's rural and paternalistic past until recently rigorously restricted such practices and, in fact, relegated drinking among women, except under carefully stipulated conditions, to women of doubtful moral character.

The general tone, character, and underlying conception of drinking as a recreational practice has been almost wholly masculine-dominated in American life. Women now, however, have access to precincts heretofore regarded exclusively as the province of the male: this constitutes a significant transition in domestic social patterns. That this development is producing a new problem in American life may be seen in the recent rise of the number of female patients admitted to mental hospitals for alcoholism, an increase from 6.3 to 17.3 per cent during a period of a little more than a decade, according to the psychiatrist, Robert V. Seliger.

In Europe, joint drinking of the sexes preceded the so-called liberation of women. As an intimate phase of family life, it frequently served to curb excesses. In America, on the other hand, the intensified, organized drive toward the liberation of women, gaining momentum during the latter decades of the past century, *antedated* by far masculine tolerance toward the woman's right to drink, and, above all, masculine willingness to accept her as a drinking partner. As a typical American paradox, it is ironic to note that the emancipation of women in this country gained its chief impetus from those feminine groups whose original, essential purpose was to outlaw liquor.[12]

(8) HISTORIC CULTURAL FACTORS AND LEISURE-TIME VALUES

Leisure-time values in any culture reflect the underlying values of the ethos of that culture, while these in turn reflect the basic clash and strain of the major institutions and the social values striving for social supremacy. Or, put in another way, the underlying character of the culture, as reflected in the need for power, the need for self-aggrandizement, the need for wealth or the need for exploitation, permeates those activities which are sought as recreational activities in themselves. Ruth Benedict and other anthropologists have illustrated the pervasive social amalgam which holds such cultures together in the recognized concept of "patterns of culture." To cite but one illustration of how this process functions in American recreational life, we need only refer to the American craving for changeful experience induced by the highly mobile and changeful

[12] For an interesting analysis of this phase of the problem, see Grace Coyle, *Social Process in Organized Groups* (New York, 1930).

nature of American culture itself. Thus, the necessary conditions of American cultural life make change and continual readaptation essential, creating thereby among Americans habit patterns congenial to change. In examining the frenetic and ebullient recreational values which characterize Americans' leisure, such underlying influences must continually be sought.

If the American culture pattern is examined from this perspective, we may observe the impact of contradictory social and economic forces producing those secondary values of the ethos described above. From the nineteenth century we have inherited (1) a diversity of cultural backgrounds, (2) the Puritan-Calvinistic negations of the New England hierarchy, (3) the unprecedented population growth and development of urbanism, with (4) the spread of commerce and industry on an unheralded scale. Out of this background have been generated habit-patterns just as zealously pursued by Americans in leisure as they are in the marketplace. Such integrated recreational patterns, reflecting the contradictions in American life itself, have stultified the bodily and psychological self-invigoration which occurs in the orderly expression of that "spontaneity and freedom" to which Erich Fromm refers in his recent works on neurosis and modern society.[13]

(9) SECONDARY EFFECTS OF CULTURAL FORCES

The fundamental values of the ethos maintained in recreational patterns are the inevitable results of the broad historical forces enumerated above. Thus, leisure-time activities have for the most part, and until very recently, neglected the strong community function of recreation which is found in the Czech Sokol and the Scandinavian communities. The attitudes (now well imbedded because of our speedy and extensive urban adaptation) of (a) repression of spontaneous expression, (b) passivism, and (c) acceptance of the priority of commercial values as earmarks of recreational merit, have ground themselves deeply into the American temperament. Such attitudes find concrete expression in the need for (i) changeful experience, (ii) a mechanized routine of recreation (closely correlated to what Lewis Mumford has so aptly called "life by the clock"), (iii) passive entertainment (evoking the various forms of the mass-spectacle) and (iv) an emphasis upon sensationalism and commercialized recreational media which always seek the lowest threshold of emotional experience.[14]

The necessities inherent in the impersonal logic of modern industrial

[13] Cf. *Escape from Freedom* (New York, 1941).

[14] An excellent analysis of a "clock-dominated" culture can be seen in Lewis Mumford, *Technics and Civilization* (New York, 1934), Chap. VI; see also his *Culture of Cities* (New York, 1938).

society control the time-budget of each individual's life, impelling the use of each parcelled-out moment of time in strict accordance with the needs of the given occasion.[15] Thus, the prevalent emotional undertone during the budgeted times allotted for recreation is frequently expressed in the grim determination to have a good time "even if it kills you" and the amazing American propensity to "kill time." In our generation, we have even witnessed an amazing American growth of industry and advertising catering to the eradication of "that tired feeling" on Saturday night. When the rhythmic compulsions of the human organism can find outlet only in accordance with the dictates of the clock, the tension-relieving devices are likely to be explosive, rather than salutary, destructive, rather than creative and healthfully cathartic.

Because of the passivism which has become so much a part of our American recreation, we more commonly refer to the state of "being entertained" than to the act of participating in the entertainment itself. Finally, the competitive nature of commercialized recreation in the United States impels the development of such forms of recreation as will have survival value on the basis of changing appeal. The result is to implant in the public expectant attitudes of speed, change, and sensationalism, to which the entrepreneur not only caters, but upon which he is *forced* to capitalize in order to survive.

From the foregoing, it seems reasonable to conclude that despite sporadic reform movements and conscientious efforts to modify the country's drinking habits, our customary outlooks are so entrenched that immediate success in transforming our habits is rather dubious. That some success in ameliorating the problem for the pathological or extreme drinker may be possible, as claimed in many quarters, is not disputed here. But any mass reformation of drinking habits suggests the need for concerted attack upon the personality-producing tensions in American life and for the modification of certain phases of the entire recreational complex reflective of our culture.

(10) THE SOCIAL DRINKER

Not all who drink become excessive drinkers or alcoholics. In fact, the majority do *not* become pathologically addicted to the use of alcohol. Moreover, as Myerson has said: "The synthesis of temperance, of the wise use of alcoholic beverages, is a necessary part . . . of the battle

[15] The relationship between the time-factor and the organization of the individual's life has been well shown in the special example of the railroader by W. F. Cottrell. Cf. "Of Time and the Railroader," *American Sociological Review* (April, 1939), pp. 190–8.

against alcoholism. Against unwise hedonism, against extravagant asceticism, we need to build up the code of temperate hedonism, and successful self-control."[16]

Although the prevalence of drinking is high in the United States—in a survey made in 1946 almost two out of three adults twenty-one years of age and over reported that they drank—this large volume does not necessarily result in a high rate of alcoholism among all groups.[17] The development of excessive drinking in any group in the population depends upon special psycho-cultural factors involving educational status, sex, family pattern, religion, ethnic background, and economic position. Thus, Jewish groups in the United States, although presenting one of the highest prevalence rates of drinking in America, yield the lowest incidence of excessive drinkers.[18] On the other hand, the increased drinking of women in this country, particularly since the Prohibition era, has resulted in a higher rate of pathological alcoholism among certain classes of women.[19]

Starling indicates that people drink because of (a) fashion, (b) ignorance, (c) economic conditions, or (d) inherent nervous defects.[20] All of these reasons may be valid within certain broad limitations. Exposed to a cultural milieu where drinking is common and is frequently identified with manliness, many individuals find difficulty in withstanding the pressure to drink. Moreover, in keeping with a long-standing workingman's tradition in Europe and the United States, alcohol, as a stimulant and source of nourishment is often considered necessary for the completion of a hard day's work. The "misery drinking" of the poor, which W. I. Thomas and F. Znaniecki have described in their *Polish Peasant in America*, frequently arises as an accompaniment of the grinding poverty of many elements in the population. Finally, that certain individuals are afflicted with nervous defects or psychopathological states of mind, inherent or acquired, may account for a certain volume of both normal *and* pathological drinking. Such reasons are frequently given by students of the subject, though it must not be forgotten that the enjoyment which controlled drinking may afford, as indicated by the entire tradition of drinking patterns in Western life, is fundamental to the whole problem.

[16] A. Myerson, "Alcohol: A Study of Social Ambivalance," *Quarterly Journal of Studies on Alcohol*, I, 1940, 13–20.

[17] The American Institute of Public Opinion reported in September, 1946, that 67 per cent of the total population declared that they drank. See also John W. Riley and C. F. Marden, "The Social Pattern of Alcoholic Drinking," *Quarterly Journal of Studies on Alcohol*, VIII (Sept., 1947), 266.

[18] Cf. R. F. Bales, "Cultural Differences in Rates of Alcoholism," *Quarterly Journal of Studies on Alcohol*, VI, 1946, 480–99.

[19] Riley and Marden, "The Social Pattern of Alcoholic Drinking," p. 267.

[20] E. H. Starling, *The Action of Alcohol on Man* (London, 1923).

(11) PATHOLOGICAL DRINKING

The causal patterns that motivate the pathological drinker have been in part brought to light only within the last two decades. Pathological drinking may take a number of forms but all are symptomatic of a disorganized personality. That extreme drinkers are fundamentally disorganized personalities, for whom drinking has become a contributory cause, symptom, or result, is a point to be recognized from the very outset. Thus, we frequently encounter (a) the *excessive* drinker, who, although drinking to extreme, manages, on most occasions, to keep his habit under control; (b) the *episodic* drinker, who periodically engages in excessive drinking bouts, frequently with rhythmic regularity; and (c) the *problem* drinker, who is completely victimized by his alcoholic habit.[21] The first and second types bear close resemblance to sufferers from certain cyclothymic forms of mental disorder. The last type represents the most common and possibly the most difficult problem of all. This last type of drinker, despite the best intentions and the most effusive professions of good faith, may be set off by even one drink on a completely uncontrolled orgy.

Very few controlled studies of the causes of alcoholism have been made. Most investigations have been analyses by psychiatrists of selected individuals or groups, with very little effort made to locate the precise causal syndromes and to assess adequately the various physiological, psychological, or socio-cultural factors. Most psychiatrists have regarded alcoholism as closely allied to repressed sexuality, frequently with latent homosexual manifestations, or as related to specific neurotic or psychotic patterns. That such relationships exist in many cases, there can be no doubt. Abraham in 1908 sought to show the relationship between alcoholism and certain forms of repressed sexuality in the excessive drinker. In 1913, Juliusberger illustrated the role of unconscious homosexuality in certain forms of alcoholic excess. Sachs, in 1925, attempted to show that both drug *and* alcoholic cravings were due to the tendency to suppress certain perversions and the associated condition of a compulsion neurosis. Weijil in 1928 attempted to ally this condition to distorted expressions of the Oedipus complex, while Chambers, in 1937, indicated that the basis of alcoholism is a special form of compulsion neurosis.

More recent studies, particularly those by Wall and the commendable psycho-cultural investigation by Harriet R. Mowrer, have sought to delineate the precise personality and socio-cultural characteristics that predispose to excessive drinking.[22] These recent studies, and the suggestive investigations of the Yale Laboratory of Applied Physiology, appear

[21] Joseph Hirsh, *The Problem Drinker* (New York, 1949).

[22] Cf. Harriet R. Mowrer, "A Psychocultural Analysis of the Alcoholic," *American Sociological Review*, V (August, 1940), 546–57.

to confirm in part the causal hypothesis of the psychogenetic pattern. In many alcoholics certain readily discernible traits are observable. Selden D. Bacon, in his discussion of the "compulsive drinker," indicates that such persons are characterized "(1) by being in continual and awful pain, (2) by a set of responses which may be summed up as immaturity, and (3) by an over-all attitude of extreme egocentricity." [23] That the origin must be found in the basic family pattern of the alcoholic is stressed by Wall, who indicates in his analysis of 100 male and 80 female alcoholics that a significant percentage of his subjects suffered from the ambivalent relationships of a doting, oversolicitous mother and a stern, forbidding father.[24] Confirming Bacon, he indicates that a high percentage of the alcoholics he studied were marked by such traits as emotional immaturity, instability, infantilism, and excessive passivity and dependence. This last factor suggests the possibility of latent homosexuality—a fact brought out by a number of the earlier psychiatric investigations.[25]

Latent possibilities of alcoholic addiction may be produced by sudden and severe crises affecting emotionally insecure individuals. This point has been stressed by the French psychiatrist Dr. Pierre Janet who illustrates it in the lives of precariously adjusted people such as the newly arrived professional, the writer, and the parvenu.[26]

Mowrer's study gives us a comparative analysis of three groups of twenty-five married couples, contrasting an alcoholic group with a "normal" group and with another group characterized by non-alcoholic "escape-response" patterns. Conspicuous in the findings of Mowrer are the following facts:

(1) The alcoholic was frequently the youngest, next to the youngest, or next to the oldest child in the family, with marked attachment to the mother or older sister and strong animosity to the father or some favored older brother. The ambivalent mechanism of rejection plays a prominent part in such situations, producing powerful strivings to maintain status. In the alcoholic groups, ordinal position in the family is a particularly striking factor as brought out by comparison with the "normal" non-alcoholic "control" group, where the majority of subjects studied were the oldest or middle children of the family. As Mowrer points out, this is largely significant because of the dependent and infantile role as the "baby" of the family which our culture tends to force upon certain children.

[23] Selden D. Bacon, "Alcoholism: Nature of the Problem," *Federal Probation*, XI (Jan.–Mar., 1947), 3–7.

[24] Cf. Mowrer, "A Psychocultural Analysis of the Alcoholic."

[25] Dr. Walter Miles, for example, has demonstrated a relationship between the personality traits of the alcoholics studied by Wall and the characteristics of homosexuals in groups examined by L. M. Terman and C. C. Miles in their standardization of the masculinity-femininity test.

[26] Pierre Janet, *Psychological Healing* (New York, 1925), Vol. II, p. 1083.

H. deB. Nachlas, Ph.D.

(2) Significant is the fact that less alcoholism existed among the fathers of the alcoholic group studied than among the non-alcoholics. If true, this would confirm the psychiatric hypothesis that excessive alcoholic habits are acquired through familial-environmental factors rather than through hereditary mechanisms, a point of view supported by the findings of Knight of the Menninger Clinic, although disputed by many physiologists and physicians. Doctors Robert J. Williams, L. J. Berry, and Ernest Beerstecher, for example, upon the basis of experimental tests performed upon white rats, have attempted to show that basic metabolic patterns may be transmitted through heredity, creating a B-vitamin deficiency which may conduce towards drinking.[27] In either event, it seems reasonable to expect that alcoholism will not result unless propitious cultural and environmental factors are present. The advocates of inherited patterns frequently overlook the fact that only structural characteristics are transmitted and not behavior patterns. This would apply to nutritional and dietary behavior as well as to other forms of acquired adjustment behavior.

(3) Occupationally and vocationally, the alcoholic group appeared for more restless and dissatisfied than the normal group, although similar characteristics were found by Mowrer among those in her "escape-response" group who developed fictive ailments and other neurotic escapes. In addition, artistic and intellectual traits were frequently found by Mowrer among the alcoholics she studied, a fact supported as well by the observations of Strecker and Chambers.[28]

(4) Testifying to the generally disorganized characteristics of alcoholic personalities was the high percentage who had sexual experiences before marriage, frequently with prostitutes, and generally of a demoralized nature, as compared with the less than half of the "normal" group who reported such experiences.

(5) Generally evidenced in the Mowrer study, as elsewhere, is the fact that failure in marital adjustment, while common, is the result of the same factors that produce alcoholism, and not the cause of alcoholism itself.

Significant in its conclusions is the final summation of the study of alcoholics, in its stress upon the infantile and dependent role of the dipsomaniac. Mowrer states: "Alcoholism provides a way of recapturing at least temporarily the attention-receiving role of the early familial group." [29] The claimed success of Alcoholics Anonymous in the treatment

[27] R. J. Williams, L. J. Berry, and E. Beerstecher, *Annual Proceedings* (National Academy of Science, Washington, D. C., 1949).

[28] Cf. Edward A. Strecker and Francis T. Chambers, *Alcohol: One Man's Meat* (New York, 1938).

[29] Mowrer, "A Psychocultural Analysis of the Alcoholic," p. 264.

of alcoholics may in part be due to the concentrated attention that is focused upon each individual subject.

(12) PROGRESSIVE NATURE OF ALCOHOLISM

Acute alcoholism is a progressive condition. The course of its development may be rapid or extremely slow. An individual may experience a period of ten to fifteen years of relatively controlled drinking before the characteristics of genuine alcoholism become fixed. During the early period, occasional intoxication may produce the drunkard's "blackouts." The danger signs of early morning drinking and solitary drinking may manifest themselves anywhere from four to seven years after original drinking and the early blackouts. Frequently at this period, the "vicious circle" process of remorse, deep anxieties, and attempts towards reformation is instituted, but leads only in the end to increased isolation of the individual. This may occur seven to ten years after the first "blackout" and fifteen years after the first drink. By this time, the individual has usually become a genuine alcoholic. Nevertheless, the entire process may be telescoped within a period of three years.[30]

(13) TYPES OF COMPULSIVE DRINKERS

An appraisal of recent findings on alcoholism suggests that behavioral characteristics of pathological drinkers fall into fairly well-defined patterns. These patterns may be seen in two recognized alcoholic types, the *primary* and *secondary* types of compulsive drinkers.[31] Although seemingly different in their overt characteristics, they reveal, nevertheless, certain striking basic similarities. In their final form, even these outer manifestations are highly similar. The *primary* type of compulsive drinker appears to have many of the characteristics of the neurotic. He tends to be isolated, frequently apathetic, marked by social ineptitude and recessiveness, and by a general sense of inadequacy. This last is not only conspicuous in ordinary social relationships, but is manifested in his vocational life and even in the intimacies of his sexual life. Such alcoholic personalities, apparently, because of early psychogenetic difficulties, not only are distinguished by a sense of inadequacy and insecurity (reflecting the "need-phase" of the p.g.p.), but manifest this insecurity in their failure to have developed the minimal skills essential for normal social relationships (the "functional" phase of the p.g.p.). The progressive course of their drinking simply accentuates the downward process of their neurotic tendencies.

[30] Cf. E. M. Jellinek, "Phases in the Drinking History of Alcoholism," *Memoirs of the Section of Studies on Alcoholism*, No. 5 (New Haven, 1946).

[31] Selden D. Bacon, "Alcoholism: Nature of the Problem," pp. 5–7.

The *secondary* type of compulsive drinker presents an outer appearance quite diametric to the type just described. In contrast with the recessiveness of the previous type, his behavior is marked by excessive exuberance and vitality, considerable striving and extroversion. He is frequently the "life of the party" and the ebullient, outgoing "good sport." This may account for the fact, as Dr. Robert Fleming has shown, that so many alcoholics are salesmen, are frequently highly successful, and appear to be extroverted.[32] Fundamentally, however, the secondary type may conceal the same sense of inadequacy as the primary type—an inadequacy covered by an inordinate compensation, expressing itself functionally by highly extroverted behavior. Since this type of drinker, despite his basic insecurity, has developed certain social facilities and skills in his relations to others, the prognosis for his potential rehabilitation appears more favorable than in the first type. However, through the progressive course of drinking, he may, "when he has achieved the full status of an alcoholic, seem not a whit different from the primary type." [33]

A causal hypothesis. Certain conclusions may now be drawn. In the first place, on the basis of recent evidence, even assuming the possibility of an inherited neurological pattern, acute alcoholism does not occur unless certain conditions in the family life and the general socio-cultural environment foster it. Moreover, irrespective of the specific basis, alcoholics are marked by distinct personality defects, foremost among which are insecurity, dependence, passivity, inadequacy, and infantilism. These traits appear to stem from strong ambivalent strivings within the personality, reflecting early family conditions and suggesting the general pattern of rejection. There is, however, one point which, although implied, has not been strongly stressed by many students: the powerful stimulus of the "ideational pattern." Alcoholics rarely learn to drink excessively unless exposed to an environment which in some way has presented powerful stimulating conditions conducive to drink. The "ideational pattern," as presented here and elsewhere in this volume, suggests that at various times in his career, the individual has been suggestible to an environment in which drinking and drinking companions have played a prominent part. This may partially be seen in the testimony of many confirmed drinkers that the mere drinking and the very taste of alcohol itself are, in themselves, distasteful. Other alcoholics have maintained that their early drinking was fostered by the fact that it focused attention upon them. Still others have suggested that their need for identification and companionship with certain groups where drinking was habitual, in a corner tavern or elsewhere, prompted them to drink regularly. In accordance

[32] Report by Dr. Robert Fleming to 27th Annual New England Hospital Assembly, Boston, March 1950, based upon an area study of alcoholic behavior.

[33] Bacon, "Alcoholism," p. 7.

with the causal theory of the psychogenetic pattern, the following schema may be suggestive:

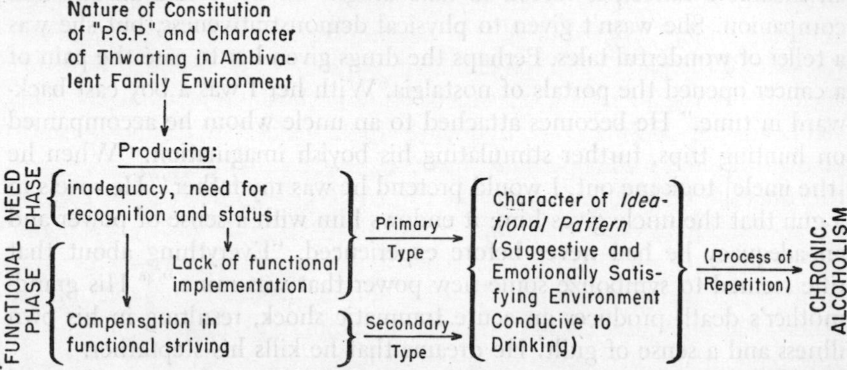

The analysis of an alcoholic life-history. An interesting application of these causal principles is afforded in the autobiography of an acute alcoholic, described in the volume, *If a Man Be Mad.*[34] A sense of insecurity and inadequacy, mingled with strong feelings of ambivalence towards his father and later his stepfather, leading to a feeling of rejection concerning his mother, is strongly underscored in the very earliest recollections of the alcoholic. Of his father, who was accidentally killed while he was a very young child, he writes: "My father was a forceful man, sure of himself, and successful in business and politics. Mother loved him deeply, and everyone respected him." Throughout the writer's recollections lurk these powerful memories, stirred by the comments of well-meaning friends and neighbors: "The son of a father like that. . . . You couldn't be your father's son. . . . If you're half the man your father was. . . ." Of his stepfather, a minister, the rival for his mother's divided affections, he writes: "I believe he loved my mother but I do not believe that he loved anything else in the world. . . . I only knew that to have my mother I had to win his approval. I had no way of knowing that he would have considered approval a personal weakness which he could not condone in himself. I had nightmares in which I was constantly trying to attract the attention of the one figure who could save me. He always indifferently let doom descend on me. . . . I lost contact with my mother through the fear that to be intimate with her would block me forever from my stepfather's approval. I would have been isolated had it not been for my grandmother, who came to live with us."[35]

This same grandmother provides a necessary imaginative stimulus

[34] Harold Maine, *If a Man Be Mad* (New York, 1947). Quotations reprinted by permission of Doubleday & Company, Inc.
[35] Ibid., p. 5.

and a surrogate parent upon whom he leans heavily. Possibly, an early ideational pattern is provided through the grandmother who, because of an incurable cancer, is forced to take drugs. "In her I had an ally and companion. She wasn't given to physical demonstrativeness, but she was a teller of wonderful tales. Perhaps the drugs given her to ease the pain of a cancer opened the portals of nostalgia. With her I was a boy cast backward in time." He becomes attached to an uncle whom he accompanied on hunting trips, further stimulating his boyish imagination. "When he [the uncle] took me out, I would pretend he was my father." He revels in a gun that the uncle gives him; it endows him with a sense of power and an adequacy he had never before experienced. "Everything about that rifle seemed to symbolize some new power that was mine." [36] His grandmother's death produces an acute traumatic shock, resulting in his own illness and a sense of guilt. He dreams that he kills his stepfather.

His sense of isolation is heightened during his adolescence, fostered to a considerable degree by the mobility of the family, making it difficult for him to secure any stable and permanent boyhood companions. "Neither my parents nor my teachers could ever know me. My life had none of the landmarks that normal youth falls heir to; it was devoid of continuity in any emotional sense. I had no loyalty but to myself." Further he writes: "I couldn't meet responsibility."

The imperceptible ideational stimulus appears in many stages of his development. While still an adolescent, he states: [37]

> During those years another thing crept into my life, almost unnoticed, but offering me unobtrusively something to replace my guns when they should fail me as a defense against fear and insecurity. While playing with another boy, I fell off an arbor and knocked the wind out of myself. The boy's mother came rushing to my rescue with brandy and water. Security gushed down my throat. Never had a woman seemed so warm, strong, and comfortable; never had a hurt healed so quickly. As a thing in itself, I didn't know what alcohol was. I only knew that something cut the sharp edges off life and threw a great tide of certainty through my flesh.

Upon still another occasion, he was injured in a neighborhood of Italian boys: [38]

> One of their mothers brought out the brandy and water. Again the inner path of peace. Shame, rage, fear, and uncertainty dissolved again. I still didn't know what brandy was. My memory of it was one of pure sensation that could be recalled only by re-experience.

[36] Ibid., p. 7.
[37] Ibid., p. 9.
[38] Ibid., pp. 9–10.

Confirmed alcoholism takes root in his personality while he is still in his teens: [39]

> I was a little over sixteen when I joined the peacetime army. Perhaps I did this because World War I had occurred when I was at an impressionable age or maybe simply because it was one way of avoiding home and school. At any rate I was soon out in the middle of the Pacific, surrounded by veterans who couldn't adjust to civil life and had returned to the army. Many were alcoholics. I was one of them before I realized what was happening. There were always meals, a bed, and another payday. The consequences of drunkenness were the same as the consequences of sobriety. I quickly learned that the need for alcohol could provide an artificial continuity to life. Getting that early morning drink became all-important; keeping a supply on hand for the day and night, a reason for living. After a year of this, with the monthly drunks running on for as much as ten days at a time, my pattern was firmly established. Before I was eighteen I could be as shaken as a Bowery bum when liquor was taken from me. I already felt that mad drive that disregards everything but the object of addiction. When drink was in me, I feared no consequences but those of being without a drink. When I was sober, I lived only toward my monthly bouts of drunkenness.

(14) ORGANIC AND SPECIAL ASPECTS OF ALCOHOL

Because of its traditional identification with strongly censured behavior, temperance groups and other adversaries have waged a steadfast campaign against the so-called "evils of drink" and the injurious effects which drinking has upon the mind and body. In some states, the temperance and prohibition advocates have been sufficiently powerful to bring about the teaching of the so-called dangers of alcoholism in the schools—teaching based upon unscientific data and embodying false or doubtful conclusions concerning the action of alcohol upon the body. Within the last two decades, our knowledge concerning the physiological and psychological effects of alcohol has improved enormously, and slowly the well-intentioned but misguided propaganda of certain prohibition zealots is being counteracted.

(15) ALCOHOL IN THE HUMAN BODY

Alcohol is a carbohydrate and, to a certain degree, may be considered in its reaction upon the body as an ordinary food. However, unlike ordinary foods, alcohol is not stored as a surplus, nor eliminated in the

[39] Ibid., pp. 11–12.

usual way. When consumed, it passes directly from the stomach and digestive tract to the blood stream, remaining there until oxidation takes place. This oxidation proceeds at a measurable rate. While in the blood stream, however, alcohol exercises a narcotic effect, producing, under certain conditions, the sensations of numbness and euphoria which have long been considered the pleasurable aspects of drinking.

In its effects upon the terminal neurons and their connecting fibres, it creates a degree of paralysis which, for centuries past, has among other purposes served man as an anodyne against pain. When the proper concentration of alcohol appears in the blood stream, three marked general effects are noted: (1) it deadens sensitivity to stimuli of the external environment and to pain; (2) it obscures the higher levels of psychical activity; and (3) it hampers accuracy of response, although it has less effect upon reaction-time, or the time-interval between external stimulus and response. The intoxicated automobile driver in an emergency may respond with sufficient speed when an object looms up before his vehicle, but may inadvertently press down upon the accelerator instead of the brake.

Contrary to popular impression, alcohol is a depressant and not a stimulant. The fallacious impression that it is a stimulant is due to the sense of well-being (euphoria) which alcohol introduces, the result of relaxation of blood-vessels at the surface of the body which creates a feeling of warmth and comfort. Slight acceleration of the heart may be occasioned during early stages of drinking, but if alcohol remains in the blood stream for any period of time, the beating of the heart is retarded and may stop altogether.[40]

Intoxication. The determination of intoxication in any given individual is a complex affair, contingent upon a variety of factors in each human organism. It depends to a considerable degree upon the concentration rate of alcohol within the organism in relation to the total fluid capacity of the human body, roughly estimated at thirteen to fifteen gallons for the average adult individual. Generally speaking, 0.2 to 0.3 of one per cent of alcohol in the blood stream is sufficient to produce recognizable signs of intoxication, the equivalent in certain cases of three to five cocktails for an average male of approximately 154 pounds in weight. In police tests applied to motorists, a concentration of no more than 0.05 per cent of alcohol in the blood is usually considered sufficient evidence of sobriety. Amounts of 0.4 to 0.5 per cent in the blood stream are sufficient to produce absolute intoxication, ranging from drowsiness to "passing out"; a concentration rate of 0.7 to 0.9 per cent, equivalent

[40] Cf. H. W. Haggard and E. M. Jellinek, *Alcohol Explained* (New York, 1942); also, "What Happens to Alcohol in the Body," Lay Supplement No. 7, *Quarterly Journal of Studies on Alcohol*, 1947; H. W. Haggard, "Metabolism of Alcohol," *Alcohol, Science, and Society* (New Haven, 1945).

to one pint of fluid alcohol consumed immediately, may, and frequently does, prove fatal. The period of intoxication depends upon the oxidation rate, proceeding at approximately three-fourths of an ounce per hour, and such factors as the size of the body, amount of food in the stomach, bodily and room temperatures, and individual tolerance rates. With some individuals, even two glasses of beer may produce discernible signs of early intoxication, while even with steady drinkers, four glasses of beer and two glasses of whiskey may be sufficient to produce some evidence of hampering of physical functions.[41]

Alcohol and sexual drives. Alcohol does not stimulate or increase the intensity of the sexual urges. The fact that sexual lapses frequently occur in conjunction with drinking bouts is due to the lowered threshold of resistence to ordinary inhibitions which alcohol produces. Actually, drinking, and especially prolonged drinking, impairs the sexual effectiveness of the individual, a fact recognized by Shakespeare in his comic characters centuries ago, when he referred to alcohol serving as a spur to lechery, but inadequate in fulfillment. From the previous discussion of the alcoholic personality, it has been seen that confirmed alcoholics frequently have deeply rooted sexual difficulties and are inadequate to normal sexual demands.[42] Investigations prior to the First World War in England indicated relatively high positive correlations, in certain selected samples of working class males, of alcoholism and syphilis. Recurrence of this association is periodically seen among alcoholic groups in the public treatment wards of some of our large city hospitals. The presence of such factors, however, is due to the general neglect incident in the lives of demoralized personalities, and not because alcohol induces hyperactive sexual drives. Drunkards make poor lovers and poor husbands.

Alcohol as narcomania. Alcoholism differs sharply from the ordinary forms of drug addiction, particularly in relation to the taking of such drugs as heroin and cocaine. In fact, in the literal sense, alcoholism may not be considered a form of narcomania. Certain resemblances, however, have been noted between habitual users of alcohol and of marihuana. The use of marihuana differs in most cases from the types of addiction induced by the other well-known drugs.[43] In general, the craving for alcohol is psycho-sociological, and while such elements may be present in the more common types of drug addiction, the persistent use of drugs affects bodily tissue in a different manner, creating an organic degeneration

[41] Cf. Haggard and Jellinek, *Alcohol Explained;* also, E. M. Jellinek, "Effects of Small Amounts of Alcohol on Psychological Functions," *Alcohol, Science and Society* (New Haven, 1945); H. E. Himwich, "The Psysiological Action of Alcohol," *Alcohol and Man* (ed. by Haven Emerson, New York, 1933).

[42] For a sensitive treatment by a novelist of certain phases of this problem, see Natalie Anderson Scott, *The Story of Mrs. Murphy* (New York, 1947).

[43] See Manly B. Root, "What the Probation Officer Can Do for Special Types of Offenders," *Federal Probation,* XIII (December, 1949), 38–39.

which complicates the problem considerably. It is not uncommon, however, to find a constant percentage of disorganized personalities who have become addicted to both alcohol and drugs. The patterns of addiction are quite distinct, however, and W. W. of Alcoholics Anonymous has even described the lack of tolerance between the two groups of addicts.[44]

Alcohol and longevity. The dire pronouncements of the early temperance leagues that continued drinking in any form would assuredly curtail life expectancy and bring about sundry other physical ills is largely without foundation. The only acceptable basis, thus far, for estimating life-spans has been the actuarial tables of life insurance companies, and even these tabulations are deficient from the standpoint of making adequate comparative judgments.[45] Upon the basis of such data, however, we may infer that moderate drinking does not appreciably curtail life expectancy, if it does so at all. In fact, Raymond Pearl has produced evidence, upon the basis of studies made upon laboratory animals, that certain groups of moderate drinkers may actually have a greater life-span than non-drinkers.[46] Some recent evidence appears to confirm this to a certain degree. If true, it is probably due to the fact that moderate drinkers are frequently more relaxed individuals than abstainers, and hence not subject to the same psychosomatic tensions.

Excessive drinking does, however, cut down the life-span of the individual. Actuarial tables do reveal higher rates of mortality among alcoholics than among moderate drinkers and abstainers, in some cases considerably higher.[47] This is not due entirely to the insidious attack of alcohol upon certain organs of the body, but due as well to the secondary aspects of physical neglect (exposure, poor diet, lack of sleep, etc.) which alcoholism creates. Recent disclosures by the Yale University Laboratory of Applied Physiology have indicated, for example, the relationship between alcoholic neglect and nutritional deficiency, created by the lack of B-vitamin content in the alcoholic constitution. This in itself is due not necessarily to the specific action of alcohol upon the body, but rather to the upsetting of ordinary vitamin balance introduced by an excessive intake of alcohol. Promising results in the rehabilitation of alcoholics are being accomplished through proper dietary care and vitamin balance.[48]

Alcoholism and the psychoses. In our previous discussion of the alcoholic personality, it was seen that alcoholics give ample evidence of neurotic tendencies. Alcohol, as a contributory factor, may accelerate the

[44] See *Alcohol, Science and Society*, p. 469.

[45] Cf. L. I. Dublin and A. J. Lotka, *Length of Life* (New York, 1936).

[46] R. Pearl, *Alcohol and Longevity* (New York, 1926).

[47] Dublin and Lotka, *Length of Life.*

[48] See "Alcohol and Length of Life," Lay Supplement No. 6, *Quarterly Journal of Studies on Alcohol* (New Haven, 1948); also, Norman Joliffe, "Alcohol and Nutrition," *Alcohol, Science and Society*, pp. 73–82.

process of complete mental collapse. The root of the problem, however, is not alcohol *per se*, but the basic disorganized conditions that have fostered general maladjustment. For this reason, the conventional psychiatric classification of "alcoholic psychosis" is being modified. The phrase "psychotic condition with alcoholic manifestations" is felt to be more nearly in accord with the facts. The only direct pathological result of excessive drinking, actually, is the temporary hallucinated state of "delirium tremens," relieved today in most alcoholic wards by use of the drug, paraldehyde. Whether specific neurotic syndromes and specific psychotic states may be linked to alcoholism has not as yet been shown.[49]

(16) CONGENITAL EFFECTS OF ALCOHOL

One of the most ominous and persistent claims made by certain temperance and prohibition groups in the past is that constant or excessive drinking affects the human germ plasm, thereby causing sterility, an increased number of stillbirths and deformed offspring, and a decreased life-expectancy among children of alcoholics. Careful recent investigations into such claims by the Yale University Laboratory of Applied Physiology and other competent scientific agencies have tended to discredit strongly such unwarranted claims. Some of these conclusions were apparently erroneously drawn from the work of C. R. Stockard upon laboratory animals, during 1909–16, which gave some slight suggestion that certain injuries to the germ plasm might be caused by alcohol. However, in the careful and cautious appraisal of tested results, the Yale Laboratory in no uncertain words states: "No acceptable evidence has ever been offered to show that acute alcoholic intoxication has any effect whatsoever on the human germ, or any influence in altering heredity, or is the cause of any abnormality in the child." [50] The investigation of the actual effects of alcohol upon the germ plasm by Miss F. M. Dunham of the National Institute for Medical Research in England in the 1920's, and a series of subsequent investigations, have tended to refute sharply earlier claims of adverse effects upon progeny in respect to (a) decrease in numbers of offspring, (b) numbers of stillbirths, (c) deformities in the issue of alcoholic parents, and (d) deterioration of the germ plasm itself. Striking have been the experiments of direct exposure to alcohol of the sperm of frogs, sea urchins, and fish, which, even when saturated in a ten per cent solution of alcohol—twenty to forty times as strong as that found in the human blood in the most severe types of intoxication—produced no harmful effects in the fertilized egg.

[49] See Carney Landis, "Theories of the Alcoholic Personality," *Alcohol, Science and Society*, pp. 129–42.

[50] Alcohol, Heredity, and Germ Damage," Lay Supplement No. 5, *Quarterly Journal of Studies on Alcohol*, p. 7.

In chronic alcoholism the body and the reproductive organs may be injured. This does not mean, however, that the germ plasm itself may be affected. Moreover, such damage to the reproductive organs is not common in men until after the age of forty-five years. (Men in this age category contribute less than 6 per cent to the annual number of births.) In the studies upon animals, the evidence appears conflicting. "Some investigators have found that rats given large amounts of alcohol daily had fewer litters than nonalcoholic rats. Another investigator found no difference in the number of litters although the number in each litter was smaller. One investigator who used 30,000 mice found that the offspring of those given alcohol for several generations showed no more abnormalities than were found in those which were given no alcohol. Still another investigator reported that the chickens hatched from eggs of hens given alcohol showed an increased vigor."[51] In viewing such studies, one is drawn to the conclusions of the Yale University investigators, who state: "When one has read all of the many reports on experiments with alcoholized animals, he must come to the conclusion that many of these experiments were badly designed; that in many others the general nutrition and health of the animal were neglected; and that in none could abnormalities of the offspring be definitely ascribed to damage from chronic alcoholism."[52]

Although the reproductive rate falls for alcoholized laboratory animals, the birth rates in alcoholic families are strikingly higher than for temperate and abstemious families. This apparently has nothing whatsoever to do with the germ plasm and reproductive powers, but is attributable almost entirely to the lack of responsibility of alcoholic parents, particularly those on the lower economic levels. The following table, based on studies made within the last two decades, illustrates these differences in birth rates.

Comparison of Average Numbers of Children in Alcoholic and Temperate Families *

	Alcoholic Families		Temperate Families	
Country	*Number of Families*	*Average Number of Children per Family*	*Number of Families*	*Average Number of Children per Family*
United States	145	2.4	150	1.5
Finland	2,461	3.9	1,551	2.4
Sweden [1]	Over 1,000	5.6	Over 1,000	4.9
France	81	4.5	245	3.2

[1] Exact figures are not known.

* Taken from compilation of studies by *Quarterly Journal of Studies on Alcohol,* "Alcohol, Heredity, and Germ Damage," Lay Supplement No. 5, August 1947, p. 10.

[51] Ibid., p. 8.
[52] Ibid., p. 9.

The higher rates of infant and child mortality, particularly before the fifth year, and the greater number of miscarriages among alcoholic families arise because of the higher conception rates and neglect, rather than because genetic factors have become affected by alcohol. Comparative studies, revealing higher fatality and miscarriage rates among illegitimate than among legitimate offspring in Germany and England during 1900–30, illustrate similar conditions of environmental neglect, and not germ damage. The equalizing of such rates within two decades was brought about by improvement in child welfare services and maternity care. That the foetus of the alcoholic mother may be injured is due not to heredity or germinal factors, but simply to the fact, as Professor Jellinek has put it, that she constitutes "a very poor intrauterine environment" for her unborn child.

The final conclusions which the Yale University researchers have arrived at are significant: [53]

(1) The use of alcohol does not injure the human germ and cause abnormalities in heredity.
(2) Excessive users of alcohol frequently come from families of poor hereditary stock.
(3) The defects they inherit are not caused by alcohol but may predispose to alcoholism.
(4) The greater incidence of disease and mortality among children whose parents are abnormal drinkers, as compared to those whose parents are temperate, is not due to germ damage. It is due to the low standards of living and to neglect in the homes of excessive drinkers.

Alcoholism and poverty. The early great classical studies of poverty and depressed urban economic conditions, such as Charles Booth's famous *Life and Labour of the People of London,* a seventeen-volume work begun in 1886 and completed in 1902, B. S. Rowntree's study of poverty in England (1901), and Robert Hunter's study in 1904, all stressed the close relationship between poverty and heavy drinking. With the trends towards increased social security and legislative efforts in the Western industrial world to alleviate the conditions of poverty, this incidence is not nearly so marked as it was formerly. Nevertheless, it appears obvious that excessive drinking may function as an extremely significant contributory factor to poverty, and, in fact, to widely extensive depressed economic conditions. When drinking begins early and leads to chronic alcoholism, stemming from egregious social and economic conditions of environment and family, it manages to keep a family on a continual marginal level of economic subsistence and poverty. When it

[53] Ibid., p. 16.

emerges later, even in families of comparatively superior economic and social conditions, it may soon lead to a condition of continual economic crisis. The alcoholic cannot maintain regular employment, he is considered a poor credit risk, and the very expense involved in his successive drinking bouts, may be enough to place his family in a perpetual condition of economic jeopardy.

Industry has long had to reckon with the problems of absenteeism of chronic drinkers and the risks involved in assigning to them duties involving serious responsibility. Of late, many large industries have come to regard this difficulty as a public health problem. In April, 1950, Dr. George H. Gehrmann, medical director of Du Pont de Nemours and Company, issued an interesting report, indicating the measures taken by this vast industrial organization to cope with the above-mentioned conditions. Planned and carried out in conjunction with Alcoholics Anonymous, the Du Pont program involves extensive work and education with supervision throughout the company, as well as among the individuals themselves, and has been credited with remarkable success. According to Dr. Gehrmann, thirty-four afflicted Du Pont workers hold important supervisory posts and 180 of the company's 76,000 workers are active in A. A. groups established by the company. For the countless alcoholics who cannot be brought into the program, Dr. Gehrmann states that if an alcoholic "cannot, or does not want to stop, he should be discharged—the sooner the better." As regards the untold numbers who fit into this category, the social and economic consequences to the drinker's family are tragically serious.

(17) CONCLUSIONS AND THE DEVELOPMENT OF SOCIAL POLICY

It is generally agreed that to achieve any type of normal pattern, within the socially defined requirements of a given culture, those conditions—organic, psychological, and socio-cultural—that tend to promote excessive forms of compensation must be alleviated, removed, or modified. As far as the drinking problem is concerned, the ideal goal is temperance and not the removal of normal drinking patterns in the United States. Recent investigations by psychiatrists have shown that serious types of tensions and pathological distortions may manifest themselves in other types of excessive imbalance, such as over-eating. Although the immediate dangers of overeating may not be so injurious as those of excessive tippling, the fact remains nevertheless that any excess lays bare the form of underlying tensions and indicates the need for widespread correctives. The admonition of the classical philosopher, "Nothing to excess," and the wise counsel of "*mens sana in corpore sano*," suggest a central principle of human adjustment extending beyond the problem of excessive drinking. Upon the assumption, therefore, that acute alcoholism is one of the symptomatic forms of maladjustment emanating from extensive and widespread disturbances in family and social life, the course of treatment must likewise be extensive, touching upon the various factors in the cultural pattern that produce tensions and imbalance. Although some of these areas may appear far removed from the central problem of the alcoholic personality, the removal of such sources of tension may do much to alleviate the general conditions productive of excessive drinking.

(1) The removal of strains upon the personality through the stabilizing of economic conditions and the further development of our already expanding program of social security have already contributed signally to a decrease of the overall alcoholic problem. Despite the continuing seriousness of this problem, Americans are beginning to drink less, as indicated by the reports of the Distilled Spirits Institute and of Edward B. Dunford, general counsel for the National Anti-Saloon League, in March, 1948. The Yale University researchers themselves have indicated the steady decline of extreme alcoholism for the country as a whole since 1900. Although our culture stresses competitive factors in much of our economic and social life, the removal of the harrowing vicissitudes and uncertainties of unemployment and the promise of social security will continue to do much in alleviating tendencies towards unrestrained drinking. Professor Bruno has pointed significantly to the sharp decrease of alcoholism in the urban industrial areas of England during the depression of the twenties with the introduction of more ample unemployment benefits and other forms of social rehabilitation.[54]

(2) The practice of adequate mental hygiene education in the schools as a mandatory measure, not solely from the standpoint of providing information, but from the necessity of applying such principles in the teaching process itself, is of undoubted significance. The anticipation of inadequate vocational adjustment through poorly planned preparation and the dangers of excessive competitive pressure must be carefully gauged and kept in mind. Dr. Pierre Janet's warning concerning the incidence of alcoholism among those precariously striving for status should serve as a reminder of the acute need for re-orienting many of our cultural objectives. The basic need for retaining the substantial values of competition in a culture which reflects their impress in all of its phases and the need for diversifying competitive objectives and reducing them to levels that may be realistically accomplished, while already a part of a contemporary cultural trend, must be fostered by deliberate social planning. Family education and the formal educational process in the schools

[54] F. J. Bruno, *The Theory of Social Work* (New York, 1936), p. 105.

may together accomplish much in preventing the common tendency of "pushing people beyond their natural capacities."

(3) While the prohibition experiment in this country has proven a fiasco, the slow tendency towards "local option" forms of alcoholic control is providing an illuminating index of a potential trend. We may be in the process of developing a "creeping" form of prohibition control. The possibility of some sort of legislative control is further shown in the prohibition and temperance programs developed through legislation in the Scandinavian countries, a fertile area for the observation of democratic social experiments. As the result of a long-standing problem of excessive drinking, culminating in a general strike in 1909, the Swedish *Riksdag* initiated a series of legislative reforms that have consistently reduced the problems of excessive drinking. In brief, the Swedish program is based upon the assumption that unlimited profits for manufacturers of alcoholic beverages and distributors, with no control over consumers, is an extremely difficult combination to overcome. Consequently, the amount of profits that distillers and distributors may make on their capital investments is sharply limited, seldom amounting to more than a three per cent annual return, with the result that there has been little incentive for investment in such enterprises. In addition, the consumer is restricted in his purchases by a combined ration system and an ingenious procedure which amounts to the "licensing" of drinkers. A *mot-bok*, or passbook, is issued to men and women when they reach ages of majority and marital status; it may be used at public liquor dispensaries, the highest quantity being issued to the amount of four and one-fourth quarts of spirituous liquors per month to married men, who must have reached their twenty-first birthdays, and to unmarried men, who must have attained their twenty-fifth birthdays. Continual intoxication may lead to the abrogation of these privileges and the rescinding of the *mot-bok*. The decline in the incidence of heavy drinking in Sweden has also been partially attributed to the remarkable adult education program developed in that country under the leadership of the renowned Swedish educational pioneer, Dr. Oscar Ollsen.

(4) Improved and prolonged education in this country, with the end in view of teaching individuals "how to live" and how to realize their own potentialities for self-fulfillment in relaxation, can aid immeasurably in curbing excessive drinking drives. The practice of "killing time" can be prevented by encouragement of participating skills in recreation and by revealing the endless capacities for self-fulfillment in leisure in our industrial culture, which increasingly is providing greater opportunities for free time. This is a challenge to which our schools, colleges, and universities have hardly as yet begun to respond.

(5) As for the compulsive drinker, modern medical, psychiatric, psy-

chological, and sociological research is beginning to reveal salient causal patterns and how they may be eradicated. As a mass movement, Alcoholics Anonymous is a significant sympton of the times, and as a hopeful area of exploration it merits continued careful investigation. Although no one knows why, and to what extent, this movement has proved successful; the explanation probably lies in the unconscious discovery of methods of group therapy which are practiced successfully elsewhere. Both from the standpoint of economy, as well as from the realistic necessity of active group adjustment, the basic principles of this group procedure, developed in other areas by S. L. Slavson and others, opens up new vistas for the potential treatment of alcoholics and other maladjusted persons.[55] The autobiographical account of Harold Maine indicates the promising nature of this process in at least one institution where he was treated—a process largely developed inadvertently because of reasons of economy and shortage of trained staff.[56]

Finally, in conjunction with intensive physical rehabilitation, adequate nutritional care, and competent psychotherapy, the new drugs give promise of considerable help to the chronic alcoholic. Using carefully prescribed dosages of tetraethyl-thiruram disulfide (antabuse), three Danish physicians, Doctors H. Jald, E. Jacobsen and V. Larsen, have met with considerable success in their treatment of certain alcoholic patients within the last two years. Antabuse, however, is no cure for alcoholism—merely a good adjunct to treatment—and if taken without adequate medical supervision can prove extremely dangerous.

Direct hormone treatment, developed independently and announced in 1949 by Dr. John W. Tinters, an endocrinologist, and Dr. Harold W. Lovell of the New York Medical College, and by Dr. James J. Smith, Director of Research in Alcoholism at the New York University-Bellevue Medical Center, also reveals considerable promise for the successful cure of alcoholism. The investigations of these scientists have disclosed that the chronic alcoholic suffers from a deficiency in the hormones secreted by the cortex, or outer layer, of the adrenal glands. By administering proper dosages of adrenal cortical extract (ACE), together with vitamin C, and in some cases, certain sex hormones, the Bellevue group claim to have achieved remarkable success in overcoming both the craving for alcohol and the after-effects of severe drinking. Doctors Tinters and Lovell rely more upon a diet high in fats, moderate in proteins, and restricted in carbohydrates. Although such methods are promising, they should, for the present, be regarded as important auxiliary methods in treatment rather than complete therapeutic procedures. What such investigators frequently overlook is that excessive drinking is part of a psychologically

[55] Cf. S. L. Slavson, *Analytic Group Therapy* (New York, 1950).
[56] *If a Man Be Mad*, Chap. 4.

rooted adjustment procedure, irrespective of its relationship, through cause or effect, to organic elements within the personality.

SUMMARY

We have considered some of the problems of personal addiction in relation to the leisure time values of the culture. (1) The use to which leisure is put in any culture sheds considerable light upon (a) the predominant end-values of the culture, and (b) the characteristic strains and distortions to which the culture is exposed. (2) In the pursuit of this problem, it was seen that certain broad social values, such as competition and pecuniary interests, as well as differing group standards and interests, play significant roles in orienting recreational objectives. (3) The character of contemporary cultural emphasis and the differential tendencies in leisure-time patterns have tended to foster habitual drinking patterns in American culture. (4) Our modern scientific and sociological viewpoints have transformed our traditional perspectives upon the problem of the excessive drinker, causing us to view such individuals as suffering from specific forms of psychopathological difficulties. (5) Recent studies indicate the wide prevalence of social drinking in the United States, with the proportion of pathological drinkers constituting a serious public health problem commensurate with such disorders as cancer and tuberculosis. (6) In analyzing the social basis for drinking, it is evident that American drinking patterns are somewhat distinct from drinking patterns elsewhere, showing differences in the matters of incidence of drinking, physical manifestations, social disorders, and customs. (7) Conspicuous in recent trends have been the increased social acceptance of women's drinking, joint drinking between the sexes, and a rise in alcoholic rates among women. (8) An appraisal of the long-range and immediate cultural factors which have played a part in affecting leisure and drinking habits indicates the effects of cultural diversity, the "puritanical complex," population expansion and urban concentration, and the dominating position of commerce and industry. (9) Resultant effects upon attitudes are manifested in loss of spontaneity in recreation, passivism, and the priority of commercial values. (10) Seen from the personal angle, conventional reasons for drinking have been sought in such explanations as fashion, ignorance, economic conditions, and inherent nervous defects. Although such reasons may in part account for certain forms of normal drinking, they tend to oversimplify and to overlook the more fundamental sociological and psychological bases for both normal and abnormal drinking. (11) Recent studies are beginning to delineate the fundamental socio-familial patterns which play a part in producing alcoholic excess, and the possible psychopathologies evidenced in the two principal types of compulsive drinkers. (12) In its onset as a pathological condition, the progressive nature of alcoholism, with considerable variations in the time-process involved for attaining this state, has been shown. (13) Compulsive drinkers indicate a causal process, linked to early psychogenetic development and the stimulus of appropriate ideational patterns, revealing pronounced patterns of infantilism, extreme dependence, inadequacy and insecurity, and, frequently, various sexual disabilities. (14) Considerable new light has been focused in recent years upon the organic and psychological results of excessive drinking, largely as a result of the work of the Yale Laboratory of Applied Physiology. (15) Foremost in these disclosures has been evidence indicating the depressant effect of alcohol upon the human organism, the complex factors involved in ordinary intoxication, the secondary relation between alcohol and the sexual urges, the distinction between alcoholism and narcomania, and the results upon longevity, psychosis, and congenital factors. (16) Conspicuous in the revelations of these modern researches are the views that normal drinking does not curtail life expectancy, contrary to the effects of prolonged excessive drinking, and that alcohol creates no intrinsic germinal damage. (17) Our new knowledge concerning the causes and pathological effects of alcoholism suggests the directions for modern social policy, in its stress upon the removal of significant areas of strain upon the personality, new orientations in alcoholic education and mental hygiene, effective use of recreation towards self-fulfillment, group therapy, and the new medical treatments of vitamin therapy and the administration of such drugs as antabuse.

CHAPTER EIGHTEEN

DRUG ADDICTION AND GAMBLING

(1) CHARACTER OF DRUG AND OPIATE ADDICTION

DRUG addiction is considerably different, psychologically and physiologically, from excessive drinking. Because of rigorous federal and state controls over the importation and use of drugs, fewer persons are afflicted by this habit than are addicted to drink. Because of the illicit nature of the traffic in drugs, addicts are usually associated with underworld elements. The effect of drugs upon the human organism and personality is quite different than in the case of alcohol. The disintegration of the addicted individual, physical and mental, assumes a different course than in the case of alcohol, and for different reasons.

The common drugs and their derivatives used by addicts do not function in the same way. The most common, and those considered by experts the most pernicious, are the opium derivatives, morphine, codeine, and laudanum. Cocaine and the ubiquitous marihuana or hashish (Indian hemp) are not considered as dangerous in their effects and addiction to them is usually easier to curb. Opium can be taken either by smoking or eating, while morphine or heroin is usually taken through injection by means of a hypodermic needle, or sniffed as a powder. The difference between the effects of heroin and morphine is expressed by Louie, the Fixer (i.e., the illicit drug dealer) in Nelson Algren's remarkable novel about drug addiction, *The Man with the Golden Arm:* "Heroin got the drive awright—but there's not a tingle to a ton—you got to get M [i.e., morphine] to get that tingle-tingle." [1]

The history of the use of drugs dates back to ancient times. Archaeologists have shown that the Sumerians, settled in Mesopotamia during the fifth millennium B.C., had developed an ideographic symbol for opium, signifying "joy" or "rejoicing"—not so far removed from the present addict's designation of the drug as "joy-pop." Terry reports that coca derivatives were employed in South America by the ancient Inca priests and

[1] Nelson Algren, *The Man with the Golden Arm* (New York, 1949), p. 58.

nobility.[2] Modern forms of these drugs date from the nineteenth century. Morphine was discovered in 1803 by Derosne, alkaloid cocaine by Niemann in 1859, and heroin by Dreser in 1898. The hypodermic syringe, the indispensable adjunct of the drug peddler's trade, was invented in 1845.

Although drugs have served an important medicinal function, their abuse is primarily a problem of modern times. It wasn't until the present century that the taking of drugs was condemned as anti-social and "immoral." During the nineteenth century, when drugs were used more extensively in Europe and the United States, victims of the drug habit were pitied rather than censured. Today, the practice seems to be localized among particular classes and groups in the various cultures where it is found. For example, in France and England drug addiction seems more common among the middle and professional classes. In Germany, the practice has been particularly extensive among physicians. In certain parts of the Orient—Formosa, for example—addiction is more common among the working classes. In the United States, narcoticism occurs largely among members of the underworld, although its practice is fairly extensive elsewhere as well. The distribution of addiction is related to such factors as ethnic background, degree of urbanization, and education. The relevance of these factors must in each case be accounted for on the basis of the cultural circumstances involved, exposure to drugs, opportunities for continuing and developing habits of addiction, contacts with distributors, and critical situations in the lives of individuals and groups.

(2) THE EXTENT OF ADDICTION

Because the taking of drugs for non-medical purposes is highly illicit, it is extremely difficult to determine precisely the number of addicts. In an interesting analysis, Ernest Mowrer has attempted to show that the pattern of drug addiction follows what he calls a "dual-crest" pattern, i.e., it has tended to rise during periods of both depression and war. This contrasts with the patterning of other pathologies, such as alcoholism, certain forms of crimes (for example, embezzlement), mental deficiencies with psychosis, and senile dementia. These disturbances follow a "dual-trough" pattern, that is, a downward trend during war and depression.[3] Particularly striking, and contrary to what we would expect, is the contrast between the patterning of alcoholism and drug addiction.

[2] C. E. Terry, "Drug Addiction," *Encyclopaedia of the Social Sciences*, Vol. 5, pp. 242–52.

[3] Ernest R. Mowrer, "Social Crises and Social Disorganization," *American Sociological Review*, XV (Feb., 1950), 64.

This contrast may be due partly to the greater laxity of control over the use of drugs during periods of crisis.

Estimates of the number of drug addicts in this country range from less than one hundred thousand to several million. Colonel Pearce Bailey, chief of the section of neurology and psychiatry in the Army during the First World War, estimated, on the basis of the number rejected for army service, that at that time there were very likely no fewer than 99,500 addicts in the entire country.[4] Estimates of Kolb and Du Mez range from a maximum of about 150,000 to 110,000, the latter figure probably being more nearly correct. Their studies point to a decrease in addiction since 1900, their report stating that prior to 1900 there may have been 264,000 addicts in this country.[5]

A report on the distribution of narcotism in 1935 by the Commissioner of Narcotics indicates wide regional differences in this country.[6] In certain areas, as this report shows, the previous estimate of one addict per thousand of the population no longer holds. In predominantly urban areas, particularly along the Atlantic and Pacific seaboards, the ratios are considerably in excess of the earlier figures.

According to Lindesmith, each major war has tended to increase the number of active and potential addicts in the population. The effects of the recent war were twofold: (1) disruption of the channels of illegal distribution probably cut down the number of addicts among the civilian population, and (2) as a result of the use of opiates in the army, there has probably been an increase in the number of addicts among the former military population.[7] The increase in the illicit distribution of narcotics in the period between 1945–50, in conjunction with the effects of the Second World War, has probably resulted in an appreciable rise over the pre-war rate of addiction. Present estimates of the number of addicts, exclusive of those who use marihuana, range between 110,000 and 125,000. However, if we include all forms of addiction, the mild and temporary as well as serious, the number may go as high as 500,000. Although it is generally believed that the number of addicts has increased significantly since the passage by the federal government in 1914 of the Harrison Act, the evidence, although suggestive, is not conclusive. It is significant to note that the fingerprint arrest records of the F.B.I. in 1948 show only 4,486 arrests for narcotic violations (exclusive of federal viola-

[4] Cf. Lawrence Kolb and A. G. Du Mez, *The Prevalence and Trend of Drug Addiction in the United States and Factors Influencing It* (U. S. Public Health Service, Bulletin No. 924, May, 1924), p. 3.

[5] Ibid., pp. 24–5.

[6] *Traffic in Opium and Other Dangerous Drugs for the Year Ended December 31, 1935* (Bureau of Narcotics, U. S. Treasury Department, Washington), pp. 2–4.

[7] A. R. Lindesmith, *Opiate Addiction* (Bloomington, Indiana, 1947), pp. 196–7.

tions), only 0.6 per cent of the total number of arrests for the year and the third smallest category in the list of all violations.

(3) EFFECTS OF ADDICTION

The effects of the continued use of drugs are highly destructive, both physically and mentally. However, contrary to popular impression, the effects are *not* direct. They are consequent upon a complex socio-psychological and physiological pattern. This pattern is associated on one hand with the need for concealment of the sources of procurement and contact with the illegal distributors, and on the other hand, with the extreme physical duress arising during the "withdrawal" period when drugs are not available. It is during the withdrawal period that the individual on occasion becomes violent and gives other evidence of severe stress. When fortified with drugs, the addict may feel perfectly normal. Light and Torrance state that "morphine addiction is not characterized by physical deterioration or impairment of physical fitness aside from the addiction *per se*."[8] As Lindesmith has pointed out, many addicts have led useful and productive lives, relatively unaffected by their habit.[9] In support of this conclusion, he cites from the work of Lawrence Kolb and others. He reports from the study of Kolb that of 119 cases who became addicted originally through medical use of drugs, 90 had good industrial records, while only 29 gave evidence of unsatisfactory job performance.[10]

> Judged by the output of labor and their own statements, none of the normal persons had their efficiency reduced by opium. Twenty-two of them worked regularly while taking opium for twenty-five years or more; one of them, a woman 81 and still alert mentally, had taken three grains of morphine daily for 65 years. She gave birth to and raised six children, and managed her household affairs with more than average efficiency. A widow, aged 66, had taken 17 grains of morphine daily for most of 37 years. She is alert mentally but is bent with age and rheumatism. However, she does physical labor every day and makes her own living.

However, the continued use of opiates over a period of time creates an irrepressible physiological need for their continuance. Discontinuance produces excruciating physical discomfort and mental anguish. According

[8] A. B. Light, E. G. Torrance, W. G. Carr, Edith G. Fry, and W. A. Wolff, *Opium Addiction* (Chicago, 1929), p. 115.

[9] Lindesmith, *Opiate Addiction*, p. 38.

[10] Lawrence Kolb, "Drug Addiction—A Study of Some Medical Cases," *Archives of Neurology and Psychiatry*, XX (1928), 178. Cited in Lindesmith, *Opiate Addiction*, pp. 38–9.

to Lindesmith: "After about three weeks of regular daily use, the abstinence symptoms apparently increase at an accelerated tempo and rapidly become very severe and even dangerous." [11] The extreme torment that such victims experience has been graphically described by A. B. Light, E. G. Torrance, *et al.*, who observed the "withdrawal" symptoms of self-committed underworld addicts at the Philadelphia General Hospital.[12]

> As the time approaches for what would have been the addict's next administration of the drug, one notices that he glances frequently in the direction of the clock and manifests a certain degree of restlessness. If the administration is omitted, he begins to move about in a rather aimless way, failing to remain in one position long. He is either in bed, sitting on a chair, standing up, or walking about, constantly changing from one to another. With this restlessness, yawning soon appears, which becomes more and more violent. At the end of a period of about eight hours, restlessness becomes marked. He will throw himself onto a bed, curl up and wrap the blankets tightly around his shoulders, sometimes burying his head in the pillows. For a few minutes he will toss from side to side, and then suddenly jump out of the bed and start to walk back and forth, head bowed, shoulders stooping. . . . He may then lie on the floor close to the radiator, trying to keep warm. . . . At the same time he complains bitterly of suffering with cold and then hot flashes, but mostly chills. . . . He has a most abject appearance, but is fairly docile in his behavior. This is a picture of his appearance during the first eight hours.
>
> Often at the end of this period the addict may become extremely drowsy and unable to keep his eyes open. If he falls asleep, which is often the case, he falls into a deep slumber well known as the "yen" sleep. It takes unusual noises to awaken him. The sleep may last for as long as eight or twelve hours. On awakening, he is more restless than ever. Lacrimation, yawning, sneezing, and chilliness are extreme. A feeling of suffocation at the back of the throat is frequently mentioned. . . . Vomiting and diarrhea appear. . . . Perspiration is excessive. . . . Muscular twitchings are commonly present; they may occur anywhere, but are most violent in the lower extremities. . . . If he is handed a cigarette to smoke, his hands tremble so violently that he may have difficulty in placing it in his mouth. . . . He refuses all food and water, and frequently sleep is unknown at this point. It is at this stage that he may one minute beg for a "shot" and the next minute threaten physical violence. . . .

[11] Alfred R. Lindesmith, *Opiate Addiction*, p. 26.

[12] Light, Torrance, et. al., *Opium Addiction*, pp. 7 ff. Reprinted by permission from the *Archives of Internal Medicine*.

> He will beat his head against the wall, or throw himself violently on the floor. Any behavior which he thinks will bring about the administration of the drug will be resorted to. . . .
>
> We believe that the height of these withdrawal symptoms is reached somewhere between the period of forty-eight and seventy-two hours following the last dose of the drug taken. . . .

The resulting physical shock to the organism may be severe in many cases, even after cure has been attained. The personal demoralization consequent on associating with the criminal procurers of drugs may be even more serious. With penetrating insight, Algren describes the entire corruptive process in his novel, through presenting the reactions of a "cured" drug-peddler, and of his victims.[13]

> [The drug-peddler—"fixer" in the addict's argot] wondered idly now where in the world his customer would get that kind of money when the day came that he'd need half a C just to taper off. He'd get it all right. They always got it. He'd seen them coming in the rain, the unkjays with their peculiarly rigid, panicky walk, wearing some policeman's castoff rubbers, no socks at all, a pair of Salvation Army pants a size too small or a size too large and a pajama top for a shirt—but with that twenty dollars clutched in the sweating palm for that big twenty dollar fix. . . .
>
> He'd taken the sweat cure in a little Milwaukee Avenue hotel room cutting himself down, as he put it, "from monkey to zero." From three full grains a day to one, then a half of that and a half of that straight down to zero, though he'd been half out of his mind with the pain two nights running and was so weak, for days after, that he could hardly tie his own shoelaces.
>
> Back on the street at last, he'd gotten the chuck horrors: for two full days he'd eaten candy bars, sweet rolls and strawberry malteds. It had seemed that there would be no end to his hunger for sweets.
>
> [He] never had the sweet-roll horrors any more. Yet sometimes himself sensed that something had twisted in his brain in those nights when he'd gotten the monkey off his back on Milwaukee Avenue.

(4) SELECTED CHARACTERISTICS OF ADDICTS

In the report published in 1935 by the U. S. Bureau of Narcotics, it was stated that the ratio of male to female addicts was approximately four to one.[14] In the nineteenth century, drug addiction was far more

[13] *The Man with the Golden Arm*, p. 59. Reprinted by permission of Doubleday & Company, Inc.

[14] Bureau of Narcotics, *Traffic in Opium, 1935*, pp. 2–4.

common among women, there being about three women addicts for every two addicted men. Studies as late as 1914 among certain regional groups still indicated a preponderance of women over men. A report by L. P. Brown in 1914 showed that 66.9 per cent of 2,370 addicts in Tennessee were women.[15] The prevalence of addiction among women during this early period was due to the lack of legal restrictions upon the distribution of drugs, and also to the widespread sale of patent medicines for women's ailments that contained habit-forming drugs.

The Bureau of Narcotics study of 1935 showed, on the basis of the analysis of 946 cases, that the average age of drug addicts was approximately forty years, the males averaging forty-one years and the females thirty-five. According to a racial breakdown, 775 (82 per cent) were white; 88 (9 per cent), Oriental; 78 (8.3 per cent), colored; and three (0.3 per cent), American Indian. The great majority, 520, had attended only grade school. It is significant that considerable percentages had attended high school (22 per cent) and college or university (16.2 per cent). This relatively high proportion of high school and college trained individuals takes on meaning when viewed in relation to the causal hypothesis presented below.

A recent analysis by Benjamin Malzberg of 135 addicts of better than average economic status, who entered private hospitals and sanitoria in New York State for treatment, brought out information about this atypical group.[16] The group studied included largely persons of means who were willing to enter private institutions, and who were diagnosed as free of psychotic disabilities. Of the sample studied, 87 were males and 45 were females. While of the previous group discussed over 38 per cent had had education beyond grade school, over 75 per cent of Malzberg's cases had attended high school and college, and 45 individuals (39.1 per cent) had had college training. The vast majority, 93.3 per cent, were urban dwellers. Because of the economic standing of this group, very few Negroes appeared in the sample, 97.8 per cent being white. However, 15.6 per cent were of foreign birth. Particularly illuminating is the distribution in relation to ethnic background, as shown in the following table. With the notable exceptions of the Hebrew and Irish categories, this distribution is proportionate to the normal population, when differences in economic level are taken into account. What seems particularly significant here is that the Jewish group, who generally show very low rates of alcoholism, should produce such a high rate of drug addiction. The reasons which may be submitted are primarily eco-

[15] "Enforcement of the Tennessee Anti-Narcotics Law," *American Journal of Public Health*, V (1915), 323–33.

[16] Benjamin Malzberg, "A Statistical Study of Some Characteristics of Drug Addicts," *Mental Hygiene News*, New York State Department of Mental Hygiene, XIX (June, 1949), 4–8.

First Admissions with Drug Addiction, Without Psychosis, to the State and Licensed Hospitals for Mental Disease in New York State, Classified According to Race (Ethnic Background) *

	Number			*Per Cent*		
Race	*Males*	*Females*	*Total*	*Males*	*Females*	*Total*
African	1	..	1	1.1	...	0.8
Chinese	1	1	2	1.1	2.1	1.4
English	3	3	6	3.4	6.2	4.4
German	3	..	3	3.4	...	2.2
Greek	1	..	1	1.1	...	0.8
Hebrew	18	5	23	20.7	10.4	17.0
Irish	7	11	18	8.1	22.9	13.3
Italian	12	..	12	13.8	...	8.9
Slavonic	1	..	1	1.1	...	0.8
Spanish	2	1	3	2.3	2.1	2.2
Mixed	21	21	42	24.1	43.7	31.1
Unascertained	17	6	23	19.6	12.4	17.0
Total	87	48	135	100.0	100.0	100.0

* Malzberg, "A Statistical Study of Some Characteristics of Drug Addicts," p. 4.

nomic. Also relevant are special features of the Jewish family organization, where considerable family pressure is exerted to safeguard the individual. Similar factors are very likely present in accounting for the extremely high rate of addiction among Irish families (22.9 per cent), although no definite conclusions may be drawn without further study of the specific causal patterns involved in the two groups concerned.

Malzberg's data and conclusions in reference to this special group are significant when seen in relation to the Bureau of Narcotics study. (1) The number of first admissions to hospitals for mental disease in New York State for drug addiction *without* psychosis is small. This is very likely the result primarily of economic factors, non-psychotic addicts not being allowed admittance to public mental hospitals. (2) The average age of the addicts studied by Malzberg was 44.6 years, the range extending from 35 to 59 years of age. As in other studies, females were younger than males. Non-psychotic female drug addicts were younger than female first admissions classified as addicted psychotics, a fact that suggests the degenerative effects of drugs. (3) This special group yielded a high rate of excessive users of alcohol. In connection with this point, Dr. Manly B. Root, in working with criminal addicts, has made reference to the large numbers of rehabilitated addicts who try drinking as a substitute, or "lesser evil." [17] (4) Psychiatric investigations reveal that approximately 40 per cent of first admissions were of normal personality. This figure is lower than we should expect and is probably due to the peculiar characteristics of this better-situated economic group. (5) Drug addiction in this group appears concentrated among the unmarried. (6) The educa-

[17] Manly B. Root, "What the Probation Officer Can Do for Special Types of Offenders," *Federal Probation*, XIII (Dec., 1949), p. 39.

tional level is high, due to the high economic status of this group. (7) Because of such factors as population concentration, wealth, and opportunity, drug addiction is primarily an urban phenomenon. (8) Certain groups, such as the Jewish category, suggest the possibility of a relatively high rate of addiction as diametrically opposed to relatively low rates of alcoholism among Jews.[18]

(5) CAUSAL THEORIES OF DRUG ADDICTION

Most of the classical theories concerning the causes for drug addiction have recently been exploded. Common among these theories has been the view that drug addicts are fundamentally emotionally disturbed, pre-psychotic, or psychotic individuals, who compensate for their disabilities by taking drugs. Some of the theories of this nature bear a strong resemblance to the theories accounting for alcoholics. Typical are the statements of Harry Elmer Barnes, in his study of social pathology, and the more specialized theories of Bingham Dai.[19] Dai's theory is particularly apposite in this connection in its stress upon "infantile" characteristics of the addict, "excessive dependence upon other people," and early abnormal relations with parents.[20] Evidence for many of these "abnormal personality" theories derives from investigations by Dr. Lawrence Kolb and Dr. C. Schultz.[21] Among the weaknesses of these studies are the following: (1) Clinical diagnoses of individuals before drug addiction were not obtainable or verifiable in many cases. Highly dubious judgments were frequently employed, such as Kolb's designation of 38 per cent of 225 addicts studied as "carefree individuals."[22] (2) Many of the evaluations of drug addicts are made after the process of addiction has produced marked effects. (3) High percentages, as indicated in the Malzberg data, are classified as "normal personalities." Why, then, should "normal" personalities become addicted? Manly B. Root's evaluation seems to confirm the normalcy of most drug addicts. (4) The majority of investigations have failed signally to develop causal hypotheses on the basis of adequate and comparable "control" groups.[23]

[18] Malzberg, *A Statistical Study of Some Characteristics of Drug Addicts*, p. 8.

[19] Cf. Harry Elmer Barnes, *Society in Transition* (New York, 1939), pp. 806–07; Bingham Dai, *Opium Addiction in Chicago* (Shanghai, 1937).

[20] Ibid., p. 174.

[21] See, for example, Lawrence Kolb, "Types and Characteristics of Drug Addicts," *Mental Hygiene*, IX (1925), 301; also, by the same author, "Drug Addiction in its Relation to Crime," *Mental Hygiene*, IX (1925), 77.

[22] Lawrence Kolb, "Types and Characteristics of Drug Addicts," p. 301.

[23] See, for example, A. R. Lindesmith's commendable critique of current causal hypotheses in his *Opiate Addiction* (Bloomington, Indiana, 1947), especially Chaps. 1, 7, and 8; also his earlier analysis, "The Drug Addict as a Psychopath," *American Sociological Review*, V (Dec., 1940), 914–20. Aside from his critique of orthodox theories, his general attack upon poor causal reasoning in sociology is especially commendable. Cf. his *Opiate Addiction*, Chap. 1.

Arthur R. Lindesmith's theory of the causation of addiction seems to us valid.[24] This view is premised on the theory that individuals to whom drugs have been administered rarely, if ever, become addicted if they do not associate physical discomfort with the withdrawal of drugs. "Addiction occurs only," says Lindesmith, "when opiates are used to alleviate withdrawal distress, after this distress has been properly understood or interpreted, that is to say, after it has been represented to the individual in terms of the linguistic symbols and cultural patterns which have grown up around the opiate habit." [25] The process of transformation from non-addiction to addiction occurs when the individual, because of linguistic and cultural identification, tends to develop altered attitudes toward himself and regards himself as victimized by the process. Supporting this interpretation is the fact that the individual rarely experiences the buoyancy attributed to the drug unless he is "taught" to expect it.

If the Lindesmith theory can be accepted, it tells us a great deal about the process of drug addiction. It indicates, in the first place, that irrespective of how drugs are first introduced into the human system, whether illicit or not, the individual's mental association with the process of relief or buoyancy constitutes the crucial factor in producing habituation. Secondly, it suggests that the basis for addiction is cultural, rather than physiological. Thirdly, the causes for its distribution among selected cultural groups would rest upon such factors as medical inadvertence, the accessibility of drugs, and the high profit to be derived from their sale, which encourages unscrupulous lawbreakers to foster its sale and to encourage its use.

Two points must be clarified before Lindesmith's theory may be proven. (1) Do all individuals who experience "withdrawal distress" and who associate it with the absence of drugs, tend, nevertheless, to become addicts? Apparently some individuals who associate distress with the withdrawal of drugs manage to overcome the tendency towards habituation. (2) Certain thrill-seekers may consciously seek the experience to be gained by the taking of drugs. For some, this quest of novelty may be the first step toward addiction. What types of individuals are likely to search for such "thrills," and what are their socio-cultural backgrounds? Further, why is it that not all thrill-seekers become addicts? Lindesmith's thesis may account for a considerable percentage of those who become addicts—and unquestionably sheds considerable new light upon methods of rehabilitation. Yet it fails to consider that certain addicts acquire the habit because of driving forces within their own personalities.

[24] Cf., particularly, *Opiate Addiction*, Chap. 8, and "The Drug Addict as a Psychopath."

[25] Lindesmith, *Opiate Addiction*, p. 165.

(6) LEGISLATION AND METHODS OF CONTROL

The present theory of control, implicit in our laws and distributive procedures, is one of repression. Effective legislative control began with the Pure Food and Drugs Act of 1906, which sought to protect the consumer from the sale of injurious and improperly represented products. However, the first specific legislation designed to curb the distribution of opiates was brought about by the Harrison Narcotic Act of 1914. This law placed stringent restrictions on the importation, manufacture, distribution, and sale of opium, coca, and their derivatives. Supplementary legislation in the form of the Jones-Miller Act in 1922, establishing a Narcotic Control Board, sought to maintain quotas of drugs to be imported, while an act passed in 1924 expressly forbade the importation of opium for the manufacture of heroin.

The net effect of such prohibitory legislation has been to drive the importation and distribution of drugs underground, necessitating the need for international control on a wide scale. International arrangements and conventions have been undertaken, beginning with the International Opium Commission at Shanghai in 1909, followed by the Hague Opium Convention of 1912, and meetings of the World Conference on Narcotic Education in New York City in 1927. The League of Nations became interested in controlling sources of supply and international distribution. The work of the former Permanent Central Opium Board and the Opium Advisory Committee has now fallen to the United Nations.

The general effects of repression in this country have been to encourage the illicit sale of drugs and to promote their use. Moreover, the high rate of crimes committed by addicts in this country is due in considerable degree to the price of the restricted supply of drugs. One British commentator, in comparing the medically regulated system of supply functioning in England with our stringent system, has stated: [26]

> It appears that not only has the Harrison Law failed to diminish the number of drug takers—some contend, indeed, that it has increased their numbers—but, far from bettering the lot of the opiate addict, it has actually worsened it; for without curtailing the supply of the drug it has sent the price up tenfold, and this has had the effect of impoverishing the poorer class of addicts and reducing them to a condition of such abject misery as to render them incapable of gaining an honest livelihood.

As long as opportunities for enormous illicit profits are present, the traffic will continue. During the recent war, when the Axis powers con-

[26] Harry Campbell, "The Pathology and Treatment of Morphia Addiction," *British Journal of Inebriety*, XX (1922–3), 147.

trolled most of the world's important sources of supply, new sources quickly arose in Iran, India, and Mexico. The cultivation of marihuana, which grows like a weed, has spread extensively in city backyards and remote rural areas, presenting a particularly difficult problem of control.

There is a need for an extensive program of education among the lay public *and* the medical profession. Moreover, the problem of addiction, if it is to be most effectively handled, must be removed from police surveillance and placed under medical supervision, both public and private.[27] Distribution of required amounts to addicts by members of the medical profession, at normal prices, would remove the incentive for criminal classes to enter into the trade. Furthermore, placing control in the hands of competent medical authorities would encourage remedial control and rehabilitation. The employment of public health facilities and clinics for the cure and treatment of drug victims would be required in such a program. Such facilities as the Public Health Service Hospital at Lexington, Kentucky, where federal prisoners and voluntary patients receive treatment, must be extended in scope and objective. Post-discharge supervisory assistance for former patients would be part of such a program and would include modern group therapeutic measures. In this connection, the development of such a new agency as "Narcotics Anonymous," patterned after the organization of Alcoholics Anonymous, may be profitably explored.[28]

(7) GAMBLING AND SOCIAL DISORGANIZATION

As an informal pastime, gambling is not necessarily an evil and may, as in the past, serve as an important form of recreation. Gambling emerges as a form of social pathology only when there is widespread feeling against it because of the psychological and social problems which it tends to create. These problems seem to take two principal forms. In the first place, the inveterate gambler frequently develops a form of addiction (like the celebrated character of Fyodor Dosteyevsky's *The Gambler*), which causes him to neglect personal, family, and social responsibilities. As might be inferred from the sociological conception of leisure developed earlier, he is condemned largely because of his failure to perform the normal functions ordinarily expected of him, rather than because of the nature of the condemned activity itself. Gambling, unlike excessive drinking, drug addiction, or sex demoralization, produces no

[27] See August Vollmer, *The Police and Modern Society* (Berkeley, California, 1936), pp. 117–18.

[28] This group approach to the problem originated in 1947 among patients at the Kentucky hospital. It was assisted in its organization by members of Alcoholics Anonymous, although the two organizations have no official connection. See the *New York Times*, Sunday, June 18, 1950, Section I, p. 25.

direct deterioration in the human organism or human social groupings. Its danger lies in the fact that it disrupts the fulfillment of normal responsibilities that organized social living compels. Moreover, gambling, like other forms of social behavior that are widely practiced in the face of taboos, becomes a social problem because of its intimate association with lawless elements within the social order.

Despite legal measures taken against it, particularly in the United States, gambling has become a significant element in modern recreational life. The ambivalence of the public attitude has made control extremely difficult. Because of this, many modern European and Latin-American countries have capitalized upon what is conceived to be an ineradicable "human weakness," diverting the profits from gambling to public revenues by means of vast government-controlled national lotteries.

(8) THE SOCIOLOGY OF GAMBLING

The psychological basis of all gambling seems to consist in the element of chance. The degree to which chance is present varies considerably from game to game. Gambling may involve strong elements of skill, as in certain forms of card-games or participation in certain forms of skilled athletic competition, or it may simply depend upon the chance throw of a pair of dice or the draw of a card, as in stud poker. In any event, the element of chance is always present.

The chance element in human life is made much of particularly in those societies where status is competitive and depends largely on pecuniary standards. A notable example of this principle is found in the United States. Here, rapid commercial expansion and industrial achievements of this country have depended to a considerable degree upon enterprises of a precarious and speculative character.

Opposing the operation of chance factors are the stabilizing and routinized mechanisms of social living that constitute the basis of the social order. In order to achieve and insure its own continuance, every society tends to reduce the scope of the unpredictable.[29]

In a society such as ours—complex, impersonal, and yet highly competitive—a great premium is placed on conformity and the need for routine. At the same time, there is great pressure to break the routine, to initiate, promote, and experiment in order to bring about the dynamic growth of our continuously expanding economy. For large masses of individuals, to respond to this pressure is difficult, if not impossible. Hedged in by stereotyped employments, the fears of insecurity, pressures of family, and the opinions of others, the average individual hesitates to "take the

[29] Cf. Wilbert E. Moore and Melvin M. Tumin, "Some Social Functions of Ignorance," *American Sociological Review*, XIV (Dec., 1949), especially 794 and 795.

chance" that may mean riches and prestige, despite the traditional assurance that the country's growth and expansion have depended upon people who *did* take chances. For the many whom circumstances prevent from taking the big step that might mean riches, substitutive betting on a small scale represents a tremendous boon. Present day gambling may be likened, in the function it serves, to the practice of magic among primitives, who entertain the notion that the unpredictable contains among its infinite possibilities the chance of good fortune for them. It is probably no accident that inveterate gamblers are among the most superstitious of men.

The escape from routine and boredom characterizes large segments of modern industrial life in which much of the creative aspect and the "instinct of workmanship" has been lost. The psychological aspect of this condition may be seen in the desire for change and new experience. Gambling and "taking a chance" dispels boredom and hence is found pleasurable, particularly in a culture where the unchanging and predictable routines of employment are sharply separated from "leisure time"—the time when the individual "really lives." This quest for thrills through new experience produces a public readily available for exploitation by professional gambling interests. Moore and Tumin have stressed the attractiveness that gambling exercises because of the factor of unpredictability: [30]

> Certainly the attractiveness of many games of chance, as well as those games and sports where chance may equalize or offset known differences in skill and performance, rests in large measure on their unpredictable outcome. In fact, there is some rough evidence that ignorance of the future in recreational activities assumes an especially significant role where routine [read: perfect predictability] and boredom are characteristic of work assignments and where there is a sharp break between working time and leisure time.

There remain to be discussed the factors of differential association, opportunity, and the large blocks of unplanned leisure that modern society creates. Games of chance are found, and even encouraged, in the play-activities of children in modern society, ranging from traditional children's guessing and matching games to the early imitation of adult gambling and card games. Among many families, on all class levels, card playing and other forms of gambling have become deeply entrenched in the pattern of recreation. It is significant to note that there are ethnic, class, and even sex differentials in these common forms of recreation. Bridge-playing is largely a middle-class diversion, poker is traditionally considered a "man's game," while the casting of dice, aside from profes-

[30] *Some Social Functions of Ignorance,* p. 794.

sional gambling interests, is favored in certain other groups, such as the Negroes. For many young men, of lower and middle-class groups, learning to play cards is part of the process of "growing up," representing identification with adult groups and standards. For the individual of few inner resources whose employment is tedious and offers little challenge, and who has witnessed gambling in some form since early childhood, the incentive to gamble is an accepted part of his existence.

In summary, gambling serves a function in well organized societies where the stress of economic competition (with its lack of predictability) is high, and where the regimen of economic and social life tends to be strict. Gambling provides an outlet for many individuals who, hedged in by social restrictions, would otherwise find no gratification for their needs for new experience and pecuniary success. The implications of the amateur gambler's attitude are twofold. (1) The risk of being a winner or loser in a game provides a marginal area of suspense, insecurity, new experience, and hope, serving an important emotional need in a society whose functions are highly regularized. (2) The belief that chance works equally in favor of any of the contestants in a gambling venture sustains the hope for status or rewards, which the individual feels he could not achieve through conventional channels. The "get-something-for-nothing" philosophy in American life has been expressed in a wide range of activities, from saving box-tops for premiums to the enormous prizes of the radio "give away" programs.

(9) THE GAMBLER AS A PERSONALITY TYPE

Gamblers, unlike alcoholics, do not seem to fit into any specific system of classification. Nevertheless, common characteristics are found in the personalities of gamblers in Western culture, irrespective of background, suggesting the configuration of a social type. Gambling, as a form of "addiction," may be said to exist when the individual consistently neglects his important primary functions and his obligations to his family, employment, and community for the sake of gambling. Studies of the life-histories of inveterate gamblers reveal a transitional period in their careers, when the regular routines of their living become disrupted and they stay away from their homes and jobs for lengthy periods of time. The inveterate gambler becomes as unpredictable and undependable as the alcoholic, as far as his home duties and employment responsibilities are concerned. For the gambler who consistently pursues his gambling interests, therefore, the sense of discipline and orderliness that guides most individuals in their conventional lives in varying degree tends to become destroyed.

The significant psychological feature of gambling is the enormous hold it finally comes to have on the individual, a hold that is comparable to that of alcohol. Once the gambler is in the addicted stage, even though he may recognize the harm his practices cause his family and associates, he will continue to follow his bent. He lives constantly in the hope of gaining in one final sweep an amount sufficient to make up his previous losses, and restore him honorably to his family and friends. The motivation to gamble, once it has achieved a "functional autonomy" of its own, may dominate other primary requirements of the personality.[31] This impetus is so strong that the individual may violate laws in order to accomplish his purpose. Thus, embezzlement is a common offense of gamblers.

The continuous suspense under which the gambler lives engenders a series of corresponding emotional tensions. The gambler is frequently an emotionally tense individual, his hypertension being sustained for lengthy periods of time. The gambler cannot afford to relax, since he is invariably in the process either of raising funds for his gambling forays or of planning for or making his bets. His inner turmoil and anxiety are frequently concealed by an affected stoical calm, evidenced in the well-known "poker face" of the inveterate card-player. Just as the alcoholic secretes liquor and funds for a future drinking bout, the gambler will retain a reservoir of funds—his "betting money"—which he will not use even for pressing personal needs or for needs of his family. Finally, there is an interesting evidence in his personality of the mechanisms of compensation and other characteristic forms of psychological tension-reducing devices. The gambler, for example, frequently boasts about his winnings, real or fictitious, to non-gamblers, while he bemoans to an exaggerated extent the amount of his losses to his fellow gamblers.

The humor of gambling and the jokes that gamblers exchange among themselves characteristically reflect the tensions they experience and the cynicism that is a sign of their awareness of the futility of gambling. Striking is the contradiction between the gambler's perennial hope that he can "beat the game" and the realistic knowledge that this is virtually impossible.

The gambler's code of ethics. A commentary upon gambling itself is the peculiar code of traditional ethics which has become associated with gambling over many centuries. Primary in this code of ethics is the principle that gambling debts must be paid and will, in fact, have primacy over other forms of obligations. This may be in part a survival of the eighteenth century attitude toward the gentleman's "debt of honor." The weight of this obligation may be so keenly felt as to cause the individual to resort to theft in order to satisfy his gambling creditors.

[31] See Gordon W. Allport, *Personality: A Psychological Interpretation* (New York, 1937), Chap. 7.

There is, however, another significant sociological element in this practice. The basic thrill in gambling is that the individual may make a "killing." This thrill-element depends upon the factor of chance, or the inability to predict with precision what the outcome of the gambling venture may be. This unpredictable factor, however, is premised upon a certainty—the certainty that the loser will pay his debts. Otherwise, the gaming venture itself has no validity. "To win" without "winning" makes no sense. Hence, to make the gambling worthwhile and profitable, there must be the continued assurance that the loser will pay his debts. The chance factor itself *becomes institutionalized* in the expectancy of certainty.

Case Study [32]

L. M., now eighty-three years of age, has for most of his adult life been an inveterate gambler. Born in Russia of a wealthy and cultured urban family, he was the youngest of four children, with a large differential in age separating him from his two sisters and older brother. Considerable attention was lavished upon the older children, particularly the oldest brother, a strong maternal influence guiding them toward eminently respectable professional careers. L. M. did not receive this same attention, largely due to the preoccupation of the mother with the family's expanding business affairs. The mother died when he was fourteen years of age. The father remarried very soon thereafter, moving away to live elsewhere. Much of the rigid discipline of the home collapsed consequent upon the mother's death and the young boy was left largely to his own resources. Rebelling against the schooling his mother had imposed, the boy was apprenticed to a skilled craftsman, a step which the rest of the family regarded with embarrassment and disfavor. Then began a series of wanderings, bringing him to the United States by the time he was seventeen.

He became a highly skilled craftsman in this country, periodically engaging in his own business as an interior decorator and painting contractor. However, he fell in with a "sporting crowd" soon after his arrival in this country. His general attitude was characterized by pride in his antecedents and the "culture" of his family. He posed as a gentleman, and had strong feelings of resentment toward authority and any tendency to impose normal restraints upon his behavior.

His wit and charm managed to disarm most of his friends and associates, even though his disabilities as a provider were soon no-

[32] This case represents a summary of a lengthy case investigation made by the author during the summer of 1940.

ticed. At the age of twenty-nine, he married a girl eleven years his junior, who had experienced a deep sense of insecurity in the large, lower middle-class family from which she had come. In partial compensation for her own background and because of an incurable illness, she attempted to impose upon her husband the same type of discipline against which he had rebelled most of his life. His characteristic traits, intensified after his marriage, were rebelliousness and irresponsibility. These were balanced by his acerbic humor, wit, and personal charm. Despite his misgivings, he gambled steadily, neglecting family, children, and his business, which soon fell away. The death of his wife, at the age of thirty-one, seemed to provide him with an excuse to cease striving. Despite periodic expressions of remorse concerning his four children, he gambled continually, eventually giving up all pretense of legitimate employment. As an old man of eighty-three, living in a nursing home and prevented from gambling largely because of the infirmities of age, he still retains his wit (although partially dulled by senescence), wry humor, and genial personality. Even now, he states, "I don't know why I did it, but gambling is like a disease; I couldn't stop it even though I often wanted to."

(10) EXTENT AND TYPES OF PROFESSIONAL GAMBLING

The extent of gambling is impossible to estimate with any degree of precision, especially if one takes into account such activities as card games played at home, bingo parties of various description, bridge playing among women's groups, and the like. However, the numbers of individuals and amounts of money involved in the various forms of institutionalized gambling, such as horse racing, the "numbers and policy" games, sporting events, and professional card games may provide us with some rough estimates. It is generally estimated that approximately 50,000,000 adult Americans participate in some form of professional gambling, involving an annual sum of approximately $30,000,000,000 and yielding an annual profit to the gambling syndicates and entrepreneurs of about $6,000,000,000. This total annual profit is unquestionably greater than the combined annual profits of our largest industrial enterprises, including such organizations as the United States Steel Corporation, General Motors, and the General Electric Corporation. One estimate places this annual volume of profits from gambling ventures as greater than the total profits of the hundred largest manufacturing companies in the United States.

One index of the enormous profit which gambling produces—and of the hold of gambling upon the American public—may be seen in the tax revenues and profits which are officially recorded in the state of Nevada, the only state which has completely legitimized gambling. On the basis of a 2 per cent gross profit tax levied upon gambling enterprises by Nevada, plus license fees, the state during 1949 collected $1,400,000, or 15.5 per cent of the entire state tax revenue. In Nevada, counties and municipalities also impose taxes and revenues upon gambling organizations, with the result that during the same year, 8.5 per cent of the budgets of counties, and 22.4 per cent of the budgets of the cities, were collected from gambling enterprises. One out of every ten workers in the state is employed by a gambling place, at an average salary, in 1949, of $4,100 a year.

Although fluctuations in the volume of gambling may be seen in relation to crisis periods, the general volume of gambling has remained at a relatively high level during the entire century. In his study of changing indexes of social disorganization, Mowrer has shown that gambling (in common with such apparently unrelated indexes as divorce, epilepsy, and somatic disease with psychosis) conforms to what he designates as a "trough-crest" pattern. This means that gambling tends to decline during depressions, but rises during periods of war.[33]

Estimates have been made of the comparative strength of certain forms of gambling and the amounts which each type contributes to the total of profits each year. Horse-racing, for example, springs up only when controlled betting and gambling are legalized. Horse-racing tracks close just as soon as betting is made illegal. *The Daily Racing Form* and the *Morning Telegraph*, well-known racing news and handicap sheets, have a claimed circulation of 1,000,000 copies a day. Taking into account the fact that more than one person has access to each purchased copy, it is estimated that very likely no less than 1,500,000 people bet on horses each day, placing bets to the amount of ten billion dollars each year. It is estimated that the annual bookmakers' profit on these bets is about 2.5 billion dollars a year.

Slot-machines constitute an especially profitable source of revenue to the professional gambling organizations. During 1949, it was estimated that there were about 200,000 such machines in active use in the United States. Conservative appraisals place the amount of profit on each machine per week at about $100 on the average, which indicates a total annual intake of about $1,000,000,000 on all machines in the country. The "*numbers and policy*" *racket*, imported into this country from England about 150 years ago, is a particularly pernicious form of gambling, preying as it does on the marginal and low income groups in our cities. In this form of gambling, the individual bets on sequences of either three,

[33] Mowrer, "Social Crises and Social Disorganization," p. 64.

four, or five numbers drawn by lottery or taken from the chance sequence of figures emerging at the end of the day from the total volume of race track bets, stock exchange, or clearinghouse figures. Even when these enterprises are honestly conducted, which is infrequent, the odds run from 345 to 26,655 to 1 against the bettor. In New York City's Harlem, there are about 175 numbers "drops" (i.e., places where bets may be placed), each one handling from $750 to $4,000 a day, bringing in a total volume of receipts each day of about $500,000. The annual volume of "numbers" bets each year is calculated at $1,000,000,000, about half of which is retained by the operators. *Betting upon sporting events* has become a large business in the United States. This form of gambling is estimated to yield an annual profit of $500,000,000 to its operators.

(11) GAMBLING AND CIVIC CORRUPTION

Gambling could not be successfully maintained without the active assistance of law enforcement officials and the police. This constitutes one of the most corrupt elements in the entire gambling situation. The attitude of the public and its law enforcement agents toward gambling is confused and ambivalent. With the collapse of bootlegging and related malpractices, following the repeal of the prohibition amendment, many of its racketeers have gravitated into the field of organized gambling. The way in which gambling interests become linked with public officials may be seen in the following case-study of Hudson County, New Jersey, the province of the former powerful political boss, Mayor Hague of Jersey City.

A Community Case Study

The powerful Hague machine, which controlled the local politics of the Democratic Party in Hudson County and the state of New Jersey for more than twenty-five years after the First World War, succeeded in organizing and regularizing the practice of professional gambling. In Hudson County, "licenses" were issued to prospective bookmakers, after careful investigation as to solvency and fitness by designated party lieutenants. Such "licenses" not only gave permission for betting operators to carry on their activities, but stipulated the areas within which they could function as well as the locations and rentals of their offices. Landlords who rented their premises for such operations, loyal cohorts of the political machine, received exorbitant rentals fixed by the party bosses, regular percentages of which were returned to the political party. During the heyday of this regime, approximately one thousand "bookies" were permitted to operate on this basis, returning about $1,000,000 annually to the party machine in the form of "kickbacks." The landlords, comprising the "hard core" of the party, were able to swing the county's electorate by approximately 125,000 carefully guarded votes. Because of the strategic position of Hudson County in the electoral system of the state, the Hague machine was frequently able to dominate the political fortunes of the state, and even to play a significant role in national elections.

Similar patterns of civic corruption can be found elsewhere. Senator Homer Fergusson, former circuit judge in Michigan, while heading an official gambling exposé in that state, showed that in the city of Detroit various civic officials were deriving approximately $1,000,000 a year from gambling enterprises. Among others, Judge Fergusson succeeded in indicting the mayor, the county prosecutor, the county sheriff, the police superintendent, ten lesser officials, and over fifty policemen. During the summer of 1950, Senator Estes Kefauver, chairman of a special senate committee investigating gambling and crime, discovered that one-third of the 1948 election campaign expenses of Governor Fuller Warren of Florida, an amount variously estimated from $100,000 to $154,000, was subscribed by William H. Johnston, a well-known race track operator in Chicago and Jacksonville.

(12) GAMBLING: A DILEMMA FOR MODERN SOCIETY

The practice and organization of gambling seems to follow a cycle in many societies. So well entrenched has gambling become as a form of recreation that, as in the case of alcohol, restrictive legislation and other forms of social control are frequently considered an infringement upon personal rights. Yet, the personal and social disorders produced by unrestricted gambling point up clearly the need for control. When controls are universally applied, they are virtually impossible to maintain because of the entrenched character of the practices they seek to eliminate. As a result, legislation and other controls are partially relaxed. The reduction of controls, however, provides an incentive for the opening up of those forms of gambling still proscribed, paving the way for socially irresponsible control by lawless and corrupt elements. This invites further legal control, virtually impossible to enforce, and leading to further corruption, with the result that considerable popular pressure is exerted to legalize all forms of gambling. When this last phase occurs, the dangers that widespread legalized gambling invites threaten the entire social structure, reintroducing the need for partial control. Thus, the cycle begins again.

In final consideration of the problem, there are two aspects to be stressed. (1) The extreme gambler, who neglects family, employment, and other social obligations, constitutes a menace to himself and to society. As a class of "addicts," such individuals merit psychiatric care. (2) In view of the obvious dangers of underworld control, gambling may either (a) be diminished or removed in relation to differential recreational patterns of the social order—a problem involving widespread social modification and reappraisal—or (b) be regulated in keeping with existent "definitions of the normal situation," through the agency of permissive and controlling legislation.

SUMMARY

Drug addiction constitutes a considerably different problem than does alcoholism with respect to causal patterns and physical effects. (1) Until the past century, the prolonged use and dependence upon drugs was not considered a social menace in the contemporary sense. In its lengthy history, dating back at least to the early Sumerian culture, the use of drugs was intimately associated with the cultural patterns of various societies. (2) Drug addiction seems to have declined noticeably since the last century, although fluctuations appear in the secular trend. Recent evidence indicates that drug addiction, unlike alcoholism, may increase during periods of war and depression. Specific analysis, however, indicates that expected wartime increases may not manifest themselves until the postwar period. (3) Contrary to popular opinion, the action of drugs upon the organism may not impair physiological and psychological functioning. Research shows many cases in which addicts of long standing have been able to lead useful and productive lives. The dangers of drug addiction are evidenced in the tormenting sensations that follow upon the withdrawal of drugs from the addict. Because non-medical use of drugs is illicit, the addict often faces difficulties in satisfying his acute need. This situation tends to bring him into contact with unscrupulous and dangerous lawless elements who have access to sources of supply. (4) Statistical studies of drug addicts reveal a preponderance of males over females, in the approximate ratio of 4 to 1—a reversal of the sex distribution existing up until the turn of the present century. An appraisal of statistical factors reveals a high percentage of misdemeanors and felonies among narcotics victims, higher average ages among males, occasional high associated rates of alcoholism, significantly high rates among certain groups. (5) In contrast to the highly generalized theories concerning the causes of drug addiction, such as those of Bingham Dai, Kolb, and others, recent theories, notably that of Lindesmith, suggest that the causes are cultural and psychological, rather than physiological. Significant in the Lindesmith theory is the stress upon the mental association between the cause of distress during withdrawal and the buoyancy attributed to drugs, a matter rooted in the culture rather than the organism. (6) Legislative controls, such as the Harrison Narcotic Act of 1914 and the Jones-Miller Act of 1922, as well as the several state enactments, have emphasized repression through stringent control upon the importation and distribution of drugs, converting a medical problem into a police problem. Effective social policy would consist in the distribution of drugs directly and forthrightly under medical supervision and control, together with the extension of public treatment facilities and post-discharge care.

Gambling is a form of recreation well-rooted in most cultures, modern and primitive, past and present. (7) It emerges as a form of social pathology in the degree to which (a) it dominates the behavior of individuals at the expense of normal obligations and responsibilities, and (b) it encourages control by illicit and anti-social agencies. (8) A sociological examination of gambling indicates that it may be fostered as a general practice in cultures which stress competition, change, and novelty, and which, at the same time, place a high premium upon orderliness and routine. (9) Although gamblers conform to no specific system of classification, certain common characteristics have been noted among gamblers, suggesting the configuration of a social type. Significant in the gambler's personality are the neglect of personal and familial obligations, the dominating functional autonomy of gambling motivations, varying degrees of hypertension and characteristic psychological tension-reducing mechanisms, tendencies towards certain types of offense, and a distinctive code of ethics. (10) The widespread practice of gambling, although illegal in varying degree in the majority of states, results in an estimated $30,000,000,000 annual turnover, yielding an annual profit of $6,000,000,000 to its operators. (11) Particularly insidious is the close association between gambling and the corruption of civic officials on local and state levels. (12) Because of the mingled social acceptance and social disapproval characterizing public attitudes toward gambling, it presents a difficult problem in social control. This lack of clear-cut definition in public attitude manifests itself in the cyclical course of control policy. Social policy in respect to the development of effectively integrated social control may only be accomplished by separating the case of the pathological gambler, the individual requiring special social therapeutic assistance, and the problem of the public's willingness to gamble in respect to recognized alternatives. Such alternatives signify revision of cultural and recreational objectives in respect to latent possibilities in the culture or the frank acknowledgment of the public's willingness to retain selected and controlled forms of gambling in keeping with existent "definitions of the situation" as normal.

CHAPTER NINETEEN

MOBILITY AND THE SOCIAL STRUCTURE

(1) THE CONCEPT OF MOBILITY

SINCE the dawn of human history, mobility has played an important part in the redistribution of human populations and has had, in consequence, effects upon cultural change and transition. These effects have been particularly marked in western Europe since the great age of discovery and exploration of the sixteenth century, and especially since the beginning of the Industrial Revolution. Some students have sought in such movements the key to all social change. Although such one-sided theories are hardly accepted to-day, there can be no doubt but that the powerful forces of mobility, irrespective of the individuated or group basis from which they spring, have played, and will continue to exercise, considerable influence upon the course of cultural development of the entire human race.

To the sociologist, the concept of mobility has proven a fruitful tool in uncovering many of the important sources of social change. Where the concept has created difficulties for the social analyst, it is usually because (1) it has largely been considered in a *generic* sense, i.e., as a broad term covering many different types of movement, and lacking in adequate discrimination of the diverse causal factors in the background; and (2) it is employed without adequate understanding of the different results it may produce within different cultural settings and upon different social levels. With respect to the first criticism, factors promoting mobility may be (a) primarily *geographic or environmental*, as in the case of extreme climatic changes or impoverishment of the soil (for example, the "dust-bowl" areas in the Western wheatlands); (b) they may be *socio-cultural*, resulting from changes in techniques of production, employment, or arising out of racial, political, or religious persecution; or (c) they may be motivated by considerations predominantly of an *individual* character. For a proper understanding of mobility, each one of these separate sets of factors should be considered individually.

As regards the effects of mobility, whether pathological or normative conditions emerge will depend upon such matters as the different types of socio-cultural barriers created, the cultural propinquity or antipathies marking the groups coming into contact, and the resiliency of the contiguous cultural systems in their capacity to bring about effective adjustment, compromise, and accommodation. Further, the degree to which physical movement may strengthen or jeopardize the individual's sense of security will depend upon the mass sanction it receives. For the individual wandering alone, the problems of disorganization may be far more acute than for large masses of individuals who travel as a group and who retain, despite the pressures of hostile and strange environments, a considerable portion of their original cultural standards and outlooks.[1]

(2) HORIZONTAL AND VERTICAL MOBILITY

Attempts have been made by sociologists to distinguish the several aspects of human mobility. In a well-known treatise, Pitirim A. Sorokin draws a distinction between *horizontal* and *vertical* mobility.[2] *Horizontal mobility* refers primarily to sheer physical or spatial movement in which a degree of readjustment may or may not be called for. From one standpoint, theoretically speaking, any type of movement involves at least a minimal degree of physical adaptation. *Vertical mobility*, on the other hand, refers to the necessity of some type of psychological reorientation, usually of a substantial nature. The relationship between these two aspects of human movement may be subtle and complex. Physical movement, for example, may involve virtually no substantial psychological change. Under certain conditions, however, it may necessitate profound revision of the personality and its standards. The distance covered in the movement, whether great or small, may be of little consequence as far as the resultant psychological effects are concerned. American tourists travelling in Europe may be almost entirely untouched by their new surroundings, despite the length of time they spend there. To the extent that these and similar cultural practices exist, we have evidence of a type of physical mobility existing quite apart from psychological mobility. Other examples of mobility without psychological re-orientation may be seen in the movement of Bedouins. These people travel over considerable areas, carrying their culture with them as they do their chattels and household paraphernalia. They live forever within a familiar environment and experience no need for psychological re-orientation despite the great distances they traverse.

Conversely, there may be movement over very little physical distance but incurring, nevertheless, extreme changes in psychological adaptation. Sudden advancement in one's economic status or changes in cultural milieu may bring about enormous demands upon the personality. In New

[1] See, for example, Margaret M. Wood, *The Stranger* (New York, 1934).
[2] *Social Mobility* (New York, 1927).

York City, the movement of one's residence from Third Avenue to Park Avenue may involve a distance of but two city blocks, but the psychological distance in such a transition may be comparable to the distance between distant countries. Moving from one side of the railroad tracks to another in a smaller community may involve an equivalent transition.

In American life, as Paul H. Landis has shown, horizontal and vertical types of mobility tend to become intimately associated under the influence of the economic opportunity and challenge that exist in this country.[3] In fact, one of the predominant influences responsible for the modification of American culture has been the result of changing status brought about by the pursuit of new economic and social opportunities. Our moving frontier in the past and our expanding economy today have impelled masses of Americans to move, and this movement in turn has created the need for constant re-adaptation. Very likely, a considerable amount of the personal and social tension experienced in American life may be attributed to this omnipresent drive toward mobility. The conditions of *social marginality* and cultural hybridism, to be discussed below, are also an effect of mobility. The degree to which mobility has produced the peculiarly American types of cosmopolitanism, secularism, casual disregard of established standards, and readiness to change, still remains to be explored.

(3) CLASS MOBILITY

In an established society, the problems associated with mobility are likely to be provoked by class barriers and the other restrictions to mobility. In their extreme form, in caste societies, the barriers may be so rigid as to prevent any kind of movement. Within common caste groupings or within relatively open-class systems, however, mobility of various types will emerge, and may even be encouraged within limits, depending on the predominant cultural values of the society. Recently, Professor W. L. Warner and his associates have shown how this mode of mobility operates within American culture.[4] According to Warner *et al.*, those principal instrumentalities in American culture for achieving vertical mobility depend upon "the use of money, education, occupation, talent, skill, philanthropy, sex, and marriage." Of these, the most important, according to the same writers, are money and skill, in conjunction with personal attractiveness, or the various combinations of these three characteristics. To win accept-

[3] Paul H. Landis, "Forces Promoting Mobility in our Modern Society," *The Transient*, V (July, 1938).

[4] W. L. Warner, M. Meeker, and K. Eells, *Social Class in America* (Science Research Associates, Chicago, 1949).

ance in upper class groups, the approval of primary, or intimate face-to-face groups must be obtained.

Certain primary requisites must be satisfied in any society if the individual is to succeed in identifying himself with the group into which he is moving. Davis and the Gardners have pointed out the instrumental role of "the clique" in relation to this function in American life.[5] The "clique," which is a highly personalized and intimate primary group, provides the incoming member, through its informal "initiatory" rites, with the powerful suggestible key-words, attitudes, and behavior mechanisms which equip him for acceptance. This may be the basis for the powerful urges toward "consciousness of kind" which the early century American sociologist Franklin H. Giddings regarded as the basis for acceptance and rejection by the group.

In such forms of mobility, the individual is in the process of either establishing or maintaining a status position. Status positions involve the operation of several appropriate role-behaviors. For the mobile individual, a certain degree of role-conflict is inevitable, although it may be largely modified by virtue of early identification mechanisms. In the case of downward movement, the problems of role-conflict may be acute. Individuals entering lower statuses may experience embarrassment as a result of the loss of status; at the same time, they may express attitudes of superiority toward those in the group of lower status with whom they are compelled to associate. Those who move upward may feel considerable anxiety as a result of their uncertainty about their new position, while experiencing annoyance and guilt toward their former associates.[6]

Newcomb has indicated the nature of the psychological barriers which class-groups establish to hinder free mobility. Rendering such groups impermeable are what he refers to as the "passwords," or the manifested forms of behavior that facilitate recognition, understanding, and acceptance.[7] Further, once class norms are well established, a circular process of strengthening barriers becomes evident in the decline of communication between groups. Norms of behavior with which the individual identifies himself closely make it difficult for outsiders to bridge the gap of class or group differences. The result is a further tightening of group or class distinctiveness. This is frequently manifested in the hostile attitudes of residents from different sides of the railroad tracks, who regard each other as "snobs" and "stuffed shirts," on the one hand, and as "nobodies," "poor white trash," and "ne'er-do-wells" on the other.

[5] A. Davis, B. B. and M. R. Gardner, *Deep South: A Social and Anthropological Study of Caste and Class* (Chicago, 1941). The use of the "clique" as an agency for investigating class structure and its characteristics in American life is becoming frequent.

[6] The author has touched upon this phase of the problem in his *The Concept of Changing Loyalties* (New York, 1934), pp. 58–60.

[7] Cf. Theodore M. Newcomb, *Social Psychology* (New York, 1950), p. 566.

(4) MOBILITY AND MIGRATION

A distinction must be drawn between the concepts of *mobility* and *migration*. Although they bear certain similarities, these movements are different in form and in their characteristic social effects. (1) Mobility refers to a continual process of movement, characteristic of the traditional hobo or gypsy, while migration suggests a single movement in space from one area to another. (2) When we refer to mobility, we usually mean the movement of individuals who proceed as individual agents without much regard for the movements of others, although they are subject to the same environmental forces or patterns of motivation. Migration, on the other hand, suggests a mass movement or movements, usually at a single time in history, with a specific purpose and frequently, a *fixed destination* in mind. Thus, such diverse movements as the trek of the Mormons across the great plains of the United States to their final place of settlement in Utah, or the pioneer settling of our Western frontier, or the mass migration of Southern and Central Europeans to this country in successive waves of immigration during the latter part of the nineteenth century, might all be considered as instances of migration. (3) Finally, mobility may be contrasted with migration from the perspective of the types of adjustments involved. Mobility may be conceived of as necessitating a series of continual adjustments, or at any rate, a style of life that is congenial to perpetual movement or mobility, while migration involves rarely more than one move, whose end is a new permanent settlement.

The perennial wanderer, tramp, hobo, gypsy, or even travelling salesman, despite his capacity to become inured to the presence of novel surroundings, may, in varying degree and upon different occasions, be confronted with the problem of continual re-adjustment. For the migratory individual or group, however, the problem of re-adjustment is usually single and of a major character. The immigrant from Europe to the United States, for example, has to contend with a new physical and cultural environment, calling upon his various capacities of adjustment. Although for the rest of his life certain minor adjustments will have to be made as a result of his migration, the problem is essentially one of a *single major adjustment* necessitated by the conditions of a novel cultural situation.

Just as these various kinds of movement involve different adjustment procedures, the problems that emerge are quite different. Marginality, or the lack of integration with any specific social group, frequently appears as a consequence of the process of mobility. The marginal person is frequently an individual without firm roots anywhere—in the popular sense, an individual "without cause, home, or country." Migration, on the other hand, brings about the problems of culture conflict and *cultural hybridism*. The cultural hybrid resulting from this process is an individual who finds himself forced to reconcile within his personality the demands of two or more different cultures. Actuated by the powerful motives of his own culture and bound by conscious and unconscious loyalties to this culture, he must nevertheless accept and participate in the forms of the predominant culture about him. The degree to which he is accepted and the degree to which he strives to become part of this dominant culture indicate the nature and severity of the problem he faces. The situation of hyphenated Americans in the past, the Italian-, German-, Scandinavian-, and Polish-American, and the more acute problem to-day of the Jewish-American and the Negro-American, indicate the types of difficulties that culturally hybrid groups have to face.

(5) INDEXES OF MOBILITY

The extent and character of mobility always afford an index of the degree and nature of socio-cultural change and transition. Societies that encourage free movement and mobility are themselves characterized by speedy change and transition, and, frequently, are marked by strains and tensions in various parts of the social structure. Mobility may manifest itself in certain types of pathological symptoms. Highly mobile peoples are continuously confronted with the problems of cultural absorption, re-adaptation, and integration.

It is possible to discover various kinds of indexes that would reveal the degree of mobility of a given culture. Such indexes of mobility would not necessarily be based solely on the physical movement of persons. Although the development of improved methods of transportation and communication have heightened the degree of cultural contact and conflict, we must recognize that *any* agency of communication may work to produce the same results. Thus, the modern press, radio, telegraph, telephone, and television, for example, must likewise be considered as extremely significant factors in the process of mobility. In the modern world, it is not always necessary for individuals to move physically in order to incur the consequences of mobility. The development of such an efficient modern technical process of communication as the moving pictures, for example, may play an instrumental role in the disorganizing or integrating phases of personality or cultural development which, in the past, were associated primarily with the processes of physical movement.

During the course of human history, the prelude to vast cultural reorganization and integration has invariably been signalized by the increase of mobility. No culture or cultural group can remain in its original form when confronted with the necessity of dealing with new ideas and cultural standards. The process that anthropologists, through the insights of

F. Boas, A. L. Kroeber, C. Wissler, and others, name *cultural diffusion*, the recognition that new ideas spread and develop in accordance with certain principles, may be advanced only through the agency of some form of mobility.[8]

Societies strategically located at geographical "crossroads," or cultures with ready access to routes of communication that encourage trade and commerce, have always been highly mobile because they are forced to deal with the emergent by-products of cultural assimilation and integration. Studies of many ancient cultures reveal this fact. In ancient Egypt, one of the salient reasons for the periodic social upheavals was the readiness of travel afforded by the natural highway of the Nile River and other trade routes. The insularity and cultural integrity of a society may not be preserved when ready access is afforded to ideas and cultural standards from without. At some stage in the process of diffusion, the individual, through the mechanisms of identification and adjustment, is compelled to absorb certain phases of cultures. This process undermines the integrity of his own outlook, and frequently invites the development of cosmopolitan and secular views. Cultural sophistication, in this sense, indicates the lapse of one's own cultural standards, and the substitution of a comparative, shifting standard of values. This type of development occurs not only as a result of contacts between alien cultures, but also as a result of contacts between different groups within the same culture. The effects which urban regions exert on rural regions in our own society are an instance of "intra-cultural" diffusion.

It is possible to devise mobility indexes on the basis of (a) measurable determinants of physical movement, and (b) the development of local and national media of communication. In connection with (a), various statistical measures have been employed to indicate per capita increase and decrease in railroad travel and the use of other public carriers, changing land values (as sensitive barometers of population movement and density), the number of state lines crossed by given groups of individuals within a stipulated period of time, and the number of changes of residence. According to a Twentieth Century Fund survey, United States railroads attained a peak operation of 98,000,000,000 passenger-miles during the height of the Second World War, as contrasted with the prewar peak of 47,000,000,000 passenger-miles in 1920.[9]

The increase in motor vehicular transportation may be seen in the fact that nearly nine out of ten passenger-miles of travel outside of cities are accomplished by automobile—despite the vast increase in railroad travel. Motor vehicles in the United States accounted for about 650,000,000,000 passenger-miles of travel in 1948—an average of about 5,000

[8] Cf. A. L. Kroeber, *Anthropology* (New York, 1923), pp. 213 ff.
[9] *Newsbriefs* (Twentieth Century Fund, No. 12, May, 1950).

miles for every individual in the nation. On the basis of the average mileage covered by each car, it is computed that the average driver spends about 500 hours a year in motoring, or about one and a half hours daily.[10] Furthermore, a survey during the summer of 1948 indicated that over 68 per cent of American families owned one or more passenger cars—28,700,000 families owning 30,100,000 cars. By the end of 1948, the United States had 33,300,000 passenger cars in use, with a sharp rise in the number of families owning more than one car.[11]

Rates of mobility, despite a rise in the secular trend, undergo periodic fluctuations. Depressions, for example, impelling individuals to seek employment, frequently bring about sharp rises in human movement, although such increases are not revealed through the figures released by public carriers. Thus, the Twentieth Century Fund survey previously cited reveals that United States railroads carried fewer passengers in 1933 than during 1895, while surveys of specific mobile groups indicate conspicuous rises in mobility. John Webb, in a study of 500 migratory-casual workers for the years 1933 and 1934, has shown that approximately two-thirds crossed one or more state lines, while about one-fourth crossed at least six state lines during the period studied. During each of the two years covered by the survey, 11 to 15 per cent crossed eleven to twenty-five state borders.[12]

Changes of residence are equally significant in reflecting the mobility pattern of selected groups and districts. Zorbaugh, in a study of a well-known rooming house area in Chicago prior to the depression of 1929, stated that the "whole population turns over every four months." [13] A study of a similar area in the middle Manhattan district of New York City west of Central Park has revealed monthly turnovers in various dwellings of 100 to 300 per cent during 1933 and 1934. Sutherland and Woodward have shown that within one Chicago neighborhood 96 of 205 upper grade children had had two or three residences, while 101 had lived in four to nine different homes.[14]

Some total perspective upon migration and mobility in the United States can be gained from data on large-scale movements over a period of time, as recorded and reported by the Bureau of the Census. During the period of 1920–9, the Census Bureau has estimated a total movement of approximately 32,000,000 people in various regional and rural-

[10] *Automobile Facts* (Automobile Association of America, January, 1949).

[11] Ibid.

[12] John N. Webb, *The Migratory-Casual Worker* (Works Progress Administration, Research Monograph VII, Washington, 1937), Chap. II.

[13] Harvey W. Zorbaugh, *The Gold Coast and the Slum* (Chicago, 1929), p. 71.

[14] R. L. Sutherland and J. L. Woodward, *Introductory Sociology* (New York, 1940), citing from M. W. Roper, *The City and the Primary Group* (Ph.D. Thesis, University of Chicago, 1935), p. 35.

urban migrations. During the war years, other than the unprecedented movement of troops and military personnel, rates of travel to and from the large industrial centers, particularly the twelve leading cities of the country, attained proportions never before equalled in our history. Further indications of mobility-migration patterns may be seen in the 3 per cent drop in the number of farm families from 1940 to 1947. Nearly 2,500,000 families left the farm areas during this seven year period. "In April, 1947, only about 17 per cent of the nation's households were on rural farms, whereas in 1940 there were 20 per cent and in 1930, at least 22 per cent," according to a report issued by J. C. Capt, director of the census in February, 1948.

International rates of mobility, accelerated by the recent war, also indicate significantly rising trends. Before the Normandy invasion, the Civil Affairs Branch of the Army estimated that there were from 12,000,000 to 15,000,000 displaced persons and refugees in central Europe. The scope of this movement may be judged from the figures on repatriation. In 1946, during a four-week period, nearly 100,000 displaced persons, principally French, were removed from the area of Linz in Austria, by plane, railroad, and trucks. In the vicinity of Kaufbeuren, Germany, during the summer of the same year, nearly 20,000 Russians were repatriated within one week's time. The problem of war refugees in Pakistan, India, Israel, Korea and elsewhere represents an intensification of the seething ferment of movement and mobility accentuated by the recent war.

The communication of ideas, images, and symbols has played an important role in the development of mobility. In an analysis of publication trends in the United States between 1920 and 1940 made by the author, it was shown that the average total percentage increase of all books published during this period attained the impressively high figure of 46.73 per cent.[15] In the study of 23 different categories of books published, it was found that every one showed a sizable absolute increase, and only one category indicated a relative percentage decrease.[16] In keeping with this mass exposure to new ideas, we have corresponding increases in the use of the telephone, radio, and, more recently, the phenomenal increase in television. The remarkable rise in telephonic communication points up this general increase. A Twentieth Century Fund study shows that in 1907 there were 6,100,000 telephone instruments in the United States; by 1917, the number was 11,700,000; in 1929, 19,300,000; in 1940, 20,800,000; and in 1944, 26,400,000. By the end of 1949, more than 40,000,000 telephones were reported to be in use.[17]

[15] H. A. Bloch, "An Analysis of National Publication Trends and Publishers' Best Sellers as an Index of Cultural Transition," *The Journal of Educational Sociology*, XXII (Dec., 1948), 290.

[16] Ibid., p. 296.

[17] *Newsbriefs* (Twentieth Century Fund, No. 12, May, 1950).

It is possible to develop composite indexes of mobility, utilizing in weighted forms the several discrete indexes that have been mentioned. These composite indexes may then be related to regional, age, and group differences, in order to determine the character and types of problems that emerge in respect to patterns of mobility.

(6) MOBILITY AND DISORGANIZATION

The process of individual and social breakdown induced by mobility has already been suggested. Howard Becker, in his discussion of the "sacred" and the "secular" types of society, has shown how some types of isolation tend to reinforce the basic forms of social control.[18] Modern forms of communication and mobility tend to foster the secular type of society. Disorganization follows on mobility in the degree to which the individual is unable to adapt himself to new conditions, ideas, and social values, on the basis of his former cultural conditioning. Since complete identification with earlier standards is hardly possible in our culture, effective compromises must be worked out which will permit each individual a degree of freedom to adhere himself to new standards. The psychological mechanism involved in this process is that of *introjection,* i.e., the process of identifying one's self with the attitudes and standards of these individuals who have contributed intimately to the early socialization and development of the personality. *Adjustment for the mobile individual or group, therefore, will be successful in the degree to which such mechanisms as introjection may be effectively employed within novel settings, and in the degree to which elements in the novel social structure reinforce or contradict basic attitudinal components and behavior tendencies within the personality.* Marginality may exist as a matter of degree, therefore, ranging from a bare minimal state in which the individual wins relatively wide acceptance to strong factors of exclusiveness which rigorously restrict the individual's capacity of adjustment within a cultural group or area.

States of marginality and disorganization manifest themselves upon distinctive social levels. Within American life, such areas of tension are commonly found in the following forms. (1) *Economic conflict* of various types is frequently brought about by the entrance of new competitive groups into an area. Mobility will produce conflict in such situations only when the incoming groups actually constitute, or are thought to constitute, a competitive threat to certain entrenched groups resident in the area. The degree of the conflict depends upon several factors: whether marked cultural differences are present, whether the incoming groups are

[18] Cf. Harry Elmer Barnes and Howard Becker, *Social Thought from Lore to Science* (New York, 1938), Vol. I, Chap. 1.

supported by dominant economic groups, the extent of the group, and the like. Violent reaction to the importation of Negro labor introduced in the large northern industrial centers at the time of the First World War was widespread among white workers, who became fearful for their jobs and the loss of their living standards. More subtle is the opposition expressed in this country and Europe against the influx of Jewish professionals (lawyers, physicians, etc.).[19]

(2) Mobility and migration, though principally the latter, frequently bring about specific forms of *cultural conflict*. This antagonism usually reflects the predominant cultural characteristics and values of the entering culture. Hence, in accordance with the principal cultural values stressed, the characteristic forms of struggle may revolve about religious issues, political differences, educational standards, recreational practices, or combinations of these. Distinctive dress or physical appearance frequently assists in throwing these differences into sharper focus. Cultural antipathy is strengthened in the degree to which there is inadequate communication and common foci of cultural interest between the contending cultural groups. Struggle may be further heightened if unstable elements existed in the dominant culture before the new group was introduced into its midst. Unstable and disorganized social groups are particularly susceptible to culture conflict.

A closely related phase of the problem of cultural conflict induced by migration is the problem of the second-generation child born within a world of two different cultures. Conflict is produced not only in relations with the dominating culture; it is also precipitated within the family circle itself in the form of sharp struggle between the different generations. The conflict of generations frequently carries with it another problem, that of intermarriage.

(3) Another type of conflict is brought about by rural-urban movement. The "flight to the city" has constituted a continuous process during the entire first half of this century. Only briefly, during the early part of the depression of the thirties, was there a slight reverse in this movement. The drop of 5 per cent since 1930 in the number of families in rural areas represents only one phase of the now continuous movement of young people who leave the rural homestead for superior economic and social opportunities elsewhere. It is characteristic of these young people to settle in the rooming-house areas of the cities to which they migrate, thus increasing the problems of their adjustment to a new environment. On a larger scale, the extent of the movement of rural and small-town families to larger industrial centers has steadily increased since 1910. The recent war has brought this movement to an unusually high level. The difficulty of adjusting to completely different surroundings, new methods

[19] Cf. Carey McWilliams, *Mask for Privilege* (New York, 1948).

of work, different living quarters, and the lack of intimate primary controls have all contributed to the development of problems among many such families. The degree to which such movements have contributed to the larger problems of pathological disorder has been demonstrated. However, there is little conclusive information about the effects of these factors on the development of national trends.

The effects of excessive mobility on personality characteristics have not been fully determined. Contrary to Elliott and Merrill's pronouncement that "all types of mental diseases result from this increased strain" there seems to be little basis for the belief that extreme mobility necessarily contributes to mental disorders, or even to acute mental strain.[20] This would depend almost wholly upon the character of the mobility, the type of personality involved, and the critical elements involved in the mobile process. Travelling salesmen may be highly mobile individuals; yet they may hardly be called disorganized personalities. Migratory workers may travel from coast to coast in a single year and yet give no evidence of mental strain.

Mobile individuals, like all other groups who live in special environments, tend to develop certain common characteristics, and these common characteristics frequently contribute to their sense of cultural normalcy. To discover the effects of mobility upon the personality would require careful study of the effects of different kinds of mobile patterns on different kinds of personalities. Thus far, such a study has not been carried out. If any general characteristic seems to emerge from an observation of mobility, it is a peculiar type of impersonality, largely developed because of the individual's incapacity to identify himself with any community and with the normal demands of family life. This impersonality, a growing characteristic of secondary and urban societies, appears among many mobile individuals. Yet it is often dissipated in the social contacts engendered by the mobile individual's own groups.[21]

(7) MIGRATORY INDIVIDUALS AND FAMILIES

Among its principal expressions, mobility manifests itself in the form of migratory individuals and families. The problem of mobility has changed considerably since the depression of 1929. During the pre-de-

[20] Mabel A. Elliott and Francis E. Merrill, *Social Disorganization* (New York, 1941), p. 305.

[21] Although mental strain may be fostered when an individual is confronted with a number of alternative choices, as in the case of Krasnagorski's famous experiments with previously conditioned and trained dogs, the analogy does *not* hold in the case of mobile individuals. Cf. Elliott and Merrill, *Social Disorganization* (New York, 1941), p. 305. Such individuals do not necessarily confront a number of equivalent choices at any given time, but are simply concerned with making a relatively simple adjustment in any environment in which they happen to find themselves.

pression era, the problem was associated primarily with the traditional seasonal worker, the hobo, and the tramp. The number of itinerant women who travelled from place to place was relatively small, and the migratory family, although not unknown, did not figure largely in the character of the mobility problem during this period. "Rickety Bill," the prototype of the classical migratory worker described by Nels Anderson, has largely disappeared in the face of the large and continuous movements of modern transients and their families.[22] Webb, in 1935, estimated that less than 10 per cent of present mobile and unattached persons could be classified as itinerant workers and hobo migrants of the predepression type.[23] Studies of contemporary homeless and unattached groups reveal these differences with respect to age groupings, intelligence, psychological factors, schooling, occupational training, marital status, and sex distribution.

(8) NUMBERS OF TRANSIENTS AND MIGRATORY INDIVIDUALS

During the brief period of operation of the Federal Transient Relief Program (1933 to 1936), it was estimated that the maximum size of the transient population was 200,000 unattached persons and 50,000 family groups. Because of the mobility of such groups, however, it is virtually impossible to arrive at an accurate estimate. In the decade prior to 1929, the author estimated that there were no less than 1,500,000 individuals travelling from one state to another during any given year in pursuit of employment. Webb has concluded that approximately 2,000,000 workers crossed state lines in the average year in order to look for work. His estimate did not include the number of non-working family members accompanying such individuals, which would make the total number of migrant individuals considerably larger. Anderson, in 1940, estimated that there were perhaps 1,000,000 people on the move, adding, however, that it may not be possible to classify all of these individuals as genuine migratory workers or transients.[24]

(9) MOBILITY AND VAGRANCY

Mobility in itself is neither a legal offense nor necessarily a breach of normal social behavior. In fact, because of the seasonal demands of industry and pressures upon individuals to find employment, it has fre-

[22] Cf. Nels Anderson, *Men on the Move* (Chicago, 1940), Chap. 1, "The Hobo Is No More." Anderson contrasts the new type of migrant with the classical figure he described in his earlier book on hobos and migratory workers, *The Hobo: The Sociology of the Homeless Man* (Chicago, 1923).

[23] John N. Webb, *The Transient Unemployed* (Works Progress Administration, Washington, Research Monograph No. III, 1935).

[24] Nels Anderson, *Men on the Move*, pp. 64–5.

quently been held to be desirable. However, as Webb has put it: "There is a popular habit of calling persons 'workers' when they are needed to harvest a ripened crop, and of referring to them as 'bums' during the slack season that follows." [25] Mobility is socially transmuted into vagrancy, a legal offense, when the individual can be shown to have no legal residence and no visible means of support. The history of vagrancy laws in Anglo-Saxon culture dates back to the famous Statute of Laborers of 1349 in England, and has been widely employed in modern communities as a means of exercising police surveillance over a range of diverse individuals whom the community regards as undesirable. In American usage, the term *vagrant* has been variously applied to beggars, strangers, individuals who appear "suspicious," prostitutes, drunkards, drug addicts, petty thieves, disorderly individuals, and many others who offend the proprieties of the community.

The category of "vagrant," thus, has served as a convenient catch-all for apprehending those individuals whom the community has occasion to fear and desire to be rid of. The antecedents for this socio-legal attitude stem from the fear of the local community for the stranger who may either become an economic burden or who, since he lacks "visible means of support," may be predisposed to predatory acts. The large mass of such itinerant individuals are law-abiding persons; yet they are commonly expelled from communities under the threat of arrest. The policy, well-defined, is to confront the individual with the choice of being arrested for vagrancy or of leaving immediately.

The F.B.I. fingerprint records reveal annually that relatively high percentages of persons are arrested for vagrancy or offenses of a similar character. In 1948, out of a total of 759,698 arrests, 49,423 (6.5 per cent) were for vagrancy, and an additional 45,135 (6.0 per cent) were on grounds of suspicion, a police charge which may be considered closely akin to vagrancy.[26] It is difficult to estimate from these records the numbers who were bona fide transients, since the charge of vagrancy may include specific acts of disorder and unspecified numbers of local unattached residents. Vagrancy, as a police charge, and transiency should *not* be regarded as the same. That a certain number of transients contribute each year to the percentage apprehended for vagrancy, there can be no doubt. However, the great bulk of transients are law-abiding individuals, most of whom are genuinely in pursuit of employment. The migratory and transient individual, particularly in the smaller community, affords a ready target for the police, however.

We are confronted with the conclusion that, exclusive of the bulk

[25] John N. Webb, *The Migratory-Casual Worker*, p. 2.

[26] *Uniform Crime Reports for the United States and its Possessions* (Department of Justice, Washington, XIX, 1949), 114.

of the migratory group, there are a number of recidivists and petty offenders who are charged with vagrancy, and that perhaps a continual, relatively small percentage of migratory individuals emerge periodically as vagrants, or are charged with related offenses. June Guild, in attempting to discover the characteristic types of offenses of such individuals, examined 858 transient males handled by the Travellers' Aid Society of Richmond, Virginia, in 1938.[27] Approximately 56 per cent of this group had previous records on file with the F.B.I., amounting to a total of 1,925 offenses. Of these, the principal offenses were, in order of frequency: drunkenness and liquor violations (589), larceny (228), suspicion (200), vagrancy (194), burglary and housebreaking (95), railroad trespassing (68), trespassing (60), assault (59), passing false checks (45), with begging (28) ranking eleven and a half in the order given. This particular group seems to include a high percentage of the older type of migratory non-worker or occasional worker, petty malefactors and pilferers who were recognized in the pre-depression classification of migratory men as "tramps."

(10) TYPES OF HOMELESS MEN

Pre-depression classifications of homeless men resembled the classification originally described by Nels Anderson. Those who are familiar with the problem of migratory workers and homeless men have recognized that such broad classifications were descriptive and loose. Anderson, too, recognized this. Although there was a basis in the past and, to a lesser extent, in the present, for the earlier system of classification, it lacks validity today.

Anderson's original classification, which he has now disavowed, included: (1) *seasonal workers*, or those who followed the seasonal demand for workers in the harvest fields, lumbering, mining, and the fishing industries; (2) the *hobos*, or migratory occasional workers; (3) the *tramps*, or migratory part-time workers or non-workers; (4) the *home-guards*, or stationary part-time workers; and (5) the *bums*, or stationary non-workers, mendicants, or persons living on public bounty.[28] Distinctions between the categories were not always clear-cut. Many of the homeless possessed characteristics of the other categories, or fell into different categories at different stages of their careers. Particularly difficult was the separation of the first two categories, many of the so-called hobos regarding themselves as bona fide seasonal workers. It was possible, in several cases, to witness the gradual deterioration of an individual over a period of years from a genuine migratory or part-time worker to the lowest rung of the ladder, the "mission stiff" or bum.

[27] "Transients in a New Guise," *Social Forces*, XVII (March, 1939), 368–369.
[28] Anderson, *The Hobo*, Chap. 1.

As long as seasonal work exists, the demand will continue for migratory workers who, in many respects, will continue to resemble their earlier forbears. However, the war and the depression years have altered the character and types of unattached individuals and migrants. The increased post-depression and war-time industrialization and calls for manpower have brought forth a migrant group who travel with hopes of permanent residence and with fixed destinations in mind. Anderson describes this new migrant pattern as follows: "They are migrating to reach a destination where they hope to settle. The hobo migrant of last generation accepted migrancy as a phase of his life-program. But whether we turn our attention to the migrants of the old style or the new, the relocation of the population has been a normal function of American life. Migrancy has ever been and will continue to be a balancer of opportunity between areas." [29] Modern transients, thus, appear to fall into two principal categories, (a) the unattached families, and (b) the unattached individuals. Unattached individuals are largely of the *homeless type* (although resident in a given area) or of the *migratory type*, and as such, may be roughly classified into the original typology of seasonal worker, hobo, home guard, and bum.[30]

There is some difficulty encountered in composing such classifications because of the fact that for some individuals the problems of homelessness and transiency are chronic and acute, while for others they are simply temporary and sporadic. The depression period swelled the ranks of the temporarily homeless, and, while some may never have been able to extricate themselves from their plight, the larger bulk eventually re-emerged with fixed residence and respectable vocational status. The Central Registration Bureau for the Homeless, organized in New York City during 1933 and 1934, registered almost 10,000 homeless during the first three months of its operation. Although the original applicants at this agency were the habitual derelicts of the metropolitan district and adjacent areas, there was a steady increase, after the first six weeks of operation in the number of unskilled workers with legal residence in the city outside of the Hobohemian district. There were, too, mounting percentages of applications from skilled and professional workers of respectable standing. For these latter groups, descent into homelessness was a bitter thing to take, even though it was but a temporary condition.

(11) CHARACTERISTICS OF HOMELESS INDIVIDUALS

In making any statistical appraisal of homeless groups, it must be remembered that they are highly inconstant in composition. Sharp dis-

[29] Anderson, *Men on the Move*, p. 5.
[30] Cf. Anderson, ibid., p. 32.

tinctions must be drawn between the habitually homeless and the genuine workers, casual and otherwise, who may find themselves temporarily classified in such transient populations. Statistical studies reveal differences in the composition of homeless groups in relation to (a) the number of bona fide workers—professional, skilled, or unskilled—who are temporarily found in them and (b) their regional and periodic emergence during periods of economic stress. Among the chief values of such investigations is the light they shed on basic disturbances in the socio-economic structure.

During the periods of chronic under-employment in the pre-depression era, when fluctuations in the business cycle were considered an inevitable and unavoidable aspect of social life, the transient groups were marked by certain persistent characteristics. The statistical profile of transient groups revealed the fact that they were predominantly male, youthful, unskilled or semi-skilled, unmarried, with little schooling, and contained a relatively high percentage of individuals suffering from physical or mental defects, or both. The degree of psychopathological elements and physical defects found present in these earlier studies was due, to a considerable extent, to the fact that the groups investigated were composed of individuals of more advanced ages. This is well demonstrated in one of the few sound original studies, the investigation by Alice W. Solenberger of 1,000 homeless transients in the Chicago Loop area.[31]

Sex distribution. Although the numbers of transient, migratory, and homeless women have increased since the time of the depression and the recent opening of opportunities for women to enter war industries, the bulk of transient individuals is still male. John N. Webb, in his survey of the transient populations during 1934–5 registered with the Federal Transient Service Bureaus in thirteen cities, found that less than 3 per cent were women.[32] This may not, however, be an accurate representation of the numbers of women taking to transiency. Women ordinarily shun the stigma and unpleasantness of seeking assistance at public shelters. Thus, a great number of women whom we would define as transients were not accounted for in this survey. Nevertheless, the percentages of women who are found without residential ties, although growing, will remain considerably less than the percentages of men. This is due to the closer cultural ties of women to home and local communities, the difficulties of travel, their lack of a tradition of mobility, and similar factors, which diminish the cultural and individual incentives to mobility. On the other hand, because of the extensive coverage of the charge of vagrancy in our culture, the numbers of women apprehended for vagrancy are quite higher in rela-

[31] Alice W. Solenberger, *One Thousand Homeless Men* (New York, 1911).

[32] Webb, *The Transient Unemployed* (Works Progress Administration, Washington, Research Monograph No. III, 1935), p. 32.

tion to the sex ratios of other categories of crime. The 1947 F.B.I. fingerprint records indicate a male to female ratio of 5 to 1, with 8 to 1 the ratio for the closely corresponding category of suspicion.[33] These may be compared with the male-female ratio for crimes of all sort, namely, 9 to 1.

Age status. The mobile group, aside from the special category of heads of families, is still primarily a youthful group. In conformity with the earlier Anderson study and other investigations, the age distribution shows a decided concentration within the categories below thirty-five years of age. In Webb's analysis, for example, the age classifications below twenty-five years show high concentrations of 37 to 42 per cent, while the older categories of forty-four years and above reveal significantly smaller percentages, 12 to 16 per cent. The charge of vagrancy, however, appears to fall on both the younger *and* the older age groups, for obvious reasons. The older derelict and transient, disorganized and demoralized by a life of vagabondage, is frequently picked up on charges of drunkenness, disorderly conduct, or begging. F.B.I. arrest data for 1948 indicate that 33.1 per cent of the arrests for vagrancy were of young men below the age of twenty-five, as contrasted with the total arrest record of this group, for all crimes, of 31.8 per cent. For the groups over thirty-nine years of age, 29.4 per cent of arrests were for vagrancy, as contrasted with a total arrest record of 27.0 per cent for the same age category.[34]

Employment. Although the pre-depression and early depression analysis revealed overwhelmingly high percentages of unskilled and semi-skilled workers among transients, investigations toward the end of the depression period showed increasingly high proportions of skilled and professional workers. During 1930, the Welfare Council of the City of New York undertook a vast spot-check of approximately 14,000 of the transient population on the Bowery during a period of less than one week. It was discovered that 74.7 per cent were unskilled or semi-skilled workers (the first to lose their jobs during economic crises), 22 per cent were classified as skilled workers, and 3 per cent as clerical, white-collar, or professional workers. Since the end of the recent war, with the continuation of unprecedentedly full employment, those who find themselves temporarily in the transient groups are increasingly likely to be of the employable and skilled categories who find themselves "between jobs," in search of jobs, or temporarily, through some personal crisis, in the ranks of the transient or homeless groups.

Marital status. The traditional migratory individual has been unmarried, or has claimed to be. During the depression years, the numbers of married individuals taking to the road showed a steady increase, although

[33] *Uniform Crime Reports*, XVIII, No. 2 (1947), p. 115.
[34] *Uniform Crime Reports*, XIX, No. 2, p. 117.

the larger number of migrant individuals still claimed to be unmarried.[35] Nevertheless, Webb's investigation in the transient shelters of thirteen cities showed that approximately 80 per cent were single (corresponding fairly closely to New York City Central Registration Bureau figures at about the same time), 10 per cent were widowed or divorced, 6 per cent were married, and 5 per cent were separated but not divorced.[36] Except for migratory families and occasional family heads who are separated from their families, the problem remains one primarily of young, unattached males.

Education. Earlier studies, such as the Solenberger investigation, gave evidence of the low educational level of transient populations studied. Modern investigations have shown that the picture has altered. Transient groups reveal increased proportions of individuals with superior educational advantages. The depression was no respecter of educational or vocational status. The Webb study exposed the fact that among persons in the federal shelter groups who had been studied, 38 per cent had completed one to four years of high school, while approximately 68 per cent had had at least an elementary school education. Improved school standards throughout the country have helped bring about this change.

Psychological factors. Studies of transients and migrants in the past included sizable proportions of unemployable, aged, resident homeless individuals, and pathological derelicts. These studies seemed to suggest a close association between homelessness, transiency, and psychological disabilities. Solenberger, for example, in examining the records of 1,000 homeless men, found 52 suffering from psychotic disabilities, 19 from feeblemindedness, and 17 from epilepsy, making a total of 89 severe mental disorders, or 8.9 per cent of the entire group studied.[37] When she separated from this group 220 genuine migrants from the resident homeless, the proportion of those suffering from some form of mental disorder was significantly less, although a large percentage of this selected group suffered from some type of physical handicap. Then, as now, one of the conclusions to be drawn was that mental disorders may serve as a predisposing factor in unemployment and transiency for selected and relatively small groups of younger men. The relationship between mental disorder and transiency among older men is even greater. The high ratio of mental disorder in this group may in part be attributed to the conditions of permanent transiency and neglect.

[35] In his work with the Central Registration Bureau for the Homeless in New York City during 1933 and 1934, the author found significant changes in the percentages of married and unmarried transients when he altered the original query of a questionnaire from "Are you married?" to "Where are your wife and children?"

[36] Webb, *The Transient Unemployed*, Chap. 1.

[37] Cf. Solenberger, *One Thousand Homeless Men.*

In view of the fact that during any period public shelter populations and groups of unemployed will include older individuals and unemployables, and those whose defects bar them from employment, it is apparent that surveys will indicate relatively high amounts of psychological defectiveness. Sutherland and Locke, in a random sample of 740 shelter residents from among the 20,000 studied, discovered, in applying the older Army Beta Intelligence Test, that only 0.4 per cent were superior, 37.7 per cent average, and 61.9 per cent inferior.[38] On the basis of comparison with army draftees of the First World War, this group was found to be decidedly inferior. Of draftees of the First World War 12.0 per cent were superior, 61.5 per cent average, and 26.5 per cent inferior. However, Sutherland and Locke make it clear that the shelter groups contained a large number of older men and men with serious defects. They showed (1) that average intelligence scores were conspicuously higher for men under forty-five than for those over this age, and (2) that Beta test scores show gradual declines for each ten-year interval in advancing age. Thus, the comparison was to an extent invalidated because of the age differentials between the two groups.

(12) CAUSES OF TRANSIENCY

It will be recalled that, in our previous analysis of leisure-time activity, it was pointed out that within any society leisure is regarded as honorable provided the individual is able to discharge satisfactorily his normal social responsibilities. The indigent and homeless individual, either through some psychological disability or through the nature of environmental circumstance, is unable to comply satisfactorily with the normal cultural demands of self-support and with family and residential identification. Migrancy and transiency are broad social phenomena, the causes for which are linked to specific group and individual differences. Men do not wander nor become homeless for the same reasons. The difficult questions we have to confront in all matters of individual and social causation are (1) why it is that individuals who are *subject to the same environmental pressures* do not react in the same way, and (2) why it is that individuals with the same psychological disabilities do not manifest their difficulties in the same way. For example, not all families and individuals confronted with the "dust bowl" crisis in the Southwest during the twenties and thirties were impelled to migrate, despite the extremity of the circumstances. Similarly, not all individuals suffering from psychotic and neurotic frustrations seek escape from familiar surroundings. The general solution, however, may be found in two broad causal patterns, suggested

[38] E. H. Sutherland and H. Locke, *Twenty Thousand Homeless Men* (Philadelphia, 1936), p. 43.

by previous analysis, *viz.*, (1) many families and individuals have been exposed to migratory environments, which make it relatively easier for migratory habits to develop; and (2) certain pathological individuals may, by a process of metamorphosis, find themselves caught up within a transient mode of life as a result of a series of personal crises.

The general conditions under which these causal processes may take place have been enumerated by Nels Anderson.[39] The broad causal categories he describes are: (1) unemployment and seasonal work, (2) wanderlust, (3) crises in the life of the individual, (4) industrial inadequacy, and (5) personality defects. In his early investigations of migratory men, the author was able to find a considerable number of cases typifying each one of these causal categories.

Certain individuals—one a former bank clerk and another a former practicing physician—had become transients as a result of crises they had encountered. Because of the nature of their psychogenetic constitutions, these crises predisposed them to a series of minor adjustments, which brought them to the life of continuous migrancy and transiency. In the case of one such individual of a seemingly respectable background, there had been no previous record of migratory behavior. However, an examination of the individual's previous life-history indicated critical factors which induced his itinerant behavior. Such extreme cases frequently reflect reluctance to assume responsibility, considerable self-doubt and anxiety (although frequently repressed), and unwillingness to bear the burden of acute personal stress or crisis. Nevertheless, it must be remembered that these are exceptional cases. For most individuals, the road to transiency is a perfectly normal development arising out of their backgrounds of marginal existence.[40]

Sutherland and Locke suggest these causal patterns toward migrancy in their analysis of what they term "roads of dependency." [41] Recognizing the complex interaction of several factors in inducing such a condition, they distinguish between the "long-term" process and the "short-term" process involved. From our standpoint, the long-term road to dependency would correspond to the gradual metamorphoses engendered by a series of personal crises in the life of the individual. Such factors as economic transitions (including marginal dependency or long periods of degeneration), marital and sexual conflicts, alcoholism, physical injuries, illness, cultural conflicts, and familial detachment are considered, in their separate and interactive effects, as strategic landmarks in the route to dependency and homelessness. The second and shorter route follows on pro-

[39] *The Hobo*, Chap. 1.

[40] Cf. *Sister of the Road: The Autobiography of Box-Car Bertha*, as told to Dr. Ben L. Reitman (New York, 1937).

[41] Sutherland and Locke, *Twenty Thousand Homeless Men*, pp. 71–84.

longed exposure to conditions of transiency and dependency or to conditions of sudden and severe personal crisis. It is characteristic of two kinds of individuals, (a) those who, because of past association, find little difference between their former existence in private "flophouses" and the public or municipal lodging houses; and (b) those who, faced with continual economic adversity, find themselves habitual clients for relief.

(13) THE MIGRATORY FAMILY

The migrating family has been a familiar and valuable adjunct of the American scene in the settling of the West and the opening of other new regions. Such families, in the past, have been stable and well-integrated, moving only in the search of better opportunities and in the hope of attaining economic self-sufficiency and independence. The modern migratory family is a comparatively new social phenomenon. They are driven largely by the whiplash of economic necessity. The goal is to find work, not only for the head of the family, but for other members of the family as well. They move from place to place seeking any kind of reasonable employment, with very little prospect of permanent residence. Lacking legal residence and the ordinary security emerging from stable community residence, they constitute a shifting army of virtually disenfranchised individuals and a relatively cheap and unprotected labor market. Prominent factors in the development of this condition have been the growing mechanization of our Western farm areas, the increase and the precarious nature of farm tenancy, the contraction in size and decline of the rural village, natural disasters such as soil impoverishment, the attraction of better paid employment in urban-industrial areas, and the special harvesting needs of perishable and other products. The industrialization of certain fruit-producing belts has made it economically necessary that large numbers of workers be brought immediately to the harvest fields when the ripened fruit is ready for picking.[42] Farm workers' families from distances as great as 2,000 miles have rhythmically been drawn to harvest the large cash crop upon which the entire prosperity of the area depends. Failure of the labor supply, and the consequent delay in the harvesting of the ripe fruits, often means catastrophic financial loss to the owner. Recently, in the Southwest, Mexican labor has been used for this purpose, while in New York State, Puerto Ricans have been flown into the grape regions of the western part of the state.

It is impossible to estimate the numbers of migrating families in the country at any given time. During the later depression years, Webb estimated that there may have been as many as 100,000 such families in the

[42] Cf. Carey McWilliams, *Factories in the Field* (Boston, 1939).

United States, although no more than 50,000 families were found registered at any time in the federal transient camps.[43]

Studies conducted by the Federal Emergency Relief Administration in 1936 revealed that migratory families tended to be relatively small in size, averaging from 3.0 to 3.2 persons per family, as compared with the size of the average relief family of 4.4 persons. The great majority of these families, almost three-fourths, consisted of two to three persons; in very few cases were there as many as six or more members. Striking was the youthful nature of these families, the vast majority of fathers being under forty-five years of age, with almost one-half under thirty-five. Also significant, particularly since it is in direct contrast to the unattached migratory groups, is the high percentage of women in such groups, the sex ratio being about 1 to 1.[44] These families are composed in large part of young married couples coming from a highly precarious and marginal rural background, who apparently lack a chance to sink their roots anywhere. For such groups, the migratory pattern has well-nigh become customary, despite its hardships. Conspicuous is the unavoidable neglect of diet, schooling, and health which the children of such families suffer.

Typical of the situation in many transient labor areas in the Southwest is the description of the wage standards and living conditions of migratory family groups in Arizona in 1937, as described in a special federal report issued in 1939.[45] Despite the fact that the group of 518 families studied experienced very little unemployment in 1937, the average cash income of these families and unattached persons from all pursuits combined amounted to $393, while the average total income amounted to $459. More than one-third of this group earned less than $300 cash during the year. Even today, sudden fluctuations in the need for employment of such workers can produce acute disaster when they are once assembled on the scene, ready for employment, after having travelled a considerable distance. As late as March 9, 1950, local state authorities were forced to rush emergency food supplies to a migratory camp, operated by the Arizona Farm Bureau Federation, where one hundred children were reported starving and living under what were officially described as "Grapes of Wrath" conditions. A sudden freeze spoiled local crops, ruining the chances for employment of the migrating families drawn there for this special harvest. Periodically, even during periods of full employment, situations of this sort occur among groups of migrant families eking out a precarious existence. The report on the condition of these destitute

[43] Webb, *The Transient Unemployed*, Chap. 1.

[44] John N. Webb and Malcolm Brown, *Migrant Families* (Works Progress Administration, Washington, Research Monograph No. XVIII, 1938).

[45] Malcolm Brown and Orin Cassmore, *Migratory Cotton Pickers in Arizona* (Works Progress Administration, Washington, 1939).

families in the vicinity of Phoenix, Arizona, portrayed a rather typical situation. As migrants, most of these families did not qualify for state relief, and local community resources were inadequate for their handling.

Because local fruit growers in such regions cannot afford to be left with a scarcity of labor during the brief period when the cash crop must be picked, the practice has been to "saturate" the area with an oversupply of workers by colorful advertising and recruitment handbills. The result is not only a guarantee of sufficient labor on hand, but an opportunity for beating down wages because of the temporary glut of labor. This practice was remarked in the 1939 report on Arizona migratory workers. There it was stated that "want ads" in widely scattered newspapers were highly effective in procuring labor, covering an enormous population at very little expense. The total cost of the 1937 newspaper advertising for harvest hands, bringing forth an excessive volume of labor on the local scene, was only about $900.[46] Typical of such advertising is the following, appearing in a wide variety of mid-western and southwestern cities during 1937.

> COTTON PICKERS WANTED
>
> 5000 Pickers Wanted near Phoenix and Coolidge, Ariz. Large acreage; Short Staple Cotton will yield 1 to 1½ bales per acre. Growers paying 75¢ hundred. Good Pickers now getting 300 lbs. to 400 lbs. daily. Come soon for several months work. Picking lasts till February. Ideal climate, warm dry, sunshine Fall and Winter days. Houses or Tents provided free. Come to any Ranch, Cotton Gin, or Farm Labor Service, 28 West Jefferson, Phoenix, Arizona.

(14) CONCLUSIONS AND IMPLICATIONS FOR SOCIAL POLICY

Leaving out of consideration the problem of special handling of those individuals whose special psychological and vocational disabilities encourage habits of mobility, the broad social policies required for the handling of other migratory groups depend upon the correction of specific abuses arising from marginal and seasonal labor. As a result of policies initiated during the recent war when manpower shortages were particularly acute, the problem of migratory families and workers, especially in areas such as the Southwest, has been rendered more acute by the importation of foreign labor, principally Mexican. As late as the spring and summer of 1950, several state governments, particularly those of California and Arizona, and the federal government, became alerted to the problem of acute social and economic demoralization of masses of migrant workers during a

[46] Brown and Cassmore, *Migratory Cotton Pickers in Arizona*, p. 69.

period of unprecedented and widespread economic prosperity. This concern came partially as a result of the exposures of shocking conditions in the rich San Joaquin Valley in California and the cotton areas surrounding Phoenix, Arizona. State and federal bodies have been actively studying the problem since 1949. Considerable pressure for the amelioration of these conditions has come from the increasingly powerful National Farm Labor Union, an affiliate of the American Federation of Labor. On June 3, 1950, President Truman appointed a special federal commission to study the social and economic conditions of migratory laborers, with a mandate to consider the following problems: (1) the social, economic, health, and educational conditions of migratory workers in the United States, and the responsibilities presently assumed by local, state, and federal agencies for such special problems; (2) the problems created by the migration into the United States of alien workers for temporary employment; and (3) the extent of illegal immigration for such purposes into the United States. The presidential commission estimates that the scope of the problem may range from 1,000,000 to 5,000,000 migratory workers.

If the problem essentially involves marginal and displaced workers, solution may be sought along the following lines: (1) Early vocational training, particularly in certain fundamental and multiple skills, enabling the individual to participate in various skilled and semi-skilled employments. (2) The provision of diversified employment in local communities and areas employing migratory and seasonal workers, and the increased industrialization of such areas. (3) Co-ordination of cycles of employment by federal and state labor exchanges; arrangement for planned movements of individuals and groups from job to job in orderly sequence. (4) Granting agricultural workers the right of unemployment benefits under the auspices of the Federal Social Security Administration. This step has already been advanced through the enlargement of the scope of the Federal Social Security Law by the Congress during the summer of 1950. (5) Reconstitution, under adequate federal and state supervision, of decent and habitable transient service camps, operating in conjunction with labor exchanges and other social services. (6) The provision for local public works projects to take up the slack of local unemployment in marginal areas. (7) Adequate supplementation, when necessary, of local relief benefits through state and federal assistance.

Many of these proposals have already been considered and are awaiting implementation. At Governor Earl Warren's special conference on unemployment in California, during December, 1949, for example, proposals for establishing industries in seasonal work areas, such as the San Joaquin Valley, were strongly recommended, as well as the development of diversification of crops in local regions and on large mechanized produce-yielding farms so that a permanent labor force might be maintained.

SUMMARY

Mobility and migration have invariably played significant roles in cultural transition and social change, although the volume and tempo of human mobility have become particularly acute since the Industrial Revolution. (1) Factors promoting mobility may stem from (a) geographical or environmental conditions, (b) socio-cultural conditions, and (c) individual psychological conditions. (2) Mobility may be conceived of as *horizontal*, i.e., through space, and *vertical*, involving change in status or psychological orientation. (3) In American culture, competition and the striving for status have encouraged considerable mobility of both types, bringing about the special problems involved in the seeking of status through class mobility. (4) Mobility may be distinguished from migration from the standpoint of (a) continuity of movement, (b) its individual character, and (c) the types of adjustment involved. (5) An examination of the special indexes of mobility in Western culture, based on the rate of use of facilities for both communication and travel, reveals the enormous heightening of mobile processes since the beginning of the century. (6) Mobility does not necessarily induce disorganization on the social or personal levels. Problems arising from the mobile process, however, may manifest themselves in (a) economic conflict, (b) special areas of cultural conflict, and (c) rural-urban maladjustments. (7) A common problem in American life, emerging from our highly mobile culture, concerns the migratory individual and the migratory family. The character and scope of this problem have changed considerably since the period preceding the depression of 1929. (8) Numbers of migratory individuals and families are extremely difficult to estimate because of the factor of mobility itself and because of the changes induced by economic conditions. (9) A small percentage of itinerant and homeless individuals are annually arrested for vagrancy. These arrests are very likely restricted to a special type of unattached person. (10) The earlier types of homeless men, whose status was brought about, to a considerable extent, by the seasonal nature of industry and farming, are becoming supplanted by a new type of migrant. (11) These new migrants reveal their altered characteristics in sex distribution, age, employment, marital status, educational level, and psychological factors. However, modern groups still reveal their youthful character, and are similar in selected respects to migrants of previous years. (12) In ascertaining the causes of modern transiency, causal patterns are found related to two broad areas: (a) exposure to a marginal and migratory environment, and (b) critical situations in the careers of individuals as viewed from the standpoint of their special psychogenetic development. (13) The modern migratory family is different from the stable nineteenth-century pioneer type and subject to the random pressures of economic necessity. It is a disenfranchised unit, relatively small in size, and frequently suffering from acute proverty and social demoralization even during periods of prosperity. (14) Modern farm mechanization and industrialization may portend the end of the earlier type of migrant. Leaving aside the demoralized transient individuals, solutions are being sought for the plight of other migrating groups. These revolve about the need for stable employment, adequate vocational training, diversification of employment possibilities within specialized areas, and the granting to migrant groups of ordinary social security benefits.

CHAPTER TWENTY

MENTAL DEFICIENCY AND SOCIAL DISORDER

(1) PHYSICAL AND MENTAL DISORDERS IN RELATION TO CULTURE

THERE has been a remarkable recent development in the study of human society in its relation to, and effects upon, the human personality. This development consists in the recognition that personality, society, and culture may not be studied as separate entities but only in relation to each other.[1] The problems involved in the study of human personality, culture, and society are not alone those of establishing valid confirmation for hypotheses and conclusions in related fields. The problems are conceptual, integrative, and semantic, necessitating new types of approaches and the formulation of new conceptual usages in order to illustrate the virtually indissoluble relationships existing among these separate aspects of a common field.

Among the consequences of this common interest is the conclusion that disorganized personalities represent, in the *frequency* and in the *character* of their occurrence, symptoms of the underlying patterns of breakdown in the social structure. The disorganization of the personality, whether on a physical or psychological plane, can be shown to have direct socio-cultural linkages, a fact that the medical profession has tended to overlook until relatively recently. During the last few decades, these views have been given renewed emphasis and ample empirical and clinical verification through the regained perspectives of *psychosomatics*, more fittingly called *sociosomatics* or *psychosocial medicine*.[2] Physicians have long recognized the close relationship that exists between environmental stress and disorders of the body and the mind. The term, "medical sociology," long discarded, was widely known in the nineteenth century. During the early part of the present century, the eminent sociologist-

[1] Cf. The interesting and challenging symposium of specialists drawn from the psychological, psychiatric, and social science fields in S. Stansfeld Sargent and Marian W. Smith, editors, *Culture and Personality*. Proceedings of an Interdisciplinary Conference, Viking Fund (New York, 1949).

[2] See Eugene P. Link, "A Note on Sociosomatics," *American Sociological Review*, XIII (Dec., 1948), 757–8.

physician, Dr. Richard C. Cabot, in conjunction with Dr. Abraham Jacobi, clearly outlined the sociological basis of numerous physical and mental ailments.[3]

If these views are valid, the sources of many of our modern ailments, physical and mental, must be sought in various socio-cultural patterns. Moreover, it would follow that certain forms of disorder will not appear in the same degree among different cultures. That the latter is to a certain degree proven may be seen in the fact that, except for certain types of organically produced pathologies, mental disorders of the kind that are so prevalent in modern cultures are relatively unknown among primitives. When they do arise among primitive groups, it is within those recently exposed to culture conflict and the vicissitudes and tensions created by cultural antagonisms centering on the individual.[4]

There is much recent evidence to demonstrate conclusively that socio-cultural tensions produce characteristic emotional effects in the individual.[5] Not only are distinctive patterns of mental aberration produced by environmental pressure and tension, but also various types of bodily disorders which themselves are related to the psychological and physical mechanisms disrupted by difficulties in adjustment to the environment. Socio-cultural factors may produce two types of effects upon the organism: (1) mental aberrations related to standards of cultural normalcy; and (2) physical disorders, usually of a chronic type, which are related to specific personality traits. Furthermore, we may observe fluctuations in the incidence of both physical and psychological manifestations in relation to changing emphases in the socio-cultural cycle.

The prevalence of certain types of modern mental disorders, such as schizophrenia and anxiety-neuroses—disorders for which there are no discernible organic bases—suggests the extent to which the stress of modern living plays an instrumental role in producing such disabilities. Of great significance, too, is the newly adduced evidence testifying to the connections between specific chronic illness states and specific personality patterns. Dunbar, for example, has found typical personality patterns in heart disease, diabetes, arthritis, and accident proneness.[6] Dr. Irving A. Fosberg at Tulane University directed an experiment, in 1949, which revealed striking similarities in the personality patterns of patients suffering from tuberculosis and those suffering from schizophrenia. In a well-known experiment by Davies and Wilson of 200 unselected persons suffering from

[3] See Richard C. Cabot and Abraham Jacobi, "The Modern Conception of Medicine," *New York Medical Journal* (Jan. 27, 1912).

[4] See, for example, some of the illustrations given in Ralph Linton, ed., *The Science of Man in the World Crisis* (New York, 1945).

[5] See, for example, Flanders Dunbar, *Mind and Body: Psychosomatic Medicine* (New York, 1947).

[6] H. Flanders Dunbar, *Psychosomatic Diagnosis* (New York, 1943).

peptic ulcers, it was discovered that 84 per cent had given evidence of the symptoms of this disorder while undergoing serious tensions, as a result of disturbing external events such as financial, occupational, or domestic crises.[7] A report in 1921 by a British parliamentary committee commissioned to study the extensive eye disorder of miners, known as *nystagmus*, concluded that the disease was caused not by inadequate lighting in the pits but by adverse psychological conditions induced by economic stress.[8] Alexander found positive relationships between respiratory disorders and personality types, while Rubin, French, and others have uncovered evidence revealing the relationship between asthmatic disorders and personality similarities.[9] Gottesman and Menninger have indicated clearly the relationship between specific types of skin disorders and emotional states induced by environmental stress, while Kersten has shown the connection between chronic diarrhea and psychic conflict.[10] The serious disorder of coronary occlusion has been shown to arise in many cases as a result of ambitious strivings.[11] Mittleman and Wolff have discovered common personality traits in individuals suffering from gastric ulcers.[12]

The recognition that the variations in certain personality syndromes and physical disorders are related to the changing stresses in the cultural cycle has caused the concept of psychosomatic medicine to be supplanted, in part, by the concept of *psychosocial* or *sociosomatic* medicine. Wolff, for example, believes there is a relationship between hyperacidity and the woman's rights movement; he suggests that the increase in ulcers in men seems to be associated with the greater independence of women! Far more effective and substantial correlations between psychosomatic disorders and changing socio-cultural conditions are revealed in the carefully detailed studies by James L. Halliday.[13] In carefully drawn tabulations, Halliday shows the acute increases in such chronic illnesses as peptic ulcer and gastritis ("the ulcer of modern civilization"), exopthalmic goiter, diabetes, and hypertensive cardiovascular disorders between 1911

[7] D. T. Davies and A. T. M. Wilson, "Observations on Peptic Ulcer," *Lancet*, II (1937), 1353.

[8] *Reports of Nystagmus Committee* (1922 and 1932, H. M. Stationery Office, London, England).

[9] F. Alexander, *Psychosomatic Medicine*, II (April, 1940), 110; S. Rubin, *Psychosomatic Medicine*, II (Jan. 1944), 31; D. French, *American Journal of Psychiatry*, LXXXXVIII (July, 1939), 638.

[10] A. H. Gottesman and Karl Menninger, "The Dermatologist and the Psychiatrist," *Bulletin of the Menninger Clinic*, XIII (July, 1949), 119–23; Paul Kersten, "Chronic Diarrhea with Psychic Conflict," *Bulletin of the Menninger Clinic*, XIV (July, 1950), 143–5.

[11] Howard Williams, "Coronary Occlusion in Relation to Ambitious Strivings," *Bulletin of the Menninger Clinic*, XIV (May 1950), 108–10.

[12] Bela Mittleman and Harold Wolff, "Emotions and Gastro-Duodenal Function," *Psychosomatic Medicine*, IV (Jan. 1942).

[13] James L. Halliday, *Psychosocial Medicine* (New York, 1948).

and 1936 in England and Scotland. He calls these disorders "psychosomatic affections," and indicates that "during the early 1930s their prevalence was equivalent to an epidemic."[14] Even more revealing are the reversals in sex and age distributions which he shows. The ratio of diabetes cases among men as against women was 2 to 1 during the late nineteenth century, while in the thirties of this century the balance was reversed, with women falling victim to the disease two or three times more frequently than men.[15] Variations in rates of such psychosomatic affections can be found in relation to rural-urban differences, occupational classes, and stratified groups. There is strong suggestion that physical and mental states respond to the structural and cultural characteristics of society as they vary in space and time.

Modern perspectives in sociology indicate that the study of mental and physical disorders must be carried on from the standpoint of total organic responsiveness to peculiar sets of evocative socio-cultural configurations. Although human *behavior* in its infinite variety has long been understood as a peculiar response to special sets of environmental conditions, both physical and cultural, it has not been readily acknowledged that *emotional states* are also affected by social conditions. The reason for this seems to lie in the confusion produced by the ancient mind-body dichotomy. This view, still widely held by medical practitioners and certain psychiatrists and clinical psychologists, tends to encourage the traditional belief that the mind is somehow enclosed by the human body and is largely rooted in the neurological structure and the cerebral cortex. The modern view emphasizes the relational and dependent aspects of human behavior, suggesting that what we ordinarily describe as physical and mental traits are simply special phases of total human responsiveness to conditions within certain situational contexts. These situational contexts are conditioned not only by a special type of organism, but also by specific conditions of human interaction defined by cultural processes.

(2) MENTAL DEFICIENCY AND MENTAL DERANGEMENT

Thus far we have stressed the close relationship between physical and mental disorders as conditions evoked within particular socio-cultural contexts. The degree to which physical or mental defects are induced by environmental stress on the one hand and by predisposing organic conditions on the other hand is a problem which must be discussed. At the very outset, a sharp differentiation must be drawn between the mental defectives suffering from *amentia*, the so-called *aments*, and those suffer-

[14] Ibid., Chap. 3, pp. 64, 65.
[15] Ibid., pp. 65–7.

ing from one of the several forms of *dementia*, the so-called *dements*. *Aments* are those who suffer from deficiencies of the intellect, rendering them incapable of making effective adjustment to their environment. *Dements*, on the other hand, are those suffering from some type of emotional disorder. These may or may not be handicapped by intellectual deficiency, and may have acquired their emotional disorder through their heredity or environment.

The two conditions may be found related in many ways and under certain specific conditions, but usually they are characteristic of different categories of individuals. Feebleminded individuals may be, and frequently are, relatively sound emotionally. Conversely, emotionally deranged individuals, particularly the so-called *neurotics*, ordinarily display normal, and, frequently, lucid intelligence. On the other hand, it is not uncommon to find both states of mental imbalance present in the same individual. Various forms of idiocy and feeblemindedness may bring about severe states of emotional stress, inducing emotional derangement. Conversely, certain forms of emotional derangement will produce deficiencies of the intellect as well. In certain cases, such a degeneration may be an accompanying condition of the deteriorating emotional state. This is true of paresis (a cerebral disorder of syphilitics) where intellectual impairment frequently occurs in relation to the ordinary symptoms of pathogenesis. On the other hand, even in cases where organic or other deterioration as a progressive aspect of the disease does not occur, emotional difficulties may decidedly hamper the capacity of the intellect to function normally.

(3) HISTORY OF ATTITUDES TOWARD MENTAL DEFICIENCY

Despite the clear distinction which can be demonstrated today between mental defectives (i.e. the mentally deficient or aments) and mentally deranged individuals, lack of clarity is still evidenced in official quarters in the definition of mental deficiency and feeblemindedness. In this country, for example, the term "feebleminded" is employed in reference to the major types of mental defect, while in Great Britain, the term is used solely to describe the uppermost grade of feebleminded, the moron. At the White House Conference on Child Health and Protection in 1930, the sub-committee on problems of mental deficiency classified as mental defectives those with intelligence-test scores below established standards of normalcy as *well as those who gave evidence of feeblemindedness through social inadequacy*. The New York State Mental Hygiene Law employs a peculiar definition, indicating that those who are not adjudged insane but who, nevertheless, are incapable of managing their own affairs, may, if supervision is required, be considered mental defectives.[16]

The distinction between the two categories of mentally inadequate individuals has long been recognized, even before the time of Hippocrates. Until the present century, the term "idiot," which now refers to the lowest grade of the feebleminded, was used generically to describe all types of individuals of deficient intellectual capacity. The early English law, going back to the fourteenth century, defined an idiot as "a natural fool." As in the case of the insane, mental deficiency was regarded as a sign of divine blessing or, more commonly, as a sign of ill-omen, according to the dominant social attitudes and values of the period. Among the Greeks and Romans, mental defectives were largely regarded as undesirable, and infanticide, as an early form of negative eugenics, was widely employed to rid society of such misfits. The laws of Lycurgus expressly condoned this practice, and both Aristotle and Plato endorsed such measures, the former for economic reasons and the latter for reasons of eugenics. Among the Romans, although feebleminded individuals were sometimes procured for amusement—the forerunner of the royal jester—their elimination through infanticide was generally approved. The philosopher Seneca, in a letter to a friend, describes an idiot child of his wife as "a burdensome legacy." Both Luther and Calvin deplored the existence of feebleminded individuals and regarded them as "children of the devil."

Beginning with the great age of rational discovery and enlightenment of the eighteenth century—the age of Condorcet, Rousseau, Turgot, Montesquieu, and the Encyclopedists—the first great forward strides were taken in perceiving the peculiar nature of mental defect and the necessity for providing specialized care and education for such unfortunates. The great humanitarian pioneer in this field was Dr. Jean M. G. Itard, the medical director of the National Institute for the Deaf in Paris, who, entrusted with the care of the celebrated "Wild Boy of Aveyron" (a boy of about seventeen years of age discovered living in a forest in Aveyron, France), developed a special procedure for his training based upon the sensationalist philosophic theories of Locke and Condillac and the educational methods for deaf-mutes initiated by Jacob Rodrigues Pereire. This procedure is still basic today in the care of institutionalized feebleminded persons. It rests upon the assumption that mentally defective individuals may show progress in caring for their own needs, within the limitations of their disability, by training progressively along three graded steps: (1) the primary development of the senses and sense-organs, (2) the development of the intellectual faculties, and (3) ultimate development of the affective functions.

[16] Mental Hygiene Law, *Chapter 426, Handbook of the Department of Mental Hygiene*, State of New York, 1933, p. 94.

Itard conveyed to his disciple and successor, Dr. Edward Seguin, his compassionate concern for such defectives together with the results of his painstaking research. After 1838 his methods were amplified by his disciple and began to attract international attention. The significance of the work of Itard and Seguin was experienced not only in the care of the feebleminded but had vast repercussions upon the training of deaf-mutes and even upon the early training of school and pre-school children. In 1842, Dr. J. Guggenbühl established a special school in Switzerland for cretins, a class of defectives commonly found in Alpine areas. In the same year, a German physician, Dr. C. M. Saegart, established a custodial institution for the feebleminded in Berlin. Championed by Dr. John Connolly, famous for his early advocacy of non-restraint in the care of insane patients, private and public institutions for the care of idiots were founded in England, beginning with a private school at Bath in 1846, and followed by public institutions at Colchester in 1849 and at Earlswood in 1855. Although Esquirol, as early as 1828, emphasized the distinction between mental defect and other forms of mental disorder in his *Maladies Mentales*, not until 1886, in England, was a legal differentiation made between insanity and feeblemindedness. During the nineteenth century, in this country as well as elsewhere, when mental defectives were provided for at all, they were frequently herded into general pauper institutions, asylums for the insane, or penal institutions.

Despite the early recognition in this country of the necessity that some special provisions be made for idiots (evidenced as early as 1793 by a special enactment for the care of pauperized idiots in Kentucky), considerable resistance was shown in many states toward the passage of legislation for the public care of mentally defective persons. As late as 1856, a legislative committee on idiocy in Connecticut stated that it was "a settled conviction of a large majority of the citizens of the Commonwealth that idiots were a class so utterly hopeless that it was a waste of time even to collect any statistics concerning them." [17] Nevertheless, in 1846, legislation in New York and Massachusetts, passed almost simultaneously and very similar in scope, attempted to establish special public care for mental defective cases. Within the decade, permanent institutions for the training and supervision of defectives were functioning in Massachusetts and New York, after trial ventures and much legislative cavil concerning their need and effectiveness. Pennsylvania, Ohio, Illinois, and Kentucky also established such facilities during this period or shortly after. Today, special institutions for the care and training of different types of defectives under public auspices are well established in all states. Some of the early optimism of the late nineteenth century concerning

[17] Albert Deutsch, *The Mentally Ill in America* (New York, 1949), p. 346.

the educational potentialities of such institutions has been modified as a result of our increasing knowledge.

(4) TYPES AND CAUSES OF MENTAL DEFICIENCY

In analyzing types and causes of mental deficiency, it must be carefully stressed that mental defectiveness is *not* a unitary characteristic. There are several types of deficiency, ranging from the idiots, with "no brains at all," as Menninger puts it, to the considerable number of border-line defectives who are only problematically feebleminded. Furthermore, distinctions as to character, types, and behavior of deficients may not always be consistently maintained. The causal conditions are not single or specific—although some few extremists still regard feeblemindedness as the result of a Mendelian recessive characteristic—but are more frequently complex systems of causative factors manifesting themselves in a variety of forms which may be regarded as types of mental defectiveness.[18] The very methods of precise determination of such states involve careful examination of physical stigmata, mental retardation, and social inadequacy.[19]

In view of the fact that feeblemindedness appears early in the vast majority of cases, the causes have generally been thought to be hereditary. Nevertheless, standard practice has been to assess causes in terms of *primary*, or constitutional cases, and *secondary*, or reactional cases. Hall, who stresses that mental deficiency results chiefly from "an abnormal nervous system," indicates that the developmental error may occur in the prenatal foetus, at the time of birth, or in the postnatal period.[20] Many of the prenatal cases are hereditary or genetic in origin, but not all are necessarily so.

Primary feeblemindedness is that type which is manifested from the time of birth, and which may be hereditary or acquired during the foetal period. Such cases are marked by distinctive physical characteristics, such as extreme obesity or other abnormal weight differentials, height peculiarities, facial deformities, and glandular dysfunction. *Secondary or reactional types* develop abnormalities as a result of disorders induced by organic action involving deleterious mechanical, chemical, or bacterial factors in

[18] Cf., Abraham Myerson, *The Inheritance of Mental Diseases* (Baltimore, 1925), p. 74.

[19] See, for example, the specific procedures for observation, testing, and diagnosis in *Regulations for Determining the Number of Children Three Years Retarded in Mental Development*, Department of Mental Diseases, Massachusetts, Acts of 1931, Chap. 358, p. 10; also, the well known "Ten-point Scale Examination" devised by Dr. Walter E. Fernald (cited in Deutsch, *The Mentally Ill in America*, p. 364).

[20] Robert J. Hall, "The Modern Approach to Mental Deficiency," *Mental Hygiene News*, Department of Mental Hygiene, New York State, XIX (April, 1949), 5.

the environment. Such conditions may be brought about by a variety of causes, including traumatic shocks to the brain and nervous system, neurological lesions, glandular malfunctioning, malnutrition, and various infectious disorders. Many such cases are associated with difficulties of birth, presumed to be most common among premature births, first children, and infants born during difficult labor of the mother requiring the use of obstetrical instruments.

Certain types are particularly difficult to classify, however, such as the *cretins*. These are of three types, the *true cretins*, utterly devoid of intellectual capacity, the *semicretins*, able to speak slightly, and the *cretinoids*, responsive to certain forms of elementary training. The condition of cretins is apparently caused by a congenital thyroid glandular malfunctioning. *Mongolian idiocy*, manifesting itself in mongoloid features and characteristics, is an endocrine disorder which, as far as may be determined, is non-hereditary. It occasionally occurs in families where the parents are gifted and the other children normal. Other types of "degenerative" feeblemindedness are hydrocephalus, microcephalus and amaurotic idiocy, all of which may not, for the present, be conveniently classified into the customary primary and secondary types.

To summarize, it would appear that the fundamental causes of feeblemindedness are twofold: (1) hereditary or congenital; and (2) the exposure of the organism, which may or may not suffer from predisposing conditions, to special sets of adverse conditions. These latter conditions may be categorized as (a) traumatic shocks at birth or shortly thereafter; (b) lesions, arising from toxic agents introduced into the organism or infectious sources, such as infantile paralysis; (c) glandular malfunctioning, centering largely about the thyroid-endocrine system; (d) certain severe infectious disorders which may lead to injury of the bodily nervous mechanism; and (e) malnutrition, which, through various forms of vitamin deficiency or because of the weakened state of the organism, may lead to deleterious mental results.[21] Although hereditary factors are still considered significant, the present tendency, on the basis of recent medical opinion and research, is to recognize the considerable importance of non-hereditary factors as well. In fact, it is estimated that only 11 per cent of the feebleminded population are themselves the progeny of feebleminded parents.[22] The conclusion to be drawn, therefore, is that 89 per cent of the feebleminded at the present time have acquired this defect either through congenital causes, exposure to environmental factors which in some way have impaired neurological and intellectual func-

[21] Cf. *White House Conference on Child Health and Protection*. Report of Subcommittee on Growth and Development (New York, 1932), pp. 220–5.
[22] Ibid.

tion, or through the agency of transmitted genetic factors from parents who themselves are normal.[23]

(5) EXTENT OF FEEBLEMINDEDNESS

Estimates concerning the numbers of feebleminded in the general population are highly variable. This is largely because the considerable numbers who are not cared for in public and private institutions do not appear in official tabulations, and because certain sizable groups, such as marginal defectives, may or may not be included in census appraisals of mental defectives. Deutsch estimates conservatively that there are 1,250,000 mental defectives in the population, a ratio of about one per hundred of the general population, of which less than 80,000 are accommodated in special institutions for their care and treatment.[24] Such an estimate, however, fails to take account of considerable numbers of border-line cases who, on the basis of the test of social adequacy, might very well be included within the category of defectives. The fact remains that if we simply employ official figures of custodial cases, the total numbers afford only a partial view of the dimensions of the entire problem. Most states are still woefully backward in providing institutional care for their defective populations. Menninger estimates that no state makes custodial provision for more than 10 per cent of the group classified as imbeciles or idiots.[25] Despite this fact, the number of institutionalized mental defectives increased from 14,347 in 1904 to 20,731 in 1910, 42,954 in 1923, and almost 80,000 today. Although this rise represents a threefold increase between 1904 and 1923, and a twofold increase since the latter date, at no time have more than one-fifteenth of the total population of mental defectives received institutional care.[26]

More helpful in making precise estimates have been the surveys conducted among school children. An example is the periodic census carried out by the Division of Mental Deficiency in Massachusetts.[27] Comparing the numbers of defective children in the public schools with the annual volume of incoming pupils in the first grades during a given year, this agency found 2.8 per cent to be definitely feebleminded and 10.9 per cent to be retarded, without clinical evidence of defectiveness. Popenoe, in 1930, employing as his criterion the conventional I.Q. level of 70, ordinarily held to separate the marginal cases from those definitely

[23] This conclusion has repeatedly given rise to the claim that many cases of feeblemindedness, if not most, are the result of a recessive Mendelian genetic factor.

[24] Deutsch, *The Mentally Ill in America*, p. 369.

[25] Cf. Karl Menninger, *The Human Mind* (Third edition, New York, 1946), p. 69.

[26] Deutsch, *The Mentally Ill in America*, p. 369.

[27] *Report of the Division of Mental Deficiency* (Commonwealth of Massachusetts, 1935), pp. 33–4.

adjudged mentally defective, estimated that 5 per cent of the total population, or about six million individuals, might be judged to be mentally deficient.[28] Stevenson has attempted to show that a figure of one million represents a conservative estimate of those who may definitely be classified as feebleminded. In addition, he claims there may be another 13 per cent of marginal defectives, persons characterized by "dullness, intellectual subnormality, or retardation," but who, nevertheless, may be able to get along if they are temperamentally stable and do not face any undue environmental stress.[29] The Subcommittee on Problems of Mental Deficiency of the White House Conference, utilizing I.Q.'s of 85 or less in conjunction with "social failure" as a criterion, affirmed that 2 per cent (850,000) of the nation's children, might be classified as feebleminded, while 5,650,000 additional children, declared either unadjusted or maladjusted, suffering from special mental disabilities or special educational disabilities, might be classified as pseudo-feebleminded.[30] The general conclusion to be drawn from these several investigations is that, as far as we can determine at present, it would be hazardous to assume that more than 2 per cent of the total population might be considered feebleminded in the strictly technical sense. However, as many as 10 to 15 per cent of the population may suffer from marginal mental defects of varying intensity. These defects may be sufficiently serious to hamper effective adjustments in normal social, familial, and industrial life.

(6) THE CONSIDERATION OF SPECIAL TYPES OF AMENTS

Errors in the precise determination of mental defectiveness. It has already been indicated that precise diagnosis of mentally defective states involves careful consideration of somatic deficiencies, various facial and bodily stigmata, social inadequacy, and mental retardation, as well as evidences of subnormality as revealed by standardized intelligence testing procedures. Considerable numbers of defectives, however, give no outward indication of their defective intellectual capacity. Prolonged and careful examination is required to assess the intelligence of these persons.

In a famous experiment which Lloyd Yepsen conducted at the school for the feebleminded in Vineland, New Jersey, he submitted uniform photographs of twenty-five feebleminded boys and twenty-five normal boys to panels of trained students, many of whom had had special experience in the handling of mentally defective individuals. The purpose

[28] Paul Popenoe, "Feeblemindedness Today," *Journal of Heredity*, XXI (Oct., 1930), 421.

[29] George S. Stevenson, "Mental Hygiene," *Social Work Year Book, 1937* (New York), p. 279.

[30] *White House Conference on Child Health and Protection*, pp. 330–2.

of the experiment was to determine whether normal and defective persons could be distinguished solely on the basis of the photographs. The results indicated that the judges were no more successful in discriminating between the two categories of individuals than if their selection had been guided entirely by chance.[31] The standard intelligence test still remains a most important instrument in detecting various grades of feeblemindedness.

The intelligence test, nevertheless, despite its considerable value in diagnosing intellectual capacity (particularly from the standpoint of predicting levels of academic achievement) is suspect because of its cultural biases. It has been repeatedly demonstrated that the results of the intelligence test reflect cultural and environmental differentials, as well as innate intellectual capacity. Indeed, some question whether it reflects innate intelligence in any degree whatsoever. The reasons for cultural bias of intelligence tests are not difficult to find. The ordinary intelligence test, after all, is based upon problems and exercises, verbal and otherwise, arising within peculiar cultural environments and academic situations. The sole intent of the test, in its standardized and generalized form, is to determine the level of the individual's performance in relation to the average levels of attainment achieved by others of the same age. The intelligence quotient score represents simply the ratio between the individual's mental age (determined by judging the results of his performance in relation to his age-group) and his chronological age. Normalcy is established by the fact of the individual's achieving a score commensurate with his age-level.

This testing device, despite its great value, has frequently undergone scathing criticism for its putative failure to make allowances for cultural and social differences, and because of the arbitrary nature in which its so-called "norms" are established. Some years ago, in a series of articles, Walter Lippmann denounced such testing instruments as devious attempts to set up an arbitrary unit of measurement, such as a mile in linear measurement, and then to draw invidious and evaluative comparisons of subnormality in respect to individuals unable to attain the arbitrarily established standards. This, Lippmann felt, is somewhat equivalent to stating that the average mile is only three-fourths of a mile in length.[32] Provided we bear in mind that individuals of equal capacity exposed to differing cultural advantages and opportunities may reflect these differences in their test performance, the intelligence test may continue to serve a limited, although a significant function.

[31] It is to be noted, however, that if a moving picture record had been taken, so that stolidity of features, awkwardness of gait and muscular movement, etc., had been revealed, the selection would very likely have been far more accurate.

[32] Cf. Walter Lippmann, "The Mental Age of Americans," *New Republic*, Oct. 25, 1922, pp. 213–15.

The degree to which intelligence-test scores may be modified as a result of changes in the socio-cultural environment is highly variable. Otto Klineberg, for example, has amply demonstrated in his discussion of the factors affecting racial differences how improvements in social and economic environment play significant roles in raising the intelligence-test scores of Negro children.[33] Similar facts have been demonstrated repeatedly. Mandel Sherman, some years ago, in testing the so-called "Mountain Hollow" children of old Scotch-Irish stock in West Virginia and Tennessee, found successive improvements in intelligence-test scores as the families of these children migrated to communities offering improved economic and educational standards. Significant of his demonstration was the complete meaninglessness to his subjects of certain items in the intelligence-test inventory because they had absolutely no relevance to their day-to-day cultural experiences.

(7) BORDER-LINE CASES

A recognition of the shortcomings of intelligence tests is especially significant in the study of the cases of those whose intelligence falls immediately below the standard of normality—those whose intelligence-test scores fall between 80 and 90 (the "dull normal") and between 70 and 80 (the "border-line" cases).[34] The intelligence-test scores of these persons may be genuinely predictive of academic failure. Nevertheless, such individuals may make effective adjustments to the environment, provided too great demands are not made upon their intelligence. The mechanical skills of such individuals, particularly when they are held to routine assignments, may be quite high. Difficulties only emerge if they are exposed to social environments where they are asked to make discriminatory intellectual choices or display evidences of intellectual imaginativeness or personal initiative beyond their capacity. Such individuals may perform

[33] Otto Klineberg, *Race Differences* (New York, 1935).

[34] According to Terman's classification of the human intelligence, based upon the Stanford Revision of the Binet-Simon Test, intellectual faculties may be distributed according to the following range:

I.Q.	*Commonplace Classification*
Above 140	"Near" genius or genius
120–140	Very superior intelligence
110–120	Superior intelligence
90–110	Normal, or average intelligence
80–90	Dull normal
70–80	Border-line (sometimes classified as dull, sometimes as feebleminded)
Below 70	Definitely feebleminded
60–70	High-grade moron
50–60	Low-grade moron
20–50	Imbecile
Below 20	Idiot

their work satisfactorily when held to routine and when the responsibilities of decision rest with other persons with whom effective relations have been established.

Nevertheless, as Menninger has been careful to point out, extreme caution should be exercised in the presumptive diagnosis of such cases. Innumerable illustrations are available of children who were considered subnormal and even feebleminded during their school years, who eventually achieved positions of considerable intellectual and social distinction. The scientist, James Watt, William Lloyd Garrison, William Warburton (considered as a child to be "the dullest of all dull scholars"), and the celebrated theologian, Thomas Aquinas, characterized in childhood as a "dumb ox," are only a few of the celebrated company who, as children, were erroneously considered devoid of intellectual potentialities. Our schools today are filled with children who, because of behavioral and emotional difficulties, inadequate preparation, poor motivation, alien background, cultural conflict, or bi-lingual strain, manifest such disorders in seeming evidence of deficient intelligence.

The morons. The morons, whose I.Q.'s fall between 50 and 70 and whose mental ages are considered equivalent to those of children between the ages of eight and twelve years, are definitely classified as feebleminded. Falling within two ranges, the high-grade moron, whose intelligence quotient falls between 60 and 70, and the low-grade moron, whose I.Q. falls between 50 and 60, this class of aments can be readily detected, ordinarily, by the use of conventional tests. It is virtually impossible to make an estimate as to their frequency in the population, although their numbers are considerable. With virtually no institutional provision made for their supervision and very few special educational facilities available for their vocational needs in even our larger urban school systems—the rural schools rarely, if ever, provide such facilities—they represent special targets for personal and social demoralization in our sharply competitive social structure. Considered free agents, nevertheless, they are called upon to exercise the functions of citizenship, marriage, and self-support for which, without adequate direction, they are utterly incapable.

Left completely to their own devices, morons frequently get into serious difficulty and form an endless parade in our police courts for a continual succession of misdemeanors and petty offenses, as well as for more serious crimes. Yet, they may possess abilities which would enable them to function productively in society. Psychometric tests given to morons show many of them to have mechanical aptitudes superior to their verbal-intelligence capacities. They may display considerable mechanical efficiency in routine tasks, as Dr. Charles Bernstein has shown in revealing the 75 to 100 per cent efficiency ratings attained by feebleminded operatives trained at the Rome School (New York) for the textile industry. Psychometric test results reveal a relatively high degree of memorative skill as well, although almost completely divorced from perceptual, evaluative, and cognitive functions. The moron may memorize a multiplication table, a formula, or a homily, but he lacks the necessary intellectual ability to apply it to a concrete situation.

This type of mentality has been brilliantly portrayed by Ellen Wembridge in the case of Chuck and Flora, two wedded morons. Chuck and Flora bore all the normal demands of marital, community, and vocational responsibility, but they were utterly lacking in the normal capacities required for the fulfillment of such obligations.[35] In the light of the endless difficulties in which such a pair continually implicate themselves, Ellen Wembridge raises a pointed question which has more than rhetorical significance: "Who are the villains and who the victims—They or We?" Excerpts from the following case illustrate the *limitations of the social participation* of such individuals, their inability to grasp certain cultural, evaluative, and moral distinctions, and their woeful lack of intellectual perception in confronting the most elementary of problems.[36]

> Chuck had met Flora on the street and said "How about a show, Blondie?" to which she had replied "Oh, Boy!" With this introduction matters had gone far before she even knew his last name—a name which she was now to assume under a wedding bell of Easter lilies. We did not approve of the wedding any more than we had approved of others about which our opinion had not been asked. But both contracting parties were of legal age, however low their mental ages might be (Flora's was between ten and eleven as it happened, and Chuck who was very dull but not quite so feeble, scored a scant year higher), and they wanted to marry, so there was nothing to do but ring the wedding bells, turn on the "Lohengrin" record, throw rice and old shoes, and wait for the inevitable. Incidentally, let no one underestimate the value of an elaborate wedding for morons, if wedded they must be. The mere signing of a license is essentially too abstract and trivial a formality for those who cannot grasp the idea of law. It takes more than a scrap of paper to hold the family together after a quarrel. But if the veil is long enough, enough jokes are made by the best man, and enough shrieks uttered by the bridesmaids, the impression is made on the dimly endowed pair that something really important socially has taken place. They are helped thereby to remember that somehow the clergy and the police will see to it that the bride does not sell the household furniture behind her husband's back, and that he will not leave her with the rent to pay. So Chuck

[35] Ellen R. Wembridge, *Life Among the Lowbrows* (Boston and New York, 1931).
[36] Ibid., pp. 3–21.

married Flora (who was getting a regular salary), and they went to housekeeping in two furnished rooms.

Chuck seemed genuinely fond of his Flora, and was marrying her under no outside pressure. Ultimately, therefore, Flora must budget his [salary] to cover rent, food, clothes, movies, gas, tobacco, lipstick, chewing gum, and layette. To do this required addition, subtraction, and even multiplication, and these processes must be accurate and rapid enough to count the change before the peddler walked away with the extra dollar.

Furthermore, a certain ability to use and to understand language was necessary, because the only callers at Flora's door would be agents for hosiery, vacuum cleaners, vanishing creams and cleaning fluids, veterans selling needles, and children raffling sofa pillows for a fair. (Before her marriage) she had consorted pleasantly with Chuck and with her other acquaintances, both girls and boys, without much recourse either to her vocabulary or to her arithmetic. She had always spent her money until she was broke, and then got herself fed by her escort of the period until the next pay day. Her conversation was about as follows: If Chuck remarked, "There goes a white horse," she shouted with laughter, and said: "Hot dog!" If he said: "That's a Ford," she agreed, murmuring: "You said it," and snuggled closer. She could also say "Ain't it so?" "You're a fright" "I'll say" "Hell's bells" and "You're crazy with the heat." She could, moreover, giggle and say nothing, which worked quite as well. She was healthy and good natured, she liked company, and was normal in all but mind.

You recall, no doubt, the standard example in arithmetic which every fourteen-year-old school child is supposed to be able to solve: If two pencils cost five cents, how many can you get for fifty cents? Not only pencils, but doughnuts, dill pickles, apples, and cotton handkerchiefs are bought at about this price. But neither Flora nor any of her moron friends could master the problem. We knew they could not because we had asked them. Flora's answer was twenty-five because two into fifty is twenty-five. Her friend Lucille's, on the other hand, was a hundred, because two times fifty is one hundred. (Lucille's husband is in the penitentiary for stealing motor cars—he had to steal *something* to keep ahead of her shopping.) Another friend, Anne, ventured a still more generous estimate. She said: "Five times fifty, because five cents times fifty cents is five times fifty—whatever that is." Chuck himself answered ten, because "you get two for five, and two times five is ten." It will be observed that all of them knew that *something* must be done in the way of arithmetic, and that their arithmetic was generally correct—except for the fact that they could not select the right process to employ. A simple problem was to them as relativity is to the rest of us.

It is hard, indeed, to discover just what words convey to morons with such a background. Flora when questioned said that "lecture" means "getting hanged," while Lucille said: "It's the chair." The fact that the latter's husband is in the penitentiary, perhaps explains why both girls should associate the word "electric." Flora says "skill" is "You do it," which isn't so bad. Lucille says: "You do it to fish." "Not scale, but skill," we repeat. "In your head," she answers, which seems perhaps on the right track, until she adds "a bone." "Not skull, but skill," we insist patiently. "Fry in it," she tries again, and we give up.

Of course, uneducated people necessarily have smaller vocabularies than the highly trained. But on the other hand, children taught in American schools and confronted by the newspapers have been exposed to a good many words, and the meanings of a few of them have got to penetrate if any sermon on behavior is to be intelligible. Moreover it is impossible for good advice to be couched entirely in words devoid of some degree of abstraction. So we ask— "What is pity?" That seems easy: "You're sorry." Encouraged, we proceed, "What is justice?" "Peace," answers Lucille, "I got married by one." Envy is "enemy," or "You like them," or (hesitating), "you *don't* like them."

In what words, then, shall we express to Flora: "You must learn to keep an account of your money, not spend more than you have, and be faithful to Chuck," when she has already told us that charity is "Don't be silly," faith is "You do it," and when, to a question requiring the answer "thirty-five cents," she has answered "eighteen hundred weeks"? When it is possible to say control means "ragged" and chastity means "tricks," what hodge-podge of ideas has one's sermon produced in the good-natured mind of the moron bride?

Dr. Menninger summarizes the peculiar problems presented by morons in modern society in the following way:

(1) Morons are considerably limited in powers of adjustment; they can succeed only under favorable conditions, and hence social and economic failures are frequent.

(2) Morons frequently get caught for crimes that smarter persons "get away with." Their mental deficiency is related both to the offense and to the capture. Few judges, however, give it any consideration in the subsequent disposition of the case. Much crime would be prevented if they did.

(3) But ninety per cent of the morons are peaceful, law-abiding citizens, most of them usefully employed. Much of the simple, tedious work of the world is done by cheerful morons, and with special supervision and training they can be used even more advantageously.

Evidence concerning the authenticity of the latter claim may be found in the case of C. M., a low-grade moron who came for a brief period under the author's supervision. He was initially encountered at the age of sixteen years, seriously maladjusted as the result of a school program utterly unsuited to his limited interests and needs. By careful vocational training as an automobile mechanic, encouragement of adequate recreational pursuits, and sympathetic social companions of both sexes, this young man has made a successful adjustment in marriage (although the eugenicists may, with justification, have considerable misgivings). He operates a small business successfully under the very watchful eye of his wife, and is a local baseball player of note, although his team-mates, while praising his batting and flawless fielding, exercise considerable concern over the poor judgment he shows in making "difficult plays."

Dr. Ruby J. Kennedy, in a sociological investigation of the social adjustments of individuals with I.Q.'s between 50 and 96 conducted in Middletown, Connecticut during 1946 and 1947, showed that the great majority made very good adjustments, while some few made adjustments considerably better than average.[37] The average moron dealt with in her study, she discovered, is self-supporting, usually as a semi-skilled laborer, earning, if a male, thirty-five dollars to fifty-five dollars a week, while the typical female moron earns thirty dollars to forty-five dollars weekly.

According to Dr. Kennedy, an employer regards the moron as "a generally satisfactory worker who gets to work on time, maintains friendly relations with fellow-workers and is regularly on the job." He shows up less favorably, however, in efficiency, learning ability, accuracy, and speed. His poorest qualities as a worker consist in the unreliability of his judgment and in his learning rate. Job turn-overs were relatively low among this group for both sexes. As to background, the moron of this group generally discontinued school before the eighth grade and nine out of ten repeated at least one grade. The fathers of these morons were largely skilled or semi-skilled factory workers and most of the mothers had at some time been employed outside the home. It is significant to note that the wives of the moron males studied tended to be somewhat better educated and of higher intellectual capacity than their husbands. Indicating their promising capacity for normative adjustment Dr. Kennedy

[37] Dr. Ruby J. Kennedy, "The Social Adjustment of Morons," American Association of Mental Deficiency, Seventy-second Annual Meeting, Boston, May 18–22, 1948.

states: "The average married moron maintains a home of his own which he rents. He is saving some money, is paying for some kind of insurance, owns a radio and has a telephone in his house, but does not own a car. The typical female moron is similar in all these respects, except that she is not saving any money."

Imbeciles and idiots. The two lowest grades of feeblemindedness are technically known as imbecility and idiocy. According to the classificatory system employed by the Federal Bureau of the Census, an imbecile is a mentally defective person with a mental age of three to seven years. If the person is a child, he is classified as an imbecile if he has an intelligence quotient of from 20 to 49, inclusive. Idiots are persons whose mental age is less than three years. Children are classified as idiots whose intelligence quotient is less than 20.[38]

Unlike the higher grades of mental defectives, these groups require special supervision and intensive and protracted care. In the great majority of cases, the brain structure has definitely been impaired, although such defects in structure may not always be apparent. With many idiots, however, the cerebral cortex shows gross abnormalities. Where the brain structure does not readily reveal such deformities even under microscopic examination, it is commonly assumed, in the case of idiots, that physical defects exist nevertheless.

Despite the barrier to adjustment created for such cases by their physical impairment, considerable improvement may be noted in many of these individuals if they are given assistance. Such public institutions as the Rome State School in New York and the Laurelton State Village for Feebleminded Women in Pennsylvania, and private institutions such as the Wood School in Langhorne, Pennsylvania, have contributed notably toward the improvement of certain categories of the low-grade feebleminded. Successful care requires that cases be classified according to the nature of the defect and that treatment appropriate to the needs of the particular classes be administered. Segregated treatment of cases has provided the opportunity for research, some of the recent results of which have yielded promise of aid for special categories of the mentally afflicted. The recent experimental use of glutamic acid for mongoloid idiots (who are really "imbeciles"), for example, has helped some children to gain eight months in mental age in a period of half a year, which is "higher than the rate of growth expected of children having average intelligence . . . and more than twice the previous rate of mental development of the group." [39]

[38] *Annual Census of Institutions for Mental Defectives and Epileptics: Instructions for Filling out Schedules* (U. S. Bureau of the Census, Washington, 1936), p. 2.

[39] Frederic Zimmerman, Bessie B. Burgemeister and Tracy J. Putnam, *Archives of Neurology and Psychiatry* (July, 1949).

Nevertheless, facilities are woefully inadequate in this country for the study and care of these special cases. In many instances, where custodial treatment is provided it is still common practice either to provide common classes for "retarded children" or to place children indiscriminately in general institutions, irrespective of the special problems which their difficulties present. At the end of 1944, over-crowding in public institutions averaged 7.5 per cent above rated capacity, according to the Federal Census Bureau, while, as previously cited, it was estimated that only one-fifteenth of the nation's mental defectives were accommodated in institutions for their special care.

(8) STERILIZATION

Despite the relative paucity of information about the genetic factors involved, legislators have been forward in proposing laws permitting sterilization of the biologically unfit. "In enacting laws on sterilization," according to Deutsch, "they have frequently rushed in where scientists fear to tread."[40] Sixty sterilization statutes have been passed in this country since the pioneer statute was enacted in Indiana in 1907. Although all existing sterilization statutes include mental defectives in their scope, the confused and unscientific nature of much of the thinking behind many of these enactments may be seen in the broad provisions contained within several state bills permitting sterilization operations to be performed upon individuals believed to be suffering from hereditary mental diseases, habitual criminals, rapists, sexual perverts, drug addicts, and epileptics. As recently as 1929, a bill proposed before the Missouri legislature (which, however, did not gain passage) provided for sterilization of persons "convicted of murder (not in the heat of passion), rape, highway robbery, chicken stealing, bombing, or the theft of automobiles. . . ."

Today, twenty-eight states have laws permitting sterilization of the mentally unfit, as well as other classes of mentally diseased and habitual legal offenders. In only a few states, however, are such laws effectively carried out. Such laws ordinarily require that cases of sterilization must be reviewed by boards including institutional heads, physicians, psychiatrists, or neurologists. The consent of the individual or his legal guardian is also required. In certain instances, voluntary sterilization coverage includes non-institutional defectives as well. The constitutionality of such laws was assured in the famous Supreme Court decision of *Buck v. Bell* in 1927, upholding the legality of the Virginia sterilization statute. In a decision notable for its brevity as well as its avoidance of adequate scientific support and legal precedent, Justice Oliver Wendell Holmes made his famous pronouncement: "The principle that sustains compulsory vaccina-

[40] Deutsch, *The Mentally Ill in America*, p. 375.

tion is broad enough to cover the cutting of the Fallopian tubes. . . . Three generations of imbeciles are enough."

Although legal in many states, sterilization still constitutes a subject of heated controversy. The lengthy arguments of the protagonists for such measures may be condensed into three major points of view: (1) the sterilization of the feebleminded would cut down drastically the incidence of feeblemindedness within a few generations, and might eventually eradicate it completely; (2) it would eliminate the need for segregation and custodial care for certain defectives, and hence would prove more humane and less of a drain upon the taxpayer; (3) it would prevent the tragic occurrence of unfavorable home conditions for children created when either or both of the parents are feebleminded.

Aside from the moral and theological arguments against sterilization, which still exercise considerable influence, the scientific arguments have grown considerably in strength since the beginning of the century. Scientific opposition is not to the principle of sterilization as such, but to its application at the present time. Such arguments are usually based on the following grounds: (1) Our knowledge at the present time of the genetics of feeblemindedness is insufficient to determine the causal relationships between combinations of genetic factors and possibly resultant varieties of feeblemindedness. (2) The tendency to group together with mental defectives individuals representative of various types of behavioral disorders in which environmental stress has played a significant role, such as "habitual" criminals, sexual perverts, and the like, is dangerous, laying the basis for possible sinister developments in social policy. (3) Of particular significance, however, is the unwarranted claim that we may drastically curtail the incidence of mental defectiveness in the total population within a few generations—three generations being a particularly popular estimate. No current scientific findings would support such a contention. If all feebleminded persons were sterilized at the present time, there would result a reduction of little more than 11 per cent in the total numbers of feebleminded in the next generation. The eminent biologist and eugenicist, Professor H. S. Jennings, has shown that in subsequent generations all that could be accomplished through such measures would be to maintain the ratios attained after the current group of definitely feebleminded had been eliminated. Similar views have been expressed by other prominent eugenicists, such as H. J. Muller, Julian Huxley, and Lancelot Hogben. J. B. S. Haldane, in his *Heredity and Politics,* terming the American penchant for sterilization statutes as "barbarous" and even more ominous than its use as a positive political instrument by the Nazis, has shown by painstaking genetic calculations the negligible decreases in the numbers of various types of mental defectives and mental disorders which would be attained within the next century if all known defectives were sterilized. (4) Finally, a question of ominous proportions is raised as to who shall assume the authority of determining which individuals, under what conditions, should be sterilized.

In the last analysis, the criterion for determining who is unfit is a social one. We have only too recently witnessed the terrible example of Nazi Germany, whose officials, with a callous indifference difficult to imagine, employed this instrument in highly capricious fashion. Under the Nazi laws, nine extremely vague categories were employed to specify individuals subject to sterilization. The term "feebleminded" was distorted by Nazi officials to include even those who might be considered political enemies of the Reich, while one governmental order endorsed sterilization for even the "slightly feebleminded." The Nuremberg war-crimes trials of 1947 revealed that more than 275,000 insane, feebleminded, and physically handicapped Germans had been put to death under the official Nazi euthanasia program.

SUMMARY

(1) Within the last few decades, there has developed an integrative tendency with respect to the study of human personality, the biological organism and the cultural environment. There has been a growing awareness of the need for re-appraisal of organic and personality problems in terms of their continuous relationships within the cultural context. This regained perspective of "organic responsiveness" within given cultural milieux has given rise to the new concepts of psychosomatics, sociosomatics, and psycho-sociality. (2) In the study of personality disorders, a sharp distinction must be made between the mental defectives (aments) and those suffering from emotional derangement (dements), although relationships may be seen to exist between the two categories in certain forms and under certain conditions. (3) Previous attitudes toward mentally defective individuals fluctuated in accordance with dominant social values, although the more common attitude in Western culture was to regard them with repugnance and with a view toward their extermination. Beginning with the age of rational enlightenment of the eighteenth century, however, and under the influence of the work of Itard and Seguin, the possibility of mental defectives benefitting by specially devised educational programs was demonstrated. Special institutions for their custody, education, and treatment were established during the nineteenth century. (4) While formerly mental defectiveness was considered largely hereditary, the function of non-hereditary factors (traumatic shocks, neurological lesions, infectious disorders, etc.), particularly during foetal development and the postnatal period, is being increasingly stressed. (5) The extent

of feeblemindedness may be ascertained only approximately. It is likely that no more than 2 per cent of the population may definitely be classified as technically feebleminded, while possibly as many as 10 to 15 per cent more give evidence of various forms of mental retardation. (6) The determination of feeblemindedness involves careful diagnosis of somatic difficulties, study of facial deformities, physical stigmata, and the like, as well as proof of intellectual incapacity. In reference to the latter, it is to be noted that intelligence-test procedures frequently reflect social and cultural differentials as well as mental aptitudes. (7) The examination of special classes of the feebleminded, such as border-line defectives, morons, imbeciles, and idiots, reveals the specialized problems they present and the need for correspondingly specialized treatment and care. (8) The movement to eliminate mental defectives through sterilization appears premature at this stage, and under certain conditions may have ominous consequences.

CHAPTER TWENTY-ONE

MENTAL DERANGEMENT AND SOCIAL DISORDER

(1) EMOTIONAL DEVIATIONS AND CULTURAL PATTERNS

PROBLEMS of *mental deficiency* are strongly rooted in organic disorders. They are significant sociologically because of the peculiar problems of role fulfillment presented by the feebleminded in certain cultures and because of the attitudes which the societies of which they are members maintain toward them. Problems of *emotional derangement*, however—that is, the problems of *psychosis* and *neurosis*, disorders involving serious emotional difficulties in adjusting to the socio-cultural environment—are significant for quite different reasons. Such problems are significant to the sociologist in so far as they represent foci of severe conflict within the culture itself.

At the very outset, we should recognize that each culture, through the mediating agencies of its basic constituent groups (familial and other), tends to mould the emotional expressions of the individual's behavior in accordance with the standards of the groups in which the individual maintains membership. Expressions of joy, resentment, anger, hatred, revulsion, repugnance, equanimity, indifference, love, and fear are channelized in accordance with the peculiar slant of the given culture. As we have pointed out earlier in this volume, the group's conceptions of normalcy refer fundamentally to a series of common definitions of the situation applicable to a variety of socially structured situations. These "definitions" specify not only the forms of behavior and attitudes that are considered appropriate *for certain situations*, but also the kinds of emotion that should accompany the behavior.

From the standpoint of the science of human behavior, it is difficult to point to any standard of normalcy other than the statistical. Moreover, this statistical standard can be said to have validity only within given cultural—or sub-cultural—units. As for an absolute standard of normalcy, one that would transcend the idiosyncrasies of single cultures and serve as a norm for all mankind, none of scientific stature exists thus far. Theologians, moralists, and social philosophers have provided us with a variety of systems, but to none of them can the scientist who is cognizant of ethnology grant an unequivocal Q.E.D. Indeed, our very reflections on the question of absolute normalcy seem to be projections of the character of our existence within our own culture.

When we narrow the question of normalcy down to the single culture, we are still far from arriving on solid ground. In problems of emotional adjustment, the opinion—or even the actions—of the majority can serve as little more than a statement of statistical frequency. The term "normalcy" bears a meaning which reaches beyond the statistical; it suggests problems of hygienic desirability as well as of statistical fact. In this chapter, whose subject-matter is the varieties of emotional disturbance, the question of mental hygiene stands in the foreground.

Students of personality have provided us with the best insights into the problem of normalcy. Recognizing at the outset that the behavior of the majority by no means establishes what are desirable personality norms (desirable from the standpoint of mental hygiene), such writers as Karen Horney and Erich Fromm have argued that within our own society adherence to the standards of statistical normalcy involves the individual in ways of living that may have decidedly deleterious influences on the personality.

Easy answers to the problems of normalcy are not readily forthcoming. In examining problems such as will be discussed in this chapter, the student should bear in mind two orientations which, while not providing absolute answers, will at least facilitate sound criticism. (1) Absolute, universal standards of normalcy remain to be discovered. (2) In dealing with problems of normalcy and abnormalcy, the culture of the individual or group under study provides a first, sure frame of reference.

(2) THE RELATIVITY OF PERSONALITY NORMS

Emotional derangement, therefore, must always be viewed within the relevant cultural context. The forms which neurotic and psychotic manifestations assume reflect the cultural base of the afflicted individual. Thus, the Eastern Cree, a singularly gentle and peaceful people who live on a very low level of material existence, develop pathological forms of behavior only in relation to the deprivations brought about by fears of hunger and famine. Delusions among these people take the form of their imagining themselves incarnations of the feared *Wihtiko*, a cannibalistic demi-god. The African Bantu, who stress oratory as a prime means of gaining distinction, tend to foster considerable emotional anguish among those of their young men who lack the gift of fluent expression. Within our culture, the psychosis of manic-depression is found with higher frequency among certain groups of higher cultural and educational levels that are marked by closely integrated family patterns. This correlation suggests that particular cultural configurations may encourage manic-depression. The tendencies toward higher rates of psychoneuroses among the professional middle class, as indicated by Karen Horney, and the increased incidence of incipient neurotic disorders among middle-class children, as contrasted with children of lower educational and social levels, also direct our attention to the fact that different factors are operative within the various sectors of our own culture.[1]

The extreme paranoid hostility and suspicion of the Dobuans and the Kwakiutl and the marked quiescence of the Zuñi provide illuminating illustrations of types of emotionality which lie at the root of cultural patterns considerably different from our own. Benedict describes a Dobuan male whose geniality, kindness, and willingness to assist others—traits which we regard highly in our society—were regarded with considerable distrust and disquiet by his tribal fellows. In their eyes, he was completely disoriented and "outside the game." [2] Lowie describes a Crow Indian male of exceptional ability and with unusual knowledge of tribal cultural forms, who was completely "beyond the pale" because of his fear of physical danger. His fear marked him as a deviant person in this society, where personal courage in war is stressed above all else. Even those forms of behavior that are regarded in our society as symptoms of extreme deviation, such as the trance of the mystic and catalepsy, are regarded by some social systems as highly desirable achievements.

Emotional states serve varied functions in different cultures. These emotional states are linked to the attitudes and objects which the society regards as essential in maintaining the basic regularities of behavior. Without such regularities, there could be no society, no indication as to how individuals would react under given conditions; society would be thrust into the chaos that Thomas Hobbes describes in his *Leviathan*. Because of our ethnocentric views, however, it is difficult for us to realize that the regularities integrating other societies may be animated by emotional functions which to us appear destructive and anarchic. To individuals within such cultures, states of suspicion, hostility, fear, and love may be expressed under conditions which are not dangerous or destructive, but which, on the contrary, are based upon the individual's need to maintain a state of emotional security. The mental state of the individual may be seriously disturbed not by the seeming destructiveness of the emotion but rather by his inability to anticipate the kind of emotional state a given social situation will bring forth.

[1] Cf. Karen Horney, *The Neurotic Personality of Our Time* (New York, 1937); also, Arnold W. Green, "The Middle Class Male Child and Neurosis," *American Sociological Review*, XI (1946), 31–41.

[2] Ruth Benedict, *Patterns of Culture* (New York, 1934), p. 239.

Ralph Linton has indicated the general social framework within which normal emotional states and attitudes are brought to collective focus. Each society, according to Linton, develops broad regularities of behavior which pervade the entire social structure. These broad regularities Linton calls the *universals*. Each culture also develops optional behavior-patterns which Linton calls the alternatives.[3] While the universals are broadly descriptive of the widely practiced and generally agreed upon patterns of behavior for all individuals within the society, the alternatives depend upon the several status and role positions within the social order, which depend on age, class, sex, occupation, and the like. These status and role positions define what patterns of behavior are expected under given conditions and indicate the kinds of attitudes that are appropriate to the given forms of behavior. Pathological states of mind are evidenced when the individual reacts to a given situation with an emotional-attitudinal set inappropriate to his action. If, for example, in our society, a parent reacts to the normal display of affection by his spouse, or children with towering states of rage, we usually surmise that something is seriously wrong, and that the personality of the parent may be impaired.

The family within culture and emotional patterning. It would appear that the process of emotional patterning is conveyed in each culture by the family. The structure of the family, as determined by what the prevalent cultural conceptions in the society recognize the functions of the family to be, plays a significant role in conveying to the child his conceptions of social normalcy. This process of socializing the child within the restraining cultural conditions of the society is highly complex. Conspicuous in this process are (1) the factors of the cultural environment, economic, social, etc., which will determine whose task it is to care for the child and under what conditions; (2) the social control within the family itself; (3) the attitudes toward children and child-bearing, particularly those held by the persons who exercise principal responsibility for child-rearing; (4) the individualized attitudes toward the child, irrespective of social mandates; and (5) the conscious efforts to impose upon the child the cultural conceptions of normalcy held by his particular group, class, and society.[4]

One of the most provocative discussions in the entire field of modern sociology is the question of how these complicated social and cultural processes and patterns bring about the unique differences of individual personalities while at the same time imposing the restraints of uniform behavior. It is in the study of this problem that the source of our insights

[3] Ralph Linton, *The Study of Man* (New York, 1936), pp. 272–4; also Linton, *The Cultural Background of Personality* (New York, 1945), Chap. 3.

[4] For an interesting discussion of how these several factors interact in the psychocultural conditioning of the child, see Margaret Mead, *Male and Female* (New York, 1949), Chaps. 3–5.

concerning normal and pathological behavior is to be found.[5] A current explanation for the development of normative cultural patterns and usages is the "learning theory," initiated by Professor Clark Hull of Yale University, and widely adopted in various forms elsewhere by Margaret Mead, Geoffrey Gorer, and others. Variations of this view, with certain psychoanalytical and cultural overtones, have been expounded by other theorists, notably the psychiatrist, Abram Kardiner.[6] These views (sometimes facetiously called the views of the "diaper determinists") and particularly the conceptions of Kardiner, stress the role of the "basic disciplines" (swaddling, nursing, weaning, toilet training, indulgence or prohibition of sexual activities) in providing the initial emotional orientations of the child upon which his resultant social attitudes are based. Kardiner also affirms that these basic emotional attitudes determine the character of the social institutions as well. Thus, the paranoid tendency which is so common among Dobuan adults as to be considered a normal trait is closely related to the distrust and hostility which the Dobuan child comes to feel as a result of prolonged absences of the mother (compelled by her economic responsibilities) and his exposure to the taunting and cruel supervision of his siblings. In modern Western culture, the austere and puritanical attitudes developed in relation to sex matters in communities such as James West's *Plainville*, appear, in part, as a natural consequence of early rigorous toilet-training (reflecting the cultural emphasis upon hygienic cleanliness) and the severe taboos upon sexual expression.

(3) INDIVIDUAL AND SOCIOLOGICAL ORIGINS OF MENTAL DERANGEMENT

In our discussion thus far, we have suggested that the chief criterion of mental or emotional derangement is deviation from statistical standards of normalcy. This, however, constitutes merely the outer facade of abnormality, its external and superficial character. Such individuals as habitual criminals, beggars, migrants, etc., may depart radically from certain established norms of behavior without necessarily manifesting serious symptoms of personality disorder. If the individual is to be labeled "deranged," the departure must be of an *emotional* character—that is, the individual must consistently give evidence of emotional patterns and displays which are inappropriate to the kinds of emotional-attitudinal orientation which the situation calls for. Although this latter may constitute an essential minimal basis upon which mental deviation

[5] Cf. Clyde Kluckhohn and Henry A. Murray, "A Conception of Personality," *Personality in Nature, Society, and Culture* (New York, 1948), Part I.

[6] See, for example, his psychodynamic interpretation in *The Psychological Frontiers of Society* (New York, 1945); also, Abram Kardiner and Ralph Linton, *The Individual and His Society* (New York, 1939).

must be assessed, it still does not give us the entire picture. It presents the important characteristic of *impairment of function* in human relationships, from which both neurotics and psychotics suffer.

There is always to be considered the subjective aspect of personality disorder manifesting itself in social malfunctioning. The individual introjects his cultural and social experiences from the outside, and in "interiorizing" this process, may set up for himself antagonistic life-goals and status-positions at great emotional cost to himself. He may experience intense emotional discomfort while apparently making somewhat effective adjustments to the various standards imposed upon him. He may even, by intense discipline, conform successfully to standards to which he is violently opposed. Karen Horney, while maintaining the popular position that neurotic behavior is an "overt deviation from a statistical norm," asserts that deviant individuals may be able to maintain an inner equilibrium, and yet "be at peace" with themselves. She also states that mere deviation from a standard is insufficient to label an individual neurotic (or psychotic)—the *character* of the deviation must proceed from the general trend of the individual's personal development.[7]

Neurotic and psychotic forms of behavior cannot be envisaged as a direct result of the mode of functioning of the entire culture. This is an erroneous view which many outstanding psychiatric theorists support.[8] *Actually the source of personality disorder may be traced to the vicissitudes of the socialization process itself.* Neurotic and psychotic traits of personality are the results of *trends,* not the isolated traumatic experiences of childhood. A given childhood experience, as profoundly disturbing as it may have been, does not *directly* determine an adult behavioral process. A traumatic shock, irrespective of its seriousness, must be geared into a total personality situation, which absorbs it, modifies it, and reacts to it in its own unique way. The psychogenetic theory of personal-social and personal-cultural relationships, stressed earlier, suggests that personality aberration is a product of the continuing relationships the individual experiences *with those aspects of the social structure which directly engage him* (for example, sex differences, ethnic membership, and particularized group and class structure). The bridge by means of which cultural processes are translated into personal states of mental disorder is the process of socialization, manifesting itself in role and status positions. If

[7] Karen Horney, *The Neurotic Personality of Our Time* (New York, 1937). See also Karen Horney, "What Is a Neurosis?" *American Journal of Sociology,* XLV (1939), 431–6.

[8] See, for example, the excellent critique by Arnold W. Green of this position as held by two of the foremost "sociological" psychoanalysts, Karen Horney and Erich Fromm. "Sociological Analysis of Horney and Fromm," *The American Journal of Sociology,* LI (May, 1946), 533–43.

these positions are in conflict in the life-pattern of the individual and not in accord with particularized modes of group normality, they bring about personality disorder.

(4) SYMPTOMS OF PERSONALITY DISORDER

The pathological individual possesses the traits of the normal individual, but in distorted and extreme form. There is no clear-cut dichotomy between normal and abnormal states of mind. Rather, the two states seem to blend into each other. Pathological mental states are recognized as *matters of degree;* they exist in the extent to which an individual's adjustment-capacities are seriously impaired.

Symptomatic personality distortions are of three categories: (1) neuro-muscular disturbances, (2) chronically disturbed emotional patterns, and (3) aberrations in attitudes. These three classes of symptomatic emotional distortions are frequently inter-related, particularly the last two.

(1) Neuro-muscular disorders, although considered essentially an organic, and, hence, a medical concern, nevertheless frequently betray deep-rooted emotional sources. Our previous discussion of "organic responsiveness" has indicated that, in the adaptation of the total organism to the physical and social environment, various organic alterations may occur, manifesting themselves in somatic idiosyncrasies. Certain physical disturbances such as the convulsive seizures of epilepsy, involuntary muscular twitches, spasms, or tics, may, of course, be directly linked to organic impairment, congenital, or acquired. However, many abnormal muscular symptoms may be shown to result from tensions within the personality organization brought about by inter-personal conflicts or general difficulties in conforming to adjustment-standards. Hyperactive states, for example, or extreme inertia, are frequently accompanying conditions of profound emotional disturbance. Catalepsy and rigidity of the bodily musculature may be caused by acute personality stress. Moreover, such conditions point frequently to direct social sources (providing significant clues to the origin of the disorder) and the forceful imposition of cultural standards. Neurotic compulsions may manifest themselves frequently in symptomatic organic behavior, such as involuntary movements and holding of the breath. Speech disorders, related in many ways to manifestations of physical disturbances in the organism, may reflect serious impairment of emotional functioning. Among the South American Pilaga, persistence in infantile speech (encouraged at one stage of development) constitutes an important symptom of personal disturbances among children.

(2) Chronic and abnormal emotional patterns, as symptomatic of personality disturbances, bring us closer to the sociological sources of the problems of mental pathology. They present peculiar difficulties of analysis. When occurring in conjunction with specific attitudes, they may be frequently diagnosed in relation to personality difficulties. A given emotional trait, however, may conceal behavioral intentions and attitudinal objectives. Furthermore, emotional traits may be closely patterned to specific cultural norms. Stolidity is not necessarily the expression of an individual's genuine temperament; it may be an attained state, acquired by great discipline, as a means of fulfilling a cultural ideal. For these reasons, emotional states must be assessed in relation to cultural standards as well as spontaneous individual inclinations. (The relationship which induced emotional states may bear to neurotic and psychotic conditions has recently been dealt with in the study of war neuroses. The theory has been advanced that individuals of Anglo-Saxon background, ashamed to reveal their fears under combat conditions and rigidly inhibiting and concealing them, were much more likely to break, psychologically, than individuals of other cultures, who, while performing their military duties, readily displayed their fears.)

Such forms of emotional disorder as we are discussing commonly reveal themselves in extreme states of chronic elation, moodiness, and compulsive fears (phobias). Karl Menninger states that abnormal emotional patterns are likely to take four principal forms: (a) schizothymic states, (b) phobias, (c) anxiety states, and (d) perversions of affect and interest. It may be shown for each one of these categories that the source of the abnormal symptom is related to distorted patterning of culturally induced emotional states.

Schizothymic traits in general represent deep disharmonies within the individual who is unable to express appropriate emotions to given situations.

Phobias may be directed at an endless variety of persons, places, and things—to high or low places, cramped quarters, darkness, crowds, buildings, dirt, or unfamiliar objects. The particular focus of the fear may shed considerable light upon the personal and social source of the individual difficulty.

Chronic anxiety states are pervasive states of worry and fear, emotions which the individual is unable to attach to a specific personality or object, and for which he is unable to offer a plausible or realistic basis.

Perversions of affect and interest are intense emotional displays directed toward persons and objects (frequently trivia) which contradict the normal expression of social interest. Such displays may manifest themselves in wide varieties of fetishism.

(3) Attitudinal distortions are especially significant in so far as they reveal themselves in patterned forms of behavior linking the individual to specific groups, objects, and personalities. Such attitudes as over-domination, over-submissiveness, isolation, or over-dependence may be marked. Associated with such attitudes, which suggest disturbed motivations and objectives within the immediate social structure, are the disturbed emotional states previously referred to. Extreme suspicion or hostility, for example, may be strikingly characteristic of these peculiarities of attitudinal orientation. Abnormal attitudinal manifestations may be characteristic of individuals seemingly normal, and, in many cases, of singularly gifted individuals of public prominence.

The degree to which a distorted social attitude, or a certain configuration of such attitudes, may become the basis for normal social behavior remains an interesting problem for further sociological analysis. The recognition that attitudes which in the past were regarded as "abnormal" may eventually metamorphose into acceptable standards of normality lends some credence to the view that consensus establishes normalcy. However, the establishment of standards of normalcy is a complex sociological process. It involves the acceptance of the new standards by strategically placed levels of society, and their fostering by the power-groups which are able to legitimize them by endowing them with prestige and the quality of need.

Attitudinal distortions may be seen in the extreme attitudes of sadism and masochism. Sadistic individuals derive pleasure (considered by the orthodox Freudians to be sexual in origin) from causing pain to others, while masochistic individuals derive pleasure from having pain inflicted on themselves. Attitudes of sadism and masochism are considered to be allied to cultural differences in sex expression, sadism being a more typically masculine form of behavior, while masochism is more related to the attitudes of women. Whether these differences would obtain in societies where sex roles were reversed, as in the case of Margaret Mead's Tchambuli, is difficult to state. Certain psychiatrists suggest strongly that such traits are deeply rooted in the innate sexual characteristics of men and women.[9] Be that as it may, there can be no doubt but that certain cultures deliberately foster strong latent attitudes of sadism and masochism among their men and women. In the patriarchal, male-dominated culture typical of Western society, there are considerable evidences of the strong tendencies toward sadistic expressions by men as a consequence of their positions of dominance.

[9] Cf. Ferdinand Lundberg and Marynia Farnham, *Modern Woman: The Lost Sex* (New York, 1947), pp. 335–6.

(5) TYPES AND CAUSES OF DISTORTED PERSONALITIES

Emotional impairment of the personality may be broadly classified into three major types: (1) the *psychoses,* (2) the *neuroses,* and (3) *simple behavior-maladjustments.*

The psychoses represent the most severe of all the personality maladjustments. The psychotic is one who has lost contact with the world of reality. He suffers, in some cases, from various forms of delusions. His intellectual capacities may be impaired as a result of his emotional derangement and his general ability to respond normally is seriously hampered. Such cases are of sufficient seriousness to require institutional treatment, frequently of a prolonged and intensive nature, and are sometimes not curable.

Neuroses, theoretically curable in all cases, represent forms of mental affliction in which the individual, while retaining some awareness of the world of social reality, nevertheless encounters serious difficulties in normal human relationships and in conforming to social standards. Neurotics may experience pervasive feelings of anxiety, self-doubt, guilt, and fear. They ordinarily do not require institutional treatment, although medical psychiatric treatment is strongly urged and widely practiced. The majority of individuals suffering from such disabilities continue to perform their daily functions, some with surprising success.

Individuals suffering from simple behavior problems or personality maladjustments may express their difficulty in a wide variety of different situations. The common characteristic of this group is the fact that frequently their maladjustments refer to specific or restricted areas of social activity. An individual incapacitated in relation to one of these areas may nevertheless be able to make effective adjustments in areas other than those in which the personality deficiency comes to light.

Causative factors and conditions of emotional disorders are conventionally classified as *functional* or *structural* (*organic*). Functional causes are those relating to difficulties of adjustment to the immediate social and cultural environment, difficulties which emerge as a result of tensions and imbalance within the socialization process. Structural disorders are the result of injuries to the neurological structure or of defective neurological functioning. It is commonly recognized today that most forms of mental disorder are brought about by functional causes.

(6) MAJOR PSYCHOTIC CONDITIONS

Not until the turn of the century was some sort of classificatory order established in the veritable jungle of symptoms with which physicians and neurologists were forced to deal in apprehending the problems of mentally deranged patients. It was in this period that the illustrious Munich physician, Dr. Emil Kraepelin, succeeded in establishing the major categories which are now recognized as clinically observable states. He delineated approximately one hundred psychiatric entities, and gave his own names to some of the more commonly recognized states.[10]

The principal psychotic disorders in the United States at the present time are schizophrenia (formerly known by the Kraepelinian designation of "dementia praecox"), manic-depressive psychosis, paranoia, and paresis (brain syphilis). The first three are largely recognized to be functional disorders, while the last-named is brought about by the attack of the *spirochete* upon the cerebral cortex and nervous system. The next sections will be devoted to a discussion of the most prevalent of the functional disorders, schizophrenia and manic depression.

Schizophrenia. The most prevalent of all the functional mental disorders and one of the most serious in the contemporary period is generally recognized to be schizophrenia. In fact, it has often been termed, "the psychosis of contemporary civilization." Particularly prevalent among youthful age-groups (it centers largely in the age classification of 21 to 35 years, and hence was designated, formerly, "dementia praecox"), it is marked by lack of co-ordination between the intellectual and emotional faculties of the individual. There seems to be little relation between the schizophrenic's emotional state and the general cognitive, perceptive, and intellectual traits which his behavior calls forth. Usual in such pathological states is the successive retreat into an inner world of the individual's own. This common mental disorder is generally recognized as being characterized by three phases, (a) *the paranoid,* (b) *the hebephrenic,* and (c) *the catatonic.* These phases are not to be construed as stages in the onset of the disorder, nor do individual schizophrenics give evidence of all three types. From one standpoint, however, they may be regarded as representative of the degree of the afflicted individual's isolation from the external world. In the *paranoid* type, the individual appears aware of personalities and events about him, but reacts to them with marked hostilities and suspicion. The *hebephrenic* individual appears to represent a sort of midway position, flitting back and forth across the shadowy borderland of some inner world of his own and the world of outside reality. This behavior is characterized by sporadic awareness of outside events and individuals, manifesting itself in the form of seemingly disconnected words, phrases, and impressions; rapid changes of mood, facial expression, and emotional tone; sporadic and sometimes sustained indifference to outer surroundings; and general behavioral processes which appear mean-

[10] The Kraepelinian classification still provides the essential basis for contemporary diagnostic categories, although the American Psychiatric Association in 1917, and later in 1934, revised these categories for purposes of standardization.

ingless. A common supposition is that the flights of the individual's perceptive and imaginative processes carry him back and forth across the shadowy barriers of his internal mental state and his external awareness. Random mental associations are brought into play, occasioned by the periodic focus of attention upon the particular external event and personality which happen to be confronting him at a given time. Connective links among the apparently disjointed phrases, sentences and verbal outbursts may be present in the person's flitting imaginative processes, although only the actual overt speech and behavioral processes are discernible to the observer. Kraepelin has provided us with an excellent clinical picture of this type of disorder.[11]

> When brought into the room she lets herself slide on the ground, throws herself about, kicks with her legs, claps her hands, plucks at her hair and makes it untidy, pulls out a whole bunch of it, makes faces, hides her face, and spits round about her. She does not generally react at all when spoken to or pricked with a needle, but resists violently if you try to take her hand. She obeys no kind of orders. She will not show her tongue, and shuts her eyes as soon as you want to examine them. But, from isolated remarks, and answers quickly thrown out, it appears that she not only understands the questions, but is also pretty clear about her surroundings. But generally she calls out disconnected words, having absolutely no relation to her position, loudly and quite senselessly: "Pup—pups—moll—you know—temperature—fire insurance—water—Weinheim—water—creolin—God damn you!—twenty marks—say, what is—away with it—thank you very much—twenty marks—say what you want—God damn you!—water—not I—twenty marks—so God damn you!—dear child—so fire-shy—stay at home with your wife—treasures—oh—sow—say what you want—thank you very much," etc. Meanwhile she croaks and crows, then suddenly begins to sing a hymn with expression, changes to a street-song, laughs without restraint, and breaks off abruptly with loud sobs. She is slightly built and very badly nourished; her lips are cracked and covered with scabs; her head is flushed and her pulse hurried.

Catatonic types represent the most extreme forms of personality breakdown in schizophrenic disorder. In such cases, the individual appears to have succumbed completely to his inner world, and presents to the outside world a facade of seeming obliviousness. Such individuals frequently fail to respond at all to any outside stimulus or communication,

[11] Dr. Emil Kraepelin, *Lectures on Clinical Psychiatry* (edited by Thomas Johnstone) (New York, 1912), pp. 33–6.

will sometimes maintain for lengthy periods of time grotesque positions which the body may have accidentally assumed, and may even remain unresponsive to sharp stimuli of pain. These individuals appear to have lost "their passports to the outside world." But, as Ernest Kretschmer has intimated, although they give little outward sign of inner response, they may be likened to Roman villas shuttered against the blazing sun, austere and grim on the outside perhaps, while inside "there may be festivities."

Social and familial factors in schizophrenia. The schizophrenic may technically, as the term indicates, be a "dual" or a "split" personality, but not in the fashion of a Dr. Jekyll and Mr. Hyde. The duality, as mentioned, refers to the separation of the individual's inner experiences and reactions from the external events of social reality. The trend in personality which appears to induce this state is a gradual process of *isolation* from human contact. Schizophrenia may be viewed as a successive retreat of the individual from reality. This isolation may stem from two sources: (1) the individual may have certain constitutional incapacities which tend to create the barriers between himself and the immediate social world about him; or (2) the individual may never have developed adequate capacities for normal social contact and intercourse. The first of these possibilities indicates a possible organic factor which may play a predisposing role—something recently suggested in the studies by Kallmann on schizophrenia in the cases of identical twins. Or, it may suggest that certain organic factors predispose the individual more readily to the acquisition of a *need-phase* in the psychogenetic structure which makes isolation from others a habitual and preferred trait. Recent studies indicate that if the *need* for isolation is deep-rooted and of long standing, the prospect of successful readjustment and reorientation of the personality is considerably more unfavorable than would be the case if the individual developed recessive and isolationist qualities merely as a secondary, or *functional phase*, of his psychogenetic structure.

Hereditary factors in schizophrenia. The first possibility suggested above, that schizophrenia, a functional disorder, may have certain organic bases, is not generally acknowledged. What appears more likely, in the light of clinical evidence, is that the isolationist tendencies within the individual's personality become rooted during the early childhood career and are accentuated by the entire subsequent trend of personality development. The study of 794 schizophrenic twins by Franz J. Kallmann sought to establish the degree to which certain organic predispositions may play a part in the development of schizophrenic states.[12] This is part of a broader study covering seven thousand pairs of twins conducted

[12] Cf. "The Twin Studies," *Mental Hygiene News*, Department of Mental Hygiene, New York State, XX (Sept., 1949), 7, 8, 11. Also, Franz J. Kallmann, "The Genetic Theory of Schizophrenia," *American Journal of Psychiatry*, CIII (1946), 309–22.

under the auspices of the New York State Psychiatric Institute, involving both fraternal and identical twins. The larger study deals with associated factors in tuberculosis and schizophrenia, as well as constitutional characteristics of twins. The investigation revealed that 85.8 per cent of the monozygotic (identical) twin-siblings of the selected index cases suffered from schizophrenia, while the same condition existed in only 14.7 per cent of the cases of the dizygotic (fraternal) twins. This last percentage is very similar to the rate of schizophrenia for ordinary siblings of schizophrenic patients, a rate of 14.3 per cent. When the rates of schizophrenia for identical twins reared in the same environment and for those reared apart were compared, the similarity was found to be high. In the former case, the rate was 91.5 per cent, while in the latter case, the rate was 77.6 per cent. The conclusion of the study stated that "the chance of developing schizophrenia increases in direct proportion to the degree of blood relationship to a schizophrenic."

Although the findings of this study are impressive, there are certain significant questions which may still be raised. Careful investigation of the developmental patterns and environmental factors at different age levels still remains to be done in order to ascertain precisely the degree to which such hereditary predispositions are affected by precipitating social environmental conditions. Dr. Nolan D. C. Lewis, director of the New York State Psychiatric Institute, has indicated that the factors of precipitation and perpetuation must be taken into account. Even assuming a genetic tendency toward such an abnormal mental state, unless certain social factors tend to elicit this condition and then to accentuate it, the disease may not manifest itself. Proper understanding requires that the entire developmental pattern of the personality be adequately examined in relation to the factors that may produce such a mental disorder.

Further social considerations in relation to schizophrenia. The previous investigation suggests that, in the organization of the psychogenetic pattern, certain constitutional or organic factors may play a role in producing acute needs for seclusiveness. These may form the basis of the primary phase of schizophrenia. It is theoretically possible that a *functional* variety of schizophrenia exists in which the seclusiveness is acquired as a secondary trait. Surveys of the types of social situations in which schizophrenics develop would indicate the merit of such a conclusion. Especially relevant are the powerful contributory influences of the family and, above all, the relationship of the mother to the child. Physical illnesses and deformities may tend to isolate certain individuals, but this tendency can be fulfilled only under certain social conditions. Seclusiveness may be fostered by a wide range of contributory conditions: geography, the fact of being an only child, peculiarities in home training, poverty, wealth, religious or ethnic differences. A common subjective process accompanying such isolation is the development of an acute sense of inferiority and inadequacy in the face of social demands.

Manic-depression. Manic-depressive psychoses, or *cyclothymias,* are characterized by the violent alternation of moods. Irrespective of which mood dominates, the behavior of the individual is so extreme that the entire life-pattern appears distorted. During the depressed state of the psychosis, suicides are not uncommon, while during the manic phase, the individual's ecstatic outpourings and frenetic activity bear little relation to the objective situation.

The types of social arrangements in the families of manic-depressives tend to foster profound emotional involvements and considerable dependence upon the mother and other adult members of the family group. The "interiorizing" of socio-cultural standards through identification with the parent, usually under powerful drives to establish status-positions in accordance with the family's objectives, may tend to bring about serious anxiety-states and misgivings concerning one's fitness. Frequently associated with these features of the family are the special disciplinary instruments employed in such a family pattern, in which overprotection or rejection of the child may both play significant roles. Consequently, the individual who has developed such intense bonds of attachment may experience an acute sense of jeopardy on the occasions when he is rejected, because of his great need to preserve what constitutes for him a basic and essential emotional tie. The sense of jeopardy may produce continual states of anxiety and fear, heightened by guilt feelings. These guilt feelings, penetrating deeply into the outlook of the depressed or melancholic individual, sharpen his entire mood. They appear to result from the doubts and misgivings occasioned by the feeling of being rejected, whether real or fancied.

There can be little doubt that such family-patterns are typical on certain socially structured levels. Selected economic, cultural, class, ethnic, and educational factors may be seen to function in producing such family configurations. The urban Jewish family, the suburban middle-class and professional family, certain Italian-American families and others, appear to establish a social setting favorable to the development of incipient manic-depressive states. Certain married middle-class women, motivated by cultural considerations of leisure, the need for status, and satisfactory ego-involvements, engendered by family background and class conditions, frequently resent the coming of children, whether consciously or unconsciously. Because of the strength of our culture's standards regarding parental care, however, such attitudes may be concealed by overcompensation, in the form of excessive attachment and overprotection of children.

We may conclude that manic-depressive states develop in part from two sources: (a) a socio-cultural matrix which involves intense personal attachment and close primary relationships; and (b) a psychogenetic pattern which prompts the individual to react strongly to fancied or real rejection.

(7) THE NEUROSES

Major neuroses have long been regarded as falling into three major classifications: (a) *psychasthenia*, (b) *neurasthenia*, and (c) *hysteria*. In *psychasthenia* (anxiety hysteria, anxiety neurosis, compulsion neurosis), the individual experiences continuous intense fears, anxieties, and self-doubts for which there is no plausible external reason. Neurasthenia, commonly recognized in varying degrees of hypochondriasis, manifests itself through innumerable physical complaints and disorders, pains, aches, weakness, and fatigue for which no organic basis may be discovered. *Hysteria* manifests itself in gross physical symptoms, paralytic states, sudden and extreme changes in behavior sustained for a period of time and then dropped, and other incapacitating physical states. Although no organic basis may be found for neurasthenia and hysteria, the individual is convinced that the source of his disorder is physical. While the neurasthenic is usually highly vocal in giving expression to his complaints, the hysteric tends to let his disorder speak for itself in proclaiming his disability. The state of mind of the neurasthenic is clearly portrayed in the following letter: [13]

> Dear Mother and Husband:
>
> I have suffered terrible today with drawing in throat. My nerves are terrible. My head feels queer. But my stomach hasn't cramped quite so hard. I've been on the verge of a nervous chill all day, but I have been fighting it hard. It's night and bedtime, but, Oh, how I hate to go to bed. Nobody knows or realizes how badly I feel because I fight to stay up and out doors if possible.
>
> I haven't had my cot up for two days, they don't want me to use it.
>
> These long afternoons and nights are awful. There are plenty of patients well enough to visit but I'm in too much pain.
>
> The nurses ignore any complaining. They just laugh or scold.
>
> . . .
>
> My eyes are bothering me more.
>
> Come up as soon as you can. My nose runs terribly every time I eat.
>
> The trains and ducks and water pipes are noisy at night.
>
> Annie

[13] Menninger, *The Human Mind*, pp. 139–40.

P.S. I don't mean to be so partial by addressing this to Mother, they are for all.

The neurotic is frequently an individual who, unable to meet the demands of a desired status-position, maneuvers himself into a position where he is spared from making the requisite effort towards its fulfillment. By his fictive illness, the neurotic renders himself *hors de combat*. Further, as Adler has pointed out, he still manages to retain some degree of power and manipulation over others by virtue of his illness. His illness, thus, may become a control technique, although he may be unaware of the intention of his unconscious deceit. The role of the invalid in contemporary society stimulates attitudes of pity and beneficence, and spares the victim from the necessity of encountering the rigors of normal social life. In the dependent relationship of the individual toward others, a psychologically regressed state is produced in which the invalid is enabled to enact the protected role of the child, without, it might be added, the necessity of being a child. Thus, the prerogatives of adult social status are safeguarded along with the immunities accorded to the childhood state. It seems reasonable to expect that, in the case of the hysteric, the individual's incapacity functions auto-suggestively to produce the gross symptoms of acute physical defect and paralysis which completely remove him from the arena of social life.

The psycho-sociological pattern functioning in relation to the psychasthenic, while not as dramatic, is even more striking in its implications, however. Psychasthenics emerge with considerable frequency in middle-class and professional groups, although they are not confined to such groups. Horney and others have indicated that psychasthenics have in common social and familial backgrounds of intense sibling-rivalry and generalized striving for status. The attainment of desired positions, however, involves a nice balance between carefully regulated aggressive impulses and the exercise of restraint. The failure in the socialization process to express aggressive impulses along socially desired channels produces a sustained state of fear concerning possible retaliatory aggression. Having failed to express his aggressive impulses adequately, the individual acquires fears concerning his own status. Consequently, the entire social world about him may begin to appear threatening. The resultant state of mind is aggravated by the omnipresent competitive drives and psychogenetic impulses to fulfill expected role-positions. The fact that many psychasthenics attain successful positions does not necessarily remove the sense of disquiet. The psychasthenic is obsessed with a lurking presentiment of doom, although he is unaware of any specific element in the immediate social environment which actually constitutes such a threat to his status.

(8) EXTENT AND TREND OF MENTAL DISORDER

An analysis of the figures for admissions to mental hospitals in the United States over several decades indicates that the rise in mental disorders for the country as a whole has been continuous and precipitate since the last century. However, this rise may be far more apparent than real, in view of our increased facilities for the recognition, detention, and care of mentally deranged persons. Nevertheless, even today, almost half of all hospital beds in the United States are occupied by mental patients, of whom about one-half are schizophrenics. According to the Federal Census, 22.6 per cent of all first admissions and readmissions to mental hospitals in 1944 were schizophrenia patients (29,010 out of a total of 128,475); 9.2 per cent of all cases admitted during the same year were manic-depressive psychotics, while 46 per cent were victims of the so-called organic psychoses.

At the end of 1945, there were about 635,000 psychotic patients in all mental hospitals, which is still just a fraction of the total numbers who may be afflicted. For example, if all states maintained facilities on a level with those of New York and Massachusetts, it is estimated that the number of hospitalized psychotics would be twice as large. While the entire population of the country has doubled since 1880, the population of our mental hospitals has increased approximately twelve times.[14] In 1880, the ratio of patients in mental hospitals was 63.7 for every 100,000 persons in the population; today, it is 366.7 per 100,000—an increase of more than 500 per cent. At the present time, our mental hospital population is increasing at the rate of approximately 20,000 a year, with an annual admission rate of about 125,000. In New York and Massachusetts, because of wider hospital coverage, there is about one patient in a mental hospital for every 185 persons in the population as a whole. In other states, where facilities are not nearly as extensive, the ratio is about one out of every 272 persons. Expectation rates, based upon statistics of the New York Mental Hygiene Department, indicate that the probability of becoming mentally ill for a young man of twenty years of age is about one chance out of twelve, while for the public at large, the chances are about one out of twenty.[15] On the basis of the Federal Census Report for 1945, we may estimate that about 1,000,000 children now in public school will at some time be admitted to our mental hospitals. It should be kept in mind that all of these figures are based upon actual hospital admissions. The rates, therefore, might be considerably higher if we had adequate data on mentally disordered persons who do not enter public and private hospitals.

On the basis of these statistics, can we say that the rates of mental

[14] Albert Deutsch, *The Mentally Ill in America* (New York, 1949), p. 507.
[15] *Trends of Mental Disease*, 1945, pp. 52–3.

disorder are actually rising? While the neuroses have increased significantly in recent years, we have no conclusive evidence to indicate that this is the case with the psychoses, despite the remarkable increases of hospitalization of mental patients. It is likely, on the contrary, that there may have been no real increase in psychotic disorders, except in the case of persons fifty years of age and over. In studies conducted by Elkind and Taylor, and by Goldhamer and Marshall, it has been shown that no appreciable rise may have occurred in functional psychoses except in the case of deteriorative disorders induced by old age.[16] Such factors as improved treatment and diagnosis, less resistance on the part of the public toward acknowledging the presence of mental disorder, and the remarkable prolongation of life brought about by scientific advances, have tended to produce statistics which appear to support a rise in the number of mental defectives which may be more apparent than real. The old-age categories of the population have changed drastically since 1900, as a result of higher medical and living standards, the category of forty-five to sixty-four years showing an increase of approximately 30 per cent, while for those sixty-five years of age and over, the increase has been over one-third.

(9) AGING AND MENTAL DISORDERS

Studies of rates of admissions of specific age-categories to mental hospitals indicate the precipitate rise and concentration of mental disorders in age classifications over fifty years. This would appear to be a natural consequence of the increase in numbers of older-age groups in the general population. The two principal mental disorders of old age are senile dementia and psychosis with cerebral arteriosclerosis. Both of these disorders are commonly regarded as effects of a natural impairment to the brain tissue, resulting from organic deterioration brought about by aging. This is the orthodox view presented by most psychologists in textbooks of psychology and abnormal psychology. However, recent investigations in geriatrics—the problems of aging—have brought to light data suggesting that impairment of intellectual and emotional orientations in old age may not necessarily be a result of organic injury, but rather of the individual's changed status and orientation in relation to the problems which old age has thrust upon him. Rothschild has indicated that while we have been essentially preoccupied with the obvious factor of cerebral pathology, we have overlooked the changed statuses, roles, and requirements which the individual's senescent state brings forth.[17] Sudden transi-

[16] Cf. Henry B. Elkind and Maurice Taylor, "The Alleged Increase in the Major Psychoses," *American Journal of Psychiatry*, 1935; also, Herbert Goldhamer and Andrew W. Marshall, *The Frequency of Mental Disease: Long-Term Trend and Present Status* (Santa Monica, California, 1949).

[17] D. Rothschild, "Senile Psychoses and Cerebral Arteriosclerosis," in O. J. Kaplan, ed., *Mental Disorders in Later Life* (Stanford University, 1945).

tion to a state of helplessness from an active and vigorous life of responsibility may induce severe strains in the personality fully as disastrous as those brought about by the organic changes of advancing age. In fact, the older person's very attitude towards his own organic enfeeblement and his increased dependence upon others may produce an inordinate amount of stress.

The tendency in industrial and economic life to relieve men of their employment at a relatively early period in their careers, coupled with the fact that until recently, little provision had been made for their subsequently contributing to society, has frequently accelerated the process of mental dissolution among many of the aged. The danger of premature retirement with no subsequent plan for organized activity, as a causal factor in senile dementia, has recently been sharply stressed by the psychiatrist, Dr. Clarence A. Neymann.[18] Belknap and Friedsam, in discussing the increasing tendency toward *social isolation* of aged individuals in the United States, suggest two possible corrective courses of action, both of which must be confirmed by further empirical research.[19] (1) Mental disorders in the case of the male may be held to a minimum when "intergenerational" continuity is maintained, when spatial and social mobility are limited, and when the "status of orientation" (i.e., the period of fulfilling vocational and social functions) is carried to a maximum and involves no abrupt changes. (2) The case of the aged female is somewhat different, in view of the dominance of male status and the greater stress upon active vocational responsibilities and duties for men in our social order. For women, therefore, mental pathologies may be kept to a minimum if social and family responsibilities are prolonged.

(10) THE ECOLOGICAL DISTRIBUTION OF MENTAL DISORDER

Added evidence that mental disorders result not only from intrinsic organic or personality factors but are closely linked to socio-cultural and social structural elements, may be seen in the concentrations of mental pathologies and psychopathies and *the pattern of their distribution* in urban areas. In a well-known study by Faris and Dunham, the character of the distribution of urban mental disorders was determined on the basis of an investigation of 34,864 cases admitted to four state hospitals and eight private institutions serving the Chicago region during the period of

[18] "Your Life Cycle," an address before the Chicago Medical Society, November, 1947.

[19] Cf. Ivan Belknap and Hiram J. Friedsam, "Age and Sex Categories as Sociological Variables in the Mental Disorders of Later Maturity," *American Sociological Review*, XIV (June, 1949), 367–76.

1922–1934.[20] Similar studies, although of less extensive scope, have been carried out in the cities of St. Louis, Milwaukee, Omaha, Kansas City, and Peoria.[21] In attempting to determine the differing rates of concentration for various mental disorders in the city of Chicago, Faris and Dunham classified their cases on the basis of the several subcommunities comprising the metropolitan district in which the mentally disordered person lived prior to first admission to a hospital. Rates for each district were then computed on the basis of populations of such areas fifteen years of age and over. It is significant to note that the differences found in the pattern of distribution of mental disorders were extremely sharp. In general, the chief concentrations of psychopathies were found in the central business district, with an overall rate of 499 per 100,000. The next highest rate, 480, was found in the adjacent hotel and Hobohemian area. These rates were more than ten times as high as the rate found in the outlying residential district where psychopathies were the least frequent. The pattern of distribution was similar to that of other problem rates (delinquency, crime, etc.), with the highest concentration in the central districts of the city and a consistent decline toward the periphery of the urban area. Although overall rates were found to be high in the ten densely populated subcommunities converging upon the center of the city (the notorious "zones in transition": slums, Negro districts, and Hobohemian sections), significant differences were nevertheless found for both overall and specific rates covering these districts.

When specific rates were examined for separate psychotic conditions, differences were noted in their distribution as compared with that of the overall rates. In an examination of 7,253 cases of schizophrenia—the most frequent single disorder, comprising about 22 per cent of the total number of cases studied—the concentration was found to follow the general pattern, with highest rates in the central districts and a progressive decline in the outlying residential areas. In the case of manic-depressive psychosis, however, the scatter was considerably broader. High concentration rates for manic-depression were found in central areas and in outlying neighborhoods of different types.

One inference to be drawn is that manic-depression may occur as a result of a certain type of family structure, supporting the suggestion made in our previous analysis. The concentrations of such cases are found, in certain instances, to be associated with areas of high income and educational status. Some indication of this may be seen in the fact that a positive correlation coefficient of +0.44 was found for manic-depressive

[20] Robert E. L. Faris and H. Warren Dunham, *Mental Disorders in Urban Areas* (Chicago, 1939).

[21] Cf. Clarence W. Schroeder, "Mental Disorders in Cities," *American Journal of Sociology*, XLVIII (July, 1942), 40–7.

rates and educational status, while in the case of schizophrenia, a negative correlation of −0.47 was discovered for the same factor. That the district of residence is of greater importance, as a determining factor, than ethnic and racial membership, appears to be borne out by the fact that foreign-born rates fluctuated in accordance with areas of residence. For example, foreign-born peoples yielded a rate for schizophrenia of 126 per 100,000 in the central districts, but a rate of only 21 in the outlying neighborhoods. For Negroes, the variation in rates by district of residence fluctuated more widely than the difference between Negro rates as a whole and white rates, suggesting strongly that high Negro rates are *not* due to racial factors.

Although some criticism has been directed toward this study on the ground that hospital figures fail to give samples adequate for generalization, modifications of the data to accord with the criticism would not alter critically the basic pattern of distribution of such disorders and the conclusions to be drawn.[22] Several hypotheses may be offered to account for the presence of such differential rates. One popular hypothesis is that individuals and families facing adverse economic and social conditions productive of mental stress will, of necessity, tend to concentrate in low-rental and disorganized areas. Another possibility is that the adverse environmental conditions of such areas will tend to foster personality conflict and strain. Thirdly, high rates of psychopathy appear to be associated with certain unstable and highly mobile individuals who will frequent the highly mobile central districts catering to their residential and other needs.

High urban rates in general seem to suggest the possibility that mental disorders may be associated with communities of greater cultural and social complexity. Some basis for such a conclusion has already been presented. The studies by Sherman and Henry of the "hollow-communities" in the Blue Ridge Mountain area of Virginia indicate that the rates of neurotic disorder and mental conflict seem to increase progressively as one moves from the simple and relatively undifferentiated culture of the isolated community of Colvin Hollow to the more modern farm and industrial community of Briarsville, a comunity with established channels of communication and contact with the "outside world." [23]

(11) INDIVIDUAL AND SOCIAL REORGANIZATION

Our attack on the problem of mental disorder must be twofold: (1) the intensification of our methods of treatment and research, medi-

[22] Cf., for example, Mary Bess Owen, "Alternate Hypotheses for the Explanation of Some of Faris' and Dunham's Results," *American Journal of Sociology*, XLVII (July, 1941), 48–52.

[23] Mandel Sherman and Thomas R. Henry, *Hollow Folk* (New York, 1933).

cal, psychoneurological, and psychiatric, along extensive lines hardly approached thus far; and (2) the introduction of procedures, whenever possible, which will bring about the re-structuring of the social order as a means of diminishing provocative personal tensions. The first task is relatively easy to accomplish. The second provides a great many difficult problems in which the limitations of our knowledge and the presence of formidable cultural barriers play important roles.

In reference to medical psychiatric care, the problem is primarily one of extending, through public and private agencies, the new developments in modern psychotherapy, both *preventive* and *curative*. Wider application of the new procedures developed in the fields of operative psychoneurology and clinical psychiatry is also called for. In addition to the conventional psychotherapeutic techniques, which are continually being improved, such new surgical methods as pre-frontal lobotomy, initiated by the Portuguese surgeons, Drs. Egaz Moniz and Almeida Lima, in 1935, and a progressive advancement of the shock-therapy methods for psychotic cases require further investigation and wider opportunity for use. The promising help offered by the new drugs, such as the penicillin derivative, tolserol (myanesin), in easing tensions and anxiety strains, must be explored for further application and improvement.

It is surprising that we know so much and yet do so little. For example, the Faris and Dunham study has located the areas in which paresis and the related paralytic states are most likely to arise. Today, syphilis and alcohol are responsible for over 11 per cent of the admissions to our mental hospitals. These conditions require improvements in public administration, supervisory control, and education, which will go a long way toward diminishing the evil effect of sexual abuse and excessive drinking.

The development of treatment facilities, *along with renewed use of our general hospitals as well as specialized institutions for the treatment of mental pathologies*, represents a genuine need in mental therapy. The increasing use of general hospital facilities in New York State, with wider use of *short-term therapy*, as part of a broader program in the concerted attack upon mental disorders, indicates the beginning of a promising development in 1950. Our medical schools are still woefully deficient in providing sufficient psychiatrists for our public needs and in stressing properly to potential general practitioners the need for sound training in psychosomatics and psychotherapy. At the National Health Assembly in Washington in 1949, it was pointed out that we presently have only 4,500 trained psychiatrists in this country, a ratio of about one for every 32,000 persons, while our actual immediate need is for at least 15,000 psychiatrists.

Some significant steps toward establishing widespread and integrated services have already been initiated on both state and federal levels. On the federal level, the passage of the National Mental Health Act by the Congress in 1946 went a long way toward realizing the original goals set forth by Dorothea Lynde Dix who, a century ago, made pioneer efforts to bring about adequate help for mental sufferers. The act contains three major provisions: (a) it authorizes federal grants-in-aid for the training of psychiatric personnel, so desperately needed, and for developing facilities for prevention, care, and treatment of mental illness; (b) it authorizes monetary grants to non-profit institutions for research; and (c) it authorizes grants up to $10,000,000 annually for aid to community psychiatric services. In addition, it established a National Institute of Mental Health, now located at Bethesda, Maryland, and a National Advisory Mental Health Council, consisting of six outstanding leaders in the field to advise the Surgeon General of the Public Health Service. Certain progressive states have followed suit with parallel programs within their own jurisdictions. Since 1948, New York State has developed an elaborate program, caring for 108,000 patients annually, establishing a special Psychiatric Institute in New York City for research, and maintaining child guidance clinics in 110 communities throughout the state. The scope of this program may be judged by the fact that its operation requires more than one-fourth of the state's annual budget.

Relative to the second phase of the problem, the task is considerably more difficult. The relieving of personality tensions would involve vast alterations in the social structure. The social structure itself reflects the attitudes of personalities who comprise the social order. The social structure is not simply a vast machine which can be re-structured by tinkering. Nevertheless, if we accept the assumption that certain phases of the social structure are maladapted to man's biological needs, considerable effective work can be done in modifying conditions of strain in such spheres as child-care and training and marital and vocational relationships. Moreover, as we indicated in the discussion of old-age psychoses, the development of programs which will utilize to the utmost the capacities of older people for vital social functions may be accomplished. Studies in geriatrics, modification of employment trends, and the recasting of institutional needs may help further such objectives. Wider programs, such as legislative plans for maintaining full employment, adequate social security benefits for the unemployed and aged, and effective programs for vocational training in conjunction with general education, may all help in reconditioning those areas of tension and insecurity which impinge upon the personality. Group therapy, in its widest application, must also be considered, from the standpoint of reorienting the lives of members of local communities so as to elicit the capacities of all personalities in such forms as to find proper outlets for competitive drives and the need for personal security.[24]

SUMMARY

(1) It is apparent from our examination of the problems of mental disorder, that a close relationship exists between cultural configurations and various types of personality distortion. It is difficult, nevertheless, to generalize about the nature of normalcy in view of the extreme forms which accepted emotional states may assume within other cultures. (2) Although, from one standpoint, abnormality may be regarded as a matter of degree of deviation from common cultural practices and standards, individual patterns must likewise be considered in evaluating deviations. It is hazardous, nonetheless, to establish clear-cut distinctions between normal and abnormal behavior functioning for all phases of the personality and in all instances. (3) The sources of mental pathologies must be sought in individual patterns of behavior and in sociological frames of reference. The individual source may be traced to the character of the socialization process itself, which may tend to reinforce certain phases of the individual's psychogenetic development. The sociological source may be found within limited cultural configurations operating within specified areas of the social structure. (4) Symptoms of personality disorder, manifesting themselves in neuro-muscular disturbances, abnormal emotional patterns, and attitudinal distortions, are highly inter-related and reflect characteristics of the immediate social environment and the individual processes of personality development. (5) Major types of pathological personalities may be viewed from the standpoint of the severity of the disorder. Disorders range from the simple behavior maladjustments to neuroses and psychoses. It is widely recognized today that the major causes for such disorders are functional, rather than organic, except in such cases where direct organic impairment through disease, injury, or congenital defect may be observed. (6) Specific social, familial and hereditary factors in the functional disorder of schizophrenia, the most common and typical of contemporary psychotic conditions, have been examined. It would appear that socio-cultural conditions promoting *isolation* and, possibly, a degree of genetic predisposition toward the disorder, are responsible for its occurrence in certain individuals. Manic-depressive states, functionally derived, also give evidence of characteristic combinations of factors in the immediate social and family environment of the individual which are provocative of this disorder. (7) The major neuroses, evidenced in psychasthenia, neurasthenia, and hysteria, may be

[24] Cf. L. K. Frank, *Society as the Patient* (New Jersey, 1948).

traced in part to particular levels within the social structure. They appear to constitute "protective devices" of the individual to spare himself from the rigors of social life, competition, and the failure to achieve status and role positions. (8) Despite the increase in the numbers of hospitalized psychotics, conclusive evidence is lacking for an appreciable rise in the rate of psychosis since the last century, except in the case of the older-age categories, inducing various forms of senile dementia. The rate of neuroses appears to show a consistent upward trend. (9) It is increasingly apparent that psychotic disorders of the aged are not necessarily the result of organic deterioration alone, but a consequence, in part, of lack of integration of old-age groups within the contemporary social structure. (10) Ecological studies of the distribution of mental disorders in urban areas, where the total concentrations are heaviest, reveal characteristic patterns of distribution of mental disorders conforming to the decreasing gradient of other indexes of pathology from the center of the city outwards. (11) Programs for the re-organization of the pathological personality involve an amplification of medical psychiatric services for prevention and cure. Promising steps have been taken, recently, in the form of the National Mental Health Act of 1946 and parallel programs sponsored by certain state governments. More difficult to meet is the task of restructuring the social order in such a way as to reduce the tension-producing situations that are fundamentally the cause of most mental disorders.

CHAPTER TWENTY-TWO

THE SOCIOLOGY OF SUICIDE

(1) SUICIDE: THE PROBLEM STATED

ACCORDING to Ruth Cavan, "Suicide is the intentional taking of one's life or the failure when possible to save one's self when death threatens."[1] Such an act involves setting aside one of the most basic of all human attitudes, the deeply implanted will to live. Nevertheless, our daily newspapers present us with a continual recital of individuals who have chosen to give up their lives voluntarily, some under the most harrowing of circumstances. How can such extreme actions be accounted for? Are such individuals abnormal? Are they temporarily demented when taking such a step? Are the causes to be considered wholly innate or psychological? Or, can we find some answer to this problem through sociological investigation?

At the very outset of our discussion, two fundamental considerations should be noted. In the first place, the will to live constitutes a *social attitude*, representing the inculcation of a vast amount of social experience. To demonstrate this, we have but to make mention of the vast numbers of individuals who have chosen to face voluntary death, in accordance with their culture's prescription, when certain basic values of their living-patterns were seriously disturbed or destroyed. The willingness to accept martyrdom for some cherished cause can be the result of social implantation, even though it appears to defy the most basic of biological compulsions. Secondly, the very fact that suicide rates fluctuate in accordance with widely differing social conditions and factors, in relation to differences of ethnic, religious, occupational, age, and sex status, indicates that its explanation is to be sought on sociological rather than on psychological grounds. This, in fact, was the basis on which the classical work on suicide of the French sociologist, Durkheim, and his equally illustrious pupil, Halbwachs, was conceived.[2]

[1] Ruth Shonle Cavan, *Suicide* (Chicago, 1928), p. 3.

[2] Cf. Émile Durkheim, *Le Suicide* (Paris, 1897). The work of Durkheim was later revised and advanced by one of his foremost followers, Maurice Halbwachs, *Les Causes du Suicide* (Paris, 1930), who enlarged upon Durkheim's work and brought his statistical data forward to 1930.

To the man-on-the-street, the act of suicide always appears to be the result of either a distorted mind or the exposure to some unendurable stress. The explanations usually provided are deceptively obvious or simple. Unrequited love, loss of one's business or personal fortune, incurable illness or disaster befalling a beloved one—all appear reasonable explanations for this extreme behavior. Yet, that such explanations are naive and frequently without adequate foundation may be seen in the fact that the vast majority of individuals will not, in the face of similar experiences, be impelled to take their lives or even to consider seriously the possibility of doing so. *The individual who takes his life does so because the social situation has in some way failed him.* The taking of one's life constitutes a repudiation, as it were, of social experience.

This does not mean that individual factors may not be significant. It merely signifies that such individual factors may be understood only in relation to the types of social values which have come to convey the nature of meaningful human experience to the individual.

(2) SOCIAL AND CULTURAL VARIATIONS IN SUICIDE

Although individual motivations must be fully explored in accounting for suicide, its character appears to be essentially social. Suicide can best be understood in terms of its meaning to individuals within different cultural settings. These meanings are diverse and suggest highly dissimilar patterns of motivation. Among certain peoples, suicide appears to be entirely unknown. Ethnological accounts of Australian aborigines, African Bushmen, and Hottentots fail to reveal any evidence that these peoples were familiar with such a practice. Andaman Islanders, until their contacts with Europeans, apparently experienced difficulty in comprehending the meaning of such an act, while inhabitants of the Caroline Islands were apt to be moved to laughter at the very mention of such a strange action as suicide.

Among the Dobuans, on the other hand, suicide is well understood. In Dobu, it usually results from marital quarrels or unfaithfulness, and it is commonly employed as an instrument of vengeance. The Dobuan male may threaten to commit suicide, giving ample evidence of his intention, without actually completing the act. Frequently, the doorway of his wife's house is chosen as the dramatic setting for this act. The wife's relatives may seek to placate him, fearful of the vengeance his own kinsmen would take should his attempt be successful. To the Kwakiutl of the Canadian Northwest, suicide is comparatively common. It is usually motivated by the shame or fear induced through failure to maintain status in accordance with the powerful property-consciousness of these people. A Kwakiutl male, stripped of his possessions in gambling and unable, consequently, to use his property as a means of implementing his prestige, may have no other recourse than to end his life. Throughout this culture lurks the spectre of loss of status through property failure; the suicide pattern appears to be dominated by property considerations. The mother of a woman sent home by her husband for unfaithfulness may feel impelled to end her life, while a man, unable to finance a winter ceremonial initiatory rite for his son, may escape what he considers an unendurable disgrace by killing himself.[3]

These variations in the suicide pattern are extensive and appear in all parts of the world. Contradictory patterns, encouraging suicide, strongly disapproving of it, or showing little knowledge of its significance, may be found in common areas. In modern Western culture, although suicides have always been fairly common, the traditional attitude toward it has been strongly disapproving. The mechanisms of social control function in such a way as to implant strongly within the individual the desire to live and to make him deeply conscious of the obligation to others which may only be served by the continuance of life. When these mechanisms of social control fail, the individual may be impelled to accept the necessity of suicide as desirable or unavoidable, in the face of the limited alternatives of action open to him. In this connection, suicide may be seen as one of the unavoidable phases of the process of social disorganization and breakdown, one of the inevitable phases of the process of unresolved forces in social disequilibrium.

(3) INSTITUTIONALIZED AND INDIVIDUAL PATTERNS OF SUICIDE

In reflecting social conditions, suicides seem to follow certain specific patterns. These patterns appear to represent two extreme forms: (1) the institutionalized suicides found in highly integrated cultures, and which are still to be found among primitive communities and in parts of the Orient today; and (2) the highly individualized suicides of contemporary Western culture.

The institutionalized pattern of suicide is that type which is usually highly approved socially and seems to occur in relation to certain specific contingencies and dangers confronting the social structure and the group. Thus, the high ceremonial hara-kiri of the Japanese Samurai and the practice of suttee among the widows of high-caste Hindus are examples of these forms of institutionalized suicide. It should be noted, in considering these forms of suicide, that not only are they considered desirable by the social group, but they are actually expected in the face of

[3] See Ruth Benedict, *Patterns of Culture* (New York, 1934), pp. 107–09, 199–203, for these and other examples.

certain critical and dangerous situations. So powerful are the impulsions towards this type of suicide, that, well into the nineteenth century, the British authorities in India had to forcibly restrain the widows of high-caste Hindus from throwing themselves upon the funeral pyres of their husbands.

It should be noted in this connection that the institutionalized form of suicide tends to follow an inflexible pattern. Involved in this pattern is the conception that the individual's welfare is subordinate to the group and that his principal function is to advance the group's welfare. Thus, the Japanese Samurai held as his principal objective successful and faithful service to his emperor, who was considered divine in origin. If he found himself in a position where he could not adequately perform his duty, there was considered little else he could do than to take his life. Although this was the traditional practice of the ancient Japanese warrior class, such customs survive and may become part of the wider patterns of contemporary cultural practice. Thus, during the recent war, the practice of hara-kiri was still exercised by high and low ranking officers of the Japanese imperial forces who felt that they had been remiss in their obligations through failing to attain victory. The structured attitudes surrounding such a conception may have wide orientation, affecting many different classes in different ways, although with a common basis of meaning fundamental to all variations of attitude. Thus, veneration by the Japanese public of those who committed hara-kiri has been general during the contemporary period, even though the average Japanese might hesitate about taking his own life in this honored fashion.

The seemingly fanatic willingness of Japanese and other Oriental troops to sacrifice themselves upon the field of battle might, to an extent, be a counterpart of the tolerance toward such ceremonialized and institutionalized forms of death. The exploits of the Japanese Kamikaze, the suicidal dive bombers of the last war, implied a sacrificial casualness concerning human life on the part of victims and their superior commanders which is difficult for outsiders to comprehend. (It is noteworthy, however, that not all Japanese pilots ordered to crash their bomb-laden planes upon the decks of American vessels were willing or able to do so.)

Institutionalized patterns of suicide are frequently found in conjunction with certain other forms of powerful supporting traits—an arrangement which the anthropologist has come to recognize as the process of so-called "trait-linkage." Linked traits refer to combinations of cultural elements which play an important role in supporting some dominant practice, belief, or institutional value. Thus, in the case of institutionalized patterns of suicide found in the Orient, it is common to note that such practices are abetted by rigid and powerfully supporting caste structures. Such social structures are highly integrated, slow to change, and frequently isolated from other currents in the culture. Significant in such societies is the relative unimportance of the individual as compared with the group, and a consequent attitude of disdain for the individualized character of human life, so powerful in our Western conception of things. Such a rigid social structure tends frequently to inhibit profound feelings of identification with other individuals and tends to cause the individual to identify almost wholly with a conception of some supreme good of his own particular group.

The disdain for human suffering found so frequently in such social orders does not necessarily indicate a studied indifference or callousness concerning others, but the development of attitudes limited by the powerful considerations of the need for survival for one's own particular group, whether that group be a given caste-structure or some rigidly circumscribed family organization. Individuals in such societies impute little value to their own lives except in conjunction with some ultimate purpose or need of the larger group. Hence, the willingness of the Hindu widow to immolate herself upon the funeral pyre of her husband. Her life takes on significance only in relation to him. In one sense, without his physical presence and social function, her life exists in a void and her extinction is made necessary by his own removal from the worldly scene. In our subsequent discussion of the suicide process, we will indicate that the reason for this is the fact that the individual's capacity for social movement is highly limited in such social structures. The types of resultant attitudes, therefore, imposed upon the institutionalized suicide—and reflecting the limitations within the social structure—indicate the diminished range of alternatives for social action, other than through the agency of self-destruction.

The individualized suicide of the Western world is quite different. Great stress has been made in modern industrial culture upon the capacity of the individual to make his own choices and to more or less guide the development of his own life. Exposed as he is to complex agencies and institutions of social control, the individual, theoretically at least, is afforded great latitude for choice and for exercising his own prerogatives. The individual has the opportunity to choose from a wide range of alternatives for social action and the complexity of these choices frequently faces him with great dilemmas. Suicides in Western culture are likely to reflect intense personality stress. The character of compulsion represents the result of conflicts in "interiorized" attitudes rather than external necessities. Suicides are likely to be the result of patterns of individual motivations, reflecting the complexity of choices and dilemmas which the social environment of the individual has imposed upon him. The individualized suicide of the Western world conforms to no socially approved compulsion. Rather, he is unable to meet the demands of certain conflicting situations and consequently, because of the peculiar personality pattern developed in the socialization process, finds no other alternative than to end his life. The role of the social environment, in individualized suicide, is one of imposing a series of insoluble dilemmas; for the institutionalized suicide, the social environment provides a clearly defined course.

(4) RATES OF SUICIDE AND PREVALENCE

The general rates of suicide in the Western world appear to have been consistently upward since the early part of the nineteenth century. This rise has been particularly marked since 1880 in most European countries and the United States, and seems to follow a distinct pattern related to the rates of industrialization of the areas in question.[4] Rural areas in general seem to show rates consistently lower than industrial regions, although rural rates have also shown an upward secular trend, paralleling, somewhat, the much more precipitate rise commonly found in industrial regions. In appraising such rates, allowances must be made for fluctuations over periods of time and in relation to distinctive patterns found within given European and American areas. As Durkheim and Halbwachs have incisively shown, the number of variables operating in conjunction with any specific suicide rate is high. Generalizations concerning differing rates for occupational, religious, class, age, and sex groups must be constantly modified in relation to the specific circumstances of the group in question. Nevertheless, certain types of generalizations may be made, particularly in relation to age and sex classifications, although they must be appraised in terms of regional differences, differences in time intervals, and specific age-categories.

In the long run, suicide rates in western European countries level off at intervals corresponding to the leveling off of industrial growth. Changes in the industrial organization, as a result of their effects upon the population and social structure, inevitably produce certain modifications in suicide rates. *Suicide appears to be a sensitive barometer of social change in complex social orders.* Consequently, when countries are classified on the basis of contemporary rates, it is extremely difficult to establish common patterns on the basis of distinctive characteristics concerning their several social structures. For example, Austria and France, both predominantly Catholic countries, have relatively high rates, while Belgium, with a large Catholic population, does not appear to fit into the same category of high rates. Thus, other factors such as age distribution

[4] Cf. Maurice Halbwachs, *Les Causes du Suicide* (Paris, 1930).

in the population, social stability, degree of integration of the social structure, and industrial characteristics must be examined in order to account for such differences. Also, England, a highly industrialized country, yields a relatively low rate, as do Norway and Finland, where the indexes of industrialization are not nearly as high. The differences in such countries, therefore, must be sought in factors other than industrialization.

Violent changes in the social order, such as the contingencies induced by war, for example, must likewise be taken into consideration. Contrary to expectations, such violent changes do not necessarily induce higher rates of self-inflicted deaths, but may, on the contrary, as Durkheim has pointed out, lead to a diminution of rates. This is largely because of the necessities of integrating the social structure at such times and because of the consequent unification of social effort. Nevertheless, in the case of special groups, such as the Jews during the last war, the rates may mount precipitately and reach unusually high proportions.[5]

Prior to the Second World War, distinctive differences in rates could be found for several categories of modern European countries and the United States. Although yearly fluctuations in rates may be noticed, these differences may still be seen to obtain, despite profound changes brought about by the recent war. Certain countries, such as Germany, Austria, France, Switzerland, and Japan, with overall suicide rates of approximately 23 per 100,000, appear to fall into a leading category. Such diverse countries as the United States, Sweden, Belgium, Denmark, and Australia appear to fall in second place, with rates ranging from approximately 10 to 16 per 100,000. In third place, we find Norway, Finland, England, Scotland, Ireland, and Italy, with rates ranging from 4 to 9 per 100,000. Highly integrated communities and primitive cultures seem to give evidence of the lowest rates of all. It should be recognized again that within these broad categorical classifications, sharp differences exist in regard to the several age, sex, occupational, and regional groupings of the various populations. In such broad classifications, only comprehensive, overall, secular rates are considered.[6]

It is significant to note that high rates of suicide have tended to be maintained in the countries where they occur, despite occasional wide-ranging fluctuations in the secular trend due to domestic crises, war, or economic depressions. Switzerland, for example, having been spared the devastation of the two major wars in this century and having enjoyed a remarkably sustained high level of prosperity for over half a century, nevertheless yields one of the highest suicide rates of the modern world.

[5] See, for example, Herbert A. Bloch on suicide in relation to his study of concentration camp victims, "The Personality of Inmates of Concentration Camps," *The American Journal of Sociology*, III (Jan., 1947), 340, 341.

[6] Cf. Ruth Shonle Cavan, *Suicide*, Chap. I.

(5) SUICIDE AND AGE CLASSIFICATIONS

Statistics on suicide disclose that the rates are relatively lower for the youthful age categories than for older-age groups. Suicide appears to be associated with old age. Virtually all of the studies that have been made on suicide appear to confirm this finding. There are, however, fluctuations within these rates based upon sex and occupational differences. For example, although male rates in general are about three to four times as high as female rates, among adolescents fifteen to nineteen years of age, female rates are slightly higher than male rates.[7] Moreover, although suicide is either nonexistent or rare in early childhood, the rise during the adolescent period may be marked, although considerably lower than for age categories of forty and above. The reasons for these facts are relatively easy to establish. For older-age individuals, the sudden transition in status, frequently accompanied by the painful enfeeblement of organic disorder, bars the individual from accustomed social experiences. For other adult categories, the consistent rise in suicide rates in direct ratio to advancing years suggests that the individual has been rendered unequal in meeting the increasingly complex demands of adult status. Adolescent suicide occurs when the individual for the first time confronts a series of situations in which he is asked to assume adult roles for which he is unprepared. In the final analysis, such problems seem to emerge in direct relationship to the incapacity of the individual to fulfill certain desired objectives. When these socially inspired objectives present dilemmas or their achievement seems impossible, the individual may feel he has no other recourse than to remove himself from the social situation.

Despite the relative rarity of suicide among youthful age-groups, suicidal wishes and tendencies are common among young people. This has been shown by Ruth Cavan in her analysis of questionnaires given to young people. Their responses showed evidences of suicidal tendencies in many sublimated and direct forms, ranging from expressed wishes "never to have been born" to a direct acknowledgment of the suitability of suicides under given conditions.[8] In an unpublished study by the author of suicidal attitudes among college students on the junior and senior levels, based upon questionnaires and personal interviews with 210 students during 1938–41, he found that over 80 per cent, both of selected groups and of the entire sample, considered suicide a justifiable act. The chief significance of such an investigation has been in its demonstration that suicidal notions are not unknown among young people, although rates of actual suicide are low. The contemplation of suicide among adolescents may be linked to the barriers that stand in the way of their meaningful participation in social experiences.

[7] Louis I. Dublin and Bessie Bunzel, *To Be or Not To Be* (New York, 1933).

[8] Cf. Ruth Shonle Cavan, *Suicide*, Chap. X.

(6) SUICIDE AND OTHER CAUSES OF DEATH

The annual volume of deaths by suicide is relatively small when compared with the total number of deaths each year from all causes in the United States registration area. In 1947, out of a total of 1,445,370 deaths reported, only 16,538 were occasioned by suicide.[9] Significant is the fact that in the list of leading causes of death in the United States, suicide ranks tenth, a position which it has more or less consistently maintained since 1930, despite the fact that its average rate has tended to decline. Whereas in 1930 the suicide rate was 15.6 per 100,000 of the population, its rate in 1945 was 11.2, and in 1946 and 1947, 11.5.[10] Of some importance is the fact that in the post-war periods of both major world conflicts during this century, the rates have appeared to decline in this country while increases were noted elsewhere.[11]

When suicide is compared with other forms of violent death, the picture is somewhat different. Deaths by suicide are second in frequency only to automobile deaths. In 1924, when Cavan first pointed to this comparison, the annual rate of automobile deaths in this country was 16 per 100,000, followed by suicide, with a rate of 12 per 100,000. Deaths by homicide ranked third, yielding a rate of 8.5.[12] Despite some significant changes in absolute rates, the rank order continues to be the same. In 1947, while deaths by motor vehicle accidents mounted to an extremely high figure of 22.8 per 100,000, suicide still ranked second with a rate of 11.5, while homicide maintained third rank with a rate of 6.0.[13]

(7) SUICIDE AND THE CULTURAL CYCLE

It is significant to note that in the past history of European cultural development, those epochs of great cultural change which laid stress upon individualized values, tended to produce, as far as may be presently determined, higher rates of suicide. Such periods of doubt and confusion appear to cut away the roots of individuals, which, in the past, linked them to the conventionalized routines of social living. These individuals live in a social world which has lost significance, meaning, and value.

Although the classical cultures of Athens, Sparta, and Thebes generally condemned suicide as a violation of religious and civic responsibilities, striking changes in attitude occurred during periods of social stress and strain. The Cyrenaics, for example, a highly hedonistic sect active

[9] *Statistical Abstract of the United States: 1949* (U. S. Bureau of the Census, 7th ed., Washington, 1949), p. 73.

[10] Ibid.

[11] Walter Lunden, "Suicide in France, 1910–1943," *The American Journal of Sociology*, III (Jan., 1947), 321–34.

[12] Ruth Shonle Cavan, *Suicide*, p. 10.

[13] *Statistical Abstract of the United States: 1949*, p. 73.

about 365 B.C., although emphasizing the pursuit of pleasure as the sole end of rational beings, nevertheless accepted and followed the doctrine of self-inflicted death proclaimed by their leader, Hegesias. The Cynics, a philosophical cult of about 360 B.C., maintained that life or death was a matter largely of individual choice. The Epicureans and Stoics, while differing widely in their philosophical outlooks, seemed to support similar views, for different reasons. According to Cavan, although Grecian attitudes toward suicide did not reach a point of complete institutionalization as in the Orient, there were nevertheless tendencies in this direction.[14]

During periods of stability in the development of Roman civilization, tendencies toward suicide were diminished and attitudes toward it were in general strongly disapproving. During the period of the Roman decline, however, attitudes toward suicide were no longer so condemnatory, and the rates appeared to have increased. The Middle Ages witnessed a remarkable period of social integration and stability under the hegemony of the Church. In view of the powerfully prevailing religious philosophy, which considered the individual to be entirely subject to the will of God, the sentiment against self-inflicted death was extremely powerful. Suicide was held to be sinful since (a) it is an unnatural act, (b) it is a breach against the community, and (c) it constitutes a usurpation of divine power. This fundamental theological conception still provides one of the powerful social and ethical blocks to the act of suicide within our own culture. Despite such bitterly censorious attitudes, however, the increase of social mobility during the Renaissance produced a series of highly contradictory practices within the European social structure, paving the way for a considerable increase in the rate of suicide. Cavan, in her analysis of the shifting cultural cycle, has indicated the relationship between the factors of social disorganization during periods of rapid transition and the drastic modification of attitudes toward suicide.[15]

(8) CONTEMPORARY SOCIAL FACTORS AND SUICIDE

Religious Factors. A study of religious factors in relation to suicide provides a good instance of how difficult it is to establish a precise relationship on the basis of single factors. During the greater part of the nineteenth century, rates of suicide among the Jewish communities of Europe were extremely low. Catholic and Protestant groups ranked next, in that order. Long before the recent wave of persecution and systematic extermination of European Jews by the Nazis, however, the rates of suicide among Jews began to climb precipitately. From a rate which was approximately one half that of the Catholic population during the nine-

[14] Ruth Shonle Cavan, *Suicide*, p. 14.
[15] Ibid., Chap. VI.

teenth century, there has been a rise to twice the Catholic rate, and even higher, in certain urban areas, during the present century. This climb in rates has occurred both in Europe and the United States. Today, the overall Catholic suicide rate is generally lowest in all areas, with the Protestant rates following next, and the Jewish rates appearing as high as the Protestant rate, or higher.[16] Since 1920, in fact, from its relatively low rate of a century before, the Jewish rate has, during specific years in parts of Europe, reached unprecedented levels as contrasted with the rates of the other major religious groups.

The differences in these rates cannot be accounted for directly on the basis of religious membership and differentials. Nor can they be accounted for on the basis of the proscriptive attitudes of the separate faiths involved. All three religions strongly condemn suicide, the attitudes of organized Judaism being as strongly condemnatory as those of the Catholic Church. The fact that the rites of religious burial may be denied suicides in the Catholic Church, as well as among orthodox Jewish groups, is far from sufficient to account for such differences. In fact, Halbwachs suggests that this situation may tend to conceal the true nature of suicidal deaths in many cases, where the family is intent upon sacerdotal burial, with the result that statistical tabulations may present a somewhat distorted picture of the true facts.

The key factor to be investigated is the social cohesiveness of certain religious groups, in conjunction with such critical factors as the degree of industrialization of a given area, distribution of occupational status, and the process of urbanism. Rates of suicide in industrial and urban areas generally tend to be high. The fact that the Jews are an urban people, concentrated in highly industrialized regions, very likely accounts for their high suicide rates. The bitter persecution of the last two decades would tend to intensify such rates. Low rates in nineteenth-century Europe among Jews might be partly accounted for on the basis of the close-knit structure of the Jewish community during this period, even within urban environments. The nineteenth century ghetto provided strong bonds which helped withstand the disorganizing influences of urbanism.

That similar factors affect the suicide trends of other religious groups may be seen in the wide variations of rates that prevail among Catholics and Protestants. Catholic rates, although relatively low, have also risen rapidly in keeping with the general secular trend, and show, moreover, considerable fluctuations. One of the reasons for the relatively low Catholic rate in Europe may be that Catholic populations in various European countries are peasant populations, concentrated in rural districts and enjoying strong local communal ties. Protestant rates are also likely to be

[16] Computation of adequate comparative rates for Jews is limited in certain areas because of the sparsity of the Jewish population.

low under similar conditions. Protestant groups in our own rural South tend to yield low rates for the same reasons. Moreover, as Halbwachs has indicated, when Catholic populations are found extensively in industrialized regions, such as the Schleswig-Holstein and Brandenburg districts of Germany, the Catholic rates in these regions may exceed Protestant rates.[17]

Urbanism and Suicide

From the foregoing, it may be seen that trends in urbanism and industrialization have exercised considerable influence on rates of suicide. In this country, for example, the rates of suicide for cities of 10,000 and more in population are consistently about 50 per cent higher than for smaller communities. Ranked in order of size, highest rates are invariably found in the large cities of over 100,000 inhabitants, followed by the intermediate urban areas ranging from 10,000 to 100,000 inhabitants, with communities of less than 10,000 consistently yielding the lowest rates of all. Although overall regional rates reveal differences in this country, the rural-urban difference in rates remains constant. In the Pacific areas, where unusually high overall rates are found, the difference between rural and urban rates still stands out conspicuously.

Not only are urban rates higher, but the pattern of distribution within urban areas appears to follow a distinctive ecological arrangement, as in the case of other pathological behaviors. Chicago, for example, gives evidence of a characteristic "suicide belt," concentrated within the highly mobile areas converging upon the central business district of the city. The four principal districts involved are the "loop" and central business district containing many of the cheaper hotels on its fringes, adjacent rooming-house areas, areas converging upon the Negro district, and the Hobohemian section of cheap flophouses. Within these localities, the rates of suicide are five to six times as high as the general rates for the entire city of Chicago. Calvin Schmid has demonstrated similar patterns of distribution for the cities of Seattle and Minneapolis.[18] Similar findings have been made in the metropolitan area of New York City, with heavy concentrations of suicide occurring in the mid-town Manhattan districts. Rates below the state average were found in the four other outlying metropolitan boroughs.

Sex differentials. Virtually all of the studies on suicide for Europe and the United States indicate that the rates of successful suicide are three to four times as high for men as for women. In other cultures, however, where institutionalized patterns prevail, the female rate may closely

[17] Halbwachs, *Les Causes du Suicide.*

[18] Calvin M. Schmid, "Suicide in Minneapolis, Minnesota: 1920–1932," *American Journal of Sociology*, XXXIX, 30–48.

approach the male rate and, in some instances, India, for example, exceed it. However, in Western culture, these comparisons do not obtain on all age levels. During the adolescent and post-adolescent period, the wide disparity between male and female suicides does not hold to nearly the same degree. With advancing years, however, the gap between the separate sex rates becomes increasingly broader, so that in the age categories of fifty and above, the differences are considerably marked and, in some cases, extreme.

Marital status. The marital state appears to provide some safeguards against suicide. Rates of suicide among married individuals are lower than among the divorced, the widowed, and the unmarried of both sexes. If corrections are made for comparable age classifications, however, the distinctions are not as marked as they ordinarily appear, except for the ordinarily high rates among the widowed and the divorced. Morselli, using data of the 1860's and 1870's for sections of central Europe, Italy, and France, found that the suicide rate for married men was lowest, followed by the unmarried, the widowed, and the divorced, in that order.[19] For France, Italy, and Switzerland, however, he found that the rates of suicide for single women were lower than the rates for the married women. Miner, employing early data of the present century for many of the same European areas, was able to confirm a similar conclusion, showing that rates for married persons were considerably lower than rates for the widowed and divorced.[20] Regional studies in America, however, appear to indicate that for males, rates are lowest among unmarried persons, with the married following closely. Marked differences separate these categories from the widowed and the divorced, who have the highest rates. Women's rates for similar areas during the same period, although not as high, appear to follow the same pattern.[21]

That marriage may be seen as a partial deterrent to suicide is further augmented by the data on childlessness. Established families with children create a sense of continuing responsibility for both parents, with the result that if there are children in the marriage, the chances for suicide are considerably less for both men and women as compared with married individuals without children. Moreover, the probabilities of suicide appear to diminish in relation to the number of children in the family.

When age as well as marital status is taken into consideration, however, the picture alters somewhat. Such studies, for example, sometimes reveal that the rates for single members of the population are greater than rates for the married, while the high rates for the widowed and

[19] H. Morselli, *Suicide: An Essay on Comparative Moral Statistics* (New York, 1897). Cited in Cavan, *Suicide*, pp. 317–18.

[20] J. R. Miner, "Suicide and Its Relation to Climatic and Other Factors," *American Journal of Hygiene*, Monographic Series, No. 2, 1922. See Cavan, *Suicide*, p. 318.

[21] Cf., Dublin and Bunzel, *To Be or Not To Be*, Chap. 11.

divorced, although still obtaining in that order, are not as acute as before age-factors are taken into consideration.[22] The basic facts are not appreciably altered by such considerations, except for the fact that advancing age-categories tend to increase the incidence towards suicide. Rates for single individuals will tend to be low, therefore, because of their concentrations within youthful age-categories, while at the same time there is definite overlapping of marital age-groups and the early adult categories of twenty to forty years. Invulnerability against suicide is thus buttressed for many individuals by the factors of youthful age *and* relatively early marital status.

Ethnic and racial factors. Ethnic and racial factors in the study of suicide are complicated by many of the other factors mentioned, such as urbanism, religion, industrialization, and occupational status. In general, however, Negro rates in this country have been extremely low as compared with rates of native-born whites and the foreign born.[23] When Cavan completed her study in 1928, she discovered that rates per 100,000 for Negroes in the city of Chicago were 7.7, while for native-born whites and the foreign born, the rates were 9.5 and 28.8 respectively. Despite the tendency for Negro rates to be high in large Northern cities, as compared with low rates for this group in the rural South, rates for Negroes as a group are still considerably lower than for white groups. On the other hand, the rise in the occupational status of many Negroes in Northern cities is bringing about an increase in the rate of suicide. Low Negro rates that have been maintained thus far are the result of rural background and the communal restraints which the dominant white society has imposed on this group. Until relatively late in American Negro history, sharp competitive drives have been lacking in Negro life because of the paucity of available opportunities. When social barriers break down, we may witness an increase in Negro suicides to a level comparable to the rate among white groups in the urban population. Chinese and Japanese groups, on the other hand, in keeping with their generally high suicidal traditions, have yielded extremely high rates in this country.

Differences in rates of suicide for individuals in this country of different national backgrounds appear to follow in part the patterns of European distribution.[24] Southern Europeans of Catholic and rural backgrounds, for example, apparently tend to produce low rates in this country. Northern Europeans from urban-industrial areas and of Protestant background tend to produce relatively high rates. However, these facts are further complicated by the concentrations in urban settlement

[22] Dublin and Bunzel, *To Be or Not To Be.*

[23] Adolph D. Frenay, *The Suicide Problem in the United States* (New York, 1927), pp. 156–7.

[24] Ibid.

of both groups and the changes in occupational status which residence in America brings about. Thus, immigrants whose backgrounds would suggest a low rate might commit suicide in considerable numbers if they encounter difficulties in occupational adjustment, cultural reorientation, and the like. For the native-born children of immigrants, trends in rates of suicide appear to follow the prevailing regional patterns in conjunction with age, sex, religious, marital, and residential differentials.

(9) PSYCHOSES AND SUICIDE

Contrary to the popular belief, the majority of suicides are not insane prior to their self-destruction. When we use the term "insane," we refer to mentally pathological states which were, or could have been, clinically diagnosed as genuine psychotic states. There are, of course, sizable numbers of individuals who do take their lives while under serious emotional stress that is diagnosed as a serious pathological disorder. The majority of studies that have been made appear to indicate that from one-fifth to approximately one-third of suicide victims suffered from such conditions. Thus, Cavan, in her analysis of 291 suicides in Chicago during 1923, discovered that 58 of these victims, 44 men and 14 women (approximately 20 per cent) suffered from antecedent or active psychotic conditions. A compilation by Louis Dublin of data on suicide covering wide areas in this country at a later period revealed percentage ranges of psychotic suicides comparable to the Cavan and other estimates.[25] Earlier investigations during the first decade of the present century and shortly thereafter in Germany by such investigators as Wassermeyer and Stelzner, revealed much higher percentages of deranged persons among attempted suicides. Wassermeyer estimated that as many as 72 per cent of the women investigated in one group were possibly insane.[26] However, in these latter groups, the attempted suicides were individuals who definitely gave evidence of psychotic states before their attempts at suicide and who were brought to a mental clinic because of their obviously disturbed states. Moreover, in a great many cases, the diagnoses of mental states prior to admission to the clinic were extremely casual. Even Stelzner, however, as do other psychiatric investigators, indicates that the causes for such attempted suicides are precipitated by acute critical factors which, in many cases, would constitute legitimate reasons for individuals judged sane. The most prominent psychotic condition accompanying suicide is the depressed state of involutional melancholia, although other psychotic conditions, such as acute and chronic paranoia, senile dementia, and dementia praecox, have also been found as accompanying conditions.

[25] Dublin and Bunzel, Chap. 22.

[26] H. Stelzner, *Analyse von 200 Selbstmordfällen* (Berlin, 1906). Cited in Cavan, *Suicide*, pp. 114–15.

The fact remains, nevertheless, that the majority of suicides may not be adjudged as insane prior to their deaths, if we are to employ clinically verifiable categories as a basis for evaluation. It may be argued, of course, that no person "in his right mind" can take his own life. Further, it is frequently claimed that the suicide's behavior was strange or "queer" during the days preceding his demise. It would, of course, be surprising to discover that a person seriously contemplating taking his own life was calm and unruffled prior to the action. However, the records seem to clearly indicate that the majority of suicides cannot be considered serious pathological specimens before their deaths.

(10) COMPARATIVE POSTWAR SUICIDE TRENDS

In view of the careful tabulations on suicides in France since the middle of the last century, providing the basis for the great classical theories of Durkheim and Halbwachs, a study of recent trends in this country should shed considerable light on the insights gained thus far. In the recent examination by Lunden of suicide statistics in France from 1910 to 1943, the basic inferences and conclusions suggested by Durkheim and Halbwachs, and built upon by others, appear to find continuing substantial verification.[27]

Lunden discovered that suicide rates decreased during the First and Second World Wars, while during the depression and postwar years they increased, with a peak rate being attained during the nadir of the depression in 1934. It is interesting to note the differential rates which occur during the postwar years. The rates of suicide for officers readjusting to civilian life, for example, are considerably higher than for former enlisted men, for whom the transition is not so difficult or drastic.[28] Depressions appear to induce an increase of suicide among those in the population who are latently predisposed to suicide. However, economic difficulties may, for others, serve as an incentive to renewed efforts or toward activities in other social fields. The depression in France, as elsewhere, brought about a sharp increase in the suicide rate. The sudden increase within a given year, and then a relapse to former rates—as in Paris, where a sharp increase of almost two hundred suicides occurred in 1934 as compared with 1933—may be due to the fact that such economic and social pressures may tend to remove only the "marginal suicides," those with suicidal tendencies which may be activated by an environmental disaster.

The male-female ratio of suicide appears to have been upheld by

[27] Walter A. Lunden, "Suicide in France, 1910–1943," pp. 321–34.

[28] In this country, during 1919, the first year after the First World War, the suicide rate for former officers was 40 per 100,000, while for enlisted men, the rate was 12 per 100,000.

these recent French statistics, approximately 75 per cent of the suicides being men and 25 per cent women, despite variations for the metropolitan district of Paris.[29] Significantly, during the German occupation of France, male suicides decreased more rapidly than female suicides. This may be partly accounted for by the fact that large percentages of men were removed from the civilian population, an estimated 2,000,000 Frenchmen being used for impressed labor in various parts of central Europe. Also of interest, because of its relevance to other areas, is the fact that suicides in older age-categories increased during the war years, but decreased during the depression. Lunden's surmise is that younger age-groups may withstand wars better than the older age-groups, while older age-groups survive depressions and economic disorder better than younger groups.[30]

Hanging, drowning, and shooting appeared the most common methods for terminating one's life. Exposure to gas and suicidal leaps appeared with increasing frequency in the case of women's suicides. Shooting was to a considerable degree influenced by the accessibility of firearms and diminished, consequently, during the period of German occupation. Variations in modes of self-destruction for both sexes were quite common, however, gas being commonly employed by both men and women during the depression years, with particular concentration in urban areas. Of interest, as well, are the facts concerning suicide of married women with and without children. During the occupation by Germany, suicides of married women with children increased with relative rapidity (an increase of 55 per cent), while suicides of married women without children showed a *decrease* almost as great as the increase of suicide among the married women with children.[31] Also significant is the fact that *multiple suicides*, or suicides by pact, increased at a greater rate during the depression years than rates for the conventional single suicides. This appears due to the closely patterned relationship of family groups and married couples who, in confronting a common disaster, find themselves sympathetically motivated.

(11) THE SOCIOLOGY OF SUICIDE

On the basis of the abundance of facts which have been collected concerning suicides and their rates, it has been possible to formulate an interesting sociological hypothesis concerning the pattern of causation of suicide within different types of social structure. Durkheim's classical theory concerning types of suicide and their processes still provides a fun-

[29] Ibid., p. 323.
[30] Ibid., p. 327.
[31] Ibid., p. 325.

damental basis for the evaluation of this problem.[32] The assumption of the Durkheim theory is that suicide is affected by degrees of relatedness and the character of various kinds of social structure. Crises which tend to disrupt or sever the bonds which bind the individual to his own social groups within the wide social and cultural structure, and which tend consequently to isolate him, or characteristics which tend to identify him too closely with the social structure in the face of a common disaster, provide ample bases for the occasions of suicide. Durkheim classifies the forms of suicide into three basic types: (1) the *altruistic,* (2) the *egoistic,* and (3) the *anomique.*

Altruistic suicides occur where the individual's welfare is closely and almost indissolubly bound up with the conception of the group's welfare. Here the identity between the individual's outlook and the social perspective is extremely close and fundamental. Highly integrated societies or groups more commonly produce this form of suicide. Thus, among primitive societies where the individual feels that his action or his presence has proven inimical to the group, this way out of the difficulty may be chosen. Such suicides are in one sense acts of expiation, although they do not necessarily have to be so. Aged and feeble individuals, wives whose husbands are deceased, slaves whose masters have expired, may, because of this intimate identification with the group or the personality of the deceased individual, have few qualms about taking their own lives. In fact, such an action may follow as a matter of course.

Egoistic suicides, although also reflecting the *character* of the social structure, manifest themselves in almost the opposite manner. In this type of suicide, the bonds of relatedness between the individual and the social structure are loose. He finds no common source of social values with which he may readily identify himself and is increasingly thrust upon his own devices. The result of such a process is increasing pressure toward isolation of the individual from society, one of the conclusions of which may be suicide. The majority of suicides in the contemporary social order are of this type, according to Durkheim. On the basis of this assumption, he formulated a general principal concerning the incidence of suicide: the number of suicides varies in inverse ratio to the degree of integration of the social group.

Suicides of the *anomique* type, to use a term which is peculiarly Durkheim's, occur in conjunction with violent social crises which disrupt existent social structures and groups. The term itself suggests the inability of the individual to establish some form of rapport with the novel social circumstances confronting him. Prior to the crisis, members of the group

[32] Durkheim, *Le Suicide.* This work not only constitutes one of the most penetrating sociological studies made of a unique problem, but has wide theoretical ramifications for various other phases of sociology.

may have felt close ties to society. Having been so well adjusted, however, they are unable to find new affiliations in the contemporary social scene. Thus, every society produces a quota of "latent" suicides, who will never be impelled to take this drastic step unless confronted with a crucial change of events. Such suicides occur in connection with economic disasters and depressions, political crises, revolutions, and wars. Depending on the previous character of the social structure, and the type of emergency which the new social forces are creating, different groups are affected in different ways by such emergencies, as Lunden's recent data on France have served to reveal. Thus, *anomique* groups at one time might be the older-age groups in the population; at other times, youthful age categories, business groups, or bureaucrats; while at still other times, special categories of the marital groups in the population. The *potential* for suicide, thus, would appear to lie in the peculiar character of the antecendent social structure and the peculiar nature of the crisis which confronts it.

(12) PSYCHOANALYTICAL PATTERNS

Various psychiatric doctrines have been evolved to account for suicide. Many of these theories are overladen with Freudian concepts. With all the caustic criticisms directed towards the Freudian view, in its original and unsullied form, the classic Freudian view on suicide appears to constitute one of the weakest and most contradictory aspects of the entire Freudian system. The Freudian view is premised upon the existence of a "death wish" or instinct, present in all individuals in greater or lesser degree, the so-called "arakne" impulse. The positing of such an entity or instinct represents the weakest type of theorizing, since it makes a gross assumption of the very thing it purports to explain. According to this view, man's biological nature is actuated by two powerful motivating impulses, the "eros," or life-continuing, principle, and its opposite, the life-destroying principle. This latter may take many forms other than the sheer desire to destroy one's life, depending on the unique character of the given personality. Lurking within each individual is the latent impulse toward self-destruction which, under certain conditions, may emerge as a full-blown suicidal wish.

Karl Menninger has attempted to develop this idea in accordance with some of the more modern conceptions of psychiatry and psychoanalysis.[33] Recognizing that the will toward self-destruction may manifest itself in other forms of destructive tendencies, such as the serious psychotic and neurotic states, "accidents," and extreme alcoholism, Menninger avers that the desire to commit suicide is the product of a complex

[33] Cf. Karl A. Menninger, *Man Against Himself* (New York, 1938).

series of elements implementing the fundamental destructive wish. Thus, the perfected suicidal wish depends upon the development of three basic attitudes: (1) the desire to kill, (2) the desire to be killed, and (3) the wish to die. Unless the attitude of the person is so structured as to include all of these three elements, the final suicidal act may not take place. Before the individual can conceive of killing himself, according to Menninger, he must have developed powerful aggressive tendencies toward others. In other words, the destructive impulse must first be directed outwardly. This constitutes a type of preparatory action. Secondly, the individual must then develop the inclination, aggravated and promoted by the circumstances of his own social environment, to turn this destructive impulse upon himself. This desire for suffering—or to be hurt—may be the result of accumulated guilt feelings. However, this is not sufficient to bring about a suicidal act; the desire to be hurt may be experienced apart from the idea of death. The final state of preparedness is achieved when the individual accepts the first two attitudes and begins to experience at the same time the actual desire to die. Only then can the fully matured suicidal wish assert itself.

As with many other Freudian interpretations, the difficulty with such a view is that it proceeds from the unwarranted assumption of innate, biological impulsions, and pays little heed to the structuring of human attitudes in relation to special social circumstances. If it has any value, it is because it gives us insight into the clinical nature of certain cases, on the basis of actual observation of those whose desires to commit suicide are vague, obscure, and inchoate. That, for example, certain individuals may plan to take their lives but then lack the courage to do so, and that others may actually make genuine attempts toward self-destruction but then express fears, regrets, and strong pleadings that their lives be spared after such attempts have actually been made, is a commonly observed phenomenon in our psychiatric wards. Whether these cases constitute sufficient evidence for such a view and whether they might not be more effectively interpreted upon other grounds is a highly moot question. Certainly, the development of the suicide process in most cases appears to follow a pattern which may be far more plausibly explained on the basis of the development of structured attitudes in relation to specific social and cultural elements.

(13) THE PATTERN OF CAUSATION IN SUICIDE

A much more realistic understanding of the nature of suicide may be sought in terms of the socialization process of different individuals and in relation to the types of social structure to which they are exposed at different stages in their careers. A marked characteristic of suicidal personality types is the relative rigidity and inflexibility of the personality pattern. This rigidity may stem from two sources: (1) from the social environment, which may strongly delimit the range of mobility and social action of the individual personality; or (2) from the limitations of action which the structuring of the personality has itself imposed upon the individual.

Rigidity of personality reflecting social environment. It is the first type of rigidity, very likely, that corresponds to Durkheim's well-known formulation of the altruistic suicide. Among the classical Japanese Samurai, for example, the rigidity of the caste structure made available only a limited number of social choices for the individual, should certain fundamental values of the social structure not be satisfied. Altruistic suicide appears to occur in conjunction with the necessity of maintaining an inflexible code. When the code is abrogated, little or no opportunity is afforded for alternative social action, with the result that death at one's own hands, or at the hands of some trusted retainer, is the sole recourse. In view of the fact that the entire life-pattern of the individual in such a society appears to be dominated by highly limited and circumscribed values, life bears little significance beyond the fulfillment or the perpetuation of such values. Similar patterns may be observed in other societies or social groups which live according to a carefully prescribed and delimited code. The essential point here is that the entire significance of social living appears to revolve about the limited meanings of the code, whose conception of the purposes of group living is extremely narrow. Thus, among the Kwakiutl, who are obsessed with the necessity of achieving or maintaining status through the instrumentalities of property, the loss of possessions shuts off virtually any other possibility for meaningful social activity. Life in these societies differs drastically from our own mode of existence, in which considerable alternatives in the social expressions of human experience may be found. A tentative hypothesis may be offered: Rigidity of social structure, in restricting the meaning of social experience and in seriously curtailing the possibilities of alternative social action, tends to provide a social base for suicide.

Rigidity of personality reflecting psychogenetic growth. The pattern of inflexibility functions differently in more highly complex and flexible societies. The rigidity of the personality structure in such societies is not so much determined by the broad social environment as it is by the peculiarities of family training and psychogenetic growth. In the course of role-identification, the individual tends to fix upon a limited series of objectives within his own social experience. It is these limited social experiences to which he attaches value and which constitute the essential meanings of life. For the vast majority of modern men and women, life presents a wide range of variable choices and meanings. For the suicidal type, the meanings of life are carefully circumscribed and delimited, although this is largely a matter of adventitious socialization and personality development. In both types discussed, it is significant to note that the effect upon the socialization process is to fix limited alternatives for the individual. Whereas for one type this fixation is a result of the limitations of the social environment, in the second type the result is achieved by the accidental processes of personality development.

(14) THE FIXATION OF THE SUICIDE PROCESS

The growing rigidity of the suicidal personality structure reflects differences in sociocultural levels and methods of child-training. Thus, specific objectives and values would be highly variable for different suicidal personalities, while the essential form or pattern of the suicide process is essentially the same, irrespective of the background of the personality. Ruth Cavan has indicated this very clearly in her analysis of the suicide process. She has shown that the major factors involved in the development of suicidal attitudes center around (1) the tendency of a given interest to become *dominant* in the life of an individual, (2) the resultant trend toward *fixation* of the interest and (3) a consequent *loss of objectivity* concerning one's self and one's relations to others, as the individual becomes victimized by the all-compelling and central theme of his existence.[34]

The growth of these dominant interests in the individual's life-pattern may be seen to take certain recognized forms, appearing to signify the growing specificity of such interests in the dominance of the personality. Viewed from this standpoint, suicide may be brought about by the following: (1) unidentified cravings; (2) recognized wishes; (3) specific wishes; (4) mental conflicts (i.e., conflicts produced within the individual because of the need to satisfy two or more compelling, but opposing interests); and (5) the "broken life-organization." Of significance is the fact that in the process of growth, dominant interests become linked with the person's sense of emotional security. Dominant interests may be associated with a specific person, an idea, a given activity (such as a job, for example), or an institution. If the focus of the interest is removed or destroyed, or if it is made impossible for the individual to achieve its satisfaction, the possibility of suicide comes to the fore.

(1) The "unidentified craving" type of suicide occurs when the individual has difficulty in specifying for himself the objectives toward which he aspires. Such suicidal types are usually characterized by a low emotional tone. In one sense, the tendency toward the development of a specific interest may be observed to be in a formative or an incipient

[34] Cf. Cavan, *Suicide,* Chap. 9, "The Suicide Process."

stage. Although such individuals may not always give evidence of the specific objectives of their striving, they give ample evidence of their complete indifference and boredom concerning the normal social activities that surround their lives. Moreover, there is usually a restless striving to find something or someone in the surrounding social scene who may provide a focus of interest in compensation for the general lack of interest the individual feels. Thus, one of Cavan's cases writes, rather typically, in a suicide note: "I am going to hunt my cloud with the silver lining if there is one."[35] The suicide notes left by such individuals are grim evidences of their dissatisfaction and failure to fulfill themselves. Frequently they are written with a morbid sense of humor.[36]

(2) In suicides characterized by the "recognized wish," the individual is usually profoundly aware of what he wants but feels that there are insuperable difficulties in the way of attainment. In the case of both the "recognized wish" and the "unidentified craving" the wish has not become focused on *one* specific object, person, or status, and so some possibility for movement remains. Conceivably, the suicide may be forestalled if the individual recognizes these opportunities and acts in favor of any of them.

(3) In the case of the "specific wish," however, the picture is different. Here the individual knows not only what is the specific target of his interest, but also precisely what specialized aspect of the interest he wishes to fulfill. Thus, to be hungry is one thing (the "recognized wish"), but to be hungry for nothing but steak (the "specific wish") is another, especially, we may add, if one does not have money enough to purchase steak. This type of individual not only craves marriage, but marriage to a specific girl; this type of person not only craves successful employment, but a very specific job, and no other.

(4) Suicides impelled by so-called "mental conflicts" occur among individuals who attempt to fulfill two or more compelling, but *mutually exclusive interests*. Thus, the individual may be able to marry the girl he really wants, but if he does so, he is forced to break the bonds with his family, also a highly dominating and compelling interest. Suicides of this type may frequently be provoked by the conflicting codes of different social groups, or by the conflicts between a social ideal and social reality.

(5) Suicides characterized by a broken life-organization are frequently precipitated by some sudden or external crisis. This resembles, to a degree, the *anomique* type of suicide described by Durkheim. This type of suicide is likely to take place when the individual whose life has

[35] Cavan, *Suicide*, p. 149.

[36] The morbid humor in many suicide notes is an interesting and significant characteristic. They express the individual's sense of the futility of much of the intensified strivings of human existence in the face of the grim reality of death.

been well organized encounters some severely disorganizing experience which makes the further pursuit of his life-plan impossible. Here the dominant interest has already become fixed and firmly established, and has promoted the development of an apparently smoothly functioning personality. The individual's habit-patterns are so firmly entrenched upon this operating autonomy, however, that when such an autonomy is disturbed, there is apparently nothing in the orbit of the individual's social experience that may adequately take its place. Thus, the loss of a successful business, a respected position in society, the death of a beloved family member or spouse, may provide no adequate substitute for the deprived individual.

The Analysis of a Case [37]

The following case deals with a young woman, Marion Blake, a resident of the city of Chicago and the wife of a clerical worker. During a period of seven years prior to the taking of her own life and the life of her male companion, she kept a highly detailed diary, giving a day-to-day account of her attitudes and the events leading up to the final disaster. Her diary entries give us a picture of a highly complex personality. Significant throughout is the growth of self-destructive attitudes culminating in the act of self-execution and murder.

> Marion came from a well-to-do middle-class family in which the parents had been divorced. Prior to her marriage, she had lived with her mother and a sister. The absence of the father may have played some part in instituting the strong drives Marion experienced for affection, although she did maintain some correspondence with her father before her marriage. Prominent in the early part of the record is her continual craving for affection from her young husband, whom she married five months after her high school graduation, at the age of nineteen. Directly after her marriage, she moved with her husband to one of the highly mobile rooming-house districts of Chicago, noted for the frequency of its suicides.
>
> The inordinate craving for continual affection from her husband, amounting almost to an obsession, becomes apparent in the earliest sections of the diary record, and is sustained throughout. The impression is gained that Marion must have continual and profuse demonstrations of affection from her husband, or if not from her husband, someone else. If this affection, in which she basks and which pro-

[37] This case of Marion Blake is found in Chapter 11 of Cavan's work (*Suicide*). However, the interpretive comments are largely those of the author. Reprinted by permission of The University of Chicago Press.

vides her with remarkable ego-satisfaction is forthcoming, her life seems to proceed on a perfectly satisfactory basis. However, even the most ideal of husbands may not devote his entire career to lavishing affection upon his spouse. The slightest shifting of interest elsewhere by her husband, thus—reading the newspaper, enjoying a personal hobby from which she feels excluded, etc.—provokes acute misgivings, uneasiness, and alarm in Marion. She also expresses, as a consequence, recriminations against her husband. A few months after her marriage, she made the following characteristic entries in her diary: "Oh, I wish my husband knew how much I want to be loved. I tell him, but he does not realize that I mean all the time, every minute he is with me."

> He is breaking my heart with his cross words and indifference. Every time it simply widens the gulf between us. . . . Oh, God, wake him up, make him kind and considerate all the time. . . . Oh, I know I must be wrong, but if so, why does God let me live? Life is unbearable to me now, and if things don't get better, something happens.

Bitter quarrels occur frequently during the first year, many of them centering around Marion's indifference and behavior toward her husband's family, whom she deliberately attempts to offend. The principal reason is that this young woman resents anyone, her husband's family included, who might detract from the attention she demands from her husband. Because of her compelling need to be in the forefront of her husband's affection, the matter of an abortion which she undergoes is treated with casualness. She does not wish to risk the possibility of rivalry from children. The operation results in compensated displays of affection by the husband which momentarily appease her.

She resents the need to work to supplement the limited earnings of her husband; the willingness of the husband to accept the fact of her employment suggests to her a casualness in his attitude toward her which she finds intolerable. (Note: The regressed juvenile attitude of this type of suicide, who builds her life upon the affection of some other person. It indicates a lack of emotional maturity and the desire to retain the status of childhood, spared of the necessity of initiating her own decisions and occupying normal adult roles.) Determined to consolidate her relationship with her husband, she finds it relatively easy to steal articles for him in the store where she is employed—a type of childish "bribe" for his affections. The dishonest nature of her conduct is a matter of little or no concern to her.

> I asked Tom what he wished to do, if we could go on, and he suggested separation. All of a sudden I seemed really to know what that would mean for me and I thought I would go mad.
>
> . . .
>
> Tom and I seem to be growing farther apart day by day. Whose fault is it? . . . Tom is so busy with cutting articles from newspapers concerning baseball and the president, that he does not care to spend his precious time [with] me. I just wonder a year from now what I will be writing in this book or if I shall be here to write at all.

On her birthday, two and one-half years after her marriage, she writes: "I hope that next year I won't be here to write." Despite the tensions in the married life of this youthful pair, the relationship is sustained, with great anxiety on the part of Marion. Eventually she is confronted with the fact that her husband has been unfaithful, an issue which she can in no way disguise or evade. Two days after this episode she writes: "Bichloride of mercury, cyanide of potassium, either will kill a dog."

> I am tired of living, of fighting and arguing. . . . Oh, God, if anyone needed me, was dependent upon me, if even I had work to do, I would never think of death. But I have always thought of that since I have been ten or twelve, and certainly am not made to be happy. If I had anything to do, I'd leave here and get a room and if I could I'd live decently, and if not, I'd go the limit or jump in the lake. Which is worse? I prefer the lake.

A permanent separation finally results and Marion seeks to find someone else with whom she may establish a dependent relationship. After a number of unsuccessful attempts, she finally establishes a close liaison with an older married man, who, for a while, successfully fulfills her powerful cravings for affection. However, a few months after this relationship is established, she writes: "Bert does not care for me enough, it is lightly, . . . it is not enough. I must make him care more or be utterly miserable. I long for companionship, love, and tenderness, and someone to help me live outside of myself."

After a tempestuous relationship with her lover over a period of months, in which she strives desperately to maintain the relationship on her own terms and in accordance with her own needs, she is forced to confront the possibility of eventual desertion. When he professes some affection for her, she writes: "It was good to hear him say that even if he does not mean it." And shortly thereafter, "He said . . . he does not intend to spend the rest of his life with me. I told him he would be very sorry when he gives me up. Oh, God, the end seems very near."

When she finally recognizes that the relationship is about to be terminated, after desperate attempts on her part to revive it, she makes her last entry, indicating the depths of her despair, and giving evidence of some realistic insights into the true nature of her position. On the same night, during what was to have been one of his last visits, she shot and killed her consort, and then herself.

SUMMARY

(1) An analysis of the problems of suicide reveals a well-defined sociological basis. The "will to live" itself, and the characteristic attitudes concerning the desirability of human life, reflect deeply implanted social orientations and attitudes. Variations in rates of suicide in different social structures, moreover, indicate characteristic patterns of sociological significance. (2) Social and cultural variations in the incidence and social acceptance of suicides are extremely widespread, indicating a wide range of attitudes. (3) Suicide forms range from highly institutionalized patterns, in which the act is socially condoned and expected, under certain critical circumstances, to the highly individualized types characteristic of contemporary Western society. (4) Studies of suicide in modern Western societies appear to indicate that a leveling off is attained at certain stages of development of the social structure. Suicide, thus, appears to serve as a sensitive barometer of social change in complex social orders. (5) In most modern Western societies, irrespective of overall rate differentials and distinguishing social characteristics, rates of suicide appear to be higher in older age-groups. Although suicide is far more common among the aged than the youthful (a significant commentary upon our contemporary social structure) suicidal attitudes and tendencies may be noted among the young. (6) Although the total number of suicides is negligible as compared with other causes of death in this country, it has shown a gradual secular rise since the last century and has figured as the tenth most frequent cause of death, in order of rank. In relation to violent forms of death, suicide is second only to automobile deaths. (7) Suicide has been shown to fluctuate in accordance with movements of the cultural cycle, occurring with greatest frequency during periods of rapid social transition and social disorganization. (8) Certain clearly marked differences may be noted in the rates of suicide in Europe and the United States since the middle of the nineteenth century, in relation to the differential factors of religion, urbanism, sex, marital status, and ethnic and

racial background. Such differences must be evaluated in terms of interrelated factors and comparable groups. (9) The majority of suicides may not be adjudged psychotic, although sizable percentages do suffer from various psychotic disorders. Psychotic suicides are largely of the involutional melancholic variety. (10) In recent studies of postwar suicide trends, the general characteristics of suicide rates and their accompanying patterns appear to be maintained. (11) The celebrated theory of Emile Durkheim appears to provide a plausible and substantial sociological explanation for the occurrence of suicide. This theory is based upon characteristic forms of social integration within different social structures. The three types of suicides Durkheim delineated, the *altruistic*, the *egoistic*, and the *anomique*, reflect different types of social organization. (12) Psychoanalytical doctrines concerning suicide presuppose a "death-wish," thus assuming the very condition requiring proof. They disregard the basic necessity of social implementation for suicidal attitudes. (13) In explaining the related individual and sociological bases of suicide, we find that patterns of causation appear to occur in relation to a growing rigidity and inflexibility of the personality structure. This rigidity may stem from (a) factors in the social environment, or (b) the way in which the personality itself has been structured. (14) In the study of selected life-histories of suicides, Cavan has indicated the fixation of the suicide process, manifesting itself in the forms of unidentified cravings, recognized wishes, specific wishes, mental conflicts, and broken life-organizations. Such forms operating in the lives of different individuals seem to suggest the dominance of certain interests for the suicidal individual, the fixity of such ideas, and a consequent loss of objectivity.

CHAPTER TWENTY-THREE

PROSPECTUS AND CONCLUSION

SOME GENERAL IMPLICATIONS FROM SOCIAL DISORGANIZATION

AN ANALYSIS of the problems of individual deviation and social pathology is an infinitely difficult and complicated task. In the first place, it calls for no less than to chart and comprehend the endlessly variable patterns of human motivation, emotions, physical traits, and social conditions. Secondly, it calls for an understanding of such processes under conditions that are never static. Thirdly, it demands concentration upon factors of human behavior which may not be apprehended as discrete and separate elements, but only in terms of complicated patterns of relationship. And finally, it compels us to seek explanations of normal and abnormal phases of human behavior within comprehensive conceptual frameworks which bring together in some systematic form the diverse insights and discoveries from a great many different fields.

The last two functions are particularly significant. We are very likely entering upon a new threshold in the field of human sciences. One of the most significant intellectual developments of the past three decades is the movement away from the former eclecticism by which we sought to account for the diversity of human behavior. Our reasoning in the social sciences and psychology at the turn of the century was to the effect that the problems of mankind were so complex that they could be understood, if at all, only in terms of the separable elements underlying each separate phenomenon. As a consequence of the general drift in science and the intellectual folkways of the present century, we are beginning to recognize and to stress the need for integrated explanations of such diverse phenomena, operating within comprehensive frames of reference. As Lewis Mumford has put it, we must begin to develop a new kind of mentality—and consequently a new kind of man—which will enable us to think in terms of many complex variables at the same time and to synthesize such elements in the form of comprehensive conceptual frameworks. To this we would add the further injunction that we must likewise develop intellectual tools that will enable us to take account of the endlessly shifting and mobile basis of society and social phenomena.

This appears a formidable and, in fact, an almost impossible task. The first question that appears to come to mind is "Can it be done?" One of the remarkable outcomes of the endless variety of approaches which have been used thus far in both the study of human nature and in the specialized studies of pathological processes that disrupt the individual organism and society is the apparent consensus concerning three fundamental considerations. In the first place, there is a widespread unanimity among those who may properly be called experts in the social sciences that human phenomena, whether individually or socially conceived, may be adequately studied only by *accredited scientific methods,* if amelioration is the end in view. Popular opposition is strenuous, among informed educational and political leaders, to the active promotion of scientific procedures in the study of human phenomena as a basis of social policy. This opposition is based almost entirely upon ignorance as to the proper function of science in these respects, or upon social and ideological attitudes, frequently of a doctrinal religious nature, which are distrustful of the impact of scientific theorizing and investigation. Secondly, there is the growing consensus that social problems may not be studied piecemeal, but only as phases of widespread dislocation of the social structure.[1] Thirdly, there is the heightened recognition that the problems of the individual personality, no less than the problems of society, may be appraised only in relation to the contextual whole which binds together the social situation and the individual personality. This last is a heartening development. Not only sociologists and social psychologists, but anthropologists, psychiatrists, and physiologists are drawn to the same conclusion.[2]

THE INDIVIDUAL IN RELATION TO THE SOCIAL SITUATION

From the welter of different viewpoints concerning the individual and social problems arising during the early decades of this century, cer-

[1] Cf. Lawrence K. Frank, *Society as the Patient* (New Brunswick, New Jersey, 1948, pp. 1–20). The theoretical implications of this view have been ably presented by Robert K. Merton, *Social Theory and Social Structure: Toward the Codification of Theory and Research* (Glencoe, Illinois, 1949), particularly in the group of papers dealing with his studies in social and cultural structure. See also Talcott Parsons, "The Prospects of Sociological Theory," *American Sociological Review,* XV (Feb., 1950), 3–16.

[2] A whole series of recent writings in the fields of sociology and social psychology have strongly affirmed this position and, in fact, have made it the central thesis of their points of view. Among the great number that might be mentioned are Theodore M. Newcomb, *Social Psychology* (New York, 1950), Parts IV and V; Walter Coutu, *Emergent Human Nature* (New York, 1949), Chaps. 10, 11, and 12; J. W. Bennett and Melvin M. Tumin, *Social Life: Structure and Function* (New York 1948), Part III and Chap. 32. For a stimulating essay presenting some of the ethical implications of this view, see Ashley Montagu, *On Being Human* (New York, 1950), especially Chap. 2.

tain significant concepts have emerged with striking clarity. Conspicuous in this development have been (1) the concept of social interaction; and (2) the concept of the socialized individual. The latter involves an understanding of the *sociological* basis of personal habit-patterns and the resultant fruitful concepts of status and role.[3] Such concepts, originating largely with the early work of Charles H. Cooley, George H. Mead, and John Dewey, have been profitably advanced by many of the more recent anthropological and sociological theorists, such as Ralph Linton, Margaret Mead, and Ruth Benedict in the field of anthropology, and Talcott Parsons, Ralph Merton, Kingsley Davis, and others in the field of sociology. These concepts are not only highly significant for further empirical investigation in the field of human behavior, but present wide-ranging implications for the formulation of social policy and the problems of social ethics as well.

It is now clearly perceived that human activity may be understood only in relation to specific social situations. This position was stressed in the early chapters of this book. The individual may be perceived only as an abstraction—as a tendency to respond to certain selected aspects of a given situation confronting him. Coutu has attempted to present this idea in a systematic form by his able analysis of what he calls the "tendency in situation," or to use his term, the "tinsit." The individual responds selectively to his environment, taking note of only those aspects of the situation which have value for him. In other words, he perceives certain key-elements within the situation. These key-elements of the somatic and other environmental factors which are involved produce configurated wholes of behavior, or a continual stream of emergents.

This complete involvement of the human being within given social situations, in which he perceives selected elements and responds to them, has been broken down by Newcomb into a series of independent, intervening, and dependent variables.[4] He recognizes certain basic limiting conditions of the organism and the environment, such as the physical properties of the organism itself and imposed social standards, which he calls "independent variables." The selective operation of such factors upon the peculiar eliciting circumstances of a given personality, in the form of motives and attitudes, he recognizes as the intervening variables. The conjunction of such factors, however, invariably produces a given form of completed social behavior, which, in turn, may be regarded as the dependent variable. The significant feature of this analysis is that the entire complex of factors operates as a whole within a given situation, *of which the individual is but a respondent phase.*

[3] For an analysis of the implications of such trend producing concepts, see Herbert A. Bloch, "A Synthetic View of the Social Individual as a Primary Datum in Sociology," *American Sociological Review*, VIII (Oct. 1943), 506.

[4] Newcomb, *Social Psychology*, pp. 30–4.

Human behavior is essentially *contingent* and dependent. The significance of this from the standpoint of what the individual may do in the face of critical situations and the degree to which he may alter such circumstances will be examined shortly. However, the basic fact is this: The individual may not be held entirely accountable for the types of difficulties or problem-situations in which he finds himself. These difficulties are parts of complicated and intricate process-situations. Comprehension of this basic fact must inevitably alter our perspectives concerning the nature of human problems and the degree of human culpability. Not only are we compelled thereby to examine our problems more realistically, thus achieving a better understanding of the causal processes involved in any human situation, but we are compelled at the same time to focus our attention upon the entire complex of conditioning circumstances, rather than upon the "erring" individual or deviant personality. What distinguishes one personality from another is the relative consistency with which the individual tends to respond to certain selective aspects of common social situations.

Such tendencies to respond do not exist within the personality as unattached elements. They develop in response to the peculiar eliciting circumstances of given situations. Man is intrinsically neither good nor bad, as Shakespeare put it, "except that thinking makes it so." What is "good" or "bad" depends upon certain patterned relationships, derived largely by accident, with which the behavior of individual men becomes inextricably involved. What is good or bad from the social point of view, thus, is based on the judgments we deliver concerning the tendencies to respond in ways which contradict or deny the meanings (or behavior responses) we impute to the same situation. While such judgments *may* be extremely significant from the standpoint of their reflecting the nature of normal cultural standards, they tell us little concerning the nature of the responding individual. Social judgments of censure and blame directed toward the individual and his behavior frequently do little more than to affirm and to widen the gap that already exists between the pathological person and the social group.[5]

In examining the complex wholes that comprise any form of human behavior, we must recognize that any personality tendency may be comprehended only in relation to the specific elements within the situation which have evoked it. No tendency exists by itself, but only in relation to something or someone. Human behavior, in short, may be perceived only in relation to an activating situation to which the person responds

[5] When censure and blame are employed without relevance to the configuring situation, they serve a social function largely for the individuals doing the blaming. This function is similar to the ancient practice of exorcism, the "casting out of devils" —a form of social rejection of the individual who displeases us.

selectively. Why the individual responds as he does to the key-elements of a situation and not to others depends upon the linkages he has established with the past, or specifically, with similar past situations. In a sense, if we choose to think of the individual as a self-enclosed entity (a notion which modern sociology and psychology now reject as archaic), we may accept such a concept purely on the basis of the tendency of the human organism to respond with more or less consistency when confronted with similar or identical elements of repeated situations. We are what we do, and what we do is essentially the tendency to respond to certain repeated configurated wholes in accordance with *key* evocative stimuli.

Much present-day thinking goes back to the long discarded notions of Aristotle, which Kurt Lewin, J. F. Brown, and others have so ably attacked.[6] This type of thinking, now discarded in favor of the scientific orientations of Galileo and his followers, made the serious error of thinking that objects behave because of properties or propensities contained within themselves. Thus, according to the older view, heavy objects fell because it was *part of their nature* to fall. Obviously, heavy objects fall and human beings behave in certain ways only in conjunction with situations which cause them to act in such ways. Heavy objects will *not* fall unless exposed to situations where gravitation may exert its force. Human beings will not hate, love, steal, or rebel, except in relation to specific situations which elicit these results. There is certainly nothing instinctive, generic, or innate about such behavior manifestations. A thief will not steal in all situations, even when the possibility for his doing so is amply evident.

The complex whole of human society functions on different levels and in countless varied situations which have come to signify different meanings and responsive tendencies to a myriad of individuals. It is these varied situations which are *structured* differently (that is, are organized differently) in accordance with special cultural meanings. Through a series of "chain reactions," men on any level are in some way integrated with the complex whole which comprises the social order. The social order refers to the statistical probability that certain common situations will repeat themselves and that men will respond to them in anticipated fashion—or, in other words, will impute to them the same meanings.

SOCIAL SITUATIONS AND CULTURE

When we speak of the effects of culture upon the social behavior of men, we must remember that human behavior functions in relation to recurrent situations. Men confront situations and not the broad abstractions of culture itself. What happens in respect to any social norm is that

[6] Kurt Lewin, *A Dynamic Theory of Personality* (New York, 1935); J. F. Brown, *Psychology and the Social Order* (New York, 1936).

its common meaning becomes transformed in its implications in respect to different kinds of social situations. The character of what purports to be a common social situation, thus, varies with respect to those distinguishing social characteristics we refer to as class, age, sex, and specialized group differentials. In his recent novel on Negro life in this country, *Without Magnolias*, Bucklin Moon portrays accurately how the same factor of racial discrimination enters differently into the lives of each separate individual involved. The compromises which some of his leading characters make, the open rebellion of others, the efforts of still others to maintain positions of dominance over others of their own race, and a variety of other reactions differ fundamentally because of varying contextual situations reflecting diverse age, sex, economic, educational, and familial factors.

Culture, thus, appears to manifest itself in the observable regularities of group behavior. These regularities, however, are nothing more than the tendency to respond in specific and recognized ways to situations to which we give the same meanings. (It has been pointed out earlier in this book, however, that a characteristic overt response may conceal a wide variety of meanings.) When we interpret the culture of a given group, we are *inferring* from the observation of a number of common and repeated situations what we believe the meaning of that situation happens to be for its participants. The common meanings of certain situations, however, are continually being altered because of the intrusion within the situation of a wide variety of uncontrolled factors. Although members of a culture may have preconceived ideas as to what their behavior should be in culturally defined situations, there is never a guarantee that the actual moment of human experience will reproduce the situation in its ideal form. Consequently, since it is the human situation that the individual reacts to and *not* the culture, responses to defined situations are highly variable and subtle irrespective of the conditioned meaning. These variations in response constitute a *penumbra* or marginal area of response whose subtle contradictions or open hostility may lay the basis for individual and social disorder.

When we speak of culture operating on different levels, what we mean is that situations become differently defined as they embrace differing sex, age, and membership characteristics. Recurrent response-tendencies for men, women, and children may be noted on different age levels as they pertain to a wide variety of different situations, having to do with home, employment, schools, churches, and political affiliations. Because of the multiplicity of situations, however, and the innumerable cultural definitions applying to them, behavior in a given sphere and concerning a given sex, age, or membership group may run counter to the general pattern of meanings applying to related situations. Thus, the culturally recognized need within our own society for parents to regulate the leisure-time activities of children may be diametric to other recognized situations in which adolescent children are accorded considerable freedom in the administration of their leisure. A serious conflict may arise which is due primarily to differences in defined situations, rather than to the recalcitrance of individuals. Such illustrations could be cited endlessly in any complex culture.

(1) The principal focus of the problem in such situations may be social and *not* individual. When such conflicts in defined situations arise, we may, if we choose, tend to regard them as conflicts within the culture, provided we remember that their functional basis consists of conflicting tendencies to respond within given situations. Furthermore, if we assume that in any society there is, as William Graham Sumner put it many years ago, a "strain toward consistency"—or, in other words, a tendency for defined social situations to reinforce each other through common meanings—the operation of a conflicting behavior process may be regarded as *dysfunctional.* There is certainly no objection to this manner of stating the point. There is considerable reason to support it since it attempts to get away from evaluative judgments. The recent emphasis by the school of Harvard sociologists led by Professor Talcott Parsons in favor of analyzing social behavior systematically according to the "structure of social action" represents a highly significant development in the field of sociology away from "value judgments."[7] Such dysfunctional processes may be carefully noted in our own emphasis on regarding cultural processes as representing divergent or congruent "definitions of the situation" in respect to the actual tendencies of men and women to respond to defined situations.

When such antagonistic or dysfunctional processes arise in social situations, they come to rest within the individual. The individual, as part of the social situation to which he responds, *develops attitudes and behavior tendencies toward himself as he does toward others.* Consequently, such dysfunctions manifest themselves in contradictory and antagonistic attitudes toward himself, the subjective counterpart of social disorder.[8]

(2) In appraising social situations as representative of culture, however, we must also be mindful that pathological processes may result because of the individual's highly personalized response to a situation. This may result irrespective of whether certain group situations are congruent or dysfunctional. In *any* society, we have maladapted personalities. The

[7] The fundamental position of the functional point of view has been presented in Talcott Parsons' well-known *The Structure of Social Action* (New York, 1937); in his *Essays in Sociological Theory, Pure and Applied* (Glencoe, Illinois, 1949); and in a number of published papers by the same author.

[8] This is somewhat akin to the position stated by Professor Pitirim Sorokin in his *Society, Culture and Personality* (New York, 1947), Chaps. 19 and 48.

source of the disorder here is the peculiar structuring of the individual's attitude which, in given instances, expresses itself in forms antagonistic to accepted meanings. The key to the understanding of this process is through the mechanism of socialization, or the way in which the individual learns to assume certain social roles. It is to this process that we now turn briefly.

ROLES, SOCIAL SITUATIONS, AND CULTURE

The group, as we have learned, is prior to the child. The child is born into a world where the values of the several groups in which he claims membership have already been established. Because of accidents of rearing, organic and hereditary differences, and the multiplicity of groups claiming his attention, he can never fully identify himself with any group, even his own family. The result is that a marginal area of group association exists for every individual, i.e., his interest and behavior in any group can never fully coincide with the "definitions of the situation" which each separate group imposes. The individual tends to identify himself with the several groups comprising his own limited social world through the acquisition of roles. Only through his roles can the individual's behavior be made meaningful to the group and to himself. Without roles, the individual remains unsocialized and, in a sense, non-humanized. What we recognize as human nature are the meanings we attach to the roles that individuals assume in the complex social situations comprising social life.[9]

The basic principles in the development of roles appear to revolve around the significant symbols of speech in early childhood, as Mead has illustrated. Also relevant is the tendency of the child to identify himself with the attitudes and behavior-patterns of those in his early childhood who are directly concerned with his growth, the so-called primary groups, of which the family and early play-groups are signally important. In encountering his early situations, the child takes account of the imputed meanings and behavior patterns which others entertain toward him. By introjecting this experience, he identifies himself with the behavior of others, and the significance of human behavior is borne in upon him and

[9] Although constituting the central portion of modern sociological theory, this phase of our subject-matter has to a considerable extent been neglected. While the basic theoretical postulates concerning the nature of role-taking were admirably stated by George H. Mead and Charles Horton Cooley three decades ago, the actual research concerning the functioning of roles within defined situations has been relatively slow in developing. Ironically, we know considerably more about the role-taking of several primitive groups than we do about the specific factors governing role-taking in contemporary American society. If we are to make significant advances in our understanding of problems of human pathology within the next few decades, we must concentrate upon this important phase of our research.

he becomes conscious of himself as a socially participating individual. Such acts are really acts of self-incorporation and self-enclosure. The individual, so to speak, incorporates the behavior of other individuals within his own person, sealing it within himself. Because such behavior-patterns are repeated in identical situations, the meanings of the situations become generic and he develops attitudes towards what Mead referred to as the "generalized other." [10] The "generalized other" becomes a kind of universal symbol for the meaning of society as it functions within specific, repeated, and *expected* social situations.

The limitations of the role that the child will play are determined by the cultural characteristics that are operative in specific situations. One of our common mistakes in attempting to comprehend human problems is to assume that role-taking specifications are much alike for the entire range of society. This is the error of so many of the broader anthropological studies—particularly when they attempt to interpret human behavior in complex modern societies. An instance is Geoffrey Gorer's otherwise stimulating analysis, *The American Character*. What Gorer does in this study is to analyze specialized phases of the socialization process as they pertain to the American middle class, and a rather specific aspect of the upper middle class. Similar limitations may be found in the studies of the so-called sociological psychiatrists, such as Karen Horney (*The Neurotic Personality of Our Time*) and Erich Fromm (*Escape From Freedom*). Although such interpretations are occasionally penetrating, they deal largely with either restricted situational elements descriptive of circumscribed cultural situations, as in the case of Horney's discussion of the middle class, or with broad historical determinants of cultural processes which are presumed to operate with considerable similarity among all social segments, as in Fromm's sweeping cultural studies. Even in the more incisive sociological studies of role-determinants, the distinctions in role ascription and assumption are suggested and implied rather than empirically demonstrated. Thus, Talcott Parsons penetratingly reveals the generic functions of age and sex status in the social structure of the United States, but does little more than suggest the patterned structural elements of such statuses within varying social situations.[11]

Role-formation is the process by which the individual assumes his place within his society and his culture, and by which he learns to apprehend the significance of his own behavior. Such roles vary in relation to age and sex, and in accordance with the kinship structure of society, as well as other structural elements of society, such as educational practice

[10] G. H. Mead, *Mind, Self and Society*, edited by C. W. Morris (Chicago, 1938), pp. 193–4.

[11] Cf. Talcott Parsons, "Age and Sex in the Social Structure of the United States," *American Sociological Review*, VII (1942), 604–16.

and economic positions. Within all societies, there are common meanings which, with little substantial alteration, exist throughout certain groups. Thus, in American society, there are certain recognized differences in expected behavior for boys and girls irrespective of educational and economic level. However, other distinctive group-differences may be seen. In certain segments of society, the attainment of certain roles is optional, while for other groups it is mandatory. Finally, there are highly distinctive and specialized patterns randomly distributed throughout the entire society. The roles which a child takes will reflect all of these possibilities in differing combinations.

The pursuit of such specialized investigations will advance considerably our insights concerning the problems of human behavior and the capacity and incapacity of individuals to adjust to specific situations. In the meanwhile, promising beginnings have been made in such studies as Arnold Green's analysis of the neurosis of the middle-class child. Our understanding of social pathology will require increasing concentration upon studies of how specific kinds of family situations determine role-formation and resultant social attitudes. The research in this field, although still meagre, is steadily growing, and is emanating from several different fields. Ada Sheffield, for example, in evaluating case-work procedures for social workers, has shown repetitions of certain patterns, such as the specific configuration which she calls "the home as the cushioned retreat for the father." [12] Such repeated configurated situations, operating upon different levels, may be considered analogous to the syndromes of traits the psychiatrist discovers on the personality level. Study of the operation of these traits in conjunction with differential structural elements of the social order will do much to clarify our insights concerning the entire process of socialization, role-formation, and attitudinal tendencies. Recently, James Bossard and Eleanor Doll have indicated the variety of family patterns which emerge in American life, each distinctively patterned and operating within differential situational contexts.[13] Such specific family-types as The Neglectful Home, The Over-Indulgent Home, The Mother-Controlled Home, The Father-Dominated Home, The Suddenly-Wealthy Family, The Disgraced Home, etc., must be studied within *actual behavioral contexts* and in conjunction with distinctive structural elements to give us clearly delineated portraits of role-processes and propensities for individuals reared in these environments. The situational elements not only represent the cultural meanings of status-positions within different structural forms but shed considerable

[12] Ada Sheffield, *Social Insight In Case Situations* (New York, 1937).

[13] James Bossard, *The Sociology of Child Development* (New York, 1948); James Bossard and Eleanor S. Doll, *Family Situations: An Introduction to the Study of Child Behavior* (Philadelphia, 1943).

light upon the procedures of child-rearing which, through the direct impact of the structured personalities of parents upon the child, indicate the idiosyncratic and highly charged emotional content of role behaviors and strivings.

THE PRIMACY OF THE FAMILY IN DETERMINING ROLES

In the last analysis, thus, we are always driven back to examining the family in order to understand the basic structuring of personality in relation to those social situations which will mitigate or aggravate tensions for the individual and his group. This point of view has been highlighted once more in the most recent of the remarkable studies on delinquency and crime by Sheldon and Eleanor Glueck.[14] Culminating ten years of intensive research on the causal factors of delinquency, this celebrated research team concluded that the character of the family situation had far more to do with creating delinquency than residence in a slum area, or exposure to "conflicting cultures," or membership in a large family. The basic components of role-forming attitudes are inculcated during early childhood, as the Gluecks have attested in the following conclusion: "Their tendencies toward uninhibited energy-expression are deeply anchored in soma (body) and psyche (mind) and in the malformations of character during the first five years."

Comparing carefully the developmental patterns of five hundred delinquent boys from the slum areas of Boston with a control group of five hundred non-delinquent boys coming from the same areas, the Gluecks discovered that if the child's family life was adequate, the chances were only three in one hundred that he would turn out to be a delinquent. On the other hand, if the family situation was poor, the chances were ninety-eight out of a hundred that the child would become a delinquent. Significant from the sociological view is the presence of factors in the structured family situation reflective of limiting social conditions in the environment, and manifesting themselves in the attitudes of the parents. Thus, commonly noted in the backgrounds of the delinquent group were such factors as over-severe or lax or erratic discipline administered by the father, lack of concern by the mother as to how the child's leisure was employed, and rejection by both parents. The presence of such attitudinal factors may be shown to be related to the structural characteristics of certain types of homes. It is significant that the chief character traits manifested by the delinquent child were marked willfulness, assertiveness, general defiance, suspicion and unreasoning hostility, and the desire to injure and destroy others as well as himself, all emo-

[14] Sheldon and Eleanor Glueck, *Unraveling Juvenile Delinquency* (New York, 1950).

tional by-products of inadequate role-formation. The fact that these boys were found with high frequency to be restless and energetic, impulsive, extroverted, aggressive, and sadistic seems to suggest strongly that their emotional drives were never channelled in the direction of positive role-identifications. In their homes, bickering between parents and lack of concern for their offspring were common. "It is clear," say the Gluecks, "that in the home and in the parent-child relations are to be found the crucial roots of character which make for acceptable or unacceptable adjustment to the realities of life in society."

FAMILY DISORGANIZATION

The family is the crucible within which the human personality and social institutions are created. As the institutional patterns of the family break down, so do we find an increase in the incidence of disorganized personalities. Conversely, the presence of a vast number of disorganized personalities testifies to the present and potential failure of our social institutions.

The disorganization of the family, so significant from the standpoint of the impairments it creates in the *socialization* process, may not be adjudged solely by divorce statistics. In fact, despite the enormous increase in the trends of divorce since 1880, and culminating in the peak rates of 1944 to 1946, divorce may be considered as only the readily recognizable and tangible end-result of certain types of disorganized homes. The fact that approximately two-thirds of divorces are granted to childless couples testifies still further to the fact that divorce in itself may not be considered a general index of family disorganization *per se*. Only a relatively small percentage of divorces occur in families where there are two or more children (approximately 15 per cent).

Family disorganization must be regarded from two standpoints: (1) the success or failure of the famliy in adequately fulfilling the personality needs of its members and the normal functions expected of it, and (2) the *degree* to which the basic social demands of the family are being fulfilled. Thus, it may be seen that family disorganization is a matter of degree and not necessarily a specific and definitive end-result. A family that apparently fulfills outward social requirements which society imposes upon it may, nevertheless, be highly inadequate in fulfilling the peculiar needs of personality development of its several members. Family disorganization must be regarded as a process and must be viewed in relation to the degree to which it satisfies both social functions and the personality needs of its members. "Failing families" in contemporary society must be judged from the standpoint of the character of the internal personal relationships with which they either impede or promote the development of integrated personalities. The process and character of family disorganization may be stated in a series of formal propositions or principles.

(1) *Marriage and family forms are sensitively responsive to changes in the social structure.* In a sense the family may be seen to be one of the most sensitive barometers of social change. There is hardly a facet of family life which is not affected by social change. Conversely, extensive and pervasive changes in the family-patterns must of necessity have certain repercussions upon the social system. Although we have been in the habit of taking this truism for granted for some years, we are just beginning to appreciate its obverse (at least in its research implications), viz., that the psychodynamic patterns laid down in family life have far-reaching and profound effects upon the type of institutional patterns and values surrounding the family. One result of this is that the structure of the family itself may be apprehended as a form of "cultural lag" in the face of changing social patterns.

(2) *The accepted pattern of family organization during a given period, supporting a specific structure and certain specific functions, affords an index whereby family disorganization may be appraised or measured.* The "structure of the family" refers to the framework of the member-roles of the family in their relationship to each other, resulting in a distinctive pattern or a coherent set of relationships. These status-roles are invariably defined by the social structure. Not only are they supported by strong customary sanctions, but in all modern states they are strongly fortified by the legal code which tends to give them permanence as well as a high degree of rigidity and fixity. In general, these member-roles and the defined social prescriptions attendant thereon, fall into three major categories: (a) the husband-wife relationship, (b) the parent-child relationship, and (c) the sibling relationships. These sets of relationships, as part of the major structure of the family, provide an index of the degree to which certain *social* functions are being satisfied, such as economic support, childhood care, and affection between members.

It should be recognized at the same time, however, that individual members of the family develop certain expectancies toward the family *other than those culturally prescribed.* Within the framework as defined, there are certain cultural expectancies which each member of the family, by conditioning, comes to hold toward it; in addition, there are closely interwoven with these expectancies certain highly individualized accents expressive of the unique character of each family. *The well-structured family unit, therefore, not only satisfies these broad, basic cultural conditions, as prescribed by the social order, but at the same time provides an integral unit within which individual personality needs may be satisfied.* To effectively subserve the "interwoven needs" of its members, a certain type of family organization results which may be viewed as a "unity of interacting personalities."

The pattern of family organization, therefore, invariably involves this dual aspect: first, the formal structure as defined by the social roles; and second, those individual variations in behavior, expectancies, and attitudes which the operating of the structure has elicited and sanctioned. Disorganization or family breakdown thus may be viewed as emanating from both sources: (a) as a departure from the socially accepted patterns of behavior which the community and the individual have come to expect as normal for compliance with social needs, and (b) as a departure from the structural needs set up by the aforementioned "unity of interacting personalities." Breakdowns resulting from the first type of deviations are ordinarily of more concern to the community. Involving a denial of community standards and values, they necessitate intervention by organized agencies and official groups. Breakdowns of the second type are more elusive and difficult for the outsider to comprehend in view of the highly personalized values involved in the disorganizing process. In a rapidly changing society, characterized by extreme mobility and the intrusion of major secondary institutions upon the lives of all individuals from childhood to adulthood, disorganization of the second type comes to assume an ominous significance.

(3) *The character of family disorganization will depend upon the peculiar typology of its structure.* The peculiar structural forms described previously, such as the matriarchal-dominated home, the over-indulgent home, the father-dominated home, the sibling-dominated home, the neglectful home, etc., are significant in determining patterns of breakdown and *effects upon the socialization process of the child.* Such patterns may frequently be assessed in terms of the internal power-relations within the family, i.e., by determining who exercises the principal controls in shaping and regulating the behavioral processes of family members.

(4) *The primary factors determining the disorganization of the family will depend upon its peculiar typological structure.* Factors which may weaken or endanger the structure of one family may actually strengthen and consolidate the structure of another. A factor which may jeopardize the status of the father in an autocratic family may have little effect upon a family in which the father's position in the power-pattern may be of inconsiderable importance. Cavan and Ranck, in their study of the effect of the depression of 1929 upon American families, showed that circumstances which militated against the maintenance of one family actually constituted factors of strength for others.[15] Consequently, whether or not the family is able to maintain itself will depend upon the

[15] Cf. Ruth S. Cavan and Katherine H. Ranck, *The Family and the Depression* (Chicago, 1938), Chap. 7.

nature of the critical factors to which it is exposed and the way in which such factors enter into the particular patterned structure. Such disorganizing influences may be either circumstantial or factors of personality stress, depending on the nature of the family organization. In general, factors causative of family disintegration or imbalance may be classified into four major categories: (a) circumstantial or non-personality factors, (b) personality defects, (c) personality differentials, and (d) incompatible roles.[16]

The Process of Family Disorganization. Involved in every family structure is its uniquely related psychological basis, consisting of the underlying complex of attitudes of its members. This psychological basis or attitudinal complex of the family situation consists of the expectancies which individual members entertain toward each other on the basis of the needs which the family has generated and which the parents have brought into their marriage. These expectancies manifest themselves in the attitudes that are channelized through the given family structure and its special type. A given structure-type determines the attitudes and conditions the responses of its members to an awareness of the type of expectancies involved in the family pattern. It is for this reason that different types of family patterns satisfy different individuals. Furthermore, stresses which appear in the life of one family may be wholly or partially disregarded in another.

The pattern of breakdown may now be seen to fall within a conceptual schema whose essential and minimal requirements may be diagrammed as follows:

THE PATTERN OF FAMILY BREAKDOWN

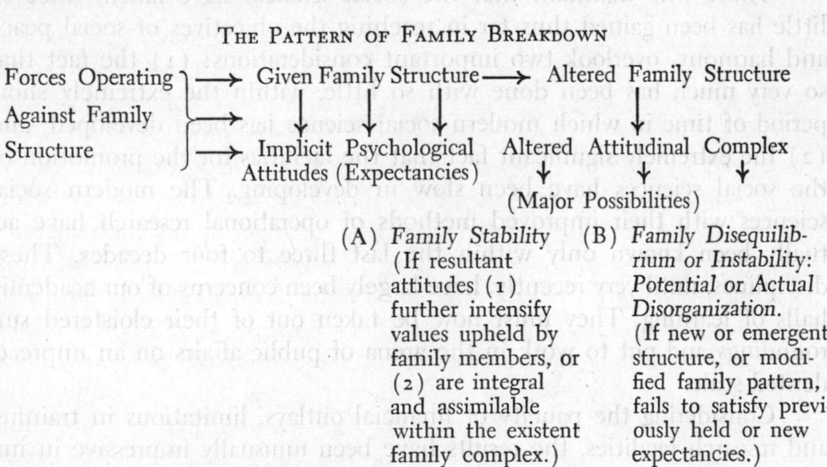

[16] Cf. J. K. Folsom, *The Family: Its Sociology and Social Psychiatry* (New York, 1934), pp. 440–6; also, by the same author, *The Family and Democratic Society* (New York, 1943), Chap. 13.

CAN SCIENCE SAVE US?

In our summary thus far, we have tried to track down the relationships existing among culture, the social situations comprising society, and the individual. We have indicated two primary conditions for the understanding of human behavior, in both its normal and its pathological aspects. They are first, the indissoluble relationship of the individual to the culturally defined situations in which he actively and continually participates; and second, the basic function of the family in generating and giving direction to these fundamental attitudes of the individual. A fundamental premise of our entire outlook is that such problems can be effectively dealt with only through the agency of scientific method. In our contemporary world, where the problems we daily face upon the domestic and international scenes appear overwhelming, the urgency of dealing effectively with them is great. Our fears of the atomic bomb continually remind us that "it may be later than we think."

Can science save us? "Yes," says George Lundberg, "but we must not expect physical science to solve social problems."

> We cannot expect penicillin to solve the employer-employee struggle, nor can we expect better electric lamps to illumine darkened intellects and emotions. We cannot expect atomic fission to reveal the nature of the social atom and the manner of its control. If we want results in improved human relations we must direct our research to the solution of these problems.[17]

Those who maintain that the social sciences have failed, since so little has been gained thus far in reaching the objectives of social peace and harmony, overlook two important considerations: (1) the fact that so very much has been done with so little, within the extremely short period of time in which modern social science has been developed; and (2) the extremely significant fact that the facilities for the promotion of the social sciences have been slow in developing. The modern social sciences with their improved methods of operational research have actually been known only within the last three to four decades. These disciplines, until very recently, have largely been concerns of our academic halls of learning. They must now be taken out of their cloistered surroundings and put to work in the arena of public affairs on an unprecedented scale.

Considering the paucity of financial outlays, limitations in training and research facilities, the results have been unusually impressive in improving policies in various fields of public, social, and industrial administration. The remarkable series of studies by Samuel Stouffer and his staff

[17] George A. Lundberg, *Can Science Save Us?* (New York, 1947), p. 104.

during the Second World War on the effects of military life, organization, and war upon army personnel should do much to illuminate these hitherto completely unknown aspects of social life and, in fact, are already providing a highly workable basis for army personnel policies. Work of a similar character performed for naval aviation units during the recent war by Jenkins and others made clear the reasons for effective co-operation and morale in certain combat units and the deterioration of the morale of others.[18] The series of epoch-making studies on industrial organization and labor appearing in Roethlisberger and Dickson's *Management and the Worker* in 1940, including the famous Hawthorne experiments for Western Electric, have demonstrated the highly practical results which adequate research in industry may produce, in terms of higher productivity and improved manager-employee relationships. Since then, a multitude of studies in industry have been performed which are amply justifying the confident expectations of these pioneer investigators.[19] Despite public skepticism as to the validity of public opinion polls following the presidential election of 1948, the accuracy of public opinion polls on a myriad of other issues and trends has been repeatedly demonstrated.[20]

The bibliographies of scientific investigations extending into family, economic, political, educational, and cultural life are already assuming enormous proportions. If there is any doubt concerning the vast range of these studies and their value for practical application to innumerable aspects of social living, we have merely to examine any one of the recent texts in the fields of experimental social psychology. Yet, despite this progress, fostered largely under academic auspices, the actual application of what we know as a basis for formulating social policy has barely gotten under way. It may be, as Lundberg has suggested, that only when the public is prepared to support social research as it does the great foundations of the physical sciences (with institutions comparable to the Massachusetts Institute of Technology and the California Institute of Technology and with facilities comparable to the research laboratories of Bell Telephone, General Electric, and General Motors), will advances comparable to those of the physical sciences be made.

The scientific method is the only system of analysis available at the present time to give us substantial help in our social dilemmas. In specific

[18] Cf., for example, J. G. Jenkins, "Nominating Technique as a Method of Evaluating Air Group Morale," *Journal of Aviation Medicine*, XIX (1948), 12–19.

[19] Cf., for example, the effective investigation by L. Coch and J. R. P. French of techniques for overcoming job-resistance of workers: "Overcoming Resistance to Change," *Human Relations*, I, 512–32.

[20] Cf., H. Cantril, *Gauging Public Opinion* (Princeton, New Jersey, 1944); also, Stuart Chase, *The Proper Study of Mankind*, Chaps. 15 and 16. For an interesting analysis as to why the polls have failed upon significant occasions, and what must be done to improve them, see D. Katz, "Polling Methods and the 1948 Polling Failure," *International Journal of Opinion and Attitude Research*, II (1949), 469–80.

instances, such as the information we have compiled concerning the causation of delinquency, enough is already known so that the major portion of our delinquency problem could be liquidated within the foreseeable future, if we were so minded. Why then, the student may ask, do we not proceed to eradicate what everyone recognizes as a dangerous social evil? The reasons may be twofold. In the first place, the costs in financial outlay and human effort may be greater than the public is prepared to make, in the face of other pressing demands. Second, our lack of interest in actually achieving such practical results may be due to forms of cultural resistance. This latter is itself a matter of sociological investigation and study. We know today, for example, why the early scientific discoveries of the pioneers of the physical sciences, Galileo, Giordano Bruno, da Vinci, and others, were rejected by early European society. We may discover today the specific areas in the social system which are resistant to the acceptance of social science discoveries; these areas of resistance themselves are amenable to scientific investigation and correction.

Adequate scientific methods as applied to human society can do two things: (1) they can tell us what the possible alternative courses of human action may be in relation to a given problem; and (2) they can assess the costs of these alternative courses of action and indicate their probable effects upon men. Such studies of future effects and possibilities science can carry out with a precision available to no other known human agency. Can science tell us *what* to want? Not entirely. The answer to this problem for the present must remain a conditional and a qualified negative. What science can tell us is whether or not what we want is *possible* of attainment and, second, it can tell us *what* the cost in human effort may be. However, it may partially answer the question by indicating whether human wants are incompatible. In indicating the possible alternatives to human action, it may suggest the directions which human striving should take. A knowledge of scientific methods in the study of human phenomena may enable us better than any other known instrumentality to drive our own vehicles along charted roadways and highways, instead of being random hitch-hikers into an unknown and unmapped future. Thus, science may provide us with a compass and a point of orientation in controlling our own destiny.

The immediate goals, however, must be charted in terms of the universal goals which all men appear to want—the eradication of war, of human suffering and illness, the catastrophes of economic disorder, and political chaos. The carefully delineated and subsidiary objectives which such broad goals suggest must be reformulated on the basis of the innumerable secondary goals and objectives of a proximate nature which can be scientifically stated in operational and carefully stipulated terms. Where do we want to go from here? Where we want to go is largely determined by where we will be able to go in accordance with the limitations of environmental, social, and psychological conditions. When Alice asks the Cheshire Cat: "Would you tell me, please, which way I ought to go from here?"—the cat answers: "That depends a good deal on where you want to get to." Whether we can get to our social destinations will depend upon our natural limitations and these may be determined only by science. In time, as science narrows down the limitations available to us, it will partially frame the proper answer.

Religionists frequently become concerned about the possible effects of widespread and concentrated use of the scientific method in the study of human problems. The use of the scientific method is falsely identified with "scientism" and the veneration of what is called "materialistic values" and a "materialistic culture." Actually, they need have no concern. Science is certainly *not* the only frame of reference in life, nor does it pretend to be. Science is a method, the most effective method that men have yet devised for adapting themselves to the natural and social world in which they live. When the religionist claims that a change of attitude and a change of heart are sufficient to bring about the surcease from human suffering which all men crave, he must recognize that such changes of attitude and sentiment depend on our ability to determine why it is that men have been unable to effect such changes thus far. What science can do for religion is to indicate how religious ideals and capacities may be made more effective and meaningful. It can also cause organized religion to examine itself in order to apprehend the extent to which religious teachings and strivings are actually functional in the lives of their followers. Far from destroying the humanities or religion, science may, in fact, actually strengthen religious aspirations and make them capable of realization.[21]

Finally, there is an important ethical consideration in the understanding of science, if scientific method is truly apprehended. It is, very likely, no accident that truly great scientists have so often been men of great humility, understanding, and compassion. For science, after all, from the standpoint of its most fundamental principles, attempts to give insight and knowledge through understanding and critical analysis of our universe. Science is analytical, and critically and comparatively perceptive. The scientific mind does not function on the basis of random impulse and prejudice. Science is evaluative only after all known factors have been carefully appraised and weighed. This type of delaying judgment and intellectual discipline runs sharply counter to the prejudicing and impetuous evaluation of people and things. This type of scientifically trained

[21] An interesting commentary on this point of view, from the standpoint of modern psychiatry, may be found in Erich Fromm's recent essay, *Psychoanalysis and Religion* (New Haven, 1950).

intelligence avoids the easy generalization and the ready imputation of blame. The very impersonality of the true scientific judgment is in itself a guarantee against unwarranted prejudice. This is a profound type of understanding and is akin to the attitude which Ludwig Lewisohn has described when he said: "I no longer thought of people as good and bad or desirable or undesirable, but I saw in all faces the struggle and the passion and the sorrow, sometimes ugly, unheroic enough always by the old, foolish tests, but full of endless fascination. . . ."[22]

Coupled with our understanding of individual behavior caught up within the matrix of culturally defined social situations, scientific insights may tend to free us from the ready casting of blame upon others. Such a view, in making us focus our attention upon the complex factors of each social situation, tends to give us a considerably wider area of orientation in which we can operate and in which we can manipulate causal factors of dysfunction with some degree of competence and assurance. From the archaic notion of sheer personal responsibility for pathological conditions, we may turn fruitfully to the therapeutic concept of accountability, as Coutu suggests.[23] In the last analysis, the casting of blame on others is evidence of our own inability to correct a difficult situation, and a projection of our sense of inadequacy. Such a projective tendency on our part is virtually an admission of our own culpability. We only blame others when we ourselves are insecure and have no means of meeting an existent situation of tension and emergency.

The proper study of mankind is man, to paraphrase Stuart Chase's striking use of Pope's *Essay On Man*. The immediate hope for man's salvation at the present time may be sought only in the detailed studies of the complicated patterns that bind men to the myriad social situations that comprise the social order. Although the scientific study of such patterns affords us no universal panacea or sudden revelation whereby all of man's ills may suddenly disappear, it does in its slow, day-to-day growth, afford us concrete improvements—however meagre they may appear—which may justify our faith in its eventual achievements.

[22] Ludwig Lewisohn, *Upstream* (New York, 1926).
[23] Coutu, *Emergent Human Nature*, pp. 406–17.

GLOSSARY

ACCOMMODATION The conscious and purposeful adjustment of individuals and groups to each other.

ADJUSTMENT, ADAPTATION The condition of harmonious association between the individual and his environment, social and natural.

ADJUSTMENT-CAPACITY The capacity of the individual to respond to the shifting demands of his environment.

ADJUSTMENT-EFFORT The effort expended by the individual toward gaining adjustment to his environment.

ADJUSTMENT-SITUATION The conditions of the natural and social environment to which adjustment must be made.

ALCOHOLISM Addiction to alcohol such that daily drinking is a necessity for the individual.

ALTERNATIVES The culture elements with respect to which the members of a given society may express a choice as regards their participation or non-participation.

AMENTIA Mental deficiency present from birth or acquired within a few months after birth.

ANOMIE The state of normlessness.

ANTISOCIAL TYPE The psychopathic personality type, associated with persons who tend deliberately to violate the mores of their societies.

ANXIETY An affective state, similar to fear. Anxiety differs from fear in that its intensity is generally disproportionate to the circumstances that provoke it, and it usually lacks a sharp focus.

ASCRIBED STATUS The status that an individual occupies irrespective of his abilities or innate characteristics.

ASSIMILATION The unconscious absorption of individuals and groups within a common area of patterned social behavior.

AUTISM The condition of extreme preoccupation with one's self, associated with the tendency to translate outer events so that they will fit with egocentric fantasies.

BASIC DISCIPLINES The fundamental disciplines imposed upon the child in early training and socialization with significant bearing upon subsequent socialization and personality development, and revolving around such concerns as food disciplines, sphincter control, and sexual indoctrination.

BASIC PERSONALITY STRUCTURE The pattern of personality traits which has a high degree of "fit" with the institutions of the given society and is more or less modal for the society.

BEHAVIORISM The school of psychology that deals only with observable and overt behavior, to the exclusion of the phenomena of consciousness and unconsciousness that are revealed by introspection.

CLASS A group within society distinguished from other groups in accordance with characteristics which the nature of the social organization—or the interests of the investigator—define as significant.

COMMUNICATION The transmission of ideas, values, beliefs, and emotions through the medium of imagery or symbols.

COMPENSATION Substitute satisfaction, sought for unconsciously when the successful response to an earlier drive is thwarted.

COMPETITION Viewed sociologically, the impersonal and unconscious struggle for limited goods or services, in which the gain of one party bars another party from gaining the same object.

COMPULSION The irresistible impulse to perform certain actions which serve no apparent function except to forestall the anxiety that would occur were the compulsive act not performed.

CONFLICT The personal and conscious struggle for power over another individual or group, or for goods or services which might otherwise rest in the opponent's possession.

CRETIN A mentally deficient person whose defectiveness is due to a thyroid deficiency. There are characteristic physical accompaniments of this disorder.

CULTURE The social transmission of acquired human capabilities, and the artifacts which are the products of these capabilities.

CULTURE AREA A geographical area within which subsist social units whose cultures are similar to a significant degree.

CULTURAL CONFIGURATION The pattern composed by the interlocking and interdependent parts of a given culture.

CULTURAL HYBRIDISM The condition under which the individual falls between two or more sets of cultural standards.

CUMULATIVE CRISIS A situation in which, by the process of slow accretion of events, the social situation is thrown into a state of precarious imbalance.

CYCLOID TYPE Persons who experience violent fluctuations in mood, ranging from mania to depression.

CYCLOTHYMIA The condition of undergoing alternating moods of depression and joy.

DELINQUENCY Deviation from the mores of the social order, legally punishable only in some cases.

DEMENTIA Emotional disturbance, inherited or acquired, with or without intellectual deficiency.

DIFFERENTIAL ASSOCIATION A basic concept in the theory of crime causation developed by the criminologist E. H. Sutherland, in which criminal behavior is regarded as learned behavior produced by a preponderance of associations with individuals and groups characterized by lawless and anti-social activities.

DIFFUSION The passage of culture traits and complexes from area to area and group to group as a consequence of borrowing and migration.

ECOLOGY The study of the mutual adjustment of types of organisms to each other and their habitat.

EGO A Freudian concept referring to the sector of the personality, partly conscious and partly unconscious, that is in touch with reality and reconciles the demands of the id and the superego with reality.

EMERGENCE The occurrence of a new state of affairs which arises, unpredictably, out of the combination of a number of factors which are understood individually but not conjointly.

ETHNOLOGY The comparative study of cultures.

ETHOS The distinctive patterning of the basic values of a given society.

ETIOLOGY The statement of the causal factors of disorder.

EXTROVERSION The tendency to turn one's interests outside the self.

FEEBLEMINDEDNESS Mental deficiency, inadequacy of intelligence and learning ability.

FETISHISM The investment of erotic affect in an object which is taken to stand for the beloved person.

FIELD THEORY A gestalt approach to the problems of psychology and sociology, which holds that the behavior of an individual or other entity must be examined in terms of the "field of forces" operating upon it.

GLOSSARY

FOLKWAYS The customary behavior of a people, sanctioned by tradition, generally failing of specific formulation.

FRAME OF REFERENCE (1) The standpoint from which individuals understand and relate themselves to their own and other groups and the world about them.

(2) An intellectualized standpoint, in accordance with which the investigator relates facts in order to achieve understanding.

FREE-FLOATING ANXIETY The state of anxious expectation, in which the individual is prepared to invest any situation or object with anxiety, according to the circumstances that present themselves.

FUNCTIONAL DISORDER A mental disorder for which there is no evidence of an organic etiology.

FUNCTIONAL-PHASE OF THE P.G.P. The established modes of action through which the individual gains satisfaction of his needs.

GERIATRICS The study of disorders that occur among the aged.

HOMOSEXUALITY The adoption of certain traits of the opposite sex, including, in some cases, the preference for members of one's own sex as love or sexual objects.

HORIZONTAL MOBILITY The movement of an individual or group from one position on a given level of a social hierarchy to another position on the same level.

HYPOPHRENIC TYPE The intellectually deficient type of person, suffering from one or another form of amentia.

HYSTERIA A category of extremely diverse psychoneurotic disorders.

ID A Freudian concept referring to the sector of the personality that is the source of instinctual drives and the site of the unconscious.

IDEAS OF REFERENCE The morbid delusion that all the actions of other persons in one's environment have reference to oneself.

IDENTIFICATION The process of acting, feeling, and thinking in accordance with one's mental image of an exterior object that has been incorporated.

IDIOT A mentally deficient person of the lowest grade who is unable to care for himself and usually has a physical deformity.

INDETERMINATE SENTENCE A sentence imposed upon a convicted person whose duration depends, within limits, upon his behavior while in prison.

INDEX A number which represents the magnitude of the variations in the appearance of certain phenomena.

INSTITUTIONS The patterned groupings of personal agents, values, artifacts, and behavioral practices that represent the major departments of societies.

INTROVERSION The tendency to turn one's interests in on the self.

INTROJECTION The form of identification that involves the incorporation of the image of the exterior object within the ego.

INVERSION Playing the role of the opposite sex; homosexuality.

ISOLATION TYPE The personality-type of individuals who tend to remove themselves from normal social contact.

LATENCY A prior adjustment-technique which has been previously effective and which is employed in the present.

LATENCY-STRUCTURE A concept referring to the composite of the structured attitudes of the individual, the procedures of adjustment of which he avails himself, and the conditions under which adjustment is being sought.

LEARNING THEORY A modern view which stresses the fact that the *socialization* of the individual is a form of learning based upon the key-elements of drive, cue (stimulus), response, and reinforcement (reward).

MANIC-DEPRESSION A psychotic state in which the individual experiences moods of elation and melancholy.

MARGINALITY The condition under which an individual exists more or less beyond the pale of the dominant culture, failing thereby to receive certain of its rewards and prerogatives.

MASOCHISM A sexual perversion involving submission to acts of cruelty at the hands of the loved one as a devious means of obtaining erotic satisfaction.

METHODOLOGY The logic of inquiry.

MONGOLIAN IDIOT A mentally deficient person of middle or low grade, bearing a superficial resemblance in some physical features to the Mongolian race.

MORES Those folkways which, by virtue of being defined as important to the social welfare, are more mandatory than optional. Their violation generally involves some emotional reaction.

MORON A mentally deficient person whose mental age is between seven and twelve years.

NARCISSISM The turning of the libido in upon the self, extreme self-love.

NARCOTISM Addiction to narcotic drugs.

NEED-PHASE OF THE P.G.P. The organic needs of the individual which have become modified and channelized through the conditions of response set up by the environing adults.

NEURASTHENIA A type of neurotic disorder, characterized by extreme fatiguability, general weakness, pains, paresthesias, and other sensations.

NEUROTIC TYPE The personality-type of individuals who react to frustrations with inefficient and ill-adapted protests.

OVERCOMPENSATION In Adlerian psychology, the tendency to compensate for a sense of inferiority by attempting to attain an overwhelming dominance.

PAROLE Release of a convicted person from a penal institution before the termination of his sentence under the surveillance of parole authorities.

PERSONALITY The characteristic organization of the individual's habits, attitudes, values, emotional characteristics, and other individualized responses which imparts consistency to the behavior of the individual.

PHOBIA A morbid fear accompanied by anxiety. Phobias may have a general reference for the individual, or a highly specific focus.

PRECIPITATE CRISIS A crisis that appears with great suddenness and over which the individual has little or no control.

PRIMARY RELATIONS Those intimate face to face contacts that exert a controlling influence upon the personality.

PRIMITIVE (1) Referring to the men or proto-men who were the beginners of human culture.

(2) Referring to the contemporary peoples whose cultural development is held to be retarded.

PROBATION The suspension of the sentence of a convicted person, with the provision that good behavior be maintained under the penalty of the sentence becoming active, such supervision being maintained under accredited probation authorities.

PROJECTION The attribution to other persons of attitudes and impulses of one's own that are unacceptable to the self.

PSYCHASTHENIA All psychoneuroses that may not be classified as hysterias are sometimes called psychasthenias. These include phobias, anxieties, and compulsions.

PSYCHOGENETIC PATTERN (P.G.P.) The organized habitual response-tendencies of the personality by means of which the basic needs of the personality are fulfilled.

PSYCHOGENIC (PSYCHOGENETIC) Related to a trait or disturbance which is conceived of as being derived from the psyche, and its development.

PSYCHOMETRICS The application of quantification to conceptualized psychological phenomena, with a view to their definition in operational terms.

PSYCHONEUROSIS (NEUROSIS) A functional disturbance of the psyche. In some cases, psychoneuroses intergrade imperceptibly with psychoses, though in general they are far less incapacitating.

PSYCHOPATHOLOGY Any type of mental disorder. The term is usually restricted to neuroses.

PSYCHOPATHY A behavioral disorder associated with a lack of the moral sense. Psychopathic individuals are frequently recidivists.

PSYCHOSIS Severe mental disorder either of the functional or organic type usually calling for institutionalization.

PSYCHOSOCIAL A behavioral manifestation in which socially patterned behavior is viewed in its varying linkages to individually motivated and separable psychological elements.

PSYCHOSOMATIC Pertaining to phenomena which are the products of the union of the psychical and physical features of the individual being, or the union itself.

PSYCHOSOMATIC AFFECTION Affects or feeling-states held in conjunction with specific interrelated bodily and mental conditions and characteristics.

PSYCHOTHERAPY The treatment of disorders, mental and somatic, by non-physical means: suggestion, hypnosis, psychoanalysis, etc.

SADISM The sexual perversion involving acts of cruelty toward the loved one as a devious means of obtaining erotic satisfaction.

SCHIZOID TYPE Persons similar to the isolation type, who tend to lose contact with the world of external reality.

SCHIZOPHRENIA A personality disorder characterized variously by introversive tendencies and loss of emotional rapport with the outside world, hallucinations, autistic thinking, and a highly individualized type of logic.

SCHIZOTHYMIA A condition which bears some resemblance to schizophrenia, while differing importantly in not being so extreme.

SECULAR TREND A statistical tendency which persists over a long period of time.

SOCIAL PATHOLOGY The study of social maladjustments, or the maladjustments themselves.

SOCIAL STRUCTURE The pattern of the relationships which exist among the members of a group.

SOCIOMETRICS The application of quantification to conceptualized sociological phenomena, with a view to their definition in operational terms.

SOCIOSOMATICS The relationship between socio-cultural conditions and organic, bodily manifestations, sometimes expressed in characteristic disease and morbidity rates of groups and classes in society.

SOCIUS The individual regarded as the focal center upon which the institutional patterns of society converge.

SOMATIC TYPE The type of person who experiences difficulty in achieving normal adaptation because of illness acquired as a consequence of his distinctive personality.

STATISTICAL PROFILE The statement in statistical terms of the various features of a problem under consideration.

STATUS The various positions occupied by the individual in relation to others within the social structure.

STRUCTURAL (ORGANIC) DISORDER Disturbances of mental or emotional functioning that are the result of tissue defects in the neurological system, whether inherited or acquired.

SUBCULTURE A sector of a larger, unitary culture which, while partaking of the greater part of the characteristics of the larger unit, nevertheless retains distinctive characteristics of its own which set it somewhat apart.

SUPEREGO A Freudian concept referring to the sector of the personality that has internalized the inhibitions on action first imposed by the individual's parents. The superego is comparable to the conscience, and in that capacity serves with the ego to control the impulses of the id.

SYNDROME The pattern of symptoms which together indicate the presence of a disorder.

UNIVERSALS The culture elements in which all normal adult members of a given society participate.

VERTICAL MOBILITY The movement of an individual or group from one level up or down to another level of a social hierarchy.

VOLUNTARY CRISIS A crisis that is the result of a sudden alteration of circumstances which the individual brings about through some act of volition.

VOYEURISM The derivation of sexual pleasure from looking at the sexual features of another person.

WHITE-COLLAR CRIME Crime committed by members of the upper socio-economic classes that is peculiarly related to their professional activities.

INDEX OF NAMES

INDEX OF NAMES

INDEX OF NAMES

INDEX OF SUBJECTS

INDEX OF SUBJECTS

INDEX OF SUBJECTS

A NOTE ON THE TYPE

The text of this book was set on the Linotype in Electra, a type-face designed by W. A. Dwiggins. The Electra face is a simple and readable type suitable for printing books by present-day processes. It is not based on any historical model, and hence does not echo any particular time or fashion. It is without eccentricities to catch the eye and interfere with reading—in general, its aim is to perform the function of a good book printing-type: to be read, and not seen.

The book was composed, printed, and bound by Kingsport Press, Inc., Kingsport, Tennessee.

A NOTE ON THE TYPE

The text of this book was set on the Linotype in ELECTRA, *designed by* W. A. DWIGGINS. *The Electra face is a simple and readable type suitable for printing books by present-day processes. It is not based on any historical model, and hence does not echo any particular time or fashion. It is without eccentricities to catch the eye and interfere with reading—in general, its aim is to perform the function of a good book printing-type: to be read, and not seen.*

The book was composed, printed, and bound by KINGSPORT PRESS, *Inc., Kingsport, Tennessee.*